THE HAPPY COUPLE

Law and Literature

THE HAPPY COUPLE

Law and Literature

Editors:
J Neville Turner
Pamela Williams

The Federation Press
1994

Published in Sydney by

The Federation Press Pty Ltd
PO Box 45, Annandale, NSW, 2038.
3/56-72 John Street, Leichhardt, NSW, 2040.
Ph (02) 552 2200. Fax (02) 552 1681.

National Library of Australia Cataloguing-in-Publication

The happy couple: law and literature.

Bibliography.
ISBN 1 86287 094 2

1. Law and literature. 2. Law in literature. 3. Law - Language. I. Turner, J. Neville. II. Williams, Pamela.

340

Typeset by The Federation Press, Leichhardt, NSW.
Printed by Ligare Pty Ltd, Riverwood, NSW.

Contents

Contributors

KJA ASCHE AC QC, BA, LLM (Melb), FACE, Hon LittD (Deakin), Hon LLD (NT University). Austin Asche practised as a Barrister from 1951 to 1976, becoming a Queen's Counsel in 1972. From 1976 to 1986 he was a judge of the Family Court of Australia and an Acting Chief Judge from 1985 to 1986. In 1986 he was made a judge of the Supreme Court of the Northern Territory and was appointed Chief Justice in 1987. Since 1993 he has been Administrator of the Northern Territory.

JEFFREY BARNES teaches law in the School of Law and Legal Studies at La Trobe University, having formerly taught at Monash University and the University of NSW. His teaching and research interests include statutory interpretation, the legislative process and administrative law. Before commencing an academic career he had a wide experience of the legislative process. After graduating he worked as a legislative drafter in the New South Wales Parliamentary Counsel's Office. He later worked for the Australian Law Reform Commission as Associate to the Chairman and as a Law Reform Officer, followed by a term at the Administrative Review Council as a Project Officer. He is a member of the Law and Literature Association of Australia and of Clarity, an international organisation which promotes the use of good, clear English by the legal profession.

ELAINE BARRY is Associate Professor of English, and Director of the Centre for American Studies, at Monash University, Clayton, Victoria. A graduate of the University of Queensland, she did her postgraduate degrees in the United States. She has been the recipient of awards from the Fulbright Commission, the Rockefeller Foundation and the American Council of Learned Societies. She is the author of books on the American poet Robert Frost and the Australian novelist Jessica Anderson, as well as many essays and reviews in scholarly journals. Her main field of interest is American Literature.

RICHARD ALEXANDER BAUMAN BA, LLB (S Africa), PhD (Witwatersrand), was born in South Africa and moved to Australia in 1965. He is a Fellow of the Australian Academy of the Humanities and Life Associate, Clare Hall, Cambridge. In 1984 he retired as Reader in Ancient History, University of Sydney, and since 1985 he is

Visiting Professor, Faculty of Law, University of New South Wales, where he has introduced courses on Roman Law and Modern Civil Law. He has published seven books, two monographs and 60 articles, mostly on Roman legal and political history, with some attention to Greek legal history. His two current fields of research are crime and punishment, and law reform and nationalism.

PETER BOSS worked for ten years in England in the child welfare field. In 1961 he joined the social science department at Liverpool University as a lecturer and later as senior lecturer at Leicester University. In 1973 he was appointed Foundation Professor of Social Work at Monash University, Melbourne. He retired from Monash in 1986 and since then has worked in research for the National Children's Bureau of Australia. He has published widely both in the United Kingdom and in Australia. His most recent books include, *On the Side Of The Child – An Australian Perspective On Child Abuse,* 1980; *Child Welfare – An Introduction,* 1981 (with Cliff Picton, and *Adoption Australia – A Comparative Study of Australian Adoption Legislation and Policy,* 1992.

ANDREW BUCK teaches in the Department of Economics, University of Newcastle. He has published a number of articles on the social history of law and the idea of property in England and Australia. He is currently working on a study of the historical relationship between property law and the English aristocracy entitled *The Aristocratic Tenure: Land Law and Social Structure in English History*.

LLOYD DAVIES OAM LLB is a barrister and author. Born in Cottesloe, Western Australia, in 1922, he served in the AIF from 1941-1946. In 1948 he graduated in Law at the University of Western Australia. Admitted as a practitioner in 1949, he conducted sole practice in Fremantle until 1970, and then joined the Independent Bar in Perth. He served as in-house counsel for the Aboriginal Legal Service WA from 1979-88. Currently, he operates as part-time itinerant prosecutor for the DPP, specialising in child sex-abuse cases. His publications include two collections of short stories, one novel, one autobiographical monograph (relating to the Hewett libel actions), and numerous articles on legal, social and literary topics. He edited the first edition of the *WA Duty Counsel Handbook* (Law Society of WA, 1979). In 1979 he was awarded the Medal of the Order of Australia for services to the Aboriginal people.

ALAN DILNOT has taught at Monash University since 1973, and is especially interested in nineteenth-century fiction. His most recent publications include several articles in *Directions 1993* and *Directions 1994,* annual collections of essays for English students, which he edits. He has also scripted and presented 50 educational video programs, the latest of which are on *Othello, King Lear, Hard Times* and the work of the Australian novelist, Tim Winton.

KIERAN DOLIN is an associate lecturer in the English Department at the University of Western Australia. His chapter forms part of a larger study of representations of law in nineteenth and twentieth century fiction, from which articles on Melville, Forster and Hasluck are published.

PAUL ELLIOTT LLB(Hons) (Melb), LLM (Lond) is a practising barrister at the Victorian Bar and is joint editor of the *Victorian Bar News*. He was formerly a lecturer in Law at London University.

GRAHAM FRICKE is an occasional United States Supreme Court and Australian High Court watcher. In his daily avocation, he operates at a much lower level in the hierarchy, in the County Court at Melbourne. As a trial judge, he regards appellate court judges as enemies, who characteristically come in after the battle, in order to shoot the wounded. His main hobby is writing, and he has had published, in addition to text books, *Libels Lampoons and Litigants* (1984, Hutchinson), *Judges of the High Court of Australia* (1986, Hutchinson), and *Profiles in Power* (1990, Houghton Mifflin). He has degrees in Law (Melbourne and Pennsylvania) and Criminology (Melbourne).

DONAT GALLAGHER teaches English Literature at James Cook University of North Queensland in Townsville. In 1983 he edited Evelyn Waugh's essays, articles and reviews. Since then he has written extensively about Waugh, with emphasis on the basic thinking underlying his polemical and other topical utterances.

ARTHUR GLASS is a graduate of the University of Sydney in Arts and Law. He later completed a Doctorate of Philosophy on the subject of law and hermeneutics. He has written in the field of legal theory, especially on the topic of legal interpretation, and in the area of constitutional law. He has published articles in *Rechtstheorie, Ratio Juris* and the *Australian Journal of Law and Society*.

COLIN GOLVAN is a barrister and holds the degrees of LLM from Monash University and LLB and BA Honours from Melbourne University. He is also co-author of *Writers and the Law* (LBC 1986) and author of *Words and Law* (Penguin 1989) and *Introduction to Intellectual Property Law* (Federation Press 1992). He is the editor of the *Intellectual Property Law Bulletin* and the *Arts and Entertainment Law Review*, and has had published and produced a number of other books and scripts. Colin is also a literary agent.

STEPHEN GRAY BA, LLB(Hons) lectures in Jurisprudence, Aborigines and the Legal System, and Legal Process at the Northern Territory University. He is interested in legal avenues for the protection of Aboriginal art, and more broadly in avenues for the recognition of Aboriginal law: this has tended recently to include a consideration of the philosophical differences of perspective between the two systems of law. A first draft of his chapter appeared in (1992) 66 *LIJ* 46. His other publications include: "Planting the Flag or Burying the Hatchet: Sovereignty and the High Court decision in *Mabo v Queensland*", (1993) vol 2 no 1, *Griffith Law Review* 41; "Wheeling, Dealing and Deconstruction: Aboriginal Art and the Land Post-Mabo", *ALB* vol 3 no 63, August 1993, 10; "Enlightenment or Dreaming?: Attempting to Reconcile Aboriginal Art and European Law", paper delivered at the 1994 Law and Literature Annual Conference.

JOE GRIXTI is currently senior lecturer in the Humanities at the Queensland University of Technology, Australia, where he teaches introductory courses in textual and cultural analysis, as well as more advanced units in popular culture and comparative European literary studies. He was educated at the Universities of Oxford and Bristol, and has held teaching appointments at the Universities of Warwick, Malta and Bristol. His previous publications include *Terrors of Uncertainty: the Cultural Contexts of Horror Fiction*, Routledge, 1989.

HON MR JUSTICE PETER HEEREY was educated in Hobart. From 1967 to 1990 he practised at the Victorian Bar. He was appointed a judge of the Federal Court of Australia in 1990. While at the Bar he had a general retainer from the Herald & Weekly Times Ltd for defamation and contempt of court. He has published a number of articles in legal journals on defamation topics.

CHRISTINE HIGGINS is a lecturer in the School of Humanities in the newly formed Faculty of Arts at the Queensland University of Technology in Brisbane. Her major teaching interests are nineteenth and twentieth century English and Australian Literature and Literary Theory. Earlier work in Media/Cultural Studies has contributed to her current interdisciplinary research project, which involves an exploration of the uses and significance of Gothic Horror motifs and tropes in the reportage of violent crime in the Queensland press in the 1890s and 1980s. A number of earlier publications have focused on the Radio medium – *Sounds Real: Radio in Everyday Life* (co-authored with Peter D Moss) University of Queensland Press, 1982; "Radio Voices", *Media, Culture and Society*, 6/4, 1984 (pp 149-65). More recently, she has developed a research interest in interdisciplinary explorations of literary theory, language study and legal texts.

PETER HUTCHINGS BA(Hons), PhD (Sydney) lectures in film studies and cultural theory in the Department of Comparative Literature, University of Hong Kong. He has published widely in the areas of cinema, literature and the visual arts, and is currently writing a study of violence and the arts, editing a collection of essays on Hong Kong cinema, and co-editing (with Maryanne Dever) *Austral-Asian Image Cultures* for Curzon Press. His doctoral thesis addressed issues of narrative, death, romanticism and postmodernism. Other research interests include French and German philosophy, popular culture and contemporary visual art.

STEPHEN A JAMES BA(Hons) (Melb), MA (Princ) is a PhD candidate in the Department of Politics, Princeton University, where he was a Princeton Wilson Fellow in 1992-1993 and a Lecturer in the Fall, 1993-1994. He is working on his dissertation on human rights law and philosophy while completing an LLB at the University of Melbourne. He has also taught at Melbourne and La Trobe Universities.

ROSANNE KENNEDY teaches Women's Studies and English at Australian National University. She has edited, with Katherine T Bartlett, *Feminist Legal Theory: Readings in Law and Gender* (Westview Press, 1991). She is interested in developing a cultural studies approach to law, and has published articles on *LA Law* and on legal trials. She is currently doing research on how evidence functions in a range of historical and contemporary discourses.

MICHAEL MEEHAN is Associate Professor and Head of English at Flinders University, South Australia, and was formerly Head of the Discipline of Legal Studies. He has a BA from Monash University, and LLB from the University of Adelaide, and a PhD from the University of Cambridge, on eighteenth century English political theory and aesthetics. He is currently writing on relations between law and literary theory in the eighteenth century, and on the "poetics" of Australian legal discourse.

SIDRA KRANZ MOSHINSKY is a tutor in the History Department of the University of Melbourne and is researching literature written during the Holocaust for her Master of Arts degree.

SIMON PETCH teaches English at the University of Sydney, and is a past president of the Law and Literature Association of Australia. He has written a book on the poetry of Philip Larkin (1981), and has co-edited a volume of centenary essays on the poetry of Browning (1989). In addition to literary and legal studies, his major research interest is in autobiography.

Contributors

PENELOPE PETHER lectures in Law at the University of Wollongong and is President of the Law and Literature Association of Australia. Her published research focuses on the literature of the late nineteenth and twentieth centuries, and she specialises in interdisciplinary research and teaching in law/literature/language; her approaches to this work are feminist and poststructuralist. Formerly a practising lawyer, she has lectured in American Literature at Macarthur Institute of Higher Education, and taught English Literature at the University of Sydney 1988-92. She has also taught courses in Australian Studies for Boston University in its Australian program.

MAURIE SCOTT is Senior Lecturer in the English Department, University of Wollongong, specialising in Theatre, Screen, Communications and Cultural Studies. He helped to devise and present the "Perspectives on Law: English" for the Law Faculty, dealing with the various aspects of the interfaces of law with literature and the other media. An active member of the Law and Literature Association, he is presently involved with developing a specialist journal in the field.

JOHANNA SUTHERLAND BA/LLB(Hons), MA(IR) (ANU) is a lecturer in law at James Cook University of North Queensland. In June 1993 she was granted leave to undertake a Research Fellowship on Reconciliation Projects at the Australian Institute of Aboriginal and Torres Strait Islander Studies in Canberra. She is currently working on a PhD on international environmental law and indigenous peoples in the Department of International Relations at the Australian National University.

TERRY THREADGOLD is Professor of English at Monash University. Her research interests include critical legal studies and performance studies and issues related to critical and feminist pedagogy. Her publications include (with E Grosz, Gunther Kress and MAK Halliday) *Semiotics – Ideology – Language* (1986), *Feminine/Masculine and Representation* (1991) (with Anne Cranny Francis). Her book *Feminist Poetics* will be published by Routledge in 1995.

J NEVILLE TURNER teaches at the Faculty of Law, Monash University. He was a founder member of the Law and Literature Association of Australia, of which he is now a Vice-President. He has lectured and published several papers on law and literature, including articles on the trial scene in Dostoevsky's *Brothers Karamazov* and the legal wit of WS Gilbert. Neville's other special interests are Family Law, Child Law, Comparative Law and the Law of Sport. He is the Vice-President of Oz Child, a large Melbourne organisation providing service for children and advocating on children's issues.

JAMES BOYD WHITE was educated at Amherst and Harvard. He practised law in Boston and has taught at the University of Colorado, the University of Chicago, and the University of Michigan. His primary interest has been in the analysis of legal thought and speech, which he has pursued in part by tracing connections between law and ordinary language, on the one hand, and the classic texts of the Western humanistic tradition, on the other. His books include *The Legal Imagination* (1973); *When Words Lose Their Meaning* (1984); and *Justice as Translation* (1990). A book on the poetry of George Herbert, *"This Book of Starres": Learning to Read George Herbert,* was published earlier this summer by the University of Michigan Press; and *Acts of Hope: Creating Authority in Literature, Law, and Politics* has just been published by the University of Chicago Press.

DR GEOFF WINDON'S undergraduate studies and doctorate were undertaken at the University of Sydney. He is currently working at Macquarie University and is preparing a study of the relationship between representations of aesthetic experience and concepts of history in the literature of the Romantic period.

Preface

In Sir Walter Scott's *Guy Mannering*, the eponymous hero calls at the office of his advocate, Counsellor Pleydell. Surprised that his bookshelves contain books of classical literature rather than law reports, Colonel Mannering questions the counsellor, and receives this reply: "These are my tools of trade. A lawyer without history or literature is a mechanic, a mere working Mason: if he possesses some knowledge of these, he may venture to call himself an architect".

Although the connexion between the two disciplines was manifest to Scott, a lawyer and novelist, it was only recently that serious study of the nexus has been attempted. The United States has pioneered this movement. Today many American Law Schools offer 'Law and Literature' as a subject in their courses. Australia can now claim to be the foremost disciple of the Americans. It has happened in the last five years, following the formation of the Law and Literature Association of Australia in 1989.

Already five annual conferences of this association have been held. The corpus of scholarly writing, both by lawyers and by literati, is growing apace. A journal has been formed, devoted exclusively to the subject. A few courses have been initiated, notably at the Universities of Sydney, Wollongong and Monash. The movement has attained academic respectability.

This volume is the first Australian book devoted to Law and Literature. It emanates from a conference at Monash University held in 1991, the second annual conference of the Association. At it, 35 papers were presented.

At the end of the conference, it was resolved that the papers be published as a collection. It transpired, however, that some of the presentations had been intended to be speeches, and did not lend themselves to a written form. Some of the presenters had published their work elsewhere. Others, for various reasons, declined an invitation to contribute to the book. It also became apparent that, in order to present a work of thematic homogeneity, it was desirable to supplement the book with selected papers from other conferences of the Association.

Accordingly, this book seeks to contain what the editors consider to be a representative collection of the work of leading Australian scholars, together with essays from a number of foreign visitors who have exercised some influence on Australian scholarship.

Apart from seeking to ensure uniformity in matters of punctuation and citation, the editors, for the most part, have not sought to modify the style of each author. After all, from those who claim to be *litterateurs*, the editors are entitled to expect literacy. The result is that there is a great diversity of types. This, we feel, is an asset, not a detriment. The eclectic nature of the subject-matter and the heterogeneity of writing styles offer, as it were, something for everyone. The voices of the papers are as varied and individual as their topics.

We have, however, informed this book with a structure into which we feel that the essays comfortably fit. The First Part consists of four essays of diverse historical import in chronological order. It thus fulfils the first limb of Counsellor Pleydell's mandate! The Second Part looks at particular illustrations of the law in action as portrayed and analysed in literature. And, for this purpose, the word, 'literature', bears a connotation in keeping with its literal meaning — that which is written. The Law and Literature movement is by no means restricted to classical writing, or even fine writing. Indeed, certain essays treat the law as it appears in the electronic media.

The Third Part of the book encompasses a number of issues in which the law impinges on art forms, and will be of particular importance to professional writers.

The Final Part covers a variety of literary matters raised by legal writing. The common law's genius is that it allows for expansive writing. Unlike in civil law jurisdictions, the 'codeless science' of the common law encourages judicial individuality.

Chapters by Graeme Fricke, Arthur Glass and the influential American scholar, James Boyd White, explore elements of style in legal writings. Jeffrey Barnes contemplates whether statutes can be said to have literary quality. Chapters by Terry Threadgold and Rosanne Kennedy will be of special interest to those who are beguiled by the applicability of modern theories of linguistics and semiotics to legal texts. Can the techniques of the professional scholar of literature be profitably applied by law? Can legal writings – statutes, case law, even pleadings and solicitors' letters – be read anew so as to discover new meanings? Can a modern draftsperson find insight from literature which will facilitate his or her seemingly chimerical attempts to write the law in “plain” English? These, and other jurisprudential and semantic issues of great fascination, may for some provide the ultimate justification, indeed the academic inevitability, of the Law and Literature movement.

We have also included a delightful quiz on Dickens, prepared for the conference dinner by the Hon Austin Asche.

We have sought to produce a protean collection, which will stimulate and provoke legal and literary readers alike. Perhaps this book will serve to encourage the initiation of further courses on Law and Literature at tertiary institutions.

Preface

Editing a collection of essays is a multifarious task. There are so many persons to whom thanks are due. First and foremost, however, tribute must be paid to Pamela Williams, who has single-handedly edited the text. Without her enthusiasm, skill and patience, the manuscript would never have reached the publishers. Federation Press Ltd, and especially the persons of Christopher Holt and Liz Halley, have been magnificently supportive in what, to more timorous publishers, would have seemed a doubtful commercial venture.

I should also like to thank my colleagues, Bernadette McSherry and Jeffrey Barnes (now on the staff of La Trobe University), for assisting in the organisation of the conference from which this collection emanated, and for their constant support.

The Publications Committee of Monash University has provided financial support for the book, in effect underwriting it. Again, I must thank that committee, and especially its chair, Professor Richard Fox, for its enthusiastic assistance.

Finally, I should like to express my gratitude to all the authors of the chapters in this book. Each one, I think, may venture to call himself, or herself, an architect.

J Neville Turner
Vice-President
Law & Literature Association of Australia,
and Chair of the Editorial Committee.

I would also like to thank my colleagues [illegible] and [illegible] now on the staff of [illegible] University [illegible] for their [illegible] and for their constant support.

[illegible]

[illegible] President

[illegible]

PRELIMINARY EXERCISE

1
A Dickens of a Legal Quiz

KJA ASCHE

1. For what offence was Fagin convicted and hanged?

2. From the same novel – the phrase much beloved of disgruntled litigants – "the law is an ass". Mr Bumble said it. But what particular doctrine of the law, as it then existed, made him say it?

3. After his mother's death, David Copperfield, ill-treated by his stepfather Mr Murdstone, fled to his aunt's house. Murdstone followed and demanded his return. The aunt refused, and Murdstone, probably because he had no more use for David, did not press the matter. But suppose he had pressed his claim in the courts, would he have succeeded?

4. Magwitch, the convict, befriended by young Pip in *Great Expectations*, and later Pip's unknown benefactor, was transported to Botany Bay, served his sentence and became free and prospered in the colony. For what subsequent crime was he sentenced to death before he cheated the gallows by dying?

5. In that same trial, the lawyer Jaggers, who was known as a fearsome advocate and had an immense criminal practice, clearly had the confidence of Magwitch. Did Jaggers appear for Magwitch? If not, why not?

6. What unusual course did Mr Pickwick insist on taking with his counsel, Serjeant Snubbin, before the trial of *Bardell v Pickwick*?

7. During the trial of *Bardell v Pickwick,* Mr Pickwick's counsel formally admitted that Mr Pickwick was "a gentleman of considerable independent property". When he lost the case, and refused to pay damages and costs, he was arrested at the suit of Dodson and Fogg, attorneys for the plaintiff, and committed to the Fleet prison as a debtor. He still refused to pay. Why did not Dodson and Fogg execute upon his property and get the damages and costs in that way?

8. One more question about the famous trial. Since Mrs Bardell could not give evidence on her own behalf it was necessary to prove Mrs Bardell's case by other witnesses. The witnesses who had found Mrs Bardell in the arms of Mr Pickwick were Mr Snodgrass,

Mr Winkle and Mr Tupman. They were called for the plaintiff and were "driven to the verge of exasperation by excessive badgering" by plaintiff's counsel. Mr Winkle, for instance, is mocked, bullied, told not to evade questions and reminded that his thoughts "would be of little service to honest straightforward men" (ie the jury). This appears to be pretty plain cross-examination of one's own witness. Why was it permitted? (No application was made to have the witness declared hostile).

9. In *The Old Curiosity Shop* Daniel Quilp committed suicide. Furthermore, he died intestate. Yet his widow appears to have inherited the whole estate. Was this possible at that time?

10. What, in one word, was the remedy devised by the promoters of the Anglo-Bangalay Disinterested Loan & Life Assurance Company after their coffers had been enriched by insurance premiums but when many of the insurances began to fall due?

11. Finally, one to which I have found no answer. In *Our Mutual Friend* Mortimer Lightwood & Eugene Wrayburn are respectively solicitor and barrister. They are together in Mortimer's office when a client (Riderhood) arrives to see Mortimer. Eugene, at Mortimer's request, takes down Riderhood's statement. Was this a breach of ethics?

For answers to these questions, see page 392.

1

HISTORIES

2

The Language of Roman Statutes

RICHARD BAUMAN

A little-noticed feature of Roman legal language is the sharp distinction, not in the early stages but later on, between the language of the jurist, or jurisconsult, and the language of statutes. The jurists, employing the uniquely Roman method of making law through the opinions of those learned in the law, delve carefully into all the *minutiae* of a problem, but they express themselves in plain Latin without embellishment. The short, sharp bark of the *responsum*, or counsel's opinion, is so terse that, at least in the earlier period, it does not even give reasons for the view that it enunciates. The authority of the enunciator was all the backing that it needed. The jurists' meticulous attention to form and detail did not fail to attract criticism and parody, as Cicero never fails to point out:

> A suit could have been brought as follows: "The Sabine property is mine." "No, it is mine." The trial should follow. But this was too simple for the lawyers. "A property which is situate in the district which is designated as Sabine." That is bad enough, but look what follows: "This I affirm to be my property by Quiritary title." Then: "From this place I formally summon you to that place yonder to join issue with me according to law." Then the same lawyer goes over to the defendant's side, like a flute-playing accompanist: "From the place whence you have summoned me to join issue, from thence I summon you to that place yonder." The judge joins in: "The witnesses for both parties being there present, I formally indicate yonder road. Proceed on that road." Even our hairy ancestors would have thought it ridiculous that men having duly presented themselves at a place should be told to leave it, only to return at once to the place from which they had gone. (Cicero *Pro Murena* 26, adapted)

But Cicero does not suggest that the meaning is difficult to uncover. The lawyers were prolix but not obscure.

Cicero's position in legal matters is anomalous. He classified himself as an orator, who conducted cases in court, not as a jurisconsult who advised on the law to be applied in such cases, yet Cicero's legal knowledge was so extensive that he is by far our most important source for the law of the Republican period (up to the first century BC). But at the end of the day he is an orator, a pastmaster in flowery language and tricks of rhetoric. He himself complains that Rutilius Rufus, prominent both as a lawyer and as an orator when Cicero was a young man, delivered court speeches in the same dry-as-dust fashion as his legal opinions.

The essentially factual nature of the lawyers' jargon survived virtually unchanged throughout the life of classical jurisprudence, that is, until circa AD 250. But the language of Roman statutes was destined to undergo some drastic changes over the long history of Roman law stretching from the fifth century BC to the sixth century AD. I omit the venerable Twelve Tables of 450 BC which, even in the second edition of circa 300 BC of which we have some knowledge, is cast in archaic Latin whose subsequent linguistic influence was minimal, whatever its impact on subsequent substantive law. I therefore take up the story from circa 200 BC, when Rome had already taken the first giant strides on the road to empire and began acquiring sophistication in all cultural spheres, including – and indeed for the *Rechtsvolk* primarily including – the law.

From circa 200 BC to circa AD 300 the language of statutes – exclusively *leges* of the popular assembly until the end of the Republic (27 BC) and thereafter decrees of the senate and the emperor – is on a par with the jargon of the jurists. The following passage is from a *lex* of the late second century BC regulating the recently established jury-court for the trial of provincial governors accused of extorting money from the locals:

> If from anyone of the allies either of the Latin name or of foreign nations, or from anyone of those dependent on the discretion, dictation, power or friendship of the Roman people in any single year property amounting to more than . . . sesterces in value has been taken, seized, exacted, procured or appropriated from such person himself or from his king, his people or his father, or from anyone who is or has been in his or his father's family . . . by a person in the exercise of his command or power who was dictator, consul, praetor, master of the horse, censor, aedile, plebeian tribune, quaestor, triumvir capitalis, triumvir for assigning lands, military tribune . . . or who is a senator or the son of a senator, with regard to this matter let a complaint be lodged with the praetor having jurisdiction and let the adjudication, judgment and assessment of damages be by those who constitute the court in terms of this law. (*Lex Acilia Repetundarum* 1-3)

The statute is in plain Latin, painfully winkling out the smallest differences of detail in order to cover all possible contingencies, but avoiding all embellishments.

The trend continued in the first century BC, despite the increasing influence of rhetoric not only on court oratory but even, marginally, on some positive law. As early as the nineties BC the famous *Causa Curiana* saw a Roman court apply one of the rhetorical canons of construction by reading an orator's interpretation of the testator's intention into an ambiguous will. This extreme application of the notion of *voluntas*, intention, might have been expected to flow on into statutes, and indeed did so, but contemporary legal draftsmen remained basically true to their craft by devising a typically casuistic, Roman application of *voluntas*.

This next extract is from a *lex* which was passed less than a decade after the *Causa Curiana*. The law was designed to meet the threat of *sicarii*, footpads, who stalked the streets armed to the teeth in search of people to rob:

> It is laid down by the first chapter of the *lex Cornelia de sicariis* that the praetor presiding over the jury-court concerning cut-throats shall investigate with the jurors appointed under that law capital charges against anyone who has gone about with a weapon for the purpose of killing someone or committing theft. (*Mosaicarum et Romanarum Legum Collatio* 1.3.1)

As it shows, the crime over which a new jury-court was to have jurisdiction was defined not in terms of what an accused did, but in terms of the intention with which he carried out certain acts of preparation. In other words, you were not charged with robbing someone with violence; you were charged with going about in public armed with the intention of committing murder or theft. Cast in this form, the definition of the crime opened the way to refinements in construction not previously accessible. It was desirable in the interests of equity that carrying or using a weapon in self-defence be not accounted culpable, but under laws making actual performance the criterion of liability the introduction of an exclusion was difficult. Now, however, carrying a weapon with the intention of defending oneself provided a usable defence. At some later point of time the statute was amended by adding as an additional case the actual performance of the act of killing, but even then the lawyers interpreted *voluntas* into the picture, "The emperor Hadrian ruled as follows: In crimes the intention is looked at, not the result" (*Digest* 48.8.14). It is interesting to note that the other intention in the original statute, namely committing theft, was not included when actual performance was added. The reason was that theft was not a crime in Roman law; it was a delict (tort). An intention to commit armed robbery could quite logically, as the Romans saw it, be brought under the criminal law, but the accomplished act could not.

The foundation of the system of one-man rule known as the Principate did not immediately end the career of the *lex*. The first emperor, Augustus, used legislation of the popular assembly as the vehicle for his program of reform, but despite the flowering of schools of rhetoric to levels undreamt of in Cicero's day, legal draftsmen kept their feet firmly planted on the ground. Augustus created a new public crime, adultery, and established a new jury-court for it. The language remained as dry-as-dust and factual as before, "Let no one hereafter commit fornication or adultery knowingly and with wrongful intent" (*sciens dolo malo*) (*Digest* 48.13). The only advance on Republican forms was that scope for excluding responsibility was framed in a somewhat different fashion. The accomplished act, committing fornication or adultery, was the basis of liability, but the rider that it be done *sciens dolo malo*, knowingly and with wrongful intent, left ample scope for exclusionary factors. The accomplished act which had only been an afterthought in the homicide law was now the primary criterion, but *voluntas* had been neatly incorporated. The contrast between this and the rhetorical absurdities which disfigure later legislation on the same subject of sexual morality is one of the clearest indications of a fundamental change as Rome moved from the Principate into the Later Empire.

By the end of the first century AD the *lex* of the popular assembly had ceased to be the instrument of legislation. The new legislative organ was the senate, soon to be joined (and ultimately supplanted) by direct legislation by the emperor. The *senatus consultum*, or resolution of the senate, was in Republican constitutional theory no more than a recommendation to a magistrate, but in the Principate it acquired full normative efficacy. The language remained true to Republican precedents. This passage, changing the name of the eighth month to Augustus in honour of the emperor, contains more material appropriate to a preamble than a *lex* would have done, but the language is still limpid and precise:

> Whereas in the month of Sextilis the emperor Caesar Augustus entered on his first consulship, celebrated three triumphs, brought legions down from the Janiculum and placed them under his auspices and protection, brought Egypt under the power of the Roman people, and ended the civil war, and whereas for these reasons this month is and will be most favourable to this empire, now therefore it pleases the senate that this month be called Augustus. (*Fontes Iuris Romani Antejustiniani* 1.280-1)

There is an interesting contrast between the senate's language when it is legislating in the sense of laying down permanent rules, and its language when it is blatantly politicising. In the latter case the influence of rhetoric sweeps aside the sober approach of the legislator proper. Thus in 192 after the murder of Commodus the senate damned the memory of the deceased emperor in language that it would not have employed in a run-of-the-mill statute, "From him who was an enemy of his country let honours be taken away, let the honours of the murderer be taken away, let the murderer be dragged in the dust, let him be dragged with a hook, a foe, a murderer, verily, verily" (*Augustan History, Commodus Antoninus* 19). It had used similar language in 96 when Domitian was murdered; we have this from the biographer Suetonius, in his *Domitian* (23.1). The resemblance to 192 is clear, though he only gives us the effect of the senate's decree. Although mainline legislation was still couched in measured terms, rhetoric was beginning to erode the dividing-line between legislation and propaganda.

Direct legislation by the emperor took the form of edicts, rescripts in reply to petitions, and judgments in cases tried by the emperor. The sobriety of this decree of Marcus Aurelius and Commodus, "The emperor Marcus Aurelius and the emperor Commodus ordered these markers to be set up because of disputes that had arisen between traders and contractors so that they might precisely demonstrate the boundaries for tax purposes" is in marked contrast to the senate's outburst against Commodus a few years later. Rhetoric had not yet infected the emperor's own legislation. But it would.

Legislation by the emperor, already the major source of new law since the mid-second century AD, was the sole source by the time the fourth century dawned. And from then on a drastic change of pattern in the language of statutes manifests itself. Rhetoric runs wild, reaching heights of absurdity that would have been anathema to Cicero, so remote are they from the stately cadences of the great Republican orator. Our first example, from a law of Constantine, deals broadly with the same subject of corruption as that encapsulated in the extract the *Lex Acilia Repetundarum* quoted earlier. Constantine was dealing with the endemic problem of judicial corruption – here is an extract from his law:

> The rapacious hands of the apparitors shall cease immediately, they shall cease, I say. For if after due warning they do not cease, they shall be cut off by the sword. The judge's curtain shall not be venal. Entrance shall not be gained by purchase, the council chamber shall not be infamous on account of the bids. . . There shall be no despoiling on the occasion of escorting persons inside, no employment of extortion on litigants. The intolerable onslaught of the centurions and others who demand money shall be crushed, and the insatiable greed of those who deliver the records of a case to litigants shall be restrained. (*Theodosian Code* 1.16.7)

The tone of the document is almost querulous, as if the speaker fears that his words will fall on deaf ears, "The rapacious hands . . . shall immediately cease, they shall cease, I say". One wonders if the ruler is trying to convince his subjects or himself. These laws were, of course, written in Latin, but a kind of Latin that even an honours graduate in Classics approaches with trepidation. It is more of a stylised Byzantine mosaic than a language that anyone spoke. After the fall of the Western Roman Empire the Germanic successor kingdoms could not come to terms with it. In their edition of the Theodosian Code the Visigoths attached Interpretations to many of the laws. These are not so much juristic constructions as desperate attempts to get at the meaning. The Visigothic Interpretation of the above extract from the Theodosian Code reads as follows, "Interpretation. The apparitors of no judges shall dare to be venal or to require a price either for the entrance or for the egress of those persons who come for an audience or for litigation" (*Theodosian Code* 1.16.7).

Only Gilbert and Sullivan could have done justice to another law of Constantine's. The emperor wished to discourage girls from eloping in order to marry without their parents' consent. His law includes a special punishment for the nurse who assists her charge to elope:

> Since the watchfulness of parents is often frustrated by the stories and wicked persuasions of nurses, punishment shall first threaten those nurses whose care is proved to have been detestable and their errands bribed, and the penalty shall be that the mouths and throats of those who offered incitement to evil shall be closed by pouring in molten lead. (*Theodosian Code* 9.24.1.1)

There is no doubt about the genuineness of this decree; whatever changes to the texts of laws the compilers of the Theodosian Code may have made, they did not cut fictitious penalties from whole cloth. But the literary sources were not quite as circumspect. A pastiche which, I believe, was aimed at the molten lead decree is included in the Augustan History's Life of Macrinus. It was a habit of the Augustan History, which was compiled in the late fourth century AD, to retroject contemporary or near-contemporary events to earlier periods, and this hilarious episode is such a case:

> Some soldiers had had relations with a maid-servant of doubtful reputation. The emperor, after questioning them and establishing their guilt, ordered that two huge oxen be cut open while still alive and that the soldiers be thrust one into each, with their heads sticking out so that they could talk to each other. Such a punishment had never been inflicted before, even for adultery. (*Augustan History*, *Opellius Macrinus* 12.4-5)

The episode has no point unless it is satirising something like the molten lead law, which had been passed some 60 or 70 years before the pastiche appeared; the interval may have been even shorter if the author of the Augustan History took the item from a work going back to Constantine's day.

This next example is my final one of bloated rhetoric. It is an interpretation by Constantine's sons of Augustus's adultery law. That law penalised *stuprum*, fornication in general, in addition to adultery. The following pronouncement is based on *stuprum*, though only careful scrutiny is able to reveal that fact:

> When a man "marries" in the manner of a woman, a "woman" preparing to renounce men, what does he wish when sex has lost its significance, when the crime is one that it is not profitable to know, when Venus is changed into another form, when love is sought and not found? We order the statutes to arise, the laws to be armed with an avenging sword, that those infamous persons may be subjected to exquisite punishment. (*Theodosian Code* 9.7.3)

The world of Lewis Carroll and Gilbert and Sullivan did not dominate Roman legislation for ever. There was a reaction in the sixth century, when the Eastern Empire – by then the only Roman Empire – experienced an intellectual renaissance. There was a conscious move by jurisprudence to return to the great classical tradition. This included the language of the law, and the imperial bureaucracy broke away from the stultifying influence of rhetoric and returned to the plain Latin of the past. Under the guidance of Justinian the new trend extended not only to the Digest but also to the Code, which is a collection of emperors' laws since Hadrian. The collection includes numerous laws which we also have in the Theodosian Code, and some significant comparisons can be made. This is because Justinian's compilers were told to bring those laws up to date, and took the mandate to include "modernising" the language – in other words, restoring the intelligibility of the past. An example of this comes from Justinian's version of Constantine's law which had included the molten lead penalty, "We subject to capital punishment all those who are convicted of being accomplices in or of having in any way assisted in such a crime, whether men or women, of whatever status or dignity" (*Justinian Code* 9.13.3a). Justinian's version simply lays down that the girl's accomplices suffer capital punishment. In accordance with the language used in the Republic and Principate, there was no need to define the penalty any more closely; it meant execution (by whatever means) and confiscation of property.

The rhetorical phase of Roman legislation is a high calorie filling between two slices of plain bread. It is often asked why the meat in the sandwich was distorted in this way. Some would ascribe it to the Christian ethic, given that Constantine, whose laws mark the start of the process, was the first Christian emperor. But although this might explain the motivation, it does not explain the obfuscation. Others simply blame it on the imperial chancellery without suggesting why it was done. Others, again, argue that Constantine and his successors were simply the end-result of a process that had been going on, albeit in an accelerating fashion, ever since the first century AD. But then why did Justinian think that the classical approach, which had been in vogue until circa AD 250, had *preceded* the avalanche of rhetoric?

The solution that I have developed (Bauman 1980) and favour was first suggested by Honig (1960). It is, briefly, that rhetoric is a reflection of the uncertainty and instability of the fourth century. The empire had barely survived the shattering political, social and economic chaos of the third century, in which weak leadership had been an important factor. The authority and prestige of the ruler was at an all-time low, and rhetoric was employed to bolster the emperor's faltering authority. The heavier the padding surrounding one's words, the less easily could one's inability to enforce one's commands be detected.

BIBLIOGRAPHY

Archi, GC,1970, *Giustiniano Legislatore*, Mulino.

Bauman, RA, 1980, "The *leges iudiciorum publicorum* and their interpretation in the Republic, Principate and Later Empire", *Aufstieg und Niedergang der Römischen Welt*, vol II 13, Walter de Gruyter, pp 103-233.

Daube, D, 1956, *Forms of Roman Legislation*, Clarendon Press.

Dupont, C, 1953-55, *Le droit criminel dans les constitutions de Constantin*, Morel & Corduant.

Gaudemet, J, 1954, "L'empereur, interprète du droit", *Festschrift Rabel*, Mohr, p 169.

Honig, RM, 1960, *Humanitas und Rhetorik in spätrömischen Kaisergesetzen*, Schwartz.

Jolowicz, HF & Nicholas, B, 1972, *Historical Introduction to the Study of Roman Law*, 3rd edn, Cambridge University Press.

Schulz, F, 1936, *Principles of Roman Law*, Clarendon Press.

Schulz, F, 1946, *History of Roman Legal Science*, Clarendon Press.

Vonglis, B, 1968, *La lettre et l'esprit de la loi dans la jurisprudence et la rhétorique*, Sirey.

Wesel, U, 1967, *Rhetorische Statuslehre und Gesetzesauslegung der römischen Juristen*, Heymanns.

3

Rhetoric and The Law of Property in Early Sixteenth Century England

ANDREW BUCK

The sixteenth century in England was a period of great political turmoil and religious upheaval – but it was also an age which produced such important works of rhetoric and innovative literature as Thomas More's *Utopia,* Thomas Smith's *De Republica Anglorum,* Thomas Elyot's *Boke named the Governour,* Richard Morison's *Remedy for Sedition,* and Thomas Starkey's *Dialogue between Reginald Pole and Thomas Lupset.*[1] Starkey's *Dialogue* was written at some time in the early 1530s. The title is actually an invention of its nineteenth century editor, as the original was untitled and (as the only surviving manuscript in the author's own hand reveals) unfinished.

The book's growth in stature due to its importance to modern scholars is in large measure owing to its first publication in 1871 by JM Cowper. Interest in the rise of humanism in renaissance England, and the study of early forms of rhetoric, for example, have ensured the continuing interest in Thomas Starkey. A second edition of the *Dialogue* with modernised spelling was produced in 1948 by Kathleen Burton and a third, more exacting transcription, was published in 1989 by the prolific Starkey scholar, Thomas Mayer (1989a). Because the interest in Starkey's *Dialogue* has, by and large, been the province of literary and historical scholars interested in the question of English humanism, the prevailing interpretations of Starkey and his *Dialogue* have been influenced heavily by this focus.

Consequently, a wide range of scholars have seen in Starkey a remarkably tolerant, modern and liberal exponent of English humanism. The interpretation lies in FL Baumer's 1936 article on

1 For a useful survey of the relationship between literature and politics, see Fox (1989); also Halpern (1991) for a particularly interesting analysis of the relationship between literature and economic development in the sixteenth century.

Starkey, Fritz Caspari's 1954 study, *Humanism and the Social Order in Tudor England*, and Arthur Ferguson's 1965 examination of *The Articulate Citizen and the English Renaissance.* The orthodox interpretation can still be seen in Alastair Fox's 1986 reassessment of the Henrican Age. The source of this interpretation of Starkey as modern and liberal is the undeniable fact that, in the course of his Platonic *Dialogue*, opposing views are given a fair and equitable hearing. A spirit of intellectual pluralism seems to pervade the *Dialogue* that does, indeed, seem modern. Joel Altman (1978 p 38) pointed out in his study of sixteenth century rhetoric that:

> His method of counsel through a form that allows him to propose radical measures, then to modify them and supply more practical alternatives – suggests how constructively the spirit of debate, exercising its ethical neutrality, may be applied to public business.

Recently, however, a revisionist interpretation of Starkey has emerged from Thomas Mayer, who, in a relentless stream of articles and books in recent years, has argued for a less liberal, more conservative interpretation of Starkey.[2] Mayer, like his predecessors, has focussed on those elements of Starkey's writings, particularly his reflections on kingship, which seem so obviously relevant to the context of sixteenth century politics.[3] In this chapter, I would like to shift the focus to a critical but hitherto neglected topic in Starkey's *Dialogue* – the law of real property.

Starkey was born some time between 1495 and 1500. His family were wealthy Cheshire gentry, and he was educated at Magdalen College, Oxford. It was there he took his MA and met Reginald Pole, grandson to the Duke of Clarence. Starkey was to see in Pole the potential leader of a re-invigorated nobility who would reform and improve English political and social life, but it was to become clear that Pole was unwilling to take on this burden of responsibility – preferring the contemplative life of the emigré.[4]

In the early 1530s Starkey drafted his *Dialogue*, where issues relevant to the day were outlined and discussed. He used the nomenclatures of Reginald Pole and Thomas Lupset (a contemporary of Pole's who died in 1530) as the pegs upon which to hang his own ideas. This was a common literary device and does not necessarily reflect the views of either man. Desiring a more active role in public life, Starkey introduced himself to Thomas Cromwell, Henry VIII's chief royal advisor from 1529 to 1540, for whom he acted as a cipher of intelligence from the emigré community in Italy and was ultimately appointed the King's chaplain in 1535. It is clear that in both his life and his *Dialogue,* Starkey tried to curry favour with both sides of the political fence – the King, on the one hand, and the faction-ridden nobility (at a time when Henry was insisting on his

---

2 Mayer (1985), (1986), (1988), (1989b).
3 See, for example, Elton (1968).
4 Mayer (1985) pp vii-ix; also (1989) ch 1; Herrtage (1878).

divorce with all its religious consequences) on the other, and was ultimately appointed one of the King's chaplains in 1535. In 1536 when Pole, with whom he was closely associated in the Court's eyes, published a damning criticism of Henry's divorce, Starkey's fortunes waned briefly and his relationship with Cromwell ended. However, Starkey retained the favour of the King, who gave him a number of preferments and offices, before he died of natural causes in 1538.

It would appear that the King never read the *Dialogue* (which is perhaps just as well, as Starkey discussed with approval, limiting the powers of a tyrannical King. Whether Henry would have understood that Starkey was referring to a hypothetical tyrant is not clear). But Cromwell did read it and many of its intended aristocratic audience would have read or discussed it. In the *Dialogue* Starkey has Pole represent the voice of reason and theory, while Lupset argues practically, empirically and pragmatically. At the point we come in there has been an exchange on the question of whether the Crown should be hereditary or elective; a question which has deflected the attention of scholars from the fascinating reflections on primogeniture which follow. Pole argues:

> A like faut is in the succession of private men. You know by the order of our law, the elder brother succeeds, excluding all the other from any part of the inheritance. This is a thing, as me seemeth, far out of order; utterly to exclude the younger bretheren out of all part of the heritage, as though they were not children to the father or bretheren to the heir. Reason and nature utterly requireth that the children, which be as parts of the father and mother, should also be admitted to parts of the patrimony, that, even as they have brought them forth into the light, so their goods might maintain and succour them after in their life. Wherefore utterly to exclude them from all, as though they had committed some great offence and crime again their parents, is plainly again reason, and seems to minish the natural love betwix the father and the child, and also increase envy and hate betwix them which nature hath so bounden togidder. For betwix bretheren undoubtably this thing harms much of the brotherly love which nature hath planted and rooted. (Burton 1948 p 105)[5]

Obviously, Pole is pointing out the inequality of the law and custom; that it is contrary to both reason and nature. But this is, of course, a dialogue. So Lupset replies:

> Sir, as touching, this, I marvel at what you mean. Meseemeth you are about to utterly take away our policy and whole order of our ream. You note such things to be fauts wherein resteth all the honour of our country, and which is the ground for all good order and civility. (p 106)

Obviously Lupset is referring to the *political* realities of the law of primogeniture and it is the dominance of the political aspects of the primogeniture which inform the *Dialogue*. But this has not occurred

5 I have quoted from Burton's (1948 p 105) modernised edition rather than Mayer's more exacting 1989 transcription of the *Dialogue*, as Burton's edition, while less exact, is more readable.

to some critics, as we shall see. To return to the *Dialogue,* Pole then asks for Lupset's views on the matter:

> Sir, first, methinketh that this may be a safe and certain ground for the rest of our communication – that the laws are made for the people, and for the order of them, and not the people for the laws, to which, therefore, must be applied somewhat to the nature of them. Wherefore such laws, ordinances and statutes which contain in good order and rule are to be allowed and firstly to be received. (p 106)

Thus the laws regulate civil society:

> This, I think, was well considered by them which first institute this law of inheritance. They well considered the nature of our people, which by nature be somewhat rude and sturdy of mind, insomuch that if they had not in every place some heads and governors to temper their affects rude and unruly, there would among them be no order at all. And therefore it was not without course, as it appeareth ordained and stablished that in every great family the eldest should succeed, to maintain a head which by authority, dignity and power, should better contain the rudeness of the people. (p 106)

The turn of Starkey's mind should be obvious. But let him continue:

> For this is both certain and sure: that if the lands in every great family were distributed equally betwix the brethren, in a small process of years the head families would utterly vanish away. And so they people should be without rulers and heads, the which then by their rudeness and folly, would shortly disturb this quiet life and good policy which by many ages they have led here in our country – such should be the dissension and discord one with another. (p 107)

What would be the consequences of such a shift in the shape of civil society?

> Wherefore, Master Pole, if you take this away . . . you shall take away the foundation and ground of all our civility and besides this you shall therewith bring in the ruin of all nobility and ancient stocks. For if you from nobles take their great possessions, or minister any occasion to the same, you shall in process of years confound the nobles and the commons togidder, after such manner that there shall be no difference betwix the one and the other. (p 107)

Now here is the *real* import of the reflections on the law of inheritance. There are *political* considerations that far outweigh issues of equity, reason or the appeals to natural law. Starkey is showing, through Lupset's answer, the truly conservative bent of his mind. The people are too ignorant and too easily given to anarchy to run their own lives. They need rulers, and that is why primogeniture exists, and that is the end that is served by the consolidation of a ruling elite.

However, this has not stopped Arthur Ferguson, an influential literary critic, from interpreting these reflections on inheritance in a way that completely fails to see their political implications. Ferguson (1965 pp 375-6) argues that the appeal to reason by Pole should persuade Lupset the humanist:

> But we are here dealing with a generation of humanists who have fallen heir to the learning of a century and a half of classical scholarship and are able to go well beyond mere imitation of the ancients and to adapt classical precept and precedent to the realities of divergent cultures. Lupset accordingly presents another side of the argument. This he says is all very well in the abstract, but laws must conform to the character and conditions peculiar to any given people. Laws must, moreover, be judged to some extent pragmatically: the proof of their validity is that they work.

So Starkey has Lupset reply the way he does because of the character of humanist scholarship. Any notion that this *Dialogue* is set in a *political* context seems lost on Ferguson at this point.

Since the Platonic dialogue is a form designed to persuade the reader to a particular conclusion it is no surprise that Pole agrees with Lupset that the inequity primogeniture may cause for younger sons is far outweighed by recognition that, "the rudeness of our people requireth heads and governors to contain them in order and quietness", and the necessity that primogeniture be applied only to "great houses (as princes, dukes, earls and barons)" (Burton 1948 pp 107-8). You will note the exclusivity of the list. In order to appreciate this point, it may be useful to examine briefly the relationship between land law and social structure in early sixteenth century England in order to appreciate the debate over land law contained in Starkey's *Dialogue*.[6]

A critical point to be kept in mind with regard to the social structure in early Tudor England was that the aristocracy and the gentry were qualitatively distinct social classes. Hereditary lay peers numbered only approximately 60 in the early sixteenth century. These men were worth, on average, around £1000 per year and collectively they owned almost a fifth of all the land of England. By comparison, the gentry – so distinguished by their entitlement to a coat of arms – numbered approximately 6000. Compared to the landed wealth of the aristocracy, the landed incomes of the gentry were in general worth between £50 and £300 per year. In a very real sense, the aristocracy were a "class apart".[7]

Consequently, the ability to perpetuate estates from generation to generation was particularly important to the aristocracy with the rules of inheritance, and the extent to which the law facilitated inter-generational wealth preservation, being matters of *political* significance to them. Just as the law of primogeniture and the exclusion of the female line facilitated the perpetuation of the landed estate in the family, a similar process developed with regard to the noble title. By the fifteenth century all new noble titles were granted in tail male, whereby the title descended to the first born son alone (McFarlane 1973 p 273). By the early sixteenth century the application of primogeniture to both the descent of the landed estate

6 What follows draws to some extent on Buck (1990).
7 Mingay (1977 p 4); Cornwall (1965 p 471). See also Cornwall (1988).

and the noble title ensured the establishment of a nexus between the aristocracy and large landholding.

The implications of primogeniture were, of course, potentially worrying for younger sons. An overly strict application of the rule could lead to their impoverishment, however on the other hand, a less than strict application could disastrously affect the dynastic aspirations of the family. The temptation to favour younger sons in later medieval England resulted in impoverishing the title causing the aristocracy's distance from the gentry, as a class with access to power, to be diminished. Consequently, in the 14th and 15th centuries, testamentary practice swung back towards a more strict application of primogeniture (McFarlane pp 277-8). Simply, primogeniture was a tool, and its application a strategy of fundamental importance to the aristocracy in the consolidation and perpetuation of political and economic power. It was the scale of their landholdings moreover, which distinguished the aristocracy from the gentry. Indeed, it was the very strictness of the application of primogeniture which led to the debate over its implications for younger sons in early modern England (Thirsk 1976). With this in mind, we may better understand the subsequent reflections on inheritance in the *Dialogue*.

Pole is now in agreement with Lupset on the need to distinguish the nobility from the ordinary people. But that is not enough. Pole argues:

> For even like it is among nobles convenient to succeed after such manner, for the maintenance of the heads and of nobility, so it is again reason and all civil order to admit the same among the people commonly. But, Master Lupset, this faut sprang of a certain arrogance whereby, with the entailing of lands, every Jack would be a gentleman, and every gentleman a knight or a lord. (Burton 1948 p 108)

Here we get to the heart of the matter. Starkey was arguing that the nobility should be set apart – even from the gentry – and that all this emulation of one's betters had to stop.

Lupset agrees with Pole. This discussion of land law very clearly reveals Starkey's views on the subject:

> I have ever thought this manner of entailing lands commonly not to be allowed by just policy. Wherefore methink this is a faut worthy now to be spoken of also, for this entailing, especially after such manner only to the eldest son in every base family, maketh many reckless heirs, causeth them little to regard neither learning nor virtue, in as much as they are sure to be inheritors of entailed land, and so, by this assurance, they give themselves to all vanity and pleasure, without respect. (p 109)

In response Pole notes that the law does not command entailing but merely permits it. Lupset replies:

> Marry, that is the thing also that I reprove. For though in great houses such entailing may be suffered for the maintenance of the

> family, yet in the base families . . . surely it is nothing convenient, for as much as it bringeth in great inequality and so much hate and malice among the community. Wherefore this is no small error in the order of our law, and may well be coupled with the other. (p 109)

Due to the political implications of land law in early modern England, Starkey's words held a particularly forceful import for his contemporaries.[8] The land law was feudal in structure and in theory there was no absolute ownership of land. All rights in land rested with the Crown, and the King then distributed use-rights to his tenants (Milsom 1977). Thus, land ownership was tenurial rather than allodial. The services exacted as conditions of the tenure were originally military. A particular tenure usually required some form of military service – the exact nature of the service depending on the conditions and type of tenure. However, as the military character of feudal England receded in the late medieval period, a corresponding transformation occurred in the tenure of land (Kerridge 1969). Tenants increasingly relieved themselves of the burden of military service by way of a fixed monetary payment known as *scuttage*. The rise of scuttage highlights the move away from services as the most desirable return from the granting of the tenure towards incidents – monetary payments in one form or another – that took place from the twelfth century on.

The alienation of land, for example, involved the consent of the superior lord, and monetary *fines* were imposed for that consent. If the tenant died without an heir the land would *escheat* or revert to the superior lord, who could then grant a new and (for the lord) more profitable tenure to another tenant. If the tenant died when the heir was under age, the heir and his estate would remain in *ward* of the lord, until the heir's majority. Even if he was of age when the tenant died, before the heir could claim his inheritance, another incident was imposed known as *primer seisin* to the lord and the payment of a *relief* to the incoming tenant. By the early sixteenth century, these incidents were extremely lucrative to the superior lord (Baker 1979 pp 205-10). Yet here too, a transformation had taken place. In 1290 the practice of subinfeudination, or the creation of new tenures by the tenants of superior lords, was abolished by the Statute *Quia Emptores*. This consolidated the position of the aristocracy with respect to their tenants, and in particular the extraction of feudal incidents from their tenants. But *fines* for alienation were also abolished for all but the Crown in 1290. Consequently, only the tenants *in capite* (holding directly from the Crown) that is, the aristocracy, were subject to this incident. Indeed, in the transformation of the nature of feudal tenure from the twelfth to the sixteenth centuries away from services and towards incidents, it was the Crown which most consistently used feudal incidents as a source of revenue, and it was the tenants *in capite* who felt the burden of

---

8 What follows draws in part from Buck (1991).

those incidents most heavily. The incentive for the aristocracy to make the payment of the incidents of tenure was accordingly high.

While land was inheritable, moreover, the feudal land law did not allow for testamentary capacity. This effectively strengthened the degree of control by the superior lord, in particular the Crown, over the tenant, especially the tenants *in capite* – the aristocracy. For this reason the legal profession, at the behest of the aristocracy, developed the conveyancing practice known as "the use", in early modern England (Ives 1967). As the law did not allow for testamentary capacity in theory, such capacity had to be applied in practice. The use was a procedure in which the legal interest in the estate was divested from the owner and placed in the hands of another party (the trustees) who then held the land for the use of the owner and whoever else was indicated in the settlement which effected the use (Baker 1977). The land was thus entailed, for one purpose of the settlement was to allow for the testamentary capacity which the common law prohibited. The estate was held by the trustees on behalf of the eldest son who resettled the estate on taking up his inheritance on his majority. From the point of view of the conflicting interests of the aristocracy and the Crown with respect to the incidents of tenure, the implications of the use were profound. As the legal estate was divested from the owner, then the owner's death and the subsequent transfer of the estate to his heir did not affect the legal estate. Consequently, *fines* on alienation, *escheat*, *primer seisin* – all could be evaded. In addition, the secrecy of the transactions provided by the use, masked the identification of the owner, thus further facilitating the evasion of feudal dues.

These were the circumstances in which Henry VIII began a campaign for the reintroduction of feudal dues in the late 1520s, when Starkey was writing the *Dialogue*.[9] In 1529 an agreement was signed with some 30 peers regarding proposed legislation to grant testamentary capacity over two-thirds of the nobles' lands in exchange for payment of feudal dues on the remaining one-third. However, Henry's "great matter" slowed progress on the Bill and Cromwell may have reduced the guaranteed devisory capacity to a half. When the lords prevaricated, Henry moved the battle to the courts and successfully ensured that, with the defeat of the Dacre inheritance, the use was declared invalid. Parliament had no choice but to accept the Statute of Uses in 1535 which invalidated the use and restored all feudal incidents to the Crown by simply enacting that the equitable owner was also the legal owner (Ives 1967). This, then, was the historical and legal context in which Starkey drafted the *Dialogue* at some time between 1529 and the early 1530s.

Thus we may more fully appreciate Starkey's reflections of primogeniture and entail in the *Dialogue*. To argue as Ferguson does, that the reflections on the law of inheritance are only to be

9 The following is described in some detail in Buck (1990).

understood with reference to the intellectual framework of the English humanist seems inadequate. When Ferguson (1963 pp 376-7) reflects that Starkey's views on entailing – the appeal to reason tempered by pragmatism – are evidence of the "times when Starkey stains the white radiance of pure reason with an almost Burkean sense of historical realitivity", he seems to me to be not sufficiently cognisant of the political issues regarding property contained in the *Dialogue*. Similarly, Thomas Mayer's (1989 p 130) otherwise perceptive revisionist interpretation, which has rejected the "liberal" Starkey for a more "conservative" Starkey, is less adequate when it argues that Starkey treats the nobility and the gentry on the same level. Although Mayer himself admits that the reflections on primogeniture and entail are an exception to the interpretation, they do seem to me to be a rather large exception, considering the importance of property to power in early sixteenth century England.

Finally, as an indication of the degree to which an appreciation of Starkey's *Dialogue* is enriched by an understanding of the politics of England's land law in the late 1520s, there is evidence of a draft Bill of 1529 dealing with the law respecting landed property (Lehmberg 1970). This Bill which was never enacted, proposed the abolition of all future entails by commoners, while all existing entails were to be converted to fee simple. The aristocracy, however, under the provisions of the Bill, were to be allowed to create entails, albeit with the sale of their lands to be permitted only by royal license. Had it been enacted, such a Bill would have had the effect of distinguishing the nobility legally as a caste (Plucknett 1936). It would have not only facilitated the consolidation of aristocratic estates, but would also have made the lands of nobles virtually inalienable. If enacted, the Bill would have fundamentally altered the relationship between landownership and political power. But the draft Bill was a document of dubious origin. It was not mentioned in the Lords Journals of any subsequent session. Technically, the wording of the Bill was rather naive, and it seems to have been the work of an amateur, whose identity we do not know. When Lupset argues that, "though in great houses such entailing may be suffered for the maintenance of the family, yet in the base families . . . surely it is nothing convenient. . ." he immediately adds, "Wherefore this is not small error in the order of the law, and may well be coupled with the other" (Burton 1948 p 109). This was indeed the intention of the draft Bill of 1529.

Thomas Starkey's *Dialogue* illustrates the use of literary sources in illuminating the role of law in society, while at the same time demonstrating the absolute necessity of understanding one's legal history in order to make effective use of those sources.

BIBLIOGRAPHY

Altman, Joel B, 1978, *The Tudor Play of Mind: Rhetorical Inquiry and the Development of Elizabethan Drama,* University of California Press.

Baker, JH, 1977, "Introduction to the Reports of Sir John Spelman", *Selden Society,* 94, pp 192-202.

Baker, JH, 1979, *An Introduction to English Legal History,* Butterworths.

Baumer, FL, 1936, "Thomas Starkey and Marsilius of Padna", *Politica,* II.

Buck, AR, 1990, "The Politics of Land Law in Tudor England, 1529-1540", *Journal of Legal History,* vol 11, no 2.

Buck, AR, 1991, "English Feudalism and the Transformation of the Land Law, 1285-1290", Australian Historians of Medieval and Early Modern Europe Conference, University of Adelaide, unpublished paper.

Burton, Kathleen M (ed), 1948, *A Dialogue between Reginald Pole and Thomas Lupset,* Chatto and Windus.

Caspari, Fritz, 1954, *Humanism and the Social Order in Early Tudor England,* Teacher's College Press.

Cornwall, JCK, 1965, "The Early Tudor Gentry", *Economic History Review,* 2nd ser, 17.

Cornwall, JCK, 1988, *Wealth and Society in Early Sixteenth Century England,* Routledge and Kegan Paul.

Cowper, JM (ed), 1871, *A Dialogue between Cardinal Pole and Thomas Lupset, lecturer in Rhetoric at Oxford by Thomas Starkey, Chaplain to the King,* Extra Series, no 12, Early English Text Society.

Elton, GF, 1968, "Reform by Statute: Thomas Starkey's *Dialogue* and Thomas Cromwell's Policy", *Proceedings of the British Academy,* LIV.

Ferguson, Arthur B, 1963, "The Tudor Commonwealth and the Sense of Change", *Journal of British Studies,* III.

Ferguson, Arthur B, 1965, *The Articulate Citizen and the English Renaissance,* Duke University Press.

Fox, Alastair, 1986, "Facts and Fallacies: Interpreting English Humanism" in Fox, Alistair & Guy, John, 1986, *Reassessing the Henrician Age: Humanism, Politics and Reform 1500-1550,* Basil Blackwell.

Fox, Alistair, 1989, *Politics and Literature in the Reigns of Henry VII and Henry VIII,* Basil Blackwell.

Halpern, Richard, 1991, *The Poetics of Primitive Accumulation: English Renaissance Culture and the Geneology of Capital,* Cornell University Press.

Herrtage, Sidney J (ed), 1878, *England in the Reign of King Henry the Eighth,* Pt 1, *Starkey's Life and Letters,* Extra Series, no 32, Early English Text Society.

Ives, EW, 1967, "The Genesis of the Statute of Uses", *English Historical Review,* cccxxv.

Kerridge, E, 1969, *Agrarian Problems in the Sixteenth Century and After,* George Allen and Unwin.

Lehmberg, SE, 1970, *The Reformation of Parliament 1529-1536,* Cambridge University Press.

McFarlane, KB, 1973, *The Nobility of Later Medieval England,* Oxford University Press.

Mayer, TF, 1985, "Faction and Ideology: Thomas Starkey's *Dialogue*", *The Historical Journal*, XXViii.

Mayer, TF, 1986, "Thomas Starkey's aristocratic reform programme", *History of Political Thought,* VII.

Mayer, TF, 1988, "Thomas Starkey, an unknown conciliarist at the court of Henry VIII", *Journal of the History of Ideas,* XLIX, 2.

Mayer, TF (ed), 1989a, *A Dialogue between Pole and Lupset*, Royal Historical Society.

Mayer, TF, 1989b, *Thomas Starkey and the Commonweal: Humanist Politics and Religion in the Reign of Henry VIII*, Cambridge University Press.

Mingay, GE, 1977, *The Gentry: The Rise and Fall of a Ruling Class*, Longman.

Milsom, C, 1977, *The Legal Framework of English Feudalism*, Cambridge University Press.

Plucknett, TF, 1936, "Some Proposed Legislation of Henry VIII", *Transactions of the Royal Historical Society*, 4th ser, 19.

Slavin, AJ, 1970, "Profitable Studies: Humanists and Government in Early Tudor England", *Viator*, I.

Thirsk, J, 1976, "The European Debate on Customs of Inheritance" in Goody, J, Thirsk, J & Thompson, EP (eds), 1976, *Family and Inheritance: Rural Society in Western Europe, 1200-1800*, Cambridge University Press.

Zeeveld, W Gordon, 1948, *Foundations of Tudor Policy*, Harvard University Press.

4

Burke's Law: Edmund Burke's Politics and Aesthetics of Terror

GEOFF WINDON

At a time when the world is experiencing the apparent dissolution of Stalinist dictatorships in eastern Europe and in what used to be the Soviet Union it seems appropriate to reflect on the history of counterrevolutionary interpretations of revolution. In particular, Edmund Burke might be regarded as an important prophet of that dissolution, and as an influential example of a certain intellectual style – that of the anti-ideological ideologue. But Burke is no vulgar empiricist or apologist for some vernacular "common sense"; rather he addresses seriously and with some originality the problem of the derivation or origination of authority, of the legitimacy of the law. To what higher tribunal ought the law be subjected? How may we decide, and in whose name, whether the law is itself lawful? Of course Burke's answer is well enough known: by reference to the aesthetic, and in the name of God. Thus he will argue in his 1790 *Reflections on the Revolution in France* (*Reflections*) (Burke 1975 vol iii p 317) that a political action such as "leading a king in triumph" may be judged as if it were a theatrical representation, his assumption being that in this case good taste will also be good politics.[1]

---

1 According to Burke (1975, vol iii p 317), Dr Richard Price in his November 1789 sermon to the Revolution Society had responded to the violent abduction of the royal family from Versailles in the previous October – "leading a king in triumph" – by quoting from the "*nunc dimittis*": "Lord, now lettest thou thy servant depart in peace, for mine eyes have seen thy salvation". However, Price argued in his preface to the fourth edition (1790) of the address in question, the *Discourse on the Love of our Country* (London 1789), and Mary Wollstonecraft insisted in her reply to Burke (also 1790), that this was a misrepresentation (see Todd & Butler 1989 vol v, p 25 and n). Price claimed to have beens referring at this point (*Discourse* pp 49-50) to the king's "voluntary" submission to the National Assembly in July 1789, not to the abduction from Versailles in October of that year. This attribution bears a great deal of weight in the *Reflections*, since it concerns the occasion which more than any other is the means employed by Burke to establish his moral and political superiority to Price and to those reformers and revolutionaries – Burke does not distinguish between the two – supposed to be like him.

Aesthetic response can adjudicate in relation to the law because it is itself law-abiding: it proceeds from the nature of the body, which was made by God. To adopt a formulation which is a little more explicitly dialectical than any of Burke's we might say that the aesthetic is that representation which returns the law to itself, which reveals it to itself in its relation to a more original, divine and paternal authority. An aesthetic moment – let us say simply "literature" – is internal to and constitutive of the law to the extent that it can be adjudged legitimate and can thence command assent, can form part of a coherent social fabric or of the history and heritage of a people. The law in action, as realised or enacted, must also *be* literature or *be as* literature, in order to be itself. But to state the issue this way is to raise the question of metaphor, of this *being as*: is the relation of the law to literature literary – ie aesthetic – or is it lawful? Or is it both or neither? It is apropos of this question that Burke will introduce his great theme of revolution, which will be inseparable from a discourse on the constituting and disintegrating propensities of figures, tropes or "turns of speech", on various modalities of turning to or turning from, and of returning. In doing so, I would like to suggest, he also raises some issues which are pertinent to formalist and historicist approaches to both literary studies and the law.

Before proceeding to a discussion of Burke's major work of political philosophy it will be useful to outline briefly some relevant concepts from his 1757 *A Philosophical Enquiry into the Origin of our Ideas of the Sublime and Beautiful* (*Enquiry*) (Boulton 1968). As is so often the case, Burke's aesthetics is a politics in embryo. It attempts a derivation of the "social passions", of the affective, irrational but providential bases of social existence. This derivation involves a constellation of three main concepts. Most obviously there is sublimity, which is associated with difference, pain, terror, masculinity and the individual self; and there is beauty, which is aligned with similarity or resemblance, with pleasure and love, with femininity, and with society. We would also be justified in connecting sublimity with the law and beauty with literature, provided that we bear in mind that literature has its own laws and the law its own, perhaps austere, beauties. Lastly, there is what Burke calls *indifference* – not, as you might be tempted to think, an absence of differences, but a whole dimension of differences which fail to register on the aesthetic scale of pleasure or pain. Indifference belongs to neither the experience of sublimity nor that of beauty but is the "normal" state of the body from which they deviate and to which they return. However, this normality is not one of health or liveliness, it is rather a degenerative, disorderly drifting towards madness and death. Thus, for an argument which is grounded in the properties and potentialities of the body, there is surprisingly little in the *Enquiry* of what would conventionally be called vitalism. The aesthetic and political life of the body is to be found only in its difference from itself, in its circulation between these various states. Comparatively little is said about indifference in Burke's aesthetics but we will see shortly that this always crucial concept or one or another of its affiliates becomes much more prominent when the life of the state is on the line.

The *Reflections* argues strenuously in favour of rejecting the application of what are described variously as "metaphysical", "abstract", "speculative" or "geometric" modes of reasoning to practical political questions. The polemic is designed to interrupt a dangerous process of speculative scrutiny of the origins of political authority, and to set a limit to speculation and criticism by establishing that authority on grounds which would be unassailable by these means. More specifically it attempts to provide a refutation of and an alternative to social contract theory in its most accepted post-Lockean forms, with the conclusion drawn from it of a right residing in the people of "cashiering kings for misconduct".[2] This last was the argument of the dissenting minister, Dr Richard Price, in his sermon of 4 November 1789 to the Revolution Society, which became Burke's foil in the *Reflections*. The object here is to undo the potential havoc that Dr Price has wrought by confusing the Glorious Revolution of 1688, which it was the function of the Revolution Society to commemorate and which was the symbolic foundation of Burke's own Whig orthodoxy, with the contemporary events in France. The issue is that of the meanings of revolution.

According to Ronald Paulson (1983 p 50), Burke was the first important British writer to use the word "revolution" in the radical French sense referring to a total transformation of social relations, as opposed both to political reform and to notions of cyclical continuity:

> The conflict lay between the strictly astronomical sense of repetition, a full circle, and the sense of a single revolution as an overthrow, a half-circle, a disruption, and so an irreversible change. Already in Swift's *Tale of a Tub* (1704), a book about forms of mental, political, religious, and social subversion, the word revolution is used to refer to an enthusiast's overturning of his brain or of the state.

Burke actually employs both of these senses in the *Reflections*, the newer one in referring to the events in France, and the older in relation to the progressive nature of the English constitution. Thus he affirms that "the inheritable principle survived with a sort of immortality through all transmigrations. . . This is the spirit of our constitution, not only in its settled course, but in all its revolutions" (p 260). Clearly a certain ambiguity arises in this schematisation, one which Burke will not always be able to control, since one person's social apocalypse (or half-circle) may be a constitutive moment in another's progressive dialectic (or full circle).

Burke pointedly retains the old concept of "constitution", however, disallowing Paine's sense of a unique foundational

2 This expression, of which we hear much in *Reflections*, originated with Andrew Kippis, William Godwin's editor and formerly his tutor, in an address to the Revolution Society in 1788, to be taken up by Price the following year. See Locke 1980 p42.

document enunciating principles, or self-evident natural rights, and the conclusions drawn from them deductively. For Paine such a document would approximate to a consistent codification, a theory of true or authentic social relations which would be actualised, where necessary, by revolutionary means. Burke opposes both this speculative, deductive mode *and* empirical induction, on behalf of what might be termed "hermeneutic reason".[3] In this view the British "constitution", like any other worthy of the name, is a comprehensive implied or immanent order which is the object of an *interpretation*. The constitution is the way in which things are constituted, ultimately by divine fiat. Thus it comprises no single document, but is the necessary principle of all documentation; it has no unique beginning in the world, since it is through it that a world of social experience begins.

This also means, for Burke (Burke 1975 vol v p 169), that society is severed from nature: "The idea of a people . . . is wholly artificial; and made, like all other legal fictions, by common agreement." The severance of the law and the state from nature, from natural rights, is the condition of the constitution of civil society. Still, this discontinuity is compensated for by "philosophic analogy": "Our political system is placed in a just correspondence and symmetry with the order of the world, and with the mode of existence decreed to a permanent body composed of transitory parts" (1975 p 275). It is important to note that this naturalism is metaphorical and illustrative rather than substantial. Burke is wary of the effects of metaphor in relation to theoretical knowledge, and is careful to emphasise elsewhere that "These analogies between bodies natural and politic, though they may sometimes illustrate arguments, furnish no argument of themselves" (1975 vol v p 124), that "Parallels of this sort rather furnish similitudes to illustrate or to adorn than to supply analogies from whence to reason" (p 234).[4] The similitude is in fact,

---

3 For example *Reflections*, p 312: "The science of government . . . requires . . . even more experience than any person can gain in his whole life, however sagacious and observing he may be". That is, it requires the collective wisdom of tradition but this is not, as it might appear, simply an extended process of induction. See below.

4 Burke (1975, vol v pp 124, 234). These are the scruples which render analogy "philosophic". For a fuller discussion see Love (1965, p 184) and also Dreyer (1979 pp 77-8). Turner (1987, p 48) makes a contrary point with reference to a passage in which the young Burke states that, "Arguments concerning the Nature of any being can only be taken from the Investigation of its Properties and the Analogy they bear to each other" (Somerset 1957 p 45). But "analogy" here appears to refer to relationships obtaining within a single entity considered as a system of those relationships for the purpose of arguing or reasoning about it. The organic analogy in the *Reflections* flirts with a further assimilation of this unavoidable systematisation conferred by language to the presumed spontaneity of other types of systems with which it is not continuous, but should not be read as directly naturalising what are nothing other than social fictions, if also "true" ones. The aesthetic paths from the body to language and to politics and back do not follow the direct road of analogy, but instead the circuitous routes of reflection, idealisation, and sublimation.

as the above passage goes on to explain, between the state, presided over by an hereditary monarchy, and the patriarchal family.

Nevertheless, this is more than a mere illustration: it has a practical rather than a cognitive justification. It is imagery, primarily metaphor, which binds up in mutual reflection the beautiful fiction of a people by transporting particular, familial affections in the direction of general laws, connecting the species-life to social institutions. Whereas organic metaphors provide from a theoretical viewpoint mere "illustration" and are unreliable, metaphor is generally an indispensable organising principle, a deceit woven into the fabric of things which defines art as natural to man, as constitutive.

Burke would establish discontinuity as the sublime truth of metaphor. The visible does not imitate the invisible world, it implies or presupposes it. A history and a people are engendered when social experience is deciphered as *if* it were an instantiation of universal values. The unreliability of metaphor, which figures in the *Enquiry* in terms of the degenerative character of indifference, here necessitates both the temporal and structural differentiation, the attribution of a history and the affirmation of a hierarchy or class system – the political sublime – which constitutes a people, much as in the earlier text it had required the production of an aesthetic.[5]

Such is Burke's crucial application of the legal concept of prescription, of the principle that possession, having perpetuated itself over a period of time, amounts to "the most solid of all titles, not only to property, but, which is to secure that property, to government" (Burke 1975 vol vii p 94). The temporal, narrative or narratable origins of authority are irrelevant for Burke, since even the product of "old violence", if it maintains itself, "is consecrated by time and becomes lawful" (Copeland 1958-78 vol vi p 45). Time distances, sublimates and beautifies violence, and in doing so legitimates it. Similarly, Burke argues in jaunty defiance of the tradition of enlightened critique that prejudices can usually be demonstrated to be the repositories of a collective "latent wisdom", that they are more reliable and more efficacious than rational judgment. Because "we are afraid to put men to live and trade each on his own private stock of reason" the English cherish their prejudices: "Prejudice is of ready application in the emergency; it . . . does not leave the man hesitating in the moment of decision, sceptical, puzzled and unresolved" (Burke 1975 vol iii p 347).

Of course, the type of emergency under discussion is just such as may lend itself to puzzlement and irresolution:

5 In the *Enquiry* metaphor (substitution) degenerates because it is not finally distinguishable from metonymy (contiguity), and threatens to drag down with it other associated conceptual couples such as necessity/chance, pain/pleasure, terror/love, masculine/feminine, and individual/society. The principal objective of Burke's aesthetics is to circumvent this degeneration, to preserve and to enforce those distinctions.

> The question of . . . "cashiering kings", will always be, as it has always been, an extraordinary question of state, and wholly out of the law; a question (like all other questions of state) of dispositions, and of means, and of probable consequences, rather than of positive rights . . . The speculative line of demarcation, where obedience ought to end, and resistance must begin, is faint, obscure, and not easily definable (Burke 1975, vol 3 p 270-1).

Questions of state, those which pertain to constitutionality and to politics, are, per se, "wholly outside the law" to the extent that they concern the possibility of laws, the assumed matrix for the enunciation of juridical discourses and prejudices alike.[6] In their highest form they require an art of statecraft involving a deliberation which accordingly is not subject to theoretical determination.

The "speculative line" is here multiple or impure, it shapes no definite contour, no simple limit. This is a sphere not determinable by "abstract" reason alone, but fortunately "It is far from impossible to reconcile, if we do not suffer ourselves to be entangled in the mazes of metaphysic sophistry, the use both of a fixed rule and an occasional deviation" (Burke 1975, vol 3 p 258). This is because the rule or law is not to be thought of as mirroring a real or a possible world, as being susceptible of any direct realisation or application, any more than it is possible, as the *Enquiry* pointed out, to read a poem by visualising its imagery.[7] The speculative line is impure because the metaphoricity which constitutes the rule, which relates it to its instances or examples, is essentially discontinuous. The idea of the rule is internally incoherent, is already deviant, so is in need of a supplementary, corrective deviation. In the *Reflections* and elsewhere Burke can write as if such social upheavals as are discussed are contingent upon particular abuses and are no intrinsic part of the constitution of society. But whereas overt and massive social upheavals, like all questions of state, involve a process of factoring an immense, indeed an illimitable diversity of empirical elements, revolution is at all times immanent to the constitution because that which constitutes in the constitution, along with the various aids and supplements which it necessitates, is metaphorical discontinuity.

---

6 One effect of Burke's argument in this connection is to erode the distinction between judgment and prejudice. Judgment only maintains itself by means of a normally forgotten or concealed appeal to prejudice, in the same way that legitimacy is ultimately dependent on prescription.

7 See Burke in Boulton (1968 p 167). Burke's point here does not rely, as Boulton suggests, on the failure to recognise that "the argument about the effect of language in hurried conversation does not necessarily apply to the reading of poetry" (Boulton 1968 p lxxix). It is independent of the practical contingency expressed in such an objection. Since the verbal and the pictorial are non-symmetrical, strictly incommensurable orders associated primarily by means of conventions and by considerations of utility, each can only be subjected to the protocols of the other at the expense of the reduction, if not in large measure the destruction, of all that is specific to the subjected term. Remaining faithful to the poetic and linguistic mode means violating the orderliness and intelligibility of the sensible and its simulacra, collapsing them into a chaos or madness from which we normally and properly avert our attention.

Revolutions of one sort or another are endemic to the system, and another name for the benign concept of immanent revolution is reproduction. Upon this recognition Burke, with some justification, pins his claim to advance a progressive conservatism which would stress combining the process of social reproduction with the maximum flexibility compatible with the preservation of order and legitimacy.

Whereas in the *Enquiry* Burke's task was to police a separation of beauty from sublimity, in the *Reflections* the object is to separate the sublime Glorious Revolution from its modern counterpart as an instance of a false sublime, of what happens when beauty and sublimity (or literature and the law) get all mixed up. Beauty is epitomised in this text above all by the consciously sentimentalised and idealised figure of Marie Antoinette, an example of the "embodiment" of social institutions in persons "so as to create in us love, veneration, admiration, or attachment". But Burke is clear that "embodiment" is also concealment. Such beautiful women and other symbolic love-objects are "pleasing illusions" with which the moral imagination clothes "the defects of our naked shivering nature". Without them laws lack visible support and so are thrown back, we are told, on "their own terrors":

> These public affections, combined with manners, are required sometimes as supplements, sometimes as correctives, always as aids to the law. The precept given by a wise man, as well as a great critic, for the construction of poems, is equally true as to states. *Non satis est pulchra esse poemata, dulcia sunto. . .*[8] To make us love our country, our country ought to be lovely (1975, vol 3 p 334).

Just how such women aid the law becomes clearer when it is recognised that Marie Antoinette dominates the argument, quite eclipsing her husband, inasmuch as she is the object at once of a threat which is implicitly sexual as well as mortal, and of a chivalrous sublimation.[9] She is the screen upon which it is possible to project a threat or fantasy of revolutionary sexual violence, and which serves to conceal from itself an all too imperious, a defective masculine and constitutionalist desire, the excess of which is at once represented and mastered in its chivalrous traversal of the feminine body. Like poems and like states women should be both beautiful and

8 The quotation is from Horace, *De Arte Poetica* 99: "It is not sufficient for poems to be beautiful, they must please".

9 Such a strategy is to be observed in the symbolic stripping and rape of the queen by the mob (*Reflections*, p 325), depicted with probable historical inaccuracy by Burke – there appears to be no evidence that she had to fly "almost naked" from her bedchamber (Paulson, p 60). Here the queen's nudity serves to clothe a more complex, a less easily represented occasion. See Paulson (pp 61-2) for a discussion of Burke's conception of revolution as the destructive liberation of masculine appetite, and see also Blakemore's characterisation (pp 43-4) of Burke's thematics of male sexual exploitation. There is a good deal in the *Reflections* about the subversion of aristocratic feminine virtue by parvenu (bourgeois or marginal) males, in effect reversing the radicals' charge of immorality against the aristocracy and in particular against aristocratic women – notably Marie Antoinette.

enticing embodiments; they are "aids to the law" in as much as they are "pleasing illusions" which protect the law and masculine desire from itself, from its own terrorism. In this way terror directed specifically toward women is a constitutive moment in Burke's derivation of political authority. It is part of the constitution of things.

In the *Letters on a Regicide Peace* of 1796-97 (Copeland 1958-78), Burke gives us a glimpse of what we are to understand it is that these "embodiments" normally and properly conceal, but which he is now quite keen to exhibit to us. It involves a trope destined to be given another celebrated turn when it reappeared in *The Communist Manifesto*, but not without losing at least one particular feature of interest. This is Burke (p 237):

> out of the tomb of the murdered monarchy in France has arisen a vast, tremendous, unformed spectre in a far more terrific guise than any which ever yet have overpowered the imagination, and subdued the fortitude of man. Going straight forward to its end, unappalled by peril, unchecked by remorse, despising all common maxims and all common means, that hideous phantom overpowered those who could not believe it was possible she could at all exist .

Burke was quick to join the émigré opponents of the revolutionary government in portraying Marianne, the new symbol of France and a full sister to the goddesses of Liberty and of Reason, as a vengeful or dangerously contagious whore. We read in the *Reflections* (p 280) that, "France has not sacrificed her virtue to her interest; but she has abandoned her interest, that she might prostitute her virtue". She has become a whore, but this is a whoredom abstracted from the mitigating forms of economic intelligibility and determination, and so from the orderly cycle of production and reproduction, within which she might function as an aid or supplement to marriage. She is a whore who does not even care to get a good price. Instead there is a collapse of values to effect not a regulated exchange but an unrestrained profligacy, an uncompensated outgoing of interest *and* of virtue. Likewise, to the insurrectionary mob who consort with her without having acquired property rights in her she will communicate the diseases, but not the virtues, of wealth and power.

In the *Reflections* Burke is much, and properly, concerned with France's economic difficulties, and in particular with inflation as a consequence of a too prolific printing of money. This takes the form of a "swelling" comparable to that attributed by Longinus to the false sublime, "the direct antithesis to elevation" (Roberts 1899 p 49). In one memorable passage the operation of "the great machine, or paper-mill, of their fictitious wealth" (p 392) produces, "a process of continual transmutation of paper into land, and land into paper . . . by this kind of operation, that species of property becomes (as it were) volatilised; it assumes an unnatural and monstrous activity . . . and . . . has now acquired the worst and most pernicious part of the evil of a paper circulation, the greatest possible uncertainty in its value" (p 486).

For a very useful discussion of this aspect of the text see Furniss (1987 p 54) where Burke is characterised as a sympathiser with the new economics of Adam Smith, who "yet seems to feel that the only way to maintain the conditions necessary for its success is to introduce it in disguise" (p 69). It is clear that the rule which must cover its nakedness in order to preserve itself is, amongst other things, the rule of capitalist accumulation, which must be encumbered by aristocratic prerogative and inherited wealth. However, for Burke the disguise is not a simple dissimulation, it is constitutive of the rule. We shall see that, as Furniss also points out (pp 63 ff), Burke himself is not immune to the monstrous (*monstrare*: to show) activity of the inflationary rhetorical machine.

It should go without saying that while Burke has a practical politician's eye to utility he is not a utilitarian, any more than because he accepts consent as a criterion of legitimacy (weaker, of course, than prescription) he should be considered a social contract theorist in the Lockean sense. In the *Reflections* he argues not only that the revolution has impoverished France, but that the relation between revolution (of the French type) and impoverishment is a *necessary* one, which conclusion, as he recognises, is not subject to empirical verification. But such an observation leaves the status of the empirical in Burke rather unclear. In the *Enquiry* (Boulton 1968 p 175) we read that, "all verbal description, merely as naked description, though never so exact, conveys so poor and insufficient an idea of the thing described, that it could scarcely have the smallest effect, if the speaker did not call to his aid those modes of speech that mark a strong and lively feeling in himself".

It must be emphasised that in such passages Burke is concerned both with the persuasive and more fundamentally with the constitutive operations of rhetoric. Thus verbal description mirrors and is mirrored by corporeal indifference or anaesthesis: the purely cognitive or empirical (the "real") is self-disfiguring, denaturing, and so is uninhabitable for the being whose nature is defined by its deviance from nature (see *Appeal* p 176). In the *Reflections* the necessary, true *divine* constitution of the social body, which is the notional object of traditional wisdom, of the experience which is accrued across the generations as a form of collective intellectual capital, is a moral illusion which conceals the foundational character of a defective, arbitrary or violent, *human* fiat. Questions of empirical verification therefore remain important but at the same time are severely limited and highly problematic, are in a sense a pretext for the maintenance of a corporeal and societal vigour whose character is aesthetic, that is to say a supplementary deviation from the purely cognitive or empirical which is called forth by its radical deficiency. Empiricity is in this sense constituted and made habitable by the aesthetic, by the social, and by language, given the dependence of the social on "compounded abstract words" which are "in reality but mere sounds" (Boulton 1968, p 165) rather than empirical "essences". Discourse thus has a "mixed" character (p 167), both empirical and "transcendental", and in its circulation between these two components comprises an inflationary machine comparable to that described in the passage from the *Reflections* quoted above.

According to the *Reflections* society requires that men's inclinations be thwarted and passions controlled by a power outside themselves. But democracy means a lack of distance between agent and instrument or between subject and object. It means a lack of mediation through the hierarchisation of power, which is ultimately divine mediation provided by the constitution under which "all who administer in the government of men . . . stand in the person of God himself" (1975, vol 3 p 353). In effect there is a disappearance of the legal fiction of agency: in a democracy the law, according to Burke's hermeneutic model, becomes a message with neither sender nor receiver – incomprehensible and irrelevant. The will of all would be a fiction, but not less dangerous for that; it would be as capricious and unaccountable as a force of nature:

> where popular authority is absolute and unrestrained, the people have an infinitely greater, because a far better founded confidence in their own power. . . Their own approbation of their own acts has to them the appearance of a public judgment in their favour. A perfect democracy is therefore the most shameless thing in the world. As it is the most shameless it is also the most fearless . . . for as all punishments are for example towards the conservation of the people at large, the people at large can never become the subject of punishment by any human hand (1975, vol 3 p 354-5).[10]

This is the half-circle as interregnum or as interruption, as social dissolution. It is accordingly also the exhibiting of what should not be seen or represented, what is interdicted by "moral taste": the false because "feminine" or "democratic" sublime.[11] In the case of this

---

10 See Griffin (1981 p 22): "the old Biblical notion of whoredom speaks through the mouth of the pornographer. Just as Jeremiah tells us 'thou hast a whore's forehead, thou refusest to be ashamed,' so Juvenal tells us that Claudius' wife is a 'shameless harlot'. For shame is the essential element in the pornographic transformation of a virgin into a whore. The whore is 'shameless' because she has already been shamed. She is shame".

11 A particularly effective development of this point is offered by Neil Hertz (1985 pp 161-91). See also his reply to responses by Catherine Gallagher and Joel Fineman (pp 206-15). The article, which is mainly concerned with recollections and interpretations of incidents from the Paris Commune, discusses the attempt to map a more overtly polemical distinction between "natural" and "unnatural" modes of interpretation against a "natural", oppositional construction of sexual difference. It takes its departure from a posthumous fragment of Victor Hugo in the collection entitled by his executors *Choses vues* ("Things Seen"). This describes, with a dubious historical accuracy reminiscent of Burke's symbolic stripping of the French queen, an incident which is presented by Hugo as revelatory of the character of the insurrection and of the opposition it encountered. It concerns two young and (of course) beautiful prostitutes who, at the expense of their lives, defied the National Guardsmen from the barricades of the communards by raising their skirts and exposing themselves to them.

"false" sublime the rule is breached but without thereby being confirmed, because that breaching reveals only an absence or lack of ground. By contrast the "true" sublime breaches the rule in order to preserve or restore it, because it embodies the wisdom which recognises that the beautiful symmetry implied by the rule is, by itself, insufficient or defective, and that therefore the rule or law alone is not enough. It acknowledges, if only implicitly, that sublimation and idealisation are required to provide something more, in the form of a logic of attribution. The law must be regulated by an appeal to the province of the poets, to "the moral constitution of the heart" (1975 vol 3 p 338).

Burke's name for this turn and return from the law to literature and back again is "reflection". The objective of the *Reflections* is in a fundamental sense to trope the French Revolution, to give it another interpretive half-turn by means of which Englishmen, once properly "alarmed into reflection", could be guided into an attributive recognition and reaffirmation of their own constitution. This is appropriate because revolution is the trope which here figures the tropological as such, either as constitution or as catastrophe. Burke argues that, rightly understood, the full circle ultimately presupposes, comprehends and neutralises the half-circle. He normalises the revolution in defining it as deviate; in arguing its irreconcilability he reconciles it, negatively, to the rule.

Thus, as a component of the historical inscription which embodies the spirit of the constitution and by means of which the society reproduces itself, there is for Burke a functional impurity of the speculative line, an ultimately saving insufficiency or incoherence of the rule. This dialectical accompaniment of culture is a representation of democracy, or a demo-graphy which is also a pornography, which is to say the writing of prostitutes by and for the benefit of the sublime, of the law, and of hermeneutic reason. It is also a representation of prescription, an epiphany of the lawlessness of the law, of the violence, arbitrariness and chaos from which Burke wishes now to remind us that the law devolves.

There is here no law as such – juridical and legislative discourses are born or embodied from the hierarchical coupling of terror with love, of sublimity and beauty. This occurs via a supplementary deviation, but one which requires a carefully contrived confrontation with the illegitimacy that this coupling would conceal.[12] Burke is anxious to produce his spectre-woman in all her irresistible compulsion, since for the moral and pornographic imaginations of his constituents her principal effect will be merely to stiffen their counterrevolutionary resolve. But this is so only with the proviso that the distinction between his two feminine fictions should

12 Thus in the *Enquiry* sublimity is called forth by the seduction of beauty which would implicate the self in a deceptively pleasurable process of dissolution. Sublimity is correlated with the unmasking of the fatality of beauty. See Ferguson (1981 p 62).

count as moral truth rather than as mere pretence, that a sharp distinction should be effected between good (1688) and bad (1789), glorious and inglorious revolutions.

It appears that the degeneration of the indifferent social body yields, in some, a vitiated "moral taste" for revolution as a false sublime, for "a great change of scene . . . a magnificent stage effect; there must be a grand spectacle to rouse the imagination, grown torpid with the lazy enjoyment of sixty years security, and the still unanimating repose of public prosperity" (1975 vol 3 p 317).

To this Burke opposes a correct taste:

> when kings are hurled from their thrones by the Supreme Director of this great drama, and become the objects of insult to the base, and of pity to the good. . . We are alarmed into reflection; our minds (as it has long since been observed) are purified by terror and pity; our weak unthinking pride is humbled, under the dispensations of a mysterious wisdom. Some tears might be drawn from me, if such a spectacle were exhibited on the stage. I should be truly ashamed of finding in myself that superficial, theatric sense of painted distress, whilst I could exult over it in real life. With such a perverted mind, I could never venture to show my face at a tragedy. People would think the tears that Garrick formerly, or that Siddons not long since, have extorted from me, were the tears of hypocrisy; I should know them to be the tears of folly (1975 vol 3 pp 337-8).

Here the lesson to be learned from the downfall of kings is that which is appropriate to the true sublime: that of mortality, of the instability and the uncertainty of worldly greatness. But this is itself a "great lesson". Far from being eroded, human greatness, by means of a familiar dialectic, is preserved in the form of knowledge of negativity. Now, shame like guilt is a retrospective emotion: to be truly ashamed one must have been at some point, if only from the vantage of retrospection, shameless in some degree. Shame here means finding to have occurred in oneself something false which had appeared to be real, to have exposed a fiction and so to have also exposed what had been concealed, especially if it is the shameful fact of the lack of anything to conceal. But the operative distinction is not that between art and "real life", even in the form of a demand that life imitate art. The question is of what nature (of what gender) are the fictions which constitute the real and the merely represented or imaginary alike. Do they truly constitute or do they fragment a world and a polity?

The "feminine" or "democratic" sublime is situated in the *Reflections* as if it were a rhetorical counter in a struggle between two male antagonists. It is indispensable to the staging of the constitution of the true by means of the purging of the false. In this narrative Dr Price is the loser: the woman whom he is depicted as brandishing at Burke and through whom he would confirm his authority is, unbeknownst to him, a site of self-expenditure, is the half-circle, the abyss within which political, pedagogical, aesthetic and sexual identities are consumed. By contrast Burke's is the woman – the queen, *his* queen – who confirms relative to the other that he has what it takes. These two faces of woman correspond to the attributes and destinies of the two men. But the very efficacy of the former face, the horrors in which she is dressed and in particular her attribute of going straight forward to her end, of seeming unstoppable, cast doubt on this correspondence. The analogy may fail to constitute without accordingly being reducible to mere ornament or illustration. In this context she is the full circle, the return to the primordial violence, to the anarchy which, despite all possible purges and all the revisionary narratives, continues to threaten even as it sustains patriarchal and counterrevolutionary culture from within.

The oscillation in Burke's text between the two senses of revolution, and so between two models of hermeneutics, requires an affirmation. A rhetoric must persuade of that which cannot be demonstrated, must effect an evocation of an invisible world. But such an argument devolves inescapably in the direction of argument from authority, hence the critical importance of determining the gender of one's own sublime, of persuading us that this is indeed possible, and that the sublime is not, as Longinus once momentarily suggested, inimical to persuasion.[13]

Burke's difficulty is that his every effort to distinguish himself from and thence to vanquish his opponent appears already to have been anticipated, his every new departure acquires the semblance of having been a repetition. His antagonist, who is in large measure his own creation, seems also to be his double, and so to be his nemesis. After all, the author of the *Reflections* and his right thinking constituency no less than the degenerate applauders of revolutions seem to require "a grand spectacle" of violence and death "to rouse

---

13 Longinus I, 4, p 43. Here the effect of the sublime is "transport" (εκστασις):

> At every time and in every way imposing speech, with the spell it throws over us, prevails over that which aims at persuasion and gratification. Our persuasions we can usually control, but the influences of the sublime bring power and irresistible might to bear, and reign supreme over every hearer. Similarly, we see skill in invention, and due order and arrangement of matter, emerging as the hard-won result not of one thing or of two, but of the whole texture of the composition, whereas Sublimity flashing forth at the right moment scatters everything before it like a thunderbolt, and at once displays the power of the orator in all its plenitude.

Peter de Bolla (1989 p 37) observes the presence of a disturbing suggestion that the sublime is a discursive scattering of everything, only analeptically attributable to a subject. Considerable support for such a view is to be found in Burke's discussions of sublimity in the *Enquiry* (eg Boulton 1968, p 34).

Hazlitt, who could not be accused of sympathy with Burke's politics in the *Reflections*, defended him against the charge of substituting rhetorical subterfuge for sound argument by observing that he was operating at the limits of language and of the expressible, that "there are no words that fully express his ideas, and he tries to do it as well as he can by different ones" (Hazlitt, W, 1819, *Political Essays, with Sketches of Public Characters*, (Waller & Glover 1902-6 vol iii, p 334)). This piece was written in 1807 when, according to the author's note (p 325) "I thought I could do justice, or more than justice, to an enemy, without betraying a cause". See pp 250-3 (1817) in the same volume for another view of Burke.

the imagination". Burke is particularly aroused by the notion of a feminine mob, such as that which attended the king and queen to their captivity in Paris after their abduction from Versailles "amidst the horrid yells, the shrilling screams, the frantic dances, and infamous contumelies, and all the unutterable abominations of the furies of hell, in the abused shape of the vilest of women" (1975 p 326). This leading of the king "in triumph" through the streets of Paris was a particularly potent piece of revolutionary street theatre, and it seems that Burke was not alone in finding this type of display disturbing. In October 1793 the Convention outlawed women's clubs on the ground that direct political participation by women would result in public "hysteria" (see Hunt 1984 p 104). Further, it is possible for Mary Wollstonecraft (1989 vol 5 pp 15-16) to reply tellingly to Burke's denunciation of the "perverted mind" which weeps for theatrical representations but exults in "real" tragedies with the accusation that :

> a *gentleman* of lively imagination must borrow some drapery from fancy before he can love and pity a *man*. Misery, to reach your heart, I perceive must have its cap and bells: your tears are reserved . . . for the declamation of the theatre, or for the downfall of queens [rather than for the "vulgar sorrows" of the many]. . . "The tears that are shed for fictitious sorrow are admirably adapted," says Rousseau, "to make us proud of all the virtues which we do not possess".[14]

Burke's account of revolution is controlled in part by the conjunction of a certain politics of gender – one which even in a generally misogynist tradition can be regarded as somewhat extreme – with the exigencies of the hermeneutic model. Revolution is manifested above all as the turn of a figure, the troping which turns from literature to the law and vice versa. Where aesthesis mediates the relation of the law to itself revolution is neither lawful nor aesthetic. It is not a harmoniously constituted and constituting scription but a pre-scription which sets in place, sweeps away or transforms literary and legal institutions. It is the violence, arbitrariness, madness or ecstasy of the turning which drives politics to the aesthetic and back again; a turning which is unregulated, between literature and the law.

In the Burkean narrative revolution is the hag, the spectre, who alarms us into reflection, into self-possession, but she is the puppet of a puppet, very much a counterrevolutionary fiction, all too factitious fodder for the aestheticisation of the self and of the state. For Burke is also a revolutionary, and not only in the often remarked

14 The quotation is from Rousseau, *Lettre à Mr D'Alembert* (1758) pp 31-2, "En donnant des pleurs à ces fictions, nous avons satisfait à tous les droits de l'humanité, sans avoir plus rien à mettre du nôtre". This is a denunciation of theatrical staging and mise en scène as such. Burke expresses comparable reservations about the cognitive value of "the mind always claiming to itself some part of the dignity and importance of the things which it contemplates" in relation to the sublime (Boulton 1968 pp 50-1), but argues in general that such a propensity for self-deception is implanted by Providence to good ends.

sense which would oppose his "progressive" method and "reactionary" content to Paine's "conservative" manner of philosophising on behalf of "radical" aims. Having adopted the hermeneutic model he is led astray by its logic or illogic; he is unable to demonstrate the undemonstrable, he cannot deliver the goods, prove that his is the true sublime, when he has come so much to resemble the other, when his every move to enforce the distinction recapitulates the resemblance. He is left with only a rhetoric, with evocation. Mary Wollstonecraft scores a hit when, taking up Burke's distinction between the aesthetic and the merely theatrical, she reverses his assignment of his own position. The important point for our purposes is not the truth or falsity of Wollstonecraft's charge of hypocrisy, but the possibility of the charge which she so deftly exploits, of the further turn of his own trope to which he will always be vulnerable.

One consequence of Burke's promotion of the hermeneutic model is the conclusion that there can be no scription without prescription, no attribution of truth or lawfulness, no judgment without its admixture of fiction. In every attribution, identification, or interpretation – this last being one name for the supplementary deviation which the integrity of the rule requires – something equivocates between the "subject" and the "object" of the "act". It is both desired and feared. Burke assimilates it violently to the distinction between the false and the true when it is neither, since it is the condition of possibility of judgments, of the identification which constitutes the speaker as legislator or as judge, which must be "wholly outside the law" and can never be justified. This violence, this falsification, is that which Burke attributes to his nemesis, the revolutionary.

A further consequence of the adoption of this model is the elaboration of a certain thematisation of history – as "tradition" or "inheritance", and above all as narrative – in the service of a self-consciously "symbolic" politics. But Burke's critique of rationalist revolutionism, his constitutive turn to literature or to fiction, haunts his counterrevolutionary apologetics. His polemic suggests that to the extent that we are drawn or compelled to a like recourse, as by his arguments which touch on the concepts of regulation and legality, or to the extent that a certain interpretative labour requires to be thematised, we are likewise committed to some further, more searching conclusions. Thus "literature" and the "law", like "revolution" and the "state", are legal fictions which obscure and which fail to obscure a dimension, let us call it also historical, in their efforts to perpetuate themselves. "Prescription" then may be said to stand, amongst other things, for the insistence of this *other* history, of a history which envelops, propels, and distorts or fractures literary and legal perspectives alike without ever quite becoming one of them or one with them; whose relations with the fraternal disciplines of literature and of law are non-simple, and irreducible.

BIBLIOGRAPHY

Blakemore, S, 1988, *Burke and the Fall of Language: The French Revolution as Linguistic Event,* Brown University.

de Bolla, Peter, 1989, *The Discourse of the Sublime: Readings in History, Aesthetics and the Subject,* Basil Blackwell.

Boulton, JT (ed), 1968, *A Philosophical Enquiry into the Origin of our Ideas of the Sublime and Beautiful,* Basil Blackwell.

Burke, E, 1975, *The Works*, 6 vols, Olms.

Copeland, TW (ed) et al, 1958-78, *The Correspondence of Edmund Burke*, Cambridge University Press.

Dreyer, FA, 1979, *Burke's Politics: a Study in Whig Orthodoxy,* Wilfrid Laurier University Press.

Ferguson, F, 1981, "The Sublime of Edmund Burke, or the Bathos of Experience", *Glyph,* 8.

Furniss, T, 1987, "Burke, Paine, and the Language of Assignats", *ELH,* 54,2, Summer.

Griffin, S, 1981, *Pornography and Silence,* Harper & Row.

Hertz, Neil, 1985, "Medusa's Head: Male Hysteria Under Political Pressure", *The End of the Line: Essays on Psychoanalysis and the Sublime,* Columbia University Press.

Hunt, L, 1984, *Politics, Culture, and Class in the French Revolution,* University of California Press.

Locke, D, 1980, *A Fantasy of Reason: The Life and Thought of William Godwin,* Routledge & Kegan Paul.

Love, ED, 1965, "Edmund Burke's Idea of the Body Corporate: a Study in Imagery", *Review of Politics,* 27.

Paulson, R, 1983, *Representations of Revolution (1789-1820),* Yale University Press.

Roberts, W Rhys (ed & trans), 1899, *Longinus on the Sublime,* Heineman

Somerset, HVF (ed), 1957, *A Note-Book of Edmund Burke,* Cambridge University Press.

Turner, J, 1987, "Burke, Paine, and the Nature of Language", *ELH,* 54, 2, Summer.

Waller, AR and Glover, A (eds), 1902-6, *Collected Works,* vol iii, Dent.

Wollstonecraft, M, *A Vindication of the Rights of Men*, in Todd, J and Butler, M (eds), 1989, *The Works of Mary Wollstonecraft*, 7 vols, Pickering.

5

Children in the Industrial Revolution

PETER BOSS

At the end of 1990 Australia ratified the UN Convention on the Rights of the Child. This did not excite a great deal of notice amongst the public at large. Indeed surprise (and some resentment) has been expressed that it should have been necessary at all. Most people would assume that the child in today's society already has attained the full share of human rights. Whether this is true or not is debatable. What is beyond debate is the historical fact that the child of yesteryear had no rights at all outside the common law, and it has taken the best part of 200 years for reform and reform legislation to evolve to the point where we can now turn to the fine tuning which will still be needed in the Children's Rights debate.

It has been my duty and my privilege over the past 40 years or so to delve into the historical times of the child in English society and in the course of that I have become captivated, in particular, by the experience of the child during that turbulent period of England's history which has come to be known as the industrial revolution. Of course, this has its relevance for us in Australia too. Certain practices like transportation and child emigration had a direct effect; others, like the boarding-out system and the industrial schools system, were copies of the English counterpart. Interestingly, other policies and attendant practices like the *Poor Law*, never did take root (though some of its principles found transference) and it was the English *Poor Laws* that both reflected and shaped attitudes toward children, particularly in the nineteenth century. These laws left their mark even after the death of the Poor Law in 1948.

This chapter gives a mere thumbnail sketch of how children fared. There is, in fact, a very large body of literature on the subject and I have picked on a few facts. These comprise glances at the tenor of the times – social mores and attitudes in relation to children, children at work, children in trouble and children at risk.

First, it is necessary to pin down the period I am talking about. The time span of the industrial revolution in England can loosely be attributed to the years between 1780 and 1880, a period of, roughly, 100 years. Probably, it must be dated from the time of the modern manufacture of iron with its introduction of the rolling mill, an invention which coincides with James Watt's development of steam power. At the same time, important breakthroughs were made in the manufacture of cotton – the spinning jenny and the spinning mill. In particular, cotton manufacture was in the vanguard of this revolution and became a factory-based industry before the end of the eighteenth century. Wool and other textiles followed some way behind, but also became factory based. Steam led to railways, and transport was an indispensable part of the industrialisation process.

Industry, which had been located in the rural areas rather than urban centres, quickly led to the growth of manufacturing towns, particularly in the north of England and the midlands. The new labour which flocked to these areas, in particular for cotton manufacture, came from the ranks of agricultural labour, not least from Ireland, and the population grew rapidly. England's population in 1781 was 9,250,000. In 1831 it was 16,539,000 and it was the number of children and young people that stood out: for instance in 1821, 28 percent of the population was under nine years old. At the same time, infant mortality in the first half of the nineteenth century was such, that one child in three died before reaching the fifth birthday. Appalling living conditions, ignorance about hygiene, and a completely inadequate sanitation and safe water supply infrastructure were responsible for the cholera epidemics, particularly in 1831, 1848 and 1852, and similar typhoid epidemics were a scourge not overcome until well into the second half of the century after the great *Health Reform Act* of 1848. Much of this state of affairs could be laid at the doors of the new methods of manufacture.

In view of urbanisation, population growth, revolutionary changes in manufacture and the prevalence of old customs and mores, how did children fare? What were the social attitudes?

Up to the nineteenth century, society had taken little discriminating interest in children. So far as the law was concerned, the child was but a small adult, an adult in the making; childhood, after all, was just a transitory stage, one soon grew out of it if one survived, and survival was a matter of God's will. It was God's will too, that you were born into a particular family situation – rich and privileged or poor – to interfere with this state of affairs would be to go against God's will. The attitude, therefore, was not so much one of indifference as one of pre-determination. Of course, that this view was not wholly shared is evidenced by the many voices that were raised against such beliefs; otherwise how could social reform have ever taken place?

The child was the property of the father and his to do with what he wanted. The exception was the illegitimate child, the *"filius nullius"* of Blackstone's commentaries in the eighteenth century. In this case, it was the mother who owned the child to the exclusion of the putative father. This was little comfort to the mother for she was, in the majority of cases, poor, often destitute, and unable even to claim maintenance from the father throughout most of the nineteenth century. It was the workhouse which had to maintain these bastard children, a duty which they discharged, in the main, with the utmost reluctance. From an abundance of memorable quotations which reflect this, I have chosen two: one from an MP called Whately Cooke Taylor on non-intervention into family life, which he pronounced in 1874 in a debate on infant mortality:

> I would rather see even a higher rate of infant mortality prevailing than has ever yet been proved against the factory districts or elsewhere . . . than intrude one iota further on the domestic hearth and the decent seclusion of private life.

and a quote from Pinchbeck and Hewitt's great work, *Children in English Society* (p 584) on the illegitimate child:

> illegitimacy was an offence against Christian morality and the institution of marriage; because of the cost which was laid upon the parish and public charity, it was an offence against the well-being of society. The combination of moral failing with lack of financial responsibility was thus a sin from which the righteous might properly recoil.

Well might we add, "and boy, were they righteous"!

The workhouse, created after the *Poor Law Reform Act* 1834 and meant to drive the destitute from out-relief to prison-like conditions as a way of deterrent to all decent folk, had illegitimate children as the single largest group in their custody. The workhouse comes through in much of the literature of the nineteenth century. Oliver Twist was born there and apprenticed out to the coffin-maker; his mother died in the workhouse; so did poor little Fanny Robbins, pregnant with Sergeant Troy's child, in Thomas Hardy's *Far from the Madding Crowd*. I recall the workhouse myself, in Bristol, with its great thick walls built to last for centuries, which was still the sometimes not-so-short-term accommodation of evicted, troubled families, as recently back as the 1950s. I also recall the old Poor Law Hospital in Liverpool, which was reached by passing through the vast cemetery located in front of it.

Change in attitudes came slowly but at least improvements were made to the advantage of children in each decade. Gradually the notion of the child as the father's property gave way to the equal sharing of guardianship and custody by father and mother; gradually too, the stigma pertaining to the illegitimate child was lost, although social attitudes took longer to change and even today, vestiges of stigma remain. The Poor Law was eventually laid to rest, but not until 1948.

The great *Education Act* of 1870 did not make education compulsory, a later Act of 1876 did that (at least up to the age of 12), but even then there were provisions of exemption. Until that time, children were at work, in the home cottage or on the farm, and even more visibly in the factory.

Today, the manner in which adults exploited children in the previous century seems incredible, and it was not just the employer in factory or mine, it was parents exploiting their own children. However, it was not necessarily for love of cruelty or callousness, but rather from economic need. In the early stages of the industrial revolution there was no protection by the state or by labour unions; that came later.

In the cotton industry, small children of only three or four years of age were employed to pick up cotton waste, creeping under unguarded machines where adults could not go. The older children worked for up to 15 hours a day, and on night work too, under conditions which were often enforced by fear and brutality. The early Factory Act – *the Health and Morals of (Pauper) Apprentices Act* 1802 – was the first legislation, and pretty ineffective it was, as it did not provide for any inspectors. The first effective Act came in 1833 and the first *Ten Hours Act* (textile mills) in 1847.

Evidence to the Commission on the Employment of Children and Young Persons in Mines, 1842, said something about their plight. Children then were still employed down the mines for 12 hours a day in Staffordshire, Lancashire and the West Riding of Yorkshire. They worked as trappers, opening and shutting doors which controlled ventilation, or filling skips and carriages with coal. The pauper children suffered the most as they were sent where the miners would not let their own children go. Sarah Gooder, a pauper child, gave evidence to the Commission:

> I'm a trapper in the Gamber pit. I have to trap without a light and I am scared. I go at four, sometimes half past three in the morning and come out at five and half past (evening). Sometimes I sing when I have a light but not in the dark, I dare not sing then.

Sarah was eight years old. At least the Commission did lead to the immediate prohibition of employment of children in the mines – children under ten years of age, that is.

There were other scandalous work exploitations of children. Charles Kingsley in the *Water Babies* wrote of the plight of the chimney sweep. Little boys were sent up to sweep out the flue and a child might have a fire lit under him to spur him on to greater effort. Some children suffocated, others got stuck, and there are accounts of fire places or flues having to be dismantled to remove corpses of the little chaps. William Blake (1789) wrote poems about them:

> When my mother died I was very young
> and my father sold me while yet my tongue
> could scarcely cry weep, weep, weep,
> So your chimneys I sweep and in soot I sleep.

Children working on the land fared no better than their like in factories or mines. Until the introduction of modern farm machinery reduced the need for direct labour, small children worked hard on the land. Particularly pernicious was the practice of the gang system in the 1820s, in which a farmer requiring a piece of work done would apply to a gang master who would contract for the work. The gang master then recruited the necessary labour and sent them to the farm with an overseer. Apart from the hardness of the work, there was the added hardship of having to walk to the work location. In the summer a gang sometimes had to walk seven or eight miles to work, put in a full day, and then walk back. If rain came on after some miles had been walked, the gang returned without anything being earned, since the day was divided into four work quarters and unless at least one quarter had been worked, the gang received nothing.

A father of a child aged 11 years described these conditions to the 1843 Commission inquiring into the employment of women and children in agriculture:

> I'm forced to let my daughter go, else I'm very much against it . . . she has complained of pain in her side very often, they drive them along, force them along . . . they make them work hard . . . pulling out turnips is the hardest work; they get such a hold of the ground with their roots; when the land's strong it's as much as we can do to get 'em out, pull as hard as we can pull. It blisters their hands so that they can hardly touch anything . . . my girl went 5 miles yesterday to her work turniping; she set off between 7-8, she walked, had a piece of bread before she went, did not stop in the middle of the day, ate nothing till she left off.

Well did Dickens write of the spirit of Christmas gazing down on the half-starved urchins condemned to near savagery, roaming the streets of London and other large towns:

> This boy is ignorance, this girl is want
> Beware them both and all of their degree
> but most beware this boy, for on his brow
> I see that written which is Doom, unless the writing be erased.

It took more than 100 years and fully 100 Acts of Parliament before "the writing" could be said to have been erased, before the alarmed and disgusted and compassionate side of English society could overcome the callous, the self-interested and those who preferred to avert their eyes or thought that it was so ordained and therefore immutable.

For most of Victorian times Disraeli's classic notion of England as "two nations" applied, "For so little do we know of the state of our country, that the air of improbability which the whole truth would inevitably throw over these pages, might deter some from their perusal". (Sybil, "Advertisement")

In a small book, *The Victorian Child* (Rowe 1959), which I found in a secondhand bookshop some years ago, the author surveys the lives of the "more or less" prosperous family:

> it suggests for the most part an atmosphere of babies brought decently into a world of more or less elegant cradles, in homes not necessarily wealthy, but comfortable after their kind; a world of rattles, and loving

> relations and nannies, of metal baths placed upon towels, of coal fires burning cosily behind tall wire fenders or guards, of the hot tangy smell of newly aired linen, of gas brackets, oil lamps and candles and night lights and all the other things that meant home. Such was true of a vast number of households.

and then bethinks himself that there was another side:

> The lot of children born into the full squalor of slum life and the dregs of poverty is something one does not care to contemplate... Babies were born into a world of poverty, dirt, rags and grew up in frightful dens where human creatures of all ages swarmed like pests which beset them. The weaklings die like flies . . . it became pretty obvious that it was not only bad but (somehow) wrong to be very poor.

This state of affairs was echoed in the work of Thomas Barnardo in his famous encounter with Jim Jarvis, the street urchin who, late one evening in 1866, begged him to be allowed to stay in the Ragged School premises where Barnardo taught:

> "Come my lad, had you not better get home, it is very late, mother will be coming for you" . . . "Please sir, let me stop, I won't do no harm" . . . "Well, but had you not better get home, your mother will wonder what kept you so late" . . . "I ain't got no mother" . . . "No mother, boy, where do you live?" "Don't live nowhere."

Consequently, Jim shows him where he and his mates do live, down in Whitechapel, in hay carts under tarpaulins, and so began the great work of the famed Barnardo.

The great laws of England are the pride of their creators through the centuries. The law is impartial – the same for the greatest and the least, the highest and the lowest. So, when we learn that until about 1780 the penalty for over 200 offences was death by hanging, we naturally assume that the sentence would have been handed out impartially too, based only on proof of guilt and in the absence of mitigating circumstances. But what offences? In 1780 a little girl of seven was hanged in the market place at Norwich for stealing a petticoat. There is recorded evidence of children even younger than seven being executed. For instance, there is the pitiable case of a child on the scaffold who cried for his mother. On one day alone, in February 1814 at the Old Bailey sessions, five children were condemned to death: Fowler and Wolfe both twelve years old, for burglary in a dwelling; Morris eight, Solomon nine and Burrell eleven, for burglary and stealing a pair of shoes. As late as 1833, a boy of nine was sentenced to be hanged for poking a stick through a patched up pane of glass and stealing two penny-worth of paint, though the sentence was commuted. Later, transportation took the place of execution. In evidence to the House of Lords Committee on Juvenile Delinquency and Transportation, 1847, it was shown that 339 boys between ages 14 and 17 were transported in 1844 alone. Extracts from the Registers of Stafford Prison illustrate the sort of crimes which merited transportation in 1834:

Matilda Seymour age 10 stealing one shawl, one petticoat – 7 years

Thomas Bell age 11 stealing two handkerchiefs (silk) – 7 years

William Biglen age 14 stealing one handkerchief (silk) – 7 years

Before leaving England's shores, probably for ever, they would almost certainly undergo a period of detention in prison or in the hulks – the old men-of-war lying in the Thames, Medway and at Portsmouth. The prisons were overcrowded – full to bursting. In 1816, when the population of London was 2½ million, the prisons in town held 3000 young people under the age of 20 years, half of them were under 17 years old. Around the country:

1835 6803 nearly 1:449 of the population 10-20 years old;

1844 11,348 nearly 1:304 of the population 10-20 years old;

1853 nearly 12,000 children and young persons were sent to prison.

Transportation was finally abolished in 1857.

In the late eighteenth century and early nineteenth century reformatory efforts by Jonas Hanway (Marine Society for training lads "with daring tempers") and in the mid-nineteenth century, Mathew Davenport-Hill (recorder of Birmingham who experimented with an early form of probation with condition of residence) had begun to take the edge off imprisonment as the habitual form of sentencing after hanging and transportation had passed. But the major work was done by Mary Carpenter for the children of the "perishing classes" who were consigned to schools and the children of the "dangerous classes" consigned to reformatory schools. These two categories later came together in the "approved schools" with which I was involved whilst working as a child welfare officer in the 1950s. The treatment of children before the Law did not improve markedly until the close of the nineteenth century and did not reach its modern form until the *Children Act* of 1908, which set up the juvenile courts.

Along with the problem of juvenile crime in the nineteenth century were other social problems in relation to children. One was the notorious baby farming system under which young children were left in the care of child minders who looked after them for a day at a time or sometimes for longer periods to enable hard-pressed mothers to go to work. Another serious problem which today we call child abuse and neglect, was then known by a more down-to-earth term: cruelty to, and neglect of, children.

In his book, *In Darkest England and the Way Out*, written in 1880, General William Booth, founder of the Salvation Army, stated:

> When an English Judge tells us, as Mr Justice Wills did the other day, that there were any number of parents who would kill their children for a few pounds insurance money, we can form some idea of the horrors of the existence into which many of the children of this highly favoured land are ushered at their birth.

One would have thought that General Booth was writing some 30 years *after* the worst excesses to children had been excised from Victoria's England. Booth's book, it is said, sold a million copies.

This was an era where families were herded together in hovels, both in town and country, when beds were habitually shared by adults with children, where standards of behaviour were often bestial. To quote Booth again:

> The overcrowded homes of the poor compel the children to witness everything. Sexual morality comes to have no meaning for them. Incest is so familiar as hardly to call for a remark. The bitter poverty of the poor compels them to leave their children half fed.

Until the second half of the nineteenth century, both Parliament and the national media were largely unconcerned with the way in which parents treated their children. Although, as we have seen, mothers were slowly gaining on fathers in their struggle to secure equal rights over their children, the idea of children's rights to protection was only in the minds of a few dedicated social reformers. In a debate on the second reading of the 1908 Bill, the Judge Advocate said:

> There was a time in the history of this House when a Bill of this kind would have been treated as a most revolutionary measure; and half a century ago it would have been said that the British Constitution was being undermined.

The initial interest in the sad plight of children caused by active cruelty and pre-meditated neglect was sparked in a sensational case of baby farming by two women, Sarah Ellis and Margaret Waters. Ellis advertised for children "for adoption" and sums of money were passed in the transactions. The children were neglected to the point where most died or would have died, but for the prompt investigation of a Sergeant Ralph of Brixton (London) Police, who had been alerted by an unusually large number of dead babies found in the district. It was not uncommon to find dead babies in places such as London at that time, but not in the numbers found in Brixton. In 1870, the year of the *Ellis and Waters* case, 276 were found, the majority under one week old. In this case, the bodies of 16 babies were found about the beginning of May. Waters was convicted and executed.

The *Ellis-Waters* case created an immense sensation and was followed by that of Mary Hall, another notorious baby farmer. Despite the intervention of noted social reformer, Lord Shaftesbury, to whom the statue of Eros is dedicated in Piccadilly, and other prominent reformers, the government, being preoccupied with political matters, took no immediate action. However, an Infant Life Protection Society was formed in July 1870, and in 1871 the Infant Life Protection Bill was introduced. This Bill included in its provisions a clause so framed that, if enacted, it would have required the registration and supervision of nurses in the manufacturing districts who took children into day care. It raised a storm of protest and was accused of "interference in the most mischievous and oppressive way with domestic arrangements . . . and an infringement of the liberties of the parent".

The *Infant Life Protection Act* was passed in 1872 but excluded day care, dealing only with persons who minded two or more children under one year of age for more than 24 hours at a time. It was a mere beginning, and other cases as notorious as *Ellis and Waters*, notably the *Mrs Dyer* case in 1896, meant the legislation and control had to be strengthened. Other legislation did exist – as early as 1868 boards of guardians had been authorised to prosecute parents who wilfully neglected their children by failing to provide for them so that their health was endangered. However, this legislation was limited to children with whom the Poor Law was concerned, that is, those children in families on out-relief where the guardians paid for their upkeep.

It was not until societies for the Prevention of Cruelty to Children were formed in the 1880s that reform was accelerated. It is interesting to note that the Liverpool society, the first of a number of societies in the large cities, was formed out of an appeal by the Society for the Prevention of Cruelty to Animals, canvassing funds for a dogs' home! As Pinchbeck and Hewitt (p 622) note:

> That societies to protect animals from cruelty were established before societies to protect children is one of the better known, bizarre features of English social history . . . the Englishman's sturdy belief in the sanctity of the home and inviolateness of the family persisted for a long time so far as parental obligations to their children went. Even Shaftesbury – lifelong social reformer, battler for factory Acts and working conditions – was against legislation that might invade the home.

The 39 societies amalgamated into the National Society for the Prevention of Cruelty to Children (NSPCC), and in 1889 this society was able to get legislation passed to protect the child at risk. It was the NSPCC's secretary, Benjamin Waugh, who stood out as an impassioned supporter and advocate. A counterpart to the NSPCC was formed in Melbourne in 1894.

In conclusion I make two comments. First, social attitudes are the most important elements in the ways that children are treated by any society. In the case of the nineteenth century, these attitudes changed far more slowly than did industrial and material developments, and legislation followed attitudinal change, it did not lead it. Secondly, children can be viewed in an economic framework as another element in the supply and demand equation, as a social investment category, or as a cost-benefit equation, without any consideration for the social philosophy of childhood. The industrial revolution demonstrated both the economic value of children in terms of their exploitation and as investment for future capital. It is only today that we accept and promote the idea of childhood as having intrinsic value, something that is precious and worth protecting. Childhood is, in any case, such a fleeting phenomenon.

BIBLIOGRAPHY

Rowe, G, 1959, *The Victorian Child*, Phoenix House.

2

STRANGER THAN FICTION

6

The Poetics of Infanticide

SIMON PETCH

By examining some relationships between sources and texts in Wordsworth and Scott, this chapter explores the cultural significance of infanticide in literature. Through their engagement with statutes, with legal procedures, and with questions of evidence, these texts display an anxiety, which they do not fully acknowledge, about the place of the unmarried woman (as represented by Martha Ray and Madge Wildfire) in the social economy: infanticide is a figure for the absence of marriage. These texts emerged from a context of social and political pressure to reform infanticide law, but Shelley's comments on infanticide (in his Notes to *Queen Mab*) take the issue beyond law reform to a critique of marriage as an institution. Shelley's discriminating account of "legitimate" relationships relies on a key distinction between the prostitute and the child killer, which declares female sexuality, as figured in the illegitimate child of the prostitute, to be the victim of the law, and which acknowledges the actions of the child killer to be complicit with the social discourses governing legislation. This chapter concludes with some general comments about the poetics of infanticide in relation to the laws that regulate human sexuality.

The first of the several stories to be told in this chapter begins at about half-past-eleven on the evening of Wednesday 7 April 1779, outside the Covent Garden Theatre in London. Two women and a man come out of the theatre and make for a carriage; as they start to get into the carriage, a man dressed in black runs towards it, grabs the gown of one of the women, puts a pistol to her head, and fires it, killing her instantly. He then turns a second pistol on himself, wounding, but not killing himself. He is immediately arrested, and at a hearing convened in the early hours of the next morning is committed for trial.

On Friday of the next week, at the Old Bailey, a jury found the Rev James Hackman guilty of murder, and Judge Blackstone pronounced the death sentence. Hackman's intention, as claimed in a suicide note found in his pocket on his arrest, had been to kill himself before the eyes of the woman he loved, but who would not marry him (the offer of marriage is important). But at the committal hearing

Hackman had admitted that, at the last moment, a moment of frenzy, he had a change of plan, and tried to kill both the woman and himself. This was a fatal admission: as Blackstone pointed out, to constitute the legal crime of murder it is sufficient that there be an intention at the time. And that there were two pistols suggested a double design, although this was the occasion of much dispute. Three days later, on Monday 19 April, the Reverend James Hackman, at the age of 26, went to the gallows at Tyburn (Boswell pp 72-75, 78, 85-95; Brady p 186; Dampier-Smith p 148).

Where his story ends is where we shall leave him, and turn to his victim, whose story has not yet begun. The murdered woman was Martha Ray, a few years older than Hackman, by whom she had been amorously pursued since 1775. In that year Hackman had met her at the house of John Montagu, the Fourth Earl of Sandwich, whose mistress she had been for more than ten years. Martha Ray was the daughter of a stay-maker, but was rescued (if that is the word) from her humble lot in life at the age of 16, when the Earl of Sandwich removed her to a higher station, giving her a continental education and bringing her up to be an accomplished musician. The association was as notorious as the *crime passionel* that ended Martha Ray's life was sensational.

Martha Ray had borne the Earl of Sandwich nine children, one of whom, Basil Montagu, became a friend of Wordsworth, and it is with Wordsworth that her story begins again. Nineteen years after Martha Ray was killed she was reborn as the central character of Wordsworth's poem, "The Thorn". In the late eighteenth century the "commonest of all literary associations for a thorn tree were illegitimate birth and child-murder" (Jacobus p 240), and here the victim of murder is reincarnated in the poem as a suspect of infanticide.

The Martha Ray of Wordsworth's poem is believed by the community from which she has been cast out to have murdered her illegitimate child. Close to the thorn of the title is a heap of moss the size of an infant's grave, and beside the heap of moss can often be seen Martha Ray, whose only utterance in the poem is the oft-repeated "Oh misery! Oh misery! Oh woe is me! Oh misery!". The poem dramatises the narrator's attempt to tell Martha Ray's story of seduction, desertion, alleged infanticide, and madness. But the story cannot be told because it is not known, and in place of an authoritative version of what did or did not happen there is only malicious superstition and rumour:

> I've heard the scarlet moss is red
> With drops of that poor infant's blood
> But kill a new-born infant thus!
> I do not think she could.
> Some say, if to the pond you go
> And fix on it a steady view,
> The shadow of a babe you trace,

A baby and a baby's face,
And that it looks at you;
Whene'er you look on it, 'tis plain
The baby looks at you again.[1]

Martha Ray has not been brought to public justice, although the locals have been busy digging for evidence with their spades. Rumours persist without verification, and as the poem moves through the mazes of circumstantial evidence, its language of repetition and hearsay disturbingly blurs the lines between fact and conjecture. In a long note to the poem, Wordsworth made clear that the narrator is superstitious and credulous (Wordsworth pp 287-91). What is equally clear from the poem itself is that Martha Ray is a scapegoat.

And the name Martha Ray sets up a play between fact and fiction, between the murdered mistress of the Earl of Sandwich, who was also the murdered mother of Wordsworth's friend, and the possibly murdering mother of Wordsworth's poem. This play draws attention to both women as victims. The Martha Ray of London society was a victim in the legal sense that she was murdered by one who wished to marry her, and a victim also in that she was the property of the Earl of Sandwich, a situation from which Hackman was trying to rescue her (this second rescue mission proving fatal).

The play between fact and fiction involves some shift, not only in roles, but also in class. The Martha Ray of the legal story moved freely in high society, although her legal status as a kept woman must have been precarious. The Martha Ray of Wordsworth's poem is a deserted woman from a rural community. If Wordsworth's Martha Ray is a dark shadow of his friend's mother, her desperate lament is an echo of what the real Martha Ray never said. Behind the repeated lament of Wordsworth's poem we can hear the fictitious voice of a real person. The story in the trial was inevitably the story of James Hackman. The story in the poem makes the victim the focus and gives her a voice.

This poem comes from a context in which there was a growing pressure to reform infanticide law, which was determined by a statute of 1624:

> An act to prevent the destroying and murthering of bastard children.
>
> WHEREAS many lewd women that have been delivered of bastard children, to avoid their shame, and to escape punishment, do secretly bury or conceal the death of their children, and after, if the child be found dead, the said women do alledge, that the said child was born dead; whereas it falleth out sometimes (although hardly is it to be proved) that the said child or children were murthered by the said women, their lewd mothers, or by their assent or procurement:
>
> II. For the preventing therefore of this great mischief, be it enacted by the authority of this present parliament, That if any woman after one

1 Wordsworth 77 (II, pp 221-231). Neither Wordsworth's editors nor Boswell's can make much of the murdered Martha Ray: see Wordsworth p 291, and Boswell p 74.

> month next ensuing the end of this session of parliament be delivered of any issue of her body, male or female, which being born alive, should by the laws of this realm be a bastard, and that she endeavour privately, either by drowning or secret burying thereof, or any other way, either by herself or the procuring of others, so to conceal the death thereof, as that it may not come to light, whether it was born alive or not, but be concealed: in every such case the said mother so offending shall suffer death as in case of murther, except such mother can make proof by one witness at the least, that the child (whose death was by her so intended to be concealed) was born dead.[2]

There is an unspoken assumption here that children born in wedlock are in no danger, which presumably justifies the high moral tone. There is also an anxiety about whether or not infanticide is the same as other kinds of homicide. But the greatest worry of all is about evidence. The statute acknowledges this as a problem, but gets around it by making the quality of concealment central. This had the practical effect of making concealment of the death of a bastard child a capital offence. By putting the burden of proof on the defence, it smoothed the path to the gallows.

The severity of this statute gradually made it unworkable. As society became more attentive to maternal sentiment, and with the growth of the affective family, juries became increasingly unwilling to condemn upon mere proof of concealment (Rose p 70; Hoffer and Hull pp 65, 78). In 1772 a movement to reform this law was led in the House of Commons by Edmund Burke and Charles James Fox, who pointed out that "nothing could be more unjust, or inconsistent with the principles of all law, than first to force a woman through modesty to concealment, and then to hang her for that concealment . . . that the concealment of the birth of a bastard might proceed from the best causes, from real modesty and virtue" (Hoffer and Hull pp 85-6). The logic of this protest is inexorable: the law creates the evidence it needs to force the crime it can then punish.

Wordsworth's poem is not itself a call for law reform, although it does raise the key legal question about evidence, and the key social question about licensed sexual relationships. Marriage cannot regulate the unruliness of human sexuality, as Wordsworth himself well knew, having fathered an illegitimate child in France some years before he wrote the poem.

The story of both Martha Rays and the relationships between them is a story about the place of the unmarried woman in the social economy. Not the single woman, the unmarried woman: the intensifying force of the negative prefix is necessary here, for both Martha Rays were significantly unmarried, one bearing nine children to her keeper, one left waiting, pregnant, at the altar. What price maternity? What price marriage? Infanticide is the driving force of the poem, not as an actual crime, but as a figure for the absence of

2 21 James I, c 27 (1624), quoted in Hoffer and Hull (p 20). My chapter is much indebted to this informed and informative study.

marriage. Infanticide becomes a focus for anxieties about where lines regulating sexual behaviour can, or should, be drawn. Martha Ray's alleged infanticide, for which there is no evidence, is itself evidence of her deviance, and that is her main problem. In the poem, as her words suggest, she is a victim; to the community in the poem, she is a threat, and thus a scapegoat for the community's anxiety about its own moral standards.

Infanticide is likewise a focus of Walter Scott's novel *The Heart of Midlothian*, published in 1818, in which Scott alludes to this poem:

> The trees were a little separated from each other, and at the foot of one of them, a beautiful poplar, was a variegated hillock of wild flowers and moss, such as the poet of Grasmere has described in his verses on the Thorn. So soon as she arrived at this spot, Madge Wildfire, joining her hands above her head, with a loud scream that resembled laughter, flung herself all at once upon the spot, and remained lying there motionless. (Scott p 297)

Like Martha Ray, Madge Wildfire is a woman on the edge: the edge of sanity, the edge of society, the edge that separates the living from the dead. Madge is not guilty of infanticide, although she did indeed give birth to an illegitimate child, which was disposed of by her own mother. As the narrator tells us:

> She had been courted by a wealthy suitor, whose addresses her mother had favoured, notwithstanding the objection of old age and deformity. She had been seduced by some profligate, and, to conceal her shame and promote the advantageous match she had planned, her mother had not hesitated to destroy the offspring of their intrigue. That the consequence should be the total derangement of a mind which was constitutionally unsettled by giddiness and vanity, was extremely natural; and such was, in fact, the history of Madge Wildfire's insanity. (Scott pp 300-1)

From one of Scott's many notes we learn that the original of Madge Wildfire was one Feckless Fannie, who had been the only daughter of a wealthy squire in the north of England, who loved her father's shepherd; and whose father, believing that the family would be disgraced by the alliance of his daughter with a lowly shepherd, shot and killed her lover. There was no pregnancy, no child, but the event turned her wits, and for many years until she was finally stoned to death in 1775 Feckless Fannie roamed Scotland and England accompanied by the sheep of her dead lover (Scott p 534).

As with Wordsworth's use of Martha Ray, Scott's treatment of his source material involves transpositions of class and gender. Fanny is from the landed classes, and her lower-class lover is killed by her father, which drives her mad; Madge is of the servant classes, she is betrayed by an upper-class lover, and her child is killed by her own mother. Neither woman has any gendered identity, though each is possessed of a powerful sexuality. Like Wordsworth, Scott takes a situation which he turns around, and which he recasts: in "The Thorn", as in *The Heart of Midlothian*, the unmarried woman's role is defined in relation to suspected infanticide.

The Heart of Midlothian was written by a Scottish Tory gentleman who had himself been called to the bar, and who believed profoundly in the rule of law as represented by the Act of Union between England and Scotland (1707). The impossible task Scott set himself in this book was to prove the House of Hanover's legitimacy in Scotland. Marriage is a type or model of political union in the novel. But Madge, unmarried and unmarriageable, is a strong sexual presence who cannot be situated in the political structures of legitimate sexuality, and who therefore cannot use her sexuality to bargain as other women in the novel do. Equally alienated from the legal culture and the criminal subculture, Madge Wildfire represents threatening aspects of femininity which the book cannot finally accommodate (Thompson pp 189-00); and she has to be killed off well before its end so that out of discord may come marriage, out of infanticide may be born legitimacy, out of regicide can come union.

The Heart of Midlothian is a bloody novel. In the background there is always regicide (of the Stuart King Charles I), there is parricide, there are two hangings, there is a lynching, there is infanticide, and there is also wife-murder. Many of the significant encounters in the novel take place at Muschat's cairn, so named because here Nichol Muschat did away with his wife. Scott's note uses the language of indictment to tell us of this, the grimmest killing in the novel:

> Nichol Muschat, a debauched and profligate wretch, having conceived a hatred against his wife, entered into a conspiracy with another brutal libertine and gambler, named Campbell by which Campbell undertook to destroy the woman's character, so as to enable Muschat, on false pretences, to obtain a divorce from her. The brutal devices to which these worthy accomplices resorted for that purpose having failed, they endeavoured to destroy her by administering medicine of a dangerous kind, and in extraordinary quantities.
>
> This purpose also failing, Nichol Muschat . . . did finally, on the 17th October 1720, carry his wife under cloud of night to the King's park, adjacent to what is called the Duke's Walk, near Holyrood Palace, and there took her life by cutting her throat almost quite through, and inflicting other wounds. He pleaded guilty to the indictment, for which he suffered death. . . In memory, and at the same time execration, of the deed, a cairn, or pile of stones, long marked the spot. (Scott pp 525-6)

Muschat's Cairn is the site of several crucial encounters or confrontations in this novel, the place where the law and its opposites meet and confront each other and sometimes change places. And, as the place where a woman is most violently unmarried, for this murder is a violent undoing of a marriage, it is the site of the book's anxieties about the relationships between men and women both within and beyond the law.

It is also a favourite haunt of Madge Wildfire, for it is to Muschat's Cairn that Madge comes to talk with the dead wife of Nichol Muschat. Ailie Muschat, according to Madge, wears her winding sheet well up, to hide her torn throat, but it cannot stop the blood from seeping through it. In a kinship of blood, for she feels somehow implicated in the murder of a child, Madge Wildfire identifies with the dead wife. This kinship crosses the borderline of life and death, and sees both women, both wronged, both victims of men, enmeshed in a common guilt (see Wilt pp 136-7). Their status as victims is translated, culturally, into guilt. At Muschat's Cairn, the wife who was killed because she could not be divorced, and the seduced woman who feels implicated in infanticide, try, in Madge's imagination, to bleach their clothes clean with the light of the moon.

Madge Wildfire is not guilty of infanticide, though infanticide is central to Scott's novel. The heart of Midlothian of the title is the Tollbooth prison, Edinburgh, where Effie Deans awaits trial on a charge of murder presumptive. She is charged under a Scottish statute of 1690, which, as Scott tells us in his note:

> in consequence of the great increase of child murder, both from the temptations to commit the offence and the difficulty of discovery, enacted a certain set of presumptions, which, in the absence of direct proof, the jury were to receive as evidence of the crime having actually been committed. The circumstances selected for this purpose were, that the woman should have concealed her situation during the whole of her pregnancy; that she should not have called for help at her delivery; and that, combined with these grounds of suspicion, the child should either be found dead or altogether missing. (Scott p 528)

The similarity to the English statute of 1624 is clear.

Infanticide is proved only by presumption, and Effie Deans is as innocent of the crime as is Madge Wildfire, her dark shadow. Her illegitimate child was not killed; it was taken by Madge Wildfire as a substitute for her own, whose death she could not accept, and returns later in the novel. In the following passage George Staunton, Effie's seducer and the father of both her child and that of Madge Wildfire, ponders the possibility of rediscovering his son:

> it would be difficult to produce him, without telling him much more of the history of his birth, and the misfortunes of his parents, than it was prudent to make known. But let him once be found, and, being found, let him but prove worthy of his father's protection, and many ways might be fallen upon to avoid such risk. Sir George Staunton was at liberty to adopt him as his heir, if he pleased, without communicating the secret of his birth; or an act of parliament might be obtained, declaring him legitimate, and allowing him the name and arms of his father. He was, indeed, already a legitimate child according to the law of Scotland, by the subsequent marriage of his parents. (Scott p 486)

This is the language of the loophole, which is also the language authorising legitimacy. Scott moves into Staunton's mind, and blends the language of judicial summary with the processes of the character's thought (Shaw pp 30-1), demonstrating the rationalising process that takes place in his imagination. The law has the power to redefine its own categories so that its subjects can be redistributed in terms of the needs of the powerful. This is the language of the father, which is also the language of the patriarchal system. It is both a personal and an institutional language.

Of course it does not help Effie Deans, whose only chance is that someone might come forward and testify that she had told them of her condition, for then the quality of concealment would be removed. Effie's sister is pressured to do just this, but Jeanie Deans will not perjure herself, even to save her sister, who did not confide in her. Only a lie, a procedural fiction, can stop the juggernaut of injustice. Only a lie will prevent the judicial authorities from becoming murderers themselves. You have to join the law to beat it, to conform to it to get around it, to compromise yourself to save the law from itself.

The trial of Effie Deans is good courtroom drama, informed by Scott's knowledge of the law, but as context for this legal set-piece *The Heart of Midlothian* also carries a commentary on the law, focused on the statute and its application. Thus Bartoline Saddletree, an amateur legal pedant, says of murder presumptive that it is "a murder of the law's inferring or construction"; "The crime", he says, "is rather a favourite of the law, this species of murther being one its ain creation". To which his wife responds, comically but correctly and unanswerably, "that if the law makes murthers . . . the law should be hanged for them" (Scott pp 54-5). The novel's most persuasive subtext is in women's responses to this statute. Against the masculine force of the law Scott pits the defiant refusal of Jeanie Deans to play the legal game by perjuring herself, and the trenchant comments of Mrs Saddletree. The law makes the criminal. The law creates the conditions of its own operation, for its means to power is the self-sustaining and binding logic of its statutory presumptions. Here we should recall Burke and Fox's challenge to the logic of the 1624 statute on the grounds that you cannot morally compel women to concealment and then hang them for it. The law authorises its own operations, and what sort of evidence is concealment? As the Duke of Argyll says, "It seems contrary to the genius of British law to take that for granted which is not proved, or to punish with death for a crime, which, for aught the prosecutor has been able to show, may not have been committed at all" (Scott p 351). How can anything, in the words of Scott's note, be "found . . . missing"?

At Effie's trial, too, her counsel contests the presumption of the statute, claiming that an illegitimately pregnant woman would not naturally communicate her situation, that she would rather conceal it until the father of the child should marry her and restore her good name (Scott p 219). This indicates how the statute creates the conditions of its own operation, that the assumptions about human behaviour on which its presumptive power rests can be challenged by different assumptions.

Legal rules can thus become self-fulfilling prophecies. Shelley, in his notes to *Queen Mab*, argues that chastity as regulated through marriage is a legalised monopoly, "A system could not well have been devised more studiously hostile to human happiness than marriage" (Shelley p 303). In his attack on marriage and its evils as an institution, Shelley's own writing marries the language of the law with the language of social rejection and persecution:

> Prostitution is the legitimate offspring of marriage and its accompanying errors. Women, for no other crime than having followed the dictates of a natural appetite, are driven with fury from the comforts and sympathies of society. It is less venial than murder; and the punishment which is inflicted on her who destroys her child to escape reproach is lighter than the life of agony and disease to which the prostitute is irrecoverably doomed. Has a woman obeyed the impulse of unerring nature; – society declares war against her . . . she must be the tame slave, she must make no reprisals; theirs is the right of persecution, hers the duty of endurance. She lives a life of infamy: the loud and bitter laugh of scorn scares her from all return. She dies of long and lingering disease; yet *she* is in fault, *she* is the criminal, *she* the forward and untamable child, – and society . . . the pure and virtuous matron, who casts her as an abortion from her undefiled bosom! (Shelley p 303)

"Abortion" here is used in the sense of the imperfect offspring of a miscarriage, the implication being that marriage itself is a miscarriage of natural justice. Shelley goes on, "Society avenges herself on the criminals of her own creation; she is employed in anathematizing the vice to-day, which yesterday she was the most zealous to teach" (Shelley p 303). Writing from the radical wing of the English romantic movement, Shelley exposes a network of relationships in which prostitution, marriage, and infanticide, are logically, and legitimately (that is, through the law) related. Law is an instrument of repression and social control, and the victim is female sexuality.

Yet into this complex of social hypocrisy Shelley builds a crucial distinction between the prostitute and the woman who destroys her child to escape reproach, in which the life of the prostitute is more subversive and threatening than the death of the child-killer. This is because the prostitute lives a life of exteriority, flaunting her sexuality outside the structures of legitimation imposed by society. The child-killer may have broken the law, but she has also submitted to it by concealing the evidence of her own sexuality. In hiding this, the killer of her child makes herself a legitimate person. Killers of children are thus on the side of the law, and infanticide is a process of complicity, collaboration, and legitimation, which marries the law and crime. Transgression is translated into acknowledgement of authority. Shelley recognises that women who take their sexuality outside marriage bear the brunt of society's anxieties about its own legitimacy, but his bold and radical distinction places infanticide in a new and disturbing ideological context.

Infanticide in literature is a figure for the unmarried woman, and literature dealing with infanticide reveals the unmarried woman as a victim of and scapegoat for the disturbing and destructuring implications of human sexuality. Because infanticide is primarily a woman's crime, and particularly an unmarried woman's crime, the law of infanticide tells us much about social expectations of women at any given historical period. The poetics of infanticide are searching forms of cultural analysis that probe the relationships between the letter of the law, and the social attitudes inscribed by the law. They provide a fictional context to question the law's own fictions. This relationship between the law and social attitudes is more to do with property and power than with people, for what is at stake are succession and legal continuity. The poetics of infanticide are therefore the politics of motherhood, marriage, and legitimacy, as authorised by the laws of patriarchy.

BIBLIOGRAPHY

Boswell, James, 1977, *Boswell: Laird of Auchinleck 1778-1782*, Reed, Joseph W & Pottle, Frederick A (eds), vol 11, *Yale Editions of the Private Papers of James Boswell*, McGraw Hill.

Brady, Frank, 1984, *James Boswell: The Later Years 1769-1795*, McGraw Hill.

Hoffer, Peter C & Hull, NEH, 1981, *Murdering Mothers: Infanticide in England and New England 1558-1803*, New York University School of Law Series in Legal History 2, New York University Press.

Jacobus, Mary, 1976, *Tradition and Experiment in Wordsworth's Lyrical Ballads (1789)*, Clarendon Press.

Rose, Lionel, 1986, *The Massacre of the Innocents: Infanticide in Britain 1800-1939*, Routledge and Kegan Paul.

Scott, Walter, 1982, *The Heart of Midlothian*, Lamont, Claire (ed), Oxford University Press.

Smith-Dampier, JL, 1935, *Who's Who in Boswell*, The Shakespeare Head Press.

Shaw, Harry E, 1989, "Scot's 'Daemon' and the Voices of Historical Narration", *JEGP* 88, pp 21-33.

Shelley, Percy Bysshe, 1972, "Notes on *Queen Mab*", in Rogers, Neville (ed), *The Complete Poetical Works of Percy Bysshe Shelley*, vol 1, Clarendon Press.

Thompson, Jon, 1987, "Sir Walter Scott and Madge Wildfire: Strategies of Containment in *The Heart of Midlothian*", *Literature and History* 13, pp 188-99.

Wilt, Judith, 1985, *Secret Leaves: The Novels of Walter Scott*, University of Chicago Press.

Wordsworth, "The Thorn", in Brett RL & Jones, AR (eds), 1963, *Wordsworth and Coleridge, Lyrical Ballads*, Methuen.

7

Madness and the Law

ALAN DILNOT

Almost for as long as novels have been written in English, to fall into the hands of the lawyers has been regarded as a miserable fate; and the figures of the rascally attorney and the impoverished client were common from the early eighteenth century. In the nineteenth century, however, a new charge was brought against the law: it could not only make you poor, it could make you mad. In Dickens's *Bleak House* (1853), before we meet any of the characters, we are told: "This is the Court of Chancery; which has its decaying houses and its blighted lands in every shire; which has its worn-out lunatic in every madhouse. . ." (p 2) Soon the narrator is listing the people in court on that murky afternoon, and immediately after the lawyers and officials and clerks and reporters, first among the citizens mentioned "is a little mad old woman in a squeezed bonnet" (p 3). We later learn that she is Miss Flite; and when she introduces herself to the wards in Jarndyce, Richard Carstone whispers to Esther and Ada that she is mad. "'Right! Mad, young gentleman,' she returned so quickly that he was quite abashed. 'I was a ward myself. I was not mad at that time. . .'" (p 23) It is clear, then, that this novel is giving attention to the link between madness and the law; or, more precisely, it suggests that into the workings of a mind which is involved with the workings of the law, madness is likely to come.

Bleak House was not the first novel to investigate the relationship in detail. Earlier in the century, in Scotland, there were two: John Galt's *The Entail* (1822) and Walter Scott's *Redgauntlet* (1824). *Redgauntlet* is set in 1765, and its main historical concern is with a suppositious visit to Britain by the Young Pretender (Bonnie Prince Charlie) to raise support for another attempt to claim the throne. We may point out in passing that such an attempt in 1765, if really made, would have been madness; and if an inability to distinguish between fact and fiction is a symptom of madness, then the reader is being required to collaborate in a kind of madness for the duration of the novel. The early part of the story is narrated mainly by Darsie Latimer and Alan Fairford, who have both been law students. Scott as usual interweaves the lives of fictitious individuals with historically based public events and personages; and before the political drama is activated, we are told of the efforts of Alan Fairford's father, also a lawyer, to get his son well commenced in his profession. To that end, he appoints Alan to represent Peter Peebles in *Peebles v Plainstanes*:

> "Peter Peebles!" exclaimed I, in astonishment; "he is an insane beggar – as poor as Job, and as mad as a March hare".
>
> "He has been pleaing in the court for fifteen years", said my father in a tone of commiseration, which seemed to acknowledge that this fact was enough to account for the poor man's condition both in mind and circumstances. (Scott p 133)

Peter Peebles has become a notorious figure about the courts of justice "where he has made shipwreck of time, means, and understanding" (p 135). His case, which has already been handled by ten advocates before Alan, is extremely intricate, a lawsuit within a lawsuit, and is partly responsible for his impoverishment. But it is his fascination with the law itself which has made him mad. One sign of his madness is his assumption that he knows more about the law than do lawyers. Related to this is his use of legal terms. Every speech, on whatever subject, is laced with the jargon: "a multiple poinding is the safest remedium juris in the whole form of process. I have known it conjoined with a declarator of marriage" (p 138). A more serious symptom is his belief that his suit makes him the hero of the most significant drama in the world: "ye are a lucky man to buckle to such a cause as mine at the outset! It is like a specimen of all causes, man" (p 138). Peebles would lose his sense of his own importance if his suit were ever concluded, and he has a psychological investment in its continuation. He virtually lives in the law courts. On one occasion he is assaulted there, and a lawyer advises him that he could make it out *hamesucken*: "I dwell mair there than ony gate else, and the essence of hamesucken is to strike a man in his dwelling-place" (p 139).

On the evidence of the first part of the novel, Peebles's cause is a producer of madness. As one of the judges says to another: "This is a daft cause, Bladderskate – first, it drives the poor man mad that aught it – then your nevvy goes daft with fright, and flies the pit – then this smart young hopeful is aff the hooks with too hard study, I fancy – and now auld Saunders Fairford is as lunatic as the best of them" (p 151).

Peebles appears only twice more in the novel, and then briefly. But each appearance is made to tell thematically. The first is on the occasion of Darsie Latimer's appearance before a justice of the peace in England, where Mr Herries seeks to obtain authority for keeping Darsie under restraint as his ward. The justice, Squire Foxley, uses Darsie's alleged "cockbrained" state as one ground for complying with Herries's application. But at this point Peter Peebles makes his way into the justice's presence, seeking a warrant to restrain the movements of Alan Fairford. Darsie naturally appeals to Peebles to swear to his identity, but Peebles makes his situation worse:

> "Ou, he is just a wud harum-scarum creature, that wad never take to his studies; daft, sir, clean daft."
>
> "Deft!" said the Justice, "what d'ye mean by deft – eh?"
>
> "Just Fifish", replied Peter; "wowf – a wee bit by the East-Nook or sae; it's a common case – the tae half of the warld thinks the tither daft. I have met with folk in my day, that thought I was daft myself; and, for my part, I think our Court of Session clean daft, that have had the great cause of Peebles against Plainstanes before them for this score of years, and have never been able to ding the bottom out of it yet".

Squire Foxley asks, "what can he mean by *deft*?", and Herries replies, "He means *mad*". Peebles then recognises Herries as well, and Scott uses this to show the interpenetration of private events and history:

> I mind ye well, for ye lodged in my house the great year of forty-five, for a great year it was; the Great Rebellion broke out, and my cause – the great cause – Peebles against Plainstanes *et per contra* – was called in the beginning of the winter Session, and would have been heard, but that there was a surcease of Justice, with your plaids, and your piping, and your nonsense (p 198).

Herries would like to dismiss this as the ramblings of a crazy man, but Peebles's memory is exact: it is part of his madness that he should recall every detail that relates to his own case, and that in some sense everything *is* so related.

Scott has by this point set up a situation in which we are ready to regard lawyers and the law as being swayed by political influence and expediency, pure justice impossible to be found, and sanity a relative matter, all of us being placed somewhere on the spectrum from quirky to daft. In support of this he undermines Darsie's sense of his own identity, Darsie finding himself in situations in which he is expected to have loyalties and affinities to which he has been a stranger, and where even his name cannot be relied upon. From high to low, indeed, names are unreliable, and the plot pulls Darsie into a kind of nightmare, as tortuous as Peebles's lawsuit.

Yet in the end the novel is supportive of the law, and once more Peebles is used to focus the judgment. First, Scott shows that under the scrutiny of a first-rate legal mind, the chaos of *Peebles v Plainstanes* could be reduced to order. Secondly, the affairs of state, which threaten upheaval, misery and destruction, can be brought to a state of order where justice is tempered with mercy. Thirdly, Peter Peebles finally appears, thanks to Nanty Ewart's narrative, not as a crazed victim of the law, but as a mean, grasping, selfish coward, who was a tyrant to the poor and powerless. His madness is not a result of his victimisation, but a symptom of his selfishness, which attracted him to the law in the first place.

Scott was brought up by his lawyer father to the law, and became a successful lawyer himself. His younger contemporary, John Galt, was entered at Lincoln's Inn in 1809, but abandoned the law after only two years. Whether he was more detached than Scott in his treatment of the profession is debatable, but his satire on it in *The*

Entail is more spirited and, I think, ultimately more damaging than Scott's. Once more, a chief weapon in the exposé is a character commonly accounted mad, Watty Walkinshaw, the second son of Claud Walkinshaw. Claud, who has worked his way to wealth, has one obsession in life, to recover the lands and status of his ancestors, and then bind them on his male descendants for ever. This obsession holds him to the point of madness, in that all other considerations in his life give way before it. Having acquired one estate, the Grippy, Claud marries Girzy Hypel, the only child of a neighbouring laird, Hypel of Plealands, who is incidentally a compulsive and only moderately successful litigant. Before the marriage Claud declares that he will entail his estate on his first-born son, whereupon Hypel of Plealands says that he will entail Plealands on a second-born son, on the condition that that son take the surname of Hypel, which will otherwise die out. Girzy bears Claud four children, Charles, Walter, Margaret and George, and the entails on Charles and Walter are made. However, it turns out when Hypel of Plealands dies that his entail has not been tightly drawn up, and Walter is admitted to his grandfather's estate, without being obliged to take his grandfather's surname – "the very obligation which the old gentleman had been most solicitous to impose upon him" (p 30). This occasions the narrator (himself apparently a lawyer) to comment: "Really, when one considers how much some lawyers profit by their own mistakes, one might almost be tempted to do them the injustice to suspect that they now and then have an eye to futurity, and carve out work for themselves" (p 30). Shortly afterwards Claud decides that the family will be better served if all the lands lie together in one estate, and he therefore seeks to amend his entail to by-pass Charles, and settle all on Watty and his male heirs, or failing them to George and his male heirs, and only after the failing of them to the male heirs of Charles. Claud does this despite having declared Walter almost from infancy onwards to be an idiot, much to the annoyance of Girzy, the Leddy, who has always claimed Watty as her brightest and best. (Claud also thinks that the Leddy is weak-brained, and that Watty gets his daftness from her.) When lawyer Keelevin tries to dissuade Claud from changing the entail, (for which disinterestedness Keelevin is praised by the narrator) we learn that Watty's intellect has already been vetted in a court of law. Keelevin remarks, "the lad's truly no in a state to be called on to implement ony such agreement as what ye propose. He should na' be meddled wi', but just left to wear out his time in the world, as little observed as possible". Claud replies, "I canna say, Mr Keelevin, that I like to hear you misliken the lad sae, for did na ye yourself, with an ettling of pains that no other body could hae gane through but yoursel, prove, to the satisfaction of the fifteen at Edinburgh, that he was a young man of a very creditable intellect, when Plealands' will was contested by his cousin?" Keelevin is forced to reflect, "Waes me, Mr Walkinshaw, that ye should cast up to me the sincerity with which I did but my duty to a client. . ." (p 59)

Claud has his way, and the entail is modified. But first both Charles and Walter have to sign the alterations. It is Claud's desire that neither should know what he has done, and the quick and cheerful and supposedly intelligent Charles readily takes the pen and signs without hesitation. But the stupid and dull Walter refuses to do so: "'What am I to get by this?' said the natural. . . 'I would like to ken that. Nobody writes papers without payment'" (pp 73-74). Claud is desperately anxious that Watty's resistance will not lead to Charles knowing what has been done, and that Watty's childishness will not result in the deed being called invalid one day. On this occasion Watty is quietened by the gift of a guinea, but it is typical of Watty that in his simplicity he sometimes acts more circumspectly, or speaks more by the book, than those whose intellects are not called in question. In other words, he has a better reverence for the mysterious power of forms and codes than does Charlie. Some of this emerges in his courting of Betty Bodle, a match which his father has promoted. At first Watty objects to the project, on the grounds that he likes his mother better than any other woman, including Betty. Claud points out:"an t'ou was ance marriet to Betty Bodle t'ou would soon like her far better than thy mother." But Watty responds: "The fifth command says, 'Honour thy father and thy mother, that thy days may be long in the land,' and there's no ae word about liking a wife in a' the rest" (p 83). And after Watty gets Betty's consent, he avers "when a bargain's struck, the sooner payment's made the better; for, as the copy-line at the school says, 'Delays are dangerous'" (p 88). In all the niceties attached to the marriage ceremony, Watty is a stickler for form, so much so that the celebrant says "I did na think . . . that the creature had sic a knowledge o' the vows" (p 99).

Nonetheless, the plans of Claud and the scrupulousness of Watty are equally frail before the dispensations of God, and Betty dies in giving birth to a girl. It now becomes Claud's object that George should marry and have a son, who would in due course be forced to marry Watty's daughter, thus keeping the Plealands inheritance in the family. Meanwhile, Charles dies, after a stroke brought on by his chance discovery that his father has disinherited him. Claud remorsefully tries to repair some of the damage, by urging Watty to make provision for his bereaved sister-in-law and her two children, and at the same time make a settlement on his mother (the Leddy). But Walter refuses to sign any papers, claiming that it would wrong his new-born daughter. This leads the Leddy to change her opinion of Watty's mental power: "I'll alloo at last, gudeman, that I hae been a' my days in an error, for I could na hae believed that Watty was sic' an idiot o' a naturalist, had I no lived to see this day" (p 135).

Therefore when Claud himself dies, the Leddy supports George in his scheme to get Watty certified, so that George can have the management of the estate. Watty, apart from his refusal to sign papers, does show signs of a harmless abnormality at this time, for when his daughter dies, he claims that neither she nor his wife are really dead, but that his Betty Bodle lives on in the form of his niece Mary. Watty is therefore brought before a panel in Edinburgh, and the ensuing examination is one of the great scenes in nineteenth century fiction. The jury eventually returns a verdict on Watty of Fatuity (p 201), but it is interesting to see just what turns the scales against him. All the witnesses called to testify for or against Watty's daftness do him little damage, because they evaluate all things in terms of the possession of real property. So although the servant Jenny Purdie swears that Watty is beyond any question daft, she concedes that she would be happy to marry such a man as Watty, because "mony a better-born than me has been blithe to put up wi' houses and lan's, though wit and worth were baith wanting" (p 189). The University Professor of Mathematics, called to witness to Watty's lack of reasoning powers, surprises the court by declaring that he has changed his opinion, and that Watty is a "very extraordinary man", and again the imagery is financial: "I was trying if he could calculate the aliquot parts of a pound; and he said to me, could I tell him the reason that there were but four and twenty bawbees in a shilling?" The most important witness, the Leddy, states that Watty was not always daft, but became so only when he refused to give her an allowance; and the clergyman declares that Watty has sufficient gleams of sense because he is now providing for his sister-in-law and her children. It is only when Watty himself is cross-examined that things go astray for him. Even then he almost prevails, particularly when, after satisfactorily answering the questions of George's advocate, he himself asks the advocate one: "How muckle are ye to get frae my brother for this job?" As long as Watty seems aware that humanity's main motive in life is gain, the public is prepared to regard him as sufficiently sane. But when it is revealed that he regards his niece as the reincarnation of his dead wife and daughter, he is adjudged insane. In contrast to his father, who wished to defy death through an entail on male heirs, and to his grandfather, who wished to preserve his surname, Watty assumes the continuation of a loved female, for which he can get no legal sanction.

After the verdict, Watty virtually disappears from the novel. But the connection between madness and the law is pursued, since the effects of Claud's madness in setting up the entail are still operating in the characters' lives. In order for these effects to be remedied, the plot develops a contest centring on George, who is interested in keeping the benefits of the entail for his own descendants, even though he has only one child, a daughter. He therefore tries to marry this daughter, Robina, to James, son of Charles. George's interests begin to be opposed by his mother, the Leddy, who is disenchanted with him after she finds that he is no more willing to secure to her a generous allowance than was Watty. She reverts to her earlier estimate of Watty as sane, though it is now too late to do anything about it, and she sets herself to favour the interests of James. She always expresses herself in an illogical and inconsequential manner, and prides herself on her knowledge of the law, which she says she inherited from her father, though in fact she is very ignorant. At times she sounds very like Scott's Peter Peebles:

> "Nae doot, Sir, I could gie an evidence, and instruct on the merits of the interdict," said she learnedly; "but I ne'er hae yet been able to come to a right understanding anent and concerning the different aforesaids set forth in the respondent's reclaiming petition. Noo, I would be greatly obligated if ye would expone to me the nice point, that I may be able to decern accordingly." (p 335)

In a delicious irony we are told that Mr Pilledge, the rascally Writer to the Signet, had never heard a clearer argument, either at the bar or the bench, and as a result he gives the Leddy enough information for her to bring about with luck, courage and guile the downfall of George's designs.

George has also been challenged by another character, a Mrs Eadie, a visionary whom the narrator is willing to call mad when speaking of her shadows and gleams of lunacy. Mrs Eadie's fixation with the workings of Providence, and her preoccupation with things eternal, though gently satirised, is contrasted with the sordid and artificial worldliness of George, who is not redeemed by any spark of idealism.

Consequently, when James is placed in what we have been led to think of as his rightful, natural position, we feel that he has been placed there by women, normally disregarded under the laws of property, working against lawyers or outside the terms of the law. It is as if their benign madness has defeated a more deadly madness.

Dickens worked as a solicitor's clerk in 1827, and later actually contemplated reading for the Bar. Certainly many commentators have noted his detailed knowledge of the law and its workings. *Bleak House* incorporates perceptions of the law and madness found in the two earlier novels treated, and builds upon them. Involvement in one's own lawsuit can madden one – like Peter Peebles, there are Miss Flite and Gridley, all affording amusement to bystanders. The technicalities of law can fascinate to the point of madness – the Leddy and Peter Peebles are joined by Richard Carstone. The idea that the law can be used to adjust familial rivalries, a major theme of *The Entail*, is paralleled by Gridley's tale, and by almost all who are parties to *Jarndyce v Jarndyce*. But, surprisingly, given the popular conception of Dickens as a satirist of the law, *Bleak House* is more concerned than either of its predecessors to point out the necessity of the law. In the world of *Bleak House* almost every major crime is perpetrated. Murder, fraud and theft are there. Rape is not there, but the brutalisation and humiliation of women are. All these crimes are committed by people who think that there are special circumstances which justify their actions. It is precisely because of this assumption that the law is necessary: the capacity in human beings to view a crime as justifiable makes necessary a rectifying agency. Bad people necessitate the law; and mad people need a Lord Chancellor, or his equivalent, to watch over their interests and appoint guardians. Mr Jarndyce says of Neckett, the follower, "The man was necessary . . . If we make such men necessary by our faults and follies . . . we must not revenge ourselves upon them" (Dickens p 147). True; and how much more so do we make necessary a Lord Chancellor. Dickens indicates the unsatisfactory nature of the alternatives to law for settling disputes in the various forms of single combat which Boythorn proposes to Sir Leicester. As Dickens (1857 p 354) wrote in an essay called "Murderous Extremes", "A due respect for the Law is the basis of social existence. Without it, we come to . . . those two shining constellations among the bright Stars of Freedom, known by the names of Bowie-Knife and Revolver". Even while Dickens is exposing the waste of time and life inherent in the legal system, he is demonstrating its indispensability. It is such a realisation that makes the atmosphere of *Bleak House* at times like that of a madhouse, but Dickens indicates from the outset that this is part of the human situation, that since the human day broke, if it ever broke, we have been struggling with each other for the best grip on the slippery pavement and for the best share in the common human inheritance. The self-destructive madness of this is focussed in the absorption of the Jarndyce estate in costs. *Jarndyce v Jarndyce* looks like a family dispute, but literally it indicates ego versus self. It is very difficult in this situation to decide what would constitute sensible behaviour, but Dickens, through John Jarndyce, counsels observance of the principle of refusing to push one's claims at the expense of others. This for Dickens is the basis of sanity and the only recipe for communal health.

For Dickens one of the signs of the law's madness is its overproduction of papers and words, in its attempt to bind humanity through systematised language. Conversation Kenge takes pride in *Jarndyce v Jarndyce* as a monument of Chancery practice, and for him one of its admirable aspects is that it displays "every masterly fiction". But Dickens himself is producing reams of paper covered with words, in a supremely masterly fiction, and like Scott and Galt might be said to be binding the relationship of humanity and the law to a definition. Like them he subverts the authority of his narrators. *Redgauntlet* employed a multiple narrative to create the history of an event which never happened. *The Entail* only intermittently suggests that a lawyer is telling the tale; at other times the credentials of the narrator are concealed. In *Bleak House* Esther's relationship with the other narrator is never explained. Furthermore, she concludes with an incomplete sentence, and the words "even supposing – ", before Dickens himself appears in the Preface using language which is nearly continuous with Esther's. If the world of law weakens the hold of its clients on reality, the world of masterly fiction does likewise; and in that respect clients and readers are equidistant from madness.

BIBLIOGRAPHY

Dickens, Charles, 1853, *Bleak House*, Bradbury & Evans.

Dickens, Charles, 1857, "Murderous Extremes", Vol 1, *Household Words*, January.

Galt, John, 1984, *The Entail*, Gordon, IA (ed), OUP: The World's Classics Series.

Scott, Sir Walter, 1985, *Redgauntlet*, Sutherland, K (ed), OUP: The World's Classics Series.

8

Bleak House: *Chancery Versus Equity*

KIERAN DOLIN

The title of this chapter will perhaps sound paradoxical to lawyers and Victorianists: how can equity be pitted against Chancery? Was not Chancery the court charged with administering equity? To adopt briefly the language of pleading, I admit the paradox! The aim of this chapter is to traverse once more the well-trodden ground of Dickens's attack on Chancery; to suggest that *Bleak House* itself deploys the language of paradox to condemn the injustices created by the court; and to argue that Dickens's notions of justice and injustice are derived from the tradition of equity. I pay particular attention to the characterisation of John Jarndyce as "guardian", and argue that in performing this function for the children of the novel he fulfils duties neglected by the Chancellor. In short, the plot of the novel defies the inaction of Chancery by depicting the supplementary, corrective action of Jarndyce and Esther. *Bleak House,* it is argued, is a radical-conservative text, castigating the institution of Chancery for its dereliction of equity.

I want to begin with Dickens's reaction to his own abortive suit for an injunction and for common law damages against the piracy of *A Christmas Carol*. In a letter to John Forster he wrote:

> It is better to suffer a great wrong than to have recourse to the much greater wrong of the law. I shall not easily forget the expense, and anxiety, and horrible injustice of the *Carol* case, wherein, asserting the plainest right on earth, I was really treated as if I were the robber instead of the robbed. (Tillotson p 651)

The interest of these words is threefold: first they remind us that Dickens had personal experience of the court and the jurisdictional dispersion that he described in *Bleak House*, a fact which bears upon the still-debated question of his knowledge of the law.[1] Secondly, the subjectivity of his language recalls Sir William Holdsworth's (1929) claim that Dickens's value to the legal historian

1 See, for example, Boyer (1989).

lies in his "account of the human side of the rules of law and their working". Thirdly, and for my purposes most importantly, the assertion of "right" and its denial is accompanied by the rhetoric of inversion, "the robber instead of the robbed".

The extremity of this reaction, and the resort to a language of inversion and antinomy, are traceable in the opening chapter of *Bleak House*. Having located the court at the very heart of the fog, the narrator moralises upon the darkness of the courtroom, with its stained-glass windows that have lost their colours, its "lantern that has no light in it", and its "attendant wigs . . . all stuck in a fog-bank!" He moves from setting to institutional critique:

> This is the Court of Chancery; which has its decaying houses and its blighted lands in every shire; which has its worn-out lunatic in every madhouse, and its dead in every churchyard; which has its ruined suitor, with his slipshod heels and threadbare dress, borrowing and begging through the round of every man's acquaintance; which gives to monied might the means abundantly of wearying out the right; which so exhausts finances, patience, courage, hope; so overthrows the brain and breaks the heart; that there is not an honourable man among its practitioners who would not give – who does not often give – the warning, "Suffer any wrong that can be done you, rather than come here!" (pp 6-7)

In this passage, which functions as an overture (in the musical sense), foreshadowing the fates of Nemo, Miss Flite, Richard Carstone and others, we hear transformed into a more controlled and elevated rhetoric the catalogued outrage and the inversion of norms noted in the *Christmas Carol* letter.[2] This trope of inversion is exploited by John Jarndyce in describing the "monument to Chancery practice" to Esther as "a Witches' Sabbath":

> In the question how the trusts under [the] Will are to be administered, the fortune left by the Will is squandered away; the legatees under the Will are reduced to such a miserable condition that they would be sufficiently punished if they had committed an enormous crime in having money left them. (p 88)

No inference should be drawn from this echo of "the robber and the robbed" that Dickens's criticism of Chancery was motivated by his own disappointment as a litigant. An examination of the historical context of both the composition and the reception of *Bleak House* shows that Chancery reform had become an urgent issue in the early 1850s. The anonymous reviewer of the novel in the *Atheneum* (17 September 1853) expressed this concern by criticising Dickens for failing to keep "that mighty mystery of Iniquity and Equity perpetually before the reader" (Dyson 1969). This writer, too, uses paradox to crystallise the confusion, the discrepancy between ideal and experience, the sense of positive evil attributed to the inefficient

---

2 Jaques (1972), a monograph on the *Carol* case, also compares these two texts, and argues that the experience of litigation was the prime inspiration for *Jarndyce and Jarndyce*.

Chancery system. The campaign to reform the court was first acknowledged in 1824 with Lord Eldon's Commission of Enquiry; but the complete overhaul necessary to achieve the desired efficiency did not occur until the *Judicature Acts* of 1873. By 1851, the year in which *Bleak House* was published, protest was at its height. Butt and Tillotson, in their essay "The Topicality of *Bleak House*" (Dyson 1957), show how much Dickens drew from the public campaign:

> Dickens's indictment of Chancery . . . followed in almost every respect the charges already levelled in the columns of *The Times*. In both we read of houses in Chancery, and wards in Chancery, of dilatory and costly procedure, of wasted lives, and of legal obstructionism. (p 116)

Bleak House is not unique in its concern with such social issues as Chancery reform and urban sanitation. Between the 1820s and 1850s, when what Patrick Brantlinger (1977) calls "the spirit of reform" was dominant in English politics, novels and even poems were used in many campaigns for social and legal change.[3] The "novel of protest and reform" represented an important alliance between law and literature. As Holdsworth realised, the novel was better adapted than the official Blue Books to the portrayal of characters victimised by the cruelty or neglect of social institutions and people in authority; and to urge a case for reform by appealing to the emotions and consciences of readers. Elizabeth Gaskell, Bulwer Lytton, Harriet Martineau, and Charles Reade are only the best-known of the many novelists who tried their hands at what the barrister-critic Fitzjames Stephen (1861) disparagingly called, "novels with a purpose". Stephen condemned such novels for being ill-informed and simplistic, but he was speaking from a position within the governing class and felt that reform should be left to the experts.

This stance is illustrated by his claim that Dickens's "notions of law . . . are precisely those of an attorney's clerk" (1857 p 128).[4] His view was largely shared among the more conservative reviewers: the *Eclectic Review* (1853) wrote that Dickens "only exhibited in a stronger and more romantic light what has been pretty well made known before in the earnest prose of plainer men" (Dyson 1969 p 82). This formulation sounds like a recipe for a novel by George Eliot if not Herbert Spencer. The writer's notions of a novel, if I may adapt Stephen's words, are precisely those of a bureaucrat, whose critical norm of realism denies the "teaching and delight" that is possible through satire, sentimentality, imagination, and even invective. The reformist poetic of *Bleak House* is not concerned with technical details. On the contrary, the oppressiveness of technicality is one of the subjects of its broad-brushed, morally-outraged critique. The novel's contemporary and continuing power to inspire reformist ideals is captured by the 1949 assessment of Sir Gerald Hurst KC. In his

---

3 See also Kestner (1985).
4 Quoted by Boyer (1989 p 596).

Lincoln's Inn Essays (1949 p 113) Hurst concludes that while the legislative reform of Chancery had already begun, *Bleak House:*

> contributed in some measure at least to mould the minds of the men who mattered . . . its version, however extravagant, of the abuses of Chancery was sufficiently biting to stir even the complacency of vested interests and for this reason deserves a place among those classical works of fiction . . . which have helped practically to make a better England.

Although it sounds too blandly confident of social progress, the phrase, "a better England", is not out of place in a discussion of *Bleak House* for, as I shall argue, this is the implicit ideal which underlies its critique of Chancery. By examining the novel's usage of equity discourse, that ideal can be made explicit.

In view of the interdisciplinary nature of this topic, I shall begin with a basic account of the history of equity. The classical notion of equity, defined by Aristotle (in the *Ethics*) as, "a correction of law where it is defective owing to its universality" (Baker 1971 p 90), might be exemplified by the pardon of Effie Deans in *The Heart of Midlothian.* The residuary power of the monarch "to administer justice outside the regular system" is usually cited as the foundation of the Chancery jurisdiction in England (Baker 1971 p 84). Originally a court of conscience, the equity it administered was gradually refined into a body of principles, partly as a result of clashes with the Common Law courts and partly from the recognition that without principles, parties would not be treated equally. Equality, as Baker puts it, "was a requisite of equity". The eventual result of this development was a system rigid in its rules and procedures:

> It is the height of irony that the Court which originated to provide an escape from the defects of common law procedure should in its later history have developed procedural defects worse by far than those of the law. For two centuries before Dickens wrote *Bleak House,* the word "Chancery" had been synonymous with expense, delay and despair. (Baker 1971 p 95)

This irony is underscored by the discrepancy between Chancery practices and the principles of the Equity jurisdiction, set forth in the "maxims of equity".[5] Among the maxims, the following are particularly telling for present purposes: equity will not, by reason of a merely technical defect, suffer a wrong to be without a remedy; he who seeks equity must do equity; he who comes into equity must come with clean hands; delay defeats equities; equality is equity; equity looks to the intent rather than to the form; and, equity acts *in personam.* These illustrate the conscientious, substantive and idealistic expectations which equity imposed on those seeking its assistance and the standard of justice which it set itself. With the defects of Chancery, some of the maxims began to function ironically.

---

5 See any edition of *Snell's Principles of Equity* for the complete list of maxims. For an account of the evolution of the maxims, see Pound (1926).

The *Jennens* case, the inspiration for *Jarndyce and Jarndyce*, was begun in 1798 and was still extant in 1915, when costs amounted to £250,000 (Johnson 1952).[6] In such an example, the maxim, "delay defeats equities", ironically applies to the court's own dilatoriness, which denies its suitors justice.

The amplitude of the maxims' application was also limited by the kinds of cases able to be brought before the court. From the sixteenth century most Chancery cases concerned land or "real property" and as the court rigidified its practice, this limitation became entrenched. In consequence, the equity jurisdiction protected the land-owning class, but not others. The maxim "equality is equity" was thereby circumscribed, an outcome highlighted in *Bleak House* by the contrast between the guardianship arranged for the "wards in *Jarndyce*" and the homelessness and death of Jo. According to Blackstone's *Commentaries on the Laws of England*, the eighteenth century classic legal text, the Chancellor was "keeper of the King's conscience . . . general guardian of all infants, idiots and lunatics; and [had] the general superintendance of all charitable uses in the kingdom". This jurisdiction derives from the monarch's duty as *"parens patriae"*, a parent of the nation.[7] Douglas Hamer comments that the "basic principle of the court of Chancery, that the socially weak must have a protector-at-law in the monarch, operated only where real estate was concerned". Lord Eldon ruled, as part of a policy of "crystallising" the equity jurisdiction, that he should not exercise these powers unless a case of disputed property was before him.[8] The Chancellor is guardian-at-law to Ada and Richard because they are heirs to the Jarndyce estate. He discharges no such responsibility with respect to Jo, or Charley, or Guster, or Esther. The apostrophe following Jo's death, "Dead, your Majesty. Dead, my Lords and gentlemen" invokes the consciences not only of all "men and women", but especially the Queen as *parens patriae* and those in power under her. That the exercise of the *parens patriae* jurisdiction is seen in the Lord Chancellor's careful and kindly enquiry into the appointment of John Jarndyce as guardian of the wards serves only to emphasise the need for and existent limitations on such power. Jarndyce becomes guardian not only to Rick and Ada, but to Esther and, through her, to Charley and others. This extension of compassion and charity makes him a supplementary Chancellor-figure, one who is perhaps more effectual, though sometimes, when the "east wind" blows, as problematic as his prototype. The function of guardian is therefore drawn from the equity tradition, but is given

---

6 Cf Dyson (1969 p 145). Johnson refers to the case as "Jennings". Hurst has the name as "Jennens" and gives more information, so his version is adopted here.

7 Robert A Donovan in his "Structure and Idea in *Bleak House*" (*ELH* 19, p 181) discusses the appropriateness of a Chancery suit as a vehicle for Dickens's exploration of the theme of the human duty to care for others. On the Chancellor's *parens patriae* jurisdiction see Kerby (1890 p 225).

8 "Dickens: The old Court of Chancery", *N&Q*, 17, 1970, p 343.

a far wider range of operation than it had in Chancery. Yet even this is recognised as second best. The notion of surrogate parenthood is criticised from the beginning by Esther, "The Lord High Chancellor, at his best, appeared so poor a substitute for the love and pride of parents" (p 31). Jarndyce himself hopes that his guardianship will "heal some of the wounds made by the miserable Chancery suit" (p 43). The Chancellor's surrogacy is vitiated by its origin in *Jarndyce and Jarndyce.* As Ada writes to Richard, the suit "had its share in making us both orphans" (p 466). *Jarndyce and Jarndyce* is largely responsible for Richard's unsteadiness: when the Chancellor reproves him as a "Vexatious and Capricious Infant" who does not know his own mind, Richard's "a pretty good joke . . . from that quarter" is pertinent criticism (p 300).

Ultimately, *Bleak House* idealises responsible parenthood and family life while multiplying instances of abandonment, neglect, infertility, poverty, disease and death. Like the ideal of equity, family "love and pride" is the desired "other" in a world of broken relations. The novel seeks to inscribe the care and protection of children into the *nomos.* The power of the Chancellor over guardianship is the one room in the "bleak house" of the law adapted to the purpose. Dickens's awareness of this power may be traced to the 1850 monograph, *The Autobiography of Leigh Hunt,* wherein the model for Harold Skimpole laments the removal of Shelley's children from their father's custody by the Chancellor:

> the reader, perhaps, is not aware that in this country so justly called free on many accounts, and so proud of its 'Englishman's castle' – of the house which nothing can violate – a man's offspring can be taken away from him tomorrow who holds a different opinion from the Lord Chancellor in faith and morals (1949 pp 767-8).[9]

The interest here is not the merits of Hunt's defence of Shelley (or of Dickens's disloyalty to Hunt), but the dialectical contrast with Dickens's view of the "condition of England" in general and of the value of the Chancellor's guardianship function. The passage gives to the novel's portrayal of Skimpole as parent a special sharpness, but most importantly it links the idea of parenthood with the image of the home as sanctuary. Esther betrays a consciousness of the rights of the householder and parent when, at the Jellybys', she is "in two minds about taking [the] liberty" of bathing Peepy (p 46), but knows that nobody will notice. Further, this legal cliché is shown to function negatively in *Bleak House,* through the forcible entry into houses by bailiffs and such self-appointed moral guardians as Mrs Pardiggle. The fractured families are also those whose dwellings are most exposed or liable to invasion, which is not only a sign of the novel's socio-economic realism, but an image pattern of emotional, psychological and also political significance. Most precarious in this respect are the brickmakers' wives and children. This domestic

9 On the question whether Dickens knew Hunt's work see Altick (1985 pp 1-15).

setting is invested with political awareness: of the arrogant paternalism of Mrs Pardiggle; of the brickmakers' radical resistance; of the "triple jeopardy" of the brickmakers' wives, poor, grieving and battered; of the effects of economic depression and the lack of self-determination evident when brickmakers cannot house their families properly. The rotting of the "house of Dedlock" as a physical and social structure is well known. The disturbing scenes in which Bucket arrests Gridley and later Trooper George by disguised entry into George's and Bagnet's homes are further examples of this correspondence. By contrast, Charley's efforts to protect her siblings by locking them in is a telling image of determination and a successful adaptation, perhaps inversion, of the skills of a bailiff. Needless to say, her father has easily gained access to Skimpole's. If, according to the mythology of English law, an Englishman's home is his castle, then the novel's imagery of homes vulnerable to invasion and of "decaying houses" in Chancery forces a reconsideration of the security afforded by the law. In consequence, the decrepit slum of Tom-All-Alone's comes to stand not only for the deranged obsession of Tom Jarndyce, but for the rotting structure of Chancery. By extension, English law is not the protective walled city of Heraclitus, but a "bleak house" in which victims like Jo are "moved on" by officers of the state.

The distinction between Chancery practice and the ideals of Equity has far-reaching consequences for an understanding of *Bleak House.* A further illustration of this "pretence of equity" is afforded by the maxim, "equity acts *in personam*". Simply put, this refers to the nature of equitable remedies, which order named persons either to perform an action that, in conscience or justice, they ought to perform, or to desist from any unconscionable or unjust action. In *Bleak House* Chancery barely acts at all; instead it is presented as feeding off the estate, as concerned only with the self-maintenance of the suit and the profits to the legal officers.

Dickens begins the action of the novel at a time when the only question in dispute in the legal action is that of costs. The reader is never informed what substantive orders were made in answer to the questions originally brought before the Court. The equitable action ordered by the Court is irrelevant when there is no estate left to be distributed after lawyers' and court costs have been deducted. The late discovery of a final will, which seems to supply the details upon which the court has ruled and the money has been spent, simply confirms the futility of the Chancery action. As DA Miller (1987 p 70) suggests, *Jarndyce and Jarndyce* is not resolved, merely ended, by the exhaustion of the estate in costs. This is the only appropriate outcome for a court obsessed by procedural issues and clogged by procedural inefficiency. The objective correlative of this wasteful system is, of course, Krook's rag and bottle shop, a business without turnover much less profit, "'of so many kinds, and all, as the neighbours think (but they know nothing), wasting away and going to rack and ruin, that that's why they have given me and my place a christening'" (p 50).

The only exception to the substantive inaction of Chancery is the order appointing John Jarndyce guardian of the wards. The Jarndyce household, under the superintendance of Esther, is a model of sympathy and efficiency, in contrast to Krook and his eponym. In consequence, Jarndyce's role as supplement to the Lord Chancellor is extended, and *Bleak House* becomes an alternative Chancery. It becomes the centre of a network of fellowship and charity, in which Jarndyce's quiet generosity and Esther's unpretentious practicality provide conscientious and effective assistance to those of their acquaintance in need. The hallmark of this assistance is personal action and immediate relief. In its conversion of ideals into reality, it contrasts with the distant dream and present mess, the torrent of words and paper, of both Chancery and Telescopic Philanthropy.

What the novel repeatedly calls "Esther's Narrative" not only describes her own "progress", but also provides a new perspective from which the confusion wrought by Chancery may be judged. As autobiography, Esther's narrative represents a completely different story-telling practice from that adopted in the Court of Chancery. Evidence in Chancery was always written, not oral. Holdsworth describes the process by which Chancery obtained its formal "depositions": witnesses were required to answer, without legal assistance, "lengthy and minute" interrogatories written by the plaintiff's lawyers; their answers were written down by commissioners, not verbatim, but in the third person and often rephrased. Holdsworth concludes "that there was every chance that in the course of this transcription its effect would be materially altered".[10]

The unusual "double narrative" of *Bleak House* may be seen in part as a reaction to this artificial and indirect form of testimony, an ironic commentary on, if not an intentional disavowal of it. Esther's narrative is a first-person statement, integral to, but part of a larger document, in her own words, preserving all her significant evasions, hesitancies, qualifications and avowals. Its inclusion has provoked much comment about the relative status of the two narrators, their contrasting voices and the consequential articulation by Esther of alternative values. What an evidentiary analysis of her narrative adds to the critical understanding of the novel is a sense of the importance of the individual witness. Esther's narrative asserts the value of personal expression over the formal reconstructions of Chancery. Moreover the elevation of the individual in the narrative system is an embodiment in form of the value of personal action in the social system. Above all it endows the illegitimate orphan with the right to speak in the cause of her own life. Esther's narrative is a vindication of her identity, a proof that she is not filia nullius, the

10 *Charles Dickens as a Legal Historian*, pp 92-8.

daughter of Nemo, nobody. It is a rewriting of the repressive history of Miss Barbary. Ironically, it effectively takes the place of the deposition she could not give in explanation of her interest in *Jarndyce and Jarndyce*. With the impersonal narration it supersedes the mountainous writing and rewriting of that case.

Underlying the opposition between Chancery and Equity explored in this chapter is an assumption of the beneficent potential of Equity. This assumption can be critically evaluated by considering what is achieved through Jarndyce's role as supplementary Chancellor. The principal beneficiary of his guardianship is Esther, and while her career moves from loveless abandonment to a family of her own, there are some problematic aspects to their relationship.

Conflicts arise when Jarndyce proposes to marry Esther: conflicts of duty and desire on his part, of gratitude and dwindling hope on hers. Their engagement is itself problematic as Esther continues to call her fiancé, "guardian". Once Jarndyce observes the love of Esther and Allan Woodcourt, the engagement becomes a front behind which he manoeuvres to gain Mrs Woodcourt's approval of Esther and to build a house in which to set the young couple up for life. The ruse whereby Jarndyce "transfers" (almost in the legal sense) Esther's plighted troth from himself to Woodcourt is arrant paternalism. Indeed it clarifies their relationship from that of lovers to that of father and daughter. Further, the presentation of the new *Bleak House* constitutes a marriage settlement, a dowry, given by a father through his daughter to her husband. If, as the rationale of the Chancery jurisdiction suggests, the need for guardianship is to ensure the protection of the weak, the young, the insane, then this extension of the activities of guardian into the arrangement of marriage is, whatever its generosity, a confirmation of woman's powerlessness and a continuation of paternalistic power.

Brook Thomas (1991) has recently suggested that this paternalism is inherent in the tradition of equity, that it posits and depends on the superior vision of the monarch, or the Chancellor, or the father. Thomas hopes for a more democratic notion of equity, on which to ground a modern argument that the relationship between law and literature is analogous to that between law and equity. In some ways this chapter provides an illustration of his thesis, first by suggesting that the literary work draws on Equity to expose and supplement the rigid deficiencies of Chancery, and secondly by applying a modern ideal of equity as between the sexes to the novel. One might, in effect, extend Dickens's own political critique of the structures of Victorian society to the structures of his novel. The paternalism of this plot results from a dependence on Victorian attitudes to women and inherited conventions of novelistic resolution. Thus, the desire for reform co-exists with respect for certain existing forms; *Bleak House* may be seen as both radical and conservative.

BIBLIOGRAPHY

Altick, RD, 1985, "Harold Skimpole Revisited", *The Life & Times of Leigh Hunt,* Friends of Iowa University Libraries.

Baker, JH, 1971, *An Introduction to English Legal History,* Butterworth's.

Boyer, Allen, 1989, "The Antiquarian and the Utilitarian: Charles Dickens vs James Fitzjames Stephen", *Tennessee Law Review,* 56, pp 595-628.

Brantlinger, Patrick, 1977, *The Spirit of Reform,* Harvard University Press.

Dyson, AE (ed), 1957, *Dickens at Work,* Methuen.

Dyson, AE (ed), 1969, *Bleak House: A Casebook,* Macmillan, p 55.

Holdsworth, Sir William, 1929, *Charles Dickens as a Legal Historian,* Yale University Press, pp 6-7.

Hurst, Sir Gerald, 1949, *Lincoln's Inn Essays,* Constable.

Jaques, ET, 1972, *Charles Dickens in Chancery,* Haskell House.

Johnson, Edgar, 1952, *Charles Dickens His Tragedy and Triumphs,* Simon & Schuster.

Kerby, DM, 1890, *An Historical Sketch of the Equitable Jurisdiction of the Court of Chancery,* Cambridge University Press.

Kestner, Joseph, 1985, *Protest and Reform,* University of Wisconsin Press.

Miller, DA, 1987, *The Novel and the Police,* University of California Press.

Pound, Roscoe, 1926, "On Certain Maxims of Equity", *Cambridge Legal Essays,* Hoffer, pp 2593-76.

Stephen, Fitzjames, 1857, "The Licence of Modern Novelists", *Edinburgh Review,* 106, pp 124-56.

Stephen, Fitzjames, 1861, "The Morality of Advocacy", *Cornhill Magazine,* 3, p 447.

Thomas, Brook, 1991, "Reflections on the Law and Literature Revival", *Critical Inquiry,* pp 510-39.

Tillotson, Kathleen (ed), *The Letters of Charles Dickens,* vol IV, Clarendon Press.

9
Dickens and The Law

KJA ASCHE

I concede bias. If this were a trial I would unhesitatingly disqualify myself. I cannot be impartial where Dickens is concerned; and I do not want to be. He has given me too much sheer enjoyment.

I do not dispute some faults. He is sentimental to the point of acute embarrassment to a twentieth century reader. But he was a man of his age and Victorians revelled in sentiment. Chesterton perceptively remarks that his death scenes got worse as he got older. There is more poignancy in the death of Mrs Weller, as recited by Mr Weller senior in a few lines, than there is in the death of Johnny in *Our Mutual Friend* which goes on for several pages. As for Little Nell, I am afraid Oscar Wilde was only too correct, "He would have to have a heart of stone who could read of the death of Little Nell without laughing". But the Victorians revelled in it and thousands wrote imploring him, "Don't let Little Nell die". Daniel O'Connell, the Irish MP, reading the book in a railway carriage, burst into tears, groaned, "He should not have killed her", and despairingly threw the volume out of the train window (*Oxford Book of Literary Anecdotes* 1977 p 309).

And that is the point. He absorbed, instructed, saddened and delighted the readers of his age to an extent which would be inconceivable today. We have a surfeit of entertainment. Radio, films and television are freely accessible, and huge resources are devoted to their production and preservation. If we obtain a recording of the "Eroica" and play it three or four times we have probably heard it more often than most avid music-lovers of the nineteenth century, who had to depend upon intermittent orchestral performances. But the very diversity of entertainment disperses our attention. The Victorians had no such variety nor, apart from the wealthy classes, did they have the time.

Because the only available medium which had the advantage of permanent and easy access was reading, Londoners clamoured for each weekly instalment of the new Dickens novel; as did the citizens of New York or Sydney or the miners in California or Ballarat when the same instalment reached them weeks or months later.

But if reading was the more lasting recreation there were, nevertheless, three more transient activities in which people of all conditions took enormous interest; and Dickens was superbly equipped to describe those activities. They were theatre, politics and law. He had a profound and practical knowledge of each.

He was an excellent actor. He enjoyed producing and acting in plays which were far more than amateur productions insofar as he gave to them the same earnest and professional skills which he displayed in the novels. When he writes of the Crummles in *Nicholas Nickleby* he gives a detailed description of the acting world even to the point of letting us know how much a reasonably competent actor might earn.

As to politics, Dickens had been a reporter of parliamentary debates and a fascinated witness to the excitement and venality of the election processes of the day. Any historian of nineteenth century English politics who neglects to read of "the election of a member to serve in parliament of that ancient, loyal and patriotic borough of Eatanswill", is no historian.

Law courts had always been one of the popular sources of entertainment. The drama was heightened in criminal law because of the ultimate sanction of the death penalty. The nineteenth century commenced with Blackstone's estimate of 160 offences for which capital punishment was the penalty (*Commentaries* bk IV p 18). Certainly, in many cases, the death penalty was commuted to transportation, a fact not without significance to Australia. (See Stephen (1833) vol 1 p 471). Transportation, for instance, was the fate of Magwitch in *Great Expectations*. But it was still a bit of a lottery, and there was a sufficiency of executions to whet the appetite. Until 1868 the executions remained public (see Holdsworth vol XI p 565), so a keen student could follow his man from arrest to trial to sentence to execution; and many did.

In civil law there were fascinating actions which often had the added advantage of involving members of the nobility. People took sides and the whole affair was full of pleasant excitement. In 1836 occurred the case of *Norton v Melbourne* wherein the noble Lord after whom this fair city is named was sued for "criminal conversations" (ie damages for adultery). "The court was packed with men and women of fashion some of whom had given five or ten guineas for a seat" (Pope-Hennessy 1947 p 11). Dickens himself reported the case for the *Morning Chronicle*.

The extent of public interest in things legal can be gauged by two trials which took place, one in Dickens's childhood, and one at the very end of his career. In 1821, the trial of Queen Caroline possessed all the ingredients of a good scandal, that is: royalty, sex and mystery. Did she or didn't she? In 1868 and later into the 1870s and after Dickens's death, the country was happily and furiously divided over the validity or otherwise of the claim of a 20-stone butcher from Wagga Wagga to be the heir to the Tichborne estates. Mr Kenealy QC so far forgot his professional ethics as to campaign publicly for his client; for which he was very properly disbarred.

Such trials aroused immense interest and passion. Dickens was supremely placed to absorb the atmosphere. The workings of the law had affected him personally from an early age when his father went to the debtors' prison in the Marshalsea. Dickens was 12 and had to spend that miserable time in the blacking factory which he describes in *David Copperfield.* When things improved a little he resumed his education and then found employment as a solicitor's clerk. He learnt shorthand and became a law reporter in Doctors Commons – "a place that has an ancient monopoly in suits about people's wills and people's marriages and disputes among ships and boats", as Steerforth described it to David Copperfield. This strange miscellany was later inherited by the Probate Divorce and Admiralty Division of the High Court.

Dickens continued his reporting until *Sketches by Boz* made him known and *Pickwick Papers* made him famous. But the scenes of the law courts, the advocates and the attorneys, the suitors, the judges and the clerks were a great mine from which he was to draw some of his most notable scenes and characters.

In 1844 he entered the lists himself, when he was the victorious plaintiff in five Chancery suits against publishers who had pirated the *Christmas Carol* (see Holdsworth vol XV p 378). Unfortunately he suffered a fate not unknown to successful plaintiffs today – the defendants had no money and he had to pay his own costs. This may have soured him of legal process, but he retained friends in the law. One of these was Serjeant Talfourd, instigator of one of the first faltering steps towards allowing a married woman some rights (albeit severely restricted) of custody or access to her children. The Act itself was known as *Talfourd's Act* 1836 (Eng). Talfourd proved a great parliamentary supporter of Dickens in his battle to reform the law of copyright. Dickens dedicated *Pickwick Papers* to him.

Dickens saw the delays, injustices, and the inhumanity of the law, which were fairly conspicuous in many areas. But reform was in the air and he was part of the movement.

His books did much to speed the process despite some last-ditch opposition. Lord Ellenborough was horrified to hear that the death penalty was to be removed for stealing goods to the value of five shillings. "'I trust', said he, 'your Lordships will pause before you assent to a measure pregnant with danger to the security of property'" (Campbell vol IV p 378).

Nevertheless, Sir Samuel Romilly got that bill through, and he and his supporters fostered a great deal more legislation to mitigate the harshness of criminal law and punishment. The public support given to them was greatly stimulated by Dickensian propaganda. For he was the greatest advocate of them all. The lawyer's field is restricted to the particular case before him. Dickens's brief was

England and its inhabitants high or low, rich or poor. His voice still speaks for the present day and particularly to the modern lawyer, for he makes plain why much legislation is in its present form. At the same time he entertains us with scenes that have not changed greatly, scenes which would be understood and appreciated by lawyers today. So we can look at Dickens the reformer, but also Dickens the entertainer and purveyor of the colour and interest of legal situations still well known. Let us first glance at the reforming side.

Dickens never forgot the misery of the days when his father was committed to the Marshalsea Prison for non-payment of debt. His description of the Marshalsea can be found in *Little Dorritt* who was, you will remember, "the child of the Marshalsea". A graphic description of another debtors' prison, the Fleet, can be found in *Pickwick Papers.* Both these novels contain powerful attacks on the inhumanity of the law which permitted indefinite imprisonment for debt. A debtor, once imprisoned and unable to pay, might spend the rest of his life deprived of liberty and in appalling degradation.

Debtors who had some outside resources did not do too badly and, in fact, John Dickens lived rather well at the Marshalsea. He was still in receipt of six pounds per week, which was handsome enough in those days. He moved his family (except Charles) into his room at the Marshalsea and, "the family confessed to each other that they felt more comfortable and unmolestable there than they ever had at home" (Pope-Hennessy pp 11, 13). So, Mr Pickwick in the Fleet, having discovered that, "money was, in the Fleet, just what money was out of it", was able to procure a private room for himself.

But what of those who did not have private resources or the help of friends? Dickens takes us to the poor side of a debtors' prison "in which the most miserable and abject class of debtors is confined" and reminds his readers that:

> We still leave unblotted in the leaves of our statute book, for the reverence and admiration of succeeding ages, the just and wholesome law which declares that the sturdy felon shall be fed and clothed, and that the penniless debtor shall be left to die of starvation and nakedness.

Truly reform was needed; and it came with the *Debtors Act* 1869 (Eng) which abolished imprisonment for debt save where some sort of fraudulent dealing was proved. Hence the statute, when adopted in many Australian colonies (eg Victoria), was entitled *The Imprisonment of Fraudulent Debtors Act*, the emphasis being on the adjective.

Hardly surprising for one of his passionate nature, Dickens had matrimonial problems. No-one reading *Our Mutual Friend* can escape the view that Bella Wilfer, the young, rather artless girl who scorns, then falls in love with and marries the older man, is modelled on Ellen Ternan, the young girl whom the older Dickens courted and almost certainly made his mistress. But although Dickens could and did separate from his wife, he could not divorce her and remarry. The courtship between Bella and John Harmon carries many marks of the pain of an old/young relationship. Their ultimate marriage and happiness seem an example of wishful thinking. Dickens seems to have treated his wife rather unjustly, for she was a faithful wife and good (and productive) mother. Her fault, in his eyes, seems to have been an exceeding dullness; but it is doubtful if any wife could have coped with Dickens. He was incurably romantic. He placed the women he loved on an impossibly high pedestal and then blamed them for failing to stay there. Maria Beadnell, his first great ideal love, was probably unlucky to meet him again when she was fat and fortyish. He turned her from the beloved Dora of *David Copperfield* into the stupid Flora of *Little Dorritt.* Mary Hogarth, his wife's 17-year-old sister, had the good fortune (at least so far as her memory with Dickens was concerned) to die young. She thereby preserved the angelic image he always had of her.

While Dickens's views on divorce may have been shaped by his own experience, his sympathy was real for those who were shackled together in impossible alliances – particularly those who could not afford the one legally permissible means of obtaining a divorce by Act of parliament. So Mr Bounderby advises Stephen Blackpool in *Hard Times*:

> Why you'd have to go to Doctors Commons with a suit, and you'd have to go to the House of Lords with a suit, and you'd have to get an Act of Parliament to enable you to marry again, and it would cost you (if it was a case of very plain sailing), I suppose from a thousand to fifteen hundred pounds. Perhaps twice the money.

Stephen, a good and honourable man, tied to a drunken, adulterous wife, thus learns that there is no way he can end his marriage and marry the heroine he wishes to marry. So his comment is, "The sooner I am dead the better".

Hard Times was written in 1854. The celebrated remarks of Maule J on the subject of divorce were probably pronounced in 1844.[1] They are in very similar terms to those used by Bounderby and it seems clear Dickens must have known of them.

The first *Matrimonial Causes Act* allowing for divorce to be granted by a court was passed in 1857. Although it remedied the sort of dilemma posed by Stephen Blackpool's situation, it would have given Dickens himself no comfort if he had seriously wished to divorce his wife to marry Ellen Ternan. It allowed divorce only at the suit of the innocent party and then, only on certain specific grounds. Mrs Dickens was clearly not guilty of any matrimonial offence, so Dickens could not divorce her, and she had no desire to divorce him. In fact, the idea of divorce was obviously unthinkable to both, and they agreed on a legal separation in 1858.

---

1 There is some doubt about the date Maule J delivered his remarks. See Megarry 1955 pp 116-17.

The lot of a married woman (unless protected by elaborate marriage settlements arranged by rich and affectionate fathers) was little better than that of a servant. "By marriage", said Blackstone, "the husband and wife are one person in law" (*Commentaries* bk 1 p 442). He then makes it quite clear that that person is the husband. On marriage the husband became the absolute owner of his wife's property. This is dramatically illustrated in *David Copperfield.* On the death of her first husband, David's mother was left the house in his will. Just after her marriage to Mr Murdstone she is incautious enough to describe it as "*my* own house". Corrected by Mr Murdstone she says "*our* own house". Corrected again, she finally gets it right: "*your* own house". We know that the main object of Mr Murdstone in marrying David's mother was to get her property because, towards the end of the novel, we find him up to the same tricks with another wife. We see the law operate also in *Bleak House* where Ada Clare marries Richard Carstone somewhat prematurely so that he can gain access to her property which, of course, he dissipates in legal costs in *Jarndyce v Jarndyce.* In *Great Expectations*, Estella's fortune is wasted by her drunken husband. Ralph Nickelby's remark to Madame Mantalini is perfectly correct: "A married woman has no property".

The concept that a husband became the owner of his wife's property on marriage was based on the idea of women being inferior or weaker beings needing protection. This philosophy was not always to the husband's advantage. For the law was, at least, logical. If he owned her property, he also owned her propensities. He was responsible for her. If she ran up bills or committed a tort, the presumption was that she did so as his agent.

The situation gradually changed from 1870 onwards with the passing of a series of *Married Woman's Property Acts* which ultimately gave a married woman the full right to own and control her own property.

Nothing enraged Dickens more than the exploitation and degradation of children. Obviously his own experiences gave power to his pen. It is clear that he would have had no legal redress from his own situation as a child. He was not actually starved or savagely beaten and few people saw any injustice in putting a boy of 12 out to work. In fact, it was the normal thing for children much younger than this to be working. Certainly it was a misdemeanour to neglect to supply necessaries to a child, servant or apprentice when a person was bound by duty or contract to provide for them (*R v John Friend* (1802) Russ & Ry 20; 168 ER 662). Oliver Twist may, therefore, have had some protection against his employer had anyone sufficiently busied himself over the matter. But who was to do that? It was Dickens's argument that the *Poor Laws* were an abomination for just that reason: they gave almost unlimited power over helpless children to parish officials whose main aim was to provide for them as cheaply as possible and apprentice them out to whoever would take them.

There were some safeguards, for even Oliver is saved from the horrors of becoming a chimney sweep by the intervention of a kindly Commissioner. But the point Dickens makes is that these protections were rare and haphazard.

Similarly, it is fair to say that Mr Squeers of Dotheboys Hall was modelled on a Yorkshire schoolmaster who was, in fact, prosecuted and convicted for cruelty to his charges. But again, it was Dickens's case that this was a rare event and that many other such cases went unnoticed and unpunished. As he said in the Preface to *Nicholas Nickelby,* "Mr Squeers is the representative of a class and not of an individual".

What Dickens was really fighting against was the almost total lack of any form of legal protection for children. True, the criminal law prohibited actual murder of a child or harsh ill-treatment – a somewhat broad concept when the philosophy of "spare the rod and spoil the child" was vigorously enforced, even upon the scions of the upper classes. The floggings at the great public schools were notorious and even a matter of pride among many who survived them. Mr Murdstone in his savage beating of David was probably quite safe from any prosecution.

Equity had developed some concept of the welfare of the child. "The wards in *Jarndyce*" were brought into the august presence of the Lord Chancellor himself. But the concept was limited to children with rights or expectation of property, not the miserable little factory workers or the *Poor Law* children of the parish.

It was for children in general that Dickens spoke. He was one of the first to suggest that a child had rights to kindness, to fair treatment, to time to grow up – in short – to childhood. Because his audience was immense he was a powerful force in the reforms which followed.

Hamlet listed "the law's delays" as one of the things which might drive a person to suicide. *Bleak House* is Dickens's savage but justified attack upon the delays in Chancery, and the first chapter of that novel is one of the most powerful pieces of writing in the English language. Since that novel is the subject of K Dolin's Chapter 8, I will not trespass save for the following observations.

The delays in Chancery had reached scandalous proportions in the early nineteenth century. This was due partly to understaffing of the court and partly to Lord Eldon's habit of reserving judgments for long periods. He commenced his judgment in *Earl of Radnor v Shafto* (1805) 11 Ves 448; 32 ER 1160 with the celebrated remark, "Having had doubts upon this will for 20 years, there can be no use in taking more time to consider it".

But delays were not unknown before that. By an interesting coincidence (I have not been able to find any family connection) the case of *Dagby v Crump* (Dick 35; 21 ER 180) was reported in 1719 by one John Dickens who is described as "late Senior Register of the Court of Chancery". Although there had been some earlier proceedings, the matter really commenced in 1699. In 1719 John Dickens reports the case only on a ruling of Lord Macclesfield giving liberty to amend an answer. So presumably there were later proceedings, though I can find no further reference in the English Reports. Perhaps, as in *Jarndyce*, the costs swallowed the cause.

For a recent case of delay I refer you to *Buttes Gas & Oil v Hammer* [1980] 3 All ER 475, which commenced in 1970. By 1980 the parties were still embroiled on interlocutory matters and got to the Court of Appeal on a question of discovery. I am happy to say however that this time the wheel had turned full circle and it was the court which justly berated the litigants for delay and not the other way round. Denning MR was in fine form:

> Now ten years later the action is nowhere near trial . . . On this interlocutory point the argument before us took nine days with five leading counsel and as many juniors. We have had excursions into the law of the sea of territorial waters and the continental shelf, into sovereign immunity and diplomatic immunity, into the rules of court and goodness knows what else . . . It looks like outdoing *Jarndyce v Jarndyce* except that these litigants are not likely to run out of money.

The more serious cases of delay in Chancery in Dickens's time were ameliorated by reforms in the court itself and, ultimately, by the *Judicature Act* 1873 (Eng). Obviously *Bleak House* had much to do with such reforms, and one may assume also that Dickens's exasperation which he expresses in his Preface against some hidebound lawyers who felt he was exaggerating, may have hastened the process.

Criminal law, on the other hand, was in Dickens's day only too brutally swift. There was no Court of Criminal Appeal[2] and one suspects that many judicial mistakes were blotted out by a quick hanging.

For instance, in *Oliver Twist*, Fagin was arrested on a Tuesday, tried and convicted on Friday of the same week, and hanged on the following Monday. There was nothing particularly unusual about this, provided the courts were in session. On 11 May 1812, John Bellingham shot and killed the Chancellor of the Exchequer, Mr Perceval. He was arrested immediately and examined by the magistrates that day. He was tried on 15 May and convicted. That day was a Friday and he was executed on the following Monday. The disturbing part of this case was that the accused was pretty obviously insane.[3]

The speed of a criminal trial was to a considerable extent governed by the "one-day rule" which insisted that a criminal trial had to be finished in one day. There were very few exceptions to this

2 The Court of Criminal Appeal was not constituted until 1907. In 1904 it was established that Adolf Beck had served seven years' imprisonment for a crime which he did not commit. His case was the catalyst for reform.

3 See the account of these events given in *The New Newgate Calendar*, The Folio Society 1960 edn pp 55-84

(see Holdsworth vol XI, p 554). Dickens does not seem to have complained about this save, perhaps, for the unsavoury devices resorted to, to suppress witnesses favourable to the defence when called by the prosecution. Thus, in *The Old Curiosity Shop* during the trial of Kit Nubbles on a trumped up charge of stealing a five pound note, the prosecutor is warned in advance that Dick Swiveller was favourably disposed to Kit. He manages by innuendo to raise such a cloud of suspicion about his evidence (albeit Dick is called for the Crown) that defence counsel feels it would be unwise to ask him any questions. This may have been, at least to some extent, inspired by the desire to get the trial over quickly.

Dickens did attack the ghastly conditions of prisoners. In Chapter 24 of *Sketches by Boz* he depicts the horrors of Newgate, rampant with disease and dirt. The judges needed their nosegays when the prisoners came forth to the court.

Both civil and criminal trials suffered from something we would these days see as a strange rule and, usually, a considerable disadvantage. That was the rule that parties in a civil trial and the accused in a criminal trial could not give evidence. The rationale of the rule seems to have been to remove bias, that is, that a witness should be unprejudiced.[4] In early times the rule extended to exclude any witness who might seem to have an interest or bias in the case. The rule was abolished as to civil proceedings in 1851[5] and as to criminal proceedings in 1898.[6]

Thus, Darnay in *A Tale of Two Cities* cannot tell his own story when accused of treason. He was only saved by two other considerations which would be as cogent today as they were then; the unsavoury character of the prosecution witness, Barsad; and the doubt thrown upon the identification of Darnay when the identifying witness was confronted with the remarkable likeness between Darnay and Sydney Carton.

Dickens makes the most of the pleasing public anticipation of the result if Darnay were convicted. As a spectator in the crowded

---

4 Thus Hawkins writing in 1795 says:

> It seems to be an uncontested rule in all cases whatsoever that if a person is either to be a gainer or a loser by the event of the cause, whether such advantage be *direct and immediate* or *consequential* only he is incompetent to be a witness (1975 edn).

See also Windeyer 186. Almost certainly this rule also had a religious basis going back to the days of compurgation when the Church's teaching was almost universally accepted that false swearing on the *Bible* imperilled one's immortal soul. Looked at in this way the rule against interested persons giving evidence was a merciful measure designed to remove a terrible temptation from a desperate person.

5 *Evidence Act* 1851 (Eng). The rule excluding witnesses, other than the parties, for interest had previously been abolished by the *Evidence Act* 1843 (Eng).

6 *Criminal Evidence Act* 1898 (Eng). Not all barristers thought this was a great boon. Marshall Hall was convinced that Seddon (charged with murder) hanged himself by his arrogant behaviour in the witness box. Marshall Hall had advised him against giving evidence but Seddon insisted.

courtroom says to Jerry Cruncher, it was a "quartering case" which meant, as the same spectator gloatingly observed:

> He'll be drawn on a hurdle to be half hanged, and then he'll be taken down and sliced before his own face, and then his inside will be taken out and burnt while he looks on and then his head will be chopped off, and he'll be cut into quarters. That's the sentence.[7]

Although Dickens was admittedly writing of an earlier time (1780), even by then the more barbarous aspects of the sentence were not implemented and the spectator is indulging in a little poetic licence.

When Dickens wrote *Martin Chuzzlewit* the company law of England was in a parlous state. The *Bubble Act* 1720 passed by a "panic stricken" parliament to stop the speculation and frauds of the South Sea Bubble had not been particularly successful.[8] It was repealed in 1825 but the growth of large, unincorporated, joint stock companies led to abuses by unscrupulous promoters. "The Anglo-Bangalay Disinterested Loan & Life Assurance Company" so artfully promoted by Tigg Montague was a perfect example. Holdsworth, in his *History of English Law* (vol XV p 48) considered that the description given by Dickens of this company (really a partnership) was no exaggeration. In fact, is there not something rather familiar today in Dickens's description of this company? Let us summarise what he says about it.

The company occupied resplendent premises, and issued colourful circulars assuring no loss to investors and promising a "perpetual Christmas Box and constantly increasing bonus". It used the time-honoured device of paying dividends out of capital. It purported to accept only the "highest lawful interest" from lenders but used the equally time-honoured devices of increasing that interest in real terms by extra charges, for example, for the bond, for "expenses" and for "inquiries" – "We keep a man at a pound a week to make 'em". It granted annuities on the very lowest and most advantageous terms known in the money market and "the old ladies and gentlemen down in the country buy 'em". All this is explained to the delight of Jonas Chuzzlewit who understands, and approves. Equally interesting for a modern reader are the public meetings reported in *Nicholas Nickleby* to form "The United Metropolitan Improved Muffin & Crumpet Baking & Punctual Delivery Company". The important persons and the grand designs are all there and, as the meeting adjourned, the directors:

> went to office for lunch as they did every day at half-past one o'clock; and to remunerate themselves for which trouble (as the company was

7 By the *Treason Act* 1814 there was to be no disembowelling before death, and the beheading and quartering was only to take place after the death by hanging. In 1870 the *Forfeiture Act* substituted hanging alone. As to the old form of the sentence see Hawkins (1795 Bk 2 ch 48 p 468).

8 Maitland 1911 in *Palmers Company Law* (1976 edn p 390).

yet in its infancy), they only charged three guineas each man for every such attendance.

As *Martin Chuzzlewit* was being written, a parliamentary Select Committee formed in 1841, was examining the situation. Its report led to the Acts of 1844 and ultimately to the first *Companies Act* 1856 (Eng). So Dickens had his share in these reforms. However, how far even the most detailed legislation can cure human greed and speculation is a question which we may ask as much today, as in Dickens's time. Novels such as *Nicholas Nickleby* and *Martin Chuzzlewit* (and indeed *The Old Curiosity Shop* for a less complicated but equally disastrous example of gambling) merely reflect a still prevalent human frailty summed up in the celebrated aphorism of Mr PT Barnum.

In *Bardell v Pickwick* we have the most celebrated of Dickens's fictitious cases. Mrs Bardel sued Mr Pickwick for breach of promise. Apart from what appears to be a strenuous cross-examination by the plaintiff's counsel of some of their own witnesses, there is much in the case which would be familiar today, although we are not often favoured with a witness quite as astute as Sam Weller under hostile questioning:

> "Have you a pair of eyes Mr Weller?"
>
> "Yes I have a pair of eyes," replied Sam, "and that's just it. If they was a pair o' patent double million magnifyin' gas microscopes of hextra power, p'raps I might be able to see through a flight o' stairs and a deal door; but bein' only eyes, you see, my wision's limited."

And we must not forget how splendidly Sam led Serjeant Buzfuz on in the matter of Dodson and Fogg. He told how Mrs Bardell and her friends had spoken admiringly of Dodson and Fogg:

> "Well!" said Serjeant Buzfuz, "they spoke in high praise of the honourable conduct of Messrs Dodson and Fogg the attorneys for the plaintiff did they?"
>
> "Yes", said Sam, "they said what a wery gen'rous thing it was o' them to have taken up the case on spec, and to charge nothing at all for costs, unless they got 'em out of Mr Pickwick."

Actions for breach of promise of marriage ceased in Australia in 1976. A civil jury is now a rarity in many States and Territories. But there is still a sufficiency of sensational cases both civil and criminal, to enable barristers to display the theatrical indignation of Serjeant Buzfuz over some innocuous correspondence. "Chops and tomato sauce. Yours Pickwick. Chops! Gracious heavens! and tomato sauce! Gentlemen, is the happiness of a sensitive and confiding female to be trifled away by such shallow artifices as these?" And any lawyer with court experience may still share the agony of poor Mr Phunky, the junior barrister who asked one question too many. We still have voluble ladies like Mrs Sanders who thoroughly enjoy being in the witness box and want to tell us their life story. And we still have to remind witnesses about hearsay, "'Quite enough to get sir, as the soldier said when they ordered him 350 lashes,' replied Sam. 'You must not tell us what the soldier, or any other man said, sir,' interposed the judge; 'it's not evidence'".

Finally, although the availability of running transcript may have made it less likely, there is still a vague possibility (I dare not put it any higher than that) that a tiny minority of present-day judges, in an inexpressibly small number of cases, on the minutest fraction of occasion, might have summed up as the trial judge did here. That is to say, "'He read as much of his notes to the jury as he could decipher on so short a notice and made running comments on the evidence as he went along'".

The Bar remains a fertile field for colourful characters. Horace Rumpole may be a century-and-a-half away from Serjeant Buzfuz but, making due allowance for a little extra colouring for dramatic purposes, his original can still be found today as much as Serjeant Bompas was the model in real life for Serjeant Buzfuz.

Bardell v Pickwick remains a delight for lawyers and lay persons today as much as it ever did. The real fascination about the case is that it is still relevant. Satirical it may be, but it is firmly based on human conduct. Nothing in it is unbelievable.

Let us turn therefore to the array of personalities of the law which Dickens parades before us. It is sometimes said that Dickens did not love lawyers. This surely is far too sweeping a statement, and it is probably based on *Bleak House* which, however, is more an attack on one, albeit very large, area of the law, than on the lawyers as a class; although Mr Tulkinghorn is certainly villainy writ large. But one of Dickens's greatest friends was Serjeant Talfourd, later Mr Justice Talfourd, the original of Traddles in *David Copperfield;* and Traddles is a delightful, compassionate and decent man. Dodson and Fogg linger on the seamier side of the law (though never caught out) but Mr Perker, who is Mr Pickwick's own solicitor, is a model of the ethical practitioner. Uriah Heep is the most degraded of law clerks despite his admiration of Mr Tidd's justly renowned work on the Practice of the King's Bench. ("What an author Mr Tidd is, Master Copperfield!"). But he is, after all, unmasked by his own clerk Mr Micawber. And, in the balance, also call Mr Wemmick, that delightful eccentric with his moated house and his aged parent. Almost in the lowest circle of the Dickensian Inferno must be placed Mr Samson Brass, a totally degraded solicitor who is no more than a wretched creature of the demon Quilp despite the fact that he refers to himself as "a gentleman by Act of Parliament". But Tulkinghorn may descend yet lower because, though far more sophisticated than Brass, he uses his great talents for despicable ends. But what of Jaggers, worldly-wise and apparently unemotional? Is he not a decent man under the facade he considers necessary in his criminal practice? Serjeant Buzfuz and Serjeant Snubbin are typical advocates modelled on real life who may still be with us today. They are not painted as villains but as workmanlike counsel going about their business in their own idiosyncratic fashion. The bumptious Mr Stryver is a good enough craftsman at his trade even if he relies greatly on Sydney Carton for his forensic triumphs. There is no suggestion that he is a disgrace to his profession, and if he exudes an air of smugness and self-satisfaction somewhat above his real merits, then I fear we may meet his like in a few barristers of the present – although I hasten to say only a few. Mr Justice Stareleigh (modelled on Mr Justice Gaselee) does not come out too well; but Lord Mansfield, in his own person, gets very favourable mention in *Barnaby Rudge*. In short, in the kaleidoscope of legal characters (and I have not mentioned those on the outskirts of the law – the bailiffs, the scriveners, the bondsmen, etc), lawyers come out in all shapes and colours – as do doctors, actors, businessmen, tradesmen and all the others in the huge cast of characters assembled in the Dickensian drama. Leaving out the caricaturing, the historical differences and the sometimes over-powering sentimentality, we are left with recognisable characters and situations as apt today as they were then. The giant of the nineteenth century remains a giant in the twentieth and will continue into the twenty-first.

BIBLIOGRAPHY

Blackstone, Sir William, 1765, *Commentaries on the Laws of England*, bk IV, Oxford.
Campbell, *Lives of the Chief Justices* Vol IV
Folio Society, The, 1960, *The Newgate Calendar*.
Hawkins, 1795, *Pleas of the Crown*, 1975 edn.
Holdsworth, W, *History of English Law*, vol XI.
Maitland, FW, 1911, 3 Collected Papers, quoted in *Palmers Company Law*, 1976 edn.
Megarry, Sir Robert, 1955, *Miscellaney-at-Law*, Stevens & Sons
Oxford Book of Literary Anecdotes, 1977, Futura Publications.
Pope-Hennessy, Una, 1947, *Charles Dickens*, Reprint Society.
Stephen, JF, 1833, *History of Criminal Law*, vol 1.
Windeyer, *Legal History*.

10

The Law in the Theatre

PAUL ELLIOTT

To quote the *Bible*, "Woe unto lawyers, for yee have taken away the key of knowledge". To quote Shakespeare, "The first thing we do, let's kill all the lawyers". To quote David Williamson:

> JANE: Why are you even contemplating taking the brief?
>
> TREVOR: It's against the Bar Rules to turn down a brief you're offered. Everyone is entitled to the best legal advice they can get.
>
> JANE: A rule devised to maximise a barrister's income and minimise his conscience.
>
> TREVOR: *(Defensively)*. It's going to be an extremely interesting case.
>
> JANE: That seems a little like a German engineer saying, 'I do not go along with Genocide, but designing the gas chamber would be a hell of a challenge'. (*Top Silk*, I, vii)

Does the poor picture of lawyers depicted in David Williamson's play *Top Silk* equate to the views of Australian society in general? If so, are these views correct? Are these views different to other Western cultures such as the United Kingdom and the United States?

There is no doubt that in Australia the legal profession is under attack. The media and in particular *The Age* newspaper regularly attack lawyers. There has been a senate inquiry into the cost of justice. The Law Reform Commission of Victoria has published two discussion papers entitled "Restrictions on Legal Practice" and "Accountability of the Legal Profession". Both are critical of the manner in which the profession conducts itself.

On 11 August 1991 *The Age* printed an article with the heading, "As legal costs rise the poor have been pushed off the scale of justice. SOME CAN'T AFFORD TO PLEAD NOT GUILTY" followed by a photograph of a barrister in wig with the subtitle, "Too high a price on his head. The greed is good credo is still reverberating around the profession." *The Age* also recently published a long article emphasising the high earnings of QCs.

These anti-lawyer sentiments are clearly expressed in Williamson's play *Top Silk*. The play concerns Trevor Fredericks, a Queen's Counsel in his late thirties who is described as articulate and highly intelligent with a forceful personality. He is married to Jane, a

Legal Aid solicitor, who is described as emotional but not neurotic and very compassionate. Trevor is in a quandary. He is a member of the Labor Party and has been offered a seat in parliament with the prospect of becoming Premier. However he has also been offered a brief to appear on behalf of a newspaper tycoon character known as Paul Bradley. Bradley is described as being a media mogul, small and benign looking, polite and charming but utterly ruthless. He wants the Queen's Counsel to represent him before the Broadcasting Tribunal so that he can keep his monopoly interests in newspapers and other media.

Trevor's wife Jane is instructed to represent one of her childhood sweethearts who has become a drug-pusher. In order to do this she attempts to bribe policemen. Her ex-lover is represented as a victim of society. He is only a "small-time" drug operator who resorted to trafficking because of monetary concerns and his love of his family.

Trevor and Jane have a teenage son. The "top silk" does not relate to his son because his son is stupid. Trevor is so busy being a top silk that as well as being unable to relate fully on any emotional level with his son, he cannot, in fact, relate on any emotional level with anyone. In essence the top silk is represented as amoral, ambitious, avaricious, disloyal and contemptible.

Unfortunately for Trevor, his political opponents discover that his wife has been attempting to bribe policemen in order to get her ex-boyfriend off. It is gently put to him by the Attorney-General that, as a result of no charges being brought against his wife, he should not run for political office.

Even though Trevor leaves Jane, she then takes steps to resurrect his political career. Tony Turner, the State Attorney-General in a conservative government, is described as extremely confident, almost arrogant, intelligent, domineering, and intensely competitive. He is the one who has blackmailed Trevor into ceasing his political career by not revealing his wife's attempts at bribery and corruption. But Jane, the good-hearted Legal Aid solicitor, has one card up her sleeve: she confronts the cold-hearted Turner, also a former boyfriend of hers, who has been campaigning on an anti-abortion platform, with the reminder that when Jane fell pregnant to him he forced her to have an abortion. Jane subsequently informs Trevor of how she has resurrected his political career by blackmailing her former lover.

Trevor then has a flash of integrity because he believes he can get on in politics. He turns down the lucrative Bradley brief in order to take up Jane's challenge and represent instead Eddy, another former lover of Jane's who was caught trafficking in drugs. In a quite astonishing scene, Trevor makes such a magnificent plea that instead of going to jail for twelve years, Eddy is released on a good behaviour bond.

In the meantime Mark, our top silk's son, has left home, earning his living firstly as a builder's labourer on a poor peoples' project, and then by selling suits in a shop. At the end of the play the top silk does not go back to his wife, but there are indications that there might be some hope for a reunion.

All the lawyers in this play are portrayed as truly dreadful people. The QC will do anything to get on, however, because he is intelligent, he should go into left-wing politics. We are supposed to empathise with his wife Jane, a response which I found extremely difficult to achieve. If she is supposed to represent the warm side of the law then the writing did not succeed. Here is a woman quite prepared to bribe police in order to get a man off drug charges and the play fails to show any reason why she would do this. The explanation that the former boyfriend is a product of society is too trite. She is then prepared to blackmail another lawyer concerning an abortion he had caused her to have. In essence, although she may have been an emotional and loving mother, she was totally amoral. As amoral, in fact, as the horrendous character of Trevor Fredericks.

Is it only Australia that espouses sentiments that lawyers are totally devoid of any good and will do anything for money? It would appear that the English are not quite so hard on their lawyers. The views we are given of barristers and solicitors in English plays are not as hard as those expressed by Williamson. Perhaps this is so because some recent plays concerning lawyers have been written by a barrister, John Mortimer. *Voyage Around My Father* and the "Rumpole" series certainly painted barristers as real human beings. Although the barristers depicted have their foibles and failings, they are not shown as ruthless, greedy and totally bad.

Even Jeffrey Archer, in his recent play *Beyond Reasonable Doubt*, casts barristers in a favourable light. Archer's play was performed in Melbourne in the same year as Williamson's *Top Silk*. Although *Beyond Reasonable Doubt* can be classified as a potboiler, Archer's barristers certainly do not get the same treatment as Williamson's. The play is concerned with the Chairman of the Bar Council, Sir David Metcalfe QC, who is standing trial for the murder of his wife who was suffering from incurable cancer. He has been accused of poisoning her with her pills in order to gain her inheritance of one million pounds. He defends himself against his old arch-foe at the Bar, and is acquitted. Sir David, and indeed all the lawyers and the judges in the case, are painted as thoroughly decent people. The play continues the courtroom drama tradition of the English theatre as exemplified by Agatha Christie's *Witness for the Prosecution* or, going even further back, *Justice* by John Galsworthy. The difference in views of lawyers can be gleaned from the following dialogue which appears in scene 5 at the very end of the play. The trial has ended and Sir David has locked himself away in his large house in Wimbledon for some two weeks. Finally, his close friend, the solicitor Hamilton, manages to gain entry and speak to the QC. He congratulates Sir David on his acquittal and, of course, immediately offers him a murder trial brief:

SIR DAVID: The black magic murder case. You almost tempt me, Lionel, but I can't return to the Bar. You see, it's no longer possible.

HAMILTON: Why not?

SIR DAVID: Because I did kill my wife.

HAMILTON: It was an accident, we all realise that.

SIR DAVID: No, Lionel it was quite deliberate. That's what she wanted and I couldn't refuse her. I loved her too much.

HAMILTON: But you're the Chairman of the Bar Council. Of all people you cannot be above the law. . .

Sir David then commits suicide by swallowing the same type of pills that killed his wife, disguising them however, in a marvellous bottle of 1961 Chateau Mouton Rothschild.

Americans love to hate lawyers and yet consistently represent them as heroes in many plays. The success of "LA Law" is to the point. Even though the lawyers in this series to a degree have many failings, "Perry Mason", "Petrocelli" and even "Jake and the Fat Man" testify to an admiration for lawyers and their skills.

Why then is there seemingly a more inherent dislike of lawyers in Australian society? At first glance it is a love-hate relationship. People do not like lawyers, yet entrance to Law at universities in Australia requires the highest marks. The marks needed to become a lawyer are even higher than those required to become a doctor. This seems at odds with the general dislike of lawyers in Australian society. Is society simply amoral and greedy, wanting its children to get on the gravy train?

Perhaps the difference between Australian and American society is the puritan work ethic, which in America is extremely strong. People are openly applauded and congratulated for working hard and making money – success is viewed as a virtue. Even those in some of the most menial jobs take pride in having that job, and do not feel jealous of others who go on and become extremely successful. Inherent in American society is the view that everybody could perhaps go on and become a success. This is not to say that American society is perfect.

However, in Australia the "tall poppy syndrome" is not just a joke – it is an inherent feature in the whole of Australian society – and it is a feature which surfaces regularly in the press. There is a deep-seated resentment against success in Australia, and it may well be that "chip-on-the-shoulder" journalists really do present the views and feelings of Australian society. David Williamson regularly rails against the tall poppy syndrome. He believes that he has become a victim of it, and he believes that the critics in Australia are quick to deride but slow to applaud. However, it appears that many of his recent plays and, most importantly *Top Silk*, actually represent the tall poppy/chip-on-the-shoulder syndrome of Australian Society.

There is nothing inherently wrong with being successful. Becoming a Queen's Counsel is not necessarily a bad thing; being good at one's profession is not necessarily a bad thing; being acclaimed for professional or other talent is not necessarily a bad thing. That is not to say that materialism and professional success are the only criteria upon which to judge a human being. I am not advocating that greed is good. The problem with Australian society, and the problem as shown in Williamson's play, is that Australia has gone too far the other way. For whatever sociological and political reasons, Australians, in general, resent those who stand out. They resent people who are talented and they resent people who gain money through their work and efforts. The attacks on professions, and especially the legal profession, are an expression of these views.

Although, perhaps, this view must be modified. Could it be that Australians resent people who are intellectually and artistically talented? There seems to be no objection to a tennis player receiving $100,000 for an exhibition game. Nobody attacks Greg Norman for his gigantic earnings on the golf course. Pages of the newspapers are devoted to sports people and their earnings, yet there is no outcry for a Senate inquiry into the cost of sport. Nobody has said that the high price paid to sportsmen is necessarily passed on to the consumer. Yet those in the professions who actually solve disputes come under constant criticism should they be seen to be earning a decent living.

Why has Australia developed this way? Has it got something to do with the convict background of the country? Has it got something to do with the fact that the majority of the people who came to these shores were not conformists or particularly successful in the old country?

Whatever the reasons, things have gone too far. The view of lawyers as crooked and amoral is a tired cliché. Williamson's play fails because it expresses this cliché over and over again. The people in the play are not real people – they are tired cardboard cut-outs. They are the cardboard cut-out lawyers that are thrust down the throats of society regularly by the media. Lawyers are not perfect and the profession is not perfect. However the views expressed by *Top Silk*, even if they express the views of Australian society, must be reversed because they go further than the hatred of lawyers. They go essentially to the fundamentals of this society and unless there is more emphasis on hard work, recognition of talent, and recognition of success, then Australia faces many problems. It is up to the lawyers to help themselves change this picture. One can only hope that in the coming years with the many challenges of inquiries and reforms that they do so. Perhaps then, a playwright will come along and represent lawyers as they really are, not as others would have them.

11

Women, Law and Literature: Representations of Women and the Law in American and Australian Fiction

ELAINE BARRY

When the long-suffering heroine of Anne Bronte's novel *The Tenant of Wildfell Hall* (1848) locked the door of her bedroom against her vicious and drunken husband, the sound of that door, it was said, reverberated throughout the bedrooms of Victorian England. Like Ibsen's Nora slamming the front door of her doll's house a generation later, the action was read as more than a dramatic gesture of individual assertion. It was seen as a symbolic protest against the legal status of married women.

Such identification confirms a relationship between literature and the lived experience that the contemporary emphasis on the autonomy of texts is sometimes in danger of under-estimating. Throughout the nineteenth century, fiction provides a particularly rich record of the changing status of women, including their legal status. The range and fidelity of such a record are the result of a number of factors. One is the form of the novel itself at that time; it not only reached the pinnacle of its achievement in the realistic mode, but it focused so much of that realism on the domestic scene and private emotions. Another was the increasing number of women writers, who would deal with such domestic material because, as Jane Austen said, that was what they knew best. A third factor is that the nineteenth century was the period in which the legal status of women changed most radically. Laws in themselves, of course, do not change social practice or put an end to the kinds of discrimination that many twentieth century novelists are still concerned with. But the nineteenth century won the great legal battles concerning the very status of women as legal beings.

At the beginning of that century, throughout the English-speaking world at least, their legal status was defined in the terms that English common law had evolved from the ecclesiastical courts: women were either *femmes soles* if they were single, or *femmes covertes* if they were married. *Femmes soles* hardly needed a legal system to chart the confines of their lives. What was not determined by the laws of inheritance certainly was by the social conventions which restricted access to most professions and denied them a social identity. Only the very rich, or the very strong-minded, or the very eccentric, escaped. It is only in our own day that the single woman, in literature or in life, has outgrown the stereotype which made her a figure of pity or ridicule. But if societal attitudes rather than law *per se* denied an identity to *femmes soles*, the law explicitly denied it to *femmes covertes*. With the marriage contract, according to Blackstone's interpretation of Common Law in the eighteenth century, a woman ceased to be a legal entity at all; her existence under the laws was subsumed into her husband's. He had total legal control of her property, her earnings, the guardianship of her children. She herself became his property. Throughout the century, changes in the law gradually gave a woman the right to her own property, the right to divorce, to the custody of her children, access to the professions, and the right to a voice on public platforms. By the end of that time, women were well on the way to winning the right to vote. In dealing with so many of these issues, nineteenth century fiction provided a reflection of women's historical experience, a forum for public debate, and a powerful vehicle for consciousness-raising. That slamming door became a central metaphor, linked to the persistent metaphors of marriage as prison – a protest against all the laws, written and unwritten, which women found circumscribing their lives and constructing their identities.

This chapter is concerned with the reflection of these legal and social changes in American and Australian literature. It is heavily weighted towards the American experience because – despite the many historical and sociological similarities between the two countries – there is a great discrepancy in their fictional representation of women's roles. Where American literature presents a rich field of primary material on the subject, Australia presents a comparative desert. My consideration of the Australian scene, towards the end of this chapter, will speculate on some of the reasons for this discrepancy.

In America, in the early nineteenth century, the legal status of women was still based in English common law.[1] Despite the federal Constitution of 1789, American law still rested largely in the individual States, genetically encoded with their colonial origins. The *femme sole/femme coverte* division pertained. Women were legally under the coverture of their husbands, they were denied access to the professions or to suffrage; custody of their children was in their

1 The legal situation of women in nineteenth century America is well-summarised in Bardes and Gossett (1990). See especially Introduction.

husband's hands. By convention rather than by law they had no access to a public voice. Their only right to property was, as in England, through special provisions of the Equity Courts.

When Hawthorne complained in 1855 about that "d--d mob of scribbling women"[2] who were capturing the reading market that he himself wanted, he gave public recognition to the dominant fictional mode of the times – the domestic or sentimental novel. The staggering sales figures for such works provide some justification for his envy. They sold by the hundreds of thousands. Susan Warner's 1850 novel *The Wide, Wide World*, for instance, was the first American novel to reach the million mark. What kind of representation of women do we find in these best-sellers? Centred round the home and family matters, the sentimental novel followed well-established conventions for plot and character. An early American critic summarised the formula in this way:

> First, take a young and not-too-pretty child about ten years old. . . Make sure that the child is, or shortly will be, an orphan. If the mother is still living, put her to death very gradually in a scene of much sorrow and little physical suffering, uttering pious hopes and admonitions to the last. The father presumably died years ago under circumstances not well known. Now put the child under the care of a shrewish aunt, who resents being obliged to take care of her dead brother's brat. If it has been impossible to remove the father as suggested above, a reasonably good compromise will be to have him make a second marriage with a frivolous, heartless society woman. In an emergency a cruel housekeeper will do. The child is now unhappy, undernourished, and underprivileged. . . The child's behaviour may in fact be actually bad in the beginning. She may "sass" her aunt. She may even shy a stone through a window. But her worst sin is her "pride". Now introduce a young woman living not far away, who embodies all the Christian virtues, especially humility. Let this lady kiss, pray over, and cry with the heroine at intervals of from three to four pages. The lady may or may not be blind; at any rate she has had her sorrows and she is destined to die about two-thirds of the way through the book of badly-diagnosed tuberculosis. She will die at sunset – without a struggle. She is going home. . . The girl's only remaining friends are an eccentric teamster, and a wealthy merchant who now and then gives her a lollipop. In the meantime she has learned to subdue her pride and to submit graciously to the suffering which is the lot of all mortals in this shabby world. You may end your story here if you will, with the child on the verge of adolescence, but it is preferable to carry on a few years in order that the heroine may be menaced by a proud, handsome, moody, Rochester-like man aged about thirty who has travelled and sinned (very vaguely) in the Orient. He at first scarcely notices the meek little girl, but her bright spirit and vaguely referred to physical charms finally force him to admit to himself that he must have her. If it weren't for Queen Victoria, he would try to seduce her, but as it is he is reduced to proposing marriage. To his astonishment she refuses. This sends him darkly off on more travels. The girl meanwhile has learned to support

2 Nathaniel Hawthorne, letter to William Ticknor, January 19, 1855, p 304.

> herself by teaching, acting as governess, or writing, and she talks rather briskly about independence for women... One day the moody man comes back, and finds her sitting in a cemetery. He proposes again and is accepted. Don't be alarmed at this: his pride has been humbled too, and he is now reformed... For her part, the heroine now drops all fantastic notions of female independence, for she realises that a woman's greatest glory is wifely submission. The acid aunt either dies or experiences a change of heart towards the heroine. In the latter case she may be married off to the neighbouring teamster. The wealthy merchant turns out to be the heroine's father: he wasn't really lost at sea! Everybody is now happy in a subdued, Christian sort of way. (Cowie 1948 pp 374-5)

It is easy to be condescending about formulas. But what needs to be remembered is that such plots – however sentimentally or melodramatically they are handled – are only conceivable because they have a certain basis in legal realities. They not only assume marriage as the only viable state for women (all the classic American *heroes*, in contrast, are single), but they assume marriage under the laws of coverture. The common plot in which an heiress is married for her money and then abandoned by her opportunistic husband became obsolete after the passage of the *Married Women's Property Acts* of the mid-century. Such plots also reflect the lack of opportunities for women. If a heroine was forced to earn a living, she generally had a choice between governessing or sewing. Not for her the American myth of working one's way from rags to riches through individual enterprise. The heroine of Mrs EDEN Southworth's enormously-popular novel *The Hidden Hand* (1859) underscores this point. She gets her start in life by disguising herself as a boy and beginning her quest for the American dream in the way that Horatio Alger would later canonise. As she explains to a man who recognises her:

> Sir, I was trying to get jobs every hour in the day. I'd have done *any*thing honest... [W]hile all the ragged boys I knew could get little jobs to earn bread, I, because I was a girl, was not allowed to carry a gentleman's parcel, or black his boots, or shovel the snow off a shopkeeper's pavement, or put in coal, or do *any*thing that *I* could do just as well as *they*. And so because I was a girl, there seemed to be nothing but starvation or beggary before me...
>
> [W]hen my last penny was spent for my last roll – and my last roll was eaten up – and I was dreading the gnawing hunger by day, and the horrid perils of the night, I thought to myself, *if I were only a boy*, I might carry packages, and shovel coal and lots of jobs by day, and sleep without terror by night... And then, all of a sudden, a bright thought struck me: *and I made up my mind to be a boy!* (Southworth 1988 pp 43-6)

The legal status of women thus underpinned the narrow plot formulas of the domestic novel. But beyond this, the enormous popularity of such novels suggests that they struck a chord in the collective unconscious. One might apply to them the same kind of mythic analysis that has been applied to more "serious" novels, decoding from their surface narratives a subtext which gives a metaphorical representation of women's experience – the orphan figure for instance. The prevalence of orphan male characters in "classic" American literature is frequently commented on, but the critical emphasis is different. From Natty Bumppo through Ishmael to Huck Finn, his orphan status is seen in terms of existential loneliness, of separation from old-world social structures, of the defiance of traditional order, of saying "no, in thunder". In the domestic novel, the heroine's orphan status is seen simply as a plot device. Yet one could surely invest this with similar significance: a symbol of female disempowerment, of a dependence reinforced by economic and legal realities.

The sentimental novel, then, in its motifs of the disempowerment and submissiveness of women, of seduction and betrayal, of sickness (real or psychosomatic), above all of physical and emotional confinement, offered a metaphor if not a literal reflection of women's lives. Their sense of entrapment within apparently benevolent patriarchal structures is most chillingly recorded in Charlotte Perkins Gilman's story "The Yellow Wallpaper" (1892).

Perhaps no writer gave more dramatic expression to the status of women in mid-nineteenth century America than did Herman Melville in his diptych of stories "The Paradise of Bachelors" and "The Tartarus of Maids" (1855). "The Paradise of Bachelors" focuses on the life of men. It is set within the Inns of Court in London, where a group of lawyers are enjoying a convivial dinner. Cocooned against the outside world by tradition, by affluence, by the rituals of clubbability, it is an exclusively male world. Melville portrays it as suffocating in its exclusiveness; it is immune either to fresh ideas or to real emotions. The other part of the diptych, "The Tartarus of Maids", is a story of New England rather than Old England, a story of women rather than men, and it is totally different in tone. The setting is a lonely snow-bound valley. The narrator is a seedsman (having "scattered his seeds through most of the mid-west") who is making a journey to a paper factory to buy envelopes for his seeds. The desolate and depersonalising snow contrasts sharply with the warmth of the men's club in "The Paradise of Bachelors". The narrator enters the valley through a kind of inter-uterine pass that follows a river called Blood River, and arrives at his destination, which is a factory operated wholly by women. There are only two male characters apart from the narrator. One is the owner of the factory (a bachelor called "Old Bach"), the other an errand boy nicknamed "Cupid", who conducts the narrator on a tour of the factory. Pallid women sit behind phallic pistons along a conveyor belt. The paper begins as a semen-like liquid, is processed through the intricacy of the "great machine", and comes out the other end as a blank sheet of paper. "Nine minutes to the dot" declares the proprietorial Cupid. In the light of the Lockian ideas of *tabula rasa* that permeate the narrative, it is significant that the final product sheet is foolscap. But, particularly in the context of its companion story, "The Tartarus of Maids" offers a remarkably modern as well as a remarkably feminist picture of women's roles in mid-nineteenth century America: one that links both the industrial exploitation of women which was increasingly prevalent in mill-towns such as Lowell, Massachusetts, and their enslavement within the engendered power-structures and within the biological determinism of pregnancy. It thus confirms – via a quite different genre and with infinitely greater art – the images of imprisonment and determinism that reflect the roles of women in thousands of sentimental novels.

Yet if the early representation of women was constructed of such images in America, as indeed it was in England, particular historical forces were working to modify it in America. American women might have inherited the English Common Law, but they also inherited the Declaration of Independence. The Declaration, of course, was not a code of law, as the Constitution was, but it had tremendous symbolic value. The American Revolution forced American women to construct a new identity for themselves as *American* women and a new role for themselves within the fabric of a new American society. That they were conscious of such challenges and opportunities is evidenced by a letter written to a friend by Abigail Adams, whose husband John Adams was a member of the first Congress and was to become the second President of the United States. She pondered a domestic parallel to the political Declaration of Independence. In a letter in 1776, she records how she presented a list of female grievances to her husband to put before the new government. "As there is a natural propensity in human nature to domination", she wrote, "I thought the most generous plan was to put it out of the power of the arbitrary and tyrannick to injure *us* with impunity by establishing some laws in our favour upon just and liberal principles. . . I even threatened fomenting a rebellion in case we were not considered . . . and assured him", she continued, echoing the phrasing of the Declaration of Independence, "that we would not hold ourselves bound by any laws in which we had neither a voice nor representation".[3] The Declaration of Independence offered American women a larger and more immediate context for their battles for legal rights than the passionate pleas for natural justice made in England by the heroine of Mary Wollstonecraft's novel *The Wrongs of Women* (1797) or by the feminist Barbara Bodichon as late as 1854. In fact it becomes one of the central tropes of the women's movement in the United States throughout the nineteenth century – invoked by the first Convention for Women's Rights held at Seneca Falls in 1848, and by novelists ranging from Harriet Beecher Stowe to Louisa May Alcott.

A second factor that gave a distinctive direction to the legal role of women in American life and fiction was the nationally divisive issue of slavery. Paradoxically, the very assumptions that had set up

3 Abigail Adams, letter to Mercy Otis Warren. Quoted in Merriam, E, 1971, p 2.

conscious demarcations between the public sphere (the world of business, politics, law, which belonged to men) and the private sphere (the world of hearth and home, of family, of feelings and morals, in which women had free rein) – that demarcation in which American women had constructed their very identity – were now the assumptions that challenged this demarcation itself. If women were the real moral guardians of the nation, then they felt compelled to speak out on what they saw as issues of public conscience. They joined Temperance Societies, Anti-Prostitution Societies, and projected these concerns into dozens of novels. Many of the same women who fought for these causes joined the Abolitionist movement (just as many male Abolitionists, including Frederick Douglass, were supporters of the campaign for women's rights). In 1850, largely as a trade-off for allowing California to join the Union as a non-slave State, Congress passed the *Fugitive Slave Act*. It allowed slaves to be pursued and recaptured in Northern States, and made it illegal for northern sympathisers to aid and abet them. With the passage of this bill slavery became a northern issue as well as a southern one. Fired with moral indignation, Harriet Beecher Stowe wrote the single best-selling novel of the nineteenth century, *Uncle Tom's Cabin*. ("God wrote it", she declared.) One of the most memorable scenes in the novel occurs when the mulatto slave Eliza, fleeing north with her young son, takes refuge in the home of liberal sympathisers, Senator and Mrs Bird. But the Senator is just home from Washington after voting on the *Fugitive Slave Act*. Face to face with the particular case, torn between public duty and private morality the senator is finally persuaded by his wife to commit the illegal act of helping Eliza escape. Throughout the novel, it is the women characters who act consistently as the moral conscience.

In stressing the indirect nature of women's power (usually exercised through their husbands), *Uncle Tom's Cabin* also illustrates how closely women's discourse of power is related to that of the slaves. Both have learned to empower themselves by subverting the dominant discourse. When the slave-trader, who has just bought Eliza from the plantation-owner Mr Shelby, finds that she has escaped, Shelby feels honour-bound to order two other slaves to help in the pursuit. The two promptly fall into a standard Sambo routine: they lose the horses, mix up the saddles, direct him along a false road, and generally capitalise on their assigned role as buffoons to ensure that Eliza has the headstart she needs. All this, they know, is clearly understood and approved by Mrs Shelby, who had tried to persuade her husband not to sell Eliza in the first place.

Stowe's novel was an important landmark in women's relation to the law in America. It confirmed an alliance between women's issues and slavery issues, both politically and metaphorically. It extended women's role as moral guardian to the public sphere. Above all, it confirmed their right to a public voice. Lincoln is alleged to have said on meeting Stowe, "So you're the little lady who made this big war".

The validation of women's access to a voice in the public forum had been a contentious issue for decades. The first national women's convention at Seneca Falls in 1848 was criticised, lampooned and trivialised by most of the American press: "Insurrection Among Women: The Petticoats Revolt" screamed the headline of a leading Philadelphia paper (Bardes & Gossett 1990 p 51). A novel published in 1839 called *The Lecturess* conveyed the dangers attendant on any woman who presumed to carry her influence into the public domain (Bardes & Gossett p 45). Perhaps no American writer expressed better than Nathaniel Hawthorne the essential ambivalence felt by so many Americans toward women's access to a public voice. He himself undoubtedly had feminist sympathies. He was a neighbour and friend of noted feminist author and speaker Margaret Fuller, though he felt ambivalent about her too. "Would that Miss Margaret Fuller might lose her tongue", he wrote to his fiancée Sophia Peabody who was about to spend the day listening to Fuller speak.[4] In *The Scarlet Letter*, set in seventeenth century New England, Hawthorne projected all this ambivalence. Ostracised by Puritan society because of her adultery, living on the borderline between the town and the forest, Hester Prynne develops radically feminist ideas:

> Much of the marble coldness of Hester's impression was to be attributed to the circumstance that her life had turned, in a great measure, from passion and feeling, to thought. . . It was an age in which the human intellect, newly emancipated, had taken a more active and a wider range than for many centuries before. . . Hester Prynne imbibed this spirit. She assumed a freedom of speculation, then common enough on the other side of the Atlantic, but which our forefathers, had they known of it, would have held to be a deadlier crime than that stigmatized by the scarlet letter. In her lonesome cottage, by the sea-shore, thoughts visited her, such as dared to enter no other dwelling in New England. . . Indeed, [a] dark question often rose into her mind with reference to the whole race of womanhood. Was existence worth accepting, even to the happiest among them? As concerned her own individual existence, she had long ago decided in the negative, and dismissed the point as settled. A tendency to speculation, though it may keep woman quiet, as it does man, yet makes her sad. She discerns . . . such a hopeless task before her. As a first step, the whole system of society is to be torn down, and built up anew. Then, the very nature of the opposite sex, or its long hereditary habit, which has become like nature, is to be essentially modified, before woman can be allowed to assume what seems a fair and suitable position. . . (pp 293-4)

But Hawthorne cannot quite sustain the momentum of this characterisation. By the end of the novel, Hester has withdrawn from such radical ideas:

4 Nathaniel Hawthorne, letter to Sophia Peabody, January 13, 1841, p 511.

> Women . . . came to Hester's cottage, demanding why they were so wretched, and what the remedy! Hester comforted and counselled them, as best she might. She assured them, too, of her firm belief, that, at some brighter period, when the world should have grown ripe for it, in Heaven's own time, a new truth would be revealed, in order to establish the whole relation between man and woman on a surer ground of mutual happiness. Earlier in life, Hester had vainly imagined that she herself might be the destined prophetess, but had long since recognized the impossibility that any mission of divine and mysterious truth should be confided to a woman stained with sin. . . (p 275)

Perhaps Hawthorne could see no place for Hester to go in seventeenth century New England (her daughter goes back to the Old World) but one suspects that he himself could find no place for her in the nineteenth century either. He remained both attracted to, and fearful of, strong-minded and articulate women. By the time of his next novel he has split this character into two, falling back on the old fair lady/dark lady division of sentimental romance. The dark-haired Zenobia, strong, proud, sensual – clearly modelled on Margaret Fuller – is a passionate advocate for women's rights. Hawthorne kills her off. The fair-haired Priscilla, sweet and submissive, marries and nurtures the man she loves. Yet the novel's multiple ambivalences belie the simplicity of that "split", and project Hawthorne's own unease with it, aesthetically and symbolically. The two women turn out to be sisters; are they then complementary roles, their real connection denied by society? Although readers are clearly meant to identify Zenobia with Margaret Fuller, it is in fact Priscilla with whom Fuller's name is explicitly linked, further confusing the relationship of the roles. The fact that both women are shown to be manipulated by unscrupulous men underscores the impossibility of *any* credible life in either role. Yet their story is presented by a male narrator, Miles Coverdale, who is such a bundle of contradictions, of timid assertions and strategic retreats, that Hawthorne also denies him any real credibility or authority in interpreting their characters. Hawthorne could thus present with great sympathy the complexities and paradoxes of the "woman question". If he could see no satisfactory resolution of it, he did at least confirm the importance of the subject and raise the sophistication of the terms of the debate. By 1886, even Henry James, who was hardly a controversialist, could not ignore the subject: "I wished to write a very American tale, a tale very characteristic of our social conditions, and I asked myself what was the most salient and peculiar point in our social life. The answer was: the situation of women, the decline of the sentiment of sex, the agitation on their behalf" (James 1961 p 47). That answer gave rise to *The Bostonians*.

Some of the debates in fiction indeed revolved around specific changes in the law. In 1852, when the *Married Women's Property Act* was being hotly debated in the New York legislature, James Fenimore Cooper entered the fray with his novel *The Ways of the*

Hour, in which he attacked all the things he saw as destroying the American Republic: the jury system, the system of elected judges, democratic trends, but above all the right of married women to their own property. In his novel, the heroine who looks and in many ways acts like a traditional heroine (beautiful, cultivated, plays the harp, speaks four languages) is corrupted by modern ways and modern laws. As soon as the law gives her the right to her own fortune, she abandons her husband, manages her own financial affairs, wishes to live independently and even takes an interest in the law itself. One of the novel's spokesmen blames the whole situation on the new law: "there are runaway wives enough, at this moment, roaming up and down the land, setting the laws of God and man at defiance, and jingling their purses, when they happen to have money, under their lawful husbands' noses" (Bardes & Gossett p 84). During the novel, the heroine is on trial (wrongfully) for murder, which, it is implied, would certainly never have happened had she stayed under her husband's coverture. Although she is acquitted Cooper, in the way of authors, exercises his authorial right to the last word. Summarily declaring her insane, he states, "The lucid intervals were long... and at such times her mind seemed clear enough on all subjects but one. Divorce was her ruling passion" (Bardes & Gossett p 88).

Mrs EDEN (Emma Dorothy Eliza Nevitte) Southworth, who was, in terms of sales figures, the most popular novelist in America at the time, rallied to the defence. Her novel *The Discarded Daughter* (1853) is a direct reply to Cooper, based on an equally convoluted and drawn-out plot. It hinges not only on a woman's right to property, but extends the theme to a fuller and less paranoid consideration of the relation of property to marriage. The heroine had been forced into a loveless marriage by her father solely for the purpose of joining two large estates in Maryland. When she, in her single act of marital rebellion, encourages her only child, a daughter, to elope in order to avoid a similar fate, she comes face to face with the *Married Women's Property Act*, passed in Maryland in 1843. A friend who is a local judge explains it to her:

> "You know something, I presume, of the Maryland laws of property, of inheritance, and of marriage?"
>
> "No – no – I know nothing about it."
>
> "At least you know that when a girl marries, all the personal property she may be possessed of at the time of her marriage, or may afterwards inherit, becomes the property of her husband?"
>
> "Yes, of course I know that."
>
> "Yes – but – listen. All the LANDED property she possesses at the time of her marriage, or afterwards inherits, is hers – hers alone. Her husband can neither alienate it during his life, or will it at his death. He cannot mortgage it, nor assign it – nor can it be taken for his debts. It is hers, and hers alone. She alone has the disposal of it."
>
> "Yes. Well?"
>
> ". . . All the LANDED PROPERTY, consisting of six thousand acres of the best land on the Western Shore, which you inherited from

> your father, is yours, your own, and at your death it is your daughter's, if she survive you, and unless you can choose to will it to some one else. General Garnet can make no disposition of it either during your life or at your death. . . Your daughter Elsie has, by her marriage, grievously offended her father. He may or may not pardon her. He may discard her. Do not put it in his power to disinherit her". . .
>
> "Why do you say that to me?" . . .
>
> "Because . . . it is said that women can always be kissed or kicked out of any right of property they may happen to possess. Now do not you, my little Alice, be kissed out of your six thousand acres. . . For it makes you independent and of great importance. Don't you be kissed out of it, Alice, for you can leave it to your beloved daughter, who will need it." (Bardes & Gossett pp 89-90)

A woman's rights under the law had always to be re-negotiated through the practical difficulties of her actual experience – through the threat of physical force or the conventional submissiveness of her wifely role. In the face of those imperatives, the law remained a theoretical abstraction even more disabling than the Chancery Courts were in *Bleak House*.

Throughout the nineteenth century, then, that period of major legal change in the status of women, American literature reflected every facet of women's responses to those changes – from the metaphorical representation of her dependency and sense of imprisonment in the sentimental novels, through her alliance with the Abolitionist movement and her growing political engagement after Seneca Falls, through specific responses to such debates as the *Married Women's Property Acts*, through her attempts to break into the strongholds of the professional medical and legal establishments, through to her involvement in the suffrage movement.

When we look for a similar engagement with women's issues in Australian literature, we are confronted with a curious vacuum. What literary record there is of women's responses to legal issues here seems far more piecemeal (the work of individual writers with no sense of themselves as part of a movement) and more arbitrary, not a central thematic issue. The problem, of course, may be historiographical – a writing of our literary history that has not only marginalised women writers of the nineteenth century but obliterated them. We all, for example, read Marcus Clarke's *For the Term of his Natural Life* as the great indictment of the convict system in Australia; few of us ever heard of *The Broad Arrow* (1900), written more than a decade before Clarke, by a woman convict, Caroline Leakey – an equally fierce indictment of the system by one who had actually experienced it.

But, historiography aside, there are, I think, three possible factors that might establish a context for this comparative silence. The first is a legal one. Although in America the legal status of women was initially inscribed in the same English common law that prevailed in Australia, the hegemony of this authority there was attacked fairly early by an emerging nationalism anxious to establish its independence in fact as well as principle, by the different social needs of individual states as the frontier pushed west, by democratic pressures against the class bias of the Equity and Chancery Courts set up to rectify anomalies in the common law, and by pressures from the legal profession to tidy up the messiness of such judicial proliferation. Australia, on the other hand, politically tied to England until 1900 and legally tied until the abolition of appeal to the Privy Council under the Whitlam Government, remained largely dependent on the English legal system. England, as the centre of empire, was anxious that any changes in its laws should be enacted as soon as possible in all its colonies. So most laws affecting women were passed in Australia within a few years of their English passage. Occasionally Australia reversed that sequence. For instance the *English Marriage Law* of 1854 which, as part of the many provisions against consanguinity and affinity, forbade marriage between a man and his deceased wife's sister, was not part of the Australian law. The difference here, I suspect, was less a gesture of national independence than a practical response to a situation where men vastly outnumbered women in the population. Indeed Sir William A'Beckett, the Chief Justice of Victoria and the grandfather of Martin Boyd, married his sister-in-law after the death of his wife – which would have been illegal in England. The plot of at least one Australian novel revolves specifically around this situation (Dale, 1895). The hero marries his deceased wife's sister in Australia; back in England he wants to discard her in order to marry a third woman, and invokes the English law to invalidate his marriage. But unluckily for him the English law (perhaps in response to the Australian situation) specifically included a provision that would acknowledge such marriages where they had been made in respect of local law.

A second factor relating to the comparative absence of legal debate in relation to women's issues in Australian literature is sociological. Women were very much a minority in early Australia – outnumbered four to one by men in the first half of the nineteenth century. Although such disproportion made for a greater social fluidity and more opportunities for women than in England (WC Wentworth's mother, for example, had been a convict), it militated against the rise, until well into the century, of a substantial female middle-class – the sort of women who articulated grievances in both England and America. Nor was there in Australia anything corresponding to the long tradition of non-conformist religion in America which encouraged women to articulate their inner experience, nor a national issue on the scale of the slavery debate to project them into the public forum.

But the most potent reason for the comparative silence has to do with the nature of Australian literature itself. When the contemporary novelist Jessica Anderson explained why she felt so little influenced by previous Australian writing, she said it was because it was "too blokey and outback" (Ellison 1986 p 34). The mode of domestic realism – the kind of novel which might express a self-consciousness, or articulate a debate, about the social position of women – has not, until comparatively recently, been a significant mode in Australian literature. What dominated instead, especially in the nineteenth century, was a bush tradition, overwhelmingly male, in which the myth of Australian mateship worked to marginalise if not exclude women altogether. Although the vast majority of Australians lived in the cities, the bush myth was the central "Australian legend" that historian Russel Ward (1958) traced back to the convicts and itinerant bush workers. Whatever the historical validity of this predominantly male myth, it was certainly encouraged by the practical realities of publishing. Australia had no publishing house of its own until Angus and Robertson began in 1886. Up until then Australian writers published with English houses, and largely for an English audience who wanted – or were presumed to want – to read about the differences, not the similarities, that Australia offered.

Catherine Helen Spence in fact was one writer who worked against the prevailing bush legend. Reacting against what she saw as provincialism in the "offensively Australian" novel, she lamented the prevalence of "'the deadbeat' – the remittance man, the gaunt shepherd with his starving flocks and herds, the free selector on an arid patch, the drink shanty where the rouseabouts and shearers knock down their cheques, the race meeting where high and low, rich and poor, are filled with the gambler's ill luck" (Magarey 1985 p 56). Her own six novels turned in contrast to the domestic scene. But although in them she takes up such realistic issues as equal work opportunities for women and the nature of the marriage contract, they remained limited by the confines of the sentimental novel form. In the end she found a more direct platform than fiction for her social and political concerns. As a journalist, lobbyist and public lecturer she campaigned directly for such issues as increased educational and working opportunities for women, universal suffrage, and proportional representation. Her textbook *The Laws We Live Under* (1888) was the first social studies textbook used in Australian schools. In 1897 she herself became the first woman candidate for political office in Australia when, aged 72, she took part in the Federal Convention election. Her lecture circuit took her to the United States where she made contact with other feminists, but as a political campaigner rather than as a novelist.

It is not surprising that South Australia – the only state that did not begin as a convict settlement, that nurtured ideas of social experiment, that had comparatively little of the bush ideology – should have produced a writer like Spence, challenging the orthodoxies of legal and social conventions. South Australia also, it should be noted, gave women the vote nine years before the rest of Australia did. (And Australia was well ahead of both England and the United States on this matter.)

But by and large the accepted literary modes in Australia were not synchronised with the reform movements of the nineteenth century that brought changes in the laws affecting women. One should note in passing a play called *Whose Child?* written in 1932 by the first woman parliamentarian in New South Wales, Millicent Preston Stanley.[5] It is one of the rare examples in Australian literature of a play written in specific response to a legal judgement – a custody issue which centred on the right of the mother, a well-known actress, to a career that involved working away from home. By the time we get to the post-World War II novels, which break away from the bush mythology, setting their stories in the cities and dealing with the realities of daily living, the major legal controversies were over. Perhaps the last major issue were the 1976 changes in the divorce law, which are sensitively chronicled in several works by Jessica Anderson.

Her moving short story "The Milk" deals with a woman who is enabled to leave her loveless marriage by this law. "This was in 1976", the text specifies. "The divorce laws had been reformed the year before, sweeping away grounds such as adultery, cruelty and desertion, and putting in their place only breakdown of marriage" (p 116). Although no law can offer a panacea for the pain and the anger that the story sensitively records, the new legislation does set up quite different narrative possibilities from that of the "barbarous times" of private detectives and sexual vendettas recorded in her earlier novel *The Impersonators*, when divorce laws demanded proof of adultery. Or that recalled by Nora Porteous in *Tirra Lirra by the River*, whose husband Colin wants to marry another woman: "Colin offered me a settlement of three hundred pounds, in return for which I was to leave him and allow him to divorce me for desertion" (p 65).

The last word in this brief survey should go to Elizabeth Jolley. Her short story "A Gentleman's Agreement" not only centres on a legal issue of property and inheritance, but more particularly on the nature of that para-legal contract invested with all the values of the patriarchal order – the gentleman's agreement. In the story, a woman with slender means and two difficult children pins her hopes on the farm that she will inherit from her father. When he dies, she is forced to sell the property, though she and the children would dearly like to live there, because she has no capital to maintain it. At the signing of the legal contract, she asks, as a special favour, and as an honour to her dead father, to be allowed to plant and harvest one last crop. The buyer agrees; the gentleman's agreement is struck. Next day she begins planting a jarrah forest.

Back in Georgia, Brer Rabbit – that crafty spokesman for those disempowered by all official discourse – would surely have cheered.

---

5 See Heather Radi, "Whose Child?" in Mackinolty & Radi, 1979.

BIBLIOGRAPHY

Anderson, Jessica, 1987, "The Milk", *Stories from the Warm Zone and Sydney Stories*, Penguin.

Anderson, Jessica, 1980, *Tirra Lirra by the River*, Penguin. (Originally published 1978).

Bardes, Barbara & Gossett, Suzanne, 1990, *Declarations of Independence: Women and Political Power in Nineteenth Century American Fiction*, Rutgers University Press.

Cowie, Alexander, 1948, *The Rise of the Novel*, American Book Co. Included in Friebert, Lucy M & White, Barbara A (eds), 1985, *Hidden Hands: An Anthology of American Women Writers 1790-1870*, Rutgers University Press.

Dale, Alice Mary, 1895, *With Feet of Clay*, George Robertson & Co.

Ellison, Jennifer, 1986, "Interview with Jessica Anderson", in *Rooms of Their Own*, Penguin.

Hawthorne, Nathaniel, 1986, *The Scarlet Letter and Selected Tales*, Penguin Classics edn, Penguin Books Ltd, p 29.

James, Henry, *The Notebooks of Henry James*, Matthiessen, FO & Murdock, B, 1961, Oxford University Press.

Jolley, Elizabeth, 1991, "A Gentleman's Agreement" in Lord, Mary (ed), *The Penguin Best Australian Short Stories*, Penguin, pp 243-48.

Leakey, Caroline (pseudonym: Oline Keese), 1900, *The Broad Arrow*, J Walch & Sons. (Originally published 1859).

Magarey, Susan, 1985, *Unbridling the Tongues of Women: A Biography of Catherine Helen Spence*, Hale and Iremonger.

Melville, Herman, 1987, "The Paradise of Bachelors" & "The Tartarus of Maids", *The Writings of Herman Melville, Vol 9: The Piazza Tales and Other Prose Pieces, 1839-1860*, Northwestern University Press and the Newberry Library, pp 316-335.

Southworth, Mrs EDEN, 1859, *The Hidden Hand*, Dobson, Joanne (ed), 1988, Rutgers University Press.

Ward, Russel, 1958, *The Australian Legend*, Oxford University Press.

12

Sex, Lies and Defamation

PENNY PETHER

It was suggested in the preamble to the program for the conference at which the paper on which this chapter is based was presented that the title of its concluding session, "Old Wine in New Bottles" was perhaps, "a metaphor of the law and literature movement". Given the project of this chapter, which is to take a few risks, breach a few boundaries, in order to show how and why law and literature scholarship and teaching – and here I am quoting from the Graduation Address delivered at Yale Law School's commencement ceremony in June 1989 by Catharine MacKinnon (1990) might – "get [the voice of women] back in", it seems appropriate to initiate it by applying a little exegetical scrutiny to the convenors' borrowed metaphor.

The source of that metaphor, which has been scrambled in the process of appropriation, is, of course, a master-text of the Law of the Father,[1] the *Bible*. Specifically, it comes from chapter 9 of the Gospel according to Matthew, which is part of the portion of Matthew's teaching which deals with Jesus's miracles of healing. Those miracles were themselves employed by Jesus in the service of his teaching. It is not without relevance to this chapter that Matthew's Gospel records, shortly before Jesus's remark on wine, two occasions on which he had some troubles with lawyers, specifically in making them listen to and understand his message. The lessons to be drawn from both incidents seem to be that lawyers are depressing materialists, in that they are only convinced by that which they can actually see, and even then are only really convinced by the dramatic (see Matt 9:2-7); further, that they do not, perhaps cannot, understand the implications of doing things in new ways (Matt 8:19-20), that they deeply suspect what they see to be challenges to the authority that is sanctified by precedent (Matt 9:2-7), and that they do not think much of the voices of ordinary people.[2] I should know. I

---

1 See Grosz (1989 ch 1) for a useful introductory account of Jacques Lacan's notion of the "Law of the Father".

2 I have chosen to interpret the reference in Matt 9:2-6 to the "Son of Man" as a paradigm for "ordinary people".

have been one myself, and I suspect that while you can take the woman out of the practice of the law, you cannot take the lawyer out of the woman.

Jesus makes the remark about new wine in old wineskins (not Old Wine in New Bottles) in order to justify his new ways of doing things, evangelically speaking. And he says, when asked by John's disciples "Why do we and the Pharisees fast, but your disciples do not?":

> Can you expect the bridegroom's friends to go mourning while the bridegroom is with them? The time will come when the bridegroom will be taken away from them; that will be the time to fast.
>
> No one sews a patch of unshrunk cloth on to an old coat; for then the patch tears away from the coat, and leaves a bigger hole. Neither do you put new wine into old wineskins; if you do, the skins burst, and then the wine runs out and the skins are spoilt. No, you put new wine into fresh skins; then both are preserved.

In other words, new programs call for new ways of doing things, because they expose the threadbareness of and the flaws in the old ways in a manner which is not apparent until they are exposed to the shock of the new. So I am suggesting, rather than this enterprise being a kind of fashionable decanter for a fine old vintage which changes it not at all, as the bodgie metaphor suggested, that if the new wine or the new cloth exposes the signs of decay in the old fabric, then that exposure, that deconstruction is all to the good. And that we had better rustle up some new wineskins, find a new dispensation[3] – to quote the Poundian phrase – make it new.

I shall move very gradually now to a borrowing from another authoritative – not to say master – text, as I turn to the title of this chapter, which is determinedly heterogeneous; indeed some readers might wish to call it heterodox; others, who have noted the current high stocks of Bakhtin in both contemporary liberal humanist (Thomas 1991) and contemporary feminist (Heilbrun and Resnick 1990) law and literature scholarship, might detect traces of heteroglossia (Bakhtin 1981). The title draws, of course, from the title of Steven Soderbergh's film: *Sex, Lies, and Videotape*, in which, many of you will recall, a character uttered the immortal line about liars and lawyers, "There's only one thing worse than a liar, and that's a lawyer". It also draws from that tort which has grounded, at least in the New South Wales jurisdiction (where I have practised), a high status and remunerative – if not uncontroversial – branch of practice, whose status is perhaps reflected by the fact that it is the subject of a chapter in what I might call one of the "black letter" sections of this book, and by the distinguished writer of that chapter, on which this chapter is based, as they say, "in another place" (Heerey J's Chapter 20, "The Biter Bit – Literary Criticism and the Law of Defamation").[4] It also draws from the Australian vernacular, and

3 See TS Eliot, "The Journey of the Magi".

4 Delivered in a parallel session.

then from what, in the nineteenth century at least,[5] was a literary invention, but a literary invention which had consequences not only in literature[6] but in what is often called "the real world."[7] That place is Wessex.[8] The writer described in the title, Thomas Hardy, wrote about sex, lies, and defamation, as he did about many sites where the law in all its manifestations,[9] the word, and questions of sex, gender, sexuality and power converge. And when he wrote of those sites he wrote what Goode (1988) has called, "the offensive truth": offensive, that is, to those in whose interests it was and is to keep, "all working people . . . [and] all women" in, "their place" (MacKinnon 1990 p 299). Hardy's writings are a particularly apt subject for a chapter with a project and a title like this one's. His work dramatises a number of voices: not just those of women and the rural poor, but those of deluded, "end-of-the-age"[10] young men, those "self-made" men, the rising professional classes: architects[11] doctors,[12] clergymen[13] and above all lawyers,[14] who believed that the purchase on power they had grafted to obtain was going to make them and those whom they called theirs live happily ever after. Hardy's fictions are also a generic ferment, mixing "high" realism with naturalism, myth, symbolism, romance, pastoral: a mixture which characteristically provides a neat closure, what appears at first blush to be a realist ending but which is no ending at all, which unravels and fragments on the page.[15] They

---

5 Wessex, as Hardy notes in the Preface to *Far from the Madding Crowd*, was "disinterred" by him from "the pages of early English history" and reinvented.

6 For example, EM Forster locates part of the action of his futuristic fable, "The Machine Stops", in Wessex.

7 As Hardy notes in the Preface to *Far from the Madding Crowd*, his "dream-country" "solidified into a utilitarian region which people can go to, take a house in, and write to the papers from".

8 It is worth noting that in his Preface to *Wessex Tales* Hardy demonstrates a playfully sophisticated awareness of the interplay between "fiction", "life", and "history".

9 I have suggested in "Hardy and the Law" (1991b) how Hardy's fictions explore contract, property and tort law, and equity, and have touched on his exploration of natural law theory (discussed at some length in Pether (1985)). *Tess* and short stories like "The Withered Arm" and "The Three Strangers" offer powerful critiques of criminal law and punishment, and *The Woodlanders* is just one of Hardy's fictions which examines "the divorce question". The laws relating to title and inheritance of property are frequently dramatised by Hardy, as in "Netty Sargent's Copyhold".

10 Thomas Hardy, "On the Western Circuit", *Life's Little Ironies* (1894,) Alan Sutton Publishing, 1983, p 91.

11 Like Stephen Smith, of *A Pair of Blue Eyes*.

12 Like Edred Fitzpiers, of *The Woodlanders*.

13 Like Joshua and Cornelius Halborough, of "A Tragedy of Two Ambitions".

14 Like Charles Raye, of "On the Western Circuit", or Henry Knight, of *A Pair of Blue Eyes*.

15 *Far From The Madding Crowd* provides a good example of this. Our belief in the conventional happy ending suggested by the marriage of Bathsheba and Gabriel is undermined by the description of Bathsheba's melancholy, by the catalogue of torment and horror which has preceded this conclusion, and the questioning of marriage provided by Bathsheba's early observations about it, her humiliation at Troy's hands, and the black comedy of the description of her father's recipe for loving matrimonial ennui.

are spectacularly and disconcertingly intertextual, loaded with references to English poets, continental philosophers, their own predecessors, and the texts of the Ancients, both hebraic and hellenic. Above all, they constantly put into play the authority of the narratorial voice, advancing Marlowe's achievement in *Hero and Leander* of exposing the dubious authority of the narrator (constructed in both cases as a man of letters) on questions of sex, gender and sexuality by exposing him as pompous, scholarly, misogynist; ignorant of the ways of the world whatever the status of his professing in the world of words. Hardy's destabilised and destabilising narrators are not cardboard cutouts, fairground targets, stock comic figures like Marlowe's unworldly academic. Rather, their presentation suggests the essential partiality and "narratedness" of the narrator, his implication in the stories that he tells and the way that he tells them.[16]

But back to bush lawyers, and why I have called Hardy one. Those of you who have seen *Sex, Lies and Videotape* will imagine my delight as I leafed through the aforementioned authoritative text, GA Wilkes's (1990) *A Dictionary of Australian Colloquialisms* and found that the entry immediately under "bush lawyer" was "bush liar". A bush liar, of course, is a teller of tall stories, and Wilkes's source in Lawson[17] suggests that being one is a marker of Australianness. Soderbergh's film, like Wilkes's definition, suggests the proliferation of stories in both professions: the law and lying, or should that be the "deployment of rhetoric"? The citations for "bush lawyer" also suggest a sort of Essential Australianness in that calling (p 62): the disrespect for authority, qualifications and licenses; a belief by the bush lawyer, the "half-shrewd mug", the bloke with an eye for the main chance, that the bush lawyer's opinion is as good as anyone's – although the lawyer in me is reminded of the dictum about the value of free legal advice – coupled with a paradoxical belief in the power and influence of the law, at least insofar as its capacity to generate income is concerned. I have catalogued elsewhere[18] Hardy's assiduous attempts to master the vocabulary and concepts of the law, and argued that this drive was part of his own project of making himself, turning himself into a nineteenth century success story. However, in his novels and stories Hardy, the bush lawyer, deconstructs the fictions of equality and empowerment on which were based the beliefs of the middle and working classes of the past century (Peter and Favret 1982 pp 175-99) as to the legal liberation they thought they had gained, "equality of rights, status of citizens" (p 180), and which were symbolised both by the capacity to contract, and by the adherent of the faith who, "identified himself with the

16 As when in *Far from the Madding Crowd* the narrator shares Gabriel's voyeurism.
17 "Every true Australian bushman must try his best to tell a bigger outback lie than the last bush-liar".
18 In "Hardy and the Law".

being of the contract, alienated himself in it, and lost himself in it" (p 180).

Hardy's critique of the law, however, is not confined to an argument as to the illusory nature of the idea that the law confers anything more than comparative and contingent power on those men who do not possess the real power which is conferred by influence or control over the levers which manipulate capital and the word: the power to tell the stories that tell us, and to which Gerbner (quoted in Glass (1990)) referred when he said "If you can control the storytelling, then you do not have to worry about who makes the laws". Everywhere in Hardy's texts he shows us how the law in all its branches (contract, land law, tort, equity, and criminal law) purports to protect women but privileges powerful men. Two of the more striking examples of this pattern are found in Tess Durbeyfield's statement, "Once victim, always victim: that's the law",[19] and in Sue Bridehead's judgment:

> I think I could be afraid of you, Jude, the moment you had contracted to cherish me under a Government stamp, and I was licensed to be loved on the premises by you – Ugh, how horrible and sordid! Although, as you are, free, I trust you more than any other man in the world.[20]

More importantly, Hardy's fictions mark the associations between law and discourse, and demonstrate how women's voices are produced, or controlled, or silenced, or rendered inaudible by the law, paradigm in Hardy's texts of the discourses of power: showing, as Bathsheba Everdene says, that, "It is difficult for a woman to define her feelings in language which is chiefly made by men to express theirs".[21] I want to focus particularly on some of Hardy's stories of sex, lies, and defamation, and I want to do this in order to demonstrate how these stories expose the way in which the law as exemplum of the power of the word, the power of naming, of signifying, of deciding what the materiality of the signified means, writes women's lives. I want to show how he plays the bush lawyer, demonstrating the power of the law at the same time as making a case for its democratisation, for its re-construction as a site for the telling of stories which is characterised by dialogism and heteroglossia, "Different texts. The same texts read differently. Other voices included in the conversation. Different behaviour" (Heilbrun and Resnick p 1948). Hardy's fiction suggests that if the law, as paradigm of the discourses of power, admits other voices, it will tell other stories. At which point I should make explicit what will already be clear to most readers; that is, if you adopt Stanley Fish's (1989) adoption of Lanham's distinction between "Serious Man" and "Rhetorical Man", you can regard me as writing from the position of

19 In chapter XLVII of *Tess of the d'Urbervilles*.
20 Part Fifth, Chapter One of *Jude the Osbscure*.
21 Chapter 50 of *Far from the Madding Crowd*.

"Rhetorical Woman". That position has been exemplified, by the satirist David Lodge (1988 p 293), as holding that, "We aren't essences . . . We aren't individual essences existing prior to language. There is only language".

Thus, the stories that we tell, and the language which we use to tell those stories, in law and in literature, are crucially important.

Defamation is a tort, a civil wrong: most readers will know that. But let us consider the implications of that definition. James (1972 p 290) differentiates tort law from criminal law on the one hand, and the law of contract on the other, and goes on to say:

> A crime is, as we have seen, a wrong which, by means of punishment or otherwise, the state inhibits. A tort is a *civil* wrong which entitles a person who is injured by its commission to claim damages for his loss, whether purely by way of reparation or as a way of bringing home to the defendant *the anti-social nature* of his act. An injunction is also a proper remedy in some circumstances.
>
> A breach of contract is, like a tort, a civil wrong; but it is different from a tort. Whereas contractual duties are imposed by the parties to the contract themselves, the duty to refrain from committing torts is imposed by the general law of the land, independently of the wishes of the plaintiff or of the defendant. It was only by an accident of history that breaches of contract were originally remedied by a tortious action.

The law of torts, then, reflects community standards about social responsibility; its normative and naturalising force is suggested by the idea that it is "imposed by the general law of the land", that it is a kind of natural law, benign, inevitable, not cultural. Defamation's particular connections with the socially normative (which is, of course, soon naturalised) is suggested by his version of the standard definition of it, "Defamation may be broadly defined as 'the publication of a statement which tends to lower a person in the estimation of right-thinking members of society generally'" (p 314) and by the fact that since 1792 juries have decided libel cases (Fleming 1987 p 508). Defamation's association with questions of gender and sexuality was well-established by Hardy's lifetime – in his 1812 *Law of Libels,* Holt recorded that:

> A young lady, nine years since, recovered 4000*l* damages for reflections upon her chastity, published in a newspaper, though she could not, without alleging special damage (as loss of marriage), have maintained an action for verbal slander, containing the grossest assertions on her honour (p 205).

It is still with us today, as any acquaintance with *Gypsy Fire v Truth Newspapers Pty Ltd* (unreported, Sup Ct NSW, 1986) will confirm. A look at standard texts on the subject will show that cases like *Hulton v Jones* [1910] AC 20, *Newstead v London Express Newspapers Ltd* [1940] 1 KB 377, *Cassidy v The Daily Mirror* [1929] 2 KB 331 – all cases to do with reputation as to sexual "misconduct" – are repeatedly cited as authority for key features of the operative law. While these cases suggest that imputations of adultery are deemed defamatory whether made about men or women, some of the material that I wish to quote to you will suggest the particular and specific inequity of defamation law as it applies to women. I quote from the definition of defamation used in Fleming's (1987) text, set in 1991 in the Torts course at Sydney University, where I trained as a lawyer, and where I taught between 1988 and 1992. It has not changed in this regard from the version given in the fourth edition, which I used as an undergraduate student in 1979, "A defamatory statement may be defined as one which tends to lower a person in the estimation of his fellow men by making them think the less of him" (p 501). For Fleming, although not for James (p 314) a reputation is implicitly a matter of concern to men, not women. It is "men" who set the standard. And yet, women who are raped are cited by Fleming as having been defamed by a publication of the fact of the crime committed against them (p 502).[22]

The same discursive construction of what is "dishonouring" to women is at work in Fleming's material on identification: "For instance, to say that A (a married man) is a bachelor defames his wife. But to allege that A's father became a psychiatric patient does not injure A's reputation, however it may injure his filial feelings" (p 509). I do not have space to go into the question here, but the choice by Fleming of madness – in father or self (p 502) – as the indicator of what is dishonourable to men and that of the status of rape victim or de facto wife as indicators of what is dishonourable to women is signal. One of the things it signals is a catch-22: actionability of defamation as to acts of sexual intercourse in which a woman has been involved – consensually or not – is related to notions of "purity", which in turn are related to ideas about exclusive sexual possession of women by men, which ideas are deemed to be norms, and thus made normative, and thus deemed to be natural. And what the norm does in both cases is blame the victim. They are normative because they relate to "reputation", to "name". And "naming", under patriarchy (Moi 1985 pp 158-9), in the symbolic order[23] is an exercise of power which marginalises or constrains women, and to which they have no access (p 158).

Hardy dramatises the effects of the way in which women are "named" in *Tess*, and signals this in his title. Is she Tess Durbeyfield, or Teresa d'Urberville, or Tess of the d'Urbervilles? Is she Tess d'Urberville the daughter of Sir John, or Teresa, daughter of Joan, and like her a victim of the law,[24] or doubly trapped by both of these heritages,[25] as the title suggests? Does she have the right – and, more

22 He is of course citing case law. But he does not note that the case is old (1934), and other examples would make his particular point effectively.
23 Moi gives a helpful analysis of Kristeva's notion of the symbolic order in chapter 8.
24 Joan Durbeyfield and her children are evicted from their home when the death of John Durbeyfield terminates the family's lifehold tenure of their cottage.
25 Both of which place her disadvantageously in both gender and class terms; she is in a sense doubly disinherited.

importantly, access[26] to what is signified by the name "Mrs Angel Clare" – that is, to upkeep and to what if she were a man would count as consortium? Whether she does so depends on what "original" sexual possession signifies. Angel's response to her account of her rape by Alec d'Urberville and his begetting of an "illegitimate child" is to say, "You were one person: now you are another" and to dismiss her from her post.[27] He asks, "How can we live together while that man lives? – he being your husband in Nature, and not I". Elsewhere in the text, Hardy makes it clear that Angel's notion of "Nature" is profoundly cultural, when the (differently acculturated) narrator says, with reverberative irony:

> She became what would have been called a fine creature; her aspect was fair and arresting; her soul that of a woman whom the turbulent experiences of the last year or two had quite failed to demoralize. But for the world's opinion those experiences would have been simply a liberal education;

and later:

> Let the truth be told – women do as a rule live through such humiliations, and regain their spirits, and again look about them with an interested eye. While there's life there's hope is a conviction not so entirely unknown to the "betrayed" as some amiable theorists would have us believe.

Naming subjects the woman named to being inscribed with and placed by cultural norms which, in their turn, are reinscribed over time as natural. Hardy points up the force and durability of such naming and norms, and their association and complicity with patriarchy and the symbolic order:

> The mixed, singular, luminous gloom in which they walked along together to the spot where the cows lay, often made him think of the Resurrection-hour. He little thought that the Magdalen might be at his side. Whilst all the landscape was in neutral shade, his companion's face, which was the focus of his eyes, rising above the mist-stratum, seemed to have a sort of phosphorescence upon it. She looked ghostly, as if she were merely a soul at large. In reality her face, without appearing to do so, had caught the cold gleam of the day from the north-east; his own face, though he did not think of it, wore the same aspect to her.
>
> It was then, as has been said, that she impressed him most deeply. She was no longer a milkmaid, but a visionary essence of woman – a whole sex condensed into one typical form. He called her Artemis, Demeter, and other fanciful names, half-teasingly – which she did not like because she did not understand them.
>
> "Call me Tess," she would say askance; and he did.

---

26 Tess's severest economic trials (which ultimately lead to her becoming Alec's mistress) occur when Angel is physically "beyond the jurisdiction", when his silence puts him beyond the reach of communication, and when Tess's delicacy about what may appear to be mendicity deter her from seeking financial assistance from his parents. And see note 37 below.

27 Tess's despairing response is to offer to live with him as his servant.

The most interesting case on woman's "name" is a key case on the question of the actionability of slander, as against libel. And the difference at common law is, and was in Hardy's time, that slander is not actionable without proof of special damage, unless it imputes the commission of a crime, or "loathsome disease", or unfitness for profession, trade or office. In 1891, by the *Slander of Women Act* (Eng), words, "imputing unchastity or adultery to any woman or girl" were added to the list of slanders actionable without proof of special – that is, pecuniary – damage. 1891 was also, of course, the year of publication of *Tess*. The case is *Lynch v Knight* (1861) 9 HLC 577. The story behind the case is apparently this – and I should stress that I am reading here in part from traces and interstices in the text, rather than just from the story which the text tells – James Lynch was accused by his stepsister, Jane Knight, of "seducing" her. The accusation was made by her to her husband, William Knight. William threatened to shoot James, and he responded with what follows:

> Jane is a notorious liar, and she will do her best to annoy you, as she takes delight in creating disturbances wherever she goes, and I advise you not to introduce her into society. Any singularity of conduct which you may have observed in your wife must be attributed to a Dr Casserly of Roscommon, as she was all but seduced by him; and I advise you, if Casserly comes to Dublin, not to permit him to enter your place, as he is a libertine and a blackguard; I have no other object in telling you about her conduct, and in speaking to you as I have done, but your own welfare. She is an infamous wretch, and I am sorry that you had the misfortune to marry her; and if you had asked my advice on the subject, I would have advised you not to marry her. . .
>
> She is a horrid young villain, and a notorious liar. Her brother, one Thomas Jones, is also a liar, but his lies are of the most harmless kind, whereas hers are of the most dangerous. In face, she is such a dangerous character to have in the house, that I was obliged to have the back door in the yard nailed up.

William refused to live any longer with Jane, and returned her to her father. It was not in issue that the allegations made by James were false. Jane sued James for slander, claiming that her loss of consortium provided the special damage necessary to found her action. She was, in the event, unsuccessful, because it was held that, as the allegation was of near-seduction before marriage rather than of adultery during it, William was not reacting reasonably in sending her back to her parents. This was not the "natural result" of the slander. The matters alleged by slander, if true, would not have entitled him to divorce her. Lord Cranworth noted that William, "might have been compelled to take back his wife". The Lord Chancellor, however, invited the speculation that she would have evidentiary problems in obtaining an order for the restitution of conjugal rights. Catch-22 again; and there is a certain irony in the fact that, as a necessary matter of form, necessary because of women's lack of legal status, William's name had to be joined with Jane's in order for her to bring her suit against James.

The case is notable, too, for some obiter dicta which reveal the gender-based inequities which produced this judgement, and their origins in the fetishisation of exclusive and original possession of women. Lord Campbell, the Lord Chancellor's, judgement read in part:

> The wife is not the servant of the husband, and the action for criminal conversation by the husband does not, like the action by a father for seduction of a daughter, rest on any such fiction as a loss of the services of the wife. The better opinion is that a wife could not maintain or join in an action for criminal conversation against the paramour of her husband who had seduced him. But I conceive that this rests on the consideration that, by the adultery of the husband, the wife does not necessarily lose the *consortium* of her husband; for she may and, under certain circumstances, she ought to condone and still enjoy his society; whereas condonation of conjugal infidelity is not permitted to the husband, and, by reason of the injury of the seducer, the *consortium* with the wife is necessarily for ever lost to the husband.

We can see the source of Angel Clare's double standard, then; it is reflected from the "real world"; or at least the world constructed by the Lord Chancellor.

Lord Wensleydale's view differed somewhat from the Lord Chancellor's, but was equally revelatory of the inferior position of women in Victorian society. Having questioned the viability of Jane's cause of action by saying that it "is certainly an objection of the greatest weight to such an action that there is no precedent or authority in favour of it", he went on to record that:

> I agree with Baron Fitzgerald, that the benefit which the husband has in the *consortium* of the wife, is of a different character from that which the wife has in the *consortium* of the husband. The relation of the husband to the wife is in most respects entirely dissimilar from that of the master to the servant, yet in one respect it has a similar character. The assistance of the wife in the conduct of the household of the husband, and in the education of his children, resembles the service of a hired domestic, tutor or governess; is of material value, capable of being estimated in money; and the loss of it may form the subject of an action. . . It is to the protection of such material interests that the law chiefly extends.
>
> The loss of . . . [domestic] service of the wife, the husband, who alone has all the property of the married parties, may repair by hiring another servant; but the wife sustains only the loss of the comfort of her husband's society and affectionate attention, which the law cannot estimate or remedy. She does not lose her maintenance, which he is bound still to supply; and it cannot be presumed that the wrongful act complained of puts an end to the means of that support without an averment to that effect.
>
> And if there were such an averment, the recovery of compensation must be by joining the husband in the suit, who himself must receive the money, which would not advance the wife's remedy. The wife is, in fact, without redress by any form of action to an injury to her pecuniary interests.

Both Lord Campbell and Lord Brougham criticised the then current law on this issue, the former calling it "unsatisfactory", the latter "barbarous", both noting that it meant that the:

> imputation by words, however gross, on an occasion, however public, upon the chastity of a modest matron or a pure virgin, is not actionable without proof that it has actually produced special temporal damage to her.

Thirty years later, their criticisms were responded to.

So the lessons of *Lynch v Knight* are these: that a wife, a sort of superior servant, has a material value to a husband which he does not have to her – perhaps because she has no property at common law; that a wife's adultery occasions loss of consortium to a husband while in the case of his adultery she does not necessarily lose consortium, and indeed in some such circumstances she should condone his actions and enjoy his society. And yet Jane could not recover for the damage suffered by her because of this defamation, because her husband had overreacted to it. The questions hang in the air: Did Jane continue to live with her parents? Did William continue to maintain her? If not, did she bring another action, and was he then compelled to do so by the law? And would this have compensated her? It is some reflection on the way that the law tells women's stories that the allegation of incest is lost in the matter, whereas the allegation as to "unchastity", as to near-seduction and its proclivity to produce a woman who "lied", who spoke in ways and of things that were unacceptable to society, takes centre stage. It is another such reflection that when I told the story to a woman colleague she asked, "What happened to Jane?" and I was unable to tell her.

But then, of course, in 1891 the *Slander of Women Act* redressed the situation of women like Jane. An advance, you think? Only insofar as it provided some women, "modest matrons", and "pure virgins", or at least those among them who could afford to bring a defamation action, with a bandaid solution to a harm caused by patriarchal society, which dictated that "chastity" – virginity or marital fidelity – was the commodity which alone entitled women to acquisition or maintenance of the "benefits" bestowed by marriage[28] and to the protection of the law. Women's domestic labour in marriage, the case makes clear, while a valuable commodity for their husbands, was not such a commodity in the hands of the domestic labourer herself.

---

28 To quote the Lord Chancellor and the Solicitor General:

Lord Chancellor: Suppose she had brought a suit for restitution of conjugal rights, would the proof of the utterance of these words be a justification to the husband of his conduct?

The Solicitor General: After such charges the Court might refuse to order a restitution of conjugal rights. There is a great difference in the proof required in a suit by a husband asking for a separation, and in one by a wife asking for restitution of conjugal rights. There is no process known to the common law by which the husband is compelled to keep his wife. If he refuses to receive her, the only remedy she has is in the spiritual court.

The court and the legislature clearly saw themselves as pronouncing community values and providing for their enforcement. But whose community? The community which values wife as servant, endorses the double standard, and only recognises and compensates those types of economic loss which patriarchy deems "natural".

Between 1861 and 1891 Hardy wrote the three fictions which I am going to examine: *A Pair of Blue Eyes,* "The Melancholy Hussar of the German Legion", and *Tess*. The first of these is an early, relatively little-read novel, chiefly regarded of interest because of its evident sources in Hardy's courtship of his first wife, and a scene where a lawyer battles for his life, gripping to a cliff composed of fossils. The central female character, Elfride Swancourt, is established early as a woman who (transgressively) seeks a voice. What she gets is "a reputation", and it is significant that one meaning of "chaste" is "decent (of speech)".[29]

Elfride writes her clergyman father's sermons and a novel. The first of these activities is sanctioned by the admiration of her father and her lover, Stephen Smith; but her father easily forgets the authorship of his sermons, and Stephen is a working-class boy making good through professionalism, and this gives him an affinity for the (illusory) belief in advancement through the appropriation of discursive power. The second is treated as harmless affectation by the text's representative member of the ruling class, the wealthy aristocrat, Lord Luxellian; or as presumptuous, by the lawyer, Henry Knight, against whom Elfride's representative and doomed struggle for power is conducted. Her worldly and thoroughly socialised step-mother sees it as a substitute for experience[30] – almost a guarantee of inexperience – and says, "Publish it, by all means. All ladies do that sort of thing now; not for profit, you know, but as a guarantee of mental respectability to their future husbands" although, "it rather resembles the melancholy ruse of throwing loaves over castle-walls at besiegers, and suggests desperation rather than plenty inside". In short, its transgressive power neutralised, it becomes an emptied gesture.

Elfride engages her two lovers, Stephen Smith and Henry Knight, in games of chess in which skill is associated with class and gender power. The second of these encounters makes explicit its function as sexual contest which puts gender roles into question, but which occurs within a format which militates against Elfride: she is, literally, like Belinda[31] before her, playing a man's game. And sexuality as site of contest and argument about gender roles and their normative force is always evident in the text, as when Elfride and Stephen first kiss:

---

29 "Chaste", *The Concise Oxford Dictionary,* 1990 ed.

30 She tells Elfride, "You should write a novel. The regular resource of people who don't go enough into the world to live a novel is to write one".

31 The heroine of Pope's *The Rape of the Lock.*

> It was Elfride's first kiss. And so awkward and unused was she; full of striving – no relenting. There was none of those apparent struggles to get out of the trap which only result in getting further in: no final attitude of receptivity: no easy close of shoulder to shoulder, hand upon hand, face upon face, and, in spite of coyness, the lips in the right place at the supreme moment. That graceful though apparently accidental falling into position, which many have noticed as precipitating the end and making sweethearts the sweeter, was not here. Why? Because experience was absent. A woman must have had many kisses before she kisses well.
>
> In fact, the art of tendering feminine lips for these amatory salutes follows the principles laid down in treatises on legerdemain for performing the trick called Forcing a Card. The card is to be shifted nimbly, withdrawn, edged under, and withal not to be offered till the moment the unsuspecting person's hand reaches the pack; this forcing to be done so modestly and yet so coaxingly that the person trifled with imagines he is really choosing what is in fact thrust into his hand.
>
> Well, there were no such facilities now; and Stephen was conscious of it – first with a momentary regret that his kiss should be spoilt by her confused receipt of it, and then with the pleasant perception that her awkwardness was her charm.
>
> "And you do care for me and love me?" said he.
>
> "Yes."
>
> "Very much?"
>
> "Yes."
>
> "And I mustn't ask you if you'll wait for me, and be my wife some day?"
>
> "Why not?" she said naively.
>
> "There is a reason why, my Elfride."
>
> "Not any one that I know of."
>
> "Suppose there is something connected with me which makes it almost impossible for you to agree to be my wife, or for your father to countenance such an idea?"
>
> "Nothing shall make me cease to love you: no blemish can be found upon your personal nature. That is pure and generous, I know; and having that, how can I be cold to you?"
>
> "And shall nothing else affect us – shall nothing beyond my nature be a part of my quality in your eyes, Elfie?"
>
> "Nothing whatever," she said with a breath of relief. "Is that all? Some outside circumstance? What do I care?"
>
> "You can hardly judge, dear, till you know what has to be judged."

And, of course, she cannot. She does not have the vocabulary. She is speaking of Stephen's "personal nature", but the language which she uses suggests what it is that passes in these transactions as "personal nature" in women: reputation for chastity. Stephen's problem, in fact is that he is the son of a tradesman and a domestic servant. In this society, "name" for women means sexual reputation; for men it relates to caste.

The fuss about Elfride's unpractised kiss arises because Stephen has been told, by his mentor Henry Knight – a character based on Hardy's mentor, Horace Moule – (who teaches him chess and the classics by correspondence, thus symbolically inducting him into the caste to which he aspires) that not "kissing nicely" "is an excellent fault in a woman". What this means is made clear when Stephen reminds Knight of the advice:

> "You remember what you said to me once about women receiving a kiss. Don't you? Why, that instead of our being charmed by the fascination of their bearing at such a time, we should immediately doubt them if their confusion has any grace in it – that awkward bungling was the true charm of the occasion, implying that we are the first who has played such a part with them".

This question of who "has" a woman first is what the text turns on; who enacts the appropriation by the paradigm of the symbolic order of this deemed tabula rasa, making the bloody trace of "lost virginity" inscribe a story dictated by patriarchy, employing woman's substance against her interests: which story certifies her his "new-found-land". Before her love affair with Stephen, Elfride has been loved by a young farmer, Felix Jethway. When Stephen asks, "And had you really never any sweetheart at all?" the following conversation ensues:

> "None that was ever recognized by me as such."
>
> "But did nobody ever love you?"
>
> "Yes – a man did once; very much, he said."
>
> "How long ago?"
>
> "O, a long time."
>
> "How long, dearest?"
>
> "A twelvemonth."
>
> "That's not very long" (rather disappointedly).
>
> "I said long, not very long."
>
> "And he did want to marry you?"
>
> "I believe he did. But I didn't see anything in him. He was not good enough, even if I had loved him."
>
> "May I ask what he was?"
>
> "A large farmer."
>
> "A large farmer not good enough – how much richer than my family!" Stephen murmured.
>
> "Where is he now?" he continued to Elfride.
>
> "Here."
>
> "Here! what do you mean by that?"
>
> "I mean that he is here."
>
> "Where here?"
>
> "Under us. He is under this tomb. He is dead, and we are sitting on his grave."
>
> "Elfie," said the young man, standing up and looking at the tomb, "how odd and sad that revelation seems! It quite depresses me for the moment."
>
> "Stephen, I didn't wish to sit here; but you would do so."
>
> "You never encouraged him?"
>
> "Never by look, word, or sign," she said solemnly. "He died of consumption, and was buried the day you first came."
>
> "Let us go away. I don't like standing by *him*, even if you never loved him. He was *before* me."

Elfride's and Stephen's desire to marry is thwarted when her father finds out that, although a trainee architect, Stephen is not connected with the "county family" of Smiths, but son of a couple in the employ of the local lord of the manor. They arrange to marry in secret in Plymouth. The plan miscarries because of Stephen's ignorance of the law: the licence he obtains can only be used in his London parish. The lovers take the train to London. When they arrive, Elfride has "cold feet", and they rush for the return train and catch it. The real catch, of course, is that all the journeying means that Elfride is away from home over night, unchaperoned. As Stephen says, "I don't like to say it, Elfride – indeed I don't; but you must be told this, that going back unmarried may compromise your good name in the eyes of people who may hear of it." Elfride comes to share his perception, saying, "Appearances are woefully against me. If anybody finds me out, I am, I suppose, disgraced". Stephen replies, "Then appearances will speak falsely; and how can that matter, even if they do? I shall be your husband sooner or later, for certain, and so prove your purity". In doing so he both enunciates the portentous truth, and suggests the staggering crudeness which underlies the valuations of patriarchal society, constructed here as articulations of its law. The necessary evidence will be provided for Stephen by proof of "deflowerment" and, in the community's eyes, by the fact that someone with an intimate knowledge of the circumstances has seen fit to marry Elfride, thus warranting her "undamaged goods."

Stephen is later supplanted in Elfride's affections by his mentor, Knight, a lawyer and literary critic. Knight's first "encounter" with Elfride occurs when he reviews her novel, scathingly and patronisingly, condemning it on the grounds that she has stepped beyond the bounds of what is deemed to be her proper sphere, and that the sphere which is properly hers is not a fit subject for literature:

> We are far from altogether disparaging the author's powers. She has a certain versatility that enables her to use with effect a style of narration peculiar to herself, which may be called a murmuring of delicate emotional trifles, the particular gift of those to whom the social sympathies of a peaceful time are as daily food. Hence, where matters of domestic experience, and the natural touches which make people real, can be introduced without anachronisms too striking, she is occasionally felicitous; and upon the whole we feel justified in saying that the book will bear looking into for the sake of those portions which have nothing whatever to do with the story.

Elfride's response[32] reveals that while Knight trades in judgments, appearances, representations, she is concerned with

32 She says, "I think he is right in some of his arguments, though wrong in others. And because he has some claim to my respect I regret all the more that he should think so mistakenly of my motives in one or two instances. It is more vexing to be misunderstood than to be misrepresented; and he misunderstands me" and later it is noted that she, "did not adopt a masculine pseudonym in vanity or conceit, but because she was afraid it would be thought presumptuous to publish her name, and that she did not mean the story for such as he, but as a sweetener of history for young people..."

understanding informed by her experiences of the social order in which she lives. This conflict between word and fact becomes acute later in their relationship. The first meeting between Elfride and Knight dramatises Knight's thoroughgoing internalisation of the importance of "feminine reputation" and emphasises how Elfride's writing marks her as transgressive. They "fall in love"; their love is delineated as a species of power relation.[33] Knight, like Stephen, values her because he believes himself to be "the first", and Hardy tips his hand in satirising this:

> Knight argued from Elfride's unwontedness of manner, which was matter of fact, to an unwontedness in love, which was a matter of inference only. *Incrédules les plus crédules*. "Elfride", he said, "had hardly looked upon a man till she saw me."[34]

Knight, lawyer and critic, the great interpreter, has an utterly naive and utterly unjustified belief in his own skills, and in the importance of what the application of those skills leads him to believe is fact. Hardy emphasises the normative effect of the products of Knight's skills when, closely and critically questioned by the worldly Mrs Swancourt about his effusions on the subject of feminine experience, Knight says:

> I do believe that remark to be perfectly true, and, having written it, I would defend it anywhere. But I do often regret ever writing it, as well as others of the sort. I have grown older since, and I find such a tone of writing is calculated to do harm in the world. Every literary Jack becomes a gentleman if he can only pen a few indifferent satires on womankind: women themselves, too, have taken to the trick; and so, upon the whole, I begin to be rather ashamed of my companions.

Hardy later sketches the violence and perversity of Knight's beliefs in two telling cross-examinations. In the event, the embittered mother of Farmer Jethway writes a defamatory note to Knight about Elfride's "reputation", and then dies (dramatically removing such possibility as there exists of a legal solution for Elfride.) The note reads:

> SIR – A woman who has not much in the world to lose by any censure this act may bring upon her, wishes to give you some hints concerning a lady you love. If you will deign to accept a warning before it is too late, you will notice what your correspondent has to say.
>
> You are deceived. Can such a woman be worthy?
>
> One who encouraged an honest youth to love her, then slighted him, so that he died.

33 See, for example, their first encounter, in chapter XVII, or their conflict on the tower of West Endelstow Church in chapter XVIII.

34 As he does later, when Knight, "read[s] her refusal [of a gift of earrings] so certainly as the bashfulness of a girl in a novel position that, upon the whole, he could tolerate such a beginning". The narrator then comments, "Could Knight have been told that it was a sense of fidelity struggling against new love, whilst no less assuring as to his ultimate victory it might have entirely abstracted the wish to secure it".

> One who next took a man of no birth as a lover, who was forbidden the house by her father.
>
> One who secretly left her home to be married to that man, met him, and went with him to London.
>
> One who, for some reason or other, returned again unmarried.
>
> One who, in her after-correspondence with him, went so far as to address him as her husband.
>
> One who wrote the enclosed letter to ask me, who better than anybody else knows the story, to keep the scandal a secret.
>
> I hope soon to be beyond the reach of either blame or praise. But before reclaiming me God has put it in my power to avenge the death of my son.

Knight breaks off his engagement to Elfride after the last of a series of cross-examinations[35] which, for all their judgmental intensity, never ask the real question; the final question and answer are, "'Did you return home the same day on which you left it?' 'No'".

Knight's parting advice to her is:

> Elfride, I have been speaking too roughly to you; I have said what I ought only to have thought. I like you; and let me give you a word of advice. Marry your man as soon as you can. However weary of each other you may feel, you belong to each other, and I am not going to step between you. Do you think I would – do you think I could for a moment? If you cannot marry him now, and another makes you his wife, do not reveal this secret to him after marriage, if you do not before. Honesty would be damnation then.

It is terrible and ironic that this advice underscores the fact that "appearances" and "reputations" are all in representation and yet nothing in fact. This point is reinforced by the account of Elfride's desperate train journey to London to plead with Knight; like Tess after her, she says, "Harry, if I am not good enough to be your wife, I wish I could be your servant and live with you, and not be sent away never to see you again. I don't mind what it is except that". As on Tess's "honeymoon", and during Elfride's abortive elopement with Stephen, intercourse does not, of course, take place, and yet Knight is shown as incapable of seeing what it means when he says, "Yet it is wrong for you to stay. O Elfride! What have you committed yourself to? It is ruin to your good name to run to me like this! Has not your first experience been sufficient to keep you from these things?" and she replies:

> My name! Harry, I shall soon die, and what good will my name be to me then? O, could I but be the man and you the woman, I would not leave you for such a little fault as mine! Do not think it was so vile a thing in me to run away with him. Ah, how I wish you could have run away with twenty women before you knew me, that I might show you I would think it no fault, but be glad to get you after them all, so that I had you! If you only knew me through and through, how true I am, Harry.

35 In chapters XXXI and XXXII.

Not only does this show (what Knight does not see) that going to London to be with a man does not mean the loss of virginity, and that the fetishisation of women's chastity is the product of a discourse which is both antipathetical and incomprehensible to women. It also reminds us – although not Knight – that Elfride has literally saved Knight's life, on that cliff of fossils, by taking off the voluminous Victorian underwear – without which she ceases to have a recognisably feminine shape – in order to fashion him a lifeline. If we apply Kristeva's notion of the semiotic[36] to what Elfride becomes at this point we see that the survival of the species depends upon a rejection of the symbolic order, dominated by the Law of the Father; upon the choice of the semiotic *chora*, linked to the mother, ceaselessly heterogeneous; Kristeva sees the choice of the semiotic as potentially restorative, as, "rend[ing] and renew[ing] the social code."

Elfride is taken back to Endelstow by her father, nearly dies of an illness brought on by grief, and subsequently has her life at home made impossible by her father's judgmental coldness. She marries Lord Luxellian, who needs a mother for his children, and has long desired her sexually. The text makes it clear, however, that she is still sick with love for the imperfect, ungentle Knight. She dies during a miscarriage, apparently due to her weakened state. Her death provides another occasion for the rendering ironic of Knight's judgments on feminine chastity, and original possession. Standing with Stephen in Elfride's tomb, observing her grief-stricken widower, Knight says, "'Come away,' . . . 'We have no right to be there. Another stands before us – nearer to her than we'". It also emphasises the stakes involved in marriage and sexual relations for women: questions of gender and sexuality are made literal and metaphorical matters of life and death under patriarchy.

The radical argument – embodied in the delineation of Stephen's education at Knight's hands – that Knight's views about "chastity" and womanhood are "unnatural", is taken up in *Tess*. But I should first like to explore briefly the way in which the issues of reputation, community and the law are taken up in "The Melancholy Hussar of the German Legion". In that tale Hardy dramatises the defamation laws' paradoxical failure to protect women's "honour", and their complicity with patriarchy in protecting masculine "dishonour". The text is striking in the way it identifies the sites where patriarchy is strongly symbolically present: the army, the church, and the state;[37] its critical positioning in relation to these institutions is strongly marked, as is its consciousness of the ethical risks inherent

36 See Moi, chapter 8, for a lucid account of this.

37 "It was nearly ninety years ago. The British uniform of the period, with its immense epaulettes, queer cocked hat, breeches, gaiters, ponderous cartridge-box, buckled shoes, and what not, would look strange and barbarous now. Ideas have changed; invention has followed invention. Soldiers were monumental objects then. A divinity still here and there; and war was considered a glorious thing".

in retelling, appropriating, a woman's story.[38] The narration, too, marks the force of Phyllis's narrative[39] and identifies her as authoritative – because of age, because of her class placing (she is "a lady" when the reteller of her story is "a lad") and because she is the recorder of community history (a privileged position in Hardy's canon). Phyllis's tragedy – to live alone, her lover having been executed before her eyes, and to live as a woman with a "reputation" – is the product of two things. The first is her own inevitable acceptance of her society's discursive construction of femininity, which leads to the failure of her brief rebellion against a loveless marriage at a crucial moment. The other is the way in which patriarchal society bruits abroad her presumed unchastity to her detriment,[40] while her father declines to proceed on the basis of "hearsay" to the effect that her promised husband, "had been heard to say in Bath that he considered his overtures to Miss Phyllis Grove to have reached only the stage of a half-understanding; and in view of his enforced absence on his father's account . . . he thought it best that there should be no definite promise as yet on either side. He was not sure, indeed, that he might not cast his eyes elsewhere". The reason for Phyllis's father's failure to act is his fear that, "it should be deemed an imputation on that bachelor's honour" – that is, defame him, and expose Mr Grove to the law's sanctions.

The text signals that for men, honour has to do with one's word; for women, honour has to do with one's name, that is, on the construction of women's bodies and sexuality by men's words. At the tale's end transgression of the law is symbolically punished – but only some transgressions. The woman and her beloved: a foreigner, and of inferior class – those placed outside the law's zone of privilege but subject to it – have been ruthlessly subdued: one by literal violence, one by figurative violence; both sorts of violence normative.

In the case of Tess, of course, whose story, as I have said, was published in 1891, that year of momentous reform in defamation law,

38 "Phyllis told me the story with her own lips. She was then an old lady of seventy-five, and her auditor a lad of fifteen. She enjoined silence as to her share in the incident till she should be 'dead, buried, and forgotten'. Her life was prolonged twelve years after the day of narration, and she has now been dead nearly twenty. The oblivion which, in her modesty and humility, she coveted for herself, has only partially fallen on her, with the unfortunate result of inflicting an injustice upon her memory; since such fragments of her story as got abroad at the time, and have been kept alive ever since, are precisely those which were most unfavourable to her character".

39 "[O]ne [story] I have never repeated, and assuredly can never forget".

40 See note 38. Phyllis is induced to abort her plans to elope with her beloved upon overhearing her (faithless) fiance remark of her, "It cannot be that she is so bad as they make out. I am quite sure that a girl of her good wit should know better than to get entangled with any of those Hanoverian soldiers. I won't believe it of her, and there's an end on't". This remark and its ilk are said to reveal "to her, as by a sudden illumination, the enormity of her conduct" and to render her "conscience-stricken". But she has done no more in fact than converse with the "Hanoverian soldier" and hold his hand, all the while being separated from him by a garden wall.

the occasion of slander which Hardy dramatises is one on which there is a defence to the action: truth. The incident is dramatic:

> In the evening they returned to the inn at which they had put up, and Tess waited in the entry while Angel went to see the horse and gig brought to the door. The general sitting-room was full of guests, who were continually going in and out. As the door opened and shut each time for the passage of these the light within the parlour fell full upon Tess's face. Two men came out and passed by her among the rest. One of them stared her up and down in surprise, and she fancied he was a Trantridge man, though that village lay so many miles off that Trantridge folk were rarities here.
>
> "A comely maid, that," said the other.
>
> "True-comely enough. But, unless I make a great mistake -" And he negatived the remainder of the definition forthwith.
>
> Clare had just returned from the stable-yard, and confronting the man on the threshold heard the words, and saw the shrinking of Tess. The insult to her stung him to the quick, and before he had considered anything at all he struck the man on the chin with the full force of his fist, sending him staggering backwards into the passage.
>
> The man recovered himself, and seemed inclined to come on, and Clare, stepping outside the door, put himself in a posture of defence. But his opponent began to think better of the matter. He looked anew at Tess as he passed her; and said to Clare, "I beg pardon, sir: 'twas a complete mistake: I thought she was another woman, forty miles from here."
>
> Clare, feeling that he had been too hasty, and that he was moreover to blame for leaving her standing in an inn passage, did what he usually did in such cases; gave the man five shillings to plaster the blow; and thus they parted, bidding each other a pacific good-night. As soon as Clare had taken the reins from the ostler, and the young couple had driven off, the two men went in the other direction:
>
> "And was it a mistake?" said the second one.
>
> "Not a bit of it. But I didn't want to hurt the gentleman's feelings – not I."

It also dramatises the selective binary readings which patriarchy imposes on women's bodies, for which process Hardy later provides a vivid image, "The sun was so low on that short last afternoon of the year that it shone in through a small opening and formed a golden staff which stretched across to her skirt, where it made a spot like a paint-mark set upon her". For all his enlightenment, the "sun/son", Angel, like the Father, and Angel's clergyman father, can only read her in terms dictated by the symbolic order: blemished/spotless; whore/virgin.

In all but one relevant sense, though, the sense "virgin", Tess *is* a maid: a girl, a young unmarried woman, a servant.[41] But there is only one meaning of "maid" which signifies in this circumstance, where her value as object of desire and marker of Angel's prestige vis-a-vis other men is at issue. Tess is, after all, as he says later, "his

41 "Maid", *The Shorter Oxford English Dictionary*, 1985 ed.

fellowship", the confirmatory sign that his self-deluding and patronising version of pastoral has not all been for nought.

Hardy goes on to show how otiose the idea of this defence to slander, and the idea of the slander itself, and thus the Law of the Father, are, when, on Angel and Tess's wedding night, they tell each other the stories of their pre-marital sexual encounters: his "eight-and-forty hours' dissipation with a stranger"; her rape by Alec. Tess says that the stories are "just the same". On a couple of levels they are, of course, although Hardy leaves us in no doubt as to an essential difference between the two events – which is not the difference that Angel perceives. At the same time he emphasises the degree to which Tess has internalised stories about the damaging effect of rape on women's reputation, and thus on her value, her nature, her self; Hardy also interrogates the symbolic difference between the stories. This symbolic difference is starkly emphasised by Angel's responses to Tess in the following passages:

> Tess followed him to the middle of the room where he was, and stood there staring at him with eyes that did not weep. Presently she slid down upon her knees beside his feet, and from this position she crouched in a heap. "In the name of our love, forgive me," she whispered with a dry mouth. "I have forgiven you for the same." And as he did not answer she said again; "forgive me, as you are forgiven. I forgive you, Angel."
>
> "You, – yes, you do."
>
> "But you do not forgive me?"
>
> "O Tess, forgiveness does not apply to the case. You were one person: now you are another. My God – how can forgiveness meet such a grotesque – prestidigitation as that!"

and:

> "I thought, Angel, that you loved me – me, my very self! If it is I you do love, O how can it be that you look and speak so? It frightens me! Having begun to love you, I love you for ever – in all changes, in all disgraces, because you are yourself. I ask no more. Then how can you, O my own husband, stop loving me?"
>
> "I repeat; the woman I have been loving is not you."
>
> "But who?"
>
> "Another woman in your shape."

and, "He looked upon her as a species of impostor; a guilty woman in the guise of an innocent one". The text, then, exposes the gendered inequity which the 1891 statute does nothing but reinscribe in the belief that what it is doing is equitable. Perhaps, though, "equitable" is precisely what it is.[42] As Eisenstein (1988 p 224) says, "Often law only affords women protection of their present engendered status". And what happens if a law is changed in the name of a (gendered) equity, while the practice of gendered inequity which it thinks it addresses persists? That for women Tess's reading, "Once victim, always victim: that's the law", will not always be the law requires

42 See Graycar and Morgan (1990 p 116), and Pether (1991a pp 71- 82).

that we take the opportunity necessitated by the fermenting of new wine to make some new bottles. Literary texts can help in the process, but not, in my view, by being placed on law school syllabi as "case studies". From the point of view of a literary studies practitioner it is both crude and naive to suggest, as Carol Sanger (1989 p 1365) has, that realist texts are relevant because they "provide a whiff of what's out there for women interacting with law". Analyses of transcripts of cases, of the language and structure of judgments and statutes, as *Lynch v Knight* suggests and as Terry Threadgold (1991 pp 39-70) has shown, show what is happening to women in the practice of the law. If your aim is to demonstrate the utility and necessity of feminist jurisprudence and of the translation of its insights into practice, you are on safer and more persuasive and more ethical ground with the artefacts of practice. To suggest that what Hardy's stories tell reflects some opaque and absolute reality, and that they can be appropriated as evidence of what goes on in "the real world" is a discredited view in my present profession; it also replaces the voices of real witnesses with the effusions of those granted authority by their inclusion in a literary canon. Where literary texts seem capable of fitting into the enterprise is, somewhat problematically, as ethical exempla – because, to quote a writer who was a lawyer, they provide, "Instruction . . . [and] [e]ntertainment".[43]

More importantly, some literary texts demonstrate the similarities between the way law and literature tell stories, and the persuasiveness and pervasiveness of the stories that they tell. They offer, to quote Raymond Williams (1983 p 189), opportunities for the study of, "Language in history: that full field", sites where we can study, "language produced in works through conventions and institutions which, properly examined, are the really active society". Sites where our studies can make a difference. But sites where we can expect resistance. To quote Thomas Hardy on the critics of *Tess:*

> they may have causes to advance, privileges to guard, traditions to keep going; some of which the tale-teller, who writes down how the things of the world strike him, without any ulterior intentions whatever, has overlooked, and may by pure inadvertence have run foul of when in the least aggressive mood. Perhaps some passing perception, the outcome of a dream-hour, would if generally acted on, cause such an assailant considerable inconvenience with respect to position, interests, family, servant, ox, ass, neighbour, or neighbour's wife. He therefore. . . cries "Shame!" So densely is the world thronged that any shifting of positions, even the best warranted advance, galls somebody's kibe. Such shiftings begin in sentiment, and such sentiment sometimes begins in a novel.

43 Henry Fielding, Preface to *Joseph Andrews*.

BIBLIOGRAPHY

Bakhtin, M, 1981, "From the prehistory of novelistic discourse", Emerson, C and Holquist, M (eds), *The Dialogic Imagination: Four Essays*, University of Texas Press.

Eisenstein, ZR, 1988, *The Female Body and the Law*, California University Press.

Favret, J and Peter, J-P, 1982, "The Animal, the Madman, and Death", Foucault, Michel (ed), *I, Pierre Riviére, having slaughtered my mother, my sister, and my brother*. . . University of Nebraska Press.

Fish, S, 1989, *Doing What Comes Naturally: Change, Rhetoric and the Practice of Theory in Literary and Legal Studies,* Duke University Press.

Fleming, JG, 1987, *The Law of Torts,* 7th edn, The Law Book Company Limited.

Glass, DM, 1990, "Portia in Primetime: Women Lawyers, Television, and LA Law", *Yale Journal of Law and Feminism*, vol 2, no 2, Spring.

Goode, J, 1988, *Thomas Hardy: the Offensive Truth*, Basil Blackwell.

Graycar, R and Morgan, J, 1990, *The Hidden Gender of Law*, The Federation Press.

Grosz, E, 1989, *Sexual Subversions*, ch 1, "Modern French Philosophy", Allen & Unwin.

Heilbrun, C and Resnick, J, 1990, "Convergences: Law, Literature, and Feminism", *The Yale Law Journal*, vol 99.

Holt, FL, 1978, *The Law of Libel*, Garland Publishing Inc.

James, PS, 1972, *Introduction to English Law*, 2nd edn, Butterworths.

Lodge, D, 1989, *Nice Work*, Penguin.

MacKinnon, C, 1990, *Yale Journal of Law and Feminism*, vol 2, no 2, Spring.

Moi, T, 1988, *Sexual / Textual Politics*, Routledge.

Pether, P, 1985, "Endogamy and Compatibility as Natural Laws: Marriage, Mating and Community in the Short Stories of Thomas Hardy", University of New England, (diss).

Pether, P, 1991a, "Fiduciary Duties: Congreve's *The Way of the World*", 7, *Australian Journal of Law and Society.*

Pether, P, 1991b, "Hardy and the Law", *The Thomas Hardy Journal,* vol VII, no 1, February.

Sanger, C, 1989, "Seasoned to the Use", 87, *Mich L Rev.*

Thomas, B, 1991, "Reflections on the Law and Literature Revival", vol 17 no 3, *Critical Inquiry*, Spring.

Threadgold, T, 1991, "Legal Practice in the Courts: Discourse, Gender and Ethics", 7, *The Australian Journal of Law and Society.*

Wilkes, GA, 1990, *A dictionary of Australian colloquialisms*, 3rd edn, Sydney University Press with Oxford University Press.

Williams, R, 1983, "Cambridge English, Past and Present", *Writing in Society*, Verso.

13

Holy Deadlock and a Handful of Dust: AP Herbert, Evelyn Waugh and Divorce Law Reform in the 1930s

DONAT GALLAGHER

AP Herbert's *Holy Deadlock* and Evelyn Waugh's *A Handful of Dust* both appeared in 1934 during the agitation for divorce law reform that led to the *Matrimonial Causes Act* 1937 (UK).[1] Despite uncanny similarities, there are marked differences between the novels. *Holy Deadlock* is a frankly polemical attack on divorce laws that simultaneously provoke and capriciously punish collusion, perjury, deceit and humbug. *A Handful of Dust* describes the same situations. But it is by no means clear that Waugh's intention is the same as Herbert's. Is *A Handful of Dust* comic or satiric? And, if satiric, what is its object? Might Waugh be attacking the divorce laws from the viewpoint of a Roman Catholic upholder of monogamy? Or is he attacking the laws with a view to their liberalisation?

Although a literalistic Roman Catholic in later life, Waugh was less predictable when young. Committed to monogamy as an ideal, he was equally committed to liberal divorce laws. Surprising though it may seem now, his early articles on marriage and divorce were influenced not only by Roman Catholic doctrine, but by two very active divorce law reformers, Bertrand Russell and Judge Ben B Lindsey. His journalism thus provides a double perspective on many of the issues that figured in the debate leading up to the Act of 1937 and creates an informative context for reading both *A Handful of Dust* and *Holy Deadlock*.

---

1 For the contribution made by *Holy Deadlock* to the passing of the Act, see Herbert's Introduction to the 1955 edition of the novel, pp 7-12. See also Stone (1990 pp 398-99).

Marriage and divorce cannot be seriously discussed without reference to anthropology, law, psychology, philosophy, and religion. It is with diffidence, therefore, that I direct attention to several short polemical articles written by a young comic novelist for the "popular" press. On the other hand the articles reflected an intensely serious controversy going on at higher levels. The clergy were defending the status quo from their pulpits; reformers were demanding liberalisation of the divorce laws from lecture platforms. The literature was vast. Powerful lobby groups of women, such as the Mothers' Union, opposed divorce, and hosts of "modern" doctors, lawyers, novelists and artists promoted it. Parliament was deeply divided. I am therefore at a loss to understand why Lawrence Stone says in *Road to Divorce* (1990 p 397) that "between 1923 and 1937, the question of reform of the divorce laws was allowed to slumber". The reality, of course, is that between 1923, when women were first allowed access to divorce on an equal footing with men, and 1937, when the *Matrimonial Causes Act* extended the grounds for divorce beyond adultery to desertion and cruelty, a "massive shift in public opinion" (p 400) had taken place. Veronica's cry in *A Handful of Dust* – "Now I understand why they keep going on in the papers about divorce law reform" (p 152) – reflects the fact that it was in the newspapers that the "shift in public opinion" was largely aroused and shaped into political pressure.

Waugh (1928 pp 59, 86) favourably reviewed Bertrand Russell's *Sceptical Essays* in 1928 (Gallagher 1983 pp 40-3); and evidence was given during his annulment hearing that he had been a follower of Judge Ben B Lindsey's *The Companionate Marriage.*[2] Russell's ideas on marriage and divorce are scattered throughout countless books, essays, newspaper articles, lectures, public debates, broadcasts and letters. But *Marriage and Morals* (Russell 1929) is a good summary. Lindsey gained world-wide fame when he was dismissed from his Juvenile Court in Denver for granting divorces and annulments to young couples on an unprecedented scale. Lindsey and Evans's *The Companionate Marriage*, was first published in New York in 1927 and republished in London with a preface by the Hon Mrs Bertrand Russell in 1928. When he deals with the civil marriage law, Waugh draws upon Russell and Lindsey.

The contest was between Christian Marriage and Divorce Law Reform. Christian Marriage was defended by all the major churches, by their allies in parliament, and by several powerful organisations of women. In fact the major Christian denominations competed to express their hostility to Reform. Thus many Protestant critics

2 Alec Waugh told the Marriage Tribunal that "*M Arthur* [ie Arthur *Evelyn* Waugh] *et Mme Eveline* [ie Evelyn Waugh's first wife, Evelyn Gardner] *avant et après leur mariage appartenaient à un milieu qui avait les idées avancées plus tard par le juge (américain) Lindsey, dans son livre* Companionate Marriage. . . *Sacrae Romanae Rotae Decisiones seu Sententiae quae prodierunt anno 1936*", Vol XXVII (Vatican City: Typis Polyglottis Vaticanis, 1944), p 446.

attacked the Roman Catholic system of annulments as a threat to the stability of marriage.[3] Later, the Roman Catholic Church regularly attacked non-Catholic clergy who supported liberalisation of the divorce laws. The reasons are instructive:

> She [the Roman Catholic Church] stands apart from the laxity of other Churches because she . . . knows by divine wisdom what is the right attitude . . . Her prohibition of divorce safeguards . . . the married; prevents thoughtless marriages and easy separations; protects women . . . and benefits the children . . . by securing for them a permanent home and continuous education. Divorce is bad for society, for individual morality, and for human life in its totality. (Rumble 1952 p 234)

This pronouncement is significant because the reference to "divine wisdom" implies that the Christian churches have a duty to oppose divorce, not only for their own members, but for all citizens. Indeed the Roman Catholic Church taught explicitly that its prohibition of divorce extended to the civil sphere. This followed from the premise that Christ's pronouncement on the subject invoked, not ecclesiastical law, but divine and natural law, and was therefore universally applicable.[4]

Evelyn Waugh's first article on marriage in *The Daily Mail*, "Let the Marriage Ceremony Mean Something", obliquely attacks the Churches' insistence on enshrining Christian monogamy in civil law. Writing in 1929 when still a nominal member of the Church of England, Waugh argues that a church has the right "to impose any obligation it thinks fit on its own members", thus implicitly denying that it has the right to impose obligations on citizens who are not its members. Circumspectly making the state the villain, he goes on to say that, as the state exists only "for the convenience of its citizens", and since most citizens desire the right to divorce, the state's prohibition of divorce is an attempt "to usurp spiritual powers". Marriage is "a bare civil contract, which should logically, like all other civil contracts, be dissoluble by mutual consent".

There was nothing oblique or circumspect about Waugh's "Home Life Is So Dull". Written in 1935 when Waugh had been a Roman Catholic for five years, it trenchantly denounces the

3 An editorial in *The Times*, "So-Called Marriage", used the Marlborough-Vanderbilt annulment to "disillusion those who might have been tempted to extol the Church of Rome as the one consistent champion of indissoluble marriage" (18 November 1926, p 15d). Several letters warned (incorrectly) that in the Roman Church impediments to marriage were so "numerous", and so easy for the unscrupulous to exploit, that they rendered all marriages "precarious" (TA Lacey, 18 November 1926, p 10c).

4 In the 1930s Roman Catholic marriage was still governed by the 1917 Code of Canon Law. The Code recognised two kinds of marriage law, one divine, the other ecclesiastical. Divine law prohibited, for example, an impotent person from contracting marriage. Ecclesiastical law dealt with formalities, such as the requirement that marriage normally take place before a priest and two witnesses. The Church claimed the sole right to declare "authentically" what divine law was. It also declared itself unable to vary, or dispense from, divine law.

Churches' opposition to divorce. As Waugh saw it, they confused "legality with morality". "The Churches," he says, "all . . . forbid things to their adherents that are perfectly legal by the law of the land. For example Catholics may not cremate their dead nor eat meat on Friday, Buchmanites may not smoke. . . [But] no policeman enforces these rules". Liberalisation of the divorce laws would not affect church members, since "Catholics refrain from polygamy in countries where it is legal, just as Buchmanites refrain from smoking where cigarettes are being sold under their noses". Yet in the case of "the intolerable muddle of the marriage laws" church members fight tooth and nail to prevent others enjoying something which they themselves do not want.

The Roman Catholic Church would have strenuously denied the parallel drawn between the prohibition of cremation and the prohibition of divorce. In its view the prohibition of cremation was institutional and variable at the will of the institution; the prohibition of divorce, on the other hand, was a divine and natural law that the Church had no power to tamper with. In the event the Catholic Church made resistance to liberalised divorce a central feature of its stand against modern "materialism" and Waugh's articles, which publicly contradicted the official policy, appeared not only unorthodox but disloyal. He nevertheless persisted in condemning the Churches for using their political power to keep monogamous marriage embodied in legislation.

But while Waugh condemned the Churches' opposition to easier divorce, he differed from many divorce law reformers in believing that lifelong monogamy was valuable in personal and sexual terms. Nor did he deny that the Churches had every right to impose monogamy on their own members and to offer it to society as an ideal.

"Let the Marriage Ceremony Mean Something" admits that all the prima facie evidence seemed to prove that the advantages of marriage are temporary:

> There are stages in the life of every man or woman when some woman or man is necessary for its full development, but the chances are extremely small that the same man and woman will be permanently valuable to each other at all stages; we all know numerous cases of marriages which started delightfully and have become a burden, the prolonged relationship undoing all the good that it originally did for both parties. From these observations many reasonable and virtuous people . . . have decided that indissoluble marriages are undesirable.

In short, experience and commonsense suggests that marriage should be dissoluble and divorce legal.

A later article, "Tell the Truth about Marriage" (Waugh 1930; Gallagher 1983 pp 94-6), develops this point. It acknowledges several tendencies in modern life that seemed to be changing the economic and social bases of marriage: the drift towards a propertyless population, which was undermining the importance of inheritance and thus the need to ensure that paternity be certain; the increasing reliability of contraception, which was destroying the assumption that marriage produced children who needed the protection of a permanent relationship; and the growing economic independence of women, which was destroying the assumption that women required marriage to secure financial support from men.[5] Waugh in this 1930 article, was uncertain about the final result of these tendencies, because "we have no knowledge of what hidden tendencies may be present to frustrate them". Nevertheless he conceded that it was "the state's job to sanction a change in marriage arrangements if the material basis for marriage altered".

But in all human affairs commonsense has its limits. "Let the Marriage Ceremony Mean Something" therefore attempts to state a truth on a higher plane than the demonstrably sensible arguments for divorce. The "best" advantages of marriage, the article argues, can be secured only if marriage is regarded as permanent. But in putting forward this argument, Waugh acknowledges that he has moved into a realm where things are "not as simple as they seem". "Tell the Truth about Marriage" goes further, explicitly attempting to reach "beyond reason" to the "spiritual basis" of monogamy. This spiritual basis was "guarded by the Church" and rested "deep in man's nature . . . on two great truths".

The first of these great truths was that the "sex life is only part of . . . general activity" and it should not supplant the obligation owed to the rest of the community. This truth rested on an appraisal of sex instinct as "in most cases a . . . controllable appetite which would never cause serious trouble if it was not being continually agitated by . . . hint and suppression" (Waugh 1930). Waugh's view corresponds with that put by Russell in Chapter XX of *Marriage and Morals*, "The Place of Sex among Human Values", and with that of Lindsey throughout *The Companionate Marriage*.

The second "great truth" about marriage, which also harmonises closely with the views of Russell and Lindsey, was that the "sex nature . . . is most fully satisfied, not in variety, but in the intensity of experience. By developing and broadening a relationship with one mate, [a man or woman] can achieve a relationship which, when it ceases to be sexual, does so by becoming something more important".[6] In short, Waugh respected the ideal of monogamous marriage and could see the wisdom of the Churches in framing marriage laws for their own members based upon the ideals of permanence and fidelity.

---

5 Russell expresses similar views in *Marriage and Morals,* pp 303-307.

6 Evelyn Waugh, "Tell the Truth About Marriage" and CFR Russell, *Marriage and Morals*, pp 142-3: "A marriage which begins with passionate love and leads to children . . . ought to produce so deep a tie between a man and woman that they will feel something infinitely precious in their companionship, even after sexual passion has decayed. . . A companionship which has lasted for many years . . . has a richness of content which cannot belong to the first days of love. . ."

On the other hand, the conditions Waugh laid down for promoting permanent fidelity could not have departed much further from the prevailing canons of orthodoxy. Like Russell, Waugh argued that the Church had formerly secured obedience to its precepts by threats of hell-fire,[7] but since these threats had ceased to be terrifying, other methods had now to be employed to achieve the same result. These methods were to show young people "the unimportance of sex in its narrow sense, and the importance of marriage in its widest sense", by allowing "the greatest possible freedom to young people in finding out the truth about sex". This freedom for the young "to find out about sex" would entail first, teaching children about sex; secondly, teaching them fully about birth control and thirdly, encouraging them to obtain wide experience.

When he wrote this in 1930, Waugh was clearly under the influence of Lindsey's *Companionate Marriage* (1927 pp 175-7), which urges the state to instruct the young in the science of birth control and in the art of sex (in Temples of Venus in each city), argues that Companionate Marriage will prevent the overemphasis on sex which irregular unions create,[8] and supports monogamous marriage as the ideal.[9]

As regards civil marriage laws, the correspondences between Waugh and Lindsey are also strong. Lindsey writes: "Companionate Marriage is legal marriage, with legalised Birth Control [in the 1920s birth control was still prohibited by law in many American States], and with the right to divorce by mutual consent for childless couples, usually without payment of alimony". Later Lindsey becomes more specific: "If this form of marriage were recognised in law, people who entered it would openly profess their intention not to have children *without special license from the state*" (pp v, 175). Waugh's 1930 article is very similar in arguing that marriages should be dissoluble by mutual consent, like any other legal contract. But Waugh's 1929 article had been closer to Bertrand Russell, who saw no need for the state to interfere in sexual relationships at all unless children were involved.[10] So Waugh (1929) wrote: "Perhaps the best thing would be

7 Evelyn Waugh, "Tell the Truth About Marriage" and CFR Russell, *Marriage and Morals*, p 84: "The motive of . . . virtue in the past [was] chiefly the fear of hell-fire; [this] was removed by the decay of theological orthodoxy. . . For some time traditional morality managed to hold out through the force of custom and mental inertia, but the shock of the war caused these barriers to fall."

8 *Companionate Marriage*, pp 159 and passim: "Above all [companionate marriage] would tend to keep young people from placing on sex a greater emphasis than sex should have in their lives . . . our sex code crowds other things off the stage and makes sex the whole object of their thought and intention."

9 *Companionate Marriage*, p 267 and passim: "I am for monogamy and against divorce. . . I recognize divorce as a great social evil. . . But I would provide against divorce by so changing the status of marriage that fewer persons would want divorce."

10 Russell, *Marriage and Morals*, p 165: "I think that all sex relations which do not involve children should be regarded as a purely private affair . . . no marriage should be legally binding until the wife's first pregnancy. . ." Again on p 77: "But for children, there would be no need of any institution concerned with sex. . ." And passim.

to abolish the civil marriage contract altogether, but make a licence necessary for the producing of a child".

In the light of the above, I clearly cannot agree with Martin Stannard (1986 pp 352-3), Waugh's most recent biographer, when he writes: "[Waugh's articles on marriage] are perfectly in keeping with his later beliefs". As Stannard regards Waugh's "later beliefs" as narrowly traditionalist, his meaning must be that the early articles conform to Roman Catholic teaching in the 1930s. I hope I have shown that Waugh's advocacy of dissoluble civil marriage was contrary to Roman Catholic teaching of the time; while his advocacy of birth control and sexual freedom for the young flagrantly contradicted the sexual morality then taught by all of the major Christian churches.

Returning to *A Handful of Dust* and *Holy Deadlock*, mention might first be made of three odd coincidences that link the two novels and the two authors.

In each novel the hero consents to "act like a gentleman", that is to fabricate evidence of adultery and allow himself to be sued for divorce rather than subject the wife to the indignity of a contested action. Both heroes therefore resort to Brighton with a professional partner to provide evidence of "infidelity" for a "hotel-bill case". Both provide this evidence by getting into bed with their partners while fully dressed, with a dressing gown over day clothes, and are so dressed when detected in "intimacy" by the maid who brings breakfast. A comic turn of events in *A Handful of Dust* requires Tony Last to eat not one, but two, breakfasts. He explains this to his partner's wondering child: "When you're a little older you'll understand these things. It's the Law!" (p 143).

Evelyn Gardner, Waugh's first wife, left him for John Heygate. Heygate worked for the BBC and was compelled to resign after being named as the co-respondent in the subsequent divorce. In *Holy Deadlock* Mary, after separating from John Adam, falls in love with Martin Seal. Seal works for the BBC and must resign after being named in the court proceedings.

Finally Mr Boom, the solicitor who acts for John Adam in *Holy Deadlock*, was closely and admittedly modelled on the well-known solicitor and divorce law reformer, ESP Haynes.[11] Boom's interviews with John Adam take place in a restaurant where they eat oysters and drink white wine. ESP Haynes handled Waugh's divorce, and in "Max Beerbohm: A Lesson in Manners", Waugh wrote of the experience: "He gave me far more in oysters and hock during its transaction than he charged me in fees" (Gallagher 1983 p 514).

11 Herbert acknowledges his debt to Haynes in the Introduction to the Penguin (1955) edition of *Holy Deadlock*, p 11: "The character of 'Mr Boom' was founded on that untiring, unselfish reformer, the late ESP Haynes, who taught me more than anyone in this complicated and difficult affair".

Despite these superficial coincidences, which can be explained by ESP Haynes's friendship with both Evelyn Waugh and AP Herbert, the novels are very different in tone.

In *A Handful of Dust* Tony and Brenda Last appear the perfect couple: "What with Brenda's pretty ways and Tony's good sense [they] were pre-eminently successful in solving the problem of getting along well together" (pp 24-5). But Brenda frivolously chooses to have a "walk-out" with a contemptible young man, falls in love with him, and seeks a "collusive" divorce from Tony. At the instigation of her lover, however, she attempts to use the legal fiction of Tony's "infidelity" to extract an unaffordable settlement. Tony thwarts the plan, implausibly as will appear. Nevertheless Tony ends up trapped in the jungle reading Dickens aloud to a religious maniac. He is a victim of civilised savagery and of the inadequacy of his own humanist values.

Only Chapter IV of *A Handful of Dust*, "English Gothic – II", is devoted to the mechanics of the attempted divorce. The action is comic, for Tony's professional partner insists on bringing her daughter, the Awful Child of Popular Fiction, to Brighton. The theme is betrayal and the tone is bitter. Tony "acts like a gentleman" against the advice of his solicitor, who warns that, as the technically guilty party, he will be open to a claim for substantial alimony (p 128). Tony rejects the warning saying, "Lady Brenda's word is quite good enough", for he "had contracted the habit of loving and trusting Brenda" (p 129). Finding later that Brenda has agreed to the scheme for extracting ruinous alimony, Tony abandons the agreed settlement and declares that he will contest the divorce, using the presence of the Awful Child to render the evidence of adultery worthless. But it might not have been so easy. Had he read *Holy Deadlock*, Tony would have known that revealing his part in fabricating evidence would have exposed him to charges of collusion, conspiracy, attempting to pervert the course of justice, and of aiding and abetting perjury – *and* his solicitor could have been struck off.

Is *A Handful of Dust* merely funny? Or is it satire? And, if satire, does it ridicule the divorce laws with a view to condemning modern divorce, or with a view to liberalising the law? The answers to these questions must be mixed. Evelyn Waugh's fundamental thinking was conservative but was tempered, in youth particularly, by an "ultra-modern" style and by unpredictable opinions on topical matters. He was also a Roman Catholic convert who had been born into a literary family and later gained entry to the world of fashion. Understandably he was embarrassed by, and sometimes openly opposed to, aspects of 1930s Roman Catholic clericalism as the articles cited above demonstrate. He was therefore entirely capable of accepting monogamy as a personal obligation flowing from the comprehensive theological and philosophical system which he had embraced; and even of championing monogamy as an ideal. He was equally capable of attacking laws, supported by the Churches, that imposed monogamy on unwilling fellow citizens. In the light of the early journalism *A Handful of Dust* should be read as a novel that, in satirising infidelity, implies commitment to fidelity; but that at the same time ridicules oppressive divorce laws with a view to their reform.

In *Holy Deadlock* John Adam and Mary Eve are almost unrealistically honest folk who married not wisely but too young, and who, without fault or animosity on either side are unable to live together. Separated for some years, each wishes to marry an entirely suitable new partner. Mary asks John Adam to "act like a gentleman" (ie to allow her to divorce him on account of an act of fabricated adultery) because, as has been pointed out, her fiancé, Martin Seal, is a popular announcer at the BBC and will lose his job if named as co-respondent. Adam attempts divorce twice. The first attempt fails comically when the elderly maid who had served breakfast at his Brighton hotel, and who is inexperienced in divorce cases, will not identify him in court as the man she saw in bed – because she likes him. The second attempt easily succeeds up to decree nisi, even though Adam's partner on this occasion develops measles during the "adulterous" weekend and Adam, the "husband," has to keep up appearances by visiting his "wife" daily for some weeks. But after the decree nisi, Mary makes love to Martin Seal, once; a hostile acquaintance sends an anonymous letter to the King's Proctor; and the King's Proctor "shows cause" why the decree nisi should not become absolute. Mary fights the case, but the judge, who is entitled to exercise discretion in her favour, declines to do so. He has a boil on his bottom, his wife has just lost money at cards, and he does not wish to favour a pretty woman. Named in the proceedings, Martin must resign from the BBC.

Mary's failure to secure a divorce leaves her, an actress, and Martin, a former wireless announcer, without the legal right to marry but with the social choice of living together. John Adam, however, has no such choice. As a respectable publisher, he may not live with the woman he loves. Nor, as a respected headmistress, may the woman he loves continue to associate with him. Ruined and desolate, John is found at the conclusion of the novel picking up a prostitute.

Holy Deadlock is about an admirable couple whose need to divorce is overwhelming, but who can find no way to be free except by resort to the collusion, perjury, deceit and humbug involved in evading the then divorce laws. Their attempts to divorce fail, but in describing the failed attempts AP Herbert, through his lawyer mouthpieces, Boom, Freebody and Barter, manages to instruct his readers both in the intricacies of the law as it was written, and in the even greater intricacies of the law as it applied in practice. Above all he makes clear the human costs involved in the workings of the law, and highlights a commonsense view of the law's absurdities.

What Herbert does not do is explore the social and sexual issues involved in fundamental changes to the institution of marriage. In his novel only self-righteous bigots and nice old clergymen incapable of reason oppose reform. Waugh's articles, though slight, give a glimpse of some of the issues debated by reformers and traditionalists that find no place in *Holy Deadlock*. Herbert's single-minded concentration on the absurdities of the law was nevertheless exactly what his reform project required.

Holy Deadlock is a classically excellent exposition of a complex law within the framework of fiction. Indeed, it once possessed textbook status. As a work of polemics it is distinguished, not only by a clear and openly stated purpose, but by laughter, tears and all the heart needed to change minds. It succeeded in winning votes for a change in the law because it combined virtuoso clarity and accuracy in explaining legal technicalities with an appeal to warm good feelings. Even the lawyers are wise, disinterested, committed to their clients' happiness, and possessed of seemingly limitless time to talk. In all of this it contrasts with *A Handful of Dust*, which is funny, bitter, allusive and ambivalent. But both novels made a significant contribution to the massive shift in public opinion which led to the historic reform of the divorce laws in the 1937 *Matrimonial Causes Act*.

BIBLIOGRAPHY

Gallagher, Donat (ed), 1983, *The Essays, Articles and Reviews of Evelyn Waugh*, Methuen.

Herbert, AP, 1955, *Holy Deadlock*, Penguin. (First published 1934, Harmondsworth).

Lindsey, Judge Ben B & Wainwright, Evans, 1927, *The Companionate Marriage*, Brentano's Ltd. (With an introduction by the Hon Mrs Bertrand Russell).

Rumble, Rev Dr, 1952, *Radio Replies*, 2nd series, Missionaries of the Sacred Heart.

Russell, Bertrand, 1929, *Marriage and Morals*, Liveright Publishing Corporation.

Stannard, Martin, 1986, *Evelyn Waugh: The Early Years 1903-1939*, Dent.

Stone, Lawrence, 1990, *Road to Divorce: England 1530-1987*, Oxford University Press.

Waugh, Evelyn, 1928, “Turning Over New Leaves”, *Vogue*,17 October.

Waugh, Evelyn, 1929, “Let the Marriage Ceremony Mean Something”, *The Daily Mail*, 8 October, p 12.

Waugh, Evelyn, 1930, “Tell the Truth About Marriage”, *John Bull*, 48, 7, 23 August.

Waugh, Evelyn, 1935, “Home Life Is So Dull”, *Sunday Express*, 1 December, p 4.

Waugh, Evelyn, 1959, *A Handful of Dust*, Penguin. (First published 1934, Harmondsworth).

14

Jakob Wassermann's Der Fall Maurizius *(The Maurizius Case): A Neglected Masterpiece of Legal Pathology*

J NEVILLE TURNER

German literature has a long tradition of *Juristendichter* – writer/lawyers, of whom Goethe, Brentano, Theodor Storm, von Kleist and Friedrich Dürrenmatt spring to mind. There are many more. Indeed German literature boasts one remarkable man who was a judge, writer and composer – an *Universalgenie* – ETA Hoffmann, who is immortalised in Offenbach's opera, *Hoffmann's Erzählungen* – "The Tales of Hoffmann".

While Jakob Wassermann does not belong to this band – for he was not legally trained – his preoccupation with themes of justice and moral responsibility places him at the forefront of writers in the tradition of Balzac, Edgar Allan Poe, Dickens, Tolstoy and especially Dostoevsky as a "legal pathologist".

Indeed, at the height of his fame, he was often referred to as the "German Dostoevsky"![1] Jakob Wassermann was a world figure in literature, a contemporary of Hermann Hesse, Thomas and Heinrich Mann, Döblin, Rilke and Musil in a fertile period of German literature – the first 30 or 40 years of this century. He was more renowned in his day than any of them. Today, he is almost forgotten. But a TV adaptation of *Der Fall Maurizius*, shown on SBS some three years ago, may signal a revival of interest in this neglected world figure. It was this program that drew me to Wassermann.

Wassermann, like the Manns and Döblin, was Jewish. He was born in 1873 in the industrial city of Fürth, Middle Franconia, not far from Nuremberg. He tells in his autobiographical treatise, *Mein Weg*

1 See Martini (1960 p 544).

als Deutscher und Jude (My Journey as German and Jew) (1921 ch 1), that his father belonged to one of the oldest Jewish communities in Germany. His father was an unsuccessful businessman, who went bankrupt. After his mother's early death, Wassermann's relationship with his father was an ambivalent one – which may explain a dominant theme of the novel.

In 1898 Wassermann left Germany and settled in Vienna, where he found less intolerance of Jews. He lived in Austria for the rest of his life and was there attracted to Freud's psychoanalytical theories. He died in Vienna in 1934.

Between 1897 and 1934, he published 13 novels and many novellas, as well as biographies of Columbus and the explorer, Stanley. He was twice married. Photographs reveal him as an intense and earnest man, lacking humour and warmth. Although he edited a literary journal, *Simplizissimus*, he had few friends in the world of literature. He belonged to no acknowledged school. One of his few close friends was the composer Ferruccio Busoni, to whom he devoted *Mein Weg Als Deutscher und Jude.* Thomas Mann once described him as a *"Welt-star des Romans"*. In February 1933, the *Preussische Akademie der Künste* – a united front of the SPD and KPD, compelled him and several other Jewish writers, including the Mann brothers, to resign from the Academy. His books were amongst those burned on the infamous night of 13 May 1933. He did not live to see the events of *Hitlerzeit.*[2]

Wassermann's most famous novel is perhaps *Caspar Hauser*, a work based on a strange character of the early nineteenth century who mysteriously appeared in society at about the age of 18, having apparently been brought up without any previous contact with any human being. Caspar Hauser is a child-like figure, rather like "The Idiot" or Jean Valjean in *Les Miserables.* Werner Herzog made a film based on this novel. Significantly this novel is sub-titled *Die Trägheit des Herzens* (Hardness of Heart).[3]

However *Der Fall Maurizius*, written in 1929, is now regarded widely as his masterpiece.[4] Henry Miller, who in 1946 wrote a monograph on it, wrote that he had pondered over *Der Fall Maurizius* more than over any book he had ever read. "I forget about

---

2 For a detailed account and criticism of the life and work of Wassermann in English, see Blankennagel (1942). See also Emmeil (1984 pp 260 et seq). Robertson (1959 pp 554-5) proffers an unusually unfavourable critique arguing that, "it is doubtful whether any of Wassermann's work is of more than transient value, save his early novellas".

3 This phrase occurs periodically throughout *Der Fall Maurizius,* and might almost be considered its *Leitmotiv.*

4 This view is not that of the great critic, F Martini, who regards the *Bildungsroman, Christian Wahnschaff,* as Wassermann's greatest work. And others have greatly praised *Der Gänsemann,* an Expressionist novel about an avant-garde composer, which must certainly have been the inspiration of Thomas Mann's *Doktor Faustus.*

it for a while", he wrote, "and then it comes back, insistently and invidiously".

It is the first part of a trilogy, the second novel of which is entitled *Etzel Andergast* (the name of the hero of *Der Fall Maurizius*). The third part, which was not completed by Wassermann, is entitled *Jospeh Kirkhovens Dritte Existenz*. The second and third novels deal with metaphysical and spiritual concepts of justice, contrasting with the forensic and criminological concerns of *Der Fall Maurizius*. This format is the direct converse of *The Brothers Karamazov*, but the parallels with that work are otherwise almost exact.[5]

Der Fall Maurizius is the story of a miscarriage of justice. At the age of 24, Leonhart Maurizius, an art historian and academic, was found guilty of the murder of his wife, Elli. She was 15 years older than he, and he had married her for money. The motive for the murder was found to be Maurizius's love of her beautiful younger sister, Anna Jahn.

Maurizius was condemned to death, but his sentence was commuted to life imprisonment. The prosecution was skilfully and ruthlessly conducted by the public prosecutor, Freiherr von Andergast. Maurizius was poorly represented by a weak and ineffectual barrister.

Maurizius's father, convinced that his son has been wrongly convicted, dedicates his life to proving his innocence. When the story begins, 18 years after the trial, old Maurizius has already had several meetings with the prosecutor, von Andergast, to no avail. But von Andergast's 16-year-old son, Etzel, is intrigued by the old man. He gleans the story from his grandmother, von Andergast's mother, who tells him that the case created a sensation. There was a strong doubt about Maurizius's guilt, but the prosecutor had succeeded in obtaining a conviction on the circumstantial evidence.

Etzel clandestinely searches his father's office for the petition for a pardon that Father Maurizius had lodged. A naive but passionate document, it is based on the alleged perjury of the key witness, Waremme.

Etzel devotes himself to ascertaining the truth. He leaves home, and travels to Berlin, where he traces Waremme, who is living there under an assumed name, Warschauer.[6] Eventually he extracts a confession from Waremme that he did commit perjury. The murderer was Anna Jahn herself. She had killed her sister out of a passionate love of Leonhart Maurizius – a love which Maurizius had never perceived.

In the meantime, Etzel's flight has caused his father to reconsider the petition. Freiherr von Andergast never previously had any doubt as to the justice of the decision. He is a blind believer in

5 For an analysis of the trial scene in *The Brothers Karamazov* see Turner (1985).

6 In fact, Warschauer is the real name of Waremme. He was born a Jew, but had assumed a more Germanic name to further his career. On his return from the United States to Berlin, he reverted to his original name.

the infallibility of the forensic system. But now he is seized by an irresistible compulsion to see Maurizius. He visits the jail. Maurizius and he enter into a lengthy dialogue – which is a masterly condemnation of the penal system – and eventually Freiherr von Andergast is convinced that Maurizius did not commit the crime. He then secures a release for Maurizius.

Etzel returns home, thrilled by his discovery, to find that his father has independently reached the same conclusion. Etzel is bitterly angry that Maurizius has only been "released" rather than completely exculpated (*rehabilitiert*).[7] In a scene of incredible violence, Etzel lacerates himself and his father suffers a fit and is taken to a sanatorium for insane persons. We learn from the later novels that he never recovers.

In the meantime, Maurizius, on leaving the prison, seeks out his father. The old man's excitement is such that it causes his death. Maurizius travels to Trier to find Anna Jahn. She has married and become a bored, bourgeois housewife. She is a commonplace woman, irritated by having to meet Maurizius again. "I have broken with the past", she says to him. She has no qualms of conscience. "Just leave me in peace!"

Maurizius, aware that he has sacrificed 18 years for an unworthy woman, wanders aimlessly around Switzerland. He is depressed by the inconsequentiality of his actions. "Whether I turn right or left or buy an English or Egyptian cigarette" is of no significance to anyone. He travels to Berlin, where he makes love to an attractive woman, but the sex leaves him indifferent. He is no longer a sentient being. Finally, he takes a train from Berlin and throws himself from the carriage as it passes over a viaduct.

It is worth noting perhaps that the German word *Fall* may mean in German either "legal case" or "fall" (or indeed "downfall") – an ambiguity which is typical of the *Zweideutigkeit* of this novel.

Der Fall Maurizius is a realistic novel. It is typical of Wassermann's *oeuvre*, in mixing a sensational plot and powerful characterisation with profound philosophical argument (usually in dialogue form). But always, in Wassermann, the psychological is subordinated to the narrative. This rather unfashionable traditional technique may offer some explanation of the demise of his popularity.

The novel is written in lucid prose, with refreshingly short sentences and crisp dialogue. It is easy to read and to translate. This indeed was a key to his success as a world figure. The famous German critic, Fritz Martini, praised Wassermann as a "virtuoso of belletristique story-telling".[8]

Detective novels have always been popular in German, but the genre has not been considered a literary art form. Until Wassermann, there was virtually no serious German criminal or criminological

7 The "release" in fact was for a probationary period of 17 months (ch 15).
8 Martini, F, *Nachwort* to J Wassermann, *Der Fall Maurizius,* p 544.

novel – and there have been few since then (with the possible exceptions of Döblin's *Berlin Alexanderplatz* and some of Heinrich Böll's novels).

Wassermann used the novel for pedagogical purposes. Without once referring expressly to the state of contemporary Germany, *Der Fall Maurizius* is a parable of that nation's political fragility. Etzel, whose name indeed is the pseudonym of "Attila", represents a type of strange, Messianic but pathological young idealist who was compulsively drawn to National Socialism. Significantly, in the subsequent novels, Etzel's idealism is transformed into perversion.

Der Fall Maurizius is an attack on the bourgeois society which predominated in the Weimar Republic. Freiherr von Andergast is a symbol of bourgeois *Korrektheit* – the preoccupation of form over substance. He believes in an absolute pure justice, unsullied by concepts of mercy. To him, the legal system is infallible. It is disastrous, he argues, to confuse justice and sentiment. That, to him, meant, *"Das Unbedingte ins Joch des Ungefährs zu sparren"* (ch 2) – to place the absolute at the mercy of the accidental.

We learn that Freiherr von Andergast never took a walk, never went to the theatre or a concert. He worked on Sundays and on holidays. Human relationships were to him less important than professional ones. Conversations with his son were exercises in dialectic. His wife had left him, and his mother was frightened of him. His son grew up to loathe him.

This father/son duality is a recurrent *motiv* of the novel. The obverse of the Andergast relationship is that of Father Maurizius and his son Leonhart. The father had lost his wife and four children through typhus, and he devotes himself to Leonhart. As a result, Leonhart is spoiled, and, despite his precocious success as an academic, is an immature and weak character. He sponges off his father. But his father refuses him money after his marriage, of which the father strongly disapproves (because Elli Jahn is a Catholic – says Wassermann, hinting no doubt at local religious bourgeois intolerance not atypical of provincial Germany).

Father Maurizius illogically blames himself for the fact of his son's conviction. He is obsessed with the desire to obtain his son's pardon. But when the son eventually meets the father, their reunion is cut short by the father's immediate death.

In each case, as K Schetzler (1968 p 14) has shown, *"Es kommt zum entgültigen Bruch zwischen Vater und Sohn"* – there occurs an ultimate breach between father and son. The parallel with *Brothers Karamazov* is striking. It is arguable that the breach symbolises the ideological gap between the bourgeois society of Weimar and the *Hitlerjugend*.

Etzel himself represents the new German Youth. Significantly, in the light of Wassermann's penchant for symbolism, he is short-sighted. He is an idealist but shows decisive will. His flight from home is a retreat from the present in search of a more hopeful future.

He is an uncritical admirer of a pseudo-philosopher, called Melchior Ghisels (almost certainly a symbol for the medieval painter, Mathias Grünewald,[9] the subject of Hindemith's opera, *Mathis der Maler*). But when he meets Ghisels in Berlin, he turns out to be a nonentity, with no answer to Etzel's metaphysical dilemmas except resigned fatuity, "Justice and love were originally sisters – in our own civilisation they are no longer even distant relatives" (ch 11).

Yet this unhelpful rejoinder is the key to Wassermann's credo. For Wassermann the novel had a didactic purpose. In his diary, he wrote, *"Ich will erschüttert sein und andere erschüttern"*[10] – "I want to be shocked and I want to shock others". His remedy was a *Gesetz des Herzens* – a law of love which sees the man rather than the deed, without which abstract justice is a chimera and without which all juridical institutions will incite a thirst for vengeance. Indeed it can be argued Etzel's search for justice is motivated by the desire to destroy his father.

Wassermann was heavily influenced by the psychoanalysts, Freud, Jung and Lévy-Brühl. All his novels abound in symbols. *Der Fall Maurizius* is no exception. Mood is often conveyed by symbolic events. Sometimes the symbols are blatant. Thus, when Etzel quarrels with his father, an out-of-tune piano sounds (ch 3). As Father Maurizius was waiting in dread at a hotel for the verdict on his son, heavy boots sound on the stairs, "as if death were walking" (ch 14).

At other times, the symbols are more obscure. The weather is a sure indicator of moods in Wassermann. When von Andergast first goes to Kressa prison, it is stormy (ch 9). It is a rainy morning when Etzel leaves home (ch 5), and stormy during the last, fateful chapter. When von Andergast re-reads the protocol of the Maurizius case, it is midnight (ch 5). And it is night when Waremme reveals the true secret of Anna Jahn's guilt (ch 14). But when Maurizius leaves the jail, the sky is cloudless (ch 15).

A subtle musical allusion occurs when Elli, Maurizius's wife, having remonstrated with Maurizius for his abandonment of her, throws the door-key into the Rhine (ch 6), a river which for Germans has mystical, foreboding associations. When her suspicions had first been roused, Elli had heard Anna playing Schumann's *Carnival* on the piano (ch 7). This extraordinary work, with highly irregular time-signatures, was a product of that tortured composer's febrile nature. Robert Schumann threw himself in the Rhine in an attempt at suicide, and finished his life in a sanatorium.

Schetzler (pp 51 et seq) has pointed out the significance of *rooms* in the novel. Von Andergast's study is neat and ordered, but gloomy and impersonal (ch 5). Waremme lives in a large room, with

9 Indeed, Ghisels is tormented by the painting of the Cricifixion by Mathias Grünewald, which hangs on the wall of his flat in Berlin (ch 11).
10 See Schetzler (1968) p 49.

dirty windowpanes, more like an institution (ch 10). The dialogues between Maurizius and von Andergast take place in a gloomy prison-cell, with Maurizius pacing up and down (ch 9). And when the final dénouement takes place, a mirror breaks, symbolising for Etzel the harsh reality of the adult world, in which perfect justice can never be attained (ch 15). Mirror imagery is prominent throughout Wassermann's work.

But perhaps the most potent symbols are ocular. The eyes of each major character are carefully described by Wassermann, and are revelatory of the prototype that the character represents. Von Andergast's gaze is fixed and pitiless. Waremme has cold, pale-blue eyes, and wears dark glasses, which break just before his confession to Etzel. And Etzel himself is short-sighted, which, to Schetzler represents his ability to see (*sehen*) but not to perceive (*schauen*).[11]

As rich as this novel is in symbolism, in drama, in characterisation and in plot, what makes a most lasting impact are the remarkable dialogues that take place between the prisoner Maurizius and the prosecutor, van Andergast; and between Etzel and the perjurer, Waremme, both of whom are using an assumed name. These both take place in the second part of this arched, three-part novel. The parts are entitled: "The Preciousness of Life", "Interregnum" and "The Irrevocability of Death".[12] Wassermann's scheme in this middle part (contrary to the first and third parts) involves the juxtaposition of the two narratives into alternate chapters.

The conversations between Maurizius and von Andergast traverse the human misery, futility and ineffectiveness of imprisonment. The graphic description of the prison is unparalleled in literature:

> Kressa towers high between wooded hills, an old fortress, the ancestral estate of a royal house. That the nation should keep the dregs of humanity confined for expiation where the cradle of its princes formerly stood is a ghastly commentary on the passage of earthly glory. . .(ch 9)

Speaking of an attempted escape, the superintendent of the prison says:

> One does for the escapees whatever is possible, they have their regular meals, their regulated hours of sleep, their religious services, their recreation and rest . . . and yet they have no insight; they never cease plotting and conspiring in culpable collusions (ch 9).

The prison is described luridly:

> The smell was of musty clothes, of warm mildewed glue, of rancid fat, of musty walls, of human perspiration. About 150 men are moving

11 For a thorough and fascinating interpretation of the symbols in *Der Fall Maurizius,* see Schetzler (1968 pp 51 et seq).

12 *Die Kostbarkeit des Lebens; Zwischenreich; die Unwiderruflichkeit des Todes.*

> about, some free, others crammed into pens. . . They are weaving straw mats (ch 9).

Maurizius has remembered every word of van Andergast's speech to the jury, and recites it verbatim to the astonished prosecutor. Van Andergast, struck by the trite platitudes that his words now seem to be, mouths the usual defence apology about the presumption of innocence, and receives this reply from Maurizius:

> From the first, [the judge] is the enemy [of the accused]. For him the deed has been done, he takes the human being at his lowest. The accuser is his God, the accused his victim, punishment his goal. If one has gotten to the point of appearing before a judge, one is done for . . . I have known people who have told me that at every trial they have the same horrible feeling in the testicles that one has if one suddenly stands over a deep abyss (ch 14).

Maurizius describes the various stages of emotions that affect the prisoner as the time passes – angst, hope, despair and ultimately the respite of sleep. But always the period of imprisonment is a torture of time. There is no past, no future – it is always the *present* for one serving a life sentence.

The eloquence of Maurizius's sincerity leads von Andergast at last to have doubts about the justness of his conviction. Maurizius is confused by this. The first human being to speak to him on his own level is the one who had him put away.

Maurizius knew that Anna had done the murder, but never raised this possibility, either at his trial or during his 18 years in prison. Why? Because of his abiding love for her (ch 12).

Waremme, who had changed his name from Warschauer in order to hide his Jewish origins, has resumed his original name. The Jewish problem in *Der Fall Maurizius* is mentioned many times, but only obliquely. This very obliqueness serves to dramatise the importance to an understanding of this novel of Wasserman's credo of German Jewishness, which is explored in *Mein Weg als Deutscher und Jude*.

Waremme/Warschauer is one of the most complex, unlikeable yet compelling figures in German literature – a Mephistophelian opportunist whose evilness (contrasted with Etzel's innocence) is perhaps signified most cogently by his love of jazz – which Etzel hates. Says Warschauer to Etzel, "The saxophone is worth a three-volume history of civilisation'" (ch 14). This is a rare example of irony in a writer who is the epitome of humourlessness.

The satanic nihilism of the possibly bisexual Warshauer is, however, assuaged by compassion for Etzel when he becomes ill. And ultimately, Etzel succeeds in extracting a confession from Warschauer that he perjured himself, not so much to save Anna (whom he had once raped) but to gain revenge over Maurizius. His hatred of Maurizius was based on the jealousy of the successful career that the mediocre Maurizius had enjoyed because of his bourgeois, Aryan connections. For Warschauer had no doubt of his own genius. The parallel with Raskolnikov in *Crime and Punishment* is unmistakable.

CONCLUSION

Having read *Der Fall Maurizius* in German and also in an excellent contemporary translation by Caroline Newton (1929), like Henry Miller, I find this novel compelling and hypnotic. It is surely one of the most underrated works of this century and like all great novels, it can be read at different levels.

In the first place, it is a dramatic and exciting mystery story. The plot is intriguing and the dramatic tension heightened by Wassermann's skill as a narrator. The technique of flashback, of alternate chapters describing the parallel discoveries of Etzel and his father, the surprising dénouement, which does not occur until chapter 14, and the harrowing events that follow Maurizius's release, maintain the reader's curiosity throughout the work.

Moreover, Wassermann possesses a Balzacian power of character description. All the main characters in *Der Fall Maurizius* are closely portrayed, and they present rich studies of humanity. Waremme/Warschauer is one of the most complex characters in literature. A Jew who converted into a devout Catholic, but then was divorced, a talented actor, dramatist and scholar, Waremme is variously described as a homosexual and a possible paedophile. Yet he is kind to Etzel during his sickness. He wrote a good review of a book by Maurizius, but at the same time spread rumours that Maurizius had plagiarised his own work!

The complexity of the characterisation is typified in the dialogues between Etzel and Waremme – each of whom at the time is using an assumed name – each a *Doppelgänger*, symbolising the essential ambivalence of human nature.

Moreover, the narrative style of Wassermann is attractively simple and readable – qualities not altogether universal in German prose writing!

Der Fall Maurizius, however, may be read as a powerful tract against the administration, and indeed the concept, of justice.

In *Der Fall Maurizius*, as in *The Brothers Karamozov*, there is a total miscarriage of justice. Wassermann examines the reasons for this, as does Dostoevsky in the latter work. There is a grave disparity in the quality of the legal representation. In contrast to the thorough and professional public prosecutor, von Andergast, Maurizius is represented by a "quibbler and dry little provincial" (ch 6). The judge himself is described as a "moderately temperate alcoholic" and "a mixture of epicurean laziness and general contempt for mankind" (ch 5).

The formalities of court procedure are mocked, especially by Waremme. "The scale of justice is not a delicate instrument, but a very coarse lever" (ch 12). "The oath is nothing more than a question of poise and a technical consequence" (ch 14).

Blind faith in the legal system is the life-force of von Andergast. He regards his own protocols as "jewels of legal art" (ch 6). The law is a perfect instrument, "not an agreement between two parties, to be modified at will, but a sacred and permanent form" (ch 2).

When ultimately, von Andergast realises that his perfect pleadings have led to a total injustice, his world collapses and he becomes insane.

But even Etzel, the crusader, becomes disillusioned by the fallibility of human justice.

Wasserman's attack on the legal system may itself be read in two ways. On the surface, it is directed at the bourgeois system prevailing in the Weimar republic. But there is no doubt that it has a cosmic message. Wasserman is surely saying that formal legal mechanisms are incapable, in any society, of ascertaining truth. He is, in a sense, pleading for a kind of equity to replace formality – *das Gesetz des Herzens* (the law of the heart). This plea is most eloquently framed in the remarkable dialogue between Maurizius and von Andergast (ch 9). Maurizius repeats word for word von Andergast's address, and turns the latter's admiration for his own oratory into disgust. "The justice of a punishment cannot be measured by how subjectively bearable it is, or by the behaviour of the organs which dictate it". Wassermann convinces us that no human has the capacity to judge another.

The penal system is also futile. The mysterious complexity of human nature will never permit of a system of condign punishment. Prisons are totally ineffective and indeed counter-productive. Human judgment is not merely fallible, it is by nature hypocritical. For, "everybody, even the most irreproachable and unassailable, has a corner in his soul which contains the germ of a crime" (ch 5).

BIBLIOGRAPHY

Blankennagel, C, 1942, *The Writing of Jakob Wassermann,* Little, Brown & Company.

Emmeil, H, 1984, *History of the German Novel,* Wayne State University.

Miller, H, 1946, *Reflections on the Maurizius Case,* Capra Press.

Robertson, JG, 1959, *A History of German Literature,* 3rd ed, Little, Brown & Company.

Schetzler, K, 1968, *Der Fall Maurizius – Jakob Wassermann's Kunst des Erzählens,* I European University Papers, no 14, H Lang and Co.

Turner, J Neville, 1985, "Dostoevsky – The Trial in Brothers Karamazov", 8 *University of Tasmania Law Review,* 62.

Wassermann, J, 1921, *Mein Weg als Deutscher und Jude,* S Fischer Verlag.

Wassermann, J, 1929, *The Maurizius Case,* Newton, C (trans), Liveright.

Wassermann, J, 1960, *Der Fall Maurizius,* Sigberg Mohn Verlag.

15

Literature of the Holocaust: The Testimonial of the Witness[1]

SIDRA KRANZ MOSHINSKY

The writing that was written by Jews during the Holocaust in the hiding places, ghettos and concentration camps of Eastern Europe poses difficulties for me, a literature student. In one sense, I acknowledge the literary and artistic value of this writing and wish to give it recognition as literature. On the other hand, this is not literature in the same way as Shakespeare's sonnets or Woolf's novels are "literature". These texts were produced in extreme conditions by men and women on the brink of death. Recorded here are acts so evil that if they had not occurred in the middle of Europe in the middle of this century we would say that such deeds were unimaginable. How to read and respond to such writing is a question with which I am grappling. This writing is quite unlike anything I have come across in my literature studies; I find myself searching for a way of reading these texts that will allow for its unique place in the literature of the twentieth century.

In this chapter I wish to explore the possibility of reading the literature of the Holocaust as quasi-legal documents. These texts will be analysed in terms of the philosophies of both law and literature. It seems appropriate to situate these texts at such a juncture, for those who wrote during the Holocaust were *authors* yet they were also victims of, and *witnesses* to, crimes of unprecedented horror. The work they generated comes to us in the form of poems, diaries and letters, but given that they were frequently produced for the purpose of providing evidence for the tribunal of the future and were written under the death sentence they can also be described as testimonials, wills and dying declarations.

By way of introduction, it is interesting to discuss the relationship between the Holocaust and language, for it was when

1 I would like to thank Professor KK Ruthven, of the English Department of the University of Melbourne, for his valuable comments on drafts of this chapter.

thinking about this that the idea of understanding Holocaust literature as almost legal documents first occurred to me.

Much discussion of the Holocaust and in particular discussion of its literature focuses on this question of language: how is it possible to represent the events of the Holocaust; how can one express in words experiences for which there are no words? These questions are real ones, felt by all who write on the Holocaust; for example, a line taken from a text discovered in a milk-can buried underneath the Warsaw ghetto reads as follows, "Documents and a cry of pain . . . do not fit together" (Kermish 1986 p 703). Certainly if any occurrence can be said to have destabilised the language, forms, culture and philosophies on which our society rests, the planned and partial fulfilment of the extermination of world Jewry and other people chosen for destruction is surely such an occurrence.

Admittedly there are real difficulties in communicating and writing the Holocaust but, to a certain extent, this predicament is but an extreme example of something we have known for a long time now: that language and reality, texts and experience, are not equal. If this is so, and only the most insistent realists would disagree, the next step is to address the question of what one is to do with such knowledge. One may anguish over the lack of correspondence, discuss endlessly the impossibility of describing what one wishes to describe and point out the failure of others to do so – such an approach characterises much discussion of Holocaust literature. It was impatience with such an approach that led me to look further afield. An alternative way of responding to the lack of match between word and world is to acknowledge that language is indeed limited but nevertheless to proceed to examine issues beyond that of signification.

The pragmatic approach to language being advocated here is perhaps more characteristic of the legal system than literary establishments. In both institutions the issue of communication is uppermost and the question of how to articulate experience central. In the sphere of literature these questions are laboured over; in legal settings they are resolved, as suggested, more pragmatically. In almost all cases presented before a court, especially those involving people who have experienced bodily injury or abuse, the act of successfully and accurately translating this experience into words is fraught with difficulties. How can the victim of assault or rape, to use two examples, fully describe the details of the act and express the humiliation and pain? Clearly there are problems but it would be absurd to suppose that those conducting a case would abandon it because language was found to be too powerful an intervention in the giving and testing of evidence.

In war-crimes trials the same issue arises with the same practical response. The edited transcript of a trial held in Belsen shortly after the war contains many examples of witnesses vexed by the formidable task of articulating and communicating experiences to those who were not there. One witness states: "the conditions which were found in that camp were quite indescribable; I know of no words which would begin to paint the picture"; another: "no description or photograph could really bring home the horrors that were there"; and yet another: "The conditions were so bad that it is impossible to find words in this world" (Phillips 1949 pp 19, 31, 85). What is important about each of these statements is that they are said by way of preface; each witness goes on to describe what was just said to have been indescribable. This double move can be seen as a practical response to the fact of a trial: namely, that if it is to achieve any measure of justice the question "Would you describe in your own words the general state of the camp?" must be answered. And to answer with a treatise on signification, however interesting, will not serve this end – only a description will do.

As in the trials in its aftermath, so too does the literature written during the Holocaust exemplify this pragmatic response. There is a recognition that one cannot fully articulate experiences yet at the same time there is an unswerving commitment to achieve such an articulation. A determination to make the facts known is present. This does not mean that in responding writers were not conscious of the contradictions embodied in the writing act – it would seem they were; for example, an anonymous text written in Warsaw in 1942 during the deportations from the ghetto contains the following lines:

> The desire to write is as strong as the repugnance of words. We hate them, because they too often served as a cover for emptiness or meanness. We despise them, for they are pale in comparison to the emotions tormenting us. And yet, in the past the word meant human dignity and was man's best possession – an instrument of communication between people. (Kermish p 704)

This notion of the word as a valued possession, as "an instrument of communication between people", is one that must be emphasised in a discussion of Holocaust literature. Whatever the shortcomings of language – linguistics, psychoanalysis, deconstruction and post-structuralism have taught that there are many – it was during the Holocaust and, despite advances in technology, continues to be, the form of communication upon which people rely. In its treatment of language we find the first sense in which the literature of the Holocaust shares features with the philosophies and approaches of the legal system.

The commonalities, however, go further than this. If Holocaust literature and legal documents merely shared pragmatic attitudes vis-a-vis communication then it would not be wholly appropriate to position the writing in a legal context. As we shall see, however, Holocaust literature can meaningfully and sensibly be read as quasi-legal documents. The combination of author and witness, literature and testimony, mean that the distinctions between the disciplines of literature and law are lessened.

In order to examine the ways in which this literature crosses disciplinary borders it is necessary to set out some details of the history of the writing produced during the Holocaust. This historical perspective is important; without this it is impossible to appreciate the significance of the writing. Only when one knows something of the conditions and pressures under which people were writing and the efforts expended to produce and preserve documents is it possible to understand the weight this literature has upon post-Holocaust readers. Only with historical knowledge does one begin to sense that before one's eyes is literature that is amongst the most compelling of this century: testimonies left by soon-to-be silenced witnesses.

It is important to emphasise from the outset that to record was an illegal act. This was in accordance with the policy of the Nazis that the extermination of Jewry was to have no reference; in Himmler's words, the annihilation was a "never-to-be-written page of glory". Official Nazi documents, therefore, are infamous for their "abstractions, weak and intransitive verbs, passive constructions", a peculiar jargon that came to be known as Nazi Deutsch (Dawidowicz 1987). Not surprisingly, there is no single document ordering the annihilation of European Jewry, instead one finds euphemistic words such as "resettlement", "forced emigration" or "Final Solution" (p 160). This prohibition of naming the facts barred identification of murderers, their brutality, and the specific locations where mass murders took place. To write or gather documents was punishable by death, with the effect that archival and artistic work had to be done in secrecy (Aaron 1990 p 126). Fear prevented many from writing and those who wrote did so strategically: writing notes in the margins of books; camouflaging a diary as a letter; substituting the words "Nazi" or "German" with less specific identifications; and avoiding recording any information that might betray people or the work of the resistance. Given the risks involved and given that it added a further crime to the already criminal act of existence, to write was a political act requiring some commitment.

Of course, it was not only the illegal nature of the activity which prevented people from writing; other, perhaps more decisive, factors prevented production. Such factors include: hunger, disease, lack of materials, exhaustion and belief that writing was a futile task which meant that one channelled one's energy either into other acts of resistance or into the day-to-day struggle for existence. These factors operated with more or less force depending on circumstance: they were more compelling later in the war than in its early stages; more compelling in the labour camp than in the ghettos; and more compelling in the death camps than in the labour camps. The amount of texts produced is almost proportional to these conditions: relatively, quite a few people wrote in the ghetto; hardly anything was produced in the death camps.

Despite these extreme physical conditions, people did write. While "thriving" would be an exaggerated description of the state of the various literary communities, the amount of activity is nevertheless remarkable. In the Warsaw ghetto, for example, poets gave readings at gatherings, there were prizes offered to encourage people to write, the demand for books – especially ones that offered hope, such as books about the rise and fall of Napoleon or the fate of Germany during World War One – was great; there was a flourishing of street and folk poetry and mobile libraries, literary cafés, theatre groups and clandestine journals all operated. People who had never written before began to do so; a commentator on life in the Warsaw ghetto writes in December 1942, "the Jews started to write. Everyone did: journalists, authors, teachers, community workers, young people, even children. Most people kept diaries where daily events were reflected through the prism of personal experience" (Kermish p 4).

Even in the concentration camps there was some measure of literary and artistic endeavour. The chronicles written by members of the *Sonderkommando*, a group of prisoners whose job it was to work in the gas chambers of Auschwitz, were discovered after the war; they had been buried underground. There is also a substantial collection of artwork from the camps which has survived. Materials were scarce and were obtained by theft, bribery or on the black market and there was much improvisation: people wrote or drew on the backs of SS circulars, on logs, on walls, even on perforated blank margins of postage stamps; if pencils could not be obtained materials such as charcoal, rust or food dyes were used (Milton 1990).

One of the largest sources of documentation comes from milk cans dug up from the rubble of Warsaw shortly after the end of the war. These documents are the product of an underground archival group in the Warsaw ghetto, code-named "Oneg Shabbat" (meaning "Pleasures of the Sabbath"), whose purpose it was to collect, disseminate and preserve documentation of "the martyrology of Polish Jewry". The material was collected originally in the hope that it would influence the events of the war; Emmanuel Ringelblum, one of the leaders of the group, writes jubilantly about the BBC broadcast on Polish Jewry in his *Notes* in June 1942:

> The OS [Oneg Shabbat] has fulfilled a great historical mission. It has alarmed the world of our fate, and perhaps saved hundreds of thousands of Polish Jews from extermination. (Naturally, only the immediate future will prove whether or not the last is true.) I do not know who of our group will survive. . . But one thing is clear to all of us. Our toils and tribulation, our devotion and constant terror, have not been in vain. (1974 p 295)

Ringelblum goes on to say that even if the information does not prevent annihilation, his group has "struck the enemy a hard blow. We have revealed his Satanic plan to annihilate Polish Jewry, a plan he wished to complete in silence" (p 296). Written three years before the war ended, on the eve of mass deportations of Jews from the Warsaw ghetto, we see this optimism to have been misplaced. Nevertheless, it was the belief of those working on collecting and distributing information that their task had value. If it did not preserve their lives it at least made their deaths meaningful.

Although this is but a brief outline of literary work during the Holocaust, it indicates something of the extraordinary nature of this writing. The conditions in which the texts were produced, the experiences they record and their miraculous existence confer on them a status quite different to those works which originate from "emotion recollected in tranquillity" – to quote a well-known Romantic. How to approach and respond to this writing poses something of a challenge if one wishes to preserve its radical nature. A reading which aligns Holocaust literature with legal documents is adopted here because this interdisciplinary approach allows one to preserve the unusual nature of this writing.

The commonalities between writing of the Holocaust and evidence given on oath become important in this context. There can be little doubt that these two forms share characteristics. The similarity in vocabulary and tone are striking. For example, Israel Lichtenstein, one of three workers in Oneg Shabbat whose task it was to bury the archives, adds his own document: "I know we shall not last. It is not possible to live through, to survive such horrible murders, such massacres. This is why I write this my *testament* ". Gelle Seckstein, an artist, deposited her paintings in the archive and places her will with them: "I *bequeath* [my italics] my works to the Jewish Museum which will be established in the future in order to recreate pre-war Jewish cultural life up to the year 1939" (Kermish pp 58, 672-3). In each of these documents the use of legal language is not accidental; the author seems fully aware of the nature of a will or a testament and adopts the appropriate language and demonstrates the requisite serious intention.

There is a form of evidence known as "dying declarations". It is appropriate to read certain Holocaust documents in light of the principle which admits this type of testimony. The law teaches that dying declarations are those statements made by the victims of homicides when all hope of survival is gone. These declarations are not made under oath and, strictly speaking, are hearsay. Nevertheless such statements made on the brink of death have come to be accepted by courts. The rationale for this was laid down in the eighteenth century case of *R v Woodcock* (1789) I Leach 500:

> The principle on which this species of evidence is admitted is, that they are declarations made in extremity, when the party is at the point of death, and when every hope of this world is gone; when every motive to falsehood is silenced, and the mind is induced by the most powerful considerations to speak the truth; a situation so solemn and so awful is considered by law as creating an obligation equal to that which is imposed by a positive oath in a court of justice.

Not all Holocaust writing is written under the certainty of death; people who wrote earlier in the war cherished beliefs in survival. But for those who continued to write over a number of years, it became more and more certain that death was imminent and this sense of foreboding is registered in the literature. In extreme, but nonetheless frequent cases, there is nothing sensory about this perception of death; the end was literally at hand and statements made at such moments can appropriately be termed "dying declarations". David Elster was one of many Jews who, on 15 September 1942, were concentrated in the synagogue of Kovel before being taken to be killed; he carved into the wall the following fragments:

> A chill passes through us . . . here come our murderers, dressed up . . . their filthy hands adorned in white gloves, they herd us two-by-two . . . tender-hearted brothers and sisters. . . O how hard it is to part from this beautiful world forever . . . let no one who remains alive ever forget – Jewish boys and girls from our Jewish street, innocent of any wrong-doing. Wreak vengeance on our murderers. (Reimer & Stampfer 1983 p 79)

Another poignant example of writing that can be read as a dying declaration comes from a document unearthed at the end of the war from the Oneg Shabbat archives. This is an anonymous piece, written during the deportations from the Warsaw ghetto, probably by someone involved in the work of the archival group:

> We want to believe that there is some sense in still being alive among the shambles, among human hyenas and jackals who live by stripping the dead. These documents and notes are a remnant resembling a clue in a detective story. I remember from childhood such a novel by Conan Doyle, in which the dying victim writes with a faint hand one word on the wall containing the proof of the criminal's guilt. That word, scrawled by the dying man, influenced my imagination in the past. The records left by us, whose survival is so uncertain, remind me of that stereotype image that once so moved me. We are noting the evidence of the crime. (Kermish p 704)

This passage is indicative of how Holocaust writing moves in two directions: it is a document belonging to both the literature scholar and the lawyer. Although this particular section does not give facts, such as names, dates and places, these details can be found in other parts of this text and they give the whole a documentary value. Lines such as "dying victim", "proof of the criminal's guilt" and "evidence of the crime" reinforce the evidentiary aspect of the text. On the other hand, one could read and analyse this passage in much the same way as one would any piece of literature. One could note the rhetorical devices, the inter-textual references, the narratorial voice. Admittedly, approaching these texts from legal and literary perspectives are but two of many: national, temporal, historical and theological discourses also contribute to our understanding of these texts.

What is important, and particularly so in the context of this volume on law and literature, is to stress the necessity of taking a truly interdisciplinary position vis-a-vis these texts. To approach writing of the Holocaust looking either for literary or evidential information but not for both is, in my opinion, misguided. Misguided because to bracket off the reality of mass murder or to ignore the weight of language and form is to fail to account for the literature in its fullest sense. As readers we need to be aware of the *type* of literature we have before us and must react accordingly.

This call to pay attention to "type" of literature, simple as it sounds, does not accord with much of contemporary practice. The tendency is to analyse biblical material in the same way as one analyses a novel. Popular romances, advertisements, legal documents, medieval tales are all there to be dissected using whatever theoretical terms are chosen. The problem with this practice is that it implies a kind of equivalence, these theoretical terms make it difficult to distinguish between different kinds of writing. While such methodologies do have a place and do serve important purposes, they tend to obscure *differences* between texts, and for the purposes of this chapter, the difference being effaced is in the bibliographic history of the text. A piece of literature can be distinguished on the basis of how, where, when and under what conditions it was written and produced. It makes a difference to our reception of a text depending on whether it was sent off to a publisher for perusal, or in the case of Holocaust literature, whether it was buried underground in milk cans in the hope that even when the author had literally gone up in smoke the document would survive to be read. What is at stake here is the difference between the text which begins "Once upon a time" and the one which begins "What can I say and ask at this moment? Poised on the border between life and death, more certain that I won't live than that I shall" (Kermish p 672).

Six million witnesses to crimes against humanity died – the opportunity to give post-war testimony never arose for them. Nevertheless a fraction of these witnesses committed to paper – or wall or log, as the case may be – what they would never have the opportunity to say formally under oath and a fraction of these texts survived and have been found. Holocaust literature has not been used as literal evidence in courts. Nevertheless, in the wider court of history this writing constitutes an invaluable source of evidence. In many cases, these documents provide historians with the only source of information on life (if one can call it that) during the Holocaust from the perspective of its victims; the diaries and testaments are often quoted in history books. The commitment to recording the facts and the pledge of truth contained in much of Holocaust writing has meant that it has indeed become, as one writer/witness hoped it would, "the mourner's richest material . . . the avenger's strongest substance" (Kermish p 672).

What needs to be considered finally is how we, as readers and critics, respond to this literature. Do we need to reciprocate in some way to the pledge of truth writers offer by making a pledge as readers? Some would say no: they would give freedom to the reader to approach the text in any possible way. Writing is open to any number of readings, interpretation is infinite, criticism need not be anchored in authorial intention.

Perhaps these scholars have a point. On one hand, I do not agree with George Steiner (1984 p 258) when he writes of Holocaust literature that it is not open for review, unless if by review one means, as he suggests, to copy the text out word for word. Discussion, interpretation and criticism are as useful in approaching this body of writing as any other. On the other hand, an untempered critical practice, taken to extremes, sanctions the work of so-called historians who seek to deny the accepted facts of the Holocaust. They read looking for inconsistencies, falsities and errors in the text and infer from these that there are also falsities in the event. In some way, this project corresponds structurally to a hermeneutics that does not anchor the word of the text in a material world and that allows for interpretation without bounds (Norris 1988). Yet there is a clarity in a number inscribed on an arm that not even the most skilful commentary can confuse.

This anxiety about interpretation is abated somewhat by locating Holocaust literature at the juncture of literary and legal discourses. It is at this intersection that the truths and experiences to which the writing attests can be accounted for. But this need not be done at the expense of ignoring the equally compelling historical questions of how did these people write, what forms did they adopt, what were their attitudes to language, what purposes did they see their writing fulfilling? And having considered the writing we must also consider our reading practices. It is hoped that by bringing to the text sufficient knowledge and understanding the chasm separating those witnesses who swear they saw it with their own eyes, and those who become witnesses on the basis of what they read, may be lessened.

BIBLIOGRAPHY

Aaron, FW, 1990, *Bearing the Unbearable: Yiddish and Polish Poetry in the Ghettos and Concentration Camps*, State University of New York Press.

Cross, R & Tapper C, 1987, *Cross on Evidence*, 6th edn, Butterworths.

Dawidowicz, L, 1987, *The War Against the Jews: 1933-45*, 10th anniversary edn, Penguin Books.

Felman, S & Laub, D, 1992, *Testimony: Crises of Witnessing in Literature, Psychoanalysis, and History*, Routledge.

Kermish, J (ed), 1986, *To Live with Honor and Die with Honor! . . . Selected Documents from the Warsaw Ghetto Underground Archives "OS" ("Oneg Shabbath")*, Yad Vashem.

Milton, S, 1990, "Art of the Holocaust: A Summary", *Reflections of the Holocaust in Art and Literature*, Braham, R (ed), Social Science Monographs & Cangeri Institute for Holocaust Studies: 147.

Norris, C, 1988, "Postmodernising History: Right-Wing Revisionism and the Uses of Theory", *Southern Review*, 123.

Phillips, R (ed), 1949, *Trial of Josef Kramer and Forty-Four Others (The Belsen Trial)*, William Hodge & Co.

Reimer, J & Stampfer, N (eds), 1983, *Ethical Wills: A Modern Jewish Treasury*, Schocken Books.
Ringelblum, E, 1974, *Notes from the Warsaw Ghetto: The Journal of Emmanuel Ringelblum*, Schocken Books.
Steiner, G, 1984, *George Steiner: A Reader*, Penguin Books.

16

Tales of Gothic Horror: Queensland's "Vampire" Murder

CHRISTINE HIGGINS

My purpose in this paper is to attempt to demonstrate that the discourse form of horror fiction (especially that of nineteenth century short fiction with which I am most familiar) is, in essence, legalistic, foregrounding testimony to provide verisimilitude, making frequent use of corroboration to authorise the "facts" of the narration, and is often interrogatory or confessional in form. This is further borne out by the strategy of "the strange case" which is a much favoured framing device in such writing.

I would then like to reverse this process and examine the Tracey Wigginton murder, the so-called "Vampire" murder case, which took place in Brisbane in October 1989, as a horror narrative of the non-fictional variety, which employs many of the same conventions of story telling, and draws upon similar codes for the transmission of its messages as its fictional counter-parts – "the strange cases" of nineteenth century fiction. Certainly, there is no difficulty in doing this so far as content is concerned, as the case involves a particularly brutal murder of a male passer-by totally unknown to the perpetrator, a self-confessed lesbian. Alleged elements of vampirism and witchcraft are associated with the crime, and the case has added complexity because of the multiple personality disorder apparently suffered by Tracey Wigginton, which has, of course, associations in the public mind and the press with Dr Jekyll and Mr Hyde.

While doing this, I want to argue that horror writing has broad cultural frames of reference which cannot be restricted to the literary genre into which such writing is usually classified. That such writing is a cultural response was recognised by eighteenth and early nineteenth century commentators, even if not by many of today's critics of the genre. The Marquis de Sade, for instance, notes that the writings of "Monk" Lewis and Mrs Radcliffe were, in essence, responses to the political upheaval of the French Revolution: "the necessary fruit of the revolutionary tremors felt by the whole of Europe" were his words (Sage 1988 p xi). This suggests, rightly, I think, that the explanation or interpretation of the significance of this form (and indeed of all literary forms) is best done by considering its relationships and interconnections with the whole of the culture that produced it.

One major aspect of this relationship is evidenced in textuality itself. In *Elements of Semiology* (1967), Barthes argued that all discourses are equally fictive, and that none stand apart as the voice of Truth. In "The Death of the Author" (1968) Barthes goes further to reject authorisation for the status or origin of a text, and reduces the author rather to a locus where language with its infinity of associations, repetitions, echoes and citations cross and recross. The reader, he argues, is free to enter the text from any point and can connect it, at will, with any other system of meaning, without reference to the author's intention – thus rejecting or defying the signified in the process.

Each text, he argued later in *S/Z* (1970), refers back differently but indefinitely to the infinity of the already written. The "I" which reads is itself already a multiplicity of other texts. Even an apparently closed text such as the realist novel, or a court transcript, which has specific reference, cannot prevent the reader from connecting such texts with "the vast sea of the already written" (1970 p 38); thus producing his or her own text with its own unique reverberations and associations.

The text is then "a galaxy of signifiers" (1970 p 46); we can gain access to it by several entrances, none of which can be authoritatively declared to be the main one. The codes it mobilises extend as far as the eye can see. The text's polysemy, therefore, depends not so much on the possible ambivalence of its content, but on "the plurality of its weave of signifiers" (Barthes 1977 p 159). Whatever meaning systems we choose to apply to it can only activate one of its infinite voices. As the reader adopts different perspectives, or reading codes, unique meanings may be generated.

I am regarding the text I am about to analyse – the transcript of the Mental Health Tribunal of Queensland hearing in respect of Tracey Avril Wigginton – as a species of interrogative text which discourages identification with a unified subject of the discourse. Equally, in such texts, the reader is distanced from the events of the narrative, rather than being interpolated into the world of the text. However, because such texts invite answers to questions posed, the reader is actively engaged in attempting to provide answers (or alternative answers) to them.

It is difficult to site an author in such a text as the transcript of the hearing; rather, the text is generated by multiple text makers, as is common in some forms of oral discourse. There are also multiple third person narrators: expert witnesses – the four or five psychiatrists who are advising on the case; friends and relatives of Tracey's whose affidavits form part of the evidence; Tracey herself and her "alters" in and out of hypnosis as first person narrator(s). All of these are in possession of certain fragments of Tracey's life story, and the events of the murder.

As the above suggests, while this is primarily an interrogative text, it does emerge as a pastiche of confessional/autobiographical writing and third person narration and evaluation, in addition to interrogation. Unlike the closed text, this text refuses a single point of view and rather brings numerous points of view into unresolved conflict or contradiction. In this instance, such conflict or contradiction occurs between the medical experts, but also between these witnesses and learned counsel, and, in a more bizarre way, between Tracey as host personality and her "alters" who surface under hypnosis. There are also ambiguities and contradictions between the various affidavits tendered as evidence. Clearly, there is no authorial sign-posting here; indeed, there is no single position which is the site of coherent meaning in this text. Whereas many court transcripts would seem almost by definition to be closed texts, this is a particularly open-ended example. After the final addresses containing the various summings-up of the positions of the medical witnesses (which reach no consensus) by learned counsel who themselves speak from different positions and persuasions, the reader (or listener if one considers the oral nature of the original hearing) is left without any sense of resolution of the many issues the text raises – even to the basic question – the reason for the generation of the discourse: whether Tracey Wigginton at the time of the alleged offence was suffering from unsoundness of mind as defined in s 27 of the criminal code. The decision on this matter is located in another text generated under different circumstances at another time.

This text, which begins in enigma and uncertainty, remains so at its conclusion, resisting an ideology which preaches that logical deduction and scientific method render all mysteries illuminated and command coherence from chaos.

Reading such a text involves a recognition of its incompleteness, its omissions, its contradictions and lack of coherence. These the text itself acknowledges but cannot resolve. Through its absences, and the multiplicity and diversity of its potential meanings, as well as through the clash of two powerful and divergent ideologies – medical and legal – the text contains its own inbuilt critique in that it admits of multiple meaning-making by a reader/listener. The text allows (or cannot prevent) the reader from re-enacting at will some of the text's mythical archetypes – the vampire, the witch, the siren, Jekyll and Hyde. Such an imaginative re-enactment is, obviously, the very antithesis of the explicit function of such a text! However, the mythical elements are so powerful, because so fully realised, that the facts of the case tend to be submerged by the power of the myths they generate!

Clearly the local press's reading or construction of the case foregrounded some of its mythic elements:

> Lust for Blood: There is a kind of sullen violence in her past and spasmodic periods of obsession with religion – the weirder the better. . . But the eyes are what people remember most about her. 'Very dark, almost black,' recalls a Rockhampton mother and family friend. . . 'When she looked at you it was almost as if you didn't exist', says Det Sgt Glenn Burton of South Brisbane CIB. . . 'It was a stare that went right through you'. Det Sgt Burton had only brief but uncomfortable meetings with Wigginton. He scoffs at suggestions that she had hypnotic powers, except upon much weaker associates. But he was impressed with the strength of her personality, a voice which – using only two or three words at a time – suggested a commanding presence from which feminism by its very nature was excluded. . . The dark eyes of Tracey Avril Wigginton, man-killer and lesbian lover, are now but an unpleasant, sometimes chilling memory for most of those who knew her. (*Courier Mail* 16 February 1991)

Even in this one sample of press reportage, despite its obvious sensationalism, one can see that the writer is assuming a shared pool of cultural understandings about witchcraft and black magic in his or her readers. Even though most of us have little first-hand experience of such things, our "knowledge" of them is almost unconsciously acquired from our reading and viewing and listening, which all draw on or rework an almost infinite number of old tales, myths, legends or popular superstitions from time immemorial.

Levi Strauss and other cultural anthropologists, have pointed out that myths prolong their lives, Dracula-like, by being re-presented in fresh guises and in new applications in each generation.

Certainly, the evidence presented to the Medical Tribunal hearing as well as that tendered in the later trials of Tracey Wigginton and her co-accused has wide-ranging mythic connotations and associations. I cannot hope to comment fully on all of these, but would like to make mention of some of the most striking examples contained in the Mental Health Tribunal of Queensland hearing transcript (1990).

The hearing does not seem able to escape engaging with the evidence of witchcraft. Affidavits from numerous friends and family members constantly refer to Tracey's fascination and involvement with witchcraft from adolescence onwards. Some of this evidence follows.

Tracey always dressed completely in black and frequently wore jewellery featuring occult symbols. She had long ago cut a pentagram into the back of one hand and tattooed over the scar. It is alleged that she also had other tattoos on her body which had magic or occult significance.

She read widely in the area of demonology, and affidavits attest to her interest "in devils and human sacrifice" (Transcript p 36). At the time of the murder she was corresponding with and receiving instruction from a white witch in Adelaide. There is also considerable mention of alleged involvement with animal sacrifices and blood-letting, with hints of various strange rituals in cemeteries. Police claim evidence of animals killed and mutilated at Mt Archer. Her drawings in recent times feature "mummy-like bats, vampires and scenes associated with death" (p 36). She often drew patterns in blood drawn from her own cuts and scratches.

After her arrest, she was found to possess a number of items – feathers, four candles, tarot cards and a large animal rib bone burned at one end – all wrapped in a series of black silk cloths, which apparently form part of the ceremonial apparatus of witchcraft. When burned by her flat mate, they gave off "a thick cloud of acrid white smoke" (p 36).

The mentions of her preoccupation with the occult go on and on and cannot but trigger off in readers of the transcript (and the newspaper reportage) associations with endless tales from childhood of "wicked witches", or more sinister horror stories involving black masses and satanic rituals; to say nothing of the historical associations with the demonological world view of the Middle Ages and its obsession with witch hunting.

Such associations are strengthened by comments from psychiatrists such as Dr Quinn, who at one point in the hearing defines three levels of witchcraft which he claims are relevant to Tracey's involvement. These range from an earlier "sanitised" dabbling with the occult – reading myths and legends and the like – to the present, where there are "strong hints of something a lot more sinister – the stuff of hard, cold Medieval witches" (pp 192-3).

Before the murder, Tracey cut her hair very short and dyed it "midnight black" (p 171). Again, one psychiatrist informs us that "the priestesses in the old cult religions were wont to cut their hair very short before certain religious rites" (p 171).

Finally, on the murder night there are confused references to Lisa or Kim going down to the murder site dressed in white, like an initiate, and returning to the car in black. No explanation is offered for this occurrence, but it has further occult implications.

Without apparently deliberate attempts to do so, Tracey is being constructed here it seems to me, as a witch, in keeping with the definition given in the *Malleus Maleficarum* of 1486 :

> Depraved human beings, chiefly women, who made a covenant with the Devil for the purpose of inflicting. . . all sorts of injuries to their fellow men's body, life, possessions. . . human beings who participated in the nocturnal Sabbat presided over by the Devil, who appeared in the flesh and to whom they paid homage; who. . . flew swiftly through the air to this Sabbat and to the places of their harmful activities and who committed sexual excesses of the worst kind among themselves and with the Devil. (Caputi 1988 p 97)

Perhaps this sort of construction is meant to help make "sense" of, or provides a rationale for her premeditated killing of an unknown passer-by: she is possessed by evil spirits!

Much has been made of the "alters" who inhabit Tracey's psyche, who, it is claimed, "behave as entities in their own right". It is claimed by some of the consultant psychiatrists that the tough, aggressive "Bobby" is responsible for the actual killing while another "alter", who may have disapproved of it, left the key card where it could easily be discovered by police – in an attempt to punish "Bobby" for his/her evil deed.

Apart from all the myths (even Biblical archetypes) of demonic possession and exorcism that this conjures up, there are parallels also with transformation myths here – well exemplified in Dr Jekyll and Mr Hyde. *The Picture of Dorian Gray* also comes to mind here, as does Faust or Dracula, or even Frankenstein and his "creature". Tracey's bewildered statement "that's not me, that's not the way I am" (Transcript p 137), when shown video taped evidence of her hypnotised self re-experiencing the murder (to which she had confessed), add further weight to the idea of possession or transformation.

All the vampire myths and Dracula, as literary archetype, spring to mind when reading of the alleged blood-drinking from the murdered man. There is strong evidence that this did take place, judging from the co-accused statements. The girls speak of this very soon after the arrest. The press had a field day with these statements! Tracey Waugh, for instance, claims that "she has to drink blood. She bought butcher's blood. She didn't eat, she only drank blood" (p 425). Lisa claims that at times she fed Tracey with blood via nicks in her own veins. Just before the murder, Tracey is claimed to have warned the others "if you come down to see me while I am feeding, I'll tear your limbs off. Nobody is going to see me but Kim" (p 294). (What is interesting is that Tracey the host has a genuine blood phobia, so a blood drinking "alter" is hypothesised to account for this!)

Revivification myths are echoed by Tracey's remarks under hypnosis, again while re-experiencing her murder, that "Faza", Tracey's childhood name for her adoptive father, George Wigginton, (whom she alleged had persistently sexually abused her as a child) "was there to be killed". The video tape presents her screaming: "I can't stop, I can't stop, I can't stop him" (p 350).

Finally the brutality of the murder and other earlier violent episodes mentioned in the hearing, in association with Tracey's fascination with knives, have "Jack-the-Ripper" connotations.

It is worth pausing to reflect upon the likely significance of such an array of allusions to mythic archetypes in this text. While most people no longer believe in the reality of vampires, werewolves and devils, they still exist, transformed, in much popular literature and film, and still, I believe, exert a powerful force on our (collective) cultural consciousness. They present images of the monstrous, the proscribed and the alien which can influence our perceptions of and responses to happenings in the real world.

To the reader, such aspects of Tracey Wigginton's life and actions as those just outlined, I would argue, provide a terrifying portrait of "Otherness" and its associated perversities, and point up the connection between criminality and sin – or evil in a theological sense – which still apparently abound in a secular age. They seem to point up the fact that there is nothing of which human beings are not capable.

I will not elaborate further on the mythic significance of this case, because I would like to turn now to another aspect: the correspondences between this murder case and the "strange cases" of the fictional canon which appropriate a legal format as fictional frame.

Much (short) Gothic fiction, in particular, is presented in this way. Very many short stories (detective and horror) contain in their titles the reference to "case": *The Strange Case of Dr Jekyll and Mr Hyde*, *A Case of Identity*, *Sherlock Holmes' Case-Book*. The use of the word "case" with its inbuilt medico-legal ambiguity produces an expectation in the reader that the story will involve an objective set of facts which are to be ascertained, and that certain records or other documents, such as letters or diaries or spoken forms of testimony, eye-witness accounts and so on, will be produced in the narrative to attest to the truth of these facts. The reader is posited as one engaged in sorting and assessing the evidence and coming to conclusions about it – a much more active process than simply following a narrative.

A partial narrative of Tracey Wigginton's past is provided by the testimony of those tendering affidavits to the hearing. The irony is that this testimony, as often occurs in horror fiction, does not necessarily contain its own explanation. What these witnesses have seen or heard is fragmentary, often contradictory, and riddled with gaps and ambiguities. These difficulties throw out a challenge to the reader to provide a convincing alternative explanation for such confusing or enigmatic testimony.

Such a reader expectation (that facts are to be presented and assessed) is effectively demonstrated in the opening of Edgar Allan Poe's story, "The Facts in the Case of Monsieur Valdemar" (1845):

> Of course I shall not pretend to consider it any matter for wonder, that the extraordinary case of M Valdemar has excited discussion. It would have been a miracle had it not – especially under the circumstances. Through the desire of all parties concerned, to keep the affair from the public, at least for the present, or until we had further opportunities for investigation – through our endeavours to effect this – a garbled or exaggerated account made its way into society, and became the source of many unpleasant misrepresentations; and, very naturally, of a great deal of disbelief. . . It is now rendered necessary that I give the facts – as far as I comprehend them myself. They are, succinctly, these. . . (Colum 1968 p 216)

The first person narrator casts himself in the role of the reliable eye-witness (and expert medical witness) able therefore to provide the authentic version of the events as opposed to "the garbled or exaggerated account" that heresay might let loose on society.

I choose this story particularly not only because it is almost a text-book illustration of the use of the legal frame in horror fiction, but also, of course, because "the case", here is a case of mesmerism, and draws on an understanding of the medical debate in the 1840s about the status of mesmerism as a legitimate medical procedure (as a possible anaesthetic).

The Tracey Wigginton Medical Tribunal hearing in many senses could also be seen to be dealing with a case of mesmerism in that much of the hearing is concerned with the current status of hypnosis as a legitimate diagnostic tool, and the status of evidence gained from a witness under hypnosis. Further, heated debate between psychiatrists and counsel, and amongst the psychiatrists themselves, concerns the likelihood or otherwise of Tracey's multiple personality disorder actually being induced by the processes of hypnosis; that is, whether or not it is an iatrogenic disorder. (This would disprove the theory strongly supported by the hypnotists – Doctors Clarke and Quinn – that one of Tracey's "alters", the aggressive masculine "Bobby", actually committed the murder unbeknown to the host (Tracey) which is, they believe, supported by her extensive amnesia about the events of the night of the murder.)

As the case of Monsieur Valdemar progresses, the narrator emerges as more than an expert witness, and rather as scientific investigator; so his testimony is prompted not just by a desire to set the record straight, but also by a desire to clear his own name of possible charges of fraud or quackery. Similarly, there is a considerable amount of overt self-justification by the hypnotists in the *Wigginton* case – prompted by fairly aggressive cross-examination – because of the above concerns about the validity and reliability of hypnotism. The strength of the reaction of those who oppose hypnosis and its use here can be judged by the Professor of Psychiatry's remarks: "this is secular demonology! The calling out of alters, the calling out of creatures within the person under the guise of modern medicine" (Transcript p 421). In both cases, Valdemar and Wigginton, there is a barrage of medical evidence in suitably technical language as to the physical and mental states respectively, of the subjects to be hypnotised; in both, the legal implications of the "experiment" are carefully considered – permission from the subject is gained before hypnosis takes place, and all hypnotic sessions are undertaken in the presence of medical personnel for expert corroborative testimony.

In "Monsieur Valdemar" the narrator is at pains to inform us that his account is drawn "either condensed or copied verbatim" from the "memoranda" of one such eye witness – thus reinforcing the illusion that the story is but a factual record of this strange case.

The reader is virtually positioned therefore as a jury member, engaged in evaluating the credibility of the evidence presented to him or her. Just before the climax of the story, the narrator, expecting a sceptical reaction from readers to what follows, breaks into his story to issue what amounts to a challenge to force the "suspension of disbelief" in readers, as well as indicating to them that a climactic point in the story has been reached. In keeping with the legalistic frame of witnessing, the narrator works hard to achieve precision and appropriate detachment in his account of Monsieur Valdemar's being induced to speak after death through hypnosis:

> There were two particulars, nevertheless, which I thought then, and still think, might fairly be stated as characteristic of the intonation – as well adapted to convey some idea of its unearthly peculiarity. In the first place, the voice seemed to reach our ears - at least mine – from a vast distance, or from some deep cavern within the earth. In the second place, it impressed me (I fear indeed, that it will be impossible to make myself comprehended) as gelatinous or glutinous matters impress the sense of touch. . . I have spoken both of "sound" and of "voice". I mean to say that the sound was one of distinct – of even wonderfully, thrillingly distinct – syllabification. M. Valdemar spoke – obviously in reply to the question I had propounded to him a few minutes before. I had asked him, it will be remembered, if he still slept. He now said: "Yes – no, – I have been sleeping – and now – now – I am dead." No person present ever affected to deny, or attempted to repress, the unutterable shuddering horror which these few words, thus uttered, were so well calculated to convey. (pp 221-2)

In the *Wigginton* case, Dr Clarke the hypnotist, strives, on several occasions, to describe objectively his reaction to the absolute unexpectedness of Tracey's abrupt personality switch which takes place under hypnosis, when she is being caused to re-experience the events of the murder night. On seeing the victim Baldock, "Bobby" speaks. Clarke's impressions of this are: "I have never in my life experienced a surge of fright as I experienced when she said in a deep and powerful voice, that I couldn't begin to emulate 'I want him'. She said it in a deep profundo voice". He returns to this experience several times, mentioning "the deep, deep voice, about an octave lower, which shifted me back in the seat" (Transcript p 131).

Dr Clarke's personal admission of surprise and fear and belief not only creates a corresponding frisson of horror in the reader, but works effectively to dispel any scepticism the reader may have felt about the likelihood of multiple "alters" inhabiting the mind of Tracey Wigginton.

Poe's narrator/witness relentlessly continues his testimony to its rather revolting conclusion:

> all in the room were prepared to see the patient awaken. For what really occurred, however, it is quite impossible that any human being could have been prepared. . . As I rapidly made the mesmeric passes, amid ejaculations of "dead! dead!" absolutely bursting from the tongue and not from the lips of the sufferer, his whole frame at once – within the space of a single minute, or less, shrunk – crumbled – absolutely

> rotted away beneath my hands. Upon the bed, before that whole company, there lay a nearly liquid mass of loathsome – of detestable putridity. (p 223)

It can be seen that he offers several overlapping forms of testimony. He is a legal witness – almost a defendant – it is implied in the case. He is also the expert medical witness, as mesmerist, and he is the scientific investigator who provides an apparently objective report of his experiment. In a further sense, he is witness to the (almost) miraculous, in a theological sense, the raising of the dead to life. These overlapping frames and their resultant ambiguities make for a text that hovers freely between a number of cultural contexts: legal, medical, scientific and theological.

The existence and consequences of various frames of witness deserve comment also in the *Wigginton* case. The incompatibilities of medical and legal discourse further problematise the interpretation of this case, bearing in mind the inbuilt ambiguity already attendant upon the word "case" itself, as discussed earlier.

Legal discourse appears to demand precision, clarity, and certainty in its attempt to discover facts and evaluate evidence. Ambiguity or ambivalence threatens this process and is thus to be avoided at all costs. It is evident that counsel are striving to proceed by means of rational argument and logical deduction in this case: trying to force short, precise unqualified answers to questions they ask.

However medical testimony, particularly psychiatric evidence, is not easily accommodated into this precise methodology. The psychiatrists' evidence tends to be heavily qualified, tentative, diffuse, relying rather on inductive methods and intuitive judgment. Discussions of other case histories and relevant text-book literature make their testimony anecdotal and somewhat circumlocutory.

These inbuilt oppositions apparent in this discourse militate against a simple, unambiguous process of sifting, explaining and proving the evidence for the reader of the text, and also, I imagine, for the judge on the bench! Difficulties are magnified by the procedural disagreements between the five or six medical experts and their unresolved debate about the existence of such a condition as multiple personality disorder, let alone their disagreements as to whether or not it is the appropriate diagnosis for Tracey Wigginton's personality problem!

The forward drive of a legal case viewed textually is not so much narrative but the need, harnessed to the evidential form, to recover the facts. What I am arguing here is that the interplay of these conflicting frames when applied to the labyrinthine nature of the evidence, greatly increases the text's density and polysemy as well as the difficulties of its resolution.

As with Poe's case of "Monsieur Valdemar", the reader can ask of the *Wigginton* case whether what takes place is:

- a medical experiment – associated with the use of hypnosis for diagnosis?
- about the uses and abuses of mesmerism? Is it simply quackery?
- exorcism or demonology – the calling out of "alters" or spirits – a theological case, perhaps?
- a latter-day real-life Gothic horror case involving a Lesbian Vampire murderess inhabited by evil "tormentors" who force her to commit evil acts?
- a legal inquiry into the mental health of a confessed murderer? Is she fit to stand trial?
- a case study of the consequences and resulting psychological trauma of severe sexual and physical abuse in childhood - victimology perhaps?
- an ethical case involving issues of the morality of causing someone to re-experience what is emotionally very painful? (Tracey's reliving the events of her childhood including the incidents of sexual abuse, as well as re-experiencing the murder under hypnosis.)

First person narration and confessional autobiography are popular in nineteenth century horror literature because of their evidentiary potential. The final explanatory chapter of *Dr Jekyll and Mr Hyde* entitled "Henry Jekyll's Full Statement of the Case" is one such example. Confession is seen as the best evidence, the strongest testimony that is possible in the courtroom. Yet there is an ambivalence of attitude in much English Gothic writing concerning the reliability of evidence gained via confession, associated with the wider Protestant mistrust of Catholic practices. Justine's (false) confession in *Frankenstein* points up the potential for duplicity in such situations.

The *Wigginton* case also includes an element of interior witnessing or confessional discourse, which gives it a further (theological) frame of reference. Tracey Wigginton provided police with a confession during their third interview with her and exonerated her companions.

The Medical Tribunal hearing also provides details of Tracey vividly re-experiencing the events of the murder night under hypnosis (which were shown on video tape in court) and also partially transcribed and discussed during the hearing. This is a variant on the process of interior witnessing. When shown the videos of these re-experiencing sessions, Tracey seemed bewildered. She says (as quoted earlier) "That's not me. That's not the way I am", while still admitting to having killed Baldock. The scientific explanation seems to be that Tracey, the host, does not necessarily have knowledge of the actions of all of her "alters" all of the time! Perhaps the theological explanation might be that she is not aware of being possessed by demons.

Sin and evil seem inextricably linked in the mind of Western human beings and here is an effective example of the legalistic frame supporting a theological theme – the existence of the devil within us. Especially in the light of Professor Varghese's comment quoted earlier about "secular demonology", one can see how the hypnotists are akin to white magicians or exorcisers, calling out alters or spirits (demons perhaps?) in ever increasing numbers – certainly a twist to the usual empirical means of presenting forensic evidence! I find it most ironic that modern psychological practice should re-kindle ancient superstition associated with exorcism – the removal of devils or evil tormentors from the soul or mind of the afflicted. Bobby, we are told by one psychiatrist, is "an omnibus term for a number of persecutors" (Transcript p 120). There are inescapable reverberations here of the Literature of Horror, once again illustrating how such a text unavoidably impinges on a number of cultural contexts. This is in every way, I would argue, a transgressive text: it seems to challenge the boundaries between truth and fantasy, fiction and non-fiction, the plausible and the implausible.

Gothic texts are those where events cannot occur according to realistic probability, yet inordinate effort is expended in them to provide the semblance of the real, to insist on their actuality. This, I believe, is achieved by bringing the materials of fantasy into collision with the techniques of realism. In the process, the reader moves from scepticism to belief.

In contrast, the content, the stuff of real life in the *Wigginton* case, is virtually overwhelmed by the power of the myths or the fantasy it generates. It is easier to place this text within the context of fiction – as part of the horror canon – than to apprehend it as a sample of everyday life. In this case, the reader moves from belief (in the fact of the murder) to doubt about almost everything else!

If the Gothic text is to be seen (as it often is) as a means of ironically interrogating the nineteenth century realist work, then is a text such as the Wigginton hearing an interrogation of real life? Does it expose life as a fiction?

BIBLIOGRAPHY

Barthes, R, 1967, *Elements of Semiology*, Lavers, A & Smith, C (trans), Cape.

Barthes, R, 1968, "The Death of the Author", *Image – Music – Text*, Collins.

Barthes, R, 1970, *S/Z*, Miller, R (trans), 1975, Cape.

Barthes, R, 1977, *Image – Music – Text* , Heath, Stephen (trans), Collins.

Caputi, J, 1988, *The Age of the Sex Crime*, The Women's Press.

Poe, EA, 1845, "The Facts in the case of M. Valdemar", *Tales of Mystery and Imagination*, Colum, P (ed), 1968, Dent.

Sage, V, 1988, *Horror Fiction in the Protestant Tradition*, St Martin's Press.

17

Censorship, Violence and the Law

PETER HUTCHINGS

> For the observation that prison fails to eliminate crime, one should perhaps substitute the hypothesis that prison has succeeded extremely well in producing delinquency, a specific type, a politically and economically less dangerous – and, on occasion, usable – form of illegality; in producing delinquents, in an apparently marginal, but in fact centrally supervised milieu; in producing the delinquent as a pathological subject. (Foucault 1979)

Similarly, for the observation that censorship fails to eliminate pornography or violence, one should perhaps substitute the hypothesis that censorship – considered as a field which includes State and Federal laws, decisions of the Office of Film and Literature Classification (the Office), of the Film and Literature Board of Review (the Board), and also media attention, and submissions from the public – censorship has succeeded extremely well in proliferating pornography and violence through its discourses.

In the past few years, books and films involving violence have provoked renewed debate over censorship. Brett Easton Ellis's novel *American Psycho* was classified as a Restricted publication. John McNaughton's film *Henry: Portrait of a Serial Killer* had some difficulty in obtaining an "R" certificate. Jonathan Demme's film *The Silence of the Lambs* had some trouble achieving an "M" certificate, and became involved in the debate surrounding *American Psycho*. And at a time when these texts have been the subject of extensive public debate, other, comparably "violent" texts have been largely ignored: for example, Helen Zahavi's novel *Dirty Weekend*[1] (for which the Office had no record at all), and Martin Scorcese's film *Cape Fear*.

---

1 "She struck him again, and it was like cracking an egg, like hitting a shell with a spoon, like having an early breakfast in Brighton. She pulled the claw out of his skull, and chewed her lip, and pounded him. She hammered her message home the only way she could. She bludgeoned him for all her silent sisters. She battered the bones that protected his brain, and she almost cried as he almost died" (Zahavi 1991).

By examining the decisions of the Office on a number of books and films, I wish to raise certain questions concerning the relationship between censorship, law, and violence in art, and to suggest that certain forms of censorship take their own place in the violence about these texts. I would wish to see, utilising concepts adapted from the work of Michel Foucault and Gilles Deleuze, what conceptions of violence inform censorship decisions. In essence, my argument is that censorship debates are structured by a paradox that may be conceived of as operating between considerations of law and equity.[2] These legal distinctions appear in the distinction in Film and Literature Classifications between lists of offending elements – language, sex, violence, and (among others) treatment of drug abuse – and considerations of artistic merit and context which may affect perceptions about these elements.

A reading of the Office of Film and Literature Classification files suggests a widespread tendency to engage with cinematic and literary texts at the level of content, on the part of both the censors and the public (including reviewers and critics). The most notorious example of this has been *American Psycho*, a text subjected to a critical violence only rivalled by the kinds of violence found in that book's own descriptions. Quite simply, the debate over *American Psycho* began with the publication of fragments or textual excerpts – an extreme case of this being a phone service organised by an American women's group which allowed callers to have "offending passages" read to them in lieu of reading the book in its entirety. The constraints of a chapter of a book will require my own analysis to engage in its own violence vis-a-vis the texts it interrogates.

At this point it is worth explaining the system of Literature Classification. The classification of printed matter is a voluntary scheme, unlike that of film and video. Under the guidelines, based on the *Classification of Publications Ordinance* 1983 (ACT), material may be submitted by the publishers or by members of the public. During 1990-1991, the statistics on complaints received were: 67 written and 35 oral complaints. Of those oral complaints, two concerned *American Psycho*. Those two complaints were then joined by a third, resulting in the book being submitted by the complainants for classification, along with a letter which reads as follows:

> We, the undersigned, are submitting a copy of "American Psycho" by Brett Easton Ellis, for review and classification.
>
> We find the content of this publication deeply disturbing and do not believe that it is in the public interest that such material should enter the mainstream culture.

The book was then read by the Chief Censor and four members of the Office, and the majority decision was that it be classified as

2 As much as this chapter's conceptual structure is informed by Foucault's *Discipline and Punish* and Deleuze's *Masochism*, it is informed by the idea of a tension between law and equity that I first encountered in Penelope Pether's reading of Arthur Miller's *The Crucible* (unpublished paper, 1992).

Restricted – Category 1 (sale restricted to persons 18 years and over, to be displayed in a sealed wrapper). Of all the reports, the minority report (recommending unrestricted status) was alone in noting the uncertain diegetic status of the text's violence:

> It was not clear . . . if the murders and mutilations actually occurred or if they were merely products of Bateman's disturbed mind. What was clear was that Bateman was a mentally ill psychopath whose depredations (as distinct from his lifestyle) were not depicted in any glamorous or pleasure achieving manner.

The same reader also noted that:

> Children under 18 are not likely to plough through the book at all. If they did, whilst they would no doubt be somewhat nauseated (as would adults) if they read the violent passages, I cannot believe that it would cause them harm or even distress them to any marked degree.

This report went on to state that "The book is just not believable".

This most equitable interpretation of the book still does not quite get its point: that it is "not believable" precisely because its "events" are "merely products of Bateman's disturbed mind". It is also quite realistic in its assumption that people under the age of 18 were unlikely to persevere with a reading of the book, an assumption that any high school teacher could confirm. However, the very style and form of censorship debates guarantees and reinforces just that fetishised reading of the book which would be the likely form of reading by minors. The debate, then, precipitates the very risk which it would seek to eliminate both by the attention it draws to a text such as *American Psycho*, and the reading practices involved in that attention.

Central to the textual strategy deployed by Easton Ellis is an attention to description. Description is also the method employed in censorship decisions, where description is used as the basis for an opinion about a text's relationship to the guidelines.

Description, as a linguistic register, involves the itemising and anatomising of things. In one sense, to name is to know, and to own. It is the register which may express the desire of possession, and the potential (or power) to possess, and *American Psycho* is crucially concerned with a depiction of just this linguistic operation; made rich and strange by Patrick Bateman, whose only purchase upon the world and its people is his psychotic, private use of elaborate, repetitive description. As Deleuze (1971 p 20) has argued of the function of description in the texts of de Sade, through description we see:

> that reasoning itself is a form of violence, and that he is on the side of violence, however calm and logical he may be. He is not even attempting to prove anything to anyone, but to perform a demonstration related essentially to the solitude and omnipotence of its author. The point of the exercise is to show that the demonstration is identical to violence.

Further, Deleuze argues that this violent quality, which is inherent in description and the demonstrative use of language, "accounts for the endless repetitions, the reiterated quantitative process of multiplying illustrations and adding victim upon victim, again and again retracing the thousand circles of an irreducibly solitary argument".

Description functions at the level of the law, defining the features of a text with reference to legal categories. It is an itemising process found in all of the Office's files, initially in the form of viewing or reading notes which then are included in the reports of classification decisions. One report on *American Psycho* features three paragraphs of synoptic description, supplemented by one and a half pages of notes on "some of the stronger elements", followed by an opinion on whether, and in what way, the text ought to be classified:

> In my opinion some of the material could justify refusal to classify if contained in an exploitative sex novel. In my view the detailed descriptions are necessary in this book, to some degree, to show the depths to which Bateman sinks. In a written work mere allusion may not sufficiently stress the dark side of the characters.
>
> Having said that I consider *some of this material* is unsuitable for perusal by a minor, including 16 and 17 year olds, and offensive to the reasonable adult person to the degree it should be restricted.

The debate aroused by *American Psycho* is an effective example of a "beat up" in more ways than one. It was characterised by a moral and aesthetic mugging of the public, and of the book, as one literary commentator pointed out:

> The scandal of Ellis's novel is a product not of the book itself, but of the mass media, with their infinite need for excitement.
>
> *American Psycho* first saw the light when *Spy* magazine published an unauthorised excerpt.
>
> "Almost universal outrage" followed. At the excerpt, not the bootlegging! *Hypocrite lecteur!*
>
> So, *American Psycho* never stood a chance of being read seriously. *Gutted*, it became a media scandal, at the hands largely of those who had not read it, or – worse still – had read excerpts only. (Anderson 1992) (my italics)

Anderson has chosen his words with characteristic consideration: as a description of the reading practices deployed against *American Psycho*, the word "gutted" clearly marks a repetition or displacement of what is complained of in the text to the level of readings of the text, including the surreal proposition that it was a "snuff" book. As if Hannibal the Cannibal had become an author or a librarian rather than a psychologist.

Locked in a solitary world in which almost no one seems to know his name, Patrick Bateman is an exemplary participant in the modern, disciplinary obscenity of itemising description, an individuation which eventually undoes itself through its own excesses, much as Patrick's narrative increasingly does toward the end of the novel. Such a disciplinary mania for itemisation is the expression of that "indefinite discipline: an interrogation without end, and investigation that would be extended without limit to a meticulous and ever more analytical observation", which Foucault characterises as the modern disciplinary régime par excellence. And, along the lines already suggested, Foucault's notion that "penality does not simply 'check' illegalities: it 'differentiates' them, it provides them with a general 'economy'" (1979 p 272) can be extended to a model of a differentiating censorship which both constitutes an economy of representations of language, sex, violence, and so on, and of community standards – a censorship which in turn constitutes its judgments by reference to that economy.

It is at this point that we return to considerations of law and equity. Censorship decisions are involved with differentiations between the various representations of language, sex, violence, and so on, and a crucial and vexed differentiation often obtains between sex and violence. As the Guidelines put it, "The closest attention is paid to the portrayal of violence and, in particular, sexual violence".

The classification of *Cape Fear* turned upon just such differentiations (and it might also be noted that, although there were some complaints about its "M" classification, the general reception of the film treated its sexualised violence as unproblematic even within the context of its rating). In arriving at a revised "M" classification it was considered that, "No sexual activity occurs and the violence is not sexualised by visuals of nudity". In this case, the equitable questions of artistic merit featured very crucially in the deliberation upon the film's status.

One report in favour of an "R" recommendation argued that:

> The suspense is of course integral to the film's genre nature and it should be noted that its self-conscious references to the film noir works of the 1950s does place its realism in cultural quotation marks. Nonetheless, at this level it remains a film for adults and this is underscored by the depictions of violence which go far beyond the conventions of the work's reference points.

While a report in favour of an "M" recommendation suggested that:

> Much of this sequence [ie the film's climax] fits neatly within the genre and is not naturalistic in the true sense. It is my opinion that this film fits both within the Thriller genre and the "art house" market and that the kind of action included would allow an M classification for this film.

Here, then, aesthetic considerations obtain on the equity side of the argument in a way which suggests that "community standards" allow a special licence for "artistic" material which might be denied to that deemed inartistic or unrecognised as a "work of art". This is not to suggest that special rules apply, but to note the notions which intervene in censorship decisions from the always unstable, uncodifiable considerations of equity.

While *Cape Fear* had a relatively untroubled classification, *The Silence Of The Lambs* was the subject of a reviewed classification (also from "R" to "M") which then caused some public concern after the film became guiltily associated with the *American Psycho* debate. The initial report is an interesting example of the descriptive regime brought to bear upon the assessment of a film's status, "The Board considered that coarse language which was both sexually explicit and assaultative together with highly realistic and impactful violence were appropriate to a RESTRICTED classification". Particular elements referred to in the Board's report included:

> – Two uses of "I can smell your cunt" which was used by a male and then asked to be repeated by a female as a means of intimidating her.
>
> – A post mortem scene where the results of violence are shown in very graphic detail with explicit depictions of wounds.
>
> – A violent attack on two guards with very heavy and impactful beatings. One victim's body is hung up with a detailed view of his opened torso revealing entrails. The other victim receives a blood burst bullet wound shown in medium close-up.
>
> – The Board felt the impact of these violent scenes was further heightened by the theme of serial killers who flay or eat their victims and frequent detailed verbal descriptions of such actions.

Again, the Board of Review decision involved considerations of "artistic and technical merit" including the idea that, "We thought it unlikely that the film's audiences would see it purely as a spectacle of gratuitous horror; the feelings of pity and terror evoked by the film may well stimulate deeper reflections".

Upon the film's release, the Office received an extremely detailed, descriptive correspondence from a man arguing for an "R" classification for the film, by way of a replication and elaboration of the descriptive, differential techniques of the decision-making process. Reading this lengthy correspondence I got a niggling sense that the author's language was not all that far from Patrick Bateman's, with the same obsessive attention to detail. But what that writer has in common with the gay lobby against the film is that both engage in the violence of silence: here, the silence of women. One consequence of the itemising descriptive regime applied to the film was that it took an inordinate time for anyone to begin to refer to the film's engagement with its formal violence: that of the gaze.

One of the remarkable achievements of *The Silence of the Lambs* is its combination of a directorial style that has been astutely described by Meaghan Morris as "a critique of feminist film theory" with what Foster described in her Oscar acceptance speech as "an incredibly strong and beautiful feminist hero" (the latter comment needing to be taken in the context of the roles available to women in Hollywood).

Anthony Hopkins's performance in the role of Dr Hannibal "The Cannibal" Lecter is integral to the film's explicatory rebuttal of feminist theories of the cinematic gaze as possessively masculine. Demme counterposes scenes of startling, eyeline-matched close-ups between Clarice and Hannibal with scenes of the diminutive Foster surrounded by towering, gawping FBI agents and policemen, making a feminist point by allegedly masculinist means. The film's most violent scenes involve this kind of inter-subjective violence, this essentially cinematic intrusion of the gaze, rather than the suggested forms of explicity, simulated physical violence about which so much fuss has been made, and which would be the forms of demonic violence so easily recuperable by what Joe Grixti discusses in Chapter 18 "Coming to Terms with Villainy" as consumerist taming of the threatening.

In this instance, itemising descriptions rendered silent the film's feminism, by taking it apart, and I am reminded of Naomi Wolf's (1991 p 59) contention that, "Since the fourteenth century, male culture has silenced women by taking them beautifully apart. The catalogue of features [the blazon], developed by the troubadours, first paralyzed the beloved woman into beauty's silence". But it is more than just a case of silence and paralysis: the atomising and anatomising of women has more serious consequences, as can be seen in Andrew Marvell's seventeenth century lyric "To His Coy Mistress":

> My vegetable love should grow
> Vaster than empires and more slow;
> An hundred years should go to praise
> Thine eyes, and on thy forehead gaze;
> Two hundred to adore each breast,
> But thirty thousand to the rest;
> An age at least to every part,
> And the last age should show your heart.
> For, lady, you deserve this state,
> Nor would I love at lower rate. (1681, ll 11-19)

Marvell's courtly blazon contains its own coyness concerning masculine power: not only is the poem's rhetorical strategy dependent upon silencing its addressee – and, thus, a demonstration of rhetorical and political omnipotence – but it conceals a bloody threat encoded within the blazon's literal effects. It too, if not preeminently, is a "taking beautifully apart" of his mistress: if her coyness betrays his sovereign desire *then* she will be dismembered in a poetic replication of a treason execution, concluding with a tearing out of her heart.

It is clear that women may be the objects of descriptive violence and that such a violence is consequent upon a fetishistic, itemising and disciplinary apprehension of the body's gendered text. This descriptive regime has the power to make silent: on the other side of silence is violence.

I opened with the hypothesis that censorship has succeeded extremely well in proliferating pornography and violence through censorial discourses: that certain forms of censorship take their own place in the violence of these texts, through a practice of discursive violence located in the operations of descriptive language. There are extremely vexed problems in the operation of equity with regard to censorship caused by the model of textuality and reading embedded in the law and its apprehension of texts through a discursive perspective of a "blazon" gaze. Categories of artistic quality, while the most frequently applied equitable concerns, do not offer the most reliable means of tempering legislative judgment with textual politics.

BIBLIOGRAPHY

Anderson, Don, 1992, "Don't judge a book by its shrink-wrapped cover", in *Real Opinions: Polemical and Popular Writings*, McPhee Gribble, p 185.

Deleuze, Gilles, 1971, *Masochism*, George Braziller.

Ellis, Brett Easton, 1991, *American Psycho*, Pan Books

Foucault, Michel, 1979, *Discipline and Punish: The Birth of the Prison*, Sheridan, Alan (trans), Vintage.

Wolf, Naomi, 1991, *The Beauty Myth: How Images of Beauty Are Used Against Women*, Vintage.

18

Coming to Terms with Villainy: The Fictionalisation of Mass Murderers and Serial Killers

JOE GRIXTI

> There is no longer any such thing as fiction or nonfiction, there is only narrative.
>
> *EL Doctorow*[1]

Early in 1992, a series of newspaper articles announced that Jeffrey Dahmer had been made the "main hero" of a comic book biography. A Milwaukee court of law had recently found Dahmer guilty of a string of violent murders involving rape, dismemberment and cannibalism. One article in the *Weekend Australian* (16-17 May 1992 p 13) headlined "Dahmer now a comic book hero", reported that the book contained "pictures of Dahmer slicing the throats of his victims and having sex with the corpses", that it had sold out immediately in Milwaukee, Wisconsin, and neighbouring States of the American Midwest, and that a sequel was being planned. Another article, again in *The Weekend Australian* (13-14 June 1992 p 16), reported that, in his response to protests from the relatives of Dahmer's victims, the book's publisher had insisted that he had only made $200 from the first comic-book, and that the relatives would be better off "directing their wrath at those who are writing books and making movies about the killer because they will be making thousands of dollars". In implying that levels of moral responsibility should be judged according to the amount of financial profit generated by representations of disturbing atrocities, the assertion provides a forceful reminder of the extent to which our perceptions of and

1 Cited in Fishkin (1985 p 207).

reactions to mass murder and serial killing have become inseparable from the orientations of consumerism.[2]

Jeffrey Dahmer's elevation to the rank of ambiguous monster-hero in the iconography of contemporary consumer culture forms part of a noteworthy tradition. Interest in mass murderers and serial killers is not restricted to readers of popular "true crime" paperbacks and comics, of course. Accounts involving such figures are very frequent and prominent in the mass media – in news and current affairs programmes, as well as in a range of popular entertainments. As Jane Caputi (1990) puts it, serial killers of the late 20th century tend to "generate legends and attract cult-like behavior" in that they are "celebrated (sometimes covertly, sometimes overtly) along a cultural gamut including made-for television movies, rock'n'roll songs, horror fanzines, jokes, pornographic magazines such as *Hustler,* and extreme sadist publications". Such celebrations in a sense usher figures like Dahmer into a hall of fame where historical murderers acquire mythical proportions (frequently reinforced by the ascription of evocative names like Jack the Ripper, the Hillside Strangler, the Vampire of Düsseldorf or the Night Stalker) and rub shoulders with a long line of fictional figures created over the centuries in the course of variously loaded attempts to come to cognitive terms with evil by visualising and personifying its threats and horrors in reassuringly recognisable forms. Within the popular cultural domains which underlie the construction of this chamber of horrors, boundaries between fact and fiction often tend to become blurred.

Criminals, psychopaths and murderers have consistently attracted the attention of writers and readers of all levels of fiction, but it is in popular literature that bloodthirsty murders have been most frequently contemplated. Murderers have here tended to be depicted in terms which frighten and disturb, and they have frequently (consciously or unconsciously) been made to serve ideologically weighted functions like those of providing challenging reminders about the need for constant vigilance, or of offering reassurance about the ultimate rightness of structures of law enforcement as guardians and embodiments of the social and moral order. As a number of commentators have pointed out, Jack the Ripper is perhaps the most influentially mythologised murderer of recent history, and fictional recreations of his crimes have dressed him up in guises ranging from that of streetcleaning avenger of decadence to blood-curdling challenger of any smug belief in the prevalence of sanity or security in advanced urban societies. Other historical mass murderers and serial killers whose exploits have been re-imagined and variously re-interpreted in fiction include Vlad the

2 Don Davis's (1991) popular "true crime" biography of Dahmer also appears to have joined the ranks of best-selling paperbacks when it was reissued shortly after Dahmer's widely publicised trial. See also: Masters (1993), *The Shrine of Jeffrey Dahmer*.

Impaler (mythologised as Dracula), Gilles de Rais (accused of sadistically torturing and murdering between 140 and 800 children as well as murdering six of his seven wives, and around whose life grew the legend of "Bluebeard"), and Elizabeth Bathory, the Hungarian Countess (fictionalised as "Countess Dracula" in a 1960s Hammer horror film) who in 1611 was convicted of killing up to 650 girls and bathing in their blood in order to halt the aging process.

Recent years have also seen a growth in the number of criminologists attempting to identify patterns in order to place such crimes within some sort of coherence – partly in response to an alarming growth in the incidence of "recreational killings" and murders involving a single killer claiming large numbers of victims. Significantly in this context, the semantic distinction between *mass murder* and *serial killing* was only developed in the 1980s. In the preface to his *Annotated Bibliography of Mass Murder* (1988), Michael Newton notes that with official recognition of a growing problem in the 1980s, "jargon raced ahead of understanding, and a host of experts quarrelled among themselves about the proper terminology for this or that atrocity". Serial sex murders have also been the focus of attention among feminist social theorists, a number of whom have unequivocally designated the phenomenon as a symptomatic sin of patriarchy. The evidence presented in this regard is challenging and damning, in that the fascination exerted by mass and serial sex killings in late capitalist consumer societies is clearly entangled with some of the more sinister aspects of phallocentrism and fear or hatred of women.[3] This is perhaps most obvious in the thrust and orientations of sado-masochistic publications which celebrate violence as sexual titillation – or *gorenography,* to borrow a phrase coined by United States traders to describe such specialty magazines as *Gore Gazette, The Splatter Times, Bill Landis' Sleazoid Express, Confessions of a Trash Fiend, Scarephanalia,* and *Fangoria* (Caputi 1988 p 216).

But the moral and cognitive problems raised by popular interest in horrific murders are wider and more complex than is suggested by the sensational and exploitative nature of many of the narratives which focus on them. According to Brian Masters (1986 p 26):

> The murderer takes his place in the jumbled kaleidoscope of the human condition. So, too, does his audience. For them to enjoy the display of crime, detection, retribution, while refusing to be drawn into a steady contemplation of themselves as audience, and the subterranean echoes which the case disturbs, would be fruitless and arid.

Masters draws attention to the moral tightrope which writers and readers have to negotiate while trying to make sense of the serial killer and of the disturbing issues which he raises. Sympathy with

3 See Caputi (1988); Smith (1989); Morgan (1989); Jouve (1986).

murder is unthinkable, Masters points out, but to avoid the pain of trying to understand is an abnegation of responsibility.

Perhaps the most widespread popular reactions to the recounting of horrific crimes are the more socially respectable ones of bafflement and incomprehension. "There is murder in cold blood, and murder in hot blood", declared *Newsweek* magazine in its report, "The Secrets of the Farm" (50, 2 December 1957, pp 30-1) on the bizarre crimes of Edward Gein:

> both, at least, can be explained in human terms. But there is also a kind of murder that springs from the deep recesses of a mind so twisted that it passes human understanding. This can be murder in its most terrible, sickening form.

The impact which violent acts have on society at large is powerful not only because they produce fear but also, and perhaps more importantly, because they produce disorientation. In this relation, Clive Bloom (1988) has suggested that the "legendary power" of the violence of a figure like Jack the Ripper "acts as a gaping maw into which perception of order and rightness are sucked". One way of dealing with this uncertainty is to affirm that mass murderers and serial killers are neither civilised nor really human – that is to stress their monstrosity so as to perceive them as belonging to the realm of the *other*. The tendency is well illustrated in the tone and imagery which dominate the following excerpt from a "true crime" account of the atrocities committed in the mid-1980s by Richard Ramirez, the Los Angeles "Night Stalker":

> The public, even the police, can understand a crime of passion, perhaps sympathize with the killer, even if they do not approve. . . But this bloody rampage was different. It was the sadistic, systematic slaughter of innocent people. Someone with a vampire's taste for human blood was creeping into houses in middle-class neighborhoods after dark to work nightmarish evil. And the ghoulish intruder was not satisfied simply to kill his victims; he added torture, rape and mutilation. He dehumanized his victims. It was villainy beyond ordinary comprehension; evil that truly chilled the soul. (Linedecker 1991)

The reaction is peculiarly modern in its implications, and it will be useful to briefly locate it in its historical context before we go any further. According to Randall McGowen (1989), the modern tendency to construct violence as the domain of the other owes a lot to nineteenth century reforms in the English penal system. By reducing the harshness and violence of the state's patterns of punishment, McGowen suggests, the legal reformers helped to bring an end to the use of violence as a means of legitimating the state's power. Violent acts could no longer be officially attributed to God's righteousness when reformers were campaigning to circumscribe and eliminate violence from the life of their society. The demands for reform, in other words, encouraged the development of a world view in which the existence of violence in civilised societies could be attributed exclusively to criminals – outsiders whose violent acts came to be designated as being beyond rational comprehension. We now like to believe, McGowen points out, that we cannot understand what makes one person harm another:

> Yet one consequence of the puzzle over the violence criminals do becomes an uncertainty about ourselves and our neighbors. The violent act comes to define a character as different from us, as criminal. This person appears to be outside of human community, perhaps less than human. But this boundary, seemingly so secure, begins to erode when we become aware of a neighbor's violence, or that of the police. We draw away from these offenders but remain uneasily aware that the violence we thought we had excluded from the community has found its way back into our midst. At such time we turn away or deny the characterization of the act because otherwise our very identity seems in doubt. (p 140)

The events surrounding the execution of Ted Bundy, one of the most notorious *and* celebrated serial killers of recent history, in many ways illustrate some of the socio-psychological implications of this tendency. *Bundy's* case was particularly disorienting to many because he looked so decent and (as a handsome, intelligent former law student who had worked for the Republican party) he seemed to epitomise many of the most cherished American notions of wholesomeness. In the course of the television interview which he gave shortly before his execution, Bundy insisted on his fellowship in a universal brotherhood and attributed his transgressions to one of the less salutary components of consumer culture:

> Those of us who are . . . so much influenced by violence in the media, in particular pornographic violence, are not some kind of inherent monsters. We are your sons, and we are your husbands, and we grew up in regular families. (Caputi 1990 p 6)

This rejection of the label of "inherent monster" contrasts starkly with the ways in which Bundy was insistently being portrayed by others. As he went to the electric chair in January 1989, a carnivalesque crowd gathered outside the prison gates and waved banners announcing (among other things) "Bundy BBQ", "I like my Ted well done" and "Fry, Bundy, Fry". The crowd, echoing as it did some of the symbolic functions performed by the torch-waving crowds which so frequently rose to destroy the monster at the climax of horror movies in the 1930s, partly reflected a firm determination not to lose sight of the murderer as outsider – an unnatural growth which society had finally recognised for what it was and was now dealing with accordingly. This is also the way in which Bundy was constructed by his journalistic biographers, Stephen Michaud and Hugh Aynesworth (1989), who claimed inside knowledge of his mind on the basis of a lengthy series of taped (and usually circumspect) interviews which he granted them in prison. Elaborating on an assertion made by the prosecution during Bundy's trial that criminals are human beings and not, as popular stereotypes have it, "a hunchbacked, cross-eyed little monster slithering through the dark, leaving a trail of slime", Michaud and Aynesworth (pp 6, 13) assert :

> But within Ted Bundy, human being, that slithering hunchback lives, residing behind what one eminent psychiatrist has termed a psychopath's "mask of sanity." The mask is a fabrication and nothing more, but it is impenetrable by even the most skilled doctor of the mind. In Ted, the cross-eyed creature lurks on a different plane of existence and can only be seen by means of a tautology; its presence must be inferred before it can be found. . . Only by means of his astounding capacity to compartmentalize had Bundy been able to keep the hunchback from raging through the mask and destroying him. When at last it did, *Ted* became the hunchback. No longer its protector, he and the entity fused.

The imagery employed here to describe the unaccountable derives unmistakably from the literary genres of fantasy and horror fiction. The passages do not add much to our understanding of a figure like Bundy. They simply appeal to a stock of prejudices and associations based on our familiarity with fictional accounts involving things like slithering cross-eyed creatures, imprisoned gorgons or Frankenstein monsters which turn on their jailers, or horrible hunchbacked witches disguised as "normal" people. Dr Jekyll and Mr Hyde also form an important part of this cluster of connotations – particularly in terms of how Mr Hyde has popularly come to personify an alleged beast beneath the skin, what Robert Louis Stevenson called in his influential 1885 novel, "the animal within . . . licking the chops of memory [when] the spiritual side [is] a little drowsed". Designating murderers as inhuman beasts, or as having been taken over completely by the "Beast Within", is a way of distancing them from what we popularly prefer to perceive as the norm.

All this suggests that popular (and formulaic) fictionalisations of serial killers allow us to make them perform scapegoating functions analogous to those identified by René Girard (1977) in his description of sacrifice as serving "to protect the entire community from *its own violence*". But, as is indicated by Ted Bundy's rejection of the label of "inherent monster", the role is not assumed willingly. Nor is the process of ascribing it either innocent or unambiguous. According to Brian Masters (1986 p 26), "people accused of vile murders who regard themselves as a cathartic release from the accumulated wickedness of mankind . . . deeply resent the additional burden".

"No one wants to believe ever", declared British serial killer Dennis Nilsen, "that I am just an ordinary man come to an extraordinary and overwhelming conclusion". Nilsen was arrested on 9 February 1983 after human remains had been identified as the cause of blocked drains outside his north London home. Parts of the bodies of several of his male victims in various stages of dismemberment were also found inside his house. Nilsen's private life, which jarred so starkly with his public role as civil servant, attracted a lot of public attention in the days following his arrest, and

Nilsen, angry at the simplistic tone of the press accounts, even penned his own pastiche of a tabloid news report headlined: "RED MONSTER LURES YOUNG MEN TO THEIR DEATHS IN HOMOSEXUAL HOUSE OF HORROR". "I am always surprised and truly amazed", Nilsen declared at another stage, "that anyone can be attracted by the macabre":

> The population at large is neither "ordinary" nor "normal". They seem to be bound together by a collective ignorance of themselves and what they are. They have, every one of them, got their deep dark thoughts with many a skeleton rattling in their secret cupboards. Their fascination with "types" (rare types) like myself plagues them with the mystery of why and how a living person can actually do things which may be only those dark images and acts secretly within them. I believe they can identify with these "dark images and acts" and loathe anything which reminds them of this dark side of themselves. The usual reaction is a flood of popular self-righteous condemnation but a willingness to, with friends and acquaintances, talk over and over again the appropriate bits of the case.[4]

Fictionalising figures like Nilsen and Bundy as inhuman monsters is one way of coming to terms with the dislocations which they generate in order to preserve the preferred contours of our own identity. Popular fiction, because of its very generic and formulaic nature, frequently acts as a frame of reassurance which allows us to safely engage in this exploratory process.[5] The process involves locating the criminal-outsiders within a tradition, and identifying their affinities with antecedents – which have in their turn been made part of a mythology. What we and our cultures are engaged in when we endeavour to contextualise serial murderers within this broader mythology is an exercise designed to allow them to be habitually perceived in the same unthreatening terms as is the case with domesticated mythic monsters like the werewolf or the vampire. It is a way of disarming threatening figures by dressing them up as circus or cinematic attractions. In other words, we are attempting to make them familiar and consumable. As Amy Taubin (1991) puts it, cinematic and other popular images of the serial killer are "a substitute and a shield for a situation so incomprehensible it must be disavowed". The argument, it bears noting, echoes Franco Moretti's (1983) account of the socio-cultural functions performed by nineteenth century horror fiction – that is that such literature takes up within itself determinate fears in order to transform them into other (unreal) fears, with the purpose of saving readers from having to face up to what might really frighten them.

The process can be briefly illustrated by drawing attention to some of the ways in which consumer culture has appropriated a mythical figure traditionally associated with obsessive, bloodthirsty and frequently sexually motivated serial killing – that of the vampire.

---

4 Nilsen cited in Masters (1986), pp 20-6.

5 The issues raised by this assertion are discussed in greater detail in Grixti (1989).

In the course of the twentieth century, vampires have been made the subject of a seemingly never-ending stream of both serious and comic representations in movies, books and television programmes. Dracula in particular has also been transmogrified into manifestations like that of the Count in "Sesame Street" (where the craving for blood has been replaced by a craving for counting numbers); Count Duckula and Quackula the Vampire Duck in children's television cartoon programmes; (in the United States) a "vitamin enriched vampire cereal" called Count Chocula as well as "vampire-shaped" ice-lollies; and (on Queensland's Gold Coast) a tourist attraction in the shape of "Dracula's Cabaret Restaurant" located (if one is to believe the publicity) "just a blood squirt from the Casino". Within a cultural context which engages in this type of transmutation, the exercise of designating serial killers as monsters can be read as little more than the first step towards making them less threatening by locating them within a multi-layered entertainment industry. We do not so much worry any more about being taken over and eaten by vampires and other monsters; our consumer oriented societies have taught us how to neutralise, eat, suck, consume *them* instead. We have, in other words, learned to transform ideas and images which might challenge our everyday securities and expectations into a means of actually reaffirming them.

The implications of this assertion call for systematic unpacking, and to this end, it will be worth focusing more directly on the fascination exerted by a selection of fictional serial killers which have captured the public imagination in recent years. The figures I have chosen to discuss here are of primary interest because of the manner in which they are cognitively and culturally located at a narrative intersection between fact and fiction. They can be shown to be based on real-life murderers but they are also fictional and appear in texts which project themselves as crime-thrillers – a genre which combines the literary conventions of realism (in its emphasis on verisimilitude, meticulous logic and hard-nosed accuracy of detail) and romance (in its focus on adventure and a hero's quest to overcome daunting odds and save or win a maiden in distress). The serial killers in question are Francis Dolarhyde, Jame Gumb and Dr Hannibal Lecter, the three villains who appear in the popular novels *Red Dragon* (1982) and *The Silence of the Lambs* (1988) by Thomas Harris, a former crime reporter for the Press Association turned bestselling novelist.

Harris approaches the task of fictionalising serial killers by compartmentalising the phenomenon into two distinct types. The first is the psychopathic loner who turns into a vicious beast largely as a consequence of serious gender identity problems which are usually attributed to (at worst) cruel or (at best) neglectful mothering. The second is the serial killer as enigmatic devil and modern embodiment of evil. The prototypes are not Harris's invention, but appear to derive from a popular tendency to stereotype murderers as either "making sense" because they are "obviously" psychotic and sexually mixed-up, or else, when the label doesn't appear to fit, as somehow being associated with a realm of supernatural evil. The tendency is well captured in Michaud and Aynesworth's (1989 p 7) account of popular reactions to Ted Bundy's crimes:

> Against a backdrop of mass insane homicide, Ted instead emerged as a variety of criminal genius, a nearly fictive character who wasn't stereotypically a loner or a loser – because he didn't *look* like one – and so must be something else: the incarnation of Evil.
>
> Even the closer profiles of him, some well researched, others based upon presumed personal knowledge of Ted, are suffused with a variety of awe at his works.

Harris's presentation of both the loner/loser and the demonic stereotypes of the serial killer proceeds in metaphoric terms which derive much of their force from identifiable mythical and literary associations. The killers who fit the first category are broadly associated with the mythic archetype of the werewolf. Thus, as if to highlight his conception as Americanised Mr Hyde, the psychopathic serial killer on the loose in *Red Dragon* is called Dolarhyde and he commits his grisly multiple murders at full moon. The notion of beasts beneath the skin is given a bizarre twist in *The Silence of the Lambs,* where the psychopath (referred to as both "Buffalo Bill" and "Mr Hide") covers himself with an outer skin sewn from the "hide" of his female victims.

Images involving murder and mayhem striking at full moon are of course deeply embedded in folklore, legends and horror tales about werewolves and similar mutants. But, as is the case with most legends, there are also psychological and historical foundations to the imagery. It has often been noted, for instance, that serial killers frequently attack in monthly cycles. When, in the early months of 1974, the bodies of Ted Bundy's victims were being discovered at monthly intervals, the police (bizarrely) started to nickname the next expected victim according to the month – as "Miss May" or "Miss June". Similarly, Bobby Joe Long, a serial rapist and murderer arrested in 1983, associated his compulsion to attack with lunar protomenstrual cycles, which he was claimed to experience because of a congenital dysfunction of the endocrine system. When he was eleven years old, Long had had more than six pounds of tissue surgically removed from his chest in an attempt to remedy what looked like the development of female breasts. He revealed to Joel Norris (1988) in prison:

> Even now I can always tell when it's full moon; I can't sit still; I have to pace; even the smallest thing sets me off. And I'm not the only one. All over the row, you can tell when it's the full moon, even if you can't see it from this hole. People start screaming and carrying on, you just know it's a full moon.

Harris's inspiration for Jame Gumb (or "Buffalo Bill") can be traced more specifically to Edward Gein, a serial murderer from Wisconsin who made news headlines in the 1950s, and who also inspired at least two other influential updatings of the Hyde-werewolf legend, those of Norman Bates in Robert Bloch's and Alfred Hitchcock's *Psycho,* and "Leatherface" in Tobe Hooper's *Texas Chainsaw Massacre.* One of the acts in which Gein had habitually engaged before his arrest in 1957 was that of prancing around his deserted farm on moonlit evenings, wearing the face, the hair, the breasts and the vaginas of his female victims. Two reasons were given for this: a secret desire for transsexual surgery for which he lacked both the courage and the funds, and a wish to recreate the form and presence of his dead mother. Other things which Gein had fashioned out of human skin and bone included a belt of nipples, a wastepaper basket, lamp shades, bowls made of skullcaps, and upholstery for his furniture.[6] One aspect of the *Gein* case which had been found most shocking at the time of its discovery was what a photo-spread article in *Life* magazine at the time termed "the chilling discrepancy between Ed Gein's public and private life" ("House of Horror Stuns the Nation", 43, 2 December 1957, pp 24-31). It was this discrepancy which became the focus of attention in Gein's fictionalisation as Norman Bates in Bloch's bestselling 1959 novel and in Hitchcock's influential 1960 film.[7] Three decades later (after a period of escalating emphasis on the details of gory violation in popular literature and cinema), while there are still allusions to this duality in Gein's reappearance as "Buffalo Bill", the metaphoric emphasis, as the nickname suggests, has shifted more forcefully to the image of the predatory beast lurking beneath a grotesquely transparent mask or extraneous skin of civilisation.

At the climax of *The Silence of the Lambs* (p 332), as "Buffalo Bill" prepares to close in on his quarry, he considers how it "would have been fun to hunt her for a long time – he'd never hunted one armed before". Hunting imagery pervades Harris's novels, and details of the killers' methods of stalking their victims are given full metaphoric force – a point highlighted in the change of title in the 1986 movie version of *Red Dragon* to *Manhunter.* It is worth stressing that the metaphor is not a simple literary conceit, in that serial killers have often been noted to think of themselves as hunters. The preparations undertaken by "Buffalo Bill" to "harvest the hide" of his victims (Harris 1988 pp 268, 288) echo Edward Gein's bizarrely

6 The most comprehensive account of the *Gein* case has been written by the judge who presided over his trial: Gollmar (1981). See also Levin and Fox (1985 pp 3-7); Newton (1988, p 140).

7 In his novel, Bloch has the popular press comparing the (fictional) *Bates* case "to the Gein affair up north, a few years back" and "work[ing] up a sweat over the 'house of horror'" (1989 pp 209-10). *Life* magazine's sensational report of the *Gein* case on 2 December 1957 had actually been headlined "House of Horror Stuns the Nation".

systematic methods of hanging his dead victims' bodies by the ankles as he prepared to put their skin to personal and household use – in much the same way as the deerhunters in his district harvested and used the hide of their prey. But within the generic conventions chosen by Harris as frame for his narrative, fact has been domesticated and made to perform clearly delineated formulaic functions – creating suspense, shocking through surprise or grotesque association, evoking a tense but ultimately reassuring atmosphere in which we know that though the villains may look daunting, it is the heroes who always win in the end. What Harris has achieved, in other words, is a cognitive and imaginative contextualisation of a disturbing social phenomenon within a recognisable and familiar mythic tradition. The medium, to modify an old cliché, has domesticated the message, in that, as Jean Baudrillard (1990) puts it:

> the truth of the mass media is that they function to neutralize the unique character of actual world events by replacing them with a multiple universe of mutually reinforcing and self-referential media. At the very limit, they become each other's reciprocal content – and this constitutes *the totalitarian "message" of the consumer society.*

The prevalence and uses of hunting imagery in the context of mass mediated entertainments like Harris's, as well as in a substantial number of popular movies which project "recreational killing" as ritualistic hunting,[8] derive from a complex series of assumptions about human nature which deserve further elaboration. We can perhaps get closer to the implications of these assumptions and to how such entertainments serve to reinforce them with specific hegemonic purposes by considering the second type of fictionalised serial killer highlighted in Harris's novels – that of the murderer as evil genius.

Dr Hannibal Lecter (or Hannibal the Cannibal) has become a celebrity in his own right, especially after the phenomenal financial and Oscar-winning success of the film version of *The Silence of the Lambs*, which among other things turned Anthony Hopkins into what Dame Edna Everage would call a megastar. A great deal of the fascination exerted by this particular character can be argued to derive from the fact that he has been presented in terms which deliberately and evocatively associate him with some of the most resilient archetypes of western mythology. As was illustrated in the 1992 Oscar Awards ceremony (in which the audience burst into laughter and applause when an actor muzzled and strait-jacketed to look like the movie version of Lecter was wheeled onto the stage), the process has served to transform the horrors and threats evoked by this figure into something reassuringly familiar and consumable.

Lecter is described in the two Harris best-sellers in which he appears in terms which associate him with preternatural evil: ever

8 Recent popular films which fit in this category include the two *Predator* features, which tell of extra-terrestrial hunters collecting human trophies, and *The Banker*.

present, ever powerful and incomprehensible. In this sense, he can be argued to owe his appeal to what John Lanchester (1991) has called "a kernel of wish-fulfilment". According to Lanchester, precisely because he baffles comprehension, the serial murderer stands to remind us that there is literally nothing of which human beings are not capable, and in this sense he "fulfils a general desire to believe that the human psyche is not fully explicable". Even the unknown, in other words, is amenable to appropriation as fodder for reassurance. It is worth stressing again that what Harris is doing here is simply applying and extending metaphors which have become the stock clichés of popular "true crime" accounts. Such clichés are highlighted, for instance, in the title of Ronald Markman and Dominick Bosco's *Alone with the Devil* (1991), which describes a forensic psychiatrist's encounters with figures like Richard Chase (the "Vampire of Sacramento") and other killers. The publishers of this particular volume have further stressed the cliché by printing two triangular dots over the letter "v" in the word "devil" as it appears on both the title page and in the running heads throughout the volume – forming what is presumably intended as a demonic pair of umlautish horns. The images surrounding Harris's Lecter also echo passages like the following about Ted Bundy:

> The *idea* of Ted Bundy preys on the mind. He is his own abstraction, a lethal absurdity masquerading as a man. Nevertheless, there were times at the prison when I was enveloped in the charisma of his madness. He fascinated me like a viper motionless in a crevice; a black, palpable malignancy. There is a cold, poisonous luster in Bundy's unguarded gaze. . . (Michaud & Aynesworth 1989 p 103)

The first time Dr Lecter's name is mentioned in *The Silence of the Lambs,* we are told that a "brief silence follows his name, always, in any civilized gathering" (p 4). The aura he exerts disconcerts those who approach him:

> Graham wanted to see Dr Lecter asleep. He wanted time to brace himself. If he felt Lecter's madness in his head, he had to contain it quickly, like a spill.
>
> To cover the sound of his footsteps, he followed an orderly pushing a linen cart. Dr Lecter is very difficult to slip up on. (1982 p 60)

As that last sentence indicates, Lecter (unlike the other characters) is frequently described in the present tense – a technique which is presumably intended to bring him closer to the reader's present reality, as well as suggesting a timeless quality:

> Dr Lecter's eyes are maroon and they reflect the light redly in tiny points.
>
> Lecter rose and walked over to his table. He is a small, lithe man. Very neat.
>
> Dr Lecter seldom holds his head upright. He tilts it as he asks a question, as though he were screwing an augur of curiosity into your face. (1982 pp 61, 63)

The tiny red spots in Lecter's maroon eyes, and the "augur of curiosity" are just some of the ways in which Harris borrows the imagery and associations of demonology in his construction of Lecter as modern day witch-doctor and fiend. At another point we are told of Lecter's gaze that it felt as if he "was looking through to the back of [the] skull" and that his "attention felt like a fly walking around in there" (1982 p 61). The monstrous dimensions of this latter-day lord of the flies are also underlined by the fact that he exhibits "the rarest form of polydactyl": he has six fingers on his left hand (1988 pp 14, 21). Echoes of Milton's Satan are also frequent. At one point in *Red Dragon* (p 172) we are told of Lecter as he watches his jailers "from the shadowed corner of his cell" that there was "a curious grace about him, even in restraints". Lecter's thoughts, we are told in *The Silence of the Lambs* (p 164), "were no more bound by fear or kindness than Milton's were by physics. He was free in his own head".[9] He has a "cultured voice [which] has a slight metallic rasp beneath it, possibly from disuse" (p 15). Before her first encounter with him, Clarice Starling, the young heroine of *The Silence of the Lambs,* is warned that if Lecter talks to her at all, he'll just be trying to find out about her: "It's the kind of curiosity that makes a snake look in a bird's nest" (p 6). As the image suggests, Harris's story of the encounter between the young trainee FBI agent and the incarcerated demon doctor has its imaginative origins in the legend of Eve's temptation by the serpent. That the association is deliberate is suggested by the novel's frequent references to the symbols of Christianity, and by the fact that Starling is also watched over by an all-wise (God the) father figure in the shape of the FBI chief who makes her his protegée.

In an angry response to a comment by Starling about the desirability of discovering why he's in jail and what happened to him, Lecter asserts:

> Nothing happened to me, Officer Starling. *I* happened. You can't reduce me to a set of influences. You've given up good and evil for behaviorism, Officer Starling. You've got everything in moral dignity pants – nothing is ever anybody's fault. Look at me, Officer Starling. Can you stand to say I'm evil? Am I evil, Officer Starling? (p 20)

"Dr Lecter is not crazy, in any common way we think of being crazy", comments the hero of *Red Dragon* (p 53), "He did some hideous things because he enjoyed them". Harris is clearly not parsimonious in his use of references to well-known villains in order to allow the connotations they bring to rub on to his character. Besides being something of a witch-doctor, a monster and a Jungian shadow, Lecter thus also has something of the charm and enigma of Iago as well as the epic grandeur of Milton's Satan. He is also a bit of a vampire. When Starling leaves him after their first encounter, "she suddenly

9 *The Silence of the Lambs*, p 164. Cf Satan's assertion in *Paradise Lost* that "the mind is its own place", and his espousal of evil with the valediction: "So farewell hope, and with hope farewell fear,/ Farewell remorse: all good to me is lost;/ Evil be thou my good" (John Milton, *Paradise Lost,* IV, 108).

felt empty, as though she had given blood" – and this while he lies on his cot "as remote from her as a stone crusader lying on a tomb" (1988 p 23). In the course of his meeting with the Senator whose daughter is in mortal danger, Lecter, we are told, "took a single sip of her pain and found it exquisite" (p 191). On another occasion, his appearance in his cell conjures up images of Klaus Kinski's haunting portrayal of the vampiric count in Herzog's 1979 *Nosferatu* :

> Dr Lecter wore the white asylum pajamas in his white cell. The only colors in the cell were his hair and eyes and his red mouth, in a face so long out of the sun it *leached* into the surrounding whiteness; his features seemed suspended above the collar of his shirt. [emphasis added] (pp 137-8)

Observing his "sleek dark head", Starling at another point has a vision of him as "a cemetery mink [which] lives down in a ribcage in the dry leaves of a heart" (p 215). Because of her association with Lecter, Starling herself also comes to be described by the popular press in the novel as the "Bride of Dracula" (p 346).

It is precisely because of the basis of his mystery and incomprehensibility in language and inter-textuality, that Lecter and the evil he represents have been so enthusiastically appropriated by contemporary consumer societies. "We have lived so long in foggy landscapes reflected in misty mirrors", as Wayne Booth (1961) put it, "that we have come to *like* fog". If this inter-textuality constructs the demon-doctor as incomprehensible, it also encourages us to think of him as somehow supernatural and infallible. As a psychiatrist who has embraced the abyss, he is projected as knowing more about the inner depths of those around him than they care to admit to themselves. "*He sees very clearly – he damn sure sees through me*", reflects Starling at one point in *The Silence of the Lambs*. "It's hard to accept", the passage continues, "that someone can understand you without wishing you well" (pp 281-2).

Lecter-Lucifer, then, tempts his young female antagonist with the fruit of the knowledge which will gain her recognition in a vicious world where law-enforcement officers perceive themselves in the same metaphoric terms as the criminals. "Because it's the plight that drives you", Lecter tells Starling in his letter at the end of the book, "seeing the plight, and the plight will not end, ever" (p 351). Like the predatory serial killers, the police and FBI agents in the novels frequently think of themselves as being engaged in a hunt and as fighting against time to catch the predator before *he* gets to *his* prey. "The reason you caught me", shouts Lecter to taunt the police officer who had mysteriously identified him as a killer and arrested him, "is that WE'RE JUST ALIKE" (p 65). Harris's novels and the films which followed them as a whole, in fact, project a world view which is basically an extended cliché – that of the vicious concrete jungle where life and death are visualised in predatory and counter-predatory terms, and where our last memory of peace is from the time before our birth. Within this world, everything appears to be interpreted in terms of the unquestioned dictates of the "survival of the fittest", so that even problem solving (as Harris's heroine comes to realise) is hunting. The good and the bad are here projected as two aspects of an evolved "basic reptile brain" – with the difference that the bad are viewed as a virus in the social organism, while the good prefer to think of themselves as a vaccine (Harris 1982 p 319).

Consciously or unconsciously, the thrust of fictionalisations like these is to appropriate and package the serial killer with the ideological purpose of making him confirm the widespread belief that we all carry a destructive beast beneath our skins, and that it is only the controls of civilised order which stop us from regressing to the nasty, brutish and short state which allegedly typified life in the state of nature. "You, too, Steve", Ted Bundy once told one of his interviewers, "could make a successful mass killer. I really think you have it in you!" (Michaud & Aynesworth 1989 p 13). Paradoxically, this parable has become reassuring. Seeing oneself as belonging on the right side of the law is usually also associated with having had the strength to control the beast within – a feat which we are encouraged to attribute to the internalisation of the rules, demands and prohibitions of the social order. We are also reassured about the rightness of the current state of civilised society, since the monsters repeatedly emerge as the exceptions which make the rule, the chinks and cracks in the social fabric which (though they might cause momentary concern and discomfort) are actually made to remind us of the structural soundness of the fabric itself. As an exercise in social cohesion and control, this could possibly be construed as an excusable, perhaps even a necessary process. The problem, however, is that its value-laden purposes continue to reinforce some very deeply ingrained but erroneous assumptions about the roots of human nature and about how our emotions and instincts relate to the (often poorly understood) historical patterns of evolution. The thrust of such assumptions is to perpetuate the puzzles about the sources of criminality and serial killing – since it is the puzzles themselves (and not their solutions) which fit most comfortably within the orientations and demands of consumerism. In this sense, these are perspectives which perpetuate self-deluding bafflement and incomprehension, and as such they can also be argued to propagate communal helplessness.

BIBLIOGRAPHY

Baudrillard, Jean, 1990, *Revenge of the Crystal: Selected Writings on the Modern Object and Its Destiny, 1968-1983*, Foss, Paul & Pefanis, Julian (eds & trs), Pluto Press, p 89.

Bloch, 1989, *Psycho,* Tor.

Bloom, Clive, 1988, "The House that Jack Built: Jack the Ripper, Legend and the Power of the Unknown", in Bloom, C, Docherty, B, Gibb, J & Shand, K (eds), *Ninteenth Century Suspense: From Poe to Conan Doyle*, Macmillan, pp 135-6.

Booth, Wayne C, 1961, *The Rhetoric of Fiction*, University of Chicago Press, p 372.

Caputi, Jane, 1988, *The Age of Sex Crime*, The Women's Press.

Caputi, Jane, 1990, "The New Founding Fathers: the Lore and Lure of the Serial Killer in Contemporary Culture", *Journal of American Culture,* 13, 1.

Davis, Don, 1991, *The Milwaukee Murders – Nightmare in Apartment 213: The True Story*, St Martin's Press. (First London publication in 1992 by Virgin Publishing Ltd)

Fishkin, Shelley Fisher, 1985, *From Fact to Fiction: Journalism and Imaginative Writing in America*, The Johns Hopkins Press.

Girard, René, 1977, *Violence and the Sacred*, Gregory, Patrick (tr), Johns Hopkins University Press, p 8.

Gollmar, Robert H, 1981, *Edward Gein: America's Most Bizarre Murderer*, Charles Hallberg and Co.

Grixti, 1989, *Terrors of Uncertainty: the Cultural Contexts of Horror Fiction*, Routledge.

Grixti, Joe, 1989, *Terrors of Uncertainty: the Cultural Contexts of Horror Fiction*, Routledge.

Harris, Thomas, 1982, *Red Dragon*, The Bodley Head.

Harris, Thomas, 1988, *The Silence of the Lambs*, Heinemann.

Jouve, Nicole Ward, 1986, *"The Streetcleaner": the Yorkshire Ripper Case on Trial*, Marion Boyars.

Lanchester, John, "Strangers", in *London Review of Books*, 11 July, pp 4-5.

Levin, Jack & Fox, James Alan, 1985, *Mass Murder: America's Growing Menace*, Plenum Press.

Linedecker, Clifford L, 1991, *Night Stalker*, St Martin's Paperbacks, p 19.

Markman, Ronald & Rosso, Dominick, 1991, *Alone with the Devil: Psychopathic Killings that Shocked the World*, Futura.

Masters, Brian, 1986, *Killing for Company: the Case of Dennis Nilsen*, Coronet.

Masters, Brian, 1993, *The Shrine of Jeffrey Dahmer*, Hodder and Stoughton

McGowen, Randall, 1989, "Punishing Violence, Sentencing Crime", in Armstrong, N & Tennenhouse, L (eds), *The Violence of Representation: Literature and the History of Violence*, Routledge, p 140.

Michaud, Stephen G & Aynesworth, Hugh (eds), 1989, *The Only Living Witness*, Signet.

Moretti, Franco, 1983, *Signs Taken for Wonders: Essays in the Sociology of Literary Forms*, Verso, p 105.

Morgan, Robin, 1989, *The Demon Lover: on the Sexuality of Terrorism*, Norton.

Newton, Michael, 1988, *Mass Murder: An Annotated Bibliography*, Garland, p x.

Norris, Joel, 1988, *Serial Killers: the Growing Menace*, Doubleday, p 137.

Smith, Joan, 1989, *Misogynies*, Faber.

Stevenson, Robert Louis, 1978, *The Strange Case of Dr Jekyll and Mr Hyde*, New American Library.

Taubin, Amy, 1991, "Killing Men", *Sight and Sound*, May edn, pp 14-18.

3

AT THE WORKFRONT

19

The "Public Figures'" Defence: A Subversion of Democracy The Lesson of *Rose v Koch*[1]

LLOYD DAVIES

> Coming from years of editing a South African newspaper, I believe that sound defamation law is one of the most important guarantees of civil liberties.
>
> *Donald Wood: Canberra Press Club address, March 1978*

Ever since the United States Supreme Court created the "public figures" defence in *New York Times v Sullivan* 367 US 254 (1963), there has been a clamour to introduce it into the Australian law of defamation. This clamour has usually come from the employees of media owners but latterly others have been persuaded to take up the cry.

The Australian Society of Authors has recently included the concept in its proposals for law reform. More surprisingly a Western Australian member of parliament has proposed a Private Member's Bill to embody it in the law of that State. This is surprising because the essence of the "public figures" defence is to make it possible for people to lie about politicians almost with impunity. Since self-destruction has reached epidemic proportions amongst Western Australian politicians the move may perhaps be described as a unique environmental phenomenon.

In 1985 there was a similar spate of agitation led by the *Financial Review* and prompted by two celebrated American cases

1 *Arnold Rose v Gerda Koch & Christian Research Inc* Minnesota S Ct, No 79 Hennepin County Appeal filed October 20 1967. This case is the subject of Professor Rose's book *Libel and Academic Freedom* (University of Minnesota Press and Oxford University Press). That book is the source of most of the material in this chapter not ascribed to other authorities.

involving General Westmoreland and Ariel Sharon as plaintiffs.[2] This agitation inspired an authoritative paper on the subject by TEF Hughes QC, which was presented at the 23rd Australian Legal Convention in Melbourne. He expressed his objection to the concept as follows:

> some restraint upon absolute liberty of action is necessarily implicit in the very concept of "freedom". Otherwise you have the law of the jungle under which no one is really free except the largest predators . . . freedom of speech requires recognition of clear rules which impose reasonable regulation upon what one person may say about another . . . no particular class person should be the subject of a special discriminatory rule. Equality before the law is always a desirable goal however difficult it may be to achieve. Therefore it is wrong to impose upon some people particular disadvantages formulated by reference to the position they occupy in the community.

An appalling example of the sort of wrong such a disadvantage can impose upon an honest man, in violation of both truth and freedom, is demonstrated by the Minnesotan case of *Rose v Koch*.

The struggle for racial equality is one of the major undertakings of our time. Its effect on both law and literature has been profound.

In 1937 the Carnegie Corporation commissioned Professor Gunnar Myrdal to make a comprehensive study of the problems of the Black in America. Professor Myrdal was at that time economic adviser to the Swedish Government and a member of the Swedish Senate. Making liberal use of Carnegie's massive resources, Myrdal enlisted 124 experts to garner resource material. With the aid of two assistants, Richard Sterner and Arnold Rose, he produced the massive 1500-page *An American Dilemna: The Negro Problem and Modern Democracy* (*Dilemna*). The fly-leaf should have been inscribed with an introductory quotation from *Julius Caesar*:

> Now let it work: mischief thou art afoot,
> Take thou what course thou wilt!
> (act III, scene ii)

Certainly, in this act of co-authorship, Arnold Rose took a decisive first step which led him to a tragic, if heroic, fate. Again, there is tragic irony in the fact that the Supreme Court of the United States, in upholding the Civil Rights cause, frustrated his personal struggle for the right to reputation, and arguably precipitated his early death.

Dilemna is reported to have been read and approved by at least some of the judges of the United States Supreme Court seeking guidance for their deliberations in *Smith v Allwright* 63 US 1325 (1944), the case in which the Supreme Court overruled the segregationist "white primary" device. *Allwright* was the first in a historic series of cases over the next 20 years in which the court

2 *Smith v Allwright* (1944) 63 S Ct 1325.

approved and promoted the claims of the American Black to full citizenship. In the leading segregation case of *Brown v Education Board of Topeka* 347 US 348 (1954), Chief Justice Earl Warren specifically referred to the authority of *Dilemna* in a footnote to his judgment.

It is an unusual accolade for a literary work to be incorporated in a judgment of a court of such high standing. It was not appreciated by the political Right in the American South. Senator James O Eastman of Mississippi denounced His Honour's dicta in the Senate on 26 May 1955:

> The Court cited and adopted generally and without reservation, as its leading authority on modern psychology, Myrdal's book *An American Dilemna*, when it said – and I quote from Chief Justice Warren's opinion: "... and see generally Myrdal, *An American Dilemna*, 1944..." This is purely Communist propaganda, which was cited by the Supreme Court, and on which the Chief Justice of the United States based a far-reaching decision looking to the destruction of our form of government. I have often wondered what was the source of pro-Communist influence in the Supreme Court.

1955 was a significant year in the Civil Rights movement. On 1 December 1955 the struggle was taken into the streets – by way of the public transport system in Montgomery, Alabama. On that day Mrs Rosa Parks, a black seamstress, weary from her day's work, was arrested for refusing to surrender her seat to a white passenger. To quote Martin Luther King (1959 p 42): "eventually the cup of endurance runs over, and the human personality cries out, 'I can take it no longer'".

It is a matter of history that Rosa Parks' sit-down strike prodded the struggle for Black Rights into a murderous conflict which kept the Supreme Court busy for years to come.

Meanwhile, on completion of his monumental project, Professor Myrdal returned to Europe, served as a minister in the Swedish cabinet and became Executive Secretary of the United Nations Economic Commission for Europe. His co-author, Arnold Rose, interrupted his academic career for military service and thereafter eventually achieved the status of Professor of Sociology at the University of Minnesota.

In 1958 Myrdal was invited to speak at the University of Minnesota and Rose was requested by the University to chair the meeting.

At the lecture a fanatically right-wing Christian fundamentalist, Gerda Koch, attacked Myrdal because he had employed Ralph Bunche as one of his advisers for *Dilemna*. According to Koch, Bunche was a Communist. A Nobel Prize winner, Bunche was at that time United Nations Undersecretary-General, but that did not deter Ms Koch – he had been described as a Communist in an obscure right-wing paper, and that was enough for her. As chairperson, Rose told her, politely, to sit down and shut up, and thought no more about it.

In 1962 Rose ran for a seat in the State Legislature. During the course of his campaign he was subjected to an anti-Communist campaign orchestrated by Gerda Koch. The electors were not impressed by Koch and elected Rose. The election of Rose goaded Koch into a fanatical frenzy. Making use of a mimeographed broadsheet entitled "Facts For Action – To Preserve Our Christian Heritage", and quoting Luke 2:7 (with additions: "There was no room for HIM at the inn. There is no room for HIM in the UN. The Supreme Court leaves no room for HIM in the schools!"), she proceeded to lambaste Professor Rose and the University of Minnesota with a series of scurrilous anti-Communist libels:

> BACKGROUND OF ARNOLD ROSE – UNIVERSITY OF MINNESOTA PROFESSOR... It is highly important for every voter to know for whom he is voting, especially since the Communists are working to conquer enemy countries through legislation... Arnold Rose assisted the socialist Gunnar Myrdal with the book THE AMERICAN DILEMNA... The American Dilemna was written in largest part by American Communist front members... Communist front members identified with Myrdal's AMERICAN DILEMNA contributed 272 different articles and portions of the book officially adopted by the Communist Party and the Supreme Court for its racial integration decision...
>
> ARNOLD ROSE MINNESOTA UNIVERSITY PROFESSOR AND STATE LEGISLATOR, COLLABORATES WITH COMMUNISTS AND COMMUNIST FRONTIERS... In our present calamity we find the American Government ... actually serving the Communist conspiracy within our nation... Former FBI agents say again and again that our universities are the breeding places for Communists. Communists are not made overnight but the socialist professors at our universities see to it that Communists are "made" in schools which once honoured God and produced "soldiers of Jesus Christ"... Refugees from Czechoslovakia say they were amazed when Czechoslovakia turned Communist how many professors turned out to be Communists!! And today we have a collaborator at the University who is at the same time a legislator at our state capitol!

The above passages are representative samples of Ms Koch's outpourings. Fellow fundamentalists soon joined her with similar contributions and a local sensationalist newspaper, the *Minneapolis Star*, took up their cause. Because the attacks had become widespread and were directed at the University as a whole, Rose considered that he had no option but to sue. The majority of the academic staff supported him and formed a "Faculty Legal Protection Committee" which within a month raised more than double the amount quoted by Rose's attorney to conduct the case. The suit was commenced on 30 January 1964. Rose and his attorney confidently expected to win.

Alas, back in Alabama a fuse had been lit which would eventually blow Rose and the defence committee out of court. Another committee calling itself "The Committee to Defend Martin Luther King and the Struggle for Freedom in the South" had inserted an advertisement in the *New York Times* protesting the brutal treatment of demonstrating students by "the police" of Alabama, and their trumping-up of a perjury charge against King. In their enthusiasm the committee had exaggerated the brutality of the police and some of their allegations were inaccurate. Police Commissioner Sullivan sued the *Times* and had little difficulty convincing the Alabama judiciary, both at first instance and on appeal, to award and sustain a judgment of $500,000 against the paper and the committee.[3] It was an outrageous decision both because of the excessive damages and because Sullivan had not been mentioned personally in the advertisement. No court of any integrity would have held that the words "the police" implied a reference to or an identification of Sullivan.

The decision was a blatant provocation to the reforming zeal of the United States Supreme Court, and the court rose to the challenge robustly. It found that the words "the police" did not identify Sullivan. It is a pity that it did not at that stage invoke the prudent dictum of William of Occam – *Pluralitas non est ponenda sine necessitate* – and leave it at that. The finding of non-identification was patently correct both in law and in fact, and was sufficient to defeat Commissioner Sullivan and uphold the Civil Rights cause.

However, the defendant committee had also argued that certain rulings of the trial judge had abridged freedom of speech and of the press guaranteed by the First and Fourteenth Amendments of the United States Constitution. The majority of the court accepted this argument and held (inter alia) that a public official can only recover damages "for a defamatory falsehood relating to official conduct" if he or she "proves that the statement was made with actual malice" (at 266).

The decision in *Sullivan*, which was handed down within two months of Rose filing his suit in the Minnesota District Court, caused some alarm in the Faculty Protection camp as Rose was at the time a State legislator and clearly a "public officer". Nonetheless, Rose and his attorney remained confident because the intemperance of Ms Koch's outpourings was clearly indicative of malice. This increased when Koch briefed an attorney who was as unrestrainably reactionary as his client, and who introduced anti-semitism into the trial, calling Rose a "Jewish Shylock".

The *Rose* case was strengthened as Koch continued her defamatory declamations through her news-sheet almost to the date of trial, giving Rose ever fresh grounds for his claim. A particular bonus was that these attacks continued after Rose retired from the

3 *New York Times v Sullivan* 367 US 254 (1963).

Legislature and ceased to be a "public officer" (thus – it was thought – freeing himself from the application of the *Sullivan* doctrine).

Rose conducted his case with moderation and reason, applied strictly to proven facts; Koch, with irrational fanaticism, relying upon a farrago of half-truth and outright falsehood, most of it irrelevant to the issue. An example of defence counsel's tactics was his misquoting from the transcript: "Defence Counsel – 'ROSE: I am a socialist. . .'"

The plaintiff's counsel interrupted to point out that the transcript clearly indicated that Rose had simply deposed to his academic discipline: he was "a sociologist".

Dirty tricks of this sort did not go down with the jury. Even more damning to the defence was the insistence on using the trial as a platform to attack the current Democratic administration, alleging that President Johnson and the late President John F Kennedy were joined with Rose in a vast Communist conspiracy.

The trial judge directed with some care on the Sullivan concept of the special position of "public officers", holding that Rose came within the category even though he was now no longer a legislator. Even if the allegation were untrue he would have to prove malice on the part of Koch. The judge proceeded to define malice by reading the Supreme Court's definition in *Sullivan*[4] and adding, by way of guidance, some examples from cases which had been decided in the Minnesota Supreme court. The jury found malice had been proved and awarded Rose $20,000.

Subsequent to the trial but pending the appeal – which Koch wasted no time in lodging – the United States Supreme Court decided four additional appeals, two on the question of the defamation of public officers: *Associated Press v Walker* 385 US 388 (1967) and *Curtis Publishing Company v Butts* 388 US 130 (1967); and two on the question of malice: *Time Inc v Hill* 385 US 374 (1967) and *Rosenblatt v Baer* 383 US 75 (1966). In the first two cases the ambit of the public officer defence was extended to include a class known as "public figure" – Butts was a defamed university director and Walker a retired army officer. In the last two cases the court insisted that the definition of malice be strictly adhered to.

The Minnesota Court of Appeal applied these cases – as it understood them – and, in October 1967, upheld Koch's appeal, remanding the case for a retrial. According to the Appeal Court, even after Rose retired from the Legislature he was still a "public figure" – being a university professor – and should be treated as such vis-à-vis the subsequent libels.

On the question of malice the trial judge's direction was wrong because some of the directions he gave, in the hope of being helpful to the jury on the definition of malice, were not on all fours with the definition given in *Sullivan* and may have misled the jury.

4 "That is, with knowledge that it was false or with reckless disregard of whether it was false or not" (at 266).

"Malice," the court held, "is not proved merely by the existence of ill will or intent to cause harm. What must be proved is an intent to cause harm through falsehood" (Rose 1968, p 225). Rose considered that such a burden of proof was logically and psychologically unprovable and calculated he had more chance of success through an appeal to the United States Supreme Court than through enduring three weeks' retrial, most of which time would be taken up by Ms Koch trying to prove that he was part of a Communist conspiracy along with Presidents Johnson and Kennedy and the rest of the United States establishment. It was at least possible that the United States Supreme Court might use his hard case as a means of revoking some of the bad law it had created in *Sullivan*.

While waiting for his own appeal to be heard, Rose wrote a book in which he summarized the case and examined the phenomenon of right-wing extremism in the United States and the potential for mischief now open to it.

On 2 January 1968, before his appeal could be heard, Arnold Rose collapsed and died, at the age of 49. His book *Libel and Academic Freedom – A Lawsuit Against Political Extremists* was published posthumously by the University of Minnesota Press. The following extracts from Rose's Epilogue are sufficient comment upon the folly of the judge-made "public figures" defence:

> If the United States Supreme Court has not yet seen the danger it has created for the nation, it is not likely to be brought to recognition of that danger by the now-academic case of *Rose v Koch*. It will take a powerful and dramatic case in which an incumbent senator or governor is defeated by an unscrupulous challenger who invents falsehoods to undermine the personal reputation of that senator or governor, or an equally powerful and dramatic case in which a famous scientist is denied funds for research because of false charges . . .
>
> It remains to be seen what effect [the decision] will have on Minnesota particularly . . . Will the Minneapolis Star and other newspapers (including Facts for Action) consider they have unlimited license to publish any falsehoods their reporters or editorial writers might present, deliberately or inadvertently, about any public figure? Will the many decent and responsible citizens of Minnesota . . . now be disillusioned with the law? The alternative to a libel suit – as it was before libel suits were possible under European law – is some sort of violent or emotional behaviour destructive of social order. Only time will tell if these events will take place.

BIBLIOGRAPHY

King, Martin Luther, 1959, *Stride Toward Freedom*, London, Gollancz.

Myrdal, G, Sterner, R and Rose, A, 1944, *An American Dilemna: The Negro Problem and Modern Democracy*, New York, Harper, 1944.

Rose, A, 1968, *Libel and Academic Freedom – A Lawsuit Against Political Extremists*, University of Minnesota Press.

20

The Biter Bit: Literary Criticism and the Law of Defamation

PETER HEEREY

One of Australia's very greatest jurists was Sir Frederick Jordan who was Chief Justice of New South Wales from 1934 to 1949. His judgments were not only celebrated for their scholarship and lucid expression but were usually presented in striking and memorable language which argued the underlying common-sense logic of the law and its relevance to the needs of society. His judgment in *Gardiner v John Fairfax & Sons Pty Ltd* (1942) 42 SR (NSW) 171 is a classic statement of the law of the defence of fair comment in the context of literary or artistic criticism. The following passage (at 174-5) is a little lengthy but illustrates better than anything I can say why Sir Frederick held the pre-eminence that he did:

> It is essential that the defamatory matter sought to be defended as comment should be statements of opinion only. Where, however, the matter complained of is, on the face of it, a criticism of a published work or public performance, the statements are prima facie comments unless they are seen to be statements of fact or are proved to be such.
>
> The test whether comment is capable of being regarded as unfair is not whether reasonable men might disagree with it, but whether they might reasonably regard the opinion as one that no fair-minded man could have formed or expressed. The opinion must, of course, be germain to the subject matter criticised. Thus, if a critic denounced a book for its indecency it would not be beyond the bounds of fair comment if he also denounced the author for publishing such a book. But dislike of an artist's style would not justify an attack upon his morals or his manners. Whistler obtained his verdict, not because Ruskin had accused him of "flinging a pot of paint in the public's face," but because he was injudicious enough to call him a coxcomb into the bargain, and to suggest that he was guilty of wilful imposture.
>
> To establish malice, it is necessary to adduce evidence that the comment was designed to serve some other purpose than that of expressing the commentator's real opinion, for example, that of satisfying a private grudge against the person attacked. But this evidence is not supplied by the mere fact that the defendant has

> expressed himself in ironical, bitter or even extravagant language. A critic is entitled to dip his pen in gall for the purpose of legitimate criticism; and no one need be mealy-mouthed in denouncing what he regards as twaddle, daub or discord.
>
> English literature would be the poorer if Macaulay had not been stirred to wrath by the verses of Mr Robert Montgomery.
>
> In a particular case, however, the language used may itself disclose an ulterior purpose in the criticism, or may serve to support independent evidence of malice or unfairness. But ridicule alone is not sufficient. A striking example of this is supplied by the recent case of *Bergman v Macadam* (1941) 191 LT Jo 131 in which a sporting critic, in order to express the opinion that a professional boxer was past his [job of] work, said, in a broadcast, "Speaking of old men, why, just as soon as he has drawn his old age pension next Thursday, Kid Berg will totter along to Earls Court and fight Eric Boon. . . After that fight Berg is almost certain to start thinking of a better way of earning his living." In an action by Bergman for slander, malice having been negatived, the judge awarded the plaintiff £500 damages on the footing that the comment was unfair. The Court of Appeal set the verdict aside and entered judgment for the defendant, holding that the comment was not only not malicious but not unfair, notwithstanding that it was couched in language of exaggerated jocosity which seemed to characterise criticism of boxing contests.

Thomas Babington Macaulay, politician and civil servant, poet, essayist and historian, was one of the great masters of English prose. He has a double relevance to this chapter's topic. As well as providing the paradigm of libel-proof critical demolition, he played a major part in the drafting of the Indian Penal Code, which included provisions on defamation that found their way into the Criminal Code of Queensland and from there to statutory provisions in Western Australia and Tasmania.

Robert Montgomery was a popular poet in the heroic mould who wrote two epics, "The Omnipresence of the Deity", which ran to 11 editions, and "Satan: A Poem". Macaulay reviewed those works in the April 1830 issue of the Edinburgh Review. The criticism has survived long after the works which provoked it, and their author, have sunk into merciful obscurity. Macaulay opened by attacking the then fashionable means by which publishers promoted worthless authors:

> Devices which in the lowest trades are considered as disreputable are adopted without scruple, and improved upon with a despicable ingenuity, by people engaged in a pursuit which never was and never will be considered as a mere trade by any man of honour and virtue. . . We expect some reserve, some decent pride, in our hatter and our bootmaker. But no artifice by which notoriety can be obtained is thought too abject for a man of letters.

After commenting that "the praise is laid on thick for simple minded people", Macaulay observed that:

> We too often see a writer attempting to obtain literary fame as Shakespeare's usurper obtains sovereignty. The publisher plays Buckingham to the author's Richard. Some few creatures of the

> conspiracy are dexterously disposed here and there in the crowd. It is the business of these hirelings to throw up their caps, and clap their hands, and utter their *vivas*. The rabble at first stare and wonder, and at last join in shouting for shouting's sake; and thus a crown is placed on a head which has no right to it, by the huzzas of a few servile dependants.
>
> The opinion of the great body of the reading public is very materially influenced even by the unsupported assertions of those who assume a right to criticise.

Zeroing in on his target, Macaulay says:

> We have no enmity to Mr Robert Montgomery. We know nothing whatever about him except what we have learnt from his books, and from the portrait prefixed to one of them, in which he appears to be doing his very best to look like a man of genius and sensibility, though with less success than his strenuous exertions deserve. We select him, because his works have received more enthusiastic praise, and deserve more unmixed contempt, than any which, as far as our knowledge extends, have appeared within the last three or four years. His writing bears the same relation to poetry which a Turkey carpet bears to a picture. There are colours in the Turkey carpet out of which a picture might be made. There are words in Mr Montgomery's writing which, when disposed in certain orders and combinations, have made, and will again make, good poetry. But, as they now stand, they seem to be put together on principle in such a manner as to give no image of anything "in the heavens above, or in the earth beneath or in the waters under the earth".

The work which gave rise to *Gardiner v John Fairfax & Son Pty Ltd* was, to put it mildly, undistinguished. It was a detective story called "The Scarlet Swirl" written under the nom de plume "Mythrilla" and privately published by the author. Less than half a dozen copies were sold, but it attracted the idle talents of the *Sydney Morning Herald* reviewer. One of the passages complained of was:

> And when Braithwaite is not being impressive as leading detective ("he drew himself up, walked across the room to the victim, stooped down, examined him 'He's dead', he said, significantly and solemnly") the lovely Jean is making good resolutions that they could not meet again.

It had been earnestly argued on behalf of the plaintiff that this was a statement of fact and not comment and was inaccurate because it meant, literally, that the book was entirely or mainly taken up with descriptions of the matters referred to. Sir Frederick remarked (at 176):

> He is evidently using clumsily a form of expression which was used effectively by the person who said, slanderously, of Jebb that he devoted such time as he could spare from the neglect of his duties to the adornment of his person. The way of a critic would be thorny indeed if clumsiness of expression were treated as evidence of unfairness.

The only Jebbs listed in the *Dictionary of National Biography* (Smith, 1990) are Irish clerics, judges, prison reformers and physicians, all of whose extensive good works suggest they could not have provoked the attack recorded by Sir Frederick Jordan. Our research continues.

It is time for a little black letter law. We have been looking at the defence of fair comment, but of course no question of defence arises unless a plaintiff can show that what was published of him or her was defamatory, that is to say it imputes some condition or conduct which would damage the standing and reputation of the plaintiff in the eyes of members of the community generally. This need not be the assertion of a moral failing. It is defamatory to say of somebody that he or she is incompetent. However, as we shall see, what often provokes a plaintiff's claim for defamation in a critical setting is an assertion that there has been not just incompetence but a form of literary dishonesty.

In *Porter v Mercury Newspapers* [1964] Tas SR 279 the famous Australian writer Hal Porter complained of a review which he said imputed that he inserted "Anglo-Saxon" words in his autobiography *The Watcher on the Cast Iron Balcony* not with any concept of literary necessity in mind but in order to promote publicity by attracting the attention of the censor. In *O'Shaughnessy v Mirror Newspapers* (1970) 125 CLR 166 the actor and director Peter O'Shaughnessy complained that a review in *The Australian* of his production of *Othello* meant that the plaintiff, having at his disposal as good a group of players as Australia could produce, wasted their talents in a dishonest production devoted to enhancing his own role at the expense of the rest of the cast.

It can also be the critic who complains, as in *Turner v Metro Goldwyn Mayer* [1950] 1 All ER 449 where a prominent film critic complained of a letter from MGM to her employer, the BBC, complaining that she was "completely out of touch with the tastes and entertainment requirements of the picture going millions".

Such a mild reproach can be contrasted with what was said of the plaintiff in *Cornwell v Myskow* [1987] 1 WLR 630. In a column in the *Sunday People* headed "Wally of the Week" the following blast was delivered:

> Actress Charlotte Cornwell made a proper pratt of herself in Central's crude new catastrophe. No Excuses. And then she foolishly prattled about it pompously in public.
>
> This repellent rubbish about a clapped-out rock singer is without doubt the worst I have ever clapped eyes on. It bears no relation to rock and roll today – all concerned must have been living down a sewer for the last decade – or indeed to human beings.
>
> As a middle-aged star, all Miss Cornwell has going for her is her age. She can't sing, her bum is too big and she has the sort of stage presence that jams lavatories.
>
> Worse, she belongs to that arrogant and self-deluded school of acting which believes that if you leave off your make-up (how brave, how real) and SHOUT A LOT it's great acting. It's ART. For a start, dear, you look just as ugly with make-up, so forget that. And as for

ART? In the short sharp words of the series, there is just one reply. It rhymes.[1]

The imputations, that is to say what are said to be the defamatory meanings arising from the publication, were drafted by the plaintiff's counsel in the following elegant terms:

(i) that the plaintiff had taken part in a production so repellently filthy that he and the others taking part in it might have been living down a sewer,

(ii) that the plaintiff was a middle-aged failure as an actress and singer, with a stage presence that drove the audience to the lavatories,

(iii) that the plaintiff was a foolish, ugly woman whose pretensions at acting in an artistic manner were utterly bogus and unjustified,

(iv) that the plaintiff lacked any ability whatsoever as an actress and was guilty of arrogant self-delusion in presenting herself as an actress to the public.

The plaintiff was awarded £10,000 damages by the jury but the defendant's appeal succeeded on the ground of wrongful admission of evidence. It is worth noting that according to the law report, counsel for the defendant on the appeal, Mr Michael Beloff QC, "suggested that the courts were not the place to deal with someone's sense of grievance that another person had been rude in print about their bottom".

Our defamation law imposes what a very experienced judge in the field has called a "low threshold" of defamation. Thus it has been held defamatory to say of the leader of a political party that he has lost the confidence of his party (*John Fairfax & Sons Ltd v Punch* (1980) 31 ALR 624). Therefore if the case is sufficiently serious to warrant getting to court at all, the chances are that attention will be mainly concerned with whether the defendant has made out a defence, and particularly the defence of fair comment.

The defence of fair comment is important in this context because of the limitations which the common law places on the other two main defences of general application, justification and qualified privilege. To make out a defence of justification the defendant has to prove by properly admissible evidence the substantial truth of every defamatory meaning arising from the publication complained of. The defence of qualified privilege does not require the defendant to establish the truth of what was said, but it is only available if the publication was made on what the law considers a privileged occasion. It is now well established, at least since *Blackskaw v Lord* [1984] QB 1 and *Morosi v Mirror Newspapers* [1977] 2 NSWLR 749, that the mere fact of publication in the general media of matters of public interest is not in itself sufficient to constitute a privileged occasion.

1 See [1987] 1 WLR at 603.

A leading English text (*Duncan & Neill on Defamation*, 2nd edn, p 57) summarises the elements of the defence of fair comment as follows:

(a) The comment must be on a matter of public interest,
(b) The comment must be based on fact,
(c) The comment, though it can consist of or include inferences of fact, must be recognisable as comment,
(d) The comment must satisfy the following objective test: Could any fair minded man honestly express that opinion on the proved facts,
(e) Even though the comment satisfies the objective test the defence can be defeated if the plaintiff proves the defendant was actuated by malice.

The first requirement will usually not present any difficulty since the courts have held clearly that there is a public interest involved in the criticism of literary and artistic works presented to the public.

The second requirement, that the comment must be based on fact, is the legal equivalent of the old journalistic aphorism that "comment is free but facts are sacred". The rationale is that if a defendant sets out true facts and then his comment on those facts, then as long as the facts are truly stated, the reader is equally able to make up his own mind as to whether he agrees or not with the defendant's comment. However, it has been recognised that it is unrealistic to expect commentators on matters of public interest to express themselves strictly in a fact-plus-comment formula. Therefore it is sufficient if the facts, although not stated in the article, are sufficiently indicated to the reader or if they are matters of public notoriety. In the case of literary or artistic criticism of course there is the twist that the more damaging the criticism, the less likely it is that the reader will buy the book or see the play or film, with the consequence that the reader will never be in possession of the facts and able to form his own opinion. However that theoretical difficulty has not troubled the courts much.

The importance of factual accuracy was demonstrated recently by the celebrated *Blue Angel* case in Sydney where a restaurant recovered $100,000 damages. A vital issue was the question of the lobster. The defendant argued that the review did not say that the lobster was broiled for 45 minutes, only that the reviewer had waited for 45 minutes to be served. It seems the jury disagreed.

The third requirement is often of critical importance because if a statement is held to be a fact, as distinct from comment, then it has to be proved to be true, and so proved by means of admissible evidence. A comment is something "which is or can reasonably be inferred to be a deduction, inference, conclusion, criticism, judgment, remark or observation" (*Clarke v Norton* [1910] VLR 494 at 499 per Cussen J). But the law is not so ritualistic as to require a defendant to preface every comment by some formula such as "in my opinion" or "it seems to me that". A comment can take the form of fact provided it is recognisable in the context as an inference from the facts on which the comment is based (*Kingsley v Foot* [1952] AC 345 at 356-357). It was on this ground that the appeal succeeded in *O'Shaughnessy v Mirror Newspapers*. The High Court held that what at first blush might have seemed like an assertion of fact (that it was a dishonest production) was capable of being regarded by the jury as comment, and that the trial judge was wrong in withdrawing that issue from the jury.

The fourth requirement has recently become a controversial issue in the law of defamation. The defence we are considering is called fair comment, but that is a somewhat misleading label. The defendant may make out the defence even though the comment is by ordinary standards unfair, in the sense that it might be prejudiced, bigoted or unreasonable. The test usually referred to was formulated by Lord Esher MR in *Merivale v Carson* (1887) 20 QBD 275 at 281 and is in these terms, "would any fair man, however prejudiced he may be, however exaggerated or obstinate his views, have said that which this criticism has said". But does the emphasis on honesty, as distinct from reasonableness, mean that a defendant can only succeed if he establishes that he in fact held the opinion expressed in the comment? This question becomes important when the defendant is publishing a comment of somebody else, for example a letter to the editor or a review contributed by someone not employed by the publisher of a newspaper. In *Cherneskey v Armadale Publishers Ltd* (1978) 90 DLR (3d) 321 a majority of the Supreme Court of Canada held that the defendant has to satisfy two tests: the statement must be objectively a fair comment which could be made on the facts in the sense abovementioned, and it must in fact have been the real opinion of the defendant. The question arose in this way. A newspaper published a letter which accused the plaintiff of holding racist views. The writers of the letter were not called as witnesses and there was no evidence as to whether or not the views expressed in the letter were the honest views of the writers. The defendants, the publisher of the newspaper, did give evidence that the letter did not represent the editor's view or the views of the newspaper. The majority of the Supreme Court held that the defence of fair comment failed because there was no proof of the honest belief of the writers and honest belief by the defendants themselves had been denied.

This decision caused a major controversy and provoked some legislative changes in parts of Canada. The reason is not hard to see. If a newspaper were to publish conflicting views by writers of letters to the editor or other commentators, the publisher could not possibly hold an honest belief in all the views expressed. Therefore the defence of fair comment would not be available and one of the vital functions of a free press, that of providing a forum for public debate, would be gravely impaired. The decision in *Cherneskey's* case was criticised in the 2nd Edition of *Duncan & Neill on Defamation* (1983) and in *Hawke v Tamworth Newspaper* [1983] 1 NSWLR 699 (see also (1985)

59 ALJ 371). Recently the English Court of Appeal in *Telnikoff v Matusevitch* [1991] 1 QB 102 has in my respectful opinion comprehensively demolished the *Cherneskey* heresy. The court (at 119) expressly adopted as correct the statement of the law from Duncan & Neill (1983) to which I have already referred.

The fifth requirement also bears on the question of the state of mind of the defendant, but with this important difference. If the defence of fair comment is made out it will only be defeated if the plaintiff shows that the defendant was actuated by malice. Thus it is up to the defendant to establish the honesty of his state of mind. Malice in this context is a technical concept which includes what would ordinarily be considered as malice, that is to say spite or vindictiveness, but also extends to what might be called wrongful or improper motives or a lack of honest belief in the view expressed or, to use the example given by Sir Frederick Jordan, the gratification of a private grudge.

Finally, I need to mention a continuing controversy affecting the law of fair comment where the comment imputes dishonourable conduct to the plaintiff. There are, on the analysis of the cases by Duncan & Neill (p 67), three possible views:

(a) the defence of fair comment does not apply at all. Suggestions of dishonourable conduct have to be justified by showing they are correct inferences from primary fact, that is by a defence of justification;

(b) the defendant has to show that the comment was a reasonable inference from the facts;

(c) the ordinary test of fair comment applies, viz could any fair minded person express that opinion on the proved facts.

There are authorities which support each view, but I think the third is to be preferred. This conclusion is supported by a remark of the High Court in *O'Shaughnessy* where their Honours said (at 174):

> To safeguard ourselves from too broad a generalisation we would add that it is not our view that an imputation of dishonesty is always an assertion of fact. It is part of the freedom allowed by the common law to those who comment upon matters of public interest that facts truly stated can be used as the basis for an imputation of corruption or dishonesty on the part of the person involved.

It is difficult to see the logic behind the contrary views. Dishonesty is to be deplored and an imputation of it is plainly defamatory, but there are other human failings just as bad or even worse.

In conclusion I think that the literary or artistic critic is not too badly restricted by the law of defamation. As Duncan & Neill say (p 69), almost any comment is defendable as fair comment provided the contents of the work criticised is not misrepresented and no personal attack is made on the plaintiff. It remains to be seen however whether the review of a recent work in England will provoke a libel action. The book in question was *Memoirs of a Libel Lawyer* by solicitor Peter Carter-Ruck and it was reviewed in *The Spectator* by Ian Hislop, who commented:

> When journalists read a particularly dull piece about a potentially interesting subject they tend to conclude that it has been "lawyered", ie that everything of interest has been removed for legal reasons. This is a whole book that has been "lawyered" by its author and the result is that all Carter-Ruck's clients are praised extravagantly and so are all the solicitors, barristers and judges he has ever come across.

Is it defamatory to say of a libel lawyer that he has written a book which is dull because it is not defamatory?

BIBLIOGRAPHY

Smith, G (ed), 1990, *Dictionary of National Biography*, Oxford University Press.

Duncan & Neill, 1983, *Duncan & Neill on Defamation* 2nd Edition, Butterworths, London.

21

Rules of Evidence: Journalistic Documentary, Docudrama and the Law

MAURIE SCOTT

The germ of the idea for this chapter arose during discussions at the University of Wollongong concerning approaches to the framing and presentation of an undergraduate subject in Law and Literature studies in the Law Department program.[1] In considering the possible subject matter, its treatment, and appropriate texts, especially film and television texts, that would serve the various connections we intended to indicate between law and literature, I recalled the words of Leslie Woodhead, British documentary/docudrama film-maker who stated in The Guardian Lecture (1979 p 12) that his aim in his work, "getting it right after the event", had the ideal of "journalistic integrity [measured] against standards of evidence as they might be understood in a court of law".

Now, such an assertion of such an article of professional faith as this would seem to be quite brave – some might say foolhardy or naive – considering the complexities, the realities, the practicalities that have to be dealt with in the practice of law. Further, along with the pragmatics that have to be taken into account, Woodhead's comment generates several conceptual problematics applicable to the genres in which he works as well as to the comparison with the law. These will be noted below, but the analogy it asserts raises some interesting issues concerning the principles and practices of certain kinds of small-screen product – from news, through current affairs and investigative journalism, to documentary and docudrama – and the principles and practices involved in applying rules of evidence in cases in law.

The analogies that come to mind, prompted by Woodhead, are several and obvious but, at this point, it has to be admitted that, for this writer, they have been conditioned and fed by mass-media

1 With Mr Robin Handley: Perspectives on Law – English.

representations, rather than experience or study of the law. My legal education up to now has been at the feet of Rumpole and Perry Mason, along with valuable inputs from "LA Law", "People's Court" and dozens of cinematic courtroom dramas. Consequently, there is a tendency to make the obvious and convenient connections in the formation of analogies, to read for and with the easy comparisons and so compound the popular perceptions reflected in and asserted by the various media. Even so, on the most basic level – albeit an arguably simplistic one – there *are* connections: for example, the television genres under consideration are posited on the discovery, gathering, arrangement and presentation of data, of information, with the most interesting being those programs that use these data to illustrate or substantiate a proposition or premise, or actually build up a "case" which is supported by the data, even to the extent of (purported) "proof". To the layperson, current affairs, documentaries and docudramas, especially those based on investigative journalism, frequently demonstrate correspondences between the principles, practices and even procedures employed by their producers, and those of the legal process.

It is not just that the analogies apply in a metaphorical sense, nor that they remain as a layperson's exotic view of courts, trials, litigation, etc: Woodhead is not alone in his recourse to the notion of rules of evidence as they apply in law, for it is part of the rhetoric and professed ethos of the newsroom and the current affairs reporting team – if not always their actual practice. It must be pointed out, however, that such expressions of scrupulous professional practice have pragmatic as well as ethical implications. On one hand, the psychological gratification, the pleasure afforded to the audience by the logical conclusion or closure when a proposition is substantiated by the "evidence" is a factor in the viewer appeal of certain of these programs. On the other, and more apposite, the very positions of these programs as published, public documents render themselves subject to the tests of law – as in the obvious potential for libel and defamation. So, the statements of scruple are self-protective as well as idealistic: documentation as substantiation of the on-screen case is vital for this as well as proper evidential reasons.

In examining how well the analogy holds between the methodologies of the subject television programs and the processes of the law – and therefore the validity or otherwise of the claims made by Woodhead and others – this chapter will cite several examples of the rules of evidence and discuss the extent to which they are applied or embodied in the television texts, "Citizen Packer" (Paul Barry), "Police Crop" (Ken Cameron) and a segment from "Hinch". Further, the chapter will deal briefly with an issue that arises consistently from the interrelationships between the law and the media, especially television: that is, the way in which analogous procedures or, as some would have it, *shared* principles and methodologies, have led to the phenomenon of "trial by television," with instances ranging from

Chris Masters' type of investigative journalism on "Four Corners" to "The Investigators" – and not forgetting the "Hinch" style of tabloid "infotainment".

Before moving on to these matters, however, there are several points that need to be raised to clarify the concepts and principles operating in the television genres involved. The texts chosen as examples are drawn from the documentary (albeit in a current affairs series), the documentary drama and the current affairs magazine, each based on investigative journalism. They have as a popularly perceived common denominator the notion of the "factual", of "truth" that can be established, illustrated and demonstrated evidentially. In the systems of meaning generated by such texts and the ideologies inscribed in them, the *denotative* and *literal* is privileged over the *connotative* and *metaphorical* – at least in theory. This common denominator is shared by the news and current affairs programs generally, all of which purport to construct their essential semantic paradigms on "telling it like it is", on the notion of "actuality", of a non-distorting "mirror with a memory",[2] "held up to nature". In each case, the representations of the "real" the "actual" are subject to procedures of *authentication* and *verification*. And, along with these "truth claims" (Kuehl 1981) are the claims of these genres to neutrality and objectivity in their presentations. Such evidence, then, might well be thought to be unimpeachable. It's the "it must be true: Brian told me so" syndrome. Further, it should be noted that all this has been institutionalised thoroughly with the force and the power of the media institution as a factor in the acceptance of the verity of representations and assertions.

Of course, these claims are part of the mythology of these genres and just do not stand up to scrutiny. There is no need to go into detail about the ways in which the nature of television as a mass medium and the interventions of the makers of programs militate against any claims to "absolute truth", to the unimpeachable status of its forms of evidence ("real" or "testimonial") and to unambiguous objectivity. The whole process of mediation in this and other media and forms places the ultimate "received" message often at many removes from its source in actual events, with opportunity for error, distortion and misrepresentation at every point, especially in labour-intensive, co-operative and corporate media such as television with inputs from many personnel in the production process. However, while all this challenges the validity of the "truth claims" of the medium and these genres, it also involves the tacit imprecation for all concerned to be aware of the inevitable subjectivities and the impact of their interventions so that they can be avoided *or* shown for what they are *or*, in some cases, exploited. Leslie Woodhead says as much in announcing his modus operandi as a television documentary drama practitioner:

2 Michael Argyle, *Non-Verbal Communication* Film.

> To a degree, the demythologising of factual television is already well established. The delusion of absolute objectivity is almost laid to rest, and television itself has in a small way begun the job of owning up about documentary and news to point out the inescapable subjective content in every camera movement and edit. The contrivances of the documentary maker have been rumbled and there's a growing public awareness (of) the manipulative presence of the director . . . (Woodhead 1979 p 13)

And, while the voice-over reporter of the "Hinch" segment insists that "the camera does not lie",[3] it does not, cannot, according to Julian Petley, be relied on to tell the whole truth. He goes on to say that "It is the mind behind the camera which matters" having previously made the equally obvious, if nonetheless valid comment that "newsreels, documentary footage, etcetera, are by no means value free or ideologically neutral". Indeed, all contributors to the production process bring their attitudinal, emotional and ideological "baggage" to the work, which may or may not translate into overt, covert or tacit bias, but will be a factor to be taken into account.

Added to this is the concept inscribed in the very term "documentary" – the root word here is *docere,* pertaining to *teaching* or *preaching* – the *didactic* mode. The notion of documentary as indicating or denoting the *evidential,* the substantiation of a premise by various modes and forms of documentation is a later, modern usage, and now the common and accepted one. However, traces of the original meaning remain in the sense that, connotatively, the word "documentation" brings with it the notion of recourse to established authority which can authenticate properly the items of data, echoing power relations based on an educated elite which possesses the information and documentation and the subordinate group which has not.

Even if you do not buy that diluted pseudo-Marxist idea, the didactic mode remains a factor in the subject television genres and is well illustrated in the examples to be cited, for the decision by the producers that the public *needs* to know, to be informed, always includes the contingent message that it needs to know *in a certain way*. Consider the "Shock! Horror! Shame!" tone of the "Hinch" exposé, the subtext of suppressed, latent ethnophobia in "Police Crop" (along with the frisson generated by the Police/Mafia conspiracy) and the controlled but firm assertion of the "tall poppy" syndrome in "Citizen Packer", compounded by the resonances of the inter-textual connections with *Citizen Kane.* In each of these cases, the standpoint of the program-makers is clearly articulated.

Again, the positioning of the audience in relation to the subject material is obviously a function of the position taken by the reporter/documentarist et al, in relation to the topic in hand, but frequently this is notional and partial. Such manipulation is always a potentiality, of course, and adept producers/journalists can

3 "Docudrama: truth or fiction?" in *The Illustrated History of the Cinema* p 1257.

orchestrate their treatment toward intended viewer responses. But viewers should not be assumed to be passive receptors, blank sheets to be imprinted with the intended message: they may well choose to comply or to adopt a more active "reading position" – for instance, resistant or complicit readings of the televisual texts presented. The assumption that we are a population of "videots" can be attacked from both empirical and theoretical standpoints – though it is easier to sustain the charge that we are becoming a population of peeping toms or voyeurs via television in general and these subject genres in particular. The point is, however, that whether the reading position adopted (and enforced), is compliant, complicit or resistant, viewers will draw conclusions based on the documentation, the data, the evidence presented and will, in effect, "consider its verdict". It becomes, metaphorically, the tribunal or jury.

The presentation of issues to audiences for their "adjudication" (to carry on the above analogy) is based on certain assumptions:

- an issue of public interest and import is identified and promulgated;
- the issue demands investigation, research, the discovery of data or evidence – documentation. (Questions arise as to who decides this and why, of course, but note that the concentration of documentary is on the exceptional issue or event, while news and current affairs magazines generally respond to the "diurnal" flow and rhythm of events);
- an argument (or "case") is built up by the presentation of selections of relevant evidence as appropriate, which may be consequent on an inquisitorial approach but which may well involve pro- and con- arguments reflecting or embodying an adversarial mode;
- a conclusion may be drawn, a "verdict" reached, based on the evidence – or at least, one may be made available. In most cases, producers will strive for such a "closure", for the premise or proposition to be substantiated by the data.

This account is a somewhat laboured and naive attempt to assert an analogy between investigative journalistic documentary method and the structure of a case in law, but it presents a broad outline of what has become almost the classic methodology – and the "house" style of programs such as "Four Corners", especially at the hands of practitioners such as Chris Masters. The following discussion of examples attempts to deal with the possible analogies in the area of "rules of evidence" for, in each instance, the text asserts the principle of the primacy of documentation, of making "evidence" visible for scrutiny.

In this way, Paul Barry's investigative documentary, "Citizen Packer", takes as its apparent motivation, its announced raison d'être, the premise that it is in the public interest to question the practices of Packer business corporations in terms of possible tax avoidance and/or evasion. One must be wary always of a subtextual level of "messages" in such programs – hidden or latent agendas – but in this case the timing of the broadcast tends to negate such a consideration during a period of recession-driven increases in the general poverty level, and the attitudes this is likely to engender in the public to the presentation of examples of Packer's extravagantly conspicuous consumption. And, of course, there is the public interest in and attitudes to the Black/Packer bid for the Fairfax press. This program then would seem to be an instance of conscious, premeditated intervention, really "stirring the possum", a political act, in effect, with its ideology up front. Further, in its approach to the topic, it could well be characterised as "trial by television", and with a strong adversarial thrust integrated with the inquisitorial.

The presentation of the data, of "evidence" in support of the premise, is logical, thorough and forceful in ways similar to those employed by Chris Masters in pursuit of political corruption (for instance, "The Moonlight State"). It is a case such as might be built by a skilled advocate but, with this analogy, the applicability of the rules of evidence is brought into play. It is obvious that effective and exhaustive substantive research was carried out, sources cross-checked and the status and validity of documentation established.

In this case, such care is not just a matter of editorial principle or journalistic accuracy and integrity: Packer is reported in the introduction to the program as threatening legal action which covered every level of personnel in the production team. One may presume that this threat caused the ABC's backroom legal eagles to be especially scrupulous. Equally, each journalist and production person would have been fully aware that any failure to dot every "i" and cross every "t" in the substance and modes of presentation of the data in support of their premise might result in their facing complex, lengthy and expensive litigation.

Consequently, and referring once more to Leslie Woodhead's dictum, Paul Barry apparently treated his documentary data so that journalistic accuracy had, perforce, to be "measured against standards of evidence as . . . understood in a court of law". To this end, he orchestrated rather than merely compiled evidence. There is the array of "real" evidence – documents in print form as well as on film, video and audiotape (archival and new footage); there is testimony from "witnesses" – eye-witnesses, character witnesses, expert witnesses – each item of testimony presented by edited interviews in "grabs", some of these looking suspiciously like cross-examinations. It is plausible, persuasive stuff, with a plethora of items that present as "factual", apparently material, and relevant evidence with a "probative force" that "makes the desired inference more probable. It would seem to be directed ultimately to the purpose of enabling the tribunal [so the audience] to understand the questions being raised, to follow the evidence and apply it . . . rather than to prove or disapprove some fact or issue" (Aronson 1982 p 416).

Readers have probably guessed that the foregoing few sentences include quotes from a basic text concerning the rules of evidence and, in the way suggested previously, serve to illustrate the claim to the analogies indicated by Woodhead. In that simple light, this investigative documentary report seems to conform to the established format and the "rules" of procedure, its handling of evidence building up a case effectively, convincingly – even if we are asked, because of the very nature of the medium, to accept the *re*presentation of evidence as *pre*sentation. We are asked to trust the integrity of the reporter and his team and accept the pictures of places, people, and events, the quotes from sources, the grabs from interviews with witnesses, the references to documentation as authentic when, as noted above, the processes of mediation place them at several removes from their sources in actuality and little attempt is made to indicate their specific evidential status.

We do accept all this, of course. "Four Corners" has the runs on the board in this genre and the highest reputation for journalistic integrity, so that very few of us choose to exercise scepticism or an informed doubt when faced with the inherent authority of the documentary form and the investigative journalistic genres in such programs. Brian, or Chris, or Paul told us so, and would he lie to us? Further, the authority of the parent organisation and the mythology surrounding "Four Corners" as a long-term flagship for the ABC are just the obvious signs of the ideological effect of institutional mediation. And here again obvious analogies with the law come to mind.

However, in the text of "Citizen Packer" there are aspects that raise several more problematic issues about the validity of the journalistic enterprise as analogous to and actually sharing the methodologies of the law. In the text one notes frequent recourse to quite questionable evidential practices, if the analogies are to be applied strictly. For example: the testimony of some witnesses could be adjudged as hearsay and yet such testimony is not distinguished from that subject to documentation of various kinds. Again, in its recourse to "expert" witnesses that provide some verification or even legitimacy for aspects of the case – lawyers, financial experts et al – the audience is left to accept the titling below the talking heads as a sufficient credential. The expertise is assumed but not tested.

Further, there are several instances that raise a number of "collateral questions" (Aronson 1982 p 423) that do not bear directly on the "case" being developed but are tacitly associated with it by their positioning. For example, some sequences that illustrate Packer's extravagant life-style (the polo, his daughter's wedding etc) are juxtaposed with items dealing with his corporate financial activities. Certainly the possible connections and conclusions are not asserted but they remain imminent possibilities for audience construal.

Again, there is a level of reliance on circumstantial evidence intended to have an attitudinal, even emotional impact, rather than the "probative force" required of evidence in law. The procedures in general are followed but the presentation tends to play fast and loose with the strict principles: it indicates a set of circumstances as part of the array of data (eg the Hong Kong "Connection") but tacitly suggests that, by its mere existence and its mode of presentation, it should be taken as "evidence" of financial malfeasance. Add to this the related reliance on *inference* enforced and reinforced by the rhetoric of images and of the voice-over commentary of the reporter (not without its analogies in the courtroom practices of some advocates, of course) and we see a case being thrust home in "extra-evidential" ways, playing on certain socio-cultural "intersubjectivities"[4] indeed, tending to make the case by allegation and inference rather than downright proof, in a way that could well be intended to confirm the perceived prejudices of the audience for this program.

One interpretation of its methodology is that it plays on popular attitudes to the stereotype of the ruthless tycoon with a touch of megalomania, in which many media representations of Kerry Packer would fit. As such, it is an expression of one of the modes of discourse of television culture, with the signifying practices within this discourse reflecting the common modus operandi of the investigative documentary – though not in an extreme form, considering "Hinch", "The Investigators", etc. What emerges in "Citizen Packer" is great adversarial stuff in which we see a paradigm case of the clash between cultures, between ideologies, between two loci of power in our society: the culture of television, especially telejournalism, along with the "Fourth Estate" in general, opposed combatively with the culture of "high capitalism" figured in and by the public, mediated persona of Kerry Packer. On one hand we have the telejournalistic position which purports to represent and assert the "public interest" and, on the other the ethos of the free-marketeer, firmly asserted by Packer who is *alleged* to have "implied" that the business of business is no business of the media.

Both of these expressions of ideological positions – the text of "Citizen Packer" and Packer's reported responses to it even before the event of its broadcast – are particular significations within the structures of the master-narratives of each culture but at least the narrative trajectory developed by Paul Barry and the "Four Corners" unit is open and evident in substance and methodology – and so readily available for and amenable to public scrutiny and criticism in its every detail. The secrets of "Big Business" have to be winkled out and we often rely on journalists of various kinds to do this for us. The clash between these cultures could thus be seen to be virtually

4 See Fiske, J and Hartley, J, *Reading Television*, p 46.

inevitable, as it is in the case of the bureaucracy, government, police, the cultures of which seem to be predicated on a resistance to the disclosure of their affairs. There has also been a corresponding reliance on the legal profession to "winkle out" the secrets of these powerful entities, again in the public interest, and so once more there is the temptation to assert an analogy between the law and telejournalistic practices and motivations. However, the divergences from the stringent application of the rules of evidence noted in Barry's treatment of issues in "Citizen Packer" indicate the limits to the extent to which the analogy holds: in terms of the "letter of the law", Barry's practices were at least questionable and much of the "evidence" as presented almost certainly would fail legal tests of materiality, relevance and admissability. On the other hand, telejournalists are themselves subject to the requirements of the law, particularly those pertaining to defamation – which, it is well known, are particularly strict in this country generally – and this program must have had to satisfy tests in this regard, as mentioned above. Chris Masters suggests that this factor, along with the codes of conduct promulgated by professional and regulating bodies (such as the AJA and the ABT) should be sufficient.[5] To apply too strictly the "letter of the law" regarding evidential procedures could constrict and constrain telejournalistic practices – could inhibit, for example, the kind of risk-taking in the public interest demonstrated by Masters in "The Moonlight State". No matter how many analogies hold between the two domains (the law and the media) they ultimately have different "briefs" – though whether "Citizen Packer" goes beyond its brief and violates "journalistic integrity" is a moot point.

Which brings me to Ken Cameron's "Police Crop" and the associated genre of the documentary drama. This genre has found a special niche in television along with other factually or quasi-factually based fictional forms – "faction" – some examples of which are "Cathy Come Home" and "Days of Hope" in the UK and "The Dismissal" and "Scales of Justice" in Australia. It has also been a controversial genre, not only because it tends towards dealing with confronting subject matter, but also because of the very nature of the formal elements of which it is constructed. It is a hybrid, "a cross-bred mongrel" according to Leslie Woodhead (1979 p 6), an amalgam of documentary and small-screen realist fiction. It is, he states, "a form of last resort, a way of doing things when conventional journalistic documentary can't cope" (p 15). For example, when an important event, known to have occurred is not documented – or not fully and accurately, the drama documentarist will reconstruct it "so that the audience is aware that it is watching the producer's best approximation of what happened" (Woodhead 1979 p 15). In all of his work in the "documentary drama reconstruction" genre, as he terms it, Woodhead so insists on the primacy and integrity of the document

5 Chris Masters, personal conversation, 1991.

of material evidence that this concept carries over into fictional, reconstructed episodes, which in his work (eg "Strike!" "The Rise of Solidarity") functions so that these approximations have something of the quality of objective reportage and the "look" of the documentary. He also insists on "signposting" his material – informing the audience of the status of the data presented – actuality footage, newsclips, transcripts, audiotape recordings, archival material, official print documents, eye-witness testimony and opinion, dramatic reconstructions, etcetera – so that the "evidence" is structured into a "readable hierarchy" of data, which is authenticated to give a sense of authenticity to the audience. Consequently, in his and other hands, this genre delivers convincing "living histories" of the events portrayed. And such is the power of the medium and the contributing genres that often these televisual versions become accepted as the "authorised" versions of the historical events. This raises the problematic issue that the drama documentary reconstruction of events perhaps displaces other accounts, either because they may be incomplete or they do not have the narrative dynamism of the dramatic form.

In this light, "Police Crop" is an interesting example of the genre. It is also remarkable for its sensational, challenging material and high level of production values, as well as the way in which its methodology highlights the question of the "rules of evidence" not only in the documentary drama itself but in any of the genres based on investigative reportage. Ken Cameron's direction shows many signs of a subscription to Woodhead's principles and practices. He "frames" his reconstructions with "authentic" material such as television newsclips, makes reference to public and "discovered" documents and provides sequences based on the "realia" of actual locations, which are signposted by subtitles and voice-over commentaries – albeit less thoroughly than Woodhead – so that he provides an effective foundation of actuality for the subsequent investigative dramatic reconstructions. However, because the subject material is a *conspiracy* involving intense secrecy and a considerable amount of covert activity, and because it is based on several unsolved murder mysteries, full documentation is denied and confounded. Consequently, much of his "best approximation of what happened" is established by recourse to hearsay, to anonymous or privileged confidences from participants or witnesses or "informants" subject to potential retribution, and to leaks from official sources. At first sight then, the "case" he builds "measured against standards of evidence as they might be understood in a court of law", would seem not to stand up, with inference rather than "proof" being the rule in Cameron's treatment.

Despite this, the text is remarkably convincing. Of course, the content, the plot, is compelling and innately dramatic. We are introduced to conspiracies purportedly involving police and Mafiosi, to multiple murder mysteries, to corruption and betrayal – the stuff of great popular drama from way back. And Cameron's skill in the compilation of material generates a narrative trajectory, a dynamic that grabs and structures intense audience attention and involvement. Further, his dramatic reconstructions (and *con*structions) often provide a sense of our having a privileged, insider's view of private moments that bring us close to the personalities involved and make them take on a "living" reality that opens up the workings of the criminal milieu normally closed to us which generates frissons that both heighten the pleasure of the text and increase our convictions about the case being built. In a way it could be claimed that these dramatised sequences are analogous to the demonstrations and "experiments" sometimes admitted in law, especially if the reconstructions are "the best approximations of what happened" available. Again, other sequences enact a "what if?" proposition which may be related by analogy to the kind of hypothesis embedded in the "I put it to you that. . ." form of question by counsel. The relevance and materiality of such instances as "evidence" in building the "case" would depend on the particulars of each in context, but often they are related, even if sometimes tenuously, to the instances of "hard data" ("real" or testimonial evidence, documented or documentable) that punctuate the quasi-fictional narrative. Among the examples are the meetings of conspiritators at the sites of the "police crops" and the revelation of "facts" of events preliminary to the murders. And, because of the force of the connections built up, some of the reconstructed instances could stand as logically or circumstantially relevant in the "case" in point.

What is presented most often, however, are educated guesses, at best rendering "the desired inferences possible but not necessarily probable" (Aronson 1982 p 416), even though such legal niceties are commonly ignored by audiences swept up in the narrative. And, in a sense, the instinct of the audience has a certain validity. If the demands of drama impact or impinge on those of journalistic accuracy or evidential probity, the documentary dramatist can choose to privilege one over the other or to strike a balance – which could well compromise both. American "faction" usually opts for the dramatic or the melodramatic: Woodhead (1979 p 11) and the British "school" do the opposite, citing the obligations of journalistic integrity "even at the risk of inadequate drama". Cameron, along with Robert Caswell and Terry Hayes in Australia strive for a nice balance: a journalistic basis, a respect for the rules of evidence, but a knowledge that, for the issues to make the fullest impact, to work on an attitudinal and even visceral as well as a cognitive level, the dynamics of screen drama can, as Woodhead (1979 p 12) says, "refresh the debate in an important way". If, in the process, their fictions sometimes take over, they may be "lies like the truth". As Gore Vidal remarked about Shakespeare's History plays, "He is never true: but he is always truthful".[6] In texts such as "Police Crop", truth, that slippery notion, is inscribed as firmly in the fictional elements as in the authenticated evidence presented. Just as in "straight" documentary, this is the touchstone of the conventional representational codes underlying the signifying practices of the medium and the genre, notwithstanding the ideological (and other) baggage the makers bring along with them that might render "truth" ambiguous. The tension between objectivity and subjectivity is always an active factor, with the emphasis on a subscription to the former tipping the balance in most genres in which the terms and/or concepts "reportage" or "documentary" are invoked.

There are exceptions, of course, and tabloid journalism in print or on radio or screen often provides them.

The 16 September 1991 edition of "Hinch" provides, in my view, an example of journalism in which objectivity was sacrificed to sensationalism and prejudice. In the eyes of this "layman", the integrity of investigative journalism with its attendant documentation was sullied: not only did the program violate investigative procedure and the *rules* of evidence, but also the rights of privacy and of a suspected person to due legal process.

None of this seemed to concern the "Hinch" report. Hinch reiterated regularly that "the camera" (hidden for surveillance in the undergrowth) "does not lie". What the report did in this case was to be a party to "trial by television". It began with the assumption of guilt followed by the presentation of a set-up situation, with entrapment by TV camera, by public, videotaped harassment, and accusation of the subject (a policeman "suspected" of drug-dealing with a dubious informant). All this was presented in an outraged tone of "SHOCK! HORROR!" which sensationalised the tenuous case presented so that the emotional presentation of opinion and inference was forced on the audience's attention.

This, in my view, is unquestionably subjectivity gone wild and a travesty of investigative journalism. It is also a signal warning of the temptation facing those working in this and the related genres – that is, to invest the assertion of "truth" in the public interest with a crusading spirit that may overflow into a self-righteous missionary zeal. Even Chris Masters, arguably "the conscience" of investigative telejournalism, has to be careful of this, though he would never be guilty of such excess. The "Hinch" segment seemed to this writer to be excessive, not so much in the pursuit of truth or justice, but of ratings. It pushed an extreme populist line despite any consequent prejudice which might taint later legal proceedings in the "case" presented.

In conclusion, the way in which texts in these genres build their "cases" can, at worst, be manipulative, inducing or enforcing compliant reading positions for the audiences, tending to push them

6 Quoted by Woodhead (1979 p 11).

to make "desired inferences". Multiple viewpoints, multiple subjectivities and "voices" in the presentations tend to be gathered and eventually returned to a centred position to which is ascribed an authoritative status based on the reputations and assertive voices of the producers, on their institutional "home", and on the medium itself. For such cultural productions and producers, the author is not dead, but alive and living in Gore Hill or Epping.

At best, there are texts in these genres that admit and incorporate multiple and shifting subjectivities and admit and exploit the polysemic nature of subjects and medium. In such cases the reading position made available may be complicit rather than compliant, or may even invite resistant or deconstructive readings. In such instances, audiences are drawn into the process of the "building of the case" and so are more likely to be able to reach informed, balanced judgements or "verdicts". As such, the texts are more likely to be faithful to Leslie Woodhead's ideal of journalistic integrity and maybe, by analogy, to ideals of justice inscribed in the principles of evidence as "understood in a court of law".

Finally, I would add this postscript: at the presentation of this chapter, I made a passing reference, somewhat flippantly, to investigative journalism being the domain of the media "Boys' Club". Unfortunately it is no joke, for the domination of the profession by males (and white "Anglo-Celt", middle-class males at that) has to be not only at the expense of women's and ethnic minorities' professional opportunities, but also precludes to a considerable extent the points of view they could bring to the production of texts in the subject genres. Certainly the picture is changing, but only a little, with positive discrimination often leading to tokenism rather than anything like an adequate representation of societal diversity in viewpoints *and* modes of production and presentation.

BIBLIOGRAPHY

Aronson, M et al, 1982, *Litigation: Evidence and Procedure*, 3rd edn, Butterworths.

Kuehl, Jerry, 1981, "Truth Claims", *Sight and Sound*, Autumn, p 274.

Woodhead, L, 1979, "The Guardian Lecture: Dramatised Documentary", National Film Theatre. (Transcript supplied by Mr Woodhead).

22

Writers' Agreements with Publishers and Strategies for Overcoming Unfair Contracting Practices

COLIN GOLVAN

The use of writing contracts dates back to the Romans. Suetonius reports that Terence sold his drama *Eunnuchus* for 8000 sesterces, or the price of eight ordinary slaves. In the first century BC, one Quintus Hortensius commissioned a free Greek artist to produce a statue for 60,000 sesterces (Boytha 1988).

In 1667, the publisher Samuel Symons entered into a contract with John Milton concerning the publication of *Paradise Lost*. Only the Stationers Company could at that time grant the right to copy works. Nevertheless, Symons still acquired from Milton "All that Booke Copy or Manuscript of a Poem intituled Paradise Lost . . . now lately Licensed to be printed" (Masson 1946 pp 509-12). Accordingly, Milton conveyed title in the manuscript to Symons, who undertook to publish a first edition of 1300 copies and to pay five pounds, as well as five pounds for each subsequent edition. The first edition sold out in two years.

Milton's contract was perpetual. In 1709, the Statute of Anne limited the duration of any assignment of the author's "title to the copy" of a work to 14 years, after which time the sole right of printing or disposing of copies was to return to the author for another 14 years. The statute established the author's "sole right of printing or disposing of copies", going beyond mere recognition of the author's ownership of the manuscript. This step abolished the printers' monopoly, and meant that publisher-author relations, concerning the use of texts, were to be governed by contract.

The book publishing industry in Australia as a whole is large and complex. There are many hundreds of publishers producing many titles each year. The most conspicuous development in publishing, both in Australia and internationally, over the past ten years has been the massive change in the ownership of publishing houses. The business of publishing has come to be dominated by a small number of extremely powerful and broadly based corporations. During the 1980s, a number of major international publishing houses have merged, with the result that the international publishing scene for general trade books in 1991 is dominated by four key corporations: Robert Maxwell's Maxwell Communications, which also owns Macmillan of the United States; the Bertelsmann Company of Germany, which owns Transworld in the United Kingdom and Doubleday in the United States; Rupert Murdoch's News Corporation, which owns Harper Collins, being a merger of Harper and Row United States, William Collins United Kingdom and Angus and Robertson in Australia; and the Pearson Group, which owns Penguin, Longman and Addison-Wesley.

Major publishing houses are increasingly becoming part of multi-interest companies concerned with the entertainment industry as a whole. The Bertelsmann Group, for example, combines its publishing interests with a significant interest in the music recording industry, operating the BMG (formerly RCA) recording label. News Corporation and Maxwell Communications have extensive newspaper and magazine publishing interests in many countries, while News Corporation owns television stations in a number of countries as well as television and film production interests in the United States. Thus, a book published by Harper & Collins in the United States has the potential of enormous international newspaper and magazine exposure through the News Corporation chain. The television and film production interests of News Corporation may become involved in acquiring key film and television rights of the book. There is a wide range of opportunities for support and exploitation between the divisions of the company.

The Australian publishing market is heavily concentrated in the hands of six to ten major players – almost all of which were foreign owned. The leading general trade publishers in terms of Australian turnover, with income in excess of $50 million per year, are Harper Collins, Penguin and Reader's Digest. This group is followed by Octopus, Pan Macmillan, Universal, Random Century, Transworld Doubleday, Time-Life, Allen and Unwin, Lothian, Oxford University Press, Simon and Schuster, Weldon, Lonely Planet and Mills and Boon, each such publisher having annual income in excess of $10 million per year.

This chapter is concerned with issues arising from the imbalance of negotiating positions between publishers generally, particularly publishers of the size referred to above, and writers, particularly inexperienced and unrepresented writers.

There may be plausible explanations for writers willingly accepting unfair contractual terms. Such terms may provide, for example, that the writer undertakes the writing of a book with no certainty that it will be published. In that regard, most publishing agreements reserve to the publisher the option to refuse publication on receipt of a finished manuscript on grounds of unsuitability or due to circumstances beyond the control of the publisher. At the same time, the publisher will reserve an option to publish the work upon completion without paying anything for it, or by paying what is usually a small advance which is not always expressed as being non-returnable, or committing to any other obligation other than the obligation of reviewing the manuscript upon completion. This option is, in fact, a very common term in publishing agreements, and writers will embark on what invariably seems like an almost endless period of writing effort on the strength of such arrangements.

The willingness of writers to accept such a term may emanate from ignorance or a sense of helplessness in the face of the such terms being commonly adopted by publishers. Much effort can be expended for potentially no return on the part of the writer seeking to "shop around" for a better term concerning assurances about publishing upon completion of a work which is contracted while it is in progress. It is important also to consider that such terms may not be the subject of great alarm in any event. It will be fairly assumed by writers that a publisher which contracts to publish means to publish it, and little regard may be paid to the broad entitlement withheld by the publisher to withdraw from the project upon a review of the completed manuscript.

The writer in the circumstances is often in the "frame of mind" of willing his or her work into print, and will not wish to be slowed along the path by seemingly unnecessary negotiation which will probably not achieve much anyway. The example is illustrative of the need to comprehend the "frame of mind" of the parties in contracting to publish. The attributing of plausible explanations for the conduct of the parties in the contracting process in turn raises the question of whether one can knowingly contract in a free market to accept substantially less than favourable terms and yet still claim to be aggrieved by contractual unfairness. The writer participant in this process may trade a better deal against the risk of losing the publisher and not finding another publisher to publish his or her work. There may be plausible ancillary considerations for writers accepting terms of publishing agreement which are substantially to their disadvantage. They may be well aware of the terms of agreement and the meaning of such terms but believe that the terms will be construed or interpreted in a way which is more favourable to them than a literal interpretation would necessarily provide. Alternatively, they may be well aware of the literal interpretation of the agreement, and have no illusions that the agreement would be construed in anything other than a literal manner if it suited the publisher, and yet substantially disadvantageous clauses are accepted because "shopping around" may, for example, produce no better result. Writers may not even consider "shopping around", but knowingly accept substantially disadvantageous terms because of perceived benefits which have nothing to do with the terms of the contract. Such benefits may include a sense of self-esteem or professional advantage stemming from having secured a publishing contract, even if it does not oblige a publisher actually to publish a work.

The position of the writer who is aware of the content of the publishing agreement and its meaning is to be contrasted with the position of the writer unaware of such content. The issue arises of whether there is some legitimate argument about unfairness warranting, for example, the courts or legislature intervening to assist the writer, in circumstances where the market appears to be free of restrictive practices of the kind prohibited by Part IV of the *Trade Practices Act* 1974 (Cth) and the writer is not otherwise suffering from some special disadvantage of the kind considered in the leading recent Australian case on unconscionability – *Commercial Bank of Australia Ltd v Amadio* (1983) 151 CLR 447.

Should the writer have to accept the consequences of lack of knowledge and the failure to obtain advice without having a claim to some kind of legal intervention? After all, lack of knowledge is part of the normal environment of the market for "new players". No matter what is said about publishing contracts, the process of contracting remains a free one. No single publisher dominates the market for the publication and sale of books, although it will be seen that a small number of publishers are dominant, as is evidenced by overall turnover and most importantly the substantial market power such publishers exert as publishers of large quantities of books and distributors of their own as well as other publisher's books.

While the barriers to entry for new publishers wishing to challenge some of the common practices in publishing contracts are not insurmountable, they are formidable. It is not the process of publishing itself which presents the problem for the new entrant, especially in an age of desk-top publishing. There are many worthy unpublished manuscripts which no doubt may be considered for publication, albeit manuscripts which may require more marketing effort than the work of well-known writers which is readily accepted for publication by the leading publishers. The key problem for the new entrant remains that of distribution, and in particular the high cost of distribution in a country as large and relatively underpopulated as Australia.

Apart from questions of writers' call on some legal redress, the problem of writers contracting to their substantial disadvantage may be answered by the proper provision of information about the content and meaning of publishing contracts. The dissemination of such information may play a role in eliminating unfair practices through a greater awareness of contracts on the part of writers and publishers alike. The dissemination of information about contracts may be also conducive to an improved sense of competition concerning the terms of contracts. To this end, this chapter may be serving some useful purpose.

Writers' organisations in Australia and the United Kingdom have responded to perceived unfairness in publishing agreements through promoting collective negotiation or at least the recommendation of preferred terms. The challenge to respond to the problems of writers entering into poor contracts has been amongst writers' organisations for some time.

One of the most interesting responses has been that of the United Kingdom Society of Authors and Writers' Guild, both of which represent writers of books, which have advocated the adoption of a Minimum Terms Agreement (MTA), embodying certain basic contractual standards which these organisations believe ought to be endorsed mutually by the writers' organisations and publishers. The Agreement has won acceptance from a number of significant United Kingdom publishing houses, and is considered to be a most significant step toward the achievement of appropriate industry regulation.

The adoption of the MTA model followed the Caute survey of 1980. The survey carried out of 60 publishing contracts found a significant disparity between actual contracting practices and the preferred approaches of the British Society of Authors with respect to virtually every clause under review. Caute, the then Chairman of the Books Committee of the United Kingdom Writers' Guild, described the situation of the writer in the following terms:

> Free-lance writing is a solitary, self-employed occupation, a cottage industry. Beset by anxiety, the writer sees within his own profession potential rivals rather than colleagues. Suspicious of unions, he is sceptical about the value of solidarity and collective action – his talent, after all, is unique. Humbly grateful when his latest manuscript finds favour, he may grouse and grumble about the terms offered until warned that he is free to take his work elsewhere. He has only the dimmest notion of what terms other authors obtain. And when a union brings him something tangible, even though he never joined it or paid his sub. – Public Lending Right is the most conspicuous example – he'll bank his cheque with an agnostic shrug. *Sauve qui peut,* back to work.

Caute observed that the publishers:

> thrive on the writer's isolation. It keeps one end of their business comfortably in the 19th century, in Gissing's Grub Street, while they bend the 20th century part of their minds to the rigours of competition, to production, promotion and marketing. When a contract between publisher and author is drawn up, it will normally be the publisher who lays down the ground rules, who seizes the psychological advantage. The clauses of a standard printed contract are drafted by lawyers to promote the publisher's interests, not the writer's.

Caute noted that "stubborn or successful" writers will pressure publishers for satisfactory terms, but the "novice – and indeed many professional writers struggling to make a living – will meekly accept most of the terms offered. His business is writing; the small print and legal phrasing confuse him, he is not sure what 'first serial rights' or 'discounts' mean, his gaze is riveted by the amount of the advance, the one thing he really understands".

Referring to the role of literary agents, Caute stated that agents tend on questions of the territory of rights granted and financial clauses and "not all of them are equally alert to other aspects of a contract – the author's control over his own text, or his participation in the production process for example". Caute was not optimistic about the writer successfully representing himself in a contract negotiation:

> The publisher knows all about markets, Australia, America, discounts, net returns, Book Club deals, paperback splits, bookshops. The writer doesn't. Nor does he comprehend clauses like the one following – with glazed eyes he prays that, whatever it may be, will never happen:
>
> > "The failure to exercise or the delay in exercising by either party hereto any of its rights powers or privileges hereunder shall not operate as a waiver of those or any other rights powers or privileges nor shall any single or partial exercise of any rights powers or privileges preclude any other further exercise thereof or the exercise of any other right power or privilege and the rights and remedies herein provided shall be cumulative and not exclusive of any rights provided by law". (WH Allen Publishing Agreement, clause 30)

Caute reviewed 60 contracts offered by publishers, and observed that there was "uniformity as regards the non-financial conditions", and a "diversity of financial terms offered by publishers in the same line of business. This even applies to different imprints belonging to the same company . . . In short, the overall position is one of anarchy. This can only mean that many authors are getting a raw deal". Caute concluded by noting an urgent need to implement an MTA: "Only general acceptance of the principle of minimum terms agreements negotiated between publishers and unions will achieve" the desired result of publishing contracts which properly protect the interests of writers.

The two principal writers' organisations in the United Kingdom, the Society of Authors and Writers' Guild combined in drafting an MTA. The then general-secretary of the Society, David Machin, wrote in *The Bookseller* magazine in 1980:

> Many of the justifiable complaints against publishers at the post contractual stage arise from the failure to secure reasonable improvements before signature, and from publishers' unsatisfactory drafting and resulting ambiguities. Agreed basic terms would, above all, save time, in which authors and publishers could get on with their respective preoccupations, instead of becoming involved in wasteful and enervating misunderstandings and disputes.

The British Publishers' Association rejected the MTA approach as an imposition on the rights of its members to freely negotiate their own contracts. Nevertheless, it responded with a recommended Code of Practice, which the writers' organisations dismissed as inadequate. A similar Code of Practice was subsequently adopted by the Australian Book Publishers Association.

The British Society pursued negotiations with individual publishers, and received agreement on acceptable minimum terms from Hamish Hamilton, WH Allen and Journeyman Press, which all tended to have very progressive contracts anyway. BBC Publishing and Faber and Faber followed. The Australian Society of Authors has resisted the MTA approach, with the view being expressed in ASA Committee of Management meetings (attended by the author in 1989 in his capacity as a member of the Committee of Management) that in the United Kingdom it has been difficult to enforce the compliance with the MTA of the few publishers which have agreed to it on a contract-by-contract basis, and that furthermore it is better to insist upon compliance with the standard agreement, rather than accept the compromises inherent in the adoption of the MTA. As regards the fact of the few publishers who have accepted the MTA, the view expressed in ASA Committee of Management meetings is that years of effort which have gone into promoting the MTA have not justified the return of the very limited group of publishers which have responded positively. While it might be thought that these publishers would serve as "pace setters", this would seem to be somewhat optimistic given the reluctance of most publishers to respond positively to the MTA initiative. Arising from these matters, the concern has accordingly been expressed that the cost of seeking to implement an MTA in Australia are too high, given that the limited resources of the ASA would be engaged predominantly on this one task if the MTA approach was adopted and with the outcome of this allocation of resources being most uncertain. Thus, the preferred position remained of seeking acceptance for the ambit-type position set out in the recommended standard agreements, which has been almost universally ignored by publishers and in relation to which writers lack the industrial muscle to insist upon.

Publishers' organisations, for their part, have expressed concerns that publishers need to be encouraged not to unfairly exploit their dominance in the contractual relationship, especially relating to the writers' interests in the integrity of their work in its published form. Publishers' organisations in Australia and the United Kingdom have recommended the adoption of Codes of Practice to guide members accordingly. Notwithstanding the Code, few publishers appear, at least by their contracts, to pay any regard to it, and I believe that it is safe to say that this project has largely been unsuccessful.

The Continental Europeans are, as always in copyright matters, far ahead of us. In this case, the Germans, rather than the French, have led the way with a Publishing Law, which has been in existence in various forms since 1794, when the Prussians introduced the notion of *Verlagsrecht*, or a publishing right, which provided for publishing rights to be transferred by written contract. The Publishing Law in operation in Germany today, enacted in 1901, provides for terms to be read into publishing agreements where contracts are otherwise silent. The proposition that we introduce a publishing law in Australia is almost inconceivable, and I suggest that it is well to ask oneself why this is so.

I return to the information dissemination model as a preferred model for remedying defects on the contracting process. The model accords with a view that writers, and artists generally, ought to be more concerned with the process of the public realisation of their works. An indifference to the processes, as I put it, is merely conducive of unfair contracting practices. Until our writers cultivate an active interest and involvement in the legal processes attaching to publication, then I believe that the notion of contractual fairness in publishing agreements will remain altogether unachievable.

BIBLIOGRAPHY

Boytha, Gyorgy, 1988, "The Development of Legislative Provisions on Authors' Contracts", *Columbia VLA Journal of Law and the Arts*, vol 12, Winter, 2, p 155.

Masson, D, 1946, *The Life of John Milton*, Peter Smith.

23

Aboriginal Designs and Copyright: Can the Australian Common Law Expand to Meet Aboriginal Demands?[1]

STEPHEN GRAY

Since before the turn of the century[2] anthropologists and educated observers have ranged over Northern and Central Australia, recording information on the practices and beliefs of the dying culture whose pillow it was the white man's duty to smooth. Aboriginal cultures did not quite see the situation in that way. Information they divulged to the visitors was a privilege which carried with it a corresponding duty of respect. Thus Dr Charles P Mountford, who made his first exploratory field trip through Pitjantjatjara country in 1940, received information which:

> could only have been supplied and exposed in confidence, a confidence he himself, as an anthropologist, accepted, and is reminded of by these people; a confidence of secrecy, a confidence which appears to have been maintained for 35 years and which is, I believe, recognised by the distinguished author. . . (*Foster v Mountford and Rigby Ltd* (1977) 14 ALR 71 (Supreme Court of the Northern Territory) at 72-3).

Respect for Aboriginal laws governing the situations in which sacred or significant information can be disseminated has never been great. The most common recent instance of this disrespect is the commercial exploitation of Aboriginal designs without consultation with the community responsible for the design. The best-publicised

1 For his assistance with both ideas and information in the preparation of this chapter, the author would like to thank Martin Hardie, Aboriginal arts consultant and para-legal assistant in *Yumbulul v Aboriginal Artists Agency Ltd* (1991) 21 IPR 481.

2 See, for example, Spencer and Gillen (1899).

example of such exploitation is the Federal Court case of *Yumbulul v Reserve Bank of Australia Ltd* (1991) 21 IPR 48.

One legal approach to the problem might be a comparative law perspective, treating it as a conflict of laws between the law of the relevant Aboriginal community and the Anglo-Australian law. Australian law, however, accords no formal significance to the question of whether or not, in such a case, Aboriginal customary law has been broken. Rather, the remedy of the artist or community concerned lies primarily under the *Copyright Act* 1968 (Cth), the *Trade Practices Act* 1974 (Cth), and in some cases in equity. This situation continues despite the arguable possible extension to Aboriginal cultural and intellectual property rights of the recognition of Aboriginal customary rights in real property accorded in *Mabo v Queensland (No 2)* (1992) 175 CLR 1.

This chapter will seek to establish three major contentions in regard to this situation. First it will argue that the requirements of Australian copyright law and equitable relief, as they have hitherto been judicially expressed, are essentially foreign to the concerns and perspectives of Aboriginal law regarding the protection of sacred designs. Second, it will argue that, given the perspective of Aboriginal law, the recognition accorded by the Australian common law to "Aboriginal native title" in land must necessarily imply recognition of Aboriginal communal rights in sacred designs. Third, should any such logical extension of the principles enunciated in *Mabo (No 2)* not occur, it will be suggested that equitable principles according protection to confidential information, as expressed most recently in *Foster v Mountford* (1977) 14 ALR 71, are sufficiently flexible to protect communal rights in sacred designs. Protection under these principles, it will be argued, is more appropriate than any other form of protection short of legislative change, because these principles are more consistent with Aboriginal law than are any other common law principles, and are therefore more capable of affording both symbolic and practical recognition to Aboriginal law.

Before proceeding further, three short matters of definition need clarification. First, the chapter will use the word "design" to include not only physical representations on bark, canvas or other media, but also other Aboriginal intellectual property the unauthorised use of which may lead to cultural or legal conflict. Thus it may include songs, dances, sounds and sacred or significant information.

Second, the word "sacred" will be used throughout to denote designs of particular significance to their Aboriginal owners: designs on the use or dissemination of which Aboriginal law places some form of restriction. It does not imply a greater value judgment than that: in particular it does not necessarily imply that the design is of the highest ceremonial or other significance.

Third, the use of the term "Aboriginal law" is a shorthand for the purposes of this chapter. In relation to a particular design it will refer to the law of the community or communities owning or responsible for the design. When used in general it is not intended to imply that there is one "Aboriginal law" Australia-wide: rather that the distinctions between the laws of various Aboriginal communities in their treatment of designs of significance to them do not detract sufficiently from the main argument to justify discussion at length.

There are, I suggest, five situations in which, as a result of the public dissemination of sacred Aboriginal designs, a breach of Aboriginal customary law may occur. These situations are as follows:

1. A sacred design is divulged in a relationship of confidence, and then published. In this situation the speaker is authorised under Aboriginal law to divulge the design, but only on condition that the receiver respect the restrictions that law imposes on the number of people to whom the information may in turn be communicated. This was the situation in *Foster v Mountford* (1977) 14 ALR 71. It may be treated by Australian law as a non-contractual breach of confidence under the requirements summarised in *Coco v AN Clark (Engineers) Ltd* [1969] RPC 41 (Ch): these requirements will be discussed further below.
2. A sacred design is divulged by a person not authorised under Aboriginal law to do so, and is then published. An example is that of a well-known Australian rock band which received a design (a particular sound) in confidence from an Aboriginal elder purporting to be authorised to communicate it. In fact the design was common property of a number of other communities and the elder was not authorised to communicate it without prior consultation and approval. The design was published on a record. This case was never litigated.[3] Whether legal action to prevent further dissemination of the design would succeed would depend on whether the court accepted that the information had the necessary quality of confidence about it, and whether it was imparted in circumstances importing an obligation of confidence, in accordance with the requirements in *Coco v AN Clark*.
3. A sacred design, as expressed in the work of an individual artist, is appropriated after publication without authorisation of any kind. An example is the case of Johnny Bulun Bulun, an Aboriginal artist whose bark paintings, incorporating sacred design elements, were reproduced without permission on T-shirts.[4] Australian law, it would appear, treats this situation differently from that outlined in (1) above, because the element of

---

3 From an interview with Martin Hardie, arts consultant and former employee, North Australian Aboriginal Legal Aid Service, conducted by the writer on 16 August 1991.

4 This was a case set down for hearing before the Federal Court in 1989: the case, however, settled before trial. For a full discussion of the case, see Golvan (1989).

"publication" has occurred, and consequently under present requirements an obligation to keep the property in confidence cannot be shown to exist. (The view that a breach of confidence action may still arise even after publication will, however, be put below). Rather, the success or failure of legal action will depend largely on whether the Aboriginal artist or community can meet the requirements of the *Copyright Act* 1968 (Cth).

4. A sacred design, as expressed in an individual artist's work, is appropriated after publication with purported "authorisation" from the artist. This was the applicant's allegation in *Yumbulul v Aboriginal Artists Agency* (1991) 21 IPR 481. This case, widely known as the *Ten Dollar Note* case, involved the "Morning Star" totem pole or Barnumbirr, a representation of which appeared on the Bicentennial $10 note. The applicant was one of a relatively small number of people in Arnhem Land who are permitted under Aboriginal law to make Morning Star poles, which are ceremonial items of great significance. He alleged that the respondents reproduced on the Bicentennial note a Morning Star pole created by him which is on display at the Australian Museum in Sydney, without valid authority to do so under either Aboriginal or Anglo-Australian law. The defence response was that Yumbulul signed a document licensing one of the respondents to reproduce his work throughout the world, and to license others to do so. The success or failure of Yumbulul's claim depended largely on whether this document constituted a valid license of copyright under Anglo-Australian law. The fact that such an assignment, if made, was without authority and hence void under Yolngu law (the law of the Aboriginal clans of Eastern Arnhem land) was considered of no direct relevance under Australian law. This is because Australian law holds Yumbulul the sole owner of the copyright in "his" work: it lacks a notion of collective ownership of copyright (see Golvan 1989 pp 353-4).
5. Sacred designs, not the work of any identifiable individual, or combined with other designs such that the work of any one individual is not readily identifiable, are appropriated, with or without an individual's "authorisation". It is this situation which raises the most difficult philosophical or "policy" issues, and the situation in which the most difficult conflict could be expected to arise between Aboriginal customary law and the considerations underlying the limited protection accorded under copyright law to mere abstract "ideas". As yet there are no cases whose facts squarely raise such issues. In *Bulun Bulun's Nejlam Investments* case (unreported, Fed Ct, NTG3 of 1989) the defence claimed that the "substantiality" requirement of s 14(1)(a) of the *Copyright Act* was not breached because the T-shirts printed contained design elements from work other than that of the plaintiff (Golvan pp 351-2). However evidence on affidavit from Margaret West, curator of Aboriginal Art at the NT Museum, clearly invalidated

such an argument: it appeared that the design elements in the T-shirt which were not characteristic of Bulun Bulun's work had simply been obtained by flipping over several pages of two well-known Aboriginal art books (Golvan p 352).

If the respondents in this case had been a little cleverer the more difficult policy issues would have been raised. Suppose they had combined in one design, in roughly equal quantities, design elements from four or five different sacred Aboriginal designs? Or suppose a non-Aboriginal artist had produced his or her own interpretation of a sacred Aboriginal design (eg a Morning Star pole), such that the work, while obviously "Aboriginal" in style, was not obviously copied from that of a particular Aboriginal artist?

In both these situations Aboriginal laws would have been breached just as clearly as in any of the other situations outlined above. It is equally clear that it would be next to impossible to prove breach of copyright under Anglo-Australian law. A resolution to this conflict must take into account, amongst other factors, the traditional concern of copyright law to give protection to the form of expression of ideas, but not to the ideas themselves (see Ricketson p 82): an issue, again, to be discussed further below.

The following, it is suggested, are factors relevant to determining whether copyright protection will be accorded to Aboriginal designs under Anglo-Australian law:

1. Whether or not "publication" of the design has occurred before its appropriation or unauthorised use. If publication has occurred, a copyright action will arguably be more appropriate: if not, copyright in the design does not exist and a breach of confidence action will need to be mounted.
2. Whether or not purported "authorisation" exists for the appropriation. Australian law regards as extremely significant the issue of whether the individual artist gave his or her consent to the reproduction or publication of the design. It takes no account of whether or not the clan or clans which own and are responsible for the design have been consulted and have approved the publication under Aboriginal law.
3. Whether or not the design was communicated in a relationship of "confidence". Australian law regards as significant the knowledge (or lack thereof) of the receiver of a sacred design, that the communicator wishes to restrict the class of people to whom access to the material may validly be given. If there was such knowledge, then the required relationship of confidence may be held to exist: if there was not, such a relationship will not be held to exist (see *Foster v Mountford* (1977) 14 ALR 71 and Ricketson pp 817-8). Aboriginal law regards this question as irrelevant: if sacred material has been disseminated amongst people not

authorised to receive it, then ipso facto a breach of Aboriginal customary law has occurred.

4. The extent to which the sacred design has been altered or combined with elements of other designs. Australian law, again, regards this question as extremely significant. If little or no alteration has occurred, copyright or other protection may exist: if there has been substantial alteration, the disputed material will be regarded as its non-Aboriginal creator's own original work (see Ricketson pp 167-70). Aboriginal laws are likely to regard the unauthorised dissemination of sacred designs as unlawful, no matter with what else the design has been combined.
5. Whether or not the design reproduced was sacred, that is, that Aboriginal law places restrictions upon its dissemination. This is the essential question under Aboriginal law, as it will govern whether or not Aboriginal law will grant permission for the proposed reproduction or publication: under Australian law, the question has only indirect significance.

Clearly, the importance which these two systems of law place on the above factors is greatly different. An Aboriginal community aggrieved by the unlawful dissemination of sacred material has, however, no remedy against the non-Aboriginal law-breakers under their own law. They must pursue their remedy under Anglo-Australian law, and failing that, against those of their own people deemed responsible under their own law. The punishment of the Aboriginal law-breaker may to a large extent be determined by the success or failure of action in the Anglo-Australian courts.[5]

This fact alone suggests that Australian law should take account of Aboriginal law in determining a copyright action involving Aboriginal designs or materials. The failure of our law to do so stems, it is submitted, from the failure of the Australian legal system to extend the recognition of propriеary interests in land accorded in *Mabo v Queensland* to interests in cultural or intellectual property. Should such extension occur, it will follow logically that the Australian law will need to pay regard to Aboriginal law in assessing copyright issues, possibly even to the extent of according it full recognition: that is, by determining that if an Aboriginal plaintiff can show a publication breaches Aboriginal law, then this will be sufficient in itself for redress to be granted under Australian law.

This argument will be supported by showing the closeness of the connection between "real" property and "intellectual" property under Aboriginal law: a relationship so close that the two are inextricably entwined. Given this closeness, it will be argued,

---

5 See, for example, a statement of Roy Marika, a witness in the *Ten Dollar Note* case, made in an interview with Martin Hardie (Aboriginal Arts consultant, referred to above) on 17 July 1991: "Yumbulul . . . is blamed for something that he had no control over and he must set things right. The Bank and Anthony Wallis has caused the problem but it is Yumbulul who may die as a result."

recognition of the right to legal protection of Aboriginal systems of real property or land tenure logically implies recognition of the right to legal protection of the designs and sacred material which, in Aboriginal law, flow from the land.

The abbreviated argument as to Aboriginal concepts of intellectual property which follows, is taken from anthropological sources, from affidavits prepared and tendered in the *Ten Dollar Note* case, and from the transcript and judge's reasons for that decision. It will be confined for space reasons to the Yolngu of North-East Arnhem Land, since it is these people on whose behalf Yumbulul has pursued the *Ten Dollar Note* case.[6] It is submitted, however, that what holds true for the Yolngu also applies to other Aboriginal land-holding groups: that is, that their "art" flows directly from their relationship to the land, and is expressive of their rights to it.

A Yolngu painting is not viewed by the clan as the unaided product of the creative impulses of the painter. Rather the painting is owned (although not necessarily exclusively) by the clan:

> Paintings are part of the corpus of ritual knowledge, which includes the paintings, songs, dances, power names and sacred objects, that can be referred to as *madayin* ["sacred law"]. Rights in *madayin* are distributed on precisely the same basis as rights in land (Morphy 1983 p 117).

The painting is expressive of the relationship between the people and the land. The "meaning", or the story behind the painting, is an assertion of land ownership, "through clan designs, which precisely signify the clan ownership of a painting, and through representing features of the topography of the landscape itself in the form of the painting" (Morphy p 118).

Each clan across Arnhem Land "owns" a set of designs, many designs being of the same basic type, but incorporating differences which express the individuality of the clan of the creator. Thus:

> on the basis of clan design alone a knowledgeable man can tell of a particular painting which clan it belongs to, which set of Ancestral Beings it is connected with and which area of the clan's land it is associated with. Not surprisingly, Yolngu frequently refer to clan designs as marks of ownership or as "copyright" marks (Morphy pp 120-1).

The *Ten Dollar Note* case illustrates the way in which this system of design ownership operates. The design of the Morning Star pole fashioned by Terry Yumbulul and on display at the Australian Museum is not under Yolngu law "owned" by Yumbulul or even by his

6 Yumbulul gave evidence that any damages ultimately awarded would be shared equally amongst all the Aboriginal traditional owners of the Morning Star pole. His relevant responses to cross-examination, as reproduced at 98 of the transcript, were as follows:

> Now, if you get any money out of this case, are you going to keep it all? – No, it's not mine.
> What would you do with the money? – The group is going to take over and they are going to sort it out and give it to other groups and themselves.

clan, the Warramiri, or his mother's clan, the Galpu. Rather the right to make the poles is vested in certain high-ranking individuals from various clans across Arnhem Land.[7] The pole performs an important ceremonial function, being central to the Morning Star ceremony which is often performed when an important person of the Dhuwa moiety has died.[8] This is a public ceremony which is "a mode of establishing ties of friendship and gift exchange between geographically and socially distant groups".[9]

> While the ceremony is in public, the making of the pole itself only takes place in the presence of suitably initiated men . . . the restricted manufacture of the pole is important as it allows religious knowledge to be controlled by the clan elders, who ensure that the requirements of religious law are appropriately preserved and passed on through a process of strictly regulated teaching.[10]

According to Terry Yumbulul, "I am the only member of my tribe authorised to paint certain sacred designs. .. I enjoy the status of a person who is entitled to represent totems of the clan and my authorisation in this regard stems from the prominent place of my family in the clan".[11]

Thus, although the ceremony itself is in public and theoretically anyone may attend, the pole itself and particularly the secrets of its design and manufacture are matters of great significance under Yolngu law. The class of people to whom it is shown and the manner and form of its reproduction must be restricted, and subject to the approval of the elders of the various clans with rights in the Morning Star ceremony. In relation to any proposed reproduction:

> it is necessary to make sure that not only is the artist consulted properly, but also that the other people with rights in the painting or object are consulted . . . [i]f all of these people do not agree then the proposed reproduction cannot go ahead.[12]

It is acceptable therefore for an artist to make an object for sale to places such as museums "in order to educate Balanda".[13] It is

---

7 See, for example, various affidavits tendered in the *Ten Dollar Note* case, including affidavits of Galarrwuy Yunupingu, sworn 20 December 1990, and affidavit of T Yumbulul, sworn 16 July 1991. Yunupingu deposes that, "the Morning Star is an important and significant totem which plays a valuable role in uniting people across Arnhem Land. It is one of the most important ceremonies which is practised in Arnhem Land . . . [t]he different clans which practice the Morning Star ceremony have created various kinds of poles which are an integral part of such ceremonies".

8 See affidavit of Mingi, sworn 18 December 1990, and tendered in the *Ten Dollar Note* case, "After an important dhua person has died, such as a leader of the clan, we often make a morning star ceremony".

9 See affidavit of Ian Keen, Senior Lecturer, Australian National University, sworn 17 July 1991, and tendered in the *Ten Dollar Note* case.

10 See affidavit of Mingi.

11 See affidavit of T Yumbulul.

12 See affidavit of Roy Dadynga Marika, sworn 17 July 1991, tendered in the *Ten Dollar Note* case.

13 Affidavit of Roy Dadynga Marika.

not acceptable for an artist to authorise reproductions or copies without prior consultation, and such a person "is likely to suffer sanctions from those who hold him or her responsible, and who themselves have rights in the design or object".[14] This may occur regardless of whether the person could be regarded as having been "at fault", or whether he was deceived into authorising such a reproduction. In this way liability under Yolngu law for Yumbulul's actions may be strict: "Yumbulul . . . is blamed for something that he had no control over and he must set things right. The Bank and Anthony Wallis has caused the problem but it is Yumbulul who may die as a result".[15]

The differences between the Morning Star poles produced by authorised members of the various Yolngu clans thus express their differing relationships to their respective ancestral lands. Certain features of an individual pole, such as the use of cross-hatching, the position or use of feathers and/or fur, indicate to the knowledgeable which clan has produced the pole and to which land the ceremony will relate.[16] The pole will indicate what dances and songs, which in turn will relate to a specific area, will be used in the ceremony.

Many Yolngu paintings express in an even more specific way the clan relationship to the land. They may be seen, Morphy (p 121) argues, "as accounts of actions that took place on the journeys of the Ancestral Beings through the area of land concerned, and as maps of the topography of the land with reference to its mythological significance". In Yolngu law the paintings are conclusive evidence of land ownership (p 131), and even further, in a spiritual sense, the paintings *are* the land.[17]

The foregoing argument clearly has in itself no relationship to the issue of whether Australian law should accord recognition to

---

14 See affidavit of Ian Keen.

15 See note 5 above.

16 See affidavit of T Yumbulul, "From my mother's side I have inherited the right to make feathered Morning Star totem poles. My mother's country is on the mainland. This particular pole is associated with a site on Galpu land in the Blue Mud Bay area. . . I . . . painted the design of yam leaves on the pole. . . The yam story depicted on the particular Morning Star pole in issue in these proceedings is a story of my mother's clan, being the Galpu clan". See also Yumbulul's evidence in chief at trial as quoted in the official transcript at 42, in particular the following exchange with counsel for the applicant:

MR GOLVAN: Can you explain to the court, Mr Yumbulul, what is being described about each area in what you've done?

– Right. That's the yam leaves which represents the yam spiritual being, yam spirit man, right. That came up and brought a life – gave the life to Galpo [sic] tribe, right, and out of that, that's where Galpo people is today which is the yam leaves and the steam [sic] of the yams. They're significant on sacred ground. That represents these patterns here which, your Honour, I can't explain the significance because of the oath that I was given to my own old people.

17 For an argument along similar lines in relation to significant words and names, see Williams, N, 1986, *The Yolngu and their Land*, Australian Institute of Aboriginal Studies, pp 42-6.

traditional Aboriginal communal rights in sacred designs, beyond that already granted in copyright law and in equity.

It does, however, imply that the recognition of Aboriginal native title to land accorded in *Mabo v Queensland* should be extended to Aboriginal cultural and intellectual property. This would be on the basis that Aboriginal cultural property is a "nature or incident" of native title, since the question of what is a "nature or incident" of native title is to be determined by reference to Aboriginal, not European, law.[18] This question has been discussed elsewhere[19] and will not be analysed in detail here. It is enough to note that recognition by the Australian legal system of proprietary interests under customary law must logically imply recognition of those interests which are "inextricably interwoven" (Morphy p 131) with those proprietary interests under Aboriginal law. To do otherwise would not be legally impossible if a rigid separation between real property law and intellectual property law were relied upon: but it would be illogical, and its effect would be to deny that measure of respect for Aboriginal customary law which a decision recognising Aboriginal proprietary interests in land at common law would confer.

There are several broader philosophical/policy issues regarding the possible recognition of the right of Aboriginal people to exclusive control of the designs and symbols which are significant to them. These are considered in turn below.

THE EXTENT OF LEGAL PROTECTION FOR "IDEAS" AS AGAINST THE "EXPRESSION OF IDEAS"

Copyright law traditionally is not concerned to protect ideas in themselves. Thus Peterson J in *University of London Press Ltd v University Tutorial Press Ltd* [1916] 2 Ch 602 at 608 to 610 stated:

> Copyright Acts are not concerned with the originality of ideas, but with the expression of thought and, in the case of "literary work", with the expression of thought in print or writing. The originality which is required relates to the expression of the thought.

This dichotomy is the product of the traditional desire of copyright law to strike a fair balance between the interests of society and those of individuals. In Anglo-Australian society individuals have an interest in retaining exclusive control of the intellectual products of their labours. Society, on the other hand, has a legitimate interest in ensuring, "that the work should enter the broader realm of culture and ideas and be free for all to use and re-work in their own way" (Ricketson p 82). This policy requirement is translated into s 32(1) to

18 "The nature and incidents of native title must be ascertained as a matter of fact by reference to those laws and customs", Brennan J in *Mabo (No 2)* (1992) 175 CLR 1 at 58.

19 See, for example, Golvan, C, "Aboriginal Art and the Protection of Indigenous Cultural Rights", ALB Vol 2, No 56, June 1992; see also Gray, S, "Wheeling, Dealing and Deconstruction: Aboriginal Art and the Land Post-Mabo", ALB Vol 3, No 63, August 1993, p 10.

the *Copyright Act* 1968 (Cth), which provides that for copyright to exist a work must be "original".

> The issue is whether Aboriginal designs should qualify for protection under Australian law, when such designs would frequently be classified as "ideas" rather than the expression of ideas. This was a concern expressed in the Working Party Report on the Protection of Aboriginal Folklore (Department of Home Affairs and Environment, 1981, Canberra, p 45).[20] Many works of Aboriginal artists, it was felt, would not satisfy the originality requirement of the *Copyright Act* for this reason.

In fact, the problem has not arisen in the cases hitherto decided or settled. This was because in the cases of both *Bulun Bulun* and the *Ten Dollar Note* case (1991) 21 IPR 481, the artist was of high standing both in his community and in the wider art world, and his work was readily recognisable by the critic as original and individual: therefore it clearly qualified for copyright protection. However the unauthorised use of Aboriginal designs less readily recognisable as individual, as suggested above, does squarely raise the problem. The concern is whether and to what extent the freedom "for all to use and re-work the idea in their own way" would be infringed by the recognition of an exclusive legal right in Aboriginal people to significant, and identifiably Aboriginal, designs.

It might be argued by non-Aboriginal artists that such a right would be a totally unjustified interference with freedom of artistic expression. Why should a European artist be prevented from using, say, a Mimi spirit or a Morning Star pole (perhaps altered or interpreted in the artist's own way) in his or her own work? After all, European religious icons such as the Cross or the Madonna and Child have long been made the subject of interpretation in works of art (with varying degrees of controversy). The publication of some legal rule against use of such symbols might conceivably even have the counter-productive effect achieved at times in the past by laws of obscenity and seditious libel.

Part of the answer to this objection lies in pointing out the difference of perspective. Sacred Aboriginal designs are not "ideas" in the same sense as, say, Cubism or Dadaism. Rather they are "property" in its most basic sense, the distinction between real and intellectual property having no significance in Aboriginal customary law. It is thus a property right, not just a mere idea, which is infringed when a sacred design is employed in an unauthorised way: an infringement as concrete as trespass in Anglo-Australian law. It should also be noted that, just as the defence of consent is open to an alleged trespasser, a non-Aboriginal user of a sacred design would also have a defence of consent open. This would be to the effect that he or she was properly authorised under Aboriginal law to use the design in that way. A particular design could be used by a non-

20 See also Golvan (1989).

Aboriginal person familiar with at least some aspects of its significance (and therefore presumably sympathetic to Aboriginal concerns) provided he or she had sought permission from the appropriate person.

THE EXTENT TO WHICH LEGAL RECOGNITION SHOULD BE GIVEN TO COMMUNAL, AS AGAINST INDIVIDUAL, OWNERSHIP

In the *Bulun Bulun* case, the artist who created the physical work clearly did not give any form of permission for reproductions to be made. In the *Ten Dollar Note* case, the applicant based his case on the argument that what appeared to be permission to reproduce was not a valid assignment of copyright under Anglo-Australian law. In neither case is the issue of collective ownership of copyright squarely raised: nor can it be, since the law as hitherto judicially expressed does not recognise such a concept.

Golvan (1989) argues that "consideration [should] be given to the introduction of a notion of collective ownership of copyright" (p 347). He points out that it is not always possible to identify the individual who created a particular work, and suggests that "the notion of individual ownership is [also] not consistent with tribal customs which emphasise communal ownership" (p 353). The notion of tribal ownership of confidential ideas was "respected" in *Foster v Mountford* (1977) 14 ALR 71 in the sense that the "deep religious and cultural significance" (at 73) of the persons, places and ceremonies was recognised: collective ownership of ideas is also recognised to some degree in Norway and France (Golvan p 353).

Problems in the practical operation of such a concept might arise in cases of conflict between the desires of the artist creating the physical work, and the desires of the clan or clans with "ownership" of the design. In this situation the answer would presumably be to leave the Aboriginal communities' own dispute resolution mechanisms to solve the problem, with precedence being given to the desires of the collective owners if conflict remains unresolved.

A more difficult problem might be identifying the communities or clans with "ownership" under traditional law. One community might "own" a particular way in which a common design is used: another might own a different aspect of its use. A suggested approach might be to establish a record or register of "title" in which the characteristic interpretations of various communities of common designs are stored.

In any case such problems do not justify jettisoning the idea of recognising collective ownership of Aboriginal designs in a manner more consistent with Aboriginal customary law than the present approach. This would require either legislative change or an extension of the *Mabo* decision beyond its present scope: see the discussion at p 250 above. An alternative approach is the extension of an equitable remedy, as will be suggested below.

THE EXTENT TO WHICH RECOGNITION SHOULD BE GIVEN TO THE ABORIGINAL COMMUNITY'S INTEREST IN THE DESIGN EVEN AFTER PUBLICATION OR SELLING OF THE COPYRIGHT

The idea that an Aboriginal community should retain a perpetual or inalienable interest in a design is in some ways akin to the European or civil law concept of "moral rights". Moral rights are predicated on an idea of Kant quoted in Golvan and McDonald (1986 p 157), who considered that "the mere act of creation conferred on the author a personal right to the product of her or his mind". It follows from this that "writers have an interest in upholding the integrity of their work which exists quite independently of any economic or proprietary interest in the work" (Golvan and McDonald p 157).

However common law or legislative recognition of moral rights in Australia is very limited (p 157). Only ss 190 and 191 to the *Copyright Act* may be said to enact a restricted recognition of two of the rights given legal recognition in Europe (pp 163, 166). In failing to give explicit protection to the moral rights of authors, Australia is in breach of Article 6 of the Berne Convention, to which it has been a signatory since 1928 (p 158).

Clearly, express recognition of moral rights along the lines of that recognised in some civil law countries, which in Australia would have to be achieved by statute, would effectively protect the rights of individual Aboriginal artists. However, it would not protect communal Aboriginal rights in a design where an individual is prepared to authorise the proposed use of the design. Nor would it be consistent with the view that Aboriginal interests in communal designs are in the nature of proprietary interests, since, as noted above, moral rights exist independent of economic or proprietary interests. Legislative recognition of moral rights would need to be very extensive in order to provide adequate protection. Its basis would need to be an extension of Kant's dictum in a manner alien to Anglo-Australian legal culture, perhaps along the following lines: "the mere act of creation by ancestral beings conferred upon the Yolngu a collective right to the product of this act of creation". It is suggested therefore that legislative recognition of moral rights is not the appropriate means for protection of Aboriginal rights in traditional or sacred designs.

Nevertheless, some form of protection for the rights of Aboriginal people in traditional designs, even after publication, is needed. The argument which follows assumes that legislation is not passed enshrining such rights: it also assumes that the decision in *Mabo v Queensland* is not extended to protect intellectual or cultural property rights. The argument will be that it is open to the common law to recognise Aboriginal rights in designs even after publication, by an extension of the equitable action of breach of confidence.

The first case which explicitly granted a right to protection for Aboriginal secrets was *Foster v Mountford* (1977) 14 ALR 71. In this case an injunction was granted restraining the author and publisher from publishing, in the Northern Territory, a book which contained secrets of significance to the Pitjantjatjara people, the author having obtained such secrets 35 years earlier in circumstances importing an obligation of confidence. The facts of the case were unique and the approach of Muirhead J was sympathetic to the Aboriginal plaintiffs, the injunction being granted partly on the basis that "monetary damages cannot alleviate any wrong to the plaintiffs that may be established and, perhaps, there can be no greater threat to any . . . than a threat to one's family and social structure" (at 75).

Nevertheless, there is nothing legally novel about the case. Muirhead J relied for his decision on the well-established principle enunciated by Lord Justice Denning that, "No person is permitted to divulge to the world information which he has received in confidence, unless he has just cause or excuse for doing so" (*Fraser v Evans* [1969] 1 All ER 8 at 11). Clearly in *Foster v Mountford* the information was confidential and had been understood to be so by the defendant at the time it was communicated. The information had never previously been "published" under the definition of publication in Anglo-Australian law. Muirhead J did not have to consider what the situation would have been had some form of publication of the information, authorised by the plaintiffs, occurred before its communication to the defendant: nor did he have to consider whether the right on which he granted the injunction was based on a breach of faith, on contract or in property (at 74-5).

Two English cases decided before the passing of the *Copyright Act* 1911 (Eng) appear to have given some early guidance on this question. The first of these was an 1824 decision in *Abernethy v Hutchinson* (1825) 1 H and Tw 28; 47 ER 1313. Here an injunction was granted to restrain a student from publishing, in a periodical, details of lectures delivered orally by a distinguished surgeon to a group of medical students.

It is unclear precisely on what basis the injunction was granted. The Lord Chancellor appears to consider significant the period of time over which the lectures had been delivered, during which period "from the understanding and usage subsisting for a long space of time between the lecturer and the persons attending the same, no publication of lectures had ever been made by the persons attending them" (at 1313). He points out (at 1315) that the case can only be viewed as either a question of property or a question of trust, but then adds that a further ground for an injunction would be that arising out of an implied contract (at 1316). He goes on to query whether a proprietary interest can exist in such a case, "Upon the question of property in *language and sentiments* not put into writing,

I give no opinion, but only say that it is a question of mighty importance" (at 1317).

In the end he does decide that a proprietary interest can exist, for "as they [the lectures] must have been taken from a pupil, or otherwise in such a way as the Court would not permit, the injunction ought to go upon the ground of property" (at 1317). He then decides to reject the possibility he had earlier approved, that of implied contract, on the ground that as it was not clear how the defendant had procured the lectures published "there was not sufficient to establish an implied contract as between the Plaintiff and the Defendants" (at 1317).

Thus while the true reasons for Lord Eldon's decision in this case remain unclear the most likely explanation appears to be that based upon a proprietary interest in the material. The plaintiff possessed such a proprietary interest even though he had never committed the lecture to writing: and more importantly for present purposes, he retained his proprietary interest even though publication (albeit in a limited sense) had occurred.

The second English case, that of *Prince Albert v Strange* (1849) 1 H and Tw 1; 47 ER 1302 provides further support for the proposition that a proprietary interest exists in original material independent of copyright. In this case an injunction was granted to restrain the defendant from publishing copies of private etchings exchanged between Queen Victoria and Prince Albert, and also from publishing a catalogue in which enumeration and a descriptive account of the etchings was contained. The etchings had never been published or intended to be published, and although precisely how they had been obtained was unclear, the Lord Chancellor considered that the means used had plainly been improper (at 1311).

The grounds for the decision in this case are clearly in property. The Lord Chancellor explicitly recognises "the exclusive right of the author in unpublished compositions, which depend(s) entirely on the common law right of property" (at 1310).

It is arguable that the Lord Chancellor has restricted his recognition of a proprietary interest to unpublished work. He does not extend the principle on which the plaintiff based his request for an injunction: that is, a right "antecedent to any publication to the world" (at 1307), and based on the "peculiar property" which each person has in his or her own sentiments or unpublished manuscripts. He appears to have accepted the proposition that:

> as every author or proprietor of a manuscript has a right to determine whether he will publish it or not, he has a right to the first publication; and whoever deprives him of that priority is guilty of a manifest wrong, and the Court has a right to stop it (at 1307).

While no specific statement is made that a proprietary interest in work cannot continue after publication independent of copyright, it is arguable that this is implicit in the judgment.

If this is the case then it is submitted that such a conclusion would be obiter, as it would be a conclusion of law not based on the material fact that the work which was the subject of the action was unpublished. Secondly such a conclusion would be inconsistent with *Abernethy v Hutchinson*, which is not discussed in any detail, much less disapproved, in the judgment. However, as such a conclusion is nowhere expressed in the judgment, it is submitted that the law in England at the time of *Prince Albert's* case recognised a proprietary right in the creators of artistic works independent of copyright, and at least in some circumstances, even after publication.

As Ricketson (p 812) points out, such a right became actionable only in equity after the enactment of the *Copyright Act* 1911 (Eng). This fact is no bar to recognising it as proprietary in nature rather than as based on an equitable obligation of good faith. According to Ricketson (p 852), "such proprietary rights, if they exist at all, are equitable in nature and approximate that class of equitable interest described as 'undefined equities'". Equally, the fact that it is based in equity implies that there is no inconsistency with any of the *Copyright Acts* (in the United Kingdom or Australia) in the argument that it may apply after publication.

In any case (whether or not the term is misleading) the action has become known as the action for breach of confidence. Its elements have become refined in later cases, and the three elements specified by Megarry J in *Coco v AN Clark (Engineers) Ltd* [1969] RPC 41 (Ch) have received particular judicial (and academic) acceptance. It is proposed to consider these three elements briefly in order to ascertain whether there is anything in the way they have been judicially interpreted which is inconsistent with the contention that the breach of confidence action may still apply after publication.

THE NEED FOR THE INFORMATION TO BE CONFIDENTIAL

According to Ricketson (p 818), "The basic principle is that information ceases to be confidential once it is in the public domain, that is, once it has become public or common knowledge". This does not mean that merely because it is possible for members of the public to inspect or copy a finished article, confidentiality and consequent protection is thereby lost (p 819). This point has received its greatest judicial recognition in the case of trade secrets, for example, *Ackroyds (London) Ltd v Islington Plastics Ltd* [1962] RPC 97 at 104 (Havers J) and other cases cited in Ricketson (p 819). In such cases mere ability in the public to inspect the product which is the subject of protection is not sufficient to divulge the particular trade secret used to make the product.

Such a doctrine can be extended to apply equally to Aboriginal designs. Merely because an object or design has been published or is in some way open to public inspection, does not mean that the "trade secrets" or sacred information encoded within it thereby lose their quality of confidentiality. Part of this quality of confidentiality may be said to lie in the restrictions placed by the Aboriginal owners of the design upon its further dissemination. The design retains its quality of confidentiality as long as its secrets are known only to those authorised by Aboriginal law to know them. Its secrets are disseminated under Aboriginal law as soon as the design is seen by someone not authorised to see it: as soon as the design is reproduced in a manner or form not authorised under Aboriginal law.

The question arises of why Anglo-Australian law should look to Aboriginal law to determine whether in this situation a breach of confidence has occurred. The clear analogy, again, is with the law dealing with trade secrets. In the case of trade secrets the law relies on the usage and practices of the particular trade or industry (*Thomas Marshall (Exporters) Ltd v Guinle* [1979] FSR 208 at 230 (Megarry V-C) and Ricketson p 822) to determine whether the information retains its quality of confidentiality. It is thus no more than logically consistent to rely in an appropriate case on the usage and practices of Aboriginal customary law.

An illustration of the way such a doctrine might work is the case of Terry Yumbulul. Yumbulul authorised his Morning Star pole to go on display at the Australian Museum. This display, being authorised under customary law, did not detract from the confidential nature of the sacred information encoded in the pole, and thence of the pole itself. When it was reproduced in a manner illegal under Aboriginal customary law, the pole lost its quality of confidentiality.[21]

THE OBLIGATION OF CONFIDENCE

It is clear from the cases that it is not necessary that the recipient of the information know that the information is confidential, in order for the circumstances to impart an obligation of confidence (*Coco v AN Clark* [1969] RPC 41 (Ch D) at 48 per Megarry J; see also Ricketson pp 822-3). Thus it would not be necessary that the Queensland T-Shirt manufacturer know that it is breaching Aboriginal customary law in printing pirate T-shirts (the fact situation arising in the *Bulun Bulun* case): nor necessary for the Aboriginal Artists Agency to know that it was breaching customary law by allowing the Reserve Bank to use Yumbulul's design on a banknote (the fact situation in the *Ten Dollar Note* case). Equally it would seem not to have been necessary for Muirhead J's decision in *Foster v Mountford* (1977) 14 ALR 71 that he conclude, as he did, that the defendant knew at the time the secrets were told to him, that

---

21 The judgment of French J in the *Ten Dollar Note* case does not consider the issue of confidential information. However French J found at 483 that the Morning Star pole lost any quality of confidentiality it may have had once Yumbulul sold it to the Australian Museum. Note also that the judgment does not recognise any obligation on the part of Aboriginal Artists Agency to explore with the applicant or even alert him to the possible implications of the proposed publication under Aboriginal customary law: see p 490.

they were meant not to be revealed (at 73). All that is necessary is that a "reasonable man" test be satisfied.

Note also that a third party who receives confidential information may nonetheless be held liable if he or she seeks to use or disclose it (*Prince Albert v Strange* in Ricketson p 824). Thus a defendant may not claim that he or she never had any direct communication with the Aboriginal community with customary law responsibility for the design.

If no "communication" at all of the design or information is held to exist, then the Aboriginal plaintiff must rely on the old case law outlined by Ricketson under his consideration of "the position where a person obtains knowledge of another's confidential information without there having been an initial communication in confidence" (p 827). However it is submitted that in most cases arising in practice there would have been some form of communication or publication sufficient to satisfy this requirement.

AN UNAUTHORISED USE OF THE INFORMATION

Clearly an unauthorised use would be a use which was not authorised under Aboriginal law: a purported authorisation by an individual artist would not be enough. The "detriment" which it is necessary to establish (Ricketson p 831) would also need to be established with reference to the standards and effects on the Aboriginal community concerned, just as it was by Muirhead J in *Foster v Mountford*.

In conclusion, this chapter has set out to outline the ways in which Aboriginal design and copyright issues may arise, and to suggest how copyright law and the treatment of the issue in equity hitherto have been inadequate. It has been suggested that the reasons for this inadequacy lie in the different concepts of "intellectual property" under Anglo-Australian law and under Aboriginal law. It has argued that the recognition of Aboriginal interests in real property at common law (achieved by virtue of the *Mabo* decision) should logically lead to a recognition of Aboriginal proprietary interests in sacred designs, beyond that already accorded by copyright law.

It has been argued that the most appropriate basis for recognition of Aboriginal interests in sacred designs lies not in copyright, but in property. This is because the concept in Anglo-Australian law of a proprietary interest accords more closely than any other legal category with the Aboriginal conception of sacred designs. It has been suggested that the basis for such a recognition already exists in the equitable action for what is called breach of confidence, although it was submitted that the true basis for this equitable action is proprietary. It was argued that the action can without difficulty be extended to cover situations of the type arising in both the *Bulun Bulun* and the *Ten Dollar Note* cases, and indeed in other conceivable situations involving the unauthorised use of Aboriginal designs. This action possesses greater scope than any other legal remedy for taking into account Aboriginal law in making the decision, particularly as it is not restricted by the notion that only an individual artist can satisfy its requirements. As such it is the most appropriate remedy, for it gives greater formal recognition than any other legal category to the legal systems already existing in Australia before the coming of English law.

BIBLIOGRAPHY

Golvan, C and McDonald, M, 1986, *Writers and the Law* Law Book Company, 1986.

Golvan, C, 1989, "Aboriginal Art and Copyright", 10 *EIPR* p 346.

Hocking, B, 1979, "Does Aboriginal Law now run in Australia?", 10 *FL Rev* p 161.

Hookey, J, 1972, "The Gove Land Rights Case: A Judicial Dispensation for the Taking of Aboriginal Lands in Australia?", 5 *FL Rev* p 85.

Lester and Parker, 1973, "Land Rights: The Australian Aborigines have lost a Legal Battle, but. . .", 11 *Alta L Rev* p 189.

Lumb, 1988, "Aboriginal Land Rights: Judicial Approaches in Perspective", 62 *ALJ* p 273.

McNeil, K, 1990, "A Question of Title: Has the Common Law been Misapplied to Dispossess the Aboriginals?", 16(1), *MonULR*.

Morphy, H, 1983, "Now you understand: An analysis of the way Yolngu have used sacred knowledge to retain their autonomy", Langton, M and Peterson, N. *Aborigines, Land, and Land Rights*, Australian Institute of Aboriginal Studies.

Priestley, LJ, 1974, "Communal Native Title and the Common Law: Further Thoughts on the Gove Land Rights Case", 6 *FL Rev* p 150.

Ricketson, S, 1984, *The Law of Intellectual Property*, Law Book Company Ltd.

Spencer, B and Gillen, FJ, 1899, *Native Tribes of Central Australia*, Macmillan, London.

Williams, N, 1986, *The Yolngu and their Land*, Australian Institute of Aboriginal Studies.

4

ON A HIGHER PLANE

24

Literary Styles in Judgments: Paragons of Penmanship

GRAHAM L FRICKE

If language is an important weapon in the advocate's armoury, it is crucial for the judge. He must make his meaning plain, not only for the benefit of the immediate parties, but also in order to avoid inflicting needless pain on subsequent generations of lawyers and law students.

The best judges have been those who have been skilled wordsmiths. This is easier to demonstrate in the United States, where the paragons have been fine literary craftsmen, and where a background in academia has not been thought to constitute a disqualification for judicial office. Men such as Holmes, Cardozo and Frankfurter were all renowned as teachers and writers before they began to discharge the judicial art.

Oliver Wendell Holmes is our first exemplar. He was remarkable for his energy, tolerance, forthrightness, style and longevity. He was the only Supreme Court justice still sitting in the 1930s who had been wounded in the American Civil War – at Ball's Bluff, Antietam and at Fredericksburg. After being mustered out as a captain in 1864, he studied law at Harvard Law School, and commenced practice in 1867. Fourteen years later, and before Holmes had celebrated his fortieth birthday, he leapt into prominence with the publication of his *The Common Law* (based on a series of lectures he had delivered at the Lowell Institute in Boston). The opening sentence, "The life of the law has not been logic; it has been experience", was typical of Holmes's aphoristic style.

Following the publication of *The Common Law*, Holmes was appointed to a chair at Harvard Law School. A year later, he began his judicial career as a member of the Massachussetts Supreme Court. After 20 years of service, including three as Chief Justice, Holmes was appointed by Theodore Roosevelt to the Supreme Court of the United States. He served there until 1932, when, at the age of

90, he was persuaded by Chief Justice Hughes to retire. During his 50 years on the bench in Massachussetts and in Washington, he wrote thousands of opinions. He became known as the Great Dissenter, although his dissents were statistically infrequent. But they marked him as a man with an independent mind, a sympathy for freedom of speech and of enterprise, and a flair for language.

Abrams v United States 250 US 616 (1919) provides an example. The defendants, who were Russian-born aliens, had been convicted of preparing and disseminating leaflets urging munitions workers not to produce weapons that could be used in an American military intervention in Russia in 1918. America was not at war with Russia, but the trial judge had excluded evidence that the Russian intervention weakened the American war effort against the Central Powers. Upon conviction, he sentenced Abrams to 20 years' imprisonment. Abrams appealed to the United States Supreme Court, contending, first, that the requisite intent had not been proved, but secondly, even if it had, that the statute under which he was charged was unconstitutional as infringing his freedom of speech guaranteed by the First Amendment.

The majority upheld the convictions, but Holmes and Brandeis dissented. After concluding that the requisite intent had not been proved, Holmes turned to the "more important aspect of the case": the First Amendment argument. Even if he was wrong on the first argument, even if "enough can be squeezed from these poor and puny anonymities to turn the colour of legal litmus paper", Holmes considered that the punishment of 20 years imprisonment was quite disproportionate:

> [When] men have realized that time has upset many fighting faiths, they may come to believe . . . that the ultimate good desired is better reached by free trade in ideas – that the best test of truth is the power of thought to get itself accepted in the competition of the market. . . [We] should be eternally vigilant against attempts to check the expression of opinions that we loath and believe to be fraught with death, unless they so imminently threaten immediate interference with the lawful and pressing purposes of the law that an immediate check is required to save the country.

When freedom of speech was not at stake, however, Holmes was generally inclined to leave it to State legislatures to use experimental measures to control social behaviour; he was loath to find such measures unconstitutional. When the New York legislature sought to regulate the maximum prices at which brokers could sell theatre tickets, Holmes disagreed with his brethren that such legislation constituted a deprivation of property (the business of ticket brokers) without due process of law, in violation of the Fourteenth Amendment:

> a State legislature can do whatever it sees fit to do unless it is restrained by some express prohibition in the Constitution . . . and . . . Courts should be careful not to extend such prohibitions beyond their

> obvious meaning by reading into them conceptions of public policy that the particular Court may happen to entertain. . . Lotteries were thought useful adjuncts of the State a century or so ago; now they are believed to be immoral and they have been stopped. Wine has been thought good for man from the time of the Apostles until recent years. . . [Public] opinion [has] changed . . . what has happened to lotteries and wine might happen to theatres in some moral storm of the future. . .
>
> But if we are to yield to fashionable conventions, it seems to me that theatres are as much devoted to public use as anything well can be. We have not that respect for art that is one of the glories of France. But to many people the superfluous is the necessary, and it seems to me that government does not go beyond its sphere in attempting to make life liveable for them. . . [If] the people of the State of New York speaking by their authorised voice say that they want it, I see nothing in the Constitution of the United States to prevent their having their will. (*Tyson v Banton* 273 US 418 (1927); Holmes's view came to prevail in 1941; *Olsen v Nebraska* 313 US 236)

In 1932, President Hoover yielded to a groundswell of professional and editorial opinion and replaced Holmes with Benjamin Cardozo, who had sat on the New York Court of Appeals for the preceding 18 years, including five years as Chief Judge. Cardozo made a substantial contribution to constitutional jurisprudence during his remaining six years, but his most significant contributions were in the common law fields during his period in New York.

Cardozo's personality was quite different from that of Holmes, whom he greatly admired. Whereas Holmes cut the bold and dashing figure of an extrovert and former soldier, Cardozo was in the same quiet gentle mould as Owen Dixon or Wilfred Fullagar. He had the same capacity as Owen Dixon or Alfred Deakin for detached and critical analysis of the foibles of his fellows, but, like Dixon and Deakin, Cardozo tended to keep his views to himself.

Like his predecessor and role model, Holmes, Cardozo had a penchant for the pithy, but he alternated his aphorisms with complex sentences to produce an elegant mix. He also emulated Holmes in his capacity as an extra-judicial writer and educationalist. He delivered a series of lectures which were later converted into a book called *The Nature of The Judicial Process*. He developed some of his themes in subsequent lectures printed as *The Growth of the Law* and *The Paradoxes of Legal Science*.

Cardozo's pithy style is exemplified by his decision in *Wagner v International Railway Co* 232 NY 176 (1921), in which he upheld the claim of a person injured in the process of rescuing another who had been jeopardised by the defendant's conduct:

> Danger invites rescue. The cry of distress is the summons to relief. The law does not ignore these reactions of the mind in tracing conduct to its consequences. . . The risk of rescue, if only it be not wanton, is born of the occasion. The emergency begets the man. The wrongdoer may not have foreseen the coming of a deliverer. He is accountable as if he had.

In 1916, some 16 years before the House of Lords dealt with the subject in *Donoghue v Stevenson* [1932] AC 562 at 580, Cardozo rejected the notion of privity as a limiting factor in the law of torts:

> If the nature of the thing is such that it is reasonably certain to place life and limb in peril when negligently made, it is then a thing of danger. . . [The] presence of a known danger attendant upon a known use, makes vigilance a duty. . . The defendant knew the danger. It knew also that the car would be used by persons other than the buyer. . . The dealer was indeed the one person of whom it might be said with some approach to certainty that by him the car would not be used. Yet the defendant would have us say that he was the one person whom it was under a legal duty to protect. (*McPherson v Buick Motor Company* 217 NY 382 (1916))

Likewise in the *Palsgraf* case, Cardozo anticipated the House of Lords' decision in *Bourhill v Young* [1943 AC 92:

> Wrong to another cannot be the basis of the plaintiff's claim and even less a wrong to a mere property interest. . . [T]he risk reasonably to be perceived defines the duty to be obeyed and risk imports relation. The victim does not sue derivatively or by right of subrogation to vindicate an interest invaded in the person of another. (*Palsgraf v Long Island RR* 248 NY 339 (1928))

Just as Holmes was succeeded by Cardozo, Cardozo was succeeded by another great pedagogue and writer, Felix Frankfurter. Although Frankfurter had spent some eight years after his graduation practising as a government lawyer, and had advised presidents on constitutional issues, his career had been devoted principally to teaching at Harvard Law School during the quarter century preceding his appointment to the Supreme Court in 1939.

Frankfurter's professorial background sometimes showed in his performance on the bench. When a senior member of the bar and former presidential candidate, John W Davis, was arguing one of the school segregation cases in 1952, Frankfurter asked him, "Mr Davis, do you think that 'equal' is a less fluid term than 'commerce between the states'?". Davis at first equivocated. "Less fluid?", he enquired. "Yes", said Frankfurter. Davis again avoided a direct answer. "I have not compared the two on the point of fluidity", he said. "Suppose you do it now", said the former professor.

Frankfurter, who had advised President FD Roosevelt during the period in which a hostile Supreme Court had held the New Deal legislation unconstitutional, supported the notion of judicial restraint, principally on democratic grounds:

> Even where the social undesirability of a law may be convincingly urged, invalidation of the law by a court debilitates popular democratic government. Most laws dealing with economic and social problems are matters of trial and error. That which before trial appears to be demonstrably bad may belie prophecy in actual operation. It may not prove good, but it may prove innocuous. But even if a law is found wanting on trial, it is better that its defects should be demonstrated and removed than that the law should be

> aborted by judicial fiat. Such an assertion of judicial power deflects responsibility from those on whom in a democratic society it ultimately rests – the people. . . In the day-to-day working of our democracy it is vital that the power of the non-democratic organ of our Government be exercised with rigorous self-restraint. . . Judges appointed for life whose decisions run counter to prevailing opinion cannot be voted out of office and supplanted by men of views more consonant with it. . . (*Lincoln Federal Labour Union v North Western Iron and Metal Co* 335 US 528 at 538 (1949))

Like Holmes, Frankfurter was more inclined to be interventionist when one of the interests guaranteed by the Bill of Rights was involved. This applied especially to the interest in academic freedom. In *Sweezy v New Hampshire* 354 US 234 (1957), an economist who had refused to answer a legislative committee's questions about possible subversive activities was convicted of contempt. He appealed ultimately to the Supreme Court. Frankfurter concurred in a decision allowing the appeal:

> When weighed against the grave harm resulting from governmental intrusion into the intellectual life of a university, [the lower courts'] justification for compelling a witness to discuss the contents of his lecture appears grossly inadequate. . . Progress in the natural sciences is not remotely confined to findings made in the laboratory. Insights into the mysteries of nature are borne of hypothesis and speculation. The more so is this true in the pursuit of understanding in the groping endeavours of what are called the social sciences. . . [F]or society's good – if understanding be an essential need of society – enquiries into these problems, speculations about them, stimulation in others of reflection upon them, must be left as unfettered as possible. Political power must abstain from intrusion into this activity of freedom, pursued in the interest of wise government and the people's well-being, except for reasons that are exigent and obviously compelling.

When one turns to England, examples of judges with backgrounds in academia are harder to find, but the outstanding judges were nevertheless fine literary craftsmen. Foremost was Lord Atkin, who was born in Queensland in 1867, but who left the State some four years later to be brought up by his maternal grandparents in Wales. He received his early education at Friars School, Bangor, and Christ College, Brecon, before going to Magdalen College, Oxford, where he obtained second class honours in Classical Moderations and Greats. In the best English tradition, he ate his dinners at Gray's Inn, and he records his enjoyment of the experience in an autobiographical fragment. "We used to have a good dinner", he says, "Soup or fish, joint, sweet, cheese and two or sometimes three bottles of wine". He observes that the choice of the principal carver of the joint was based then on seniority, and adds, "I have seen some strange carving".

Atkin survived these stringent gastronomic tests, and was admitted to the bar in 1890. He walked the courts in his quest for a master and, finding Scrutton to be the most impressive of the barristers he observed, he persuaded his exemplar to let him read with him. Work was slow at first, and it was not until his fourth year at the bar, 1894, that he earned a three-figure sum, exactly £100. In 1897, he earned £346 in fees, after which, as he puts it, "The corner was turned". Some nine years later, at the age of 39, he took silk, and seven years later, he was appointed by Lord Haldane to the King's Bench Division. He spent the next six years as a trial judge, and these were Atkin's most enjoyable professional years.

The next nine years were spent on the Court of Appeal as its junior common law Lord Justice. From the quality of his judgments, one might have inferred that these were satisfying years, but this was the period that Atkin enjoyed least. He contemplated resigning on at least two occasions, but was rescued from the tedium in 1928, when he was appointed to the House of Lords. He remained there for 16 years until his death in 1944.

Atkin's most celebrated judgment, of course, is *Donoghue v Stevenson*, in which Atkin resorted to biblical allusion:

> The rule that you are to love your neighbour becomes in law, you must not injure your neighbour; and the lawyer's question, Who is my neighbour? receives a restricted reply. You must take reasonable care to avoid acts or omissions which you can reasonably foresee would be likely to injure your neighbour. Who, then, in law is my neighbour? The answer seems to be – persons who are so closely and directly affected by my act that I ought reasonably to have them in contemplation as being so affected when I am directing my mind to the acts or omissions which are called in question. ([1932] AC 562 at 580)

From today's perspective, the dissents of Lords Buckmaster and Tomlin seem incredible. But in 1932, the Atkin judgment represented a skilful synthesis of authority and his elegant expression of principle no doubt helped to establish the general neighbour principle in the law of torts.

An equally powerful but less happy set of pronouncements is contained in Atkin's dissenting judgment in *Liversidge v Anderson* [1942] AC 206. During a low point in World War II, the Secretary of State had detained Liversidge under Defence (General) Regulation 18B, which provided that:

> If the Secretary of State has reasonable cause to believe any person to be of hostile origin or associations . . . and that by reason thereof it is necessary to exercise control over him, he may make an order against that person directing that he be detained.

The issue was whether, in construing the words "has reasonable cause to believe" one should adopt a subjective approach or an objective approach. In other words, should the Secretary of State be allowed to judge the reasonableness of his own grounds, or was the reasonableness of his belief open to challenge in the courts?

As a matter of statutory construction, Atkin felt strongly that the objective approach was appropriate. He rejected the view that the words "if a man has" could mean "if a man thinks he has". If the legislature had intended to confer an unchallengeable discretion, it would have been easy to adopt another form of words, such as "if it appears to the Secretary of State that".

Atkin's views on the question of statutory construction have been vindicated by posterity – see *IRC v Rossminster Ltd* [1980] 1 All ER 80 – but in 1942 it required enormous courage to express them. Atkin's forthrightness in maintaining his views and in attacking his brethren led to his alienation from his colleagues, and may have contributed to his death a year or two later. For despite attempts by Lord Chancellor Simon to dissuade him, Atkin did not shrink from an attack upon his colleagues and on counsel for the Secretary of State:

> I view with apprehension the attitude of judges who on a mere question of construction when face to face with claims involving the liberty of the subject show themselves to be more executive minded than the executive. Their function is to give words their natural meaning. . . In this country, amid the clash of arms, the laws are not silent. They may be changed but they speak the same language in war as in peace. It has always been one of the pillars of freedom, one of the principles of liberty for which on recent authority we are now fighting, that the judges are no respecters of persons and stand between the subject and any attempt at encroachments on his liberty by the executive, alert to see that any coercive action is justified in law. In this case I have listened to arguments which might have been addressed acceptably to the Court of King's Bench in the time of Charles I.

As if this were not enough, Atkin concluded with the suggestion that there was only one authority for the method of construction adopted by his esteemed colleagues: that was *Alice in Wonderland* in which Humpty Dumpty asserted, "When I use a word, it means just what I choose it to mean, neither more nor less".

The judgment had an electric effect. Lord Maugham was moved to the ultimate in resolute aristocratic action, a strong letter to *The Times* deploring "so grave an animadversion" as Atkin's reference to the arguments of counsel. At the House of Lords Dining Room later that day, Atkin observed his old friend, Lord Wright, pass by him in silence. Plainly, Atkin was being sent to Coventry. Before the end of the war which had led to such passions and schisms, Atkin died at Aberdovey.

Unlike his American counterparts, Atkin was not noted as a pedagogue. Indeed, he disclaimed such a capacity. In his autobiographical fragment, he asserted proudly, "I do not pose as an 'educationalist', heaven forbid, though I have been on the government bodies or courts of about a dozen educational establishments". He added, somewhat gratuitously, "One is reminded of the definition of a jurist as a man who knows a little of the laws of every country but his own".

But Atkin had the same gift for the aphorism, the pithy phrase, as Holmes and Cardozo. Phrases such as "justice is not a cloistered virtue", "convenience and justice are often not on speaking terms", and "finality is a good thing but justice is better" decorate his judgments. He demonstrated the importance for the judges of two qualities – courage and the felicitous use of language.

25

The Ethics of Meaning[1]

JAMES BOYD WHITE

In choosing what I call "the ethics of meaning" as the subject of this chapter I bring together two of the most complex and difficult terms in our language. To begin with "meaning", few things are harder to talk about than the complex and tangled process by which what we say – or do – takes on a meaning for another. Meaning is a mixture of conscious intention and subconscious wish, of expectation and imagination, of varying and often incompatible perceptions of context, and this on the part of both writer and reader. As for "ethics": it involves nothing less than our understanding of the possibilities for goodness in human life, and how far, in a particular instance, they are achieved. Obviously, I shall not in this chapter try to work out conclusive definitions for either term or try to say anything final about the relation between them. Rather, I hope to trace out a single line of thought that connects them, less with the idea of arriving at conclusions than with the hope of defining a set of questions in such a way as to suggest how they might be worth pursuing.

I wish, that is, to draw attention to a single strand of the tangle I have described, which I shall call the ethical dimension of meaning. The thought that I wish to elaborate is a very simple one, namely that every text or utterance is a form of action, and that as such it is an ethical performance, calling for ethical judgment. This is so in at least two respects, for in every text the speaker acts both upon what I shall call her language – by which I mean all the resources of meaning her culture affords her – and upon her audience, by which I mean all those people whom her text addresses or speaks about.

However simple this thought may be, it is actually rather difficult to keep in mind, for it runs counter to many of the ways in which we habitually talk about both "meaning" and "ethics". With respect to "meaning", for example, we often talk – especially if we are

---

1 Earlier versions of this chapter were presented at Brown University and at the 1992 conference of the Law and Literature Association of Australia. For helpful comments on an earlier draft I wish to thank AL Becker, Larry Kramer, Martha Nussbaum, Joseph Vining, and Mary White. A portion of the chapter is taken from White, JB, *Acts of Hope: Creating Authority in Literature, Law, and Politics*, University of Chicago Press 1994. Copyright © 1994. Reprinted by permission.

being philosophic or analytic – as if the meaning of a text were reducible to the set of propositions it advances. The meaning is the message; everything else is a kind of surplusage. And with respect to ethics, we often talk as if ethics concerned conduct alone, and not mere talk. On this view, the radical question of ethics is how to behave oneself, or how to judge the behaviour of others: whether to obey this law or that, for example, or to approve or disapprove of abortion or the death penalty or a particular act of war. What we *say* is disregarded, as an adjunct to the real business, which is material action; our words are an epiphenomenon, or, at best, a kind of deliberation, the object of which is to lead to right action. My suggestion, on the contrary, is that we can see text-making – writing and talking – as a kind of action itself, and thus within the field of ethics; and, conversely, that we can see an important part of the meaning of a text as lying in the ethical action it performs. To take a crude example: if someone insults you, by calling you a name, say, surely you know that this is an act, not merely an idea, and you know how to judge it. Is it really any different when a political candidate, or leader, insults us all by speaking to us as if we were fools, or incapable of human sympathy? Or consider this: when someone composes an advertisement that represents a woman as a simple object of sexual desire, available to the fantasy life of the male viewer, does the writer not degrade himself, his audience, his culture, and his language, as well as women generally? This is not merely speech but action, and we can – and do – judge it ethically.

Notice that we judge it, as I suggested briefly above, in two ways, both as it affects its language and as it works on its audience. One might indeed think of each text as having two axes, the linguistic and the social, along which it could be seen to act ethically.

On the social axis every text does at least three things: first, it defines a character, or persona, for its speaker, who is present before us in the text, defined by tone of voice, quality of mind, attitude towards others, and so forth. (We know right away, for example, if someone sounds like a bully, or a salesman, and we can respond directly to that quality in his speech.) Secondly, it defines its audience in the way it addresses them – in the qualities of mind and character and knowledge it assumes they have – and thus defines a character for them too. Once again we immediately know, and respond, if we perceive someone addressing us as a bigot or an ignoramus, or – at the opposite extreme – as wise and good. Thirdly, in doing these things the text constitutes a community between speaker and audience, a relationship defined by the practices the text engages in and invites in others. This much we are taught by elementary rhetorical analysis.

But there is another axis as well, perhaps less obvious yet nonetheless real, which is linguistic and cultural in nature. For every text can be seen to act upon the language its speaker has been given to use, replicating some of its forms, modifying others, and so on, and this too can be regarded as a kind of ethical action. Whether he knows it or not, in making his text the speaker is not merely communicating a message, expressing a feeling, or trying to achieve a material or social objective, but affecting, or tending to affect, the materials for meaning in our world: perhaps to change them, perhaps to affirm that they need not, should not, be changed.[2]

As an obvious example think of a political advertisement or speech you find odious: do you not find yourself saying that such a text "degrades the process" or "cheapens the discourse of politics"? Or of a speech that you admire, that it "improves the quality of debate" or "clarifies the issues in important ways"? (Or think of the mind – one's own at times – that insists upon reiterating a set of ossified clichés.) Much the same can be said of less prominent forms of speech too, good and bad, say in a set of remarks made by a dean to her faculty or a teacher to his students or parents to their children. The text becomes a part of a community's common experience and helps shape the way conversation or thought in that world will proceed. It is a prior text that may be worked and reworked as allusions are made to it. The speaker reconstitutes her language and culture, in great ways or small, and for good or ill. This can be seen as a kind of ethical action; perhaps, indeed, one of our deepest obligations is to the language we use and to the culture it defines.

This is of course only to state, in rather conclusory terms, one way among many of conceiving of what happens when we speak to each other, and to suggest some of the questions to which it leads. In what follows I shall try to elaborate this way of thinking by way of examples.

I begin with the law, and in particular with the judicial opinion, which is for us the paradigmatic legal text, asking this: how are we to understand these texts as ethical action? How are we to express our approval and disapproval of them, and in doing so how are we to define their ethical meaning? Obviously the judgment or result reached by the court – the resolution of the case – is a form of ethical action, subject to ethical judgment. But can we also see the opinion, the text in which the judge explains that judgment, as a form of ethical action too, in some sense independent of the result?

Consider, for example, a judicial opinion upholding the constitutionality of the death penalty, say, or the right to abortion. How would we respond to and judge it? Partly no doubt as a matter of simple agreement or disagreement with its result: we are for or against these things and applaud, or disapprove, what the court does. But is that the end of it? Is it not also true that we can and do judge opinions in a different way, admiring some opinions with which we disagree, and condemning some with which we agree? What is it, in such a case, that we admire or condemn? Not just the result – in a simple sense the opinion's message – but something the opinion

2 This theme is developed at length in White (1984).

achieves as a piece of writing: the kind of action it performs with and upon its language, with and upon its various audiences.

Even if one happens not to have much experience of this kind of text, I think it is nonetheless possible to imagine how what I suggest could be true. Imagine a conservative on the Supreme Court who is joined in many opinions by a colleague who shares his general attitude towards crime, say, or abortion, or the powers of the President; yet he thinks him at bottom a fool. On the other side he is perpetually opposed by a justice whose work and mind and character he admires, but who comes out, for him, on the wrong side of question after question. Who is the better judge? For his judicial colleagues, for the world, for the litigants?

If our imaginary justice agrees that the better judge is the second, he is presented with the question, How can he begin to evaluate his colleagues' work, and his own, in ways that go beyond approval or disapproval of the result? In working out his response, such a judge would look partly, I think, to what I called the linguistic situation out of which the judge spoke. In the law this mainly consists of the set of the constraints established by the prior texts that speak to the judge with authority: the constitution, statutes, other precedents, the whole body of legal material that the parties invoke. How faithful is her opinion to that material, including to its principles of transformation and self-modification? How truthfully does she set forth the strains within it that work against her result? How adequate is the language of her opinion for future thought and argument about the issue she has decided? In asking such questions as these one would be starting off to investigate the quality of the opinion as a reconstitution of its language, and measuring this in part by seeing it as one stage in a conversation evolving over time.

To say this much is to bring us to the other axis of ethical meaning, the social, for we are already asking how the opinion constitutes, or reconstitutes, the community of which it is a part. Who is the judge as she defines herself in this text, and who are her various audiences: the litigants on both sides, future lawyers and judges, the public? How fully, for example, does her opinion recognise and reflect the experience of each of the litigants?[3] How fully does it

3 Notice that one might conclude that no opinion upholding the death penalty could meet these standards, on the grounds that the claim of meaning made by that penalty – that the defendant's life and being can be reduced to a single narrative, with a single and univocal end – is impossible. Unlike the prison sentence, for example, which recognises that the defendant has other possibilities for life, defined by his continuing rights against the state and against other individuals, the death penalty erases every aspect of the defendant except that defined by this single narrative, the story of his crime, as if it told all; and this is to deny what we know to be true. In literature we call it a form of sentimentality when the writer speaks as if a character's life could be reduced to a single act of cowardice, or bravery – think of Hemingway's "Short, Happy life of Francis Macomber" and contrast Conrad's *Lord Jim* – and the death penalty can be seen to have an analogous vice. If this is what one concluded, one would have discovered a ground for judgment "on the merits" in the ethics of meaning itself.

present and respond to what can be said on each side of the case? The goal here might be to create a text in which each party, to the greatest possible degree, sees reflected her own voice, or what she sees her case to mean. How is this to be done?

Without answering that question in detail, we know this much: that it is not just vaguely good motives that we require, but a capacity to attend to what is external to the self and its needs; to imagine the experience of another and to honour it; and to act wisely in light of one's own limitations. And these things must be made manifest and real in speech. The judge's excellence is in large part an excellence of character as that is defined in the performance that is her text; it is thus at once a matter of ethics, in the root sense of the term, and a matter of writing.

Notice that in thinking this way we are defining law, and justice itself, in ways not usual, at least in academic circles: not as an instrument of policy, or a tool of power, or a way of achieving a set of imagined results in the world, but as discursive and relational in nature. The justice that a judicial opinion achieves, or fails to achieve, can be seen as a matter of right relations – with one's language, with one's prior texts, with those one speaks to and about – at least as much as a matter of right results.

I mean all this as a way of suggesting that at least in the field of law we can conceive of the making of a text as itself an ethical activity, to some extent independent of the results or consequences of the underlying decision, and of its propositional content too, and this in both of the dimensions I have outlined, the social and linguistic. This is a thesis I have pursued at length in *Justice as Translation* (1990), and I shall not pursue it further here. Rather, I wish now to ask whether something similar can be said of other forms of literature as well: of the work of poets, novelists, politicians, historians, and perhaps even of philosophers?

Here I turn, as often, to the *Iliad*, and in particular to the beginning of the second book where, as one may remember, Agamemnon gives a long speech to his men which in effect says this, "We have been here too long; nine years, with no result; the timber of our ships is rotting; our wives and children await us; let us go home".

What is the meaning of Agamemnon's speech? His actual aim is not to encourage the men to abandon the war, as he claims, but quite the opposite, to inspire in them, by resistance to his speech – which he thinks cowardly – the desire to stay. He puts the case for quitting, that is, in terms that he thinks no one can accept, and is surprised by the men's response: they leap to their feet and start to prepare the boats for departure, and must be whipped back into line by Odysseus and Nestor, aided by the gods.

What was it that moved Agamemnon to make this speech? He had a dream, sent by Zeus, which promised the Achaeans victory, that very day; so heartened, he tried to instil anger and martial unity in his men. But as he deceived the men, he was himself deceived: the dream was in fact sent by Zeus as a trick to encourage the Greeks to engage the Trojans so that they could be beaten back to their ships; then they would be forced to honour Achilles, who, outraged at his treatment at the hands of Agamemnon, has withdrawn from battle. At one level, then, the ethics of this speech is double deception and manipulation.

Looked at as part of a larger narrative, however, this speech has a different and perhaps more positive function. It expresses directly what the men must have felt, over and over, but not been able to say, that the war was not worth the prize. In a world devoted to martial heroism, to the kind of glory that can be achieved only through arms, this speech says what cannot normally be said. And when the men have been checked in their flight by Nestor and Odysseus and moved to battle, restored to a martial energy that is now purified of boredom and lassitude, one can see the whole enterprise as a kind of therapy, in which Agamemnon was perhaps wiser than he knew: the speech brought to the surface, where they could be addressed and quelled, the fears and longings which rankled in the hearts of the men. This was in fact a way of redirecting the community towards its common goal.

But – as I have argued at length elsewhere[4] – the speech is part of an even larger design, in the poem itself: it is one of a long series of speeches and events in the first several books of the *Iliad* that throw into question the value of the military enterprise itself, and the value as well of what can only be attained by war, namely honour and glory.

As the speech addresses the reader, that is, rather than the men, it is one of a series of appeals away from the war, and from what can be attained by war, qualifying our perception of the language and motives upon which all of the male actors in the poem – except perhaps Thersites – seem to have built their lives. The effect on the reader is to work a kind of alienation from the culture of war, and from the only language available to anyone in the poem in which to describe himself and his motives. Thus it is that when Achilles, in book nine, having been injured because of a deprivation within the system of honour, speaks out in rejection of that system, and of the war, he speaks for us. To those to whom he speaks he is mad; to us he speaks a truth that we have been made to see.

In doing this Homer offers his reader a set of experiences from which we can see what no one in the imagined world can see, or keep in mind, the common humanity of both sides. From this position the values of war and heroism become, to say the least, deeply problematic. This movement receives its fullest expression in book 24 when Achilles and Priam meet, to embrace and weep together over the body of Hector, two people acknowledging their shared condition of human mortality.

---

4 White (1984), chapter 2.

My own way of describing this has been to say that Homer uses a language that was designed for the description and celebration of a particular heroic culture, the art-language of epic, to create a text that is deeply critical of that culture and of the language that makes it real. The ground of this criticism lies not in explicit statement, but in the way in which the materials of the poem are arranged to make a new meaning of their own, and in the community of understanding thus created between the text and its reader. A counter-world is constituted in the relation between text and reader upon which a criticism of the "real" world about which the text speaks can be based.

The poem is thus a form of ethical action: it acts at once upon the language and upon the reader, and its meaning lies in this action, not in any statement the poem makes. One of its achievements is to criticise its own culture; and it does this on a ground – the common humanity of all people; the impossibility of our languages to reflect that fact – upon which not only this but any culture, any public language, can be criticised. In this sense its criticism is radical, and reaches our own world.

But there is another side to this. Homer's respect for our common humanity does not translate into an anti-war tract, certainly not into a condemnation either of soldier or of general. It is rather a respect for each person, situated as he – or, believe it or not, she – actually is: for the Trojan ally, Sarpedon, when he describes the aristocratic ethic that compels his participation in war; for Diomedes, on his great day of destruction; for Helen, in her impossible position of divided loyalty and double shame; for the prize-girls, seen momentarily as people, not merely as tokens of honour. The poem respects each person as an actor in a context, from which he perceives what it is natural for him to perceive, from which he acts as it is natural for him to act. This is made plain, for example, when we think of how different the ethical meaning of Agamemnon's speech actually is to its various audiences: to the men, who think that they are being invited to go home; to Agamemnon who thinks he is manipulating them; and to Zeus, who sees it all.

The poem educates us, that is, by offering us an experience of imagination and sympathy, as we see the material of a culture rearranged to say something new about our common humanity and as we are simultaneously reminded of the reality of differing human perspectives that constitute that world. In doing this the poem offers to teach us an integrative and combinatory mode of thought, a way of imagining the world by putting its pieces together in new patterns, sequences, and combinations; a way of finding a truth by putting opposing sentiments, thoughts, visions, actors, against each other in larger patterns of significance.

This poem can thus be seen as an ethical performance in both of the dimensions referred to above, as it acts on its language – making it do the opposite of what it seems made to do – and as it acts on its reader, constituting him by offering him a set of experiences that transform the way he can imagine the world. To say this leads to a view of the *Iliad* in particular, and imaginative literature in general, that is somewhat different from the usual, namely that a large part of its meaning, and its excellence, is ethical in character.[5]

So I would say this: that all speech or writing is verbal action, and as such is ethical action, for it always involves the reconstitution both of language and of the social world. The linguistic element is central: for as there can be no expression without ethical significance, there can be no claim of ethical meaning, good or bad, without the use of a particular inherited language, with all of its possibilities for rigidity, exclusion, falseness, and cliché. We are as ethically responsible for what we do with and to our languages as for what we do with and to each other. This is true of judge and poet alike.

My next question is this: can the way I have suggested we can read judicial opinions and the *Iliad*, that is with attention to their ethical meaning, help us when we turn to overtly political texts, and political discourses, in the real stuff of political life? Can the strand of meaning I am trying to define connect, that is, the disparate fields of law, and literature, and politics itself?

One central subject of Agamemnon's speech, and of the *Iliad* itself, is how to talk about war. This is itself a contemporary issue – or nonissue – for us as well, and has been all of my life. Any such talk necessarily involves us in a definition of "us" and "them", allies and enemy, for every war has sides. To talk this way denies the fundamental human reality that the *Iliad* insists upon, our common humanity, and it erases, or trivialises, the real experience of others: dead women, maimed children, old men's bodies shattered, fifteen-year-old soldiers incapacitated with uncontrollable fear, the inner

---

5 This is also, of course, to suggest that the heart of a literary education can be ethical, though not in the currently fashionable sense – that it teaches rules or maxims of conduct, or establishes the habit of yielding to authority – but in a deeply different way: for it is here, in literature of the most powerful kind, that we can find intellectual and ethical performances that test the language the writer has inherited against other languages, other experience; performances that thus draw into question what had theretofore seemed natural, immutable. In this sense a good literary education is a radical education in cultural criticism.

Literature can offer an education in the nature of ethical thought more generally as well. For literature characteristically speaks to the question: "What are the proper standards by which to judge a text's ethical achievement?" by telling us that it cannot be answered on the terms it invites, that is, with a declaration or an exposition of a set of rules or criteria, as if there were a plane outside of culture and language on which thought of that sort could go on. Rather, it teaches us to think as these literary texts themselves do: as if we were all embedded in our languages and cultures, with no place outside of them to begin from or to withdraw to; as if the only kind of thought possible for us were the reconstitution or reformulation of what we have been given, of what we are; as if the only way to think about the kinds of character and relation we honour or approve is through comparison and contrast, as we test one experience against the other. This, after all, is how human beings grow to maturity, by putting one experience together with another, by thinking of one in light of another; this is the kind of thought that Homer teaches, and it affords us one, perhaps the best, way of thinking about ethics as well.

destruction of oneself that is caused by the killing of others, and so on. I think of the way public talk in our country erased the significance of Iraqi deaths in the recent war, for example.[6]

Who are we to be in our talk about war? How are we to define ourselves, other people, and the activity in which we are engaged? Can we talk in a way that is entitled to respect, to self-respect, or are we necessarily reduced to triviality, cliché, and empty hype? War is a moment of national self-definition, in which our way of talking defines the kind of character we have as a people and the meaning of our national experience. Can this meaning be one that we can endure, or even be proud of, or will our habits of mind and talk reduce it to emptiness and triviality? Is nobility possible here? These are ethical questions of the first importance, from the *Iliad* to the present moment.

In exploring them I will draw attention, in considerable detail, to a text that speaks about the meaning of war, at another time from our own, a text whose achievement is at once literary and political: Abraham Lincoln's Second Inaugural Address.

This text famously resists the claim of simple victory of "us" over "them". Consider, for example, these closing words:

> With malice toward none; with charity for all; with firmness in the right, as God gives us to see the right, let us strive on to finish the work we are in; to bind up the nation's wounds; to care for him who shall have borne the battle, and for his widow, and his orphan – to do all which may achieve and cherish a just and lasting peace among ourselves, and with all nations.

This is in its own way stirring and noble, but it also has, perhaps partly as a result of its decontextualised repetition, a kind of clichéd quality, at least in my country. Yet in the context in which it was originally uttered, at the end of this speech, it is not at all, I think, a set of clichés, but an enormously rich and demanding utterance. The reason is that in the speech that precedes it Lincoln remakes his language in such a way that these terms and gestures come to have a meaning that they could not have standing alone. His terms, that is, are given much of their meaning in his text, as he acts

---

6 When one thinks of what war-talk always disguises or hides, and the kind of false communities it establishes, one can ask – as we could ask of the death penalty too – whether we can *ever* talk responsibly about war except as an illegitimate violence, the infliction for ultimately selfish reasons of terrible pain and suffering on the weak and defenceless.

The pacifist part of me says yes, that is so, that there is no other way to talk about war, which is to say that there is no responsible way to justify it. That is, if we insist upon appropriate ethical standards in our talk, both with respect to the language we use and with respect to our relations with others, we shall find it impossible to speak of war as a permissible instrument of policy. But I recognise other more warlike impulses both in myself and others; there is in addition the question of the realities that pacificist talk denies; and in any event pacificism is not the present issue, for even if one accepts the necessity of war, one will still have to face the question of its meaning, that is of the meaning that our ways of thinking and talking give to it.

at once on his language and his audience. This is an example of "ethical" speech, then, in both directions, as he works with his language and as he establishes a character for himself and a community with others.

As I sketch rather quickly how Lincoln does these things, I will keep a special eye on the nouns and pronouns that define his social universe: "I", "us", "them", "all", "North", "South", "slaves", "the nation", and so forth, for this text is centrally about these terms, about the people to whom they refer, and about the kinds of relations that can be imagined to exist among them.

But first, let me briefly describe the situation Lincoln addressed, and the extraordinary difficulty of his task. His Second Inaugural was in 1865, after three years of unimaginably hideous civil war. He had been elected, of course, only by the states that remained loyal, but he wished to see the Union re-established, including the rebellious South. His object was to speak in such a way as to confirm the North's sense of the rightness of its cause and the justice of its impending victory, yet at the same time to speak to, and about, the people of the White South not as beasts or monsters deserving only death and humiliation, but, as his language of Union had asserted all along, as fellow citizens, as those who will soon share again in the process of government and in the fate of the nation. "Our" victory is good and right, he must say to the North; yet to the vanquished South, he must say you are of "us" too, and at the same time must persuade the North to accept that view. How can he possibly do these inconsistent things?

And how is he to speak to, and about, the African-American people whose enslavement was one of the causes of the war? Shall he speak to them as future citizens and equals? If so, how can he speak to the White South in terms they will regard as anything but hostile? If not, what happens to the moral basis of this war? And behind it all is a large question of principle, the deepest issue of the Civil War: why it is proper in the first place for a democratic state, itself based on the right of the people to choose their own forms of government, to use arms to resist secession?

What he said was characteristically very short, short enough in fact for me to include each sentence in the analysis that follows.

Lincoln's words of salutation, usual enough in addresses of this sort, are in this context highly problematic: "Fellow countrymen". For who is to count as a "fellow countryman" is exactly the issue he addresses: does he really speak only to the loyal North, or to the rebellious White South as well? If to the latter, in what possible terms? And to what degree will he imply, or acknowledge, that African-Americans are his fellow countrymen too?

Listen to this: "At this second appearing to take the oath of the presidential office, there is less occasion for an extended address than there was at the first". This is not a rousing start, to say the least. The awkward and official-sounding sentence reads like prose issuing from a typical bureaucratic office. The attention is all on the official occasion; the speaker is entirely erased by the impersonal construction and the absence of pronouns. The promise of this sentence is that the speech as a whole will be one of unutterable dullness.

"Then a statement, somewhat in detail, of a course to be pursued seemed fitting and proper". Seemed to whom? To be pursued by whom? This sounds more like an annual report to shareholders than a presidential inaugural address. This is a sentence, indeed this is a paragraph, that any secondary school writing teacher would criticize roundly for its passive constructions, its awkwardness, its impersonality. In an obvious sense it is very bad writing indeed, and this from the pen of perhaps the greatest master of American prose.

How can this be explained? I think the reason is that the rigorously depopulated universe of the opening paragraph creates as it were a blank space, free of people, against which the terms that do define the human actors in his drama – "me", "us", "all", "North", "South", "nation", and so forth – will be marked with greater clarity and emphasis when they emerge. It is a way of making plain that he is constructing his social universe in this text, in a kind of creation story: starting with nothing.

Listen to the cadences shift in the next sentence:

> Now, at the expiration of four years, during which public declarations have been constantly called forth on every point and phase of the great contest which still absorbs the attention and engrosses the energies of the nation, little that is new could be presented.

We still have the passive voice ("have been called forth", "could be presented") but we also have an actor and action as well: "the great contest" is the actor and it "absorbs" and "engrosses" another person, defined here as "the nation". But this is still to think of both the contest and the nation in ambivalent terms: is the "nation" on one side of the "contest", at war with another side? Or does the "nation" somehow appear on both sides of it? Upon the answer to this question much, including the success of any effort to speak to the South, will depend.

In the next sentence he seems to answer it: "The progress of our arms, upon which all else chiefly depends, is as well known to the public as to myself; and it is, I trust, reasonably satisfactory and encouraging to all". The pronouns here identify the speaker, and the audience, with the North; the "all" to whom the progress of arms is encouraging cannot possibly include the White South. But he still insists upon the impersonal and the passive, again to the point of awkwardness: "With high hope for the future, no prediction in regard to it is ventured".

He next repeats in somewhat different terms his earlier invocation of the difference between the present inauguration and his first: "On the occasion corresponding to this four years ago, all thoughts were anxiously directed to an impending civil war. All dreaded it – all sought to avert it". Who are *these* "alls", the reader asks: the North? or North and South? What of the slaves: are they included or not?

"While the inaugural address was being delivered from this place, devoted altogether to saving the Union without war, insurgent agents were in the city seeking to destroy it without war – seeking to dissolve the Union and divide effects, by negotiation". Here we learn that "all" no longer refers to the North alone, but now includes the White South, for the anxiety and dread of civil war includes both sides. But that does not mean there is no moral difference between them. "Both parties deprecated war; but one of them would make war rather than let the nation survive; and the other would accept war rather than let it perish". One side is devoted to union and the "nation," the other to secession; one side makes war, the other accepts it. Both North and South are thus included in the "all", but the moral difference between them is acute. Lincoln closes this paragraph with an allusion to the rains that flooded the earth in Noah's time: "And the war came".

He has thus raised, and left us with, a question which perhaps he will not answer, namely why maintaining the "nation" in its unified form is something worth fighting for, something indeed that entitles him to adopt his position of moral superiority to the "insurgent agents". What kind of response will this speech make to this, perhaps the central question of the war?

Perhaps none, we learn, for the next paragraph seems to treat of another subject, namely the human beings held in slavery. Here we begin to see what place they have in the "we" or "all" constituted by this speech:

> One-eighth of the whole population were colored slaves, not distributed generally over the Union, but localized in the Southern part of it. These slaves constituted a peculiar and powerful interest. All knew that this interest was, somehow, the cause of the war. To strengthen, perpetuate, and extend this interest was the object for which the insurgents would rend the Union, even by war; while the government claimed no right to do more than to restrict the territorial enlargement of it.

A lukewarm statement to say the least: in this paragraph the slaves are hardly defined as human beings at all. They do make up a certain percentage of the "population" but are more deeply defined as "constitut[ing] a peculiar and powerful interest", a phrase that analogises them to other interests, such as timber or mining. In doing this Lincoln uses the term by which White Southerners were accustomed to speak of their "peculiar institution". This part of the paragraph indeed looks at slaves very much as the White Southerners would wish; to this extent it tends to include the Southern Whites within the circle of its "we" and "all", and to exclude the African-Americans.

Notice that for Lincoln the difference between North and South is not couched in terms of support of slavery versus opposition to it. So far at least, slavery is not seen itself as an evil but simply as an issue over which the parties divide; the difference between North and South lies not in their attitudes towards slavery, but in Southern extremism versus Northern moderation. For the radical South insisted on extending "this interest" even by war; the moderate North wished only to confine it to its present boundaries. This, not slavery itself, is the moral difference between the "insurgents" and the "government".

All this works as a kind of implicit history that at once explains the war and justifies, perhaps even ennobles, the North's role in it: for the North seeks only to preserve union; the South by contrast wishes to impose a kind of tyranny upon the North. This is, so far as these things can be known, the "somehow" by which slavery was the cause of the war; not that one side thought it right and the other wrong, but that they had different ideas of what to do about that difference itself, one consistent with the premises of constitutional life and union, the other opposed to it.

But the "somehow" does a little more work even than this, for it suggests – as the rest of the speech will amplify – that despite our natural claims to understanding, claims of a kind already made in this address, the actual workings of the universe are to a large degree beyond our comprehension.

The speech has been moving towards a sense that in many respects the South and North are on an equal footing. This sense is more firmly established, with heavy emphasis, in what follows, as the syntax – "Neither . . . neither . . . each . . . both . . . each . . ." – drums it home:

> Neither party expected for the war the magnitude or the duration which it has already attained. Neither anticipated that the cause of the conflict might cease with, or even before, the conflict itself should cease. Each looked for an easier triumph, and a result less fundamental and astounding. Both read the same Bible, and pray to the same God; and each invokes his aid against the other.

This is an equality, however, of ignorance, folly, and presumption: both sides expected a shorter and easier war, neither was prepared for a result "so fundamental and astounding", each had the temerity to invoke God's aid against the other. This picks up the note sounded with "somehow" and expands upon it mightily: our common characteristic is our overconfidence, both in our capacity to understand the world and in our moral righteousness. From this perspective the differences of attitude about the Union, and about slavery, slip away; what emerges most is our common plight, not only in this, but by implication, in all circumstances.

Especially dangerous is the last thing that both sides share, a self-righteousness that dares to call on God in aid. To say this is to qualify, perhaps even to purify, the sense of Northern moral superiority – of righteousness – that Lincoln has earlier established, for its tendency is to make the Northerners in the audience feel corrected, the White Southerners feel that they are spoken to as equals.

Now comes a central sentence: "It may seem strange that any men should dare to ask a just God's assistance in wringing their bread from the sweat of other men's faces; but let us judge not, lest we be judged". The first clause of the sentence reaffirms the Northern cause, but this time it is grounded not in Union and the Constitution, but in opposition to human slavery. We are not equal, after all, he is saying; the moral issue that divides us is a real one and we in the North are right. And slavery is defined here not merely as an "interest", to be reflected in statistics, but as a deep and radical evil, a denial of the condition of equality with which humankind left Eden, condemned to make our bread by the sweat of our brows. Slavery is an attempt to deny or avoid a scarcity imposed by God on human life, and an offence therefore not only to the other men, by whose sweat one lives, but to God himself. One could hardly imagine another phrase that could capture so powerfully the heart of the matter.

Yet the second half of the sentence turns away, not from the particular judgment but from the act of judging, to a position essentially theological in character, as the use of Biblical language here and elsewhere also suggests. Lincoln's position here is one that recognises that our knowledge of our own fault, and of the fault of others, is radically imperfect. This is a point at which South and North can truly meet, space they can openly share. "The prayers of both could not be answered – that of neither has been answered fully".

It is to the vacuum of human knowledge thus established that the next line speaks: "The Almighty has his own purposes". Although Lincoln has not yet mentioned the "Almighty", as I say above the view of human life he has been enacting is a profoundly theological one: an assertion of the limits of knowledge and the corruption of the human heart, and a concern with the ultimate meaning of things. These are the recognitions that permit him to speak as he does, of the Almighty, whose point of view, as represented in the words of Jesus, he then for a moment adopts: "Woe unto the world because of offences! For it must needs be that offences come; but woe to that man by whom the offence cometh".

The war here is defined at once as an "offence" in the sight of God and man; as a necessity; and as an occasion of just punishment. Or so it seems; but the next sentence specifies and transforms the "offence" in a surprising way:

> If we shall suppose that American slavery is one of those offences which, in the providence of God, must needs come, but which, having continued through his appointed time, he now wills to remove, and that he gives to both North and South this terrible war, as the woe due to those by whom the offences came, shall we discern therein any

> departure from those divine attributes which the believers in a living God always ascribe to him?

We see now that it is slavery that is the offence, the war the punishment (or "woe") inflicted for it; and that it is inflicted on both North and South – no longer "government" and "insurgent" but another version of "all" the people – as both responsible for the offence. This is a far cry indeed from his remarks about slavery as an "interest" that "somehow" "caused" the war, where he spoke as a rather bloodless political scientist. The cause is not of that sort, it turns out, but a moral cause, and slavery is not only an interest, or even an immorality, but an abomination, an "offence".

And his sense of who we are has been transformed as well: we are no longer seen as autonomous individuals or communities in charge of our own conduct, as we were when he spoke of those who sought to "save" or "destroy" the Union without war, but actors in a cosmic drama of which we can only guess at the significance. Our knowledge of everything, everything upon which our judgments of superiority, of unity, of the meaning of our conduct depend, is drawn into question.

But all this is cast less assertively than I have so far indicated, in a conditional sentence, and as a suggestion only. For this is not the voice of a self-certain preacher who has a privileged view of God's will, but the voice of one of us, who lives in the universe he describes, one that is and will always be inscrutable.

We then get a sentence that could be recast as a poem:

> Fondly do we hope -
> Fervently do we pray -
> That this mighty scourge of war
> May speedily pass away.

This is cast in traditional hymn-tune rhymes and almost, but not quite, in traditional hymn-tune rhythms. In this sense its form makes it the kind of prayer it speaks of: the praying, that is, is not merely a practice he is describing, but one he is performing, here before us. "Fondly" here has both the modern sense of "affectionately", or perhaps "tenderly", and also Shakespeare's sense: foolishly, naively. For no hope can be justified in the world he describes except the hope that is an aspect of faith. Prayer is a different matter, and it is not only "they" who do that, but we, here and now; and this "we" is all of us, North and South, Black and White. The diction, "mighty scourge of war" and "speedily pass away" also establishes a continuity between this sentence and the Bible.

> Yet, if God wills that it continue until all the wealth piled by the bondsman's two hundred and fifty years of unrequited toil shall be sunk, and until every drop of blood drawn with the lash shall be paid by another drawn with the sword, as was said three thousand years ago, so still it must be said, "The judgments of the Lord are true and righteous altogether".

By now, slavery has changed its character altogether, from an "interest", to "wringing one's bread from the sweat of other men's faces", to an "offence", to an affirmative crime, both economic and human: the amassing of wealth by "blood drawn with the lash". And it is not only in God's mysterious ways, but in our own eyes, that we can see the justice of this war that shall sink all that "wealth piled by the bondsman's two hundred and fifty years of unrequited toil" and pay for the blood drawn by the lash with blood drawn by the sword.

In this address we move from a world divided between North and South, with one side righteously victorious over the other, to a vision of a common fate, a common and just suffering that converts the African-American – whom he earlier called "colored" – from slave into person. Lincoln never denies the rightness of the Northern cause, nor suggests anything but satisfaction at the progress of her arms. But he has located these motives and feelings in a different context, and transformed them, creating at the end a sense of actual – that is to say imagined – Union, which permits him to close as he does. Whilst reading this next passage pay attention to the pronouns:

> With malice towards *none*; with charity for *all*; with firmness in the right, as God gives *us* to see the right, let *us* strive on to finish the work *we* are in; to bind up the *nation's* wounds; to care for *him who* shall have borne the battle, and for *his* widow, and *his* orphan – to do all which may achieve and cherish a just and lasting peace among *ourselves*, and with all *nations*.

Here all sense of triumph over others is gone, all sense of self-righteousness. What is left is a sense of common humanity, common suffering, common decency, a sense that this event in our history is a mark of God's attention to us, giving us a suffering past, and present, like that of the Israelites, and defining us, with divine authority, as one nation – "among ourselves" – in a world of other nations.

This is especially vivid in the pronouns: from talking about "all" in an ambiguous or partisan way, he now plainly uses "none" and "all" in their most inclusive sense. He reaffirms his sense of the right, but equally reaffirms that his sense is necessarily partial. When he speaks directly to his audience and says "let us strive", the "us", like the "all", includes North and South, Black and White. And the nation whose wounds he has described is the entire nation for which the war was fought and to define which his speech was given. It is no doubt one measure both of his aim and his achievement that much of the North was bitterly disappointed by what he said.

In Lincoln's speech what I have called the two aspects of the ethical dimension of meaning are both highly prominent, the action upon language and the action upon the social world, and they are deeply related. For Lincoln aggressively reconstitutes his language, breaking down the natural division of "us" and "them", and in so doing he offers his readers a new way of imagining themselves, in a "Union", in which he gives a place to all. Like the *Iliad*, the ethical and intellectual force here is integrative: Lincoln finds a place, in a theological drama, from which he can put together in a single frame elements that seem impossibly opposed. And this achievement is not one that takes place at the level of theory or proposition, but is performed in the text itself, ethically, as he acts upon his language and audience.[7]

My hope in this chapter has been to draw attention to one dimension of the meaning of texts, which I call the ethical, a dimension that emerges from a sense of the text as a form of action both upon language and upon people. From this point of view what we say matters as much as what we do, indeed speaking is a form of doing; and what we do in a more material sense – even in a war – is seen to be dependent for much of its meaning upon what we say, upon what we claim that meaning to be.

To focus upon this dimension of meaning is to raise a series of questions – about the language the author is given to use; about her transformation of it; about the kind of community created with the reader – all of which carry us in the direction of seeing connections among texts that seem at first quite disparate, and connections among their concerns as well. We may come to see that the legal text, for example, is partly aesthetic in character; that insofar as it is about justice, this is a matter of the relations created in the text at least as much as it is a matter of material results; that the literary text is ethical and political in nature, at its best teaching us a mode of ethical thought and criticism which we might well try to emulate in our own thoughts and compositions; and that the achievement of a political text, like the others, can lie in the way it remakes its language and creates relations with others.

BIBLIOGRAPHY

White, JB, 1990, *Justice As Translation*, University of Chicago Press.

White, JB, 1984, *When Words Lose Their Meaning: Constitutions and Reconstitutions of Language, Character, and Community*, University of Chicago Press.

7 This may be a harder act than the *Iliad* for us to acquiesce in, for the text that includes the enemy and the slave, that recognises the humanity of both, is also used to justify a hideous war. It would be possible, I suppose, to read Lincoln's address as an attempt to cover evil with hypocrisy, saying that it never really addresses the central question of the Civil War, which is why it is right for one part of a democratic nation to go to war to prevent the secession of another part. On the other hand, one might reply, it is exactly the way this text works to define a national community, its own constitution of a world that includes all, that most persuasively justifies the war undertaken to preserve it.

26

James Boyd White and the Character of Judgments

ARTHUR GLASS

In a series of valuable books, James Boyd White has written, among other matters, of the remarkable possibilities of the court case. Our practice of adjudication is misunderstood and reduced according to him when it is treated from the stand-point of social science as, say, a form of bureaucratic dispute resolution or as a way of stabilising uncertain behavioural expectations. For the court hearing is an important opportunity for achieving cultural education and change (1984 p 274)[1] and, when seen in this light, the judicial opinion, the writing which consummates the hearing, becomes a genre of immense promise for communal self-understanding and self-education (1984 p 266f; 1990 p 174). However, this potential will only be realised, according to White, if we come to understand judgments differently. His most recent three books – *When Words Lose Their Meaning* (1984 pp ix, 4f), *Heracles' Bow* (1985 p ix, xvf, 93) and *Justice As Translation* (1990) – can be seen as an attempt by him to show lawyers a new and valuable way of reading judgments, a way of reading which he says, provocatively, already inheres within these texts.

Of course, in our professional discourse we presently have criteria for evaluating judgments. We can ask of a particular decision is its result fair or sensible or workable or, alternatively, we can consider the craftsmanship of the judgment – how well it explains and uses the relevant precedents or statutes, how convincingly it fits the particular case into the legal corpus or even how succinctly it restates its facts or summarises the legal principles it employs. But White does not have such everyday standards as these in mind. He is not interested in, or at least not directly interested in, the substance

---

1 The law is a culture of argument in which we give "experience to ourselves, individually and collectively, the experience of making and remaking language under pressure" (White 1985 p 225); see also White 1990 p 157. For White's convincing attack on an understanding of adjudication which treats it as no more than dispute resolution see White 1984 p 266f; 1985 pp x, 123ff; 1990 pp 41, 223f.

of the judgment (1984 pp 273, 282f; 1990 pp 111, 123) and he considers that what he calls the "craft tradition" has failed to provide a usable language of criticism (1990 p 94). What does interest White are the criteria for judging opinions which become available to us when we think of the judgment as establishing a textual community – with the reader and with the people it speaks about.[2] When thought of in these terms new questions emerge which can be asked of a judgment. Does it treat the reader as an equal mind ready to listen, or does it try to dominate the reader (1984 p 282; 1985 p 130)? Is it like a friend in that it encourages and educates its readers to become more fully what they are? (1984 p 227) Does it reduce or increase the reader's integration of self? (1985 p 131)[3] Can the writing be seen as opening up a dialogue with its audience or does it attempt to close off further conversation? (1990 pp 176, 223) These are strikingly unusual questions to put to judgments and just what content can be given here to such abstract notions as openness or friendship or dialogue is my concern throughout this chapter. But there is no doubt that White makes large claims for his approach. For if we live up to the standards implicit in this art form we are told:

> this will greatly limit the range of substantively permissible or reachable decisions even in hard cases. You cannot write a great novel in support of anti-semitism, says Sartre, and I think you cannot write a great opinion that denies that sense of the ultimate value of the individual person that is necessarily enacted in any sincerely other-recognizing expression. (1985 pp 107f, 131; 1990 pp 158, 140)

How can White say that his proposed standards for judging judgments are implicit in the legal texts themselves? For the most part he relies upon an account which claims to find these norms in judgments simply because they are inherent in all written compositions. Here White offers us an analysis of the author/text/reader relationship which he brings to law from literary criticism. When discussing this relationship White is concerned, of course, not with the living breathing author, or with the responses to the work by actual readers[4] but, rather, with a relationship between, as it is put, an implied author and the work's implied reader, a relationship, that is, which is defined by the text. White suggests, reasonably enough, that every text can be thought of as inviting its readers to take particular attitudes towards the people about whom it speaks and can be seen as defining a particular type of reader it would like its readers to become. And that in the experience of

2 The judicial opinion is "a form of life – a manifestation of character and an establishment of community – that can be judged ethically and politically; as authoritarian or democratic; as recognising or erasing the experience of others; as open or closed to the possibility of other voices, other languages, than its own" (White 1989 p 2046). See also White 1990 p 216.

3 "By bringing tensions and contraries into simultaneous view".

4 For the real author's intentions are irrecoverable and are uninteresting unless realised in the text and little can be said about the actual responses of real readers as these are complex and unpredictable.

reading we cannot but enter into some kind of engagement with this authorial presence in the work. Alternatively, if we consider the work from the author's side, we can see that the writer inevitably gives to himself or herself a tone of voice or character, an outlook upon or attitude towards life which the reader is invited to adopt. In this way we can think of texts as persons, as potential friends (or enemies), and can ask of the relationships which they establish with us the same kinds of normative questions which we ask of the relationships we form with people.[5] White can then say of every composition that it has an ethical dimension, in the sense that it offers the reader the opportunity to engage with another mind and become somebody different, and a social (or political) dimension in that this is an invitation which can be discussed and criticised (1984 pp 17f, 283; 1985 p 128; 1990 p 99ff).

In his books and articles White presents us with a number of apparently different standards for evaluating these textual relationships – for example, equality, friendship, conversation, humility, integration of self. But what appears central to these notions are two ways of understanding the norm of equal respect (1984 p 18). First, that the work be open to its readers, that it speaks to the reader as an equal mind, as someone who is able to judge the argument and, secondly, that in its treatment of its subject matter it respects difference, it acknowledges the equal humanity of other people. Following White, I will at times speak of these ideas of openness to the reader and tolerance for difference in its subject matter as the extent to which the text is "other-regarding".

Now there would seem to be something seriously misleading about White's claim (1984 p 17) that the normative criteria which he proposes inhere within any text, fictional or non fictional. Consider briefly how the standard of other-regarding would apply to literary works. White would appear to give us two different ways of understanding this claim. At times the claim that these works are other-regarding is no more than an observation (common to contemporary literary criticism) that if reading as we understand it is to take place then the reader, the other, must play a productive role in establishing the meaning of what is read. But an account of what necessarily occurs in all acts of reading, just because it discloses what always occurs, cannot tell us anything about how texts should be written and read. So when White (1985 p 124) tells us that, "in a life of composition and reading each of us is at least potentially present as an individual mind ready to speak and ready to listen; and between such minds recognised as such equality is the only possible relation" this is no more than a description of the structure of reading and as such it can have no normative consequences. At other times we find White drawing upon an approach known in literary studies as ethical criticism. This approach assumes, plausibly enough, that the

5 Both individual and communal.

experience of reading literary works may help us to live well and calls upon the critic to concentrate on how the work in question attempts to bring about this change in the reader.[6] This is clearly a legitimate approach to take to literary works in as much as some contemporary critics do adopt it. But White goes further and specifies just what it is that literary works may teach us, viz, to respect difference, to acknowledge the equal humanity of other people. Now these are values acceptable to most of us – though we may wonder why moral values which are clearly drawn from our culture at this time are the very values which are found to endure in the canon of classical works[7] or, again, we may be troubled that the benefits of reading literature are limited to moral education rather than some other aspect of personal cultivation – the development of aesthetic sensibilities, for instance. However, even if we grant White these points, he would appear to go too far when he directly connects the ethical significance of reading with the actual relations embodied in particular literary works. For this would produce the striking and questionable result that the more a literary work is open to its readers, the more it itself respects difference, then the better the work.[8] Now do we really want to limit the claim of greatness here to those works of fiction which treat their reader as an equal mind and which acknowledge the equal humanity of all of their characters? It is interesting to note that Wayne Booth, the principal spokesman for ethical criticism, does not go as far as White on this point. For when Booth provides a vocabulary for making discriminations between the different ways in which books may deal with us he speaks not about the moral quality of the invitation but in morally neutral terms about the quantity, the range and the intensity of the invitations offered. He makes it clear (1988 p 488) that many great works of fiction do not treat the reader as an equal and that, as he puts it, “some good friends, in life as in literature are wonderfully beneficial to my soul, even though they are clearly immoral on many a scale” (1988 p 179).

So it would seem that White's grounding of his other-regarding criteria in the textual nature of literary works is questionable for a number of reasons. First, as a discussion of what always occurs in reading it can not tell us anything about how to read. Secondly, as there is no consensus on just what makes literary works valuable or significant for us, ethical criticism remains just one approach which may be taken among many. White (1984 pp 15, 281) goes too far when

---

6 Of course, we are speaking here again of the implied reader for whether a particular reader actually benefits from a particular work depends on who the reader is at the time of reading (White 1984 p 17).

7 Stanley Fish has a criticism of White along these lines. See Fish (1982) p 502ff.

8 A more charitable way of understanding White on this point would see him as limiting this claim to the particular works which he discusses in *When Words Lose Their Meaning*: the *Iliad*, Thucydides' *History*, Plato's *Gorgias*, Swift's *Tale of a Tub*, Johnson's “Rambler” essays, Austen's *Emma,* and Burke's *Reflections*. But as I read him he does not restrict his ways of reading to these texts or these types of texts.

he claims this as the ultimate standard or the "true center of value of any text". A work of art may be considered aesthetically successful even though it says something negligible or even evil about how we should live.[9] Finally, there seems no reason for thinking that the particular moral qualities which may be cultivated through reading (tolerance for difference, for instance) will actually be embodied in the relationships which the text creates – either with the reader or between the characters it talks about.

Although White's analysis of the author/reader relationship appears to provide an unsatisfactory basis for his other-regarding criteria, it could be said that this failure has no consequences for his analysis of judgments. For whatever the position may be with other compositions, it can be claimed of legal texts, certainly of statutes and judgments, that they ought to be open to their readers and that they ought to respect the equality of persons. We expect the law to be public and followable and we assume that before the law all will be treated equally. These are important requirements of the Rule of Law which are institutionalised in many different ways in contemporary legal practice. Just to focus on adjudication, there is, as White (1984 p 273; 1985 p 174; 1990 p 216) points out, a sense of equality and openness built into the hearing. Each side is given the opportunity to tell their story publicly and it is the task of the judgment to respond impartially to these different accounts of fact and law, to the different interests that the parties represent and to apply the law equally to both sides, irrespective of race, class, religion or sex. And the judgment must give reasons, it must justify its resolution of the case openly to its readers. It would seem then that when judgments are understood as legal texts rather than as texts in general, White's standards for evaluating these works can be grounded, as far as these things can be, for we are now given some normative content, viz, a social context in which there is an institutionally imposed consensus concerning the purpose of these texts.[10] I have dwelt upon the point that White's standards find their normative basis in understandings institutionalised in legal practice – and not in their inherent textual nature – so that it can be more easily recognised that the application of these norms will not be a straightforward affair. It will not simply be a matter of encouraging lawyers to live up to these obligations. For, as I will make clearer, these demands will confront and compete with other norms, themselves grounded in present understandings, which point in other directions.

This brings me to the central question of this chapter: can we usefully apply White's criteria to judgments? It would be a mistake to let the novelty of his standards count against them for White (1985 p 242) makes it clear that he is not describing contemporary legal

---

9 Baudelaire's *Les Fleurs du Mal* and Céline's *Journey to the End of the Night* are often-used examples of this point. See also Orwell, G, 1968.

10 Something clearly missing in literary criticism.

practice but, rather, prescribing what in the right hands the writing and reading of judgments might become. But in evaluating his suggestions as prescription I think it fair to ask of White whether he has provided us with the rhetorical resources for understanding and improving legal practice or whether his proposed criteria are merely utopian or are no more than exhortations to lawyers to be well-intentioned. I should add that I am considering White's suggestions in the context of the Anglo/Australian legal tradition. White invites this approach for, while his examples are invariably American Supreme Court opinions, his discussion of judgments does not treat the work of this court as different from the work of other American courts, or of other courts in the common law family or even of courts in general.[11]

I shall consider four ways in which White directs his other-regarding prescriptions at judgments. First, his requirement that the judgment be open to the uncertainty of the future (1984 p 266; 1990 p 157). We are told, for instance, that the judge should be aware of the limits of human understanding and should speak as someone with something to learn and that a good judgment will be less assertive and more tentative (1984 p 269; 1990 pp 21, 145, 223). Now one cannot be told too often to be self-reflective or humble or less dogmatic, especially if one is a judge. But criteria such as these would appear to be of only limited use in evaluating judgments. Not simply for the reason that they are rather abstract and empty but because in the circumstances of how we presently practise adjudication there is clearly a limit as to how far a judgment can express its doubts and as to how far it can remain tentative. For we expect more of a judgment than reflection on how we should live. We expect of it that it will determine the dispute in an unequivocal way and that in doing this it will prescribe rules which are followable. When fulfilling these needs the judgment must aim not at openness but at closure; temporary closure, to be sure, for law must change as it is applied to new circumstances. But a temporary closure is still a "freezing of the legal position" for the present audience. We are also told that the judgment should be open to the importance of the past and that it should respect the prior legal texts (1984 p 266; 1990 pp 99, 222). Respect for textual authority is clearly a characteristic feature of legal interpretation but White's call to respect the prior texts is an empty demand when it is considered apart from the procedures and concerns of the "craft tradition" about which he is so dismissive. The methods of statutory interpretation and case analysis are, for White (1990 pp 94, 118ff, 123f, 133, 141ff, 171, 216, 219, 246), simply ways in which the judge closes off further discussion by resorting to false grounds of authority. No doubt these methods may be improperly used but without the criteria and standards of appropriateness they provide, concepts such as "respectful" or "proper" would have little

11 How his ideas would apply to the civilian tradition, for instance, is quite unclear.

meaning when applied to the treatment of past materials. The canon of legislative intention, for instance, should be seen as giving more concrete meaning to the demand that the legal interpreter respect the bindingness and the completeness of the relevant statutes. It directs the search for meaning into the question of what parliament could have or is likely to have meant in the circumstances and it operates as a unifying principle which holds together a number of sub-rules which delimit the appropriate context for answering this question.[12] White seriously reduces the significance of the canon when he sees its use as no more than an attempt to replace the legal question of textual meaning with a factual inquiry into the intentions of the actual authors of the legislation.[13]

Thirdly, White (1990 pp 111, 136, 172, 224) asks of a judgment that it be written in a way which opens it to the reader's scrutiny and criticism. This raises the question of just who are the readers of judgments?[14] Although the judgment is ostensibly directed at the public – for it is an important requirement of the Rule of Law that the law be made known to all citizens – non-professionals do not read judgments.[15] Law, unlike the other humanities, has at present no lay readers. No one reads legal texts for enjoyment or for guidance on how to live. It is White's point (1985 pp 123, 185, 192) that this will change once judges modify the vocabulary and style of the law reports and integrate law's language more with communal standards and ordinary speech.[16] No doubt there is something in this but the tendencies inhibiting the laicisation of the law should not be ignored. The large degree of cultural autonomy which modern law has achieved – the extent to which the content of the law and its methods are thought of as forming a special and distinct field of knowledge – seems an inescapable feature of modern life. For if the growing

12 That is, the rules concerning the internal and external aids to construction.

13 It can also be noted that at times White treats the concept of legal authority in an unsatisfactory way – as an issue of political rather than legal legitimacy (1985 p 136; 1990 pp 111, 121, 145, 216f). The authority of the judgment – that is its bindingness on the interpreter – follows from its legal validity (from its being made by a properly constituted court in the proper exercise of jurisdiction). A judgment does not have to create its own legal authority rhetorically, as White has it, and nor is it merely presumptively binding on the legal interpreter.

14 Legal (and other) professionals do read judgments and clearly they expect the judgment to be written in a way which opens the argument to their inspection. An opinion that is considered to rely on manipulative language or mere assertion or a dogmatic use of legal methods will be criticised. But the judge must at some stage close off the discussion and "find" the relevant facts and apply the appropriate law. Whether closure comes sooner or later, it will always come before all of the assumptions and premises relied on in the conclusion have been made transparent.

15 Here my remarks are not directed at the judgments of the American Supreme Court, for these do reach a non-professional audience. But the exceptional influence of these writings upon American culture only serves to make clearer the limited reception of English and Australian judgments.

16 In other words, once judgments take the ordinary reader as their ideal reader (White 1990 p 110).

complications of social and economic life are to be dealt with by the law, and dealt with in a way which maintains the continuity of the legal system, then the complexity of the law and the involvement of a specially trained caste of experts who promote its inaccessibility to the laity would appear to be in both cases a technical necessity.[17]

Whatever the possibilities may be for resisting these tendencies it seems clear that the separation of law from everyday knowledge belongs to the way in which legal practice is presently organised. White, like many other contemporary commentators,[18] can be thought of as asking us to rethink the distinction between what is internal to law and what is external. But I find him particularly unhelpful when he makes such suggestions as, the judgment should be open to all relevant considerations, or that it should be a summing up of all that can be said on the matter before the court (1984 p 248; 1990 p 136), or that the judgment should ask the reader to respond "with all that he is and knows" (1985 p 131)[19] or that judges should "make their official voices more fully their own" (1985 p 242). These claims cannot be taken at face value. Of course the judge should not reduce complexity by judicial fiat but all writing involves closure and the writing of judgments in particular is in need of techniques and an argumentation which delimit clearly the appropriate considerations. The terms of reference must be narrowed here, for adjudication is a practice in which decisions one way or another must be made in circumstances of limited time and limited knowledge. A court case cannot be a general inquiry into all the possible moral and political considerations.[20]

The postulated autonomy of the law is better questioned by White (1990 pp 81, 140, 223) when he suggests that we look at judgments from the stand-point of what they leave out – that we think of what issues and interests cannot be fully expressed in the present legal vocabulary.[21] By thinking of the legal categories from this perspective, judges and their critics can more concretely challenge the prevailing conceptions about which factors are internal and which are external to the law. One thinks here of how feminist jurisprudence has assisted in making issues like sexual harassment, domestic violence, the division of labour in the home and pornography matters of legal and public concern. And the recent judgment of *Mabo v Queensland* can be seen as the High Court expanding the legal discussion so that it can take account of the historical facts of the

17 Here I am drawing generally upon a theme associated with Max Weber's influential sociology of law.

18 Members of White's particular bogey, the Law and Economics movement, for instance.

19 Also, see generally White's discussion of "intellectual integration" in the first chapter of *Justice As Translation*.

20 Neil MacCormick puts this point well (1988 p 167f).

21 And we can think about this in a positive sense for we can think of what they rightly leave out – terms of race, for example (White 1990 p 127).

dispossession of the Aboriginal people.[22] By opening the law to these matters the court could more easily show the unworthiness of two long-accepted legal doctrines – the presumption of vacancy of the land and the doctrine that claimed all ownership of land on settlement for the Crown – for these were irreconcilable with the common law rights of Aborigines to the land.[23]

Admirable as White's suggestions are here it is important to acknowledge that they will have to be implemented in the context of numerous other normative requirements presently at work in legal practice which stipulate how adjudication should function and which help to regulate the proper relationship between the courts and other legal institutions. Just to mention some of these – the demand that the judgment acknowledge the authority of the existing law and limit itself to stating what the law means in present circumstances, the demand for readings of the law which are unambiguous, consistent and impersonal, the requirement that the judgment limit itself to what is necessary to decide the actual litigation and not attempt to settle interconnected problems and the constraints on when it is thought appropriate for judges to take responsibility for an area of the law and when they should leave it to the legislature. Now the vitality of these postulates in present legal practice is not just a matter of the profession's acceptance of an inadequate positivist ideology. For these prescriptions are an attempt to give specific and concrete meaning to certain basic aspirations of our political and legal tradition.[24]

Some of the best pages of White's books are where he speaks about a number of tensions which the writer of an opinion must address.[25] What is missing from this discussion characteristically is the tension between the interpretive freedom involved in the necessity of applying the law to new circumstances and the institutional need to do this in a way which minimises interpretive licence. The stipulations which I have briefly listed along with many other norms of legal practice work to restrict the role which personal

---

22 "[T]he darkest aspect of the history of this nation" Deane J and Gaudron J (1992) 107 ALR 1 at 82.

23 This case can be compared with another recent case, the *War Crimes Act* case (*Polyukhovich v Commonwealth* (1991) 101 ALR 545). Here the court's discussion of the relevant legal categories – the meaning of external affairs and of judicial power – seems unconcerned with the central issues raised by the public debate of this legislation, viz, its selectivity, its expense, its influence on relationships between groups within Australia and even (except for Deane J) its retrospectivity.

24 Viz, the Rule of Law, the separation of powers and judicial restraint. Ideals accepted by most legal interpreters but their abstractness, the very qualities no doubt which produce this general acceptability, make it impossible to achieve agreement upon how these concepts on their own connect up with specific understandings of the law.

25 Between the opposed stories told by the parties, between the facts as found and the available legal categories, between the discourse of law and what lies outside the sphere of law, between the rival interests and beliefs represented by the parties and between the need to justify the result and the acknowledgment that complete justification is impossible (White 1985 p 240f).

values and interests are able to play in the judgment. An aim it would seem to me as important for the writers of judgments to strive for as furthering communal education.

We owe a debt to White for making us see better the possibilities which adjudication can provide for a critical discussion of our legal and extra-legal culture.[26] For here we do have a unique social practice, available at least in principle to all, which provides the public space for recognising others, for acknowledging ignorance, for questioning prejudices and for extending the imagination (1984 pp 267, 274). But until judgments are read more widely it is hard to see how the elaboration of judicial discourse can directly influence non-legal culture.[27] However, White (1985 pp 123, 185, 191) is surely right to point out the opportunity which the judgment provides for legal professionals to develop the law in a way which helps to legitimate it to the public. For the law's long-term acceptability and its effectiveness as a means of regulating conflict will depend ultimately on its basic accord with communal standards. The critical discussion of the law by judges and their critics is one way that the practice of law can be inserted into this broader cultural context. But I question whether, as he claims, White has provided a vocabulary for this purpose which we can learn and use. For it is unclear how his suggestions for the writing and reading of judgments – unconnected as they are with the standards and criteria provided by the present legal tradition – can promote a critical rather than a merely ad hoc discussion of the law.

BIBLIOGRAPHY

Booth, W, 1988, *The Company We Keep*, University of California Press.

Fish, S, 1982, "Interpretation And The Pluralist Vision" Texas Law Rev, 60, 495.

MacCormick, N, 1988, "Why Cases Have Rationes And What These Are", in Goldstein, L (ed), *Precedent In Law*, Oxford University Press.

Orwell, G, 1968, "Benefits of Clergy: Some Notes On Salvidor Dali", *Collected Essays,* vol 3, Secker and Warburg.

White, JB, 1984, *When Words Lose Their Meaning*, University of Chicago Press.

White, JB, 1985, *Heracles' Bow*, University of Wisconsin Press.

White, JB, 1986, "Doctrine In A Vacuum", *Legal Education*, 35, 155.

White, JB, 1989, "What Can A Lawyer Learn From Literature", 102 *Harvard Law Rev*, 2014.

White, JB, 1990, *Justice As Translation*, University of Chicago Press.

26 See, among numerous discussions, White 1986 at p 165.

27 Again, I should acknowledge that this point cannot be made as forcefully against opinions of the American Supreme Court.

27

The Odd Couple: Statutes and Literature

JEFFREY W BARNES[1]

Statutes (Acts of parliament)[2] have long been subjected to biting criticism from both sides of the literary/legal divide. In a lecture to the Royal Society of Literature the noted English jurist, Sir Carleton Allen (1958 p 284) remarked, "A statute is probably the most repellent form of written expression known to man. Nobody has ever read a statute except for duty, never for pleasure".[3] The literary icon, Sir Ernest Gowers (1987) agreed, "By normal standards of good writing legal drafting is usually both cumbrous and uncouth". But he thought that legislation should not be judged by normal standards. It was in a class of its own. Legal English must be able to withstand "detailed and possibly hostile scrutiny by acute legal minds". Legislative drafters also need to be aware of the special meaning which words "have acquired by legal convention and by previous decisions of the Courts". Legal drafting must therefore aim to be "unambiguous, precise, comprehensive and largely conventional" (Gowers, 1987).

In this chapter, I wish to challenge the assumption that statutes are not literature (or greatly lacking in literary qualities), and that they should not be viewed from a literary angle.[4] I will not be putting forward the unlikely proposition that statutes make great

---

1 This chapter is drawn from a talk given to the 1991 conference of the Law and Literature Association of Australia under the title "Statutes, Literature and Critical Theory". I would like to thank Bernadette McSherry and Neville Turner for comments on a draft of this chapter, and Enid Campbell, Bruce Dyer and Andrew Goldsmith for suggestions.

2 The argument in this chapter also applies to subordinate or delegated legislation.

3 But see discussion of Allen's view re literary entertainment in statute below (p 305).

4 In this chapter I assume various "literary" qualities. I have not found it profitable to attempt to *define* what I mean by "literature". I readily acknowledge, however, that some of these qualities (such as narratives) are not universally found in what is commonly understood as literature, and some (such as openness to critical theory) are the subject of controversy.

bedtime reading for the general reader; rather I will be arguing that their literary qualities have been overlooked and underrated.

The chapter advances, in outline, the case *for* the connections between statutes and literature. Of course, in disciplines as different as law and literature the differences between statutes and literature are many, as Posner (1988 ch 5) has eloquently argued in a comparative analysis of legal and literary interpretation. On that score, Posner finds that "there are too many differences between works of literature and enactments to permit much fruitful analogising" (p 218). It is not the purpose of this chapter to focus solely on the issue of interpretation, but I note that it was Posner's admitted aim to *emphasise the differences* between the problems of literary and legal interpretation (p 211). It is submitted that it is too early to write off the connections between statutes and literature; the other side should first be heard.[5]

Posner does have a point when he says that, unlike the law, "it is not the function of literature to lay down rules of conduct" (p 242). But, for all the obvious prosaic purposes of statutes – the regulation and control of individuals, organisations and the state – statutes should not be seen, when viewed from a literary angle, as mere texts – as we might think of the weekly shopping list or a bus ticket. As will be shown, a statute is a form of literature in a non-trivial sense.

Viewing statutes from this angle has practical benefits too. Neville Turner (1985) has explained how literature can be used to give law a "three-dimensional" context. One effect of being exposed to law in this way can be the opening up of a person's mind to additional avenues for legitimate criticism of the law – or even to the very possibility of critical scrutiny. An intelligent law student once told one of my classes that we could not criticise "the law" (ie find fault in it) because law was "impersonal". In all kinds of ways literary perspectives cannot fail to *humanise* the law (Turner 1985); the familiarity of literary forms and concepts, and the accessibility of their mediums ensure this occurs. It follows that they can assist in removing misconceptions about the law and in developing our critical "eyes", even when confronted with the somewhat forbidding statute.

Even before a statute is drafted, a statute's literary qualities are evident, for legislative drafters, like their more celebrated literary cousins, must exercise their imaginations. Aided by their instructions, the drafters must constantly attempt to foresee into the future. It is not simply a case of finding words to deal with a current social problem (which is difficult enough). The drafters must frequently create new controls over industry[6] or public

---

5 See also Hackett-Jones (1988) and, for an early analysis of the links between statutes and literature with reference to interpretation, see Abraham (1979).

6 The *Privacy Amendment Act* 1990 (Cth) instituted new controls over the credit reporting industry.

officials[7] and imagine how the various actors will interact. The package of federal legislation known as the "new administrative law" illustrates some of the difficulties in exercising this creative function. In the 1970s and early 1980s the Federal Parliament passed complementary legislation which revolutionised the way that individual citizens could challenge decisions against the Federal Government. Importantly, there were few precedents in significant areas covered by the legislation. The principal statutes were the *Administrative Appeals Tribunal Act* 1975, the *Ombudsman Act* 1976, the *Administrative Decisions (Judicial Review) Act* 1977 and the *Freedom of Information Act* 1982. Even so, the legislative package was found to be deficient in failing to prescribe any steps to ensure that the citizen would be informed of their existence! (Administrative Review Council, 1987). This has now been partially remedied through an amendment to the *Administrative Appeals Tribunal Act*.[8] In requiring persons to be informed of their right to appeal to the Administrative Appeals Tribunal (where the right exists), the legislation now more fully takes account of the way in which such legislative schemes interact with the environment upon which they are superimposed.

It might be thought, however, that *the drafter* does not have a creative role in preparing new legislation; the governmental adviser is the real creator. It is true that, according to the "traditional view" of drafting, the drafter is responsible for the form of the legislation rather than the content (Hackett-Jones 1988 pp 53-4). However, several drafters, who are normally a reclusive lot, have been at pains to emphasise the reality. John Ewens, who retired in 1972 as First Parliamentary Counsel of the Commonwealth, is said by one of his successors to that position to have directed his subordinate officers to be aware that, "Anything that anyone tells you is *prima facie* wrong" (Kolts 1988 p 102). Stephen Mason (1988), another drafter, further points out that, "'Policy' is not immutable while the Bill to enact it is being drafted" and that "it is rare for the policy to remain unaltered during the drafting process".

The concern of another eminent legislative drafter, Geoffrey Hackett-Jones QC, is with the preservation of this creative role. He says that client departments are "almost inevitably . . . primarily concerned with particular instances: problems that have actually arisen or that their experience leads them to anticipate". In his view it is essential that they not attempt to dictate every element of a legislative scheme. It is the function of the drafter "to deduce appropriate principles for dealing with these problems", a function he describes as "generalising and rationalising" (1988 p 54). In fact, he

---

7 The *Crimes Amendment Act* 1991 (Cth), s 23H, set up a new system of controls over the Commonwealth police when investigating possible offences by Aborigines or Torres Strait Islanders.

8 *Law and Justice Legislation Amendment Act (No 3)* 1992 (Cth), which inserted ss 27A and 27B into the *Administrative Appeals Tribunal Act* 1975 (Cth).

sees the creative aspect of drafting as under threat by over zealous bureaucrats:

> a certain degree of artistic liberty is necessary. . . . [A] regime in which the client dictates every element of a legislative scheme . . . stifles and precludes intellectual and aesthetic functions that are indispensable if coherent and intelligible statute law is to be achieved (1988 p 56).

In a less creative (some would say non-literary) way, statutes are also acts of the imagination. For convenience, a statute may alter the normal meaning of a word and even give it a quite different meaning. For example, s 3(1) of the *Social Security Act* 1947 (Cth) included the following definition, "'unmarried person' means a person who is not married". This definition is not as silly as it sounds, for its antithesis was defined as follows:

> "married person" includes a de facto spouse but does not include -
> (a) *a legally married person* [italics added] (not being a de facto spouse) who is living separately and apart from the spouse of the person on a permanent basis; or
> (b) a person who, for any special reason in any particular case, the Director-General determines in writing should not be treated as a married person.
>
> (Eagleson 1988 p 24).

In this context a "married person" is not intended to include certain legally married persons. Posner (1988 pp 1-2) regards fictions in the law as not being literary devices. But the task of the statute writer is to give effect, in legislative language, to his or her instructions in the most convenient way possible – this will on occasion call for an imaginative use of language. Giving a word the opposite meaning it normally has seems to fit this bill!

The above example also makes clear that when the statute writer puts pen to paper or finger to keyboard, he or she is not aiming, as Gowers (1987) pointed out, for literary elegance or euphony. Most modern legislative prose is as a result "anaemic" (Hackett-Jones 1988 p 46). But elegant writing can still be found on the statute books. The original federal income tax legislation, the *Income Tax Assessment Act* 1915 (Cth), has been claimed to be a "thing of beauty and simplicity that would not have shamed Wordsworth or TS Eliot" (Finemore 1988). It is *impossible* to think of today's *Income Tax Assessment Act* 1936 (Cth) – 1597 pages in its last reprint – being thought of as lovely! Its antecedent's pocket-book size (65 sections taking up a mere 21 pages) must have been the attraction.

Statute writers have been rightly criticised for their convolution and prolixity (Eagleson, 1988),[9] but the statute books also include phrases and provisions which are simple and elegant, and

9 Some of the examples Eagleson gives are literary feats of a different kind. One sub-section of the *Credit Act* 1984 (Vic) quoted in his article runs to 345 words – all in a single sentence.

even moving. An example of a striking turn of phrase (for a statute) is the following section:

> The Social Security Appeals Tribunal must, in carrying out its functions under this Act, pursue the objective of providing a mechanism of review that is fair, just, economical, informal and quick. (*Social Security Act* 1991 (Cth) s 1246)

For emotional power, Magna Carta (re-enacted in New South Wales and Victoria) is difficult to surpass:

> No freeman shall be taken or imprisoned, or be disseised of his freehold, or liberties or free customs, or be outlawed or exiled, or any other wise destroyed; nor will we pass upon him, nor condemn him, but by lawful judgement of his peers, or by the law of the land. We will sell to no man, we will not deny or defer to any man either justice or right.[10]

Less dramatic, but still quite atmospheric, is our turn-of-the-century Constitution. Its preamble evokes an earlier era – when God and the Crown were much more a part of this country's consciousness:

> WHEREAS the people of New South Wales, Victoria, South Australia, Queensland, and Tasmania, humbly relying on the blessing of Almighty God, have agreed to unite in one indissoluble Federal Commonwealth under the Crown of the United Kingdom of Great Britain and Ireland, and under the Constitution hereby established. . . (*Commonwealth of Australia Constitution Act* 1900 (Imp))

Any cursory glance at a statute will reveal how much drafters resort to the paragraph format to reduce ambiguities, and how rigorously they observe the convention of beginning each new legislative sentence on a new line (a new section or sub-section). This of course defeats any possibility of a prose style in the body of the statute.[11] It is therefore a refreshing change to read prescriptions such as the following one, which is directed at decision makers whose decisions are subject to appeals to the federal Administrative Appeals Tribunal:

> **Plain English**
>
> 6. When you are preparing a notice of decision and of rights of review, it should be given in plain English. Everyday language should be used, wherever possible, for ease of understanding. The notice must be clear, and expressed as simply as the subject matter permits.[12]

It is a notorious fact that the result of a drafter's efforts is not always intelligible to an interpreter. Gowers (1987) is kind enough to

---

10 (1297) 25 Edward I ch 29, re-enacted in *Imperial Acts Application Act* 1980 (Vic) s 3, Pt II, Div 3. See also *Imperial Acts Application Act* 1969 (NSW) s 6. In Victoria the *Imperial Acts Application Act* 1922 s 4 had also previously re-enacted it. In the other States identifying the ancient English statutes which were "received" into Australian law is much more difficult: Crawford (1993).

11 Preambles, which are much less resorted to nowadays, are however written in a prose style. For a comment on preambles, see Allen (1958 p 285).

12 "Code of Practice for Notification of Reviewable Decisions and Rights of Review", Gazette s 174, 11 June 1993, as appearing in Pearce (1994).

say that, "If it is readily intelligible, so much the better; but it is far more important that it should yield its meaning accurately than that it should yield it on its first reading . . .".

With great respect, it is now widely held that it is not good enough for statutes to be written so that they yield their meaning *eventually*. The "plain" or "clear" English movement (Eagleson 1988 p 15; Kennan 1988; Asprey 1991) in legal drafting is perhaps the strongest rebuttal to the view that legal English should not be viewed from the normal standards of good writing. Moreover, clear English has been embraced at official levels (Turnbull 1990; Unattributed 1985). Several statutes and regulations at the Commonwealth level have recently been rewritten in a more plain English style. For example, the *Social Security Act* 1947 has been thoroughly rewritten (see the *Social Security Act* 1991). Initiatives include simpler writing; explanations by way of introductions, cross-references and examples; short sections; more headings; use of the more informal possessive case; purpose clauses; "road maps" (including an order of provisions/structure of parts, location of definitions, a reader's guide, and an outline of structure etc); step-by-step instructions; and use of graphics (Turnbull 1990).

Even when written in conventional style, statutes are not always impenetrable for the general reader, or at least considered to be so by the popular press. The Melbourne *Age* recently devoted a 4-page "lift out" to the controversial *Employee Relations Act* 1992 (Vic). It included liberal extracts from the Act as well as expert commentary (*The Age*, 1 December 1992).

Effective drafting, particularly drafting which aims to be accessible to a general audience, does not come easily. No doubt the craft of the drafter involves surmounting the many problems peculiar to the legislative process (Kolts 1988) but a characteristic of drafting which the drafter shares with other accomplished writers is a disciplined approach to the task at hand. The observation that "Writing is largely re-writing" (Watson 1987) is as true for drafters as for any other professional writer. Hackett-Jones (1988, p 55) writes approvingly of Tolstoy's 105 drafts of a particular passage. The most accomplished drafters devote great time and intellectual effort to writing effectively (Kolts 1988 p 110). We should not blame them always if the result is not successful; the problem may lie in the unfortunate "baroque style" of the instructions (Hackett-Jones 1988 p 55).

A statute is not just a verbal framework. James Boyd White (1973) memorably described it as a "way of setting up conversations among its users". Of course, many of the conversations are not anticipated, as in the case of a prescription, contained in most Australian jurisdictions, concerning the general approach which courts should take in interpreting statutes ("the purpose rule"). Section 15AA of the *Acts Interpretation Act* 1901 (Cth) is typical:

> In the interpretation of a provision of an Act, a construction that would promote the purpose or object underlying the Act (whether that purpose or object is expressly stated in the Act or not) shall be preferred to a construction that would not promote that purpose or object.

A very similar provision was proposed in England. During a debate in the House of Lords about the Bill, the promoter of the legislation, the distinguished jurist, Lord Scarman, bravely remarked that the provision was drafted in "perfectly clear terms".[13] Neither courts, nor jurists, have agreed with this assessment (Barnes 1994). Questions which have arisen have included, in what circumstances does the rule apply? Does it only apply if the statute is ambiguous on its face? What is the nature of the purposive construction which is required or permitted by the rule? How may a purposive construction be accommodated? When will a court decline to bring a purposive interpretation into account against a non-purposive interpretation? What is the status and effect of the purposive meaning once brought to account? Does the rule cater for a situation with different or competing purposes? What is the meaning of "not promote"? How is the purpose rule related to and affected by the rule permitting extrinsic evidence (ie evidence of intention outside the statute)? And finally, is the meaning of the rule the same or different to the meaning of comparable rules in State legislation? Clearly, while the section has not made statutory interpretation on balance any more certain, it has stimulated useful "conversations" about purposive interpretation.

To anyone involved in dealing with statutes on a regular basis, the constancy of interpretation might make it appear to be a kind of epic "language-game".[14] Although the meaning of many statutory provisions is not disputed, the case books are full of disputes over the meaning of apparently simple statutory words. Is the Catholic church a "profession" for the purposes of the *Bounty (Books) Act* 1986 (Cth)? (*Re EJ Dwyer Australia Pty Ltd and Comptroller-General of Customs* (1989) 17 ALD 699 (AAT)). Does rocking a motor vehicle without permission amount to "tampering" with the vehicle under the *Motor Car Act* 1958 (Vic)? (*Harris v Sumner* [1979] VR 343). Is a pre-operative male-to-female transsexual a "woman" for the purposes of the *Social Security Act* 1947 (Cth)? (*Secretary, Department of Social Security v SRA* (1993) 118 ALR 467).

The open texture of statutes also means that statutes, like "imaginative literature" (Cordner 1994), encompass a moral dimension. In an erudite essay, Hackett-Jones (1988 p 43) discusses the relationship between the lawmaker and the artist; of how "the lawmaker recognises the artist as a spiritual brother":

---

13 House of Lords, *Debates*, 1981, vol 418, p 83 per Lord Scarman.
14 An expression invented by Wittgenstein to describe a way of learning about language through concrete cases: Monk (1991).

> According to Platonic theory, the artist's function is to hold a mirror up to reality; and the ultimate reality is a world of ideal forms of which our world is itself an imperfect reflection. The lawmaker has an analogous function: to mould a social order resembling the ideal concept of a city-state.

The familiar edicts of the criminal law are obvious expressions of public morals, but there is a less certain way in which morals become merged with statutes in the act of interpretation. Consider the definition of a "homeless person" in s 5(1) of the *Social Security Act* 1991 (Cth):

> [A person who] does not live at a home of the parents, or of a parent, of the person because domestic violence, incestuous harassment or *other exceptional circumstances* [italics added] make it unreasonable to expect the person to live at such a home.

What is an exceptional circumstance which would make it unreasonable for young persons to live with their parents? In particular, what standard of family life and what cultural norms do we assume in interpreting this provision? (*Re Secretary of Department of Social Security and Tu-Nguyen Tran* (1991) 23 ALD 449 (AAT)).

While it is common knowledge that statutes are open-textured and will require authoritative interpretation to settle their meaning in many cases, it is a less well-known fact that statute writers often *deliberately* create a degree of ambiguity or a "space" (Carney 1991 p 15) within which decisions are to be made about the detail of the law. True enough, the usual style of statutes is "anticipatory", whereby the legislators' message is conveyed through detailed prescriptive rules. However, Professor Carney is inclined to overstate the case when he says that "virtually all Australian legislation has been written over the years" in this style (p 16).[15] On this issue, Francis Bennion (1990) is closer to the mark when he highlights what he calls "broad terms" – single words or phrases in which "legislative power is delegated to the processors whose function is to work out the detailed effect". The common practice for law-makers to delegate, in effect, to the courts and other interpreters was recognised long ago by Professor Julius Stone (1964) as one of the main sources of judicial "law-making":

> A second (non-usurpatory) kind is where for some reason the legislator has (in effect) consciously delegated norm-creation to the judiciary, whether because flexibility of administration is required as in the Sherman Anti-Trust Law, or because conflicting views and interests within the legislature prevent agreement on anything but vague expressions.

15 Carney later on acknowledges that a mixture of strategies is not uncommon (1991 p 22) and he goes to some length to describe these other strategies, which he calls "framework laws" and "'soft/responsive' laws". These strategies are of less interest here because they are rather more a devolution of law-making (see Carney 1991 p 22) than an engagement with the interpreter.

Numerous examples may be given of broad terms or "fuzzy" law: a tribunal "may" extend time for the making of an application (*Administrative Appeals Tribunal Act* 1975 (Cth) s 29(7)); a right of access to a public document may depend on the disclosure not being contrary to the "public interest" (*Freedom of Information Act* 1982 (Cth) s 36(1)); a requirement of "reasonable" steps may be required of a citizen before certain rights accrue (*Rooming House Act* 1990 (Vic) s 20(1)); and the concept of "proper" use and enjoyment of a room in a rooming house may be employed to define a person's rights in that area (*Rooming House Act* 1990 (Vic) s 19(1)(e)).

Therefore, Posner's distinguishing of statutes from literature on the basis that the former are basically commands by the legislature to subordinates in the governmental system (1988 p 240) is far too simplistic.[16] There is plenty of evidence that the statute writer deliberately engages interpreters as partners in the legislative enterprise.

The need for interpretation in a particular case, whether intentional or unforeseen, inevitably means that the statute is continually the site for a series of real life narratives. The outstanding example is the *Commonwealth of Australia Constitution Act* 1900 (Imp), which has provided "both plot and ramifying subplots for countless human dramas" (Stephen, 1987). For example, most Australians can recall or have heard of the *Tasmanian Dam* case (*Commonwealth v Tasmania* (1983) 158 CLR 1)[17] and the *Communist Party* case (*Australian Communist Party v Commonwealth* (1951) 83 CLR 1).[18] In the former, the High Court of Australia was called upon to determine whether Commonwealth legislation preventing the damming of the Franklin River in southwest Tasmania was valid under s 51(xxix) of the Constitution, which referred to the power to make laws with respect to "external affairs". The latter case dealt with Commonwealth legislation banning the Communist Party purportedly pursuant to the power under s 51(vi) to make laws with respect to "The naval and military defence of the Commonwealth and of the several States, and the control of the forces to execute and maintain the laws of the Commonwealth".

The nation's laws have been the basis of an unprecedented narrative in Gavin Souter's *Acts of Parliament* (1988). His bicentennial task was to compile "a narrative history of events and people connected with the Australian parliament" (p xv). This is what he found behind the 7000 or so Acts of parliament, "A tale . . . full of sound and fury, tragedy and comedy, high hope and low cunning. . . The cast is well endowed with jesters, conjurors, gladiators, a number of stars and one or two Titans" (p xvi).

---

16 Posner does recognise the use by the legislature of "general language" to permit the courts to "complete" the legislation: Posner (1988 p 251).
17 See further Coper 1987.
18 See further Marr 1980.

A favourite story concerning a Bill for an Act of Parliament would have to be the attempt to introduce an identity card for all Australians called the Australia Card, first proposed in the Australia Card Bill 1986 (Cth). The hero was Ewart Smith, a little known former officer of the Attorney-General's Department:

> Like many flashes of inspiration, Ewart Smith's came while he was shaving on the morning of Tuesday 22 September 1987. He was talking on the telephone at the same time to Senator John Stone. It was in the middle of both these activities that he read clause 32(1) of the Australia Card Bill and grasped the fundamental point that the operation of a national identification scheme based on the Australia Card depended on there being fixed a "first relevant day" on which a person must produce his or her Australia Card or become liable to a penalty – and that day was to be fixed by regulation, and regulations could be disallowed. If the Senate disallowed the regulation, the "first relevant day" could not be fixed and the Australia Card system could not operate. The certainty that the Senate would disallow the regulation forced . . . Bob Hawke . . . and his Cabinet to conclude that the Australia Card was dead. If he did not actually kill it, Ewart Smith put the murder weapon in the hands of the Opposition parties. The magpies helped. (Virtue, 1989)

Without the embellishment of such sagas, even Allen (1958, p 284) concedes that "there is a certain amount of literary entertainment, not to mention a vast amount of history, to be derived from legislation". Statutes document ancient liberties such as the right to jury trial (Magna Carta),[19] judicial independence (The Act of Settlement)[20] and freedom of speech in parliament (The Bill of Rights).[21] They have constituted modern Australia from the initial idea of transportation ((1784) 24 George III ch 56), to federation (*Commonwealth of Australia Constitution Act* 1900 (Imp)), and, most lately, legal independence from the United Kingdom (*Australia Act* 1986 (UK, Cth)). And they have ushered in momentous social changes such as no-fault divorce (*Family Law Act* 1975 (Cth)).

On a lighter note, statutes may even be humorous. Doubting readers should reach for a copy of Sir Harold Kent's memoirs (1979). Sir Harold was formerly a United Kingdom Parliamentary Counsel. In the Appendix to his memoirs, he includes extracts of Acts which he drafted accompanied by various wry comments. His annotated s 2 of the *Factories Act* 1937 (Eng) is a masterful deconstruction of the drafting process (pp 251-252). Illustrative of his approach is the following little gem (p 261):

---

19 Magna Carta; see n 10 above.

20 (1700) 12 and 13 William III ch 2, re-enacted in *Imperial Acts Application Act* 1969 (NSW) s 6.

21 (1688) 1 William and Mary Sess II, ch 2.

PERFECTLY CLEAR WHEN YOU UNDERSTAND IT

> *Section 89(8) of Civil Defence Act 1939*
>
> For the purposes of this Act, the number of persons who work in or about a mine shall be deemed to be a number ascertained as follows, that is to say -
>
> (a) by having regard to all the people employed in or about the mine and ascertaining how many of them are from time to time simultaneously present in or about the mine otherwise than below the surface, and
>
> (b) if the numbers so ascertained fluctuate, by ascertaining the highest figure below which throughout any consecutive period of fifteen minutes the numbers do not fall.

Of all the literary analogies considered so far, the one which is most remote from its reputation as a prosaic text is the statute as image or symbol (Conklin 1989). Yet, even here, examples are not hard to come by. Until recently, the Australian Constitution lacked an image, probably because a majority of the general public were simply ignorant of it. However, recent debates about whether Australia should become a republic, and if so, the kind of arrangement which would be suitable, have altered this picture dramatically. The writer Geoffrey Atherden, who created the popular "Mother and Son" television series, associates the Constitution with an image of youth:

> When I say that our culture is youth, I'm not saying that we celebrate youth, which we do, but that we behave like teenagers. Look at the republican debate. . . Despite all the arguments about Constitution and economics, to me it is all about our growing up. Against this, the pro-monarchist argument sounds like: "You can be grown up and independent and still live at home with Mum and Dad". (1994 p 14)

Finally, statutes are not immune from critical theory either (Abraham 1979; Hackett-Jones 1988; Fish 1989; Glass 1991; cf Posner 1988 ch 5). Literary theory has been used to debunk the idea that the plain meaning of a statute is free of interpretation. In the following extracts the literary theorist, Stanley Fish, attacks the classic theory of jurist, HLA Hart. According to Fish (1989 p 512), Hart had asserted that:

> a rule framed in the appropriately general terms (eg, "vehicles are prevented from entering the park") will pick out "standard instances" of its application, and that these instances will constitute a set of "central" or "plain cases" in relation to which other, less clear cases can be classified.

Fish's response is that:

> Hart's answer must be that a plain case is inherently plain, plain in and of itself, plain independently of the interpretive activities it can then be said to direct. But it takes only a little reflection to see that the truth is exactly the reverse (p 513).

Fish concludes:

> rather than being independent of perspective [the literal meaning] is a product of perspective (it is the meaning that, given a perspective, will immediately emerge); it is itself an interpretation and cannot therefore be the indisputable ground on which subsequent interpretations securely rest (p 185).

Statutes and their interpretations may be deconstructed by questioning the assumptions of the maker or interpreter and subverting them (Airo-Farulla 1991; cf Posner 1988, pp 211-20). Though there is not space here to deconstruct a statute (see Airo-Farulla 1991; Barnes 1994), it is convenient to recall one suggestion as to why statutes may lack a fundamental principle or coherent objectives:

> to see the key to the meaning of a section in the policy or purpose of the legislation is, in my opinion, to take a less than sophisticated view of the art of the parliamentary draftsmen. In many cases, the interpretation of a provision is difficult, not because the policy or purpose of the legislation is not clear, but because the section is directed, not simply to effecting that policy or purpose, but to achieving a compromise between it and other considerations. (*Metal Manufacturers Ltd v Lewis* (1988) 13 ACLR 357 at 366-367 per Mahoney JA)

The coupling of statutes and literature is not therefore as implausible as it may first sound, and the connections are numerous and in some cases quite substantial. Posner's claim that a statute is "an effort to communicate a message rather than to create a work of art" (1988 p 246) too easily dismisses the literary aspects of the statute (and may not even be true in the case of certain constitutions). In this chapter I have briefly considered several of the statute's literary analogies: its imaginative scope, literary elegance, readability, disciplined "craft", open texture, "language-game" quality, moral dimension, engagement with the reader, narratives and other entertainments, images, and openness to critical inquiry. Whether or not a statute could ever be a great work of art, in all these ways the statute reveals itself to be every much as human as more commonly acknowledged forms of literature.

BIBLIOGRAPHY

Abraham, KS, 1979, "Statutory Interpretation and Literary Theory: Some Concerns of an Unlikely Pair", 32 *Rutgers Law Review* 676.

Administrative Review Council, 1987, *Access to Administrative Review: Stage One: Notification of Decisions and Rights of Review*, Report No 27, Australian Government Publishing Service.

Airo-Farulla, G, 1991, "'Dirty Deeds Done Dirt Cheap': Deconstruction, Derrida, Discrimination and Difference/ance in (the High) Court", 9(2) *Law in Context* 102.

Allen, CK, 1958, "The Literature of the Law", *Aspects of Justice*, Stevens and Sons, p 281.

Asprey, MM, 1991, *Plain English for Lawyers*, Federation Press.

Atherden, G, 1994, "What is Australian Culture?", *The Age*, 26 January 1994: 14.

Barnes, JW, 1994, "De-construction: Statutory Interpretation, Law Reform and Sampford's Theory of the Disorder of Law", *Federal Law Review*, forthcoming.

Bennion, FAR (ed), *Bennion on Statute Law*, 3rd edn, Longman, p 237.

Carney, T, 1991, *Law at the Margins: Towards Social Participation?*, Oxford University Press.

Conklin, WE, 1989, *Images of a Constitution*, University of Toronto.

Coper, M, 1987, *Encounters with the Australian Constitution*, CCH Australia, ch 1.

Cordner, C, 1994, "Beyond Reason's Categories", *Quadrant*, March 1994, 75, pp 76-77; a review of Goldberg, SL, 1993, *Agents and Lives: Moral Thinking in Literature*, Cambridge University Press.

Crawford, J, 1993, *Australian Courts of Law*, 2nd edn, Oxford University Press, p 17.

Eagleson, R, 1988, "Efficiency in Legal Drafting" in Kelly, D St L (ed), 1988, *Essays on Legislative Drafting in Honour of JQ Ewens*, Adelaide Law Review Association, 13.

Finemore, J, 1988, "Development of the Commonwealth Statute Book 1901-1986" in Kelly, D St L (ed), 1988, *Essays on Legislative Drafting in Honour of JQ Ewens*, Adelaide Law Review Association, 28, p 38, citing Sir Robert Garran.

Fish, S, 1989, *Change, Rhetoric, and the Practice of Theory in Literary and Legal Studies*, Duke University.

Glass, A, 1991, "Interpretive Practices in Law and Literary Criticism", 7, *Australian Journal of Law and Society* :16.

Gowers, E, 1987, *The Complete Plain Words*, Greenbaum, S and Whitcut, J, 3rd edn, Penguin, p 6.

Hackett-Jones, G, 1988, "The Scar of Odysseus and the Role of Parliamentary Counsel in the Legislative Process", Kelly, D St L (ed), 1988, *Essays on Legislative Drafting in Honour of JQ Ewens*, Adelaide Law Review Association, 43.

Kennan, J, 1988, "The Importance of Plain English in Drafting", Kelly, D St L (ed), 1988, *Essays on Legislative Drafting in Honour of JQ Ewens*, Adelaide Law Review Association, 74.

Kent, HS, 1979, *In On the Act: Memoirs of a Lawmaker*, Macmillan.

Kolts, G, 1988, "The Legislative Draftsman as Problem Solver", Kelly, D St L (ed), 1988, *Essays on Legislative Drafting in Honour of JQ Ewens*, Adelaide Law Review Association, 100.

Marr, D, 1980, *Barwick*, Allen and Unwin.

Mason, S, 1988, "Law-making, Drafting and Law Reform", Kelly, D St L (ed), 1988, *Essays on Legislative Drafting in Honour of JQ Ewens*, Adelaide Law Review Association, 111, p 113.

Monk, R, 1991, *Ludwig Wittgenstein: The Duty of Genius*, Vintage, pp 330-1.

Pearce, DC (ed), 1994, *Australian Administrative Law Service*, Butterworths, p 3092.

Posner, RA, 1988, *Law and Literature: A Misunderstood Relation*, Harvard University Press.

Souter, G, 1988, *Acts of Parliament*, Melbourne University Press.

Stephen, N, 1987, "Foreword", Coper, M, *Encounters with the Australian Constitution*, CCH Australia, p v.

Stone, J, 1964, *Legal System and Lawyers' Reasonings*, Maitland Publications, p 353.

Turnbull, I, 1990, "Clear Legislative Drafting: New Approaches in Australia" 11(3) *Statute Law Review* 161.

Turner, JN, 1985, "Teaching Law Through Literature", 14, *University of Queensland Law Journal*: 61.

Unattributed, 1985, "Kennanisation", 59 *Law Institute Journal* : 673.

Virtue, B, 1989, "How Ewart Smith Stopped the Australia Card", 24(9) *Australian Law News* 14, reviewing Smith, E, *The Australia Card – the Story of its Defeat*, Sun Books, 1989.

Watson, G, 1987, *Writing a Thesis*, Longman, p 9.

White, JB, 1973, *The Legal Imagination: Studies in the Nature of Legal Thought and Expression,* Little, Brown and Co, p 215.

28

Originalism and Constitutional Interpretation in Australia: The Way Backwards[1]

STEPHEN A JAMES

The Australian and American polities and legal systems share much in common: both are former English colonies, both have written constitutions (and, of course, the Australian one drew heavily on the American model), both have systems of representative government, both have federal systems, share a common law heritage and practice, and have entrusted the ultimate power of constitutional interpretation to supreme courts. This chapter explores another feature currently common in both countries (although to a much greater extent in the United States): popular, academic and judicial controversy over the use of historical evidence in constitutional interpretation and the legitimacy of judicial review and "law-making" and, more specifically, the debate over "originalism".

Following Professor Daniel Farber (1989 p 1086), we may define originalists as those constitutional interpreters "committed to the view that original intent is not only relevant but authoritative, that we are in some sense obligated to follow the intent of the framers". As with many schools of thought, there are extremists and moderates among originalists: the former holding that *only* original intent is relevant, and that whoever wins on historical evidence should win the case; the latter that other factors may be significant, especially where original intent cannot easily be determined. There are also differences among originalists about the level of generality at which to approach original intent. Are we to focus on the framers'

---

1 Versions of this chapter were presented to the "Law in History" and "Law and Literature" conferences at La Trobe and Monash Universities (Australia), respectively, during 1991. This chapter is an abridged and edited version of an article originally published in *In the Public Interest The Buffalo Review of Law and Society,* XII (Spring 1992), pp 23-54. The author thanks those at the conferences for their comments on the chapter as well as the editorial board of *In the Public Interest* for its advice and the permission to republish the article in this book.

general principles? Their specific intent with regard to particular words or government machinery? Or linguistic conventions? But certainly a prerequisite to join the originalist club must be acceptance by the interpreter that, as Farber (1989 p 1086) says, "*clear* evidence of original intent is controlling on any 'open' question of constitutional law".

This chapter asks two main questions of originalism in Australia: can we readily ascertain original intent? And, if so, is it *in principle* the best form of constitutional interpretation? (following Farber 1989). The conclusion is that originalism is inconsistent, impracticable and no more democratic than alternative approaches. But this conclusion does not preclude the judicial consideration of historical evidence in constitutional cases. Rather, such evidence (including framers' "intentions" to the extent that these can be ascertained or (re-) constructed with any certainty) is a valid part of the social data necessary for any constitutional judgment which must resolve human disputes. Further, history can illuminate the *purpose* and fundamental principles of a constitution, and provide a degree of political and legal consistency.

Ironically, in Australia (compared with the United States) – if the issue of originalism is even debated[2] the possibility of deriving the original intent from judicially considered historical evidence is generally thought by the legal fraternity to have radical rather than conservative implications. Despite the general acceptance among Australian jurisprudents that judges *make* law and do not simply *declare* it, the notion of the judge as historian or social theorist can still make many a traditional judge or lawyer blanch as they recall what is for them the spectre of a Justice Lionel Murphy or Lord Denning.

Recent trends in the High Court toward a more explicitly political and history-conscious role[3] and new legislation promoting judicial recourse to a wider range of materials in interpreting

2 Compared with the torrents of ink that have flowed because of this issue in the United States, the Australian discussion has amounted to a mere trickle; see Thomson, 1982a, 1982b; Burmester, 1986; Cooray, et al, 1986; Coper, 1987; Mason, 1986; Dawson, 1990; Detmold, 1985. However, this chapter was written before reading Craven, 1990, which was not indexed in the Index to Legal Periodicals or Legal Trac, and escaped my notice. Since this chapter was first published in *In the Public Interest* (James, 1992), Mr Craven has written several more articles in the area (viz: 1992a, 1992b, 1992c). I do not respond to his arguments here, but see my "Craven's Constitutional Contextualism – A Critique", unpublished MS (1993).

3 Recent High Court cases indicative of this trend include *New South Wales v Commonwealth* (1990) 169 CLR 482 (the *Corporations* case) (where the majority relied on the Convention debates to hold that the Commonwealth lacked the power under s 51(xx) of the Constitution to legislate in relation to the *incorporation* of trading and financial corporations); *Mabo v Queensland (No 2)* (1992) 66 ALJR 408 (recognising native title over the land by its indigenous inhabitants, and the importance of international human rights law); and *Australian Capital Television Pty Ltd v Commonwealth (No 2)* (1992) 66 ALJR 675 (recognising, for the first time, a constitutionally "implied guarantee of freedom of communication as to public and political discussion").

statutes (notably s 15AB of the *Acts Interpretation Act* 1901 (Cth)) promise that the role of history in constitutional interpretation will become a lively issue. Questions such as whether judges should be historians, what methods they should use, and whether the intentions of the Framers should be controlling in constitutional interpretation, should become smouldering if not burning ones over the next few years. The answers one gives to these questions will significantly influence how democratically and flexibly the Constitution will operate.

The strength of legal positivism in Australia, and the correspondingly weak natural or higher law tradition in its constitutionalism (see Winterton 1986 pp 228-235), contributed to the doctrine whereby the Constitution as an Act of parliament was to be interpreted according to the ordinary rules of statutory interpretation used in English courts. As anyone who has ever been a law student would know, this approach requires the court to ascertain the intention of parliament as revealed in the words of the text of an Act. "Intention" was understood in the *artificial* sense of the "will" of the legislature "manifest" in the words of the text, not as a retrospective, and sometimes no doubt posthumous, exercise in psychological analysis of present or past parliamentarians.

As we have noted, the High Court purports to follow the English model and not without some practical effect. Until 1988, for instance, the court did not take notice of the Convention debates, records of which had been thought to be too incomplete (excluding drafting committees and so forth) or to invite dangerous distraction from the words of the text adopted in the various popular State referenda (Thomson 1982 p 314; Coper 1987 p 412; Mason 1986 p 25; Dawson 1990 pp 93-4; Burmester 1986 p 29). The text was to be construed by the court in the light of various canons of construction, including prominently the Mischief Rule and many other maxims in Latin too tedious to recite (see Dawson 1990 p 93; Thomson 1982 p 314). The Mischief Rule, for instance, is a subset of the more general *purposive* approach to statutory interpretation in England: to discover *why* parliament is changing or adding to the background of legislation, constitutional law and common law already in existence, one:

> look[s] to the overall intention of the legislature as discovered from reading the statute as a whole . . . [asking] what "mischief" [or social, legal "defect", "evil", or "lack"] this statute was intended to remedy. . . [One must ask] [w]hat social purpose was intended to be achieved by this legislation . . . [and then] read each word and phrase so as to carry out that purpose to the extent that they are capable of being so read (Derham 1977 pp 139, 138).

In *Cole v Whitfield* (1988) 62 ALJR 303, however, the High Court changed its long-standing rule excluding consultation of the Convention Debates, declaring that they and other historical materials (not specifically identified) could be consulted:

> not for the purpose of substituting for the meaning of the words used the scope and effect – *if such could be established* – which the founding fathers subjectively intended the section to have, but for the purpose of identifying the contemporary meaning of the language used, the subject to which that language was directed and the nature and objectives of the movement towards federation from which the compact of the Constitution finally emerged (at 307, emphasis added).

Thus, the court relaxed its textualist legalism but did not thereby adopt originalism as its new doctrine of constitutional interpretation.[4]

In any case, the strict theory had always been mitigated by judicial practice in a number of ways: by the recognition that it is a *constitution* being interpreted; by the influence of the common law tradition of evolutionary, judge-made law; by the court's reference to legislative history and general historical development; by purposive and structural interpretation using implied principles and extra-Constitutional notions; and by policy choices.

The court has recognised that the Constitution is not an ordinary statute; it is "a mechanism under which laws are to be made and not a mere Act which declares what the law is to be", as Higgins J once said (*A-G (NSW) v Brewery Employees Union of NSW* (1908) 6 CLR 469 at 612). His statement reflects what Sir Anthony Mason (1986 p 23) has recently called the High Court's "dynamic rule of constitutional interpretation". According to this rule, one should construe the Constitution broadly and flexibly to meet the needs of the current generation of Australians. As Sir Owen Dixon (in Mason 1986 p 23) once explained, the Constitution is:

> an instrument of government meant to endure and conferring powers expressed in general propositions wide enough to be capable of flexible application to changing circumstances.

This principle now finds more specific expression in the court's connotation/denotation distinction which means, crudely, that the essence of a word can remain the same as in 1900 but it can apply to a related concept, exemplication or new instance not foreseen in 1900 (Mason 1986 p 26). The connotation is fixed, the denotation changing. Of course, this distinction can, at times, be highly artificial.

With regard to interpretation of the Constitution, reference may be made by the High Court to the draft Bills of 1891, 1897 and 1898 (*Tasmania v Commonwealth* (1904) 1 CLR 329 at 333, per Griffith CJ arguendo; *A-G (Cth) v T & G Mutual Life Society Ltd* (1978) 52 ALJR 573 at 583 (Aickin J)). There has been no clear explanation of why logically the court should limit itself to these particular draft Bills – why, for instance, reference could not be made

4 I neglected to discuss this seminal case in James, 1992, unfortunately wrongly characterising the High Court as committed at that time to the rule excluding consideration of the Convention Debates, and giving the misleading impression that this rule was only really diluted by the court's decision in the *Corporations* case (see James, 1992, pp 35,39-40 and n 61).

to the Bill produced at the 1899 Premiers' Conference which made seven amendments to the 1898 Bill and which was then put to the second national referendum. We may now identify the main content of these Constitution drafts. The 1891 Bill was the result of an *unelected* National Australasian (so-called because of New Zealand's early involvement) Convention of State Premiers and delegates (45 men in all) in Sydney, and was drafted principally by Sir Samuel Griffith (Premier of Queensland, a lawyer, "declared positivist", and an "arch-conservative politically" (Davidson 1991 p 231)). It embodied the main features that now exist in the Commonwealth Constitution. These features may be listed as follows: a bicameral Federal Parliament with equal representation for all States in the Senate with the House of Representatives predominating in matters of finance and the control of the executive; the *possibility* of responsible government along British Westminster cabinet lines; a federal tax uniform in all States with concurrent State tax powers; state determination of electoral boundaries; a Federal Supreme Court; free trade between the States. Commentators Quick and Garran (1901 pp 136-137) describe the impact of the Bill in the following way:

> The idea was once for all crystallised into a practical scheme. . . The real work of the Convention was now practically finished, [for] in the first draft of 1891 the whole foundation and framework of the present constitution was contained . . . [although] it was in some few respects less essentially democratic in its basis . . . [and] less definite and less elaborate in its treatment of the vexed problems. . . In those few days they [the framers] laid down the main lines from which the movement has never since wavered. On 2nd March 1891, Australian Federation was a misty abstraction; on 31st March it had definite outlines and a practical policy.

Thus the subsequent drafts of 1897 and 1898 embellished but did not substantially alter this model.

Attempts by the Framers to forge inter-colonial agreement on the 1891 Bill by parliamentary means failed. As Quick and Garran (p 144) note:

> neither the [colonial] Parliaments nor the people would accept the work of the [1891] Convention as final . . . [for] in the minds of many of the people there was a vague feeling of distrust of the Constitution as the work of a body somewhat conservative in composition, only indirectly representative of the people, and entrusted with no very definite or detailed mandate by the Parliaments which created it.

The Bills of 1897 and 1898 were the result of "popularly" elected national Conventions in Adelaide, Sydney and Melbourne. But, according to Davidson (1991 p 233), the:

> popular [pro-Federation] movement's leadership was in fact composed almost exclusively of middle-class, commercial and dependent professional interests . . . and, when finally there were elections of delegates to a further convention, the "popular mandate" which returned the old guard of 1891 to Adelaide in 1897 totalled slightly more than 55 percent of all voters.

and Queensland was not represented at all.

The 1897 Adelaide Convention, while claiming with their "democratic" mandate to "begin at the beginning", commenced by discussing leading principles, "almost exactly in the form of Parkes' resolutions of 1891 [on which the 1891 Bill was based]" (Quick and Garran p 166). Indeed, the draftsmen of the 1897 Bill had "endeavoured to treat as reverently as possible" (Quick and Garran p 166) the 1891 Bill. The 1897 Bill went through the convention's committee process (constitutional, financial, judicial and drafting committees), before being submitted to the various colonial legislatures for approval. At the Sydney session of the 1897 Convention, the framers had before them 286 proposed amendments to the Adelaide draft, suggested by the ten colonial Houses of Parliament. The session closed "before more than half of the Constitution had been considered" (Quick and Garran p 193) and it had earlier reduced consideration of the amendments to:

> four great questions: the financial problem [how to resolve conflicts of interest between "big" and "small" in terms of population states], the basis of representation in the Senate, the power of the Senate with regard to Money Bills and the insertion of a provision for deadlocks (Quick and Garran p 188).

According to Quick and Garran (p 194), the Melbourne Session of the convention in 1898 (20 January – 17 March) was "the longest and most important of all". The whole 1897 Bill was considered and reviewed clause-by-clause in the Drafting Committee; significant debate occurring on the issues of the regulation of rivers and railway rates and finance. But, relying as it did on the framework and substance of the 1891 Bill which had been developed by an *unelected* body, and failing to represent large sections of Australian society, the Constitutional framing process was only partially democratic and it does not provide the kind of legitimacy that originalists assume it does.

Can we readily ascertain the original intent of the Australian Founding Fathers? Clearly, the problem concerning the fact that the Framers will not have always turned their attention to, or debated, issues currently before the constitutional court holds equally well in the Australian as in the American situation. Nor can the Australian "originalist" (actually a rather rare breed – but see Craven (1992a, 1992b, 1992c)) avoid difficulties with the completeness, accuracy and bias of the records of the national Constitutional conventions from 1891 to 1898. These difficulties are made more acute by the fact that, even after *Cole v Whitfield* (1988) 62 ALJR 303, examination of the Convention Debates can only be undertaken to elucidate the meaning of the words in the constitutional text and not to substitute for that meaning the intent of the Framers (assuming that they can be identified).

The task of identifying exactly who is to be counted a "Framer", is a difficult one in the context of the creation of the Australian

Constitution between 1890 and 1901. Were the Framers the 14 delegates to the Melbourne Conference (1890)? The 45 delegates at Sydney in 1891? The 50 delegates at the 1897-1898 Conventions? These are only some of the perplexing questions one can ask in relation to the Constitutional Conventions. Other problems involve questions of hierarchy and authority concerning which persons count and to what extent the views of long-standing active "framers" should be preferred (even when not spending much time on a particular issue)? What of the members of the committee and the relation between committees? What of the colonial parliamentary and popular interventions and interpretations (like John Quick's and Robert Garran's (1901), for example)? What of participants at Premiers' Conferences? What of members of the United Kingdom Parliament and Home Office? No adequate originalist theory has emerged to recommend how one would answer these questions and simultaneously reconcile the inevitable conflicts of opinion that would and did emerge.

In any case, what evidence of the Framers' "intentions" (remembering that this is a fiction in the sense of *fictio* – made, constructed – since we cannot "get inside" anyone's mind so as to know a person's intention as she herself does) that can be gathered seems to point *against* any notion that the Australian "Founding Fathers" intended their own intentions to be controlling in constitutional interpretation: if they were, to generalise, under the spell of an interpretive theory it was legalism not originalism (a *spell* because, as we have seen, the formal theory was often departed from or had unintended consequences). At least formally, the Australian judiciary, including the High Court, is still wedded to the "ordinary" English canons of statutory construction, despite judicial and extra-judicial statements reflecting a weakening of the bond (see, eg, Mason 1986; Brennan 1991). Additionally, progressive liberals at the Conventions "intended" that the constitution be populist and dynamic why else the power of the people under s 128 to amend the Constitution? It has also been rightly argued by Professor Tribe (1987 p 52) in relation to the United States Constitution, but certainly applicable to Australian constitutional language (if not as strongly), that:

> The very generality of many of the terms the Framers used – such as *liberty, due process* and *equal protection* – strongly suggests an intent not to confine their meaning to the specific outcomes and contexts of those who first used them, but to invite the development of meanings in the light of the needs and insights of succeeding generations.

The normative arguments in favour of originalism in the United States such as congressional democratic majoritarianism, authorial interpretation of texts and the supposed lack of principled alternatives, fare equally poorly, but for *some* different reasons, in Australia. Here I can only give a sketch of these reasons: the dubious democratic credentials of the framing process (for example,

Australian Aborigines did not take part, nor did most women); the originalist normative view underestimates the extent to which the High Court has (although erratically) promoted, and can promote a Dworkinian, humanistic, cosmopolitan notion of democracy that is concerned with treating all persons with fair and equal concern and respect[5] (especially important when a parliamentary majority uses its power to unfairly discriminate against a minority's interests); that the interpretation of texts via authorial intention is hardly the only approach to obtaining meaning and needs arguments as to how one can do it and why it is *preferable* to other "readings" (for example, textual, hermeneutic, deconstructionist and postmodernist ones); and that, in any case, the High Court, for its part, seems to prefer, as a formal approach, to derive the intention of *parliament* (not the Framers) via textual and purposive interpretation. Of course this list by no means exhausts the possibilities for a critique of originalist normative arguments, but in itself constitutes at least one demonstration of the deficiency of those arguments.

Studies by Coper (1987), Zines (1987) and Winterton (1986) amass substantial evidence that the High Court's purposive constitutional interpretation has not been confined to the text but embraced various extra-Constitutional notions such as federalism, the national interest, responsible government, separation of powers and democracy. The principle of federalism has been held by the court to imply both the necessity of judicial review to adjudge between Commonwealth and State powers, and the assumption in the Constitution that there are limits to Commonwealth power (Gageler 1987; Coper 1984; Zines 1984). The use of the concept of "nationhood" by the High Court has expanded the Commonwealth's legislative and executive power, especially via the external affairs power as enlarged in the *Dams* case (*Commonwealth v Tasmania* (1983) 46 ALR 625 in Hanks 1985 p 751; Lane 1990 p 100; also see (on nationhood) *Davis v Commonwealthth of Australia* (1988) 166 CLR 79). The choices High Court judges have to make between national needs or the federal balance are, as in the *Dams* case, inevitably value and policy choices. Unfortunately, the court has rarely been open about the choices it is making, the justification for them and how they "trump" competing considerations. This obviously reduces the accountability and democratic nature of the judiciary.

I have argued that neither strict originalism nor legalism can be decisive in questions of constitutional interpretation. In the United States the intent of the Framers, or in Australia the often absurd

5 The increasing "domestification" of international law norms in Australian municipal law, via Commonwealth treaty-making, legislation, and High Court interpretation, gives some legal reality to this moral aspiration. See, eg, *Mabo v Queensland (No 2)* (1992) 66 ALJR 408; Bailey, 1990; *Commonwealth v Tasmania* (*Dams* case) (1983) 46 ALR 625 in Hanks, 1985, p 751; *Koowarta v Bjelke-Petersen* (1982) 39 ALR 417 in Hanks, 1985, p 736. See also Dworkin (1985, 1990).

assertion of the "plain meaning of the text,"[6] has veiled the complex web of principles, policies and preferences necessarily involved in constitutional interpretation and adjudication. It is a web, however, continually being spun and re-spun even as some judges deny such activism. But, given that the United States and Australia both have written constitutions embodying a constrained democratic majoritarianism, how are we to be constitutional *and* provide adequately for the needs, desires and interests of those currently interpreting and affected by the Constitution? It is only possible here to briefly describe the theory that I argue provides the best answer to this question and adequately accommodates historical analysis in constitutional interpretation (for a fuller elaboration, see James 1992 pp 45-54). I will use Australia as an illustration. Professor Richard Fallon has argued that constitutional law suffers from a "commensurability problem". Courts admit the relevance of a number of kinds of argument all of which we have touched upon:

> arguments from the plain, necessary or historical meaning of the constitutional text; arguments about the intent of the framers; arguments of constitutional theory that reason from the hypothesized purposes that best explain either particular constitutional provisions or the constitutional text as a whole; arguments based on judicial precedent and value arguments that assert claims about justice or social policy.

Since courts must come to a single legal decision in cases before them, the commensurability problem is "to show how arguments of all these various kinds fit together in a single, coherent constitutional calculus" (Fallon 1987 pp 1189-1190).

According to Professor Fallon's "constructivist coherence theory" (pp 1192-1193) (with which I concur), judges must try to balance fairly the various antinomies that arise in considering the different kinds of argument: for example, original understanding versus authoritative current meaning; ordinary language versus "constitutional" language (for example, "due process" in American Constitutional law); and principles versus counterprinciples embodied in the Constitution. A suitably modified constructivist coherence theory of constitutional interpretation could, and, it is argued, should, operate in Australia, with the fundamental principles of the Constitution governing over other kinds of argument.

The theory I propose may be called a *text-constrained, but democratic and constitutionalist* theory of constitutional interpretation. Its main outlines can be described in a number of interlinked propositions concerning (1) the possibility of democratic judicial review; (2) the judicial consideration of historical evidence; (3) the status of the constitutional text; (4) implied constitutional principles; (5) the Mischief Rule and general constitutional principles and

6 Consider, for example, the "plain meaning" of the words "absolutely free" in the "free trade" clause of the Australian Constitution (s 92). For discussion of s 92 in this context, see James, 1992, pp 44-5.

structures; (6) the place of judicial policy and value choices. We can now examine each of these elements in turn.

(1) POSSIBILITY OF DEMOCRATIC JUDICIAL REVIEW

The judicial review of legislative and executive acts by the High Court of Australia is a duty of that court, one connected with judicial independence and the doctrine of separation of powers. Such review need not be undemocratic; rather it can bolster *constitutional* democracy, guard against legislative, majoritarian or executive tyranny (for example, through the protection of minorities), and defend fundamental constitutional principles concerning responsible government, representative democracy, federalism, political participation and individual rights. (See Lindell 1977; Bailey 1990 ch 4; Federalist nos 10, 51, in Murphy et al 1986 pp 36-7; Brennan 1991 pp 35-37; Freeman 1992).

(2) THE JUDICIAL CONSIDERATION OF HISTORICAL EVIDENCE

The High Court can consider historical evidence including the framers' intent (as far as this can ever be determined) in constitutional cases (*Cole v Whitfield* (1988) 62 ALJR 303; *Corporations* case); providing that it does not take the originalist approach that the framers' intentions are somehow *binding* and determinative of its decision (this consultation of historical evidence ought not to be regarded as heterodox, but as a legitimate part of the court's ex post facto judicial law-making in the common law tradition) (See Detmold 1985 pp 230-238; Freeman 1992).

(3) THE STATUS OF THE CONSTITUTIONAL TEXT

The court is bound to try to understand the written constitutional text (while it has the respect of the Australian polity), and is restrained by it in its decision-making. Nevertheless, the language of the Constitution is often open-textured, and, in any case, the text is not exhaustive of the "political constitution of any regime" (Freeman 1992 pp 6-7) (for instance, there is no single text governing the constitutional polity of the United Kingdom).

(4) IMPLIED CONSTITUTIONAL PRINCIPLES

Within a common law and constitutionalist tradition, and despite frequent (though less so now) denials, the High Court, as this article has demonstrated, *already* construes the constitutional text in the light of constitutional *principles* thought to be implied by it, and according to the perceived requirements of rule of law (Brennan 1991 p 40; *Australian Capital Television* case).

(5) THE "MISCHIEF RULE" AND GENERAL PRINCIPLES AND STRUCTURES

It would be a relatively small step from the court's use of the Mischief Rule to then refer to historical evidence to help *discern in the text* (original intent not being decisive in interpretation) those general principles and structures designed by the Framers which bound legitimate constitutional interpretation – such as representative democracy – whatever the specific content attributed to them by the court at any particular time. This builds on the court's connotation/denotation distinction, and is consistent with Dworkin's (1986 pp 90-96) distinction between "concepts" and "conceptions".

(6) THE PLACE OF JUDICIAL POLICY AND VALUE CHOICES

Finally, in construing the broad constitutional principles and structures that have been referred to, judges must be candid about policy and value choices being made, hear argument on all sides, and make an assessment based on their perception (as it must be) of current *community* values: this will increase the democratic basis of judicial review as well as fostering judicial accountability (since the values are placed in a public forum where they can be critically assessed) (see Mason 1986; Fallon 1987 pp 1249, 1263; Dworkin 1990).

This chapter has sought to demonstrate the impracticality, inconsistency and normative unattractiveness of originalism as an approach to constitutional interpretation in Australia. Nevertheless, I have maintained that this conclusion does not preclude the judicial consideration of historical evidence as long as that evidence is not regarded by the judge as binding upon her constitutional interpretation. Finally, the chapter outlined a *text-constrained, but democratic and constitutionalist* theory of constitutional interpretation; suggesting its merit and showing its "fit" with *existing* High Court constitutional interpretation. Thus, history can play its part in elucidating the fundamentals of the written document constituting the polity we have, but it would not be decisive. With this approach to historical evidence and a community-based model of constitutional interpretation in place, we can have some confidence in Australia, as does Dworkin (p 346) in the United States, that "democracy and constitutional constraint are not antagonists but partners in principle".

BIBLIOGRAPHY

Bailey, P, 1990, *Human Rights Australia in an International Context*, Butterworths.

Brennan, G, 1991, "Courts, Democracy and the Law", 65, *Australian Law Journal,* p 32.

Burmester, H, 1986, "The Convention Debates and the Interpretation of the Constitution", in Craven, G (ed), *The Convention Debates 1891-1898: Commentaries, Indices and Guide,* vol 6, p 25.

Coper, M, 1984, "The High Court and the World of Policy", 14, *Federal Law Review, p* 294.
Coper, M, 1987, *Encounters with the Australian Constitution,* CCH.
Craven, G, 1992a, "The Crisis of Constitutional Literalism in Australia", 30, *Alberta Law Review,* p 492.
Craven, G, 1992b, "Cracks in the Façade of Literalism: Is there an Engineer in the House?", 18, *Melbourne University Law Review,* June, p 540.
Craven, G, 1992c, "After Literalism, what?", 18, *Melbourne University Law Review*, December, p 540.
(Current Topics), 1987, "The Constitutional Doctrine of "original intent", 61(2), *Australian Law Journal,* p 51.
Davidson, A, 1991, *The Invisible State The Formation of the Australian State 1788-1901,* Cambridge University Press.
Dawson, D, 1990, "Intention and the Constitution – Whose Intent?", 6, *Australian Bar Review,* p 100.
Derham, DP, 1977, *An Introduction to Law,* Law Book Company.
Detmold, MJ, 1985, *The Australian Commonwealth A Fundamental Analysis of its Constitution,* Law Book Company.
Dixon, O, 1935, "The Law and the Constitution", 51 *Law Quarterly Review* p 590.
Dworkin, R, 1986, *Law's Empire,* Belknap.
Dworkin, R, 1990, "Equality Democracy and Constitution: We The People in Court", XXVIII(2), *Alberta Law Review,* p 324.
Fallon Jr, RH, 1987, "A Constructivist Coherence Theory of Constitutional Interpretation", 100, *Harvard Law Review,* p 1189.
Farber, DA, 1989, "The Originalism Debate: A Guide for the Perplexed", 49, *Ohio State Law Journal,* p 1085.
Freeman, S, 1992, "Original Meaning, Democratic Interpretation and the Constitution", 21(1), *Philosophy and Public Affairs,* p 3.
Gageler, S, 1987, "Foundations of Australian Federalism and the Role of Judicial Review", 17, *Federal Law Review,* p 162.
Hanks, 1985, *Australian Constitutional Law,* Butterworths.
James, S, 1992, "Original Intent: The Judicial Uses of History and Constitutional Interpretation in Australia and the United States", XII (Spring), *In the Public Interest The Buffalo Review of Law and Society,* p 23.
Lane, PH, 1990, *An Introduction to the Australian Constitution,* 5th edn, Law Book Company.
Lindell, G, 1977, "Duty to Exercise Judical Review", in Zines, L (ed), *Commentaries on the Constitution,* Butterworths.
Mason, A, 1986, "The Role of a Constitutional Court in a Federation – A Comparison of the Australian and the United States Experience", 16, *Federal Law Review,* p 4.
Murphy, WF, Fleming, JE and Harris, WF II, 1986, *American Constitutional Interpretation,* The Foundation Press.
Quick, J and Garran, R, 1901, *The Annotated Constitution of the Australian Commonwealth,* Angus & Robertson.
Thomson, JA, 1982, "Constitutional Interpretation: History and the High Court: A Bibliographical Survey", 5, *University of New South Wales Law Journal,* p 313.
Tribe, 1987, "Current Topics"
Winterton, G, 1986, "Extra-Constitutional Notions in Australian Constitutional Law", 16, *Federal Law Review,* p 235.
Zines, L, 1984, "The State of Constitutional Interpretation", 14, *Federal Law Review,* p 277.

29

Re-Writing Law as Postmodern Fiction: The Poetics of Child Abuse

TERRY THREADGOLD

For parents who were themselves abused as children, the business of parenting is an overwhelming responsibility (*The Age* "Tempo" 17 March 1993 p 15).

Victorian child protection officials expect a dramatic increase in the number of reported cases of child abuse after the State Government's decision, in the wake of the *Valerio* case, to make reporting mandatory (*The Weekend Australian* 6-7 March 1993 p 5).

A brother and sister both under the age of 10 told a jury yesterday that they and their 5-year-old brother were chained to their beds and physically abused by their mother's boyfriend (*The Age* 6 March 1993 p 3).

A mother on trial with her former boyfriend for alleged abuse of her three children yesterday denied the allegations, and said the children made their stories up because they were hurt at their lack of stability (*The Age* 11 March 1993 p 5).

But you just can't get rid of the problem of 10-year-old murderers by draconian punishments. Even the politicians conceded as much. The British Home Secretary said revealingly that the hands that bludgeoned James Bulger were "hammer blows against the sleeping conscience of the nation" (*The Age* "Opinion and Analysis" 3 March 1993 p 13).

KATY: Those words you used? Where did you get them from?
SUSY: What words?
KATY: "The twin peaks of womanhood. Soft, sweet, seductive."
SUSY: Gary. That's what he said.
KATY: No he didn't.
SUSY: *(frowning)* Are you saying I'm a liar.
KATY: Gary didn't say that. Dad did.
(Susy stares at her)
SUSY: You told me he never touched you.
KATY: He did.

SUSY: You told me I was lying.
KATY: I'm sorry. I couldn't handle it. It was like reliving what *I* went through.
SUSY: How old were you?
KATY: I don't want to talk about it.
SUSY: How old were you?
KATY: Thirteen.
SUSY: So was I. What did he do?
KATY: Same as you. It would start as a game of "chasey" and he'd end up grabbing my breasts from behind. I hated being left alone with him.
(Williamson 1993 *Brilliant Lies* pp 37-8).

> A recent landmark judgement in an American court – and an upcoming hearing in Perth – underlines a growing backlash against therapists who encourage memories of sexual abuse in their patients without regard for the truth ("Headline, Bettina Arndt" *An Abuse of Trust* "Focus" *The Weekend Australian* 28-29 May 1994 p 23).

The above are a set of fairly random quotations, fact and fiction, with the boundaries between the two often hard to maintain. They are what Roland Barthes might have called "voices" from "the multiple centres of the culture", the babble of everyday life, textual traces of a problem. They attest to the social reality and the contested nature of child abuse, the struggles over meaning and identity, and the narrativity of both. It is these things that I want to address in this chapter by looking at the legal traces of a particular case which began to be about child abuse but was sidetracked by a point of law. This sequence of events, I will suggest, is symptomatic of the difficulty of speaking the problem, of allowing it to be spoken or written, or of understanding the complexity of what we do when we speak or write it. It is also symptomatic of what a general theory of textual forms, a poetics, has to do with *poiesis*, the making of texts and meanings in everyday and expert contexts, including those which involve the law and its agents.

I speak of these things in the context of what has become known as "the crisis of representation", that postmodernist phenomenon whereby the apparent certainties of a modernist world, its carefully constructed and distinct categories, its order and coherence, its totalising theoretical narratives, seem to be being challenged on all sides by a blurring of boundaries and categories, an openness to new and multiple perspectives, and a rewriting of enlightenment, wisdom and knowledge as partial, positioned, fiction and patriarchal. The Law, as that institution which most epitomises Reason, Rationality, Order, Control, is increasingly "on trial", subject to rewriting, as the effects of poststructuralist, feminist and deconstructive theory begin to circulate within Law Schools, among those writing about the Law, and as commonsense in the media and on television.

My focus will be particularly on those aspects of the law which are brought into focus by this most recent brand of postmodernist theory – the corporeal and discursive production of the law – the genres and text-types that the law, as complex organisation, produces – and then on the way these discursive resources become technologies for disciplining, positioning and constraining the social body, including the law itself and its agencies and structures. I will argue that the law as a complex organisation is a network of signifying practices – bodies and discourses, genres and behaviours, modes of speaking and writing, reading and interpreting – all of which construct relations of power through rules of membership and meaning. It is, moreover, a complex organisation which operates at the intersections of a number of other complex organisations – the media/pedagogy/literature/the economy to name just a few. Its agents, the people who perform the law and construct it on a daily basis, move between and among these sites as sexed bodies, and their discourses, the text-types they speak and write and live, bear the traces of these daily and nomadic migrations from place to place within these organisational and private structures.

That is, in the end, it is people and their interactions, their readings and their writings, which constitute the law. And that is why the law will never accomplish its mythical goal of truth and objectivity and universal justice.

This is a different story to the one the law tells about itself. The law is an interpretive community with a complex intertextual history which has always worked with a view of language that is "realist", "referential". This is a view of language that has always argued, in the face of all the evidence to the contrary, that meanings inhere in words, that there is a "true" meaning or intention to be recovered from language, that language is a kind of container for meanings which it transmits unproblematically from sender to receiver, that language "refers" to or "represents" a reality which pre-exists it. In its language about itself the law writes the people out.

In speaking of these things here I want to refer to just two theorists of the postmodern, both of whom have questioned these taken-for-granteds about language and meaning and their relations to the social order. I believe that deconstruction and poststructuralism are actually ways of understanding the structure and the play in the institutions and the discourses that we have to deal with on a daily basis. Contrary to the masculinist reading of postmodernism, and of these theories, as a refusal of mastery, a loss or decentredness of mastery (Owens 1983), I agree with Gayatri Spivak that the value of deconstruction is precisely in its suggestion that the subject is always centred (Spivak 1989 p 214). Thus, contrary to Owens and others, I would argue that there is *no loss of mastery* in the texts of the legal institution that I want to explore today, and that despite the postmodernist scenario of competing and contradictory meanings which they seem to construct, if read in a particular way, the masculine legal subject is very much centred in these texts, at home, at attention (Spivak 1989). His centring/centredness is precisely what delimits his "others" (his woman client and her children in this case) as not at home, absent. Poststructuralism and deconstruction, contrary to popular opinion, are precisely testimony to mastery. They are testimony to the material effects of the discursive structures and the conceptual oppositions which hold the master in his dominant position.

> It is always possible one could speak the truth in a void; one would only be in the true however, if one obeyed the rules of some discursive "policy" which would have to be reactivated every time one spoke.
>
> Disciplines constitute a system of control in the production of discourse, fixing its limits through the action of an identity taking the form of a permanent reactivation of the rules.
>
> We tend to see in an author's fertility, in the multiplicity of commentaries and in the development of a discipline so many infinite resources available for the creation of discourse. Perhaps so, but they are nonetheless principles of constraint, and it is probably impossible to appreciate their positive, multiplicatory role without first taking into consideration their restrictive, constraining role. (Foucault 1971 p 224).

Foucault here speaks of the "creativity" of discourse as something that must be understood only in relation to the principles of institutional constraint that police and constrain that creativity. He is concerned, in other words, with the operation of those rules of membership and meaning which constitute the visible practices and articulated beliefs of institutions, their members, and their practices (genres), but also with those resources available for the "creation" of discourse which seem to be "in excess" of those structures, but are in fact restrictions and constraints of another kind. They are the discipline-based knowledges, the discursive formations, the narratives, the common ways of thinking and believing and talking about the world, which circulate as common sense and theory, and which discipline subjects, in ways that are not limited to the one institution or its rules and constraints. These circulate in all kinds of texts: verbal, bodily, visual, spatial; and across a wide range of institutions, in often contradictory and incompatible forms. They become embodied forms of knowing and they are just as systematic and structured and every bit as constraining as the more obvious structures of control, perhaps more so, because they are not the subject of even subjective and everyday ways of theorising, but constitute a profoundly taken-for-granted and embodied way of being in the world.

These are the kinds of resources for making texts which poststructuralism recognised as intertextual, what, in their texts, speaking subjects enact and perform because of the other texts where they have been. This is the source of the poststructuralist metalanguage of discourses (in Foucault's sense), narratives and myths, and of the notion that speaking subjects are as much "spoken by" these taken-for-granted elements as speaking and controlling them.

> I submit for your consideration the following hypothesis: a text cannot belong to no genre, it cannot be without or less a genre. Every text participates in one or several genres, there is no genreless text; there is always a genre and genres, yet such participation never amounts to belonging. And not because of an abundant overflowing or a free, anarchic and unclassifiable productivity, but because of the trait of participation itself, because of the effect of the code and of the generic mark. Making genre its mark, a text demarcates itself (Derrida 1980 p 212).

In similar vein, Derrida is arguing here that all texts must work under the constraints of genre (imposed institutional structures and rules) – and that what is not generic in texts – is not there "because of an abundant overflowing or a free, anarchic and unclassifiable productivity" but because the text is "spoken" by the social discourses (Foucault), the narratives and myths, which speak its speakers and readers.

In both texts the argument is a complex one for both freedom and constraint simultaneously, but the powers of the constraints, and the issue of mastery and control are foregrounded in both. In *Limited Inc* (1988) Derrida, the very voice of instability and plurality as he is so often read, had more to say about this:

> *If I speak of great stability* . . . Such *stabilisation* is relative, even if it is sometimes so great as to seem immutable and permanent. It is the momentary result of a whole history of relations of force (intra- and extrasemantic, intra- and extradiscursive, intra- and extraliterary, or -philosophical, intra-and extracademic etc). In order for this history to have taken place . . . there must have been a certain play in all these structures, hence a certain instability or non-self-identity, nontransparency. *Rhetorical equivocation and mobility, for instance, must have been able to work within "meaning"*. Différance must have been able to affect reference. . . *What has always interested me the most,* what has always seemed to me the most rigorous (theoretically, scientifically, philosophically. . .) *is not indeterminacy itself,* but the *strictest possible determination* of the figures of play, of oscillation, of undecidability, which is to say, of the differential conditions of determinable history, etc. . . (1988 p 145).

The emphasis in the above is my own. What both theorists are arguing here is for the need to understand and establish exactly how it is that "equivocation" and free play can and do exist under, or within, the constraints of the huge stabilities of the culture – of which the law as institution would have to be one. I want to argue that in these, the now canonised texts of malestream critical theory, this is a plea for analysing and making sense of the social construction of stability and order, and not only an argument for re-writing everything as fiction. It is this approach to understanding texts – as operating always within the huge stabilities of the culture – that I want to use in what follows.

THE TEXTS – THE LEGAL DOCUMENTS

1. Solicitor's (representing the parents) affidavit (4/6/1984) recounting events that took place in the Children's Court, Cobham, New South Wales (20/2/84). Attached, the decision of the Magistrate (27/4/84) refusing the arguments of the barrister that the mother be permitted to appear.
2. Solicitor's affidavit recounting his application for leave to appear for the children. Attached, transcript of court proceedings in which this request is debated (23/5/91). Permission given in relation to the son, but not the daughters.
3. Judgment, Cantor J, Supreme Court of New South Wales, refusing appeal and supporting the magistrate's decision (29/6/84).
4. Judgment, Court of Appeal (Supreme Court) — Kirby P, Mahoney and Priestley JJA — upholds this decision (25-26 March; 3 April; 9 August 1985). Supreme Court of NSW (Court of Appeal): *Shales v Lieschke* (1985) 3 NSWLR 65; 16 A CrimR 384, 10 Fam LR 261.
5. Judgment, High Court (on appeal from Supreme Court) — Brennan J, Dawson J, Deane J, Mason J, Wilson J — Appeal upheld. J. . . Appellant. Lieschke and others (respondents); on appeal from the Supreme Court of NSW, (1987) 162 CLR 447-65.

This set of texts constitute the legal institution's records of its own practices. As such they are part of the codification of the law by which it represents and constructs itself as discipline and profession. It should be noted that while records are kept of affidavits and court proceedings in the lower courts (viz here the magistrate's court) these are not the texts that are published in the Law Reports and used as precedent for subsequent judgments or as texts for the training of the profession. The recording and codification process is selective and partial, and matters dealt with at these "lower" levels appear in the public records as narratives told by judges, embedded in their written judgments, as part of the judgment as genre. They are incorporated and appropriated as part of the thesis (setting or introduction) of another argumentative genre, a genre which is itself part of the canon of legal pedagogic texts, and as the text-type produced by the "highest courts", has much more value and status than the embedded genre. If an appeal moves from court to court as in this case, the final judgment, the victor in this adversarial process between appellants and judges, embeds and incorporates selectively within itself in this way all the previous argumentation and process.

As with genres, so with the status and value accorded to those who speak or write them – magistrates and court officials, solicitors and barristers, delinquent parents and neglected children – are almost entirely written out of the "official" and visible legal records. Even at the "lower" levels this hierarchisation operates, so that the voices of children and parents are heard only through their legal representatives, and then what is heard is their desire to speak, not their speaking, which is refused, not permitted, by the court. This gradual filtering out and silencing of the bodies and subjectivities and events that constitute the social process, the transformation of a family trauma into a point of law, and the process of legal objectification that goes with it, are accomplished by institutionalised linguistic and semiotic means perpetrated by obedient, compliant legal subjects who are those means made flesh, embodied.

The hierarchy of legal texts so produced has one single and superordinate goal – the maintenance of the appearance of rule-governed social order, coherence and consensus. The universal values of the legal system, the truth, justice and objectivity, the absent cause of "right reason", which must be seen to ground jurisprudence, is constructed in and through the linguistic and generic strategies of its texts. These texts adhere to rules of interpretation and commentary, they refer dutifully to established authorities – the canonised texts of the law and the statutes. They quote one another in an ordered and respectful fashion. Even their disagreements are gentlemanly (the exchanges between judges in High Court Appeal). They observe, with respect, the differences in value and power which they themselves construct and reproduce.

All the texts use the register of legal discipline and operate in an apparently ordered way in relation to its conceptual and administrative constraints. Thus, in each of them in this case principles of evidence (the exclusion of hearsay), rules defining kinds of procedures (inquisitorial or adversarial, matter or charge), rules defining kinds of participant roles or the role of the court (parties, care or criminal), and general principles of jurisprudence (natural justice) are adhered to. So are the structures of legal argumentation. The typical pattern of thesis, antithesis, synthesis is everywhere apparent, even in the court proceedings. Where documents occur in a series, an affidavit for example with an annexure, the pattern is again repeated, the affidavit functioning as thesis, the annexure as antithesis or synthesis, with the same structure often replicated within its own structure. This "logical" expository or argumentative structure is one of the constant realisations of the adversarial (and masculine) nature of the law. It is always arguing a case against the hostile forces of disorder which it must hold at bay. Documents and texts thus have multiple, but ordered, functions within the system. And they are produced, and read, according to the rules of membership and exclusion (Bourdieu 1991) which determine what can and cannot constitute a legal text of a particular kind or genre.

Genres at different levels in the hierarchy exhibit different relations to the authoritative texts they must quote/interpret and refer to. As you move from "The Magistrate's Judgment" (1), through "The Appellate Cases in the Supreme Court" (2), to "The High Court" (3), the differences can be characterised as follows:

1. Obedience/compliance;
2. Reference and Scholarship (establishing the authority and knowledge of the system and its agents);
3. Legislating interpretations (constructing and asserting judicial authority by challenging the authority of the authorities, re-writing, in the light of experience, and according to personal interpretation, the meaning of legislation, and the reading of the common law).

These differences construct and maintain a mutually supportive hierarchy of legal agents and power relations.

However, at all three levels, these differences are more apparent than real. In each case the texts actually demonstrate all three things, and paradoxically, and for quite different reasons, the greatest power seems to be both at the bottom and at the top of the system simultaneously. At the top, this is because of the greater power and authority of the High Court judge, at the bottom it is because the magistrate has effective powers which allow him to bypass the entire system and act according to his own conviction as to what is appropriate, even while appearing to comply with and defer to the system. In this case, his actions are eventually re-appropriated and controlled by the system, or rather negated by it, in the High Court decision, but what this comes down to is two men's opinions in conflict, and one man – the High Court Judge – with the power to assert his as "right". It does not alter the social consequences for a family of the magistrate's ability to manipulate the system in the direction of his personal view of what is just in this case:

> The magistrate in the course of argument evinced some concern that the "complaint" might not be established if the parents intervened and that "could be said to be working very much against the interests of the children". The concern was misplaced. The magistrate's refusal to accord the parents a right to be heard lest their appearance prevented the making of an order presumed the existence of facts which would show that the children were neglected children and presumed that it was in the children's interests to prevent a parental attempt to challenge the proof of those facts. Such a presumption is at odds with the terms of s 82 which make it clear that the authority and duty of the parents or other guardians must not be interfered with by order of the court unless it is found that the child is "neglected" or "uncontrollable". Such a finding cannot be made without hearing the persons who have the authority and duty and who wish to be heard and who can practicably be heard in opposition to the making of the finding. In general the principles of natural justice must be applied however grievously the parents or guardians may be suspected to have failed (Brennan J, High Court Appeal at 457).

What I want to suggest here then is that carefully contextualised linguistic, semiotic and rhetorical analysis of the structure of these texts can tell us a great deal about the way the texts are made, and the way that they appear to function within the context of the law. It can tell us a great deal about what the agents of the law think their texts do, and what they think they are doing with their texts. These explicit aims and goals are after all what the linguistic and semiotic structures of the texts are designed to accomplish, and these we can find "in the texts", as it were, as linguistic traces and realisations of those aims and goals, so long as we have a fairly thorough understanding of the legal institution's own understandings and descriptions of its practices to make "metalinguistic" sense of our linguistic analyses. What we cannot find in this way, or interpret in this way, are the things that are in the texts that the institutional descriptions do not acknowledge, and that the generic strategies of the texts, like those of the institution, seek to contain or control. Nor can we find the things that are not in the texts at all, written out by the institutional practices and the agents who embody those practices in their making of the texts. The finished products of legal debate have a history, and they intersect with countless other stories that they do not tell. These are the aspects of this textuality that I will explore in the next section of this chapter.

READING AGAINST THE GRAIN: DECONSTRUCTION

In what follows I am going to read the texts against the grain of the institutional practices which produced them, using the strategies of Foucauldian discourse analysis and Derridean deconstruction. Here I want to read the texts another way, so as to give the lie to their coherence, their systematic differences, their clear hierarchical order, their reliance on precedent, their logic and their claims to "right reason", truth and objectivity.

In this reading I have identified passages in the legal texts which share certain discursive, narrative, generic or linguistic patterns. I have collated these passages and given them new names, new titles. I will discuss them under these headings below. What this produces is a second set of texts – a set of discursive materials which are the stuff of which the socially ratified legal genres are made – heteroglossic stuff – speaking in many contradictory voices – from many different places in the social system – quoting one another endlessly, contradicting one another – a sort of postmodernist collage, a tissue of citations, a babble of rumour and opinion, which indeed attests to instability, plurality and difference – something that might well read like a postmodernist fiction of the most nightmarish kind if you were caught up in it, if the reality of your life was part of it, or perhaps more importantly, if you were in the helpless and powerless position of being she whose life had started all this babble off, but were now somehow systematically excluded from and silenced by its considerations.

The differences between the first set of texts listed above and the groups of text fragments of which the first are made and which I will now discuss, are an illustration of the Derridean points quoted earlier about the intersections between great stabilities, hegemonies of discourse, and the rhetorical equivocation and mobility which work – via embodied and sexed subjectivity – which Derrida does not say – within meaning, genre and rhetoric.

THE DISCOURSES AND NARRATIVES EMBEDDED IN THE LEGAL GENRES

1. The absent/embedded story of the "incompetent parent" and her "neglected" children: the social construction of guilt and the institutional denial of child abuse.
2. Nonsense and Obedience: the power of the *Child Welfare Act* and the not-yet-proclaimed statute.
3. The Parent/Child – Natural Justice Discourse – embodied meanings.
4. The Enlightenment Discourse and the belief in the "plain intendment" of texts.

1. THE ABSENT STORY

What we know of this story is only what the men who represent the law chose to tell us. It is embedded in dialogue between men in the magistrate's court, and in the thesis/introductory phase of the various judgments. What they can and do tell of it is constrained by their own role as legal agents in various contexts and by the discourses of the law which seek to "define" and "label" its elements. Thus we know that there is a woman who has five children, four of them girls, only three of whom are listed in one account. There is also said to be a "very young baby" but the youngest child appears in fact to be a son aged seven in 1984. The solicitor is constantly represented as "appearing for the parents" although in fact he represents only the mother. There is a remarkable lack of attention to the details of these facts in these apparently factual documents.

We know that the woman is living apart from her husband, and that there is another man, who has an alcoholism problem, with whom the daughters are encouraged by the mother to spend the weekends. It appears that improprieties have occurred between the man and the girls, allegations of which the children "do not contest", and that other events have taken place between the man and the boy involving the mother. The mother appears to be accused of condoning the former and participating in the latter, although the court transcript of the prosecution's discussion of this is marked "(inaudible)" and this continues to be quoted as "(inaudible)" in successive texts. We also know from one of the solicitor's affidavits that by June 1984 the children are all in foster care and the mother is under psychiatric treatment "to which she is responding".

We never hear the voice of the children. In the magistrate's court there is a solicitor seeking to represent them who enters a plea of "no cause to show" on their behalf in relation to the mother's application to be heard in the case, but it is questioned whether the solicitor can represent the children because there is no-one "competent" to give the solicitor instructions, or at least the magistrate does not think there is "because the Act makes no clear distinction between infants and juveniles". This state of affairs is "deprecated" in both the High Court and the Supreme Court judgments.

It also appears that the children have been in foster care since December 1983, when the allegations, charges, complaints, were first brought against them by a police officer, presumably the one who appears in the magistrate's court transcripts as "Court Officer" and is addressed once or twice as "Sergeant". Thus although no evidence has been heard with respect to either of the charges, and no orders have been made by the magistrate to deprive the woman of the custody of her children, justice has effectively been done and without the court procedure. It has evidently been done by the local authorities dealing with the complaint, and it remains done through the long years of litigation and it is not undone by the High Court's decision to allow the woman to speak in a case which then has not yet come to court. The magistrate's decision not to allow the woman to speak transforms a case of child abuse into a legal disputation about a point of law. That disputation is what the records will show as the whole story. Generically it is structured as having a clear beginning and a clear end, but the story neither begins nor ends with those generically demarcated points.

Insofar as the charges are named at all they are remarkably non-specific and multiply ambiguous. "Sexual allegations", "moral danger", "incompetent guardianship", "(inaudible)", and numbered sections of the Act, which the magistrate himself does not know how to read, "I just can't work out what the Act was getting at" (original court transcript p 7). These issues are caught up in the ambiguities between an *inquiry* into the *complaint*, and an investigation which might lead to *criminal charges*, the different standards of evidence involved with respect to the admission or not of hearsay evidence, depending on which way you classify the proceedings (as *adversarial* or *protective* for example), and the dizzying and consequent implications for the role of the parent, as *party* to the former, or entitled by *natural justice* to be heard in the latter. The "stories" that legal agents tell one another about these points of law are called "interpretations" and it is through this storying that the discourses which reproduce and reconstruct the categories of parent, child, nuclear family, justice and truth (among others) are actually "made". (See Brennan J, High Court judgment at 459ff for a summary of the issues involved).

The uncertainties one is faced with here in the textual traces of this narrative are symptomatic. First, one does not know what they mean, and one cannot recover what they mean in relation to whatever might have been the facts of the original events; and second, the courts and their agents do not know what they mean, despite the multiplication of readings and re-readings of statutes and precedents that is evidenced in the written judgments which are supposed to determine this. Indeed their deliberations very quickly by-pass "what they mean" in my first sense (meanings they may have in relation to this woman's story), in favour of "what they mean" in the second, the meanings they may have in terms of the accumulated textual (ie verbal, written, encoded and presumably equally partial) records of the wisdom of the law. And in fact the final judgment bypasses even these written sources and relies almost entirely on the embodied wisdom of a single High Court judge. This embodied and sexed wisdom, the wisdom accumulated from the texts that he has lived, that he has been disciplined to believe and speak, the wisdom of the *habitus*, effectively ignores the legislature, authorises itself in terms of those precedents it *prefers* – "With respect, these express provisions carry no implication that the legislature intended the principles of natural justice to be excluded"; "With respect, there is no merger" (Brennan J at 459) – and calls itself "natural justice" – one of those absent causes Goodrich (1986) identifies as the ideational sources of the law (including God, Truth, Right Reason and so on).

The actual story of child abuse, and all that is involved in that, is quickly and effectively side-stepped on the pretext of dealing with a point of law – whether a parent who is accused of complying with child abuse, or engaging in it (we are never sure because of "(inaudible)", has the right to appear and to give evidence in the case where she is "on trial" as "incompetent" parent or worse. This judgment revolves around the fundamental rights of parents, not of children (this discourse effectively conflates the two), and it never addresses at all the issues that surround the troubled masculinity which has perhaps used its authority and rights (those granted it by natural justice) to abuse and do violence to children and possibly this woman.

The whole complex process of evasion and contradiction is symptomatic of a social reluctance to name or discuss, or even acknowledge, the reality of these sexual and troubling issues. It is nowhere more symbolically symptomatic than in the one place in all these texts where the name of the alleged child abuser might have been recorded – the place in the transcript of the proceedings in the magistrate's court which is transcribed "(inaudible)" and transmitted as such in all subsequent texts (original magistrate's court transcript p 8). The contents of the narrative summary dealing with the issue of child abuse and its consequences before it came to court is treated *as if it had not happened.* Throughout all the texts under discussion here magistrate and judges speak of the possible results of certain interpretations of the *Child Welfare Act* as *potentially* depriving the woman of the custody of her children – as though only their written orders, in response to dialoguing with that Act can actually effect this, when they know *it has already been done:*

> It would offend the deepest human sentiments as well as a basic legal principle to permit a court to take a child from its parents without hearing the parents when they can be heard and when they wish to be heard in opposition to the making of an order (High Court Appeal at 458).

In terms of this text alone, *what has already been done* is *both* acknowledged as constituting the deprivation of basic civil rights, *and* constructed as if it had not happened, as if this judicial process is in place to stop it happening. The denial of basic civil rights to this woman and her children is effectively elided from the discussion which constitutes in every sense a re-telling, a narrative, which can only be called a legal fiction.

The reality of the impossibly contradictory discourses of the Act and of the law in relation to these issues is born of this conspiracy of silence. A masculinity which is supposed to protect and defend women and children, but which instead does them violence, is what should be on trial here, but this is what the patriarchal institution of the law, which constructs itself in the image of that masculine protector, cannot and does not acknowledge. Instead the role of a female parent, her complicity with patriarchal violence, and her right to be heard in her own defence displaces the narrative of child abuse, and constructs her as the problem with which the courts and the common law have to deal. The issue is then again displaced from woman as problem to the "natural justice" which gives "parents" the right to be heard in any case involving their children. Thus the patriarchal structure of the law itself, and its replicated structure in the nuclear family (Yeatman 1987) and in heterosexual and homosexual relations, the right to possess, to control, and to do violence, is protected from the challenge posed by the reality, the normality and the violence of child abuse. (La Fontaine 1990 is an excellent account of the "normality", the extent of the problem in everyday life.) Like Freud, in his classic rewriting as female fantasy, of all the evidence he had of the source of female "hysteria" in childhood sexual abuse, in his refusal to acknowledge the violence to and appropriation of female bodies which is written in his theory as the story of the law of the father, as masculine protection and right reason (La Fontaine 1990; Yeatman 1987), the law also displaces and objectifies the problem. A point of law, and legal texts and arguments, troublesome as they may be, are easier to deal with than real and contradictory masculine bodies and the difficult and troubling issues around the compliance of men and women in the maintenance and transmission of patriarchy (Gatens 1991; Pateman 1988).

But this denial of the story of child abuse is a double displacement which involves the construction of boundaries and the construction of the law itself in other important ways. The records tell us, at least the High Court judgment, which will be the pedagogic tool that will be the only written trace of all of this, tells us, that these proceedings start with the events in the magistrate's court and end with the High Court judgment. This sets limits which confine discussion of the events to legally regulated and normalised procedures and agencies. Thus justice appears to be being done in an autonomous and objective way. The links with the social processes which initiate the making of these texts remain inscribed in them only in the incidental and imprecise ways that I have outlined above. But the "imprecision" is of far greater magnitude than these merely linguistic traces can possibly suggest.

These traces have a long and complex history in a whole range of other texts and practices and events which exist "outside" the limits of the law and its textual attempts to maintain social order. These texts and practices are not policed by the rules of hearsay, and if they operate according to precedent it is unwritten, embodied precedent, common sense and social practice made flesh, enacted and performed as the rhetoric of daily life. Such are the practices by which we define and recognise behaviours as "child abuse", as "mental illness", as "homosexuality" for example. They nearly always involve the construction of narratives about the behaviours of others which, to be believed, to be convincing as evidence, must match up with others' narratives of the enactment of the same categories. Thus in interpreting the behaviour of someone as signifying "mental illness", for example, one must have, as Dorothy Smith (1990 pp 15-16) points out, "a set of criteria and rules" for classifying events as, "this or that kind of social fact". This kind of narrativity constantly reappears in the carefully policed texts of the courtroom and the judgments. Discursive constructions of reality and the narrativity of evidence "invade" the domain of the law precisely because that domain is peopled by embodied, sexed subjects, whose knowledges, beliefs and goals intersect at every level with the other worlds and the other stories they inhabit and live outside the courtroom. The initial decision by the magistrate and the police officer are based on narrative constructions of this kind, so are the judgments of the High Court judges. These narratives are never questioned because the issue becomes one of arguing a point of law. The question of child abuse is thus displaced by that argumentation in ways which legitimate the legal and patriarchal doing of violence to the social and domestic body.

Whatever her story was, no evidence has been heard, and this woman and her children have been done violence, both by the complexities of child abuse itself, and by a legal system which replicates that violence in (1) constructing itself as the law of the father and (2) in never questioning the discourses and the narratives which set the father up as the protector or punisher of those over whom he has "fundamental rights and authority".

2. *NONSENSE AND OBEDIENCE*

> As is pointed out by Lord Widgery CJ in *R v Worthing Justices* [1976] 2 All ER 194, the English legislation was amended specifically to provide for an enhanced right of parents beyond that previously provided in the *Children and Young Persons Act* 1933, s 34(1). *Reform of the provisions under the principal Act have been suggested to cure the perceived deficiency in the existing legislation. The* Community Welfare Act *1982 (NSW), s 96(2), which has been enacted by the Parliament,* but *not yet proclaimed to commence*, followed the report on proposed child and community welfare legislation issued in 1978 by the then Minister for Youth and Community Services. The relevant section of the report which, in important respects, reflects the same concern about due process that was influential in the United States Supreme Court decision in *Re Gault* (above) *includes the separation or care and criminal proceedings. . .* (Supreme Court Appeal at 78). [My italics]

> DEANE J: There is one further matter which I would mention. *The argument before the Court again exposed some of the long recognized deficiencies of the* Child Welfare Act *1939 (NSW)*. The notions that a child should be "apprehended" as a neglected child on a "warrant" issued by a justice; that a child so "apprehended" should be "brought before" a court to enter a "plea" to what is commonly described as a "complaint" and was, in the present case, actually set out in a "charge sheet"; and that, if no substantive order is justified, an allegedly neglected child is to be "admonished and discharged" are reminiscent of days when the wrong done to a child who was neglected was treated as if it were an offence on the part of the child. Those notions have no place in the legal system of a mature, responsible society: cf ACT Law Reform Commission, *Report on the Law of Guardianship and Custody of Infants* (1974) p 13; Australian Law Reform Commission, *Report on Child Welfare* (1981) p 208. *It is to be hoped that there will be less room for their persistence if and when the necessary administrative action is finally taken to bring into effective operation the new system of procedure which was enacted by the Parliament of New South Wales as long ago as 1982:* see *Miscellaneous Acts (Community Welfare) Repeal and Amendment Act* 1982 (NSW) and *Community Welfare Act* 1982 (NSW) (High Court Appeal at 462). [My italics]

The texts quoted above are examples which realise the discourse of child welfare as it is inscribed in the practices of the legal system. In each of the courts to which this case proceeds the complaint is the same. The Act is impossible as a basis for judgment. There is another Act which has been enacted by parliament but not yet proclaimed, which would resolve these difficulties: but no-one can act upon it.

These impossible elements of the existing legislation have to do with the conflicting discourses which structure the *Child Welfare Act* itself – its uncertainty as to the nature of the child, the child as in need of protection or in need of control, the parent, the parent's role as guardian and protector of the child or as disciplining and punishing agent, and the nature of "being neglected" as opposed to "delinquency" (Havemann 1989). In this the Act bears witness to a long history of conflicting and incompatible discourses which have produced the impossible objects, the impossible categories, of parent and child in the present social configuration (Carmen Luke 1991; Holland 1992). The Act also participates in that typical obfuscation and denial of the business of child neglect and child abuse which I noted above, displacing patriarchal guilt onto its victims, constructing the child as "criminal", as "charged", and the inquiry into the relations between children and parents in such cases as an adversarial, party-to-party one, *as if* the child had committed some crime by being neglected or abused. This functions to avoid again the question of patriarchal violence and guilt – allowing it to masquerade as protection and control.

This legislative text has a history which would explain some of its many contradictions. Legislative texts are never monologic, they are constructed by many actual voices, emanating from many embodied subjects with different and often conflicting agendas. When such legislations are, as well, subject to successive revisions by again different subjects with again different agendas they must always be almost the paradigm case of the heteroglossic text (Bakhtin 1968), a text that speaks in tongues to confound and confuse the conflicting discourses of the social order as it attempts to synthesize them.

When this already complex textual dialogism is reactivated in dialogue with the disciplined agents of the law who believe that this text (the Act) should offer them the basis for authoritative decisions, should offer them clear guidelines for thought and action, and when these agents do not any more embody the discourses the Act speaks, but another set of more recent welfare discourses which have rewritten the paternal role of the state and the legislature as *care* and *inquiry*, not *criminality*, *accusation* and *complaint*, then the conflict is only exacerbated. These more recent discourses have also been enacted as legislation, reflecting the processes of social and institutional change, and perhaps effecting them, bringing them about as discursive and non-discursive categories, but this legislation has not been proclaimed. It can be spoken, it can be referred to, but in this legal context it cannot be acted upon. The Act in force, enforced by the obedience of these legal subjects to its statutory regulations, continues to control the debate, despite the fact that it is verbally contested as "nonsensical", "unsatisfactory", "inconsistent", "defective" and "mischievous". It is worth reflecting on the power of disciplinary and institutional technologies to instil this kind of obedience to the recognisably nonsensical in their disciplined and enacting subjects.

When the Act is finally thoroughly critiqued for its construction of the child as criminal in the High Court judgment, it is done not on the basis of recourse to the authority of the not-proclaimed statute, as it is in the other judgments, but in terms of the personal opinion of the judge, who here has the authority to offer legislating opinions, and who is to a large extent freed of the need to have recourse to textual authorities with which he does not agree. The same is true of the dismissal of earlier judgments in this document. The argument is very much *ad hominem*, addressed to earlier judges and their judgments, and based in personal opinion.

3. *THE DISCOURSE OF NATURAL JUSTICE*

It is the natural right of parents to be heard in cases affecting them and their children, which "speaks" this personal opinion, locates it, and articulates it. This judicial voice is also "spoken" by the new discourses of care, protection and inquiry, discourses which explicitly eschew, in the legal context, the rules excluding hearsay evidence in cases such as this one. This is a very considerable local freeing up of the rigidity of court procedures, and clearly important since it will function as precedent and have more than local effects. It is evidence of that judicial labour which Stone (1985) describes as enabling the continuity and change of the common law. It is the rights of parents that have been upheld, even if children have been rewritten as victims rather than offenders. There is much talk of the mutual reciprocity of the bonds of natural justice that bind parents and children together, of mutual obligations and duties to protect and to obey. But the law still has the right to "take children into custody" and hear the evidence next, and there is no talk of the denials of "natural justice" perpetrated as child abuse every day in ordinary homes by mostly male participants in these magic and time-honoured bonds. The patriarchal order is untouched by this judgment, at its core, where it might be changed, precisely because the law constructs itself in the image of the patriarch, and continues to perpetrate its own forms of violence with impunity, constructing them, like the inalienable rights of parents, as care and protection.

And to prove that nothing changes, that *"plus ça change, plus c'est la même chose"*, even after all this evidence of the impossibility of legal objectivity and disinterested justice, of the impossibility of fixing meanings once and for all in authoritative texts, the belief in fixed and determined meanings reasserts itself in -

4. *THE ENLIGHTENMENT DISCOURSE*

The general principle which governs this case is clearly established. It is stated by Barwick CJ in *Twist v Randwick Municipal Council* (1976) 136 CLR 106 in these terms:

> The common law rule that a statutory authority having power to affect the rights of a person is bound to hear him before exercising the power

> is both fundamental and universal . . . But the legislature may displace the rule and provide for the exercise of such a power without any opportunity being afforded the affected person to oppose its exercise. *However, if that is the legislative intention it must be made unambiguously clear.* (High Court judgment at 456). [My italics]

With respect, these express provisions carry no implication that the legislature intended the principles of natural justice to be excluded. As Dixon CJ and Webb J said in *Commissioner of Police v Tanos* (1958) 98 CLR 383:

> Such an intention is not to be assumed nor is it to be spelled out from indirect references, uncertain inferences or equivocal considerations. *The intention must satisfactorily appear from express words of plain intendment.* (High Court judgment at 461). [My italics]

CONCLUSION

If critical textual theory has told us anything, it has told us *why* the magistrate, solicitor, barrister and judges in the child neglect case have such difficulties arriving at any one *true* and *final* interpretation of the meaning of the Act. And it has told us why that Act is so multiply ambiguous and open to different readings. It is a heteroglossic text, a text that speaks contradictory discourses and tells stories. It does that because the society it realises and constructs cannot make up its mind about child neglect, cannot decide whether this is a criminal or family affair, cannot decide whether the family is sacrosanct or the State as parent has the right to protect its others. The discourses the Act negotiates are complicated by the metaphorical links between the body politic and the body of the father, the body politic and the family, the patriarchal power of the sexual contract which is always written as a social contract (Pateman 1988) and the violence that is always hidden in that writing. When the State steps in as father to take children from their parents on the grounds that it is "protecting" the children we have precisely the discourse of surveillance of populations, discipline of bodies, that Foucault's work was all about. It is a set of discourses that re-write power as protection, violence as pastoral care.

The legal men see these issues as "urgent". The welfare of the children is uppermost in their deliberations. But they see them as urgent for *four long years* of litigation.

The children may have been in real danger. The foster home may have been the best place for them. The mother may not have been the best person to have responsibility for their care. My only point is that whether they were or not, whether it was or not, whether she was or not, this legal violence was done to their lives in a way that gave them no choices and no voice, and no way of dealing with this interference in their lives.

Anna Yeatman pointed out, as long ago as 1987, the very recent history of the discourses which construct child abuse and their intersections with the law. The discursive constitution of child abuse, and of the child abuser as "objects", and of embodied responses to these issues as problems needs (a) to be recognised as discursively constructed and (b) to be thoroughly explored in relation to a number of key issues. What constitutes child abuse, for example, as opposed to the multiple kinds of seductive and erotic interactions between children and their "protectors", both male and female, which are never so constituted. What makes the abuser, and those who comply with that abuse? How do the discourses that construct these things selectively order and arrange the facts in accord with particular class, gender, economic and ethnic issues? How do we change the violent and patriarchal response involved in the ambiguities and fictions of the discourse of "protection" so as to deal with the troubled and damaged people, who are all of us, who enact and perform and make "real" these discourses?

What the judgments and lower court histories of the case that I am using in this account demonstrate, is a systematic distancing of texts from the realities they seek to deal with. This distancing happens in language but at the same time it constructs, supports, and maintains the institutions that are the Law and its agents, those who are trained, and have the right to speak its genres and its discourses in its different spaces. It is the constant transformation of everyday lived and spoken realities into more and more lexically dense, written, metaphorical and institutionalised realities, and the implacable failure to remember that it is all a construction from someone's perspective, that I have tried to talk about. It is also the textual practice of writing intertextually, from other texts, the practice Foucault called commentary, and the author function, and the will to truth, that needs addressing here. At the same time I want to argue for the need to train legal practitioners to think about their own production as legal subjects and literate bodies, as the intertexts and at the textual and discursive intersections of this system.

Re-writing law as postmodern fiction – a play of difference, metaphor, absence of logic and meaning – may capture something of the sense of helplessness one has when caught up in the intractable, obscure and mystifying practices of the current legal system – where the rules keep changing as in *Alice in Wonderland* (perhaps the first postmodern fiction) – and facts and justice turn out to be endless re-interpretations – often from very sexed and patriarchal positions – of endless earlier interpretations. But to do that alone is not enough. The coherence of the legal body can be called into question, not by merely calling it nonsense, or rewriting it as "decentredness, loss of mastery", – which it patently obviously is not or is not only – but by scrutinising its textual practices and its relations to other social bodies, both institutional and individual – using all the resources that critical theory, literary theory, discourse analysis, rhetoric and feminism and sociology can offer.

Legal fictions are *not* the same as literary fictions. They have real and devastating and immediate social and personal effects, which must be explored in their specificity and difference as well as in their complex intersections with the literary and other institutions. The patriarchal problem which structures all of them has to be addressed in explicit and theorised ways and the pedagogy and practice of the law has to be restructured by that explicit agenda: only then is there any possibility of real and lasting change.

BIBLIOGRAPHY

Bakhtin, M, 1968, *Rabelais and his World,* MIT Press.

Barthes, R, 1983, *Mythologies*, Granada.

Bourdieu, P, 1991, *Language and Symbolic Power*, Polity Press.

Derrida, J, 1980, "La Loi du Genre/The Law of Genre", *Glyph*, The Johns Hopkins Press, pp 176-232.

Derrida, J, 1988, *Limited Inc,* Northwestern University Press.

Foucault, M, 1971, "L'Ordre du Discours/The Discourse on Language", *Social Science Information*, April 1971, pp 7-30.

Gatens, Moira, 1991, "Corporeal Representation in/and the Body Politic", Diprose, R and Ferrell, R (eds), *Cartographies: Poststructuralism and the mapping of Bodies and Spaces,* Allen & Unwin.

Goodrich, P, 1986, *Reading the Law: a critical introduction to legal method and techniques*, Basil Blackwell.

Havemann, Paul, 1989, "Crisis justice for youth: making the Young Offender's Act and the Discourse of penalty", Maclean, B and Currie, D (eds), *The Administration of Justice*, Garmond.

Holland, Patricia, 1992, *What is a Child? Popular Images of Childhood,* Virago Press.

La Fontaine, Jean, 1990, *Child Sexual Abuse*, Polity Press.

Luke, Carmen, 1991, "On Reading the Child: A Feminist Poststructuralist Perspective", *Australian Journal of Reading, Australian Language and Literacy Research: An Overview.*

Owens, C, 1985, "The Discourse of Others: Feminists and Postmodernism", Foster, Hal (ed), *The Anti-Aesthetic,* Bay Press, p 67ff.

Pateman, Carole, 1988, *The Sexual Contract,* Blackwell.

Smith, Dorothy, 1990, *Texts, Facts and Femininity: exploring the relations of ruling*, Routledge.

Spivak, Gayatri Chakravorty, 1989, "Feminism and Deconstruction, again: Negotiating an Unacknowledged Masculinism", Brennan, Teresa (ed), *Between Feminism and Psychoanalysis,* Routledge, p 214ff.

Stone, J, AO, OBE, 1985, *Precedent and Law: Dynamics of Common Law Growth,* Butterworth.

Williamson, David, 1993, *Brilliant Lies,* Currency.

Yeatman, Anna, 1987, "The Politics of Child Abuse", paper presented to the conference "The Social Context of Child Abuse", sponsored by the SA Office of The Government Management Board and Department of Premier and Cabinet, 1 December 1987.

30

The Logic of Metonymy: Reading Catherine MacKinnon

ROSANNE KENNEDY

Anyone familiar with the literature of feminist legal theory cannot help but be struck, not only by the frequent references to Catherine MacKinnon, but by the way feminists continue to return to her work. These returns urge us to investigate the role of both the author and the reader in ordering the field of feminist discourse and, ultimately, in maintaining or disturbing that order. How does the name "MacKinnon" function within feminist (legal) theory? How should we read her texts? Do we, as feminists, have an obligation to be faithful to an author's apparent intention, when the author is a "sister"? If so, does that mean that feminists have a general obligation to respect an author's intention, or should they, in the interests of strategy, take one approach to feminist texts and another to non-feminist texts? Does feminism have, or should it attempt to develop, a theory of how texts produce meaning, and of the various levels on which a text can be read? What does it mean to read "like a feminist"?

Within law, feminists are acutely attentive to and critical of the interpretive practices of non-feminist judges and legal theorists, but we seldom reflect on the unstated protocols that moderate our readings of feminist theory, and that govern something as apparently individual as one's choice of style. Consequently, what we actually *do* when we read, how we make sense of a text, and the implications of our interpretive practices for the development of feminist (legal) theory have not been widely discussed, nor even seen as constituting an issue. To the extent that reading is not just a matter of passively consuming, paraphrasing, and reiterating the words on the page, but requires analysis of the implicit logic of a text, of its rhetoric, its contradictions, its blindspots, we are often not producing readings at all. Rather, we are providing summaries, commentaries and critiques. While these activities are important, the failure to analyse how a text produces meaning is, in my view, currently limiting the development of feminist legal theory.

Here, using MacKinnon as a case study, I will lay the groundwork for an alternative approach to reading. If I choose MacKinnon's texts as an example, it is because of their theoretical wealth and interest: the titles themselves ("An Agenda for Theory" and "Towards Feminist Jurisprudence") call attention to her attempt to ground, and simultaneously, to found feminism as theory. Yet she vociferously denounces theory. In the preface to her most recent book, she writes, "This book does not aspire to locate itself within academic literature or trends or discourse. It aspires to create, on its own terms, a feminist theory of the state" (1989 p xv). I also choose MacKinnon's texts because certain stylistic features make them particularly ripe for analysis. Perhaps most significantly, however, I choose them because of the place occupied in them by a theory of interpretation. They obliquely address the very question that I will be considering here: the question of who has the authority to speak for women and for feminism.

The bulk of my chapter will be devoted to elaborating a reading of an early but still influential text, MacKinnon's "Feminism, Marxism, Method and the State: An Agenda for Theory", published in the feminist journal *Signs* in 1982. I will also draw from another essay of the same period, "Feminism, Marxism, Method and the State: Toward Feminist Jurisprudence". In MacKinnon's oeuvre, these articles mark a shift in both scope and style. Her previous book, *Sexual Harassment of Working Women,* successfully argued that sexual harassment should be a legally actionable form of sex discrimination. While ambitious, this work was theoretically modest, and written in an "objective" style. Interestingly, as MacKinnon has entered more controversial arenas such as pornography, her rhetorical strategies have become more pronounced. Occasionally, I will refer to her later books, *Feminism Unmodified* and *Toward a Feminist Theory of the State,* to see if and how MacKinnon has changed her position, but for the most part it is fair to say that these books only marginally expand upon arguments she initially formulated in the *Signs* articles. My reading will aim to elucidate those rhetorical features of the text that are routinely praised or denounced, but are rarely analysed. By rhetorical I refer both to the traditional notion of speech intended to persuade a specific audience, which has always included the study of literary figures such as metaphor, metonymy, irony and paradox, and the newer deconstructive claim, associated with Jacques Derrida and Paul de Man, that rhetorical tropes and figures are constitutive of all language, not just literary language.

Michel Foucault's "What is an Author?" (1970) provides a provocative starting point for our inquiry into the nature of feminist returns to "MacKinnon". In opposition to those post-structuralists who proclaim the death of the author, Foucault argues that we need to understand how an author's name, which differs from other proper names, functions in discourse. Of particular interest here is the distinction Foucault draws between discursive practices such as psychoanalysis and Marxism, which he claims develop precisely through "returns" to the texts of a founding author, and sciences such as physics and chemistry, in which such returns play no significant role.

Foucault's discussion of the return to the origin implies a text-based theory of reading, and it is this theory that is pertinent to our inquiry. In his words, the return "is always a return to a text in itself" (p 137). But Foucault advises more than a positive reading of the words on the page, which is an indispensable condition for any interpretation. He advocates "particular attention to those things registered in the interstices of the text, its gaps and absences . . . those empty spaces that have been masked by omission or concealed in a false and misleading plentitude" (p 137). According to Foucault, this attention to gaps and absences is both motivated and required by the essential character of the text which initiates a discourse:

> If we return, it is because of a basic and constructive omission, an omission that is not the result of accident or incomprehension. In effect, the act of initiation is such, in its essence, that it is inevitably subjected to its own distortions; that which displays this act and derives from it is, at the same time, the root of its divergences and travesties (p 137).

One of the striking things about Foucault's notion of "the return" is its focus on the negative rather than the positive, on the absent rather than the present. This "negative" view implies that the "words on the page" only tell part of the story: they operate as an invitation to investigate the implicit logic and rhetorical strategies through which meaning is produced. It also implies that the author is not in control of his or her discourse at the time of writing, and cannot later control it, and that the author's intention should not be mis-taken for the ultimate horizon of the text's meaning. Although Foucault is not explicitly concerned with hermeneutical issues, any "return to the origin" implicitly, if not explicitly, involves a struggle for the power to determine what a text means. In the words of one critic, "interpretation is always a politically interested act of persuasion" (Mailloux 1990 p 127). The stakes of interpretation can be high, especially where a single interpretation of a foundational text dominates, and consequently shapes the development of a discursive field.

We have pursued Foucault's discussion of the "return to the origin" both because it will aid us in classifying feminist readings of MacKinnon, and because it suggests how we might begin to read her differently. As we have seen, for Foucault, a return involves attention to the gaps and absences of a text. By contrast, the majority of feminists read meaning at the level of manifest content or, in Foucault's terms, in the printed words in the text, rather than in the relations between the words. MacKinnon's critics often neutralise contradictions within her texts, by taking her use of paradox as evidence of her appreciation of women's paradoxical situation under patriarchy. This pious fidelity to the author's word grounds feminism as an epistemology: in the process of reading, critics attempt to distil some concept or theoretical principle that then, to quote MacKinnon against herself, "becomes the truth to be described".

Let me illustrate this point with an example. Rather than explain what MacKinnon might have meant by the concept of consciousness raising, how it fits into her theoretical system, and whether it continues to prevail today, feminist legal theorists often simply repeat MacKinnon's assertion that "consciousness raising is feminist method", a claim that now seems to have assumed the status of unassailable truth. For instance, Christine Littleton (1989 p 753) observes that:

> feminist method starts with the very radical act of taking women seriously, believing that what we say about ourselves and our experience is important and valid, even when . . . it has little or no relationship to what has been or is being said about us.

Littleton follows MacKinnon here, but does not question the limits or dynamics of believing what we say about ourselves.

Recently many feminists have criticised MacKinnon on the grounds that her claims about women are essentialist. However, none of her critics appears to consider that the concept of consciousness-raising is itself problematic, or might be linked to her alleged essentialism. In a typical example, Pat Cain (1990 p 196) writes:

> MacKinnon may be the feminist legal scholar who has most consistently focused on the importance of feminist method. Feminist method . . . means women listening to other women. Women, as they listen to each other, tend to discover a commonality of experience. Uncovering the fact of women's common experiences creates new knowledge.

Cain argues that, despite the widespread theoretical commitment to consciousness-raising, feminists in law do not, in fact, practise it, because if they did they would include lesbian experience in their theories. Cain appeals to the principle of consciousness-raising to insist that feminists should include lesbian experience, but, like Littleton, she does not question its limits. In a similar vein, Angela Harris argues that MacKinnon, in marginalising the experience of black women, fails to practise feminist method. Harris (1990 p 601) writes, "feminist essentialism represents not just an insult to black women, but a broken promise – the promise to listen to women's stories, the promise of feminist method". Harris implies that if MacKinnon would only listen to black women, consciousness-raising would work. And Robin West (1987) contends that MacKinnon's failure to practise feminist method leads her to the mistaken assumption that women want power and equality rather than happiness. West (p 87) argues that to find out what women really want, MacKinnon should be listening to women, rather than patterning feminism on male theory.

The continuing commitment to consciousness-raising is odd not only because it has not been practised on a large scale since the early seventies, or because its limits have been repeatedly exposed, but because the whole thrust of MacKinnon's theory is to come up with a single interpretation of women's experience. Now clearly, a single theory cannot claim both to be the final interpretation of women's experience and to value women's own interpretations of their experience. Something, somewhere, has to give. To some extent the contradiction I have been tracing – between the open-ended and necessarily revisable approach of listening to women, and the hermeneutic closure that MacKinnon promotes – is now out in the open. But, and here's the twist, the critics do not take this contradiction as being exposed, nor take themselves as exposing it. Rather, the tendency to read MacKinnon as a guide to practice has led many feminists to accept consciousness-raising as a method, while criticising the way MacKinnon practises it. In what follows, I will show that a textual analysis of MacKinnon's rhetoric will reveal that essentialism characterises not only her use of "women" but also the method of consciousness-raising, and that her essentialism is linked to a general rhetorical pattern that I call the logic of metonymy.

"Feminism, Marxism, Method and the State: An Agenda for Theory" begins by constructing an elaborate analogy between feminism and Marxism, which has since been the object of considerable dispute. We have been told, by an irate Marxist, that MacKinnon's "extremely narrow formulation of Marxism focuses on work alone" (Miller 1984 p 168). We have been told, by feminists, that, "MacKinnon claims to have made a contribution to a new feminist theory that transcends the difficulties of putting together Marxism and feminism, but the Marxist side of the equation is absent" (Acker and Barry 1984 p 178). Perhaps the analogy *would* work if only MacKinnon had got her Marxism right? These critiques, valid though they may be, typically limit themselves to documenting an isolated misrepresentation, but they stop before asking the questions crucial to a rhetorical analysis: what privilege authorises the analogy? What special bond yokes together Marxism and feminism, side by side? If MacKinnon's aim is ultimately to reject Marxism as an inadequate partner for feminism, why this intercourse first? Why not simply a critique, rather that a critique begotten of an analogy? Let us examine this analogy, attending not only to the words, but to the relations between the words. MacKinnon (1982 pp 1-2) writes:

> Sexuality is to feminism what work is to Marxism: that which is most one's own, yet most taken away. Marxist theory argues that society is fundamentally constructed of the relations people form as they do and make things needed to survive humanly. Work is the social process of shaping and transforming the material and social worlds, creating

> people as social beings as they create value. It is that activity by which people become who they are. Class is its structure, production its consequence, capital its congealed form, and control its issue.
>
> Implicit in feminist theory is a parallel argument: the molding, direction, and expression of sexuality organizes society into two sexes – women and men – which division underlies the totality of social relations. Sexuality is that social process which creates, organizes, expresses, and directs desire, creating the social beings we know as women and men, as their relations create society. As work is to Marxism, sexuality to feminism is socially constructed yet constructing, universal as activity yet historically specific, jointly comprised of matter and mind. As the organized expropriation of the work of some for the benefit of others defines a class – workers – the organized expropriation of the sexuality of some for the use of others defines the sex, woman. Heterosexuality is its structure, gender and family its congealed forms, sex roles its qualities generalized to social persona, reproduction a consequence, and control its issue.

Equation, equivalence, value. Inflation, deflation, castration. Dominance and submission. These are the themes we will discuss, the special privileges of what is ultimately a sexual analogy. The analogy posits an equivalence between Marxism and feminism. But if the analogy is not simply a fraud, there must be some common standard or shared concept that permits Marxism and feminism to be equated. The text does not disappoint us. "Sexuality" and "work", it tells us, are both "social processes", "Work is the social process of shaping and transforming the material and social worlds, creating people as social beings as they create value. It is that activity by which people become who they are" (1982 p 1). Likewise, "Sexuality is that social process which creates, organizes, expresses, and directs desire, creating the social beings we know as women and men, as their relations create society" (1982 p 1). Apparently, then, the category of "social process" organises the analogy, and, as we shall see, is the common standard by which the theoretical values of Marxism and feminism will be established and measured.

But what exactly is a "social process" and are "sexuality" and "work" social processes of the same kind? Apparently, the essence of a social process lies in its power to "create" social beings. As theoretical concepts, then, "work" and "sexuality" are apparently to be compared on the basis of two criteria: their creative power and their fundamental role in social life. However, "sexuality" and "work" have something else in common: they are both "that which is most one's own, yet most taken away" (1982 p 1). Here, work and sex are described not as social processes, but as personal property, wrongfully caught up in a circuit of exchange, violence, and force. One's most intimate property is taken away by force. But taken by whom? Process or property? There is, apparently, a certain anonymity in this force that takes. Is there also a certain force in this analogy?

Despite the prominence of the analogy, MacKinnon only addresses its status and validity obliquely, and then only in the margins of the text. In a footnote, she tells us that, "'Desire' is selected as a term parallel to 'value' in Marxist theory to refer to that substance felt to be primordial or aboriginal but posited by the theory as social and contingent" (1982 p 2). In a later text, we learn that the analogy is somewhat forced. MacKinnon tells us the "desire" and "value" are not the same kind of processes. Rather, they simply occupy "an analogous theoretical location of being the quality that is taken for a natural essence . . . but is actually created by . . . the hierarchical relations in question" (1988 p 107). For our purposes, this meta-theoretical statement is important because it reveals the logic that organises the analogy. A parallel is constructed not on the basis of any substantive similarity between the concepts "desire" and "value", but on the basis of an alleged positional similarity. However, it is important to point out that "desire" and "value" can only be represented as occupying an "analogous location" because MacKinnon has already, implicitly, accepted Marxism as the model for feminist theory. It is not really surprising that MacKinnon strives to establish feminism's theoretical credentials by drawing an analogy with Marxism. Even if it had ignored "the woman question", it did offer a model, a method, a barrage of theoretical concepts, and the claim to understand social life as a totality – all features that would appeal, not to her sense of the interrelationship between women's oppression and capitalism, but to her ambitions for feminist theory. Paradoxically, then, MacKinnon's analogy privileges Marxism, yet she objects to Marxist-feminism precisely because Marxism always retains the privileged position. Her unintended affirmation of Marxism casts some doubt upon her triumphant claim that feminism is Marxism's "final conclusion and ultimate critique" (1982 p 30).

But let us return from our musings on the legitimacy of the analogy to the text *proper,* and to the question of the implied equivalence between feminism and Marxism. MacKinnon (1982 pp 1-2) tells us:

> Work is the social process of shaping and transforming the material and social worlds. . . It is that activity by which people become who they are. Class is its structure, production its consequence, capital its congealed form, and control its issue. Implicit in feminism is a parallel argument.

The word "implicit" here carries a heavy burden. The value of "work" as a "fundamental social process" is taken for granted, while the value of "sexuality" remains to be established. Marxism's value as theory has been proved, feminism's value is only implied. We might ask, then, does this word "implicit" bear a trace of anxiety about the value of a "sexuality" conceived but not yet born as a theoretical concept, about the appropriateness of an analogy based on an inequality? If this is the case, then we should not be surprised to discover that the text will work to relieve this anxiety, by attempting to prove, over and over, that feminism is a potent rival to Marxism, not a helpmeet or subordinate.

Even before she attempts to establish the validity of sexuality as a theoretical concept, however, MacKinnon raises a series of "what if" questions concerning the coexistence of Marxism and feminism. She asks:

> What if the claims of each theory are taken equally seriously, each on its own terms? Can two social processes [work and sexuality] be basic at once? Can two groups be subordinated in conflicting ways, or do they merely crosscut? Can two theories, each of which purports to account for the same thing – power as such – be reconciled? (1982 p 3).

Although these questions imply an openness to co-existence, a few lines later MacKinnon not only answers them negatively, but she presents the impossibility of co-existence as an ontological fact. Marxism and feminism, she tells us:

> do not mean to exist side by side to insure that two separate spheres of social life are not overlooked. . . They exist to argue, respectively, that the relations in which many work and few gain, in which some fuck and others get fucked, are the prime moment of politics (1982 p 3).

Now, it is worth noting that Marxism and feminism can only be described as attempting to account for "the same thing" – "power as such" – if each is emptied of its specific content, and re-presented as a critique of the social whole, that is, if each took itself as theoretically capable of explaining all structures of oppression, be it on the basis of class, race, or gender. On this reading, what Marxism and feminism share is a will to power: according to MacKinnon, each takes itself as aiming to be *the* master social theory. Clearly, though, this description is neither inevitable nor neutral. Rather, it polemically announces MacKinnon's agenda for feminist theory, which is not to establish feminism as a mere rival to Marxism, but to replace Marxism with a totalising feminism. In other words, her claim that these theories exist to explain the same thing is precisely what sets up and justifies the displacement of Marxism.

Although MacKinnon's claim that each theory exists to account for "the same thing" suggests that one theory must take precedence over the other, at other times she implies that the theories could co-exist, if only each would confront the other "on its own ground: at the level of method" (1982 p 13). There is, then, an ambiguity here: is MacKinnon rejecting the traditional Marxist ideal of a critique of the totality, or is she advocating feminism as a better candidate for the privileged position of master theory? Which is it? Can they co-exist? Or would sexual violence, a will to mastery, a desire for recognition, inevitably get in the way? We should not be surprised that this apparently innocent comparison of Marxism and feminism involves a dynamic of mastery, because it is ultimately a sexual analogy. But to show why, we must first examine the logic of heterosexuality according to MacKinnon.

MacKinnon first mentions heterosexuality in the opening paragraph of the essay, where she claims that heterosexuality is the structure of sexuality, and by implication, of women's oppression. Her next mention of heterosexuality occurs midway through the first *Signs* essay, where she tells us that, "Women and men are divided by gender, *made* into the sexes as we know them, by the social requirements of heterosexuality, which institutionalizes male sexual dominance and female sexual submission" (1982 p 19). MacKinnon explicitly rejects the common notion of heterosexuality as a natural attraction between members of the opposite sex, to emphasise instead how heterosexuality operates as a social institution, or in her view, as a gendered structure of dominance and submission. Although many feminists, including Monique Wittig, Adrienne Rich and Judith Butler, have revealed the social and political nature of heterosexuality, MacKinnon's use of the phrase "social requirements" is perplexing. One might intelligibly speak of the biological requirements of heterosexuality, as Shulamith Firestone did, meaning that heterosexual intercourse is necessary to reproduce the species. But we must ask why the institution of heterosexuality is socially required, and why, specifically, it requires male dominance and female submission, unless heterosexuality simply is a structure of dominance and submission.

That MacKinnon sees heterosexuality exclusively in terms of dominance and submission is clarified in a long footnote in the *Signs* essay on feminist jurisprudence (1983 p 651). She writes:

> Perhaps most interchange between genders, but especially violent ones, make sense in sexual terms. However, the larger issue for the relation between sexuality and gender, hence sexuality and violence generally, including both war and violence against women, is: What *is* heterosexuality? If it is the erotization of dominance and submission, altering the participants' gender is comparatively incidental. If it is males over females, gender matters independently.

The "perhaps" and two "ifs" suggest speculation; however, by the following sentence this speculation becomes a theoretical principle. She continues, "I see heterosexuality as the fusion of the two, but with gender a social outcome (such that the acted upon is feminized, is the 'girl' regardless of sex, the actor correspondingly masculinized)" (p 651). This hypothesis leads her to conclude that:

> sexuality is violent, so violence is sexual, violence against women doubly so. If this is so, wives are beaten, as well as raped, *as women* – as the acted upon, as gender, meaning sexual, objects. It further follows that all acts by anyone which treat a woman according to her object label 'woman' are sexual acts. The extent to which sexual acts are acts of objectification remains a question of our account of our freedom to make our own meanings (p 651).

By the end of the paragraph, the text has lucidly displayed what we will come to recognise as its typical logic: it slides from a speculation on the relationship betwen gender and sexuality to a totalising assertion about the sexual nature of violence.

Let us look a little more closely at MacKinnon's logic here. The equation between sexuality and violence works as follows: both sexuality and violence are structures of dominance and submission, hence they are "the same" and therefore interchangeable. We have seen this "logic of the same" before, to be precise, in MacKinnon's discussion of feminism and Marxism. The "doubly" indicates, however, that along with sexuality and violence, there is an invisible third term in play, which is gender. Violence against women is doubly sexual because all victims of violence are feminised and women are doubly feminised, once as victims of violence and once as women. Or, to put it another way, women are doubly oppressed by violence: once as victims of violence, and once as women. This logic leads to the curious conclusion that violence against women is more violent or more sexual – it does not matter which since they are the same – than violence against men.

In the paragraph I have been discussing, MacKinnon's theoretical pretensions mask the rhetorical mechanism of her argument, which proceeds and persuades through repeated use of the rhetorical figure of metonymy. Metonymy is a figure of speech which operates through a mechanism of substitution: "thirty sails" is substituted for "thirty ships" or "the crown" stands in for "the queen". Thus a common (although not strictly correct) definition of metonymy is the substitution of a part for a whole. In the equation between sexuality and violence, MacKinnon uses dominance and submission as proxies or stand-ins for male and female. In other words, violence is gendered because it involves a relationship of dominance and submission and, in MacKinnon's view, the person in the dominant position is masculinised and thus socially male, while the person in the submissive position is feminised and thus socially female. Although metonymy may sound like an obscure literary device, understanding MacKinnon's not necessarily conscious use of it is important, for it underlies every crucial turn in her argument.

Although MacKinnon is careful to use the terms "socially male" and "socially female", she constantly takes the biological as a stand-in for the social, especially where masculinity is concerned. In fact, in a curious inversion of the usual radical feminist line, men are more constrained by their biology than women. At one point she claims that, "the defining theme of [the social] whole is the male pursuit of control over women's sexuality – men not as individuals nor as biological beings, but as a gender group characterized by maleness as socially constructed, of which this pursuit is definitive" (1982 p 18). Despite her disclaimer that masculinity is socially constructed, her description of maleness *is* the biological stereotype of the sexually aggressive male. Surely masculinity is a little more complicated than that.

MacKinnon's claim that violence is essentially gendered, so that perpetrators are masculinised and victims are feminised, has some curious consequences: it foregrounds male violence against women, thereby making invisible violence by men against men or children, violence by women against men, and violence by women against women. The twist ending of the film *Presumed Innocent* plays on the invisibility of violence by women against women: at the last moment it is revealed that the woman who was murdered early in the film was killed not by her rejected lover, but by his jealous wife. Another peculiar consequence is this: if, as MacKinnon claims, war is an example of sexual violence, then it follows that historically men, and not women, have been the primary victims, or at least equal victims, of sexual violence. I do not want to argue against the feminist claim that male violence against women is an extremely serious problem. However, I think it is crucial for feminists to clarify the problem: is it that masculinity, as socially constructed, produces male violence, including both war and violence against women, in which case violence against women is a subset of a much broader problem, or is it that women are victims, although not exclusively so, of male violence? For MacKinnon, it appears that the primary problem is not that our society is pervasively violent, but that women are victims of male violence, although they supposedly do not perpetrate violence against men. Numerous other feminists, including myself, take the problem to be the social construction of masculinity, femininity and sexuality. Obviously, how feminists analyse the problem determines their responses to it and their political agendas. MacKinnon's analysis has led to practices such as the antipornography campaign, which in the United States at least, has resulted in a regrettable alliance between some feminists and right-wing fundamentalists, and not surprisingly, has provoked division among feminists. Moreover, because MacKinnon sees women only as victims, she cannot recognise that prostitutes are workers.

Given her enthusiasm for analogy, we should not be surprised to discover that MacKinnon carries the logic of heterosexuality over into the analogy between Marxism and feminism. For, as I have pointed out, the analogy involves mastery, and MacKinnon takes mastery as the sign of a relationship of dominance and submission, which in turn signifies gender inequality. In other words, MacKinnon treats the relationship between Marxism and feminism as if it were a heterosexual relationship. Marxism and feminism cannot co-exist because mutual recognition of the sexes is impossible under patriarchy: woman is always objectified. This explains why, if feminism is not to occupy the position of the feminine in the relationship with Marxism, then feminism must displace, and ultimately subordinate Marxism. Predictably, after reviewing the hostilities between Marxism and feminism, MacKinnon concludes that in any alliance, “however sympathetically, 'the woman question' is always reduced to some other question, instead of being seen as the question, calling for analysis on its own terms” (1982 p 13). Interestingly, in her latest book she claims that in any relationship between the two, Marxism occupies and displaces feminism, a strategy which, as I have tried to show here, precisely characterises her own approach to Marxism.

But let us return to our immediate problem: how can feminism achieve mastery over Marxism when it is, theoretically speaking, in the subordinate position? Obviously, feminism must prove that it is theoretically potent. If the text began by masking (in an analogy) its anxiety about feminism's value as theory, it now embraces this anxiety as its very raison d'être. MacKinnon writes:

> Feminism has not been perceived as having a method, or even a central argument, with which to contend. It has been perceived not as a systematic analysis but as a loose collection of factors, complaints, and issues which, taken together, describe rather than explain the misfortunes of the female sex (1982 p 14).

Apparently, MacKinnon is now ready to acknowledge, at least implicitly, that she is not comparing two equally mature theories. Her use of "perceived" implies that critics have misjudged feminism, that feminism is a potential rival to Marxism. All that remains is for someone to reveal feminism's theoretical power. But "perceived" also suggests that feminism is in transition: that it has now broken with its non-theoretical past. In response to the alleged inadequacies of feminism, MacKinnon claims that, "The challenge [for feminists] is to demonstrate that feminism *systematically* converges upon a central explanation of sex inequality through an approach distinctive to its subject yet applicable to the whole of social life, including class" (1982 p 14). Notice the phrase "the whole of social life", which reminds us that MacKinnon takes feminism as aiming to become a master theory – again, we see a will to power at work. Note also that, in rhetorical terms, the idea that an analysis of women's oppression could stand in for an analysis of "the whole of social life" is an instance of metonymy.

MacKinnon's language in this passage is remarkable in several respects. On the one side, we have "method", "central argument", "systematic analysis". On the other, "loose", "complaints", "describe", "misfortunes", "female sex". While MacKinnon appears to be merely describing the way critics mistakenly view feminism, her rhetoric performs the very thing it describes: a division between Marxism, a rigorous science, and feminism – the complaints and stories of loose women. Why does she accept the traditional dichotomy between scientific and humanist discourses? I think we can find one answer in a footnote, where she distinguishes between the scientific and humanist versions of Marxism. She claims that the "scientific version", associated with Louis Althusser, has been more influential than the humanist version, associated with Lukacs and Sartre, but that the humanist version has been more hospitable to feminism (1982 pp 13-14). There are some interesting points to be made about MacKinnon's relationship to Althusser, and to Althusserian feminists, which I cannot detail here. For the moment, I simply want to note that MacKinnon banishes all discussion of the differences within Marxism to the footnotes. This allows her, in the main body of her text, to present a monolithic Marxism, which is ultimately nothing more than a caricature. Because she does grudgingly acknowledge the existence of different versions of Marxism, she cannot be accused of ignorance, but by limiting her discussion to the notes, she never has to deal with any actual Marxists. Marxist-feminists are also banished to the footnotes, where they are effectively silenced. This strategy conveniently magnifies the differences between feminism and Marxism, but has some absurd consequences. Perhaps the ultimate absurdity is that she cannot admit that Juliet Mitchell, whose work she characterises as more psychoanalytic than feminist, is a "true feminist" (1982 p 10 n 17). The problem is not that her representation of Marxism "focuses on work alone", but that her version is partial while attempting to address Marxism as a whole. By maintaining the distinction between scientific and humanist discourses, MacKinnon is able to claim, in the footnotes, that humanism is more hospitable to feminism, while nonetheless attempting, in the body of the text, to establish feminism as a scientific theory – which is thus able to compete with the more influential strain of Marxism.

Another point about this passage is the way it elevates explanation, allegedly scientific and objective, over interpretation, often considered to be subjective. MacKinnon's use of the word "demonstrate" suggests that feminism has a theoretical explanation for women's oppression, but that it has not yet been brought to the surface. Like the meaning of a dream, the meaning of women's oppression remains scrambled, buried, obscured. For feminism to be taken seriously as *theory,* then, someone would have to show that it has a distinctive method and a systematic explanation of women's oppression. In the face of this monumental task, MacKinnon places herself in the role of the analyst; she sees her task as revealing the meaning of sexuality as the process by which women are oppressed. What does it mean to be an analyst? Let us see what Freud, the master analyst, has to say. In his case study, *Dora,* Freud describes his method of analysis. He writes:

> In the face of the incompleteness of my analytic results, I had no choice but to follow the example of those discoverers whose good fortune it is to bring to the light of day after their long burial the priceless though mutilated relics of antiquity. I have restored what is missing, taking the best models known to me from other analyses; but like a conscientious archaeologist I have not omitted to mention in each case where the authentic parts end and my constructions begin (1983 p 12).

Freud's data is incomplete because Dora, his independent-minded patient, rejected his analysis and broke off the treatment. No wonder Freud acknowledges the role of narrative reconstruction. To write her case history at all, he must create a fiction based on other cases.

MacKinnon practises a similar method of narrative reconstruction. She tells a story about women's oppression, but she represses the role of interpretation, preferring to see her method as "systematic explanation". Now, as Paul Ricoeur and others have argued, the traditional distinction between interpretation and explanation does not hold up because every explanation involves interpretation (Ricoeur 1981). But MacKinnon nonetheless maintains the distinction by characterising what she does as "systematic explanation", while consigning description to the dustbin of feminism's prehistory. She attempts to provide a properly *theoretical* foundation for feminism by showing that the concept of "sexuality" provides a "central explanation of women's situation". MacKinnon dismisses the various explanations of women's oppression offered by other feminists because they take nature, law, the family and sex roles as foundations, rather than as consequences of women's oppression. In her view, sexuality is the foundation, and these other things are merely effects. Thus, like many other theorists over the past two centuries, MacKinnon locates the source of women's oppression in sexuality, while striving to differentiate her notion of sexuality from others. She writes, "The centrality of sexuality emerges not from Freudian conceptions but from feminist practice on diverse issues including abortion, birth control, sterilisation abuse, domestic battery, rape, incest etc . . . Taken together, they are producing a feminist political theory centring upon sexuality" (1983 p 15). Freud, who had much to say about sexuality, must be excluded from a feminist explanation, for feminism must prove its theoretical independence. Despite MacKinnon's disclaimers, Freud nonetheless manages to penetrate feminist barriers. For MacKinnon, sexuality as a theoretical concept depends upon a process of displacement; we are, once again, in the presence of metonymy. For if we take together (and taking together is the key) all these various feminist practices, we see that they centre upon a single signified: sexuality. By mere association with the concept of sexuality, the content of practices such as rape and abuse are transformed, to now become examples of the logic of dominance and submission. For MacKinnon, displacement leads to truth: sexuality explains women's oppression. For Freud, displacement both obscures and provides access to truth; but it does not lead directly to truth. The image or word that results from a process of displacement is precisely what has to be unravelled before truth can emerge. Is it any surprise, then, that MacKinnon must rule Freud out of bounds?

I want to quickly trace some other examples of this metonymical logic, beginning with MacKinnon's claim that one is not born but "becomes" a woman, which is meant to mark a break with naturalist accounts in which gender is equated with or viewed as an effect of biological sex. MacKinnon claims that, "'one becomes a woman' – acquires and *identifies* with the status of the female . . . through the experience of sexuality" (1982 p 17). And further, that, "Gender socialisation is the process through which women come to *identify* themselves as sexual beings, as beings that exist for men. It is that process through which women internalise (make their own) a male image of their sexuality as their identity as women" (1982 pp 16-17). Although MacKinnon relies extensively on the concept of identification, she does not explain what makes a female identify herself as one whose sexuality exists for a male. Instead, she characteristically relies on a series of metonymical substitutions to explain the transition from sex to gender, "Socially, femaleness *means* femininity, which *means* sexual availability on male terms. What *defines* woman as such is what turns men on" (1982 pp 16-17 [italics added]). In MacKinnon's theory of subjectivity, gender stands in for all other discursively produced differences: women are defined as essentially gendered subjects, rather than as subjects of race and class, which is why Angela Harris calls MacKinnon a "gender essentialist" (1990 p 585). Although Harris claims that essentialism is a problem in MacKinnon's work, I would add that essentialism is itself a metonymy in which one part of an object is taken as the essence of the whole (female biology is the essence of woman) or one trait is attributed to an entire class of objects. It may be that MacKinnon's essentialism produces a whole series of metonymies, or that her essentialism is an effect of her general strategy of metonymy.

MacKinnon's most obvious and repeated use of metonymy, and the one that has produced the most controversy, occurs in her frequent discussions of pornography. In her view, pornography is constitutive of all sexual relationships under a system of male dominance: there is no uncolonised space of sexuality. She writes, "men's power over women means that the way men see women defines who women can be. Pornography is that way" (1989 p 197). In short, MacKinnon takes the sexual objectification of women in pornography as a proxy or stand-in for sexuality as a whole. In MacKinnon's words, "Escalating explicitness . . . is the aesthetic of pornography not because the materials depict objectified sex but because they create the experience of a sexuality which is itself objectified. It is not that life and art imitate each other; in sexuality, they are each other" (1989 p 199 [footnote omitted]). Here again we see the logic that characterises MacKinnon's discussion of sexuality and violence: life and pornography are the same because each constructs and reproduces dominance and submission as the meaning of sexuality. Whereas Suzanne Kappler argues, in *The Pornography of Representation,* that all representation is pornographic, MacKinnon inverts that argument, claiming that pornography is representative of all sexuality.

In opposition to MacKinnon's monolithic interpretation of sexuality, feminists have argued that women's experiences of sexuality cannot be limited to or contained in a single meaning. Although not expressed in rhetorical terms, many criticisms of MacKinnon can be rephrased as critiques of this metonymical logic.

In their critique of the antipornography position, Carole Vance and Ann Snitow (1984) observe that:

> The antipornography analysis, even if correct, constitutes a description of but a *small segment* of sexuality, not a description of the *whole.* In fact, information about sexuality comes not from *one* source but from *many* . . . [y]et the antipornography movement has consistently presented a critique of pornography as if it were a *substitute* for an analysis of sexuality (pp 129-30 [emphasis added]).

In their view, the antipornography position mistakenly takes pornographic sexuality, which is just one representation of sexuality, as a stand in for the whole of sexuality – a rhetorical strategy that I have been referring to as metonymical. In opposition to the equation between sexuality and pornography, Vance favours a view which stresses multiplicity, claiming that, "The hallmark of sexuality is its complexity: its multiple meanings, sensations, and connections" (1984 p 5).

To return to the issue of consciousness-raising, what happens when metonymical logic encounters feminist method? Although MacKinnon implies that the extent to which we are free to make our own meanings remains open to debate, all her comments on consciousness-raising suggest that she has already determined the true source of women's oppression, the true meaning of women's sexual experience. Her claim that "Feminism turns theory itself – the pursuit of a true analysis of social life – into the pursuit of consciousness . . ." (1989 p 84) indicates that the goal of theory is to develop a true, and by implication, a single analysis of women's experience. In a theoretical climate that celebrates heterogeneity and difference, advancing a single interpretation of anything, let alone women's experience, is a contentious business. MacKinnon may not intend to represss heterogeneous meanings or ignore what women say about their experience, but within the terms of her theory, a monolithic explanation is a theoretical necessity, at least if feminism is going to compete with Marxism. Thus, it is fair to say that, within the context of MacKinnon's theoretical framework, consciousness-raising leads to hermeneutic closure, and ultimately works to shut women up rather than to validate their speech. MacKinnon's repeated use of mentonymy helps to explain why she is willing to let one aspect of women's experience stand in for the whole, or for that matter, to let one definition of feminism stand in for the whole of feminism.

So far, I have not made any distinctions in MacKinnon's use of metonymy. Rather, I have implicitly suggested that all her metonymies follow the same logical structure and that they are all bad for feminism. However, it is important to emphasise that the political resonances of her metonymies vary, depending upon the context or register in which they are employed. It is one thing to say that all sexuality is structured in dominance and submission, and another to use the category of women. Feminism itself, as a political movement that represents women is, like all representational politics, based in a logic of substitution or metonymy: one person or group stands for and speaks on behalf of the whole. It is up to us to determine, as feminists, which metonymies are valid or acceptable, and which lead to unfortunate political practices. This, of course, is both a political and a practical decision and will ultimately shape the agenda, or more precisely, the agendas for feminist theory.

Let me end by returning to a question that I raised in my introduction: what function does MacKinnon's name perform in the discourse of feminist legal theory? Is feminist (legal) theory a discipline or a discourse? To the extent that feminist legal theory adheres to MacKinnon's theoretical agenda, discipline remains the appropriate term, for, as we have seen, developing a "systematic explanation" of women's oppression ultimately involves discipline. Despite her own best efforts, however, MacKinnon's view of feminism is neither neutral nor widely shared: even in the pre-postmodern days when grand theory was considered a legitimate project, few feminists viewed feminism as either aiming to be or capable of becoming a total theory of power. At stake in MacKinnon's displacement of Marxism was ultimately the displacement of Marxist-feminism, which in the late 1970s and early 1980s posed a considerable threat to radical feminism. To be fair to MacKinnon, in the most recent version of this article, she seems to have relinquished her grand designs for feminism, now attributing exclusively to Marxism a desire for total critique. She writes:

> The aspiration to encompass all inequality within a critique of the "totality" of social life has been a central feature of Marxist theory from the beginning. . . Feminism, by contrast, has not typically regarded the existence of class, or any other social division or theory, as needing to be either subsumed or dismissed, or as a challenge to the theoretical viability or practical primacy of focus upon relations between the sexes (1989 p 60).

Although she appears to have changed her position in the seven years between the publication of her first *Signs* essay and her most recent commentary on the relationship between Marxism and feminism (1989), the earlier essays did attribute to feminism a desire for mastery. In MacKinnon's first *Signs* essay, a feminist hermeneutic is vested with disciplinary powers, specifically the power to discipline unruly feminists. For MacKinnon's aim is not to present radical feminism as just one analysis of women's oppression, but to claim radical feminism as "true feminism". In making this claim, MacKinnon inevitably set herself up both to judge other feminisms, and to police the borders of feminist discourse.

BIBLIOGRAPHY

Acker, Joan and Barry, Kate, 1984, "Comments on MacKinnon's 'Feminism, Marxism, Method, and the State'", no 1, *Signs* 10, p 176.

Cain, Patricia, 1990, "Feminist Jurisprudence: Grounding the Theories", 6, *Berkley Women's Law Journal,* p 191.

Foucault, Michel, 1970, "What Is An Author?", Bouchard, Donald (ed) and Simon, Sherry (trans), *Language, Counter-Memory, Practice,* Cornell University Press.

Freud, Sigmund, 1983, *Dora: Fragment of an Analysis of a Case of Hysteria,* Macmillan.

Harris, Angela, 1990, "Race and Essentialism in Feminist Legal Theory", 42, *Stanford Law Review,* p 581.

Littleton, Christine, 1989, "Feminist Jurisprudence: The Difference Method Makes", 41, *Stanford Law Review,* p 751.

MacKinnon, Catherine, 1979, *Sexual Harrassment of Working Women: A Case of Sex Discrimination,* Yale University Press.

MacKinnon, Catherine, 1982, "Feminism, Marxism, Method, and the State: Toward Feminist Theory", no 3, *Signs* 7, p 515.

MacKinnon, Catherine, 1983, "Feminism, Marxism, Method, and the State: Toward Feminist Jurisprudence", no 4, *Signs* 8, p 635.

MacKinnon, Catherine, 1984, "Response to Comments on MacKinnon's 'Feminism, Marxism, Method, and the State'", no 1, *Signs* 10, p 184.

MacKinnon, Catherine, 1987, *Feminism Unmodified: Discourses on Life and Law,* Harvard University Press.

MacKinnon, Catherine, 1988, "Desire and Power: A Feminist Perspective", Nelson, Cary and Grossberg, Lawrence (eds), *Marxism and the Interpretation of Cultures,* University of Illinois Press p 105.

MacKinnon, Catherine, 1989, *Toward a Feminist Theory of the State,* Harvard University Press.

Miller, John A, 1984, "Comments on MacKinnon's 'Feminism, Marxism, Method, and the State'", no 1, *Signs* 10, p 168.

Mailloux, Steven, 1990, "Interpretation", Lentricchia, Franck and McLaughlin, Thomas (eds), *Critical Terms for Literary Study,* University of Chicago Press.

Ricoeur, Paul, 1981, "What is a Text? Explanation and Understanding", Thompson, John B (ed and trans), *Hermeneutics and the Human Sciences,* Cambridge University Press.

Vance, Carole S (ed), 1984, *Pleasure and Danger: Exploring Female Sexuality,* Routledge.

Vance, Carole S and Snitow, Ann Barr, 1984 "Toward a Conversation about Sex in Feminism: A Modest Proposal", no 1, *Signs* 10, p 126.

West, Robin, 1987, "The Difference in Women's Hedonic Lives: A Phenomenological Critique of Feminist Legal Theory", 2, *Wisconsin Women's Law Journal* 81.

31

Discourse Analysis and the Nuclear Non-Proliferation "Regime"[1]

JOHANNA SUTHERLAND

During the Gulf War in 1991 much of the world witnessed the horrific and bizarre televised spectacle of the massive bombing of Iraq. The United States had required some of the bombs to destroy Iraq's suspected clandestine nuclear facilities (Albright and Hibbs 1991). But before that bombing there was not much public debate about the need to better enforce the 1968 Treaty on the Non-Proliferation of Nuclear Weapons (NPT), and the international safeguards system administered by the International Atomic Energy Agency (IAEA), in Iraq, an NPT party.

Concerns about the nuclear non-proliferation "regime" (NNPR) are at flashpoint again because of tensions in the Korean Peninsula; North Korea's 1993 threat to withdraw from the NNPR, and its equivocating over special IAEA inspections of its suspect nuclear facilities. Because the NPT Review and Extension Conference in 1995 will decide whether the NPT shall continue in force indefinitely, for prescribed periods subject to renewal, or shall continue for only an agreed period, international attention continues to be focussed on the NPT and the strengthening of the NNPR.

Ironically, such dramatic incursions into the status and credibility of the NNPR come after increased academic interest in the operation of international "regimes" and "learning" within them (Breslauer and Tetlock 1991, Modelski 1990, Haas 1980, Nye 1987). But for post-modernists and post-structuralists who eschew foundational truths and epistemological certainties, the rapidity with which the Gulf War and developments in the Korean Peninsula have

1 This chapter includes edited extracts from my MA(IR) sub-thesis, Department of International Relations, Australian National University. I wish to gratefully acknowledge significant guidance from Richard Leaver, and comment on an earlier draft of this chapter by Jim Richardson, Eric Chauvistre and Greg Manning.

eroded the credibility of the NNPR, and have undercut the notion of "learning" may not come as a surprise.

Post-structural and post-modern approaches to both international law and politics advocate a reappraisal of the central discourses and political practices of those disciplines (for example: Koskenniemi 1992, Ashley and Walker 1990, George 1994), and a lively liberal and critical debate over "regime theory" continues within the disciplines (Krasner 1983, Strange 1983, Ashley 1984, Kratochwil 1988).

This chapter aims to support the post-structuralists in the debate by demonstrating the potential for post-structural analyses of texts about international politics to open discursive space to hitherto marginalised discourses and events, and for re-historicising represented events in liberal "realist" portrayals of international politics.

This chapter analyses a small selection of texts on nuclear non-proliferation by Professor Joseph Nye Jr, including those which analyse the NNPR using regime theory. It will not attempt to deconstruct current interpretations of the legal agreements comprising the NNPR – that is a task better left to post-structural international lawyers.

Joseph Nye joined the United States administration following the 1976 election as one of the experts drawn from a Ford-Mitre study on nuclear energy, and he served as Deputy to the Under Secretary of State for Security Assistance, Science and Technology for several years. He has been Professor of Government, and Ford Foundation Professor of International Security, at Harvard University. He is also the author and editor of a large number of highly regarded works, including *Power and Interdependence* (1977) (with Robert Keohane) and more recently, *Bound to Lead: The Changing Nature of American Power* (1990). In 1994 he was working at the National Intelligence College, Central Intelligence Agency.

The texts selected for analysis should be regarded highly by virtue of the status of their author, and their "authoritative content". Foucault suggests, in part, that the author's name is not just part of a discourse, but performs a validating and classificatory "author-function", one of its discursive properties and "ideological product". "The author's name manifests the appearance of a certain discursive set and indicates the status of this discourse within a society and a culture" (Foucault, 1988). The educational and professional qualifications of speakers confer rights of entry to exclusive or privileged communication mediums such as journals, monographs and public addresses, and since these mediums tend to be limited to specialised "experts", discourses, or "knowledge practices" are generated through that interaction (Turkel pp 177-8). The power of networks of "knowledge-based experts" or "epistemic communities" who have control over knowledge and information, and influence over state policy-makers, is becoming increasingly recognised and theorised also within more liberal approaches (Haas 1992).

The chapter will seek to demonstrate that the selected texts include discursive constructions of the United States policy interests, however desirable those policy interests may be. Textual aspects to be examined include hierarchic ordering, enframing and marginalising, and notions of "learning".

The selected texts include representations of superpower, and particularly United States' dominance in shaping global policies – representations which have been evident generally in "realist" analyses of international relations until recently (Kubolkova and Cruickshank 1987, Hoffmann 1977, Smith 1989). Parts of the selected texts tend to reproduce a particular discursive formation: that of a constructed superpower dominance, or hegemony, regarding the formation, boundaries and elements, and maintenance of the nuclear nonproliferation "regime". One text argues:

> It has been said that the ultimate success of a national policy occurs when a country is able to elevate its interest to the level of a general principle. In that sense, American nonproliferation policy over the years has been surprisingly successful. The United States has helped to foster an international regime that establishes a general presumption against proliferation. . . While there are a few important exceptions, the large majority of states adhere to at least part of this set of norms (Nye 1981 p 16).
>
> Given the natural decline in American preponderance in the nuclear issue area, it was important that the burden of leadership in regime maintenance be more broadly shared. To a considerable extent, INFCE and the other initiatives of the late 1970s helped to accomplish this . . . [t]he United States persuaded others to share its agenda. . . Changed attitudes are reflected in many decisions such as the June 1977 German policy of no further exports of reprocessing plants, or the agreement about sanctions in the 1978 Suppliers Guidelines, or the French pressure on South Africa and restrained response to Brazilian inquiries about breeder technology. . . As important as the specifics is the general convergence that Lellouche describes elsewhere: . . . each of these landmarks in the history of non-proliferation policy has been the product of US policy (Nye 1981 p 38; see also Nye 1977b p 185).

Although particular United States' policies may be seen as highly desirable, the extent to which the United States can or has secured compliance with "its" norms and policy prescriptions may be overstated in the selected texts. Such textual priority can be reversed under deconstruction to better assess the role of the non-superpower, the less "developed", and in particular the non-aligned states. Other texts on the NNPR as a "regime" will not be assessed (such as Smith 1987, Tate 1990, Brzoska 1992).

"Regimes" within western liberal and neorealist theories of international relations have been defined as the set of implicit or explicit principles, norms, rules and decision-making procedures around which actor expectations converge in a given issue area (Krasner 1983a p 1; Nye 1987 p 374; Smith 1987 p 253), and "the set of rules, norms and procedures that regulate behaviour and control its effects in international affairs" (Nye 1981 p 16).

Susan Strange (1983) and Richard Ashley (1984, 1989), two critics of regime theory, suggest that the analysis of "hegemons" and "regimes" can be seen as the logocentric creation of a "sovereign voice"; an external point of reference; a hierarchical representation of the political values of strong leadership, discipline over disorder and certainty over uncertainty. The term "regime" connotes regularity, order, shared values and norms, and minimal dynamic or disruptive state and non-state behaviour.

Richard Ashley has described the foundational dualisms in international relations scholarship, including structure / superstructure, core/periphery, domestic/international and continuity /change as Derridaen "logocentricity" (Ashley 1989). These theoretical constructs create a role of "heroic practice" for the sovereign state; a construct which has a commitment to a modernist narrative of universalising progress. Logocentrism also renders "ordered" the messy and transient nature of the world disorder. This logocentrism is evident in the selected texts not only regarding the central role that the superpowers play in the NNPR, and in particular which the United States plays, but also in the use of the concept of "learning".

Dissent within the regime, evident for example at NPT review conferences, has been prevalent regarding the nuclear disarmament, nuclear testing and nuclear supply policies of mainly the United States and the United Kingdom, but this dissent is dealt with dismissively in the selected texts. Consensus under the "regime" is prioritised over dissensus, and reified. Through this reification, the perceived "regime" is represented as a tangible object capable of analysis by an objective, neutral observer. What may be better described as a dynamic, changing political process, or a world, "culturally, socially and institutionally determined; . . . messy, noisy, and full of disturbances, surprises, and instabilities" (Birch 1989 p 2) becomes an abstraction – a manifestation of universal tendencies under certain conditions. Critical, postmodern and poststructural analyses tend to emphasise the interruptions and disturbances to expected outcomes when assessing global affairs (Ashley 1984, 1989; Strange 1983; Derian and Shapiro 1989).

TEXTUAL ENFRAMING PRACTICES

The selected texts on the NNPR tend not to give a detailed analysis of the the various NPT review conferences, the work of the European Atomic Energy Agency (hereafter Euratom) nor the Treaty of Tlatelolco, all of which is indicative of the super-power-centricity reflected in the boundaries Nye draws to delineate the regime and its constituent elements. But Soviet-centricity is equally problematic in commentary on the NPT by scholars from within the former Soviet Union however (for example Shestov 1973; less so Borisov 1982).

For Nye, the NNPR comprises an array of domestic and international legal regulations and institutions, including various international treaties. He writes:

> For nonproliferation, the main regime norms and practices are found in the Non-Proliferation Treaty (NPT) and its regional counterparts like the Treaty of Tlatelolco; the safeguards, rules and procedures of the International Atomic Energy Agency (IAEA), as well as in various UN resolutions (Nye 1981 p 16; and see also Nye 1985 p 124, 1987 p 397).

Other NNPR instruments and processes such as the London Suppliers' Group and Zangger Committee's "trigger list" of sensitive export items requiring safeguards, the international fuel cycle evaluation committee (INFCE), and "special bilaterals" are also discussed in the selected texts. "INFCE helped the United States to set the agenda for other governments . . . INFCE focused other countries' attention on a US question – non-proliferation" (Nye 1981 p 25). Interestingly however, the texts do not review the role of the Coordinating Committee for Multilateral Export Controls (COCOM). This was a Cold War committee formed in 1949 to deny member countries of the Warsaw Pact access to western technology which could be used for military purposes. It was to be disbanded by 31 March 1994 (Wilson C 1994 p 31).

Nye describes the NPT as a "relatively simple treaty" (Nye 1981 p 18). Articles 1 and 11 aim to prevent assistance being transferred or accepted which could assist in the development of nuclear weaponry or explosives in non-nuclear-weapon states (hereafter NNWS). Under Article III and preambular paragraphs four and five NNWS are required to enter into nuclear safeguards agreements with the IAEA and to put their nuclear facilities under safeguards, while under the fourth and fifth Articles, and preambular paragraphs six and seven NNWS are promised access to technology and to the benefits of peaceful nuclear explosions. Under Article VI and preambular paragraphs eight to twelve, NWS should seriously continue negotiations toward ending the arms race, concluding a comprehensive nuclear test ban treaty (CTBT), attaining nuclear disarmament, and towards general and complete disarmament.

In Nye's texts, the laws, policies and institutions valued by the United States are selectively examined, while those which undercut United States' "normative hegemony" in the regime, such as Article VI, are marginalised and de-emphasised. This in effect prioritises United States Government concerns.

The fact that Nye does not review the operation of the European Atomic Energy Agency (Euratom) and its safeguards system also demonstrates a United States-centric approach, since Euratom and other European procedures are distinct (Greig 1978 pp 111-12; Muller 1993); have attracted relaxed procedures under a Presidential statutory waiver authority regarding US-origin nuclear material (Schwartz 1988 p 25, n 101); are of questionable effectiveness (Leaver 1988; Muller 1993) and they have prevented an IAEA safeguards monopoly (Shakar 1980 p 695). Unlike IAEA safeguards, which apply fully to NNWS and not automatically to NWS, Euratom members' nuclear materials are subject to safeguards if they are declared to be for peaceful use, but not if declared to be intended for military use (Shakar 1980 p 691). However, European Community members are reported to have given nuclear export laxities "unprecedented priority" attention by the end of 1992 (Muller 1993).

Another indication of "superpower-centricity" in the selected texts is Nye's description of the Treaty of Tlatelolco as a "regional counterpart" of the NPT which "helps to fill the normative gap" left by significant states not ratifying the NPT (Nye 1981 p 18; and see Nye 1988 p 336). This description does little justice to the insistance by Latin American states after the Cuban missile crisis, that the superpowers keep their nuclear weapons well away, and belittles that independent statement of abhorrence to nuclear weaponry. In 1962 Brazil had sought a United Nations General Assembly resolution for the creation of a Latin American nuclear weapon free zone, following the Cuban missile crisis (Redick 1994 p 3), and because of regional states' aversion to the "great power" rivalry in the region. Negotiations were complete in 1967 before the NPT was finalised. It was not a derivative of the NPT but followed other regional nonproliferation and weapons-free zone treaties such as the Antarctic Treaty 1959. The Tlatelolco control system is in some ways more stringent than that of the IAEA. Protocol 1 to the Tlatelolco Treaty prohibits the deployment of NW within the zone covered by the Treaty, for example, which exceeds the NPT obligations which tolerate stationed nuclear weapons.

MARGINALISED DATA

Most of the selected texts focus on slowing proliferation and fuel cycle questions, rather than on the NPT aim of encouraging disarmament negotiations : the NPT's "key injunctions" are to slow the spread of weapons-usable technologies and to place non-proliferation concerns before political advantage with allies or third parties (Nye 1987 p 396). The texts do not identify as a central obligation that nuclear weapon states negotiate seriously "in good faith" towards ending nuclear testing and disarmament as agreed in the NPT preambular paragraphs and in Article VI. This issue is important to the survival of the NPT beyond 1995.

In giving minimal attention to the failure of the superpowers to achieve substantial progress in disarmament negotiations over a period when the issue was far more pressing than today, most of the texts (except Nye 1985) down-play a major source of tension within the regime. Criticisms of the high levels of superpower armament under deterrence made at various NPT review conferences are marginalised with fleeting references (for example Nye 1981 p 26). That the failure of the United States and the Soviet Union to disarm may contribute to the collapse of the NNPR is acknowledged in the 1985 text, but it suggests that superpower alliance guarantees "indicates that their Article VI obligations cannot be interpreted as simple disarmament". The failure to disarm is justified by reference to "robust", "stable" and extended deterrence (Nye 1979 p 40; Nye 1985 pp 126, 128; Nye 1981 pp 34-5), with "security guarantees" being "some of the most important instruments of our nonproliferation policy" (Nye 1977b pp 183-4; 1977a p 559; 1979 p 40). High levels of nuclear weaponry held by the "superpowers" are preferable to even small arsenals in the "Third World" (Nye 1985 p 126). The assumptions of deterrence theory are strongly challenged by their critics however (for example, Mack 1989).

The selected texts tend to reflect the perceptions of the nuclear supplier states – that the security of processed uranium derived from the nuclear cycle and its non-diversion to military use is the most important priority of the NPT (Nye 1978b p 42). The Review Conferences on the NPT are traditionally regarded as a yardstick by which its strength can be assessed, and the final communiques of the conferences are important documents which record officially member states' assessments of the "regime". They have reflected differences in perceptions about the priorities in the treaty, and Nye tends to reflect the perceptions of the supplier states. At the NPT review conferences there has been general agreement that Articles 1 and 11 have been faithfully adhered to, but the lack of substantive progress in superpower disarmament and thus the failure to meet the demands of Article V1 have been condemned strongly (Shakar 1980 pp 581-2; Goldblat 1986 p 13; Albright and Carothers 1985 pp 8-10).

At the first review conference, concern was expressed by NNWS about the lack of progress in disarmament. In 1975 the superpowers were criticised strongly for their failure to disarm (Shaker pp 581-2). The 1980 second review conference again affirmed the success of the NPT in attracting membership and in preventing proliferation, but participants from the United Nations' Group of 77 (G-77) "developing" countries condemned the lack of progress in superpower disarmament. Some "developing" countries also objected to the restrictive export policies toward NPT members by some NWS, following the implementation of the restrictive London Supplier Group guidelines. The 1980 review conference failed to produce a consensus final document. The 1985 third review conference reflected a better consensus but again the failure of the NWS to progress with disarmament was condemned strongly. The conference affirmed the value of the NPT, IAEA safeguards, the need for stability in long-term supplies, and the need for mutual consent before the re-negotiation of supply agreements, but the United States and the United Kingdom were criticised for their refusal to negotiate on the proposed Comprehensive Test Ban Treaty (Goldblat p 13). The G-77, non-aligned and neutral participants condemned the NWS for their lack of arms reductions, increased arms spending and space race research. The non-application of full-scope safeguards (that is, IAEA supervision of all of a states' nuclear facilities) also caused concern. A final communique was issued however. The 1990 fourth review conference failed to reach sufficient consensus to enable a final communique to be issued, even though nearly all speakers stressed the importance of the treaty and some delegations strengthened their endorsement of it (Van Doren and Bunn). In the First Committee, a number of non-aligned states led by the Mexican delegation insisted on a firm commitment by the United States to ending nuclear testing, citing Article VI of the NPT, but this was contrary to the position of the United States and the United Kingdom, leading to an impasse (Van Doren and Bunn p 9). In other respects some post-conference salvaging of the conference agreement was pursued with the IAEA General Conference officially recognising the conference language on NPT Articles III, IV and V, and their preambular paragraphs.

A related and significant development which was not examined in the selected texts, probably because of their lack of focus on superpower disarmament (cf Nye 1985), escalated into a proposed fast-track method for the introduction of a Comprehensive Test Ban Treaty (CTBT) in 1991. The frustrations of a number of non-aligned states about the nuclear arms race and the failure of some Western states to agree to a CTBT led to majority support for a resolution at the 1991 Nuclear Test Ban Amendment Conference to propose an extension of the PTBT into a complete ban, as had been sought for many years (Epstein 1990). This polarisation of positions has abated for various reasons, including: testing moratoria by the United States, Russia and France, the decision in August 1993 of the Conference on Disarmament to begin negotiations for a Comprehensive Test Ban Treaty, and the record support for the annual resolution on the CTBT in the United Nations General Assembly (Wilson M 1994 p 2).

The testing issue is likely to be important at the 1995 conference, which is to decide whether the NPT is to continue in force indefinitely or for an additional fixed period or periods, since some members of the Non-Aligned Movement have proposed that unless a CTBT has been achieved by 1995, only a two-year extension would be agreed for the NPT (Bunn 1994 p 53).

HEGEMONIC DISCOURSES AND "LEARNING"

From a "realist" regime theory perspective, Krasner has argued that "regimes" become either "intervening variables" in the international order, assuming a life of their own, partially independent of fluctuations in the power exercised by states in the international system, or interactive variables, feeding back into states' assessments of their interests (Krasner 1983b p 358) by "increasing transaction flows, facilitating knowledge and understanding, and creating property rights" (Krasner 1983b p 362). Thus regimes are thought to constrain states' short-range self-interest and to contour long-term policies, with regime injunctions being the focal point around which actors' interests converge (Nye 1987 p 399). The internalisation of norms and the redefinition of interests is said to occur through "learning" – a factor which is being cited increasingly as a cogent explanation for regime formation and maintenance.

Nye argues that this learning can have various effects. If regime principles and norms are internalised by states or important domestic coalitions, the costs of defecting are raised. Information can also change perceptions of self-interest held by states. National bureaucracies can change procedures because of regimes; subnational actors and third parties may have new coalition opportunities; attitudes can be changed, and regular meetings may insulate the regime from other changes in the political relationship (Nye 1987 p 400). However, both Krasner and Nye suggest that regimes are likely to rupture if states with greater power capabilities seek to change the underlying principles and norms of the regime (Krasner 1983b p 357).

Nye argues that the NNPR owes much to the realisation by the United States and the Soviet Union that the sharing of nuclear technology with allies could not be controlled or kept from military use effectively, during the 1960s, without a multilateral "regime" (Nye 1987). The NNPR was made possible by the United States and the former Soviet Union "learning" to co-operate after the terror of the Cuban Missile Crisis, the development of Chinese nuclear capability and demands by West Germany and other NATO countries to have a greater say on nuclear matters (Nye 1988). With the decline in power of the United States, the maintenance of the regime has become difficult but the United States will share its burden among like-minded states (Nye 1981 p 20).

Following Haas, Nye argues that knowledge and learning about nuclear issues must be accounted for as factors in multilateral co-operation:

> international norms, [which] interact with domestic politics of the states in an international system so that they transform states' definitions of their interests. Transnational and interstate interactions and norms lead to new perceptions of interests and new coalition possibilities for different interests within states. (1987 p 372)

Nye uses knowledge and learning to explain significant decisions made by regime members, suggesting that both superpowers modified their short- and long-run self-interest because of the success of the regime (Nye 1987 p 383). Nye concedes that in the past he downplayed the domestic politics inherent in "learning" (Keohane and Nye p 739), but more recently he has better explored the complexities of domestic learning "structures" (Nye 1987 pp 378-80).

By "re-historicising" the formation of the regime, Nye's views on "learning" appear wanting in that the role of smaller states such as Ireland, which consistently sponsored non-proliferation resolutions in the United Nations General Assembly in the late 1950s and 1960s, is not emphasised, although referred to.

The theoretical conundrum about "learning" – "to what extent, and under what conditions, the impacts of regimes on state interests are significant enough to make much difference in world politics" (Keohane and Nye 1987 p 743) is not explored in the selected texts in relation to sanctions policies. The texts refer to "sanctions" only in passing (Nye 1979 p 41; Nye 1981 pp 27, 31-2; 1985 p 130), acknowledging both that difficulties arise when nonproliferation objectives have to be balanced with other aspects of United States foreign policy (Nye 1981 pp 31-2), and that United States "sticks" have tended not to be applied (Nye 1981 pp 20, 27).

Presidential waivers of legislative nuclear export requirements and sanctions in relation to Israel and Pakistan have been the most blatant examples of the susceptibility of United States governments' nonproliferation discourses to broader geo-political narratives. These fleeting references to sanctions seem to put "off limits" strong criticisms of governments' decisions to waive available sanctions (Smith and Cobban 1989; Schwartz 1988 pp 51-60) – measures which may be superior to those under the NPT and IAEA (Schwartz 1988 p 22; Bauser 1977). This indicates that "realist" geo-political narratives are still often paramount and that the events which evoke them, such as the invasion of Afghanistan, subvert predictive theorising about "learnt norms" under "regimes".

One of the instances of successful pressure to "enforce the regime" in the texts was the disclosure by the United States of certain information to France (an NNPR outsider) about Pakistan's nuclear ambitions, which led France to cancel its proposed sale to Pakistan of a plutonium reprocessing plant (Nye 1987 378-9). Babu argues, however, that both French and Pakistani domestic political considerations were also determinative in that instance, since President Giscard d'Estang had assumed office in 1976 and had overturned Chirac's policies, ordering a halt to the export of all reprocessing plants. For its part, Pakistan had sought the cancellation of the deal after France had insisted that the plant only produce a mixture of uranium and plutonium – rendering it unsuitable for military use (Babu 1992).

But suspicions of Israel's nuclear programs did not lead to strong United States condemnation of Israel nor to the suspension of foreign aid to that state, and the United States even withdrew its support for the IAEA temporarily in 1982 in support of Israel, hardly suggesting an apolitical, "learnt" commitment to the NNPR (Smith and Cobban 1989). The texts on the events of 1981-82 suggest political horsetrading rather than shared norms.

The notion of a learned normative consensus under the NNPR is problematic because the NNPR has been fraught with tension since its inception, and the foundation compromises between the NWS and the NNWS have been challenged at most review conferences, as discussed above. The notion of "learning" also glosses the different motivations for participation in the NNPR by states at different historical moments. This has been especially so for the less "developed" and non-aligned states who are a majority of the NPT members. The United States agenda in the Gulf War to destroy potential Iraqi nuclear capabilities, independent of NNPR procedures and processes for dealing with NNPR transgressions, ironically happened soon after Joseph Nye's publication about the United States' increasingly "soft power" (Nye 1990). The United Nations Security Council did subsequently authorise the destruction of all weapons of mass destruction in Iraq, however. Thus Keeley's argument on "regimes", purporting to use a Foucauldian framework, may be more convincing. He suggests that regimes are loci of tension: that the actors supporting the dominant discourse seek to extend its grasp to others, while those holding "subjugated knowledges" pursue resistant practices (Keeley 1990 pp 98-9).

"Learning" theory does not accommodate well the non-existence of alleged "learning" by some states because it is status-quo-centric and not focussed explicitly on social, economic, political and security interests. India, for example, has been described as a state which has exploited its ambiguous nuclear status to extract international concessions and benefits independent of NNPR "lessons" – domestic and regional dynamics being more important. Relevant decision-makers in India have seen nuclear weapons conferring status and deterrence benefits, and from their location alongside sometimes "hostile" nuclear-capable neighbours they have asserted a different "knowledge" about nuclear politics than other states in less tense regions. Thus domestic "learning" by political coalitions differs markedly depending on the region.

Liberal "learning" theory suggests that the "most learned" states participate in the NNPR thereby delineating "legitimate discourses". The knowing subscribe to the regime, the ignorant, learn. Under this view the various arguments raised by states such as India and Israel and, till the 1970s, West Germany, are not legitimate – they have just not learnt their lessons well. It can also be construed as quite paternalist: since many of the non-hegemonic powers took years to ratify the NPT, and many states still refuse to accede to it. They are being portrayed, by implication, as extremely slow-learners.

An appraisal of the creeping hegemony of modernism and of science and technology, in the tradition of Feyerabend, Habermas or Foucault, may be more appropriate or perhaps explicable as an historical phenomenon, synonymous with the spread of bureaucracy, perhaps as an elite adaptation to the encroachment of capitalism in newly industrialising economies (Girling 1984-5 p 439). The point is that pursuing or eschewing nuclear weaponry is a highly contingent political phenomena – not just a "learnt" state response.

It can also be argued that the notion of "learning" promotes the rationalist Kantian belief in progress through cumulative knowledge and learning, when in the context of the NPT it is not clear that NNWS who endorsed the treaty intended to become NWS in any event; or conversely, that signatories to the NPT did not intend to acquire their nuclear technology under the treaty while simultaneously pursuing the NW option.

CONCLUSIONS

The selected texts are likely to be regarded as authoritative because their author is a "security expert" and public figure close to Democrat government. The views may also be seen as a discursive practice: part of a broader discourse of political power. The author both constitutes part of that discursive practice and is constituted by it. The implicit nationalism in the texts also demonstrates the creation of subjects of the modern state who perceive the world as imagined political communities (Anderson 1983). Nye is an active contributor to and the subject of this discourse which portrays the United States as such an imagined community – both the sovereign protector of its citizens and a leading contributor to world "security". Nye's contributions to political discourse, although variable, contribute to the formation of identities and images which found subjectivities and public outlooks, and influence foreign policies and decisions, especially within the "security" elite. It is conceded though that public discourses are heterogeneous, and that Nye is more confident than others about the strength and effectiveness of the NNPR.

Nevertheless, Nye's works exemplify western "security" discourse which has a narrative structure that is super-power-centric, and in particular United-States-centric, as has been common in mainstream international relations journals until recently. Many of the points made could have, and in some cases have arisen in "mainstream" critiques, but this chapter has attempted to demonstrate the potential benefit of deconstructive readings of the politics of an international legal "regime".

It can be concluded that in most of the selected texts the constant criticisms that have been made about the failure of the nuclear weapon states, until very recently, to honour the spirit of the disarmament and arms control obligations on the NWS, and the grievances expressed by some less developed states that unilaterally tightened supplier restrictions were discriminatory and in breach of regime norms, are muffled or silenced. Nevertheless some predictions can be made about the future of the NPT although in only a few of Nye's texts do these issues feature (such as Nye 1985). The concerns of the eighties about vertical proliferation by nuclear weapon states, and by the United States and the former Soviet Union in particular, are unlikely to jeopardise the 1995 review conference on the NPT. Relations between the United States and Russia have improved substantially in recent years and relatively significant, if not absolutely significant, progress in disarmament talks have taken place. Nuclear testing does not appear to be the major threat to the regime, because only a minority of states seem determined to hinge the future of the NPT on the CTBT issue, and the Conference on Disarmament has agreed to re-commission debate on a nuclear test ban.

The lack of "learning" about the NNPR norms by some states problematises the notion of learning. The stability of the regime under consensual norms is overstated in the selected texts, despite the high number of regime participants. To the extent that there has been learning from the regime, it may or may not be about United States sponsored norms, as suggested by Nye, but may be because of an independent and genuine international commitment to nonproliferation by the vast majority of states, or varying degrees of interest in pursuing nuclear energy programs. The Commission on Disarmament, the United Nations General Assembly and the NPT review conferences have been crucial in challenging the disarmament and arms control policies of several NWS. It may also be that many states have so successfully entered the nuclear black market that weapons programs are proceeding undetected.

Notwithstanding the strengthening of the regime through conversions by France, China and South Africa, to the extent that some NNPR member states are pursuing nuclear capability clandestinely it clearly has not been a success. The perceived need to resort to military force to destroy partial nuclear capability, as in the case of Iraq, and as threatened in North Korea, represents a fundamental failure of the "regime", even if these are only subsidiary aspects of broader conflicts. It demonstates a weakness in the argument about the "hegemonic" norms and values of the regime espoused by regime proponents such as Nye.

BIBLIOGRAPHY

Albright, D and Carothers A, 1985, "Fragile Consensus on Non-Proliferation Treaty", 41(11), *The Bulletin of the Atomic Scientists*, p 8.

Albright, D and Hibbs, M, 1991, "Iraq's nuclear hide-and-seek", *The Bulletin of the Atomic Scientists,* 47(7) pp 14-23.

Anderson, B, 1983, *Imagined Communities: Reflections on the Origins and Spread of Nationalism*, Verso.

Ashley, R, 1984, "The Poverty of Neorealism", 38(2), *International Organisation*, pp 225-286. Reprinted in Keohane, RO (ed), 1986, *Neorealism and its Critics* , Columbia University Press.

Ashley, RK, 1989, "Living on Border Lines: Man, Postructuralism, and War", Derian, Der J and Shapiro, MJ (eds), *International/Intertextual Relations: Postmodern Readings of World Politics*, Lexington Books.

Ashley, RK and Walker, RBJ, 1990, "Speaking the Language of Exile: Dissident Thought in International Studies, 34, *International Studies Quarterly*, p 259.

Bauser, MA, 1977, "United States Nuclear Export Policy: Developing the Peaceful Atom as a Commodity in International Trade", 18, *Harvard International Law Journal,* p 227.

Babu, DS, 1992, "France and the NPT: Return of the Prodigal", *Peace Research Centre Working Paper No 116*, Australian National University.

Birch, D, 1989, *Language, Literature and Critical Practice: Ways of Analysing Text,* Routledge.

Borisov, K, 1982, "The Effectiveness of the Nuclear Non-proliferation Regime", *International Affairs (Moscow)*, pp 101-106, 129.

Breslauer, GW and Tetlock, PE (eds), 1991, *Learning in US and Soviet Foreign Policy*, Westview Press.

Brzoska, M, 1992, "Is the Nuclear Non-Proliferation System a Regime? A Comment on Trevor McMorris Tate", 29(2), *Journal of Peace Research*, p 215.

Bunn, G, 1994, "Viewpoint: The NPT and Options for its Extension in 1995", *The Nonproliferation Review*, Winter, p 52.

Derian, Der J and Shapiro, MJ (eds), 1989, *International/Intertextual Relations: Postmodern Readings of World Politics*, Lexington Books, pp 259-321.

Doren, CNV and Bunn, G, 1990, "Progress and Peril and the Fourth NPT Review Conference", *Arms Control Today*, p 8.

Epstein, W, 1990, "The Nuclear Testing Threat", 46(6), *The Bulletin of the Atomic Scientists*, p 34.

Foucault, M, 1988, "What is an author?", Lodge, D (ed), *Modern Criticism and Theory: A Reader*, Longman, p197.

George, J, 1994, *Discourses of Global Politics: A Critical (Re)Introduction to International Relations*, Lynne Rienner Publishers.

Girling, J, 1984-85, "Hegemony and Domination in Third World Countries: A Case Study of Thailand", 10, *Alternatives*, p 435.

Goldblat, J, 1986, "The Third Review Conference of the Nuclear Non-Proliferation Treaty", 17(1), *Bulletin of Peace Proposals*, p 13.

Greig, DW, 1978, "The interpretation of treaties and Article IV 2 of the Nuclear Non-Proliferation Treaty", 6, *Australian Yearbook of International Law*, p 77.

Haas, EB, 1980, "Why Collaborate? Issue-Linkage and International Regimes", 32, *World Politics,* p 357.

Haas, PM, 1992, "Introduction: epistemic communities and international policy coordination", 46(1), *International Organisation*, p 1.

Hoffmann, S, 1977, "An American Social Science: International Relations", 106(3), *Daedalus*, p 41.

Keeley, JF, 1990, "Toward a Foucauldian analysis of international regimes", 44(1), *International Organisation*, p 83.

Keohane, RO and Nye Jr, JS, 1977, "*Power and Interdependence: world politics in transition*, Little Brown.

Keohane, RO and Nye Jr, JS, 1987, "*Power and Interdependence:* Revisited", 41(4), *International Organisation*, p 725.

Koskenniemi, M (ed), 1992, *International Law*, Dartmouth Publishing Company Limited.

Krasner, SD, 1983a, "Structural causes and regime consequences: regimes as intervening variables", Krasner, SD (ed), *International Regimes*, Cornell University Press, p 1.

Krasner, SD, 1983b, "Regimes and the limits of realism: regimes as autonomous variables", Krasner, SD (ed), *International Regimes,* Cornell University Press, p 355.
Kratochwil, F, 1988, "Regimes, Interpretation and the 'Science' of Politics": A Reappraisal", 17(2), *Millenium: Journal of International Studies*, p 263.
Leaver, R, 1988, "Australian Safeguards: Can We Trust Euratom?", 1(1), *Pacific Research,* p 6.
Mack, A, 1989, "What is Wrong with Deterrence Theory?", Peace Research Centre Working Paper No 76, Australian National University.
Modelski, G, 1990, "Is World Politics Evolutionary Learning?", 44(1), *International Organisation*, p 1.
Muller, H, 1993, "Europe's Leaky Borders", 49(5), *The Bulletin of the Atomic Scientists*, p 27.
Nye Jr, JS, 1977a, "United States Policy on Nuclear Technology: Combining Energy and Security", *Department of State Bulletin*, May, p 550.
Nye Jr, JS, 1977b, "Planning a Safeguardable Nuclear Future", *Department of State Bulletin*, August, p 183.
Nye Jr, JS, 1978a, "Non-proliferation: a long term strategy", 56, *Foreign Affairs*, p 601.
Nye Jr, JS, 1978b, "Nuclear Policy: Balancing Nonproliferation and Energy Security", *Department of State Bulletin,* October, p 38.
Nye Jr, JS, 1979, "Nuclear Policy: The US Approach to Nonproliferation – Are We Making Progress?", *Department of State Bulletin,* January, p 39.
Nye Jr, JS, 1981, "Maintaining a Nonproliferation Regime", Quester, G (ed), *Nuclear Proliferation: Breaking the Chain*, University of Wisconsin Press, p 15.
Nye Jr, JS, 1985, "NPT: The Logic of Inequality", 59, *Foreign Policy*, p 123.
Nye Jr, JS, 1987, "Nuclear learning and US-Soviet security regimes", 41(3), *International Organisation*, p 371.
Nye Jr, JS, 1988, "US-Soviet Cooperation in a Nonproliferation Regime", George, A, Farley, P and Dallin, A (eds), *US-Soviet Security Cooperation*, Oxford University Press, p 336.
Nye Jr, JS, 1989, "Arms Control After the Cold War", 68(5), *Foreign Affairs*, p 42.
Nye Jr, JS, 1990a, "Soft Power", 80, *Foreign Policy*, p 153.
Nye Jr, JS, 1990b, *Bound to Lead: the changing nature of American power*, Basic Books.
Redick, JR, 1994, "Latin America's Emerging Non-Proliferation Consensus", *Arms Control Today*, March, p 3.
Schwartz, JB, 1988, "Controlling Nuclear Proliferation: Legal Strategies of the United States", 20, *Law and Policy in International Business*, p 1.
Shakar, MI, 1980, *The Nuclear Non-Proliferation Treaty: Origin and Implementation 1959-1979*, Oceania Publications.
Shestov, V, 1973, "The Non-Proliferation Treaty in Action", *International Affairs (Moscow)*, p 33.
Smith, GC and Cobban, H, 1989, "A Blind Eye to Nuclear Proliferation", 68(3), *Foreign Affairs*, p 53.
Smith, RK, 1987, "Explaining the non-proliferation regime: anomolies for contemporary international relations theory", 41(2), *International Organisation*, p 253.
Smith, S, 1989, "Paradigm Dominance in International Relations: The Development of International Relations as a Social Science", Dyer, HC and Mangasarian, L (eds), *The Study of International Relations: The State of the Art*, MacMillan/Millenium, p 3.

Strange, S, 1983, "Cave! hic dragones: a critique of regime analysis", Krasner, SD (ed), *International Regimes*, Cornell University Press, p 337.
Tate, T McMorris, 1990, "Regime Building in the Non-Proliferation System", 27(4), *Journal of Peace Research*, p 399.
Turkel, G, 1990, "Michel Foucault: Law, Power, and Knowledge", 17(2), *Journal of Law and Society*, p 170.
Van Doren, CN and Bunn, G, 1990, "Progress and Peril and the Fourth NPT Review Conference", 20(8), *Arms Control Today*, p 8.
Wilson, C, 1994, "COCOM", 7(1), *Pacific Research*, p 31.
Wilson, M, 1994, "NPT Procedural Issues and Processes", Paper presented at the Asia-Pacific Regional Seminar on the Nuclear Non-Proliferation Treaty, Canberra, 28-29 March 1994.

32

An Anatomy of Australian Law or "The Human Element In Legal Argument"[1]

MICHAEL MEEHAN

Personification of the law appears casually in most legal judgments and in much of our legal advocacy. It occurs directly – familiarly, to the point of virtual invisibility – in phrases like "the law speaks" (Cox J in *The Queen v Palazoff* (1986) 43 SASR 99 at 105 "For laws may speak in vain"),[2] "the law takes the view", or "the law demands" (Bray CJ in *The Queen v Mayne* (1975) 11 SASR 583 at 586, "The law demands of all of us when we take to the roads that we exercise at all times proper vigilance. . ."). It appears in thousands of fragments, in casual reference to the "flesh", "hand", "arm", "limbs", "organs", "face" and "heart", "soul", "spirit", "shade", "skeleton", "ghost" and "spectre", and most frequently and most evocatively, to the "eye" and to the "voice" of the law. This chapter, in assembling these fragments, proposes a new kind of legal biography. It offers a critical "Anatomy of Australian Law" in quite a literal sense. It suggests that an analysis of personification in legal argument provides access to the central mythological projections and religiose apprehensions which direct much of what we think of as legal reasoning. It proposes a reading of legal texts as cultural (even as literary) documents, and suggests that this habitual legal projection of the law as a thinking, speaking, authorising subject is one of the most powerful fictions in our culture: and that it is, in the terms Justice Lionel Murphy used in another context, yet another legal "convenient falsehood" (Murphy J

1 Apologies to Stephen Leacock's "A, B and C: The Human Element in Mathematics", from *Literary Lapses*, in Priestley, JB (ed), 1957, The Bodley Head Leacock, pp 29-34.

2 See also Winneke CJ, Gowans and Gillard JJ in *Taylor v Miller* [1969] VR 987 at 991.

in *Coe v Commonwealth* (1979) 24 ALR 118 at 138), of a kind to underwrite a far wider range of Australian cultural attitudes.

The principal function of the personification of law and the metaphoric "humanising" of its operations is, paradoxically, to *dehumanise* the processes of advocacy and adjudication, displacing human frailty and all the adjudicative ills that flesh is heir to, through invocation of the higher authoritative presence of the law, in phrases such as "the law speaks" (Jacobs J in *McCoy v Watson* (1978) 12 SASR 506 at 512); on "the sense in which the law speaks of cause and consequence" (Cox J in *The Queen v Palazoff* (1986) 43 SASR 99 at 105); "the law regards" (Barry J in *Re Galvin (No 2)* [1961] VR 740 at 753); on the "limits of what the law regards as reasonable" (Smith J in *R v Bufalo* [1958] VR 363 at 364); and even "the law regards some causes as being ones which the law takes regard of" (Hogarth, Walters and Jacobs JJ in *The Queen v Hoskin* (1974) 9 SASR 531 at 538). The law appears within Australian legal argument as a solemn magisterial presence ("the law takes a *stern* view" (Von Doussa J in *Sadler v Crossman* (1988) 47 SASR 331 at 338)) standing sufficiently beyond local time and local place to maintain authority, a satisfactory historical resonance, a posture of high disinterest and omniscience. It retains, however, a comforting array of familiar human characteristics of a kind to affirm fellowship, understanding and even empathy, in phrases such as "the law is concerned", "the law takes account" (Bray CJ in *GH Mitchell and Sons (Australia) Pty Ltd v Minister of Works* (1974) 8 SASR 7 at 13), and "the law recognises" (Jacobs J in *Venning v Chin* (1974) 10 SASR 299 at 325-26). Personification is a central rhetorical strategy in the naturalisation of the processes of law: but it is also, oddly enough, a central strategy in propagating an image of the law's comprehensive and omniscient authority, its elusiveness and unassailability.

One of the most useful functions of criticism in legal contexts is to describe how such apparently innocent "turns of phrase", ostensibly imported merely to grace the processes of legal reasoning, may actually determine their character. Language is not a neutral instrument. We do not use figures of speech, so much as that they use us: *"On est écrit!"*, and there are few forms of discourse in our society which construct and constrain the subjectivity of the speaker more potently than the heavily ritualised "turns of phrase" and "figures of speech" of the law. In this area, banality is strength: it is the very ordinariness, the sheer familiarity, of legal personification that is the hiding place of its power.

Identifying the "body" of Australian law, in its thousands of scattered allusive fragments, becomes the first step in the process of improved understanding. The second step lies in identifying the Mind, the mysterious legal author, the "eye" and the "voice" of the law. The legal comparativist, Professor Alan Watson (1985; 1988), long ago formulated the task of tracing the role of legal culture in its characteristic intervention between what he calls "social input" – the needs of a society at any given time – and "legal output", as the legal response to those needs. The personification of law is one such intervening factor, a device by which the eye of the law subverts the power of the human eye, and the voice of the law overrides the human voice. Elaborately cultivated in the great texts of the common law, and endlessly recycled in thousands of casual but highly manipulative allusions in our legal argument, this construction of law as a unified, sentient, "sensitive" yet decisive authorising entity, is the central social fantasy – the very masterfiction of our culture. As such, it is a fiction of special significance in our postcolonial environment, where this whole process of legal incarnation takes on an even more dangerously pre-emptive turn, in which the embodiment of the law may promote a reverse process of colonial cultural disembodiment, where the legal recycling of the myths, of shadowy parental presences from the imperial culture, may obliterate all independent growth in the child.

IDENTIFYING THE BODY

It is a great irony that the perennial desire to envitalise, to clothe the law with flesh and blood, should have resulted in so much dead metaphor. The phrase "a body of law" recurs with such casual frequency in our legal writing that it retains little figurative force: it is liberally "mixed in" with other metaphors, even in the most sensitive and language-conscious of our legal authors who are to be found searching, for example, for "common threads" in our various "bodies of law" (Kirby P in *Avel Pty Ltd v A-G (NSW)* (1987) 11 NSWLR 126 at 127). Metaphors of legal incarnation are not a purely lawyerly phenomenon: many, such as the "arm of the law", and the "hand of the law" occur in popular parlance, though even these surface occasionally in formal legal discourse, as in Samuel J's reflection, in *Barton v Walker* [1979] 2 NSWLR 740 at 755, that "the arm of the law would be short indeed" if judges' qualifications to sit could not be challenged, and in his ruminations on the dangers of legal "amputation" (at 756). In general, the limbs of the law, the limbs of statutes (except occasionally, when heavily "fettered"), draw little attention to themselves, whereas the "face" does retain some metaphoric force, as where the law "sets its face against a tightly rigid interpretation" (Marks J in *Pacific Seven Pty Ltd v City of Sandringham* [1982] VR 157 at 160), or "the law sets its face against the use of detention" (Brooking J in *R v Haidley and Alford* [1984] VR 229 at 255), or "the law sets its face against scatter-gun prosecutions" (Southwell J in *Davies v Waldron* [1989] VR 449 at 454).

Reference to the "heart of the law" has largely gone down the funereal path of legal "bodies" and legal "limbs", in phrases such as "the principles and standards that lie at the heart of the law" (Wells J in *Hackney Tavern Nominees Pty Ltd v McLeod* (1983) 34 SASR 207 at 214; King CJ in *Robertson v Swincer* (1989) 52 SASR 356 at 362;

Wells J in *The Queen v Hansford* (1974) 8 SASR 164 at 194), or the "heart of the common law principle" (Legoe J in *Walker v Baehnk (No 2)* (1987) 44 SASR 380 at 381). The metaphor can, however, be revitalised by the slightest extension – as in Isaacs J's reference, in *James v Cowan* (1929) 43 CLR 386 at 403, to the dangers of the Federal Constitution "stifling the heart-beat" of State legislation. At the "heart" of all such imagery is, of course, the determination to keep law on the side of the living: to ensure, in the words of Windeyer J in *Damjanovic v Commonwealth* (1968) 146 CLR 390 at 409-11, that our Constitution will continue as a "living document": that the law in general, in the words of Sachs J in *Porter v Porter* [1969] 1 WLR 1155 at 1159 (quoted in *Boshell v Boshell* [1972] 1 NSWLR 52 at 56), will persist as a "living thing moving with the times and not a creature of dead or moribund ways of thought". Animism of the kind invests the law with a wide range of physical attributes – of reproduction (for law, in our legal discourse, breeds new "creatures" continually[3]), of both physical integration and physical immunity,[4] and even, of life after death: for not only do the forms of action "rule us from their graves", as Maitland wrote, but every lawyer knows what it is to be haunted by the "ghosts", the "spirits" and the "spectres" of the law.[5]

IDENTIFYING THE MIND

Legal discourse then moves to a higher investiture – the animation of the body of the law with the attributes of mental life, as the "eye of the law" displaces the role of the human eye, and the "voice of the law" overrides the human voice. While the rhetoric of legal personification is ostensibly one of human fellowship – of the law's sympathetic participation, the law's embroilment in the human condition – the real function of such personification is one of displacement and disempowerment. Voltaire's memorable maxim "My enemies, I'll take care of. God save me from my friends" is apposite, and in legal discourse, it is when the law is at its engagingly personified, when it is at its most apparently human – most "solicitous", most "anxious", most "concerned" (Blackstone's terms[6]), that its displacement of real and local human voices is at its most insidious.

---

3 See, as instances, Hunt J in *Mirror Newspapers v Waller* (1985) 1 NSWLR 1 at 5; Rogers J in *Boyd v Ombudsman* [1981] 2 NSWLR 308 at 310; Master Allen in *ANZ Banking Group Ltd v Greig* [1980] 1 NSWLR 112 at 115; Street CJ in *Re Asiatic Electric Co Pty Ltd (in Liq) and the Companies Act* [1973] 1 NSWLR 603 at 606; Carmichael J in *Hutton v Hutton* [1972] 1 NSWLR 175 at 184.

4 "Revenue law is not a mystery separate and apart. It is an integrated part of the body of statute law" (Kirby P in *Commissioner of Stamp Duties v Permanent Trustee Co Ltd* (1987) 9 NSWLR 719 at 723).

5 For an instance of judicial valour in the face of such "haunting" and "daunting", see Jacobs J in *Venning v Chin* (1974) 10 SASR 299 at 325.

6 Blackstone (1768) III pp 265, 422 and see III, p 328 and IV, p 323.

The fictional character of legal writing (Peller 1985, Carty 1990) emerges forcefully in the local and everyday language of Australian legal advocacy and adjudication. Reference to what figures only "in the eyes of the law",[7] and specific exclusions of what the "eyes of the law" will not acknowledge, recurs with such casual frequency in Australian legal judgments as scarcely to register in the eyes of the reader.[8] The specific perceptual categories sanctioned by the law, the particular narrative categories authorised by the law, often proceed in opposition to the natural, the "lay" order of things. Of this, the concept of legal personality is the most conspicuous instance, and I quote Gowans J in *Hubbard Association of Scientologists v A-G (Vic)* [1976] VR 119 at 128, endorsing the resounding formulation of *Salmond on Jurisprudence:*

> The chief difficulty in apprehending the true nature of a corporation . . . is that it bears the same name as the natural person who is its sole member for the time being, and who represents it and acts for it. . . One is a human being, administering for the time being the duties and affairs of the office. He alone is visible to the eyes of laymen. The other is a mythical being whom only lawyers know of, and *whom only the eye of the law can perceive.*

It is the encounter between "persons of flesh and blood" and these "mythical beings whom only lawyers know of", between the order of rules and the order of things, which is the subject of most literature about law, in its exploration of conflicts between the invisible structures of the law (invisible characters, invisible stages, invisible dramas) which *only the eye of the law can perceive*, and the world as it presents itself to the eyes of mere "laypersons", to the eyes of mere "flesh and blood".

The "voice" of the Law is invoked rather less frequently than the "eye" of the law: but with its attendant metaphors of law "speaking" (Jacobs J in *McCoy v Watson* (1976) 13 SASR 506 at 512), "taking the view" (White J in *DB and AE Newman Pty Ltd v Barossa Co-operative Winery Ltd* (1981) 28 SASR 501, "The law takes an objective view. . ."), and "holding" an opinion (Hogarth ACJ and White J in *The Queen v Garrett* (1978) 18 SASR 308 at 314), it is the single most powerful figure of speech in all our legal culture. It is used, repeatedly, to articulate the furthest reaches of legal utopian fantasy – fantasies of a "unified body of law" which can speak for itself (Hogarth ACJ and White J in *The Queen v Garrett* (1978) 18 SASR 308 at 314): of a Constitution which can "speak in its own voice", which can simply tell us the answers, and instruct us in what

7 On the law's "point of view", see *Rendell v Asso Finance Pty Ltd* [1957] VR 604 at 6067.

8 See Lord Devlin, "The case of shutting the eyes is actual knowledge in the eyes of the law", in *Roper v Taylor's Central Garages (Exeter) Ltd* (1951) 2 TLR 284 at 208-9; on "fairness in the eye of the law", see Rath J in *Calvin v Carr* [1972] 2 NSWLR 308 at 341; on lists of objects "charitable in the eyes of the law", see Holland J in *A-G (NSW) v Sawtell* [1978] 2 NSWLR 200 at 204.

to think. It is one of the greatest paradoxes in Australian legal culture that the whole tradition of "literal reading" (better, of "strict and complete legalism") should have been set in motion, in the *Engineers* case, by one of the most exotic flights of figurative fantasy ever recorded in an Australian legal judgment: the admonition, by the majority, to *loyally permit that "great instrument of government to speak with its own voice"* (*Amalgamated Society of Engineers v Adelaide Steamship Company Ltd* (1920) 28 CLR 129 at 147). The figure "legal voice" is singularly appropriate for expressing an ideal of unity, of coherence, and above all, the legal fantasy of a text which somehow "contains" within itself its own meanings to the point of resonant articulation. But it is also, repeatedly, the bearer of bad legal tidings, of tales of multiple bodies of law, speaking with a "variety of tongues" (Cross J in *Challenor v Douglas* [1983] 2 NSWLR 405 at 415). It is also the image most strongly drawn upon to articulate the primal Australian legal nightmare – the nightmare of any federal system – of "deafening and conflicting voices" (Deane J in *Miller v TCN Channel Nine Pty Ltd* (1986) 67 ALR 321 at 362), of an Australia in the throes of multivocal disintegration: as (in a new "incantation" from the High Court, a resonant phrase Deane J has set in ritual motion) – a mere legal "Bedlam of a Babel" (*Breavington v Godleman* (1989) 80 ALR 362 at 414; *Thomson v R* (1989) 169 CLR 1 at 35).

FROM PERSONIFICATION TO BIOGRAPHY

Our judges play much upon the literary capabilities of "the facts". The favoured phrase is "narrative" – the particular narrative in the case – but this is occasionally enhanced one stage further in the direction of some more specific literary genre, as in "story", "history", "epic" (Fullagar J and Webb J in *Poulton v Commonwealth* (1953) 89 CLR 540 at 551 and 593), and even "satire" (Fullagar J in *War Assets Pty Ltd v Federal Commissioner of Taxation* (1954) 91 CLR 53 at 69). Occasionally, the "facts" are caught up in an extended theatrical metaphor. Our judgments are replete with images of "dramas" (Fullagar J in *War Assets Pty Ltd v Federal Commissioner of Taxation* at 69; Fullagar J in *Trobridge v Hardy* (1955) 94 CLR 147 at 151; Barwick CJ in *VosciaNo v VosciaNo* (1974) 130 CLR 267 at 273; Menzies J in *Ryan v The Queen* (1967) 121 CLR 205 at 237) – of "actors" entering upon "stages" (for theatrical metaphor, see Fullagar J in *Kain v Shelton v Virgo* (1956) 97 CLR 230 at 242, and Dixon J in *R v Wilkes* (1948) 77 CLR 511 at 517), (the phrase *dramatis personae* is one that frequently recurs[9]), of

---

9 As in Menzies J in *Truesdale v Federal Commissioner of Taxation* (1970) 120 CLR 353 at 363; Windeyer J in *Federal Commissioner of Taxation v Casuarina Pty Ltd* (1971) 127 CLR 62 at 64; Powell J in *Kurt Keller Pty Ltd v BMW Australia Ltd* (1984) 1 NSWLR 353 at 360; Hutley JA in *Aboriginal Development Commission v Treka Aboriginal Arts and Crafts Ltd* [1984] 3 NSWLR 502 at 514.

"scenes",[10] of dramatic "climaxes" – and even of tragic "denouements".[11] But in all these various legal dramas, the *dramatis personae* in question pass like walking shadows, their very names quickly appropriated, almost algebraically, to whatever legal principle they happen to have become entangled with. Who knows anything of Mrs Donoghue before the raising of the fateful glass? Who cares what happened to her thereafter? There is little chance for gleaning, from those "closely edited narrative diagrams of reality" (Geertz 1983) to be found in our legal cases, much sense either of the inner, human factors at issue, or, given the formidable prosceniums erected by the rules of evidence, the wider narrative contexts of the case. Even the judicial directors themselves strut and fret their hour upon the stage and then are heard no more. . . and it is, finally, the law itself that is the only durable legal player.

THE LAW, AS *DRAMATIS PERSONA*

There has, over the past decade, in the context of the bicentennialism and the passing of the *Australia Acts* 1986 (UK and Cth), been a lot of loose talk about the "character of Australian law". We have now collected sufficient materials for a far more literal approach. The images reviewed above are a part of the international *argot* of the common law. But we always say more than we mean, and mean far more than we intend: and while, in Australia, we may be cheerfully recycling the "sayings" enshrined in English common law culture, the "meanings" may emerge in a somewhat different guise: or to put it in the terms familiar from Australian constitutional exegesis, while we are cheerfully availing ourselves of the connotative resources of English legal language, the denotative range of that language in Australia may mean somewhat more – and in this instance of personification, somewhat less – than we intend.[12] "The Law" – in England – is a figure of speech. But it is also far more than that. It is the figure of a whole culture: a culture which, in the proper sense of the term, has grown, "organically", from the earth. English law, as Peter Goodrich (1990 p 211) has recently written, is the "peculiar elocution of a particular geography", with its iconography profoundly rooted in place – "dear, vile England" – with its ultimate origins mythologised as a form of pristine thoughtlessness (p 227), as an unwritten code of values haling from a time, in Sir William

10 Windeyer J in *Federal Commissioner of Taxation v Casuarina* (1971) 127 CLR 62 at 65, where the whole "narrative" of the facts is built upon "the theatrical metaphor".

11 See Barwick CJ in *Hungier v Grace* (1972) 127 CLR 210 at 216.

12 See Higgins J, using the notion of the "centre" and the "circumference" of a power, in the *Union Label* case (1908) 6 CLR 469 at 610, and see Barwick CJ, in *King v Jones* (1972) 128 CLR 221, reaffirming the principle that the "connotation of words employed in the Constitution does not change though changing events and attitudes may in some circumstances extend the denotation or reach of those words" (at 229).

Blackstone's (1765 I pp 67, 76) resonant phrasing, "whereof the memory of man runneth not to the contrary", from a time when thought and memory simply fade back into a physical location, into an archive that is purely geographic, from an ultimate source in physical place rather than in human reflection.

The law, as we encounter it in Coke, Hale, and Blackstone, is always far more than the sum of its disparate parts, and the addition – that which acts to metamorphose a mere list of shifting rules and procedures into an overseeing eye and a coherent voice – is an act of prolonged, aggregative national self-consciousness, formed upon that geographical archive. It is a process in which the law emerges as a putative collective *psyche*, in which – in the terms of the principal mythologers, at least – the voice of the law functions not so much by pre-emption and displacement, as by integration and elevation. It functions by a centripetal motion of running individual voices towards the centre, elevating indistinct and fragmented voices from particular points in time and place into an articulation far surpassing all the disparate legal wisdoms of the individual vocal parts.

The law has its own "interiority". Recent psychoanalytical investigations into legal authorship, in the work of the French historian Pierre Legendre and his English disciples,[13] Goodrich, Carty, Duxbury, explore both the putative *psyche* of the Law itself – the "character of English law" – and more extensively, the *psyche* which makes the imputation. It traces across a range of legal cultures the occupation, by the law and its attendant iconography, of psychic territory primordially mapped out in the micro-relationships of parent and child, with the ideology of law – the imagery of law as coherent, comprehensive, unified and authoritative – primarily underwritten in a form of psychic infiltration. The authority of the law – in the face it presents to the psychoanalyst – is founded not upon abstractions like "rules of recognition", of even the "laws of nature", but upon a long cultivation of a complementarity between "inner" psychic susceptibilites in the legal subject, and outer, social iconographies both of menace and of reassurance, with the patriarchy of law – the eye, the voice of the law, as the Lacanian *Nom du Père*, infiltrating and expanding the inner "spaces", the psychic sites of submission and obeissance. This legal psychoanalytical literature is to date mostly concerned with the foundations of authority in civil law systems. It is, however, even more illuminating in a review of the great texts of the common law, and the ways in which, in England, a

13 Legendre's psychoanalytical explorations are most extensively pursued in his *L'Amour du Censeur* (1974). For an English account of this work, see Neil Duxbury, "Exploring Legal Tradition: Psychoanalytical Theory and Roman Law in Modern Continental Jurisprudence", *Legal Studies* 9 (1989), pp 84-98. A wider review of Legendre's more recent writing on legal iconography (*Le Désir Politique de Dieu: Etude sur les montages de l'état et du droit* (1989) is found in Peter Goodrich's chapter "Law's Emotional Body: Image and Aesthetic in the Work of Pierre Legendre", *Languages of Law*.

far wider literary culture has contributed to this process of legal psychic imputation, and the ways in which this parental presence, "stern" on occasion and "solicitous" on others, has been constructed from a particular site – "this England" – and from a putative English national childhood memory.

Blackstone provides an instance of this "long cultivation". Blackstone's *Commentaries on the Laws of England* (*Commentaries*) is not just a legal textbook, not just a disposition of rules. The work is structured as an historical narrative. Nor is it just a legal history – a mere list of dates, about the development of a list of rules. Centrally, Blackstone's *Commentaries* is presented as a form of legal biography, a tale of the "inner" struggling to re-manifest itself outwardly. It is the history of a voice – the pure Anglo-Saxon common law voice, the childhood voice of a nation in its "pristine simplicity and vigour" (1769 IV p 411), successfully struggling against the incursions of Norman "chicanes and subtleties" (IV p 410) and the "new-fanglings" of statute (III p 329; IV p 86), to re-manifest itself in the present "Glory", "Unity", "Symmetry" and "excellence of our present establishment" (III p 379; VI p 323; I p 10). Blackstone's *Commentaries* is one of the great English pre-Romantic texts, prefiguring in its legal mythologising what the poet Wordsworth was to articulate, in a succeeding generation, in the form of poetic doctrine, that the "child is father to the man": that the hiding places of inventive power lie in repetitions of a process of creative regression, which interleaves the experience of adulthood continually with the freshness of childhood perception.

"THE CHILD IS FATHER TO THE MAN"

The power of Blackstone's formulations – of his "childish fictions" – is still being registered, positively and negatively, in our own courts.[14] But the question we encounter, in Australia, is whether the legal man can actually be father to a healthy child: that is, whether a legal system like the Australian legal system, the origins of which lie within historical time – at the virtual moment, indeed, of Sir William Blackstone's "present Glory" – can ever recover from quite so much good fortune. Our own legal mythologers have, it is true, been busy. The imagery of legal "transplantation" is prolific in Australia, transplants watered continually by those "unpolluted streams" – streams of power, streams of authority, streams of justice – "flowing from a higher imperial source" (Brennan J in *Kirmani v Captain Cook Cruises Pty Ltd (No 1)* (1985) 159 CLR 351 at 415). In this, unfortunately, law works against lore. Few themes are more insistent in our colonial literature, in Harpur, Clarke, Lawson, than the resistance of our landscape to its inherited forms of legal inscription, and there are few legal acts of what I earlier called "prolonged,

14 On Murphy J's attempts to exorcise Blackstone, see *Dugan v Mirror Newspapers* (1978) 142 CLR 583 at 608-10, and *SGIC v Trigwell* (1979) 142 CLR 617 at 650-1.

aggregative national self-consciousness" in Australian legal culture: far fewer, at least, than there ought to have been, and certainly, far too few for that "figure of speech", the law, to assume in Australia the character of the figure of a vital legal culture. To speak of "the law" in Australia is to invoke the pre-emptive authorial power of the figure – to intervene yet again upon that act of national self-consciousness – but without quite invoking the compensatory associations, the fruits of "long cultivation", that the figure attracts in its home culture.

So there is, in all that sheer labour of legal metaphoric incarnation in Australian legal discourse, something just a little sad. With all the plethora of limbs, bodies, breath, hearts, faces, eyes and voices, Australian law retains a fractured, even disembodied character, with our dominant legal "figures of speech" reinforcing a local authorial absence by recycling at a lost, antipodean remove, an intimidating "spectre" – the Law – which, in its home culture, did speak out of a richly articulated biography – as the spokesperson for a particular place, speaking from that place both as child and as man, and speaking within a continuing family saga. That saga was instituted in the panegyric of writers like Blackstone, and is echoed still, in our own time, even in the most sceptical of English legal criticism, claiming that the potency of English legal iconography derives from geographical and from familial contexts, from the fact that "in the end, [the common law] is a family history, a history of a domestic constitution" (Goodrich p 217).

What in England may succeed as a voice, becomes, in Australia, a creative vortex. It figures less as an intensive form of social self-consciousness than as a mode of intellectual evasion, as mere repetitions of the imputed consciousness of another. In practical terms, it promotes a situation where English law may continue to be "organic", flexible and legally creative, while Australian law lies dutiful and dormant, its adjudication frozen in postures of listening rather than speaking, the whole culture bound by widening implementation of the doctrine of *stare decisis.* The Americans, understanding something more than we do about biography and organic nature of "culture", were more inventive, extensively rewriting English legal history, through the later eighteenth and early nineteenth centuries[15] – re-issuing Blackstone in a republican version, as just one example – in order to place themselves at the living end of the law's biography, and in order to postpone the legal conclusion, to ensure that there could be legal life and legal growth, even beyond the present "Glory" and "Excellence" of the parental legal establishment. Intervention, the American experience suggests, is paradoxically the way to ensure a truly vigorous legal continuity. The instigation of a new legal childhood, a new era of "pristine

15 On such rewritings, see Bailyn, Bernard, 1967, *The Ideological Origins of the American Revolution,* Harvard University Press, and Pocock, JGA, 1972, "Civic Humanism and its Role in Anglo-American Thought", in *Politics, Language and Time: Essays on Political Thought and History,* Methuen.

simplicity and vigour", is the way to ensure a true legal adulthood. Of such intervention and such propagation, there has been little in Australian legal culture.

A note, then, on "bonds", "fetters", "shackles" and "straitjackets" – these strange, but inevitable products of a situation where lawyers seek to have their metaphoric cake and eat it: to clothe with flesh and blood, to incarnate, to keep the "living body of the law" in motion, but all in the final interests of restriction, order and control. These images of legal bondage appear in a hierarchy – a hierarchy of degrees of judicial consciousness of the literal capabilities of each metaphor. The imagery of bonds and legal "binding" is used pervasively, ritualistically, unconsciously. While the same is largely true of legal "fetterings", it is not entirely so, and in a legal literature rich in "fettered" statutory "limbs", our judges have occasionally glossed the metaphor. We hear, for example, of an appeal court's power to "strike off the fetters" (Gibbs J in *Bailey v Marinoff* (1971) 125 CLR 529 at 540-41), and judges have occasionally moved from the metaphor into wider reflection, as in Lord Davey's much recycled comment on the "effort made by men of great intelligence and sound learning to escape from the fetters forged by an earlier generation".[16] With the "shackling" of legal bodies, the metaphoric tempo increases: the image does tend to draw attention to itself, and the legal reader is, in most instances, ushered into some saga of legal liberation. We read of "the tendency in lawyers and judges to carry forward restrictions and limitations embodied in past decisions and to shackle them to new legislation" (Hutley JA in *Lake v Quinton* [1973] 1 NSWLR 111 at 136) – legal corpses, in effect, yoked to the living bodies of the law. We read of improper "shacklings" of a court's discretion (Kirby P in *Raybos Australia Pty Ltd v Tectran Corporation Pty Ltd (No 4)* (1986) 6 NSWLR 674 at 686), of the interpretative "shackles of technical rigidity" (Master Allen in *Rust v Barnes* [1980] NSWLR 727 at 729) and of a "sorry day" when administrative law might be "returned to the shackles of artificial formalism" (Kirby P in *Commissioner for Motor Transport v Kirkpatrick* (1987) 11 NSWLR 427 at 432).

The legal "straitjacket" is less common. It occurs in the same context as "shackles": as a rebuke to excessive legalism (Rogers CJ of Com Div in *Challenge Bank Ltd v Raine and Horne Commercial Pty Ltd* (1989) 17 NSWLR 297 at 306), and as an attack on "long discredited procedural straitjackets" (Deane J in *The Queen v Gray, Ex Parte Marsh* (1985) 157 CLR 351 at 391), on narrow interpretation of entities like "natural justice" (Wootten J in *Dunlop v Woollahra*

16 In *Free Church of Scotland v Overtoun* [1904] AC 515 at 544, 645, as quoted, for example, by Latham CJ in *Wylde v A-G (NSW)* (1948) 78 CLR 224 at 247. See also Wilson J on the *Colonial Laws Validity Act* 1865 (Imp) as the "removing of fetters", to "eliminate any trace of the historical subordination of the colonial legislatures": *Kirmani v Captain Cook Cruises Pty Ltd (No 1)* (1985) 159 CLR 351 at 415.

Municipal Council [1975] 2 NSWLR 446 at 470, citing Lawton CJ, *Maxwell v Department of Trade and Industry* [1974] QB 523 at 539), or on rigid interpretations depriving the courts of all "discretion" (Kirby P in *Challenge Bank Ltd v Raine and Horne Commercial Pty Ltd* at 306). Legal images gain power by repetition, by "ritual incantation".[17] The literary critic sees them surface – watches them gather momentum in our legal literature for a generation or so – and generally, sees them die by a sheer surfeit of citation. But the legal "straitjacket" is still on the move, gaining a particular momentum in the writings of that great judicial nationalist, Justice Lionel Murphy – a writer in whom legal inquiry often took on that character of national self-consciousness, who regularly tested his metaphors for more than legal content, and who was – for better or worse – little given to seeing through the "eye of the law", or speaking through the voice of the law. In the *China Ocean Shipping* case, the "straitjacket" metaphor proclaims a wider saga of legal liberation. Here, it seemed, as in *SGIC v Trigwell* (1979) 142 CLR 617, and *Dugan v Mirror Newspapers* (1978) 142 CLR 583, that the living body really was yoked to a legal corpse: in this instance, to nineteenth century English laws for the regulation of colonies. To affirm the validity of such laws, Murphy J suggested, was to bring down the threat of an Australia "doomed indefinitely to live in a constitutional straitjacket" (*China Ocean Shipping Co v South Australia* (1979) 145 CLR 172 at 235-36). Tales, indeed, of the "body" of Australian law, born into bondage – and in such a context, I suggest, the cheerful English romantic vision of legal continuity, of "binding one's days together", takes on a darker hue: and our more inquiring legal imagery in Australia reflects the temper of an earlier Wordsworth, the youthful, protesting Wordsworth, who attacked Edmund Burke's Ancient Constitutionalism as "a refinement in cruelty superior to that which in the East yokes the living to the dead", which binds us to "cherish a corpse at the bosom, when reason must call aloud that it should be entombed" (Owen and Smyser 1974).

CONCLUSION

The analysis of our legal "figures of speech" is an act of expropriation. It is about the recovery of power and authority from the very language we use, forcing it, in some measure, in Bahktin's words, to "submit" to our "own intentions and accents" (Emerson and Holquist 1981). The dismembering of the body of the law attempted here may provoke us to recover a stronger sense of "the facts" – all the facts and not merely those facts visible to the eye of the law. It may provoke us to listen, not just to the voice of the law, but to all the voices – the "inner" voices of reason, justice and compassion, as well as the "outer" voices of our own culture, our own literature, our own landscape. This

17 On the legal sway of such "ritual incantations", see Kirby P in *Raybos Australia Pty Ltd v Tectran Corporation Pty Ltd (No 4)* (1986) 6 NSWLR 674 at 685.

formula was tried, long ago, with distinguished legal results. Evatt J, in 1939, in *Chester v Council of the Municipality of Waverley* (1939) 62 CLR 1, clearly did not like the shape of the facts, as seen through the eye of the law. The case concerned a mother's inability, under the law as it then was, to recover damages for nervous shock, occasioned in this instance by seeing the corpse of her little boy retrieved from a council drain. Evatt J clearly did not like what the voice of the law was telling him to say. So he re-constructed the facts, not according to the voice of the law, but according to the inner voice of compassion: not according to the eye of the law, but with assistance from the "eye" of a similarly compassionate Australian novelist, Joseph Furphy (at 18). The law, as reconstructed by this reconstructed set of facts, was thrust into dissent – though only temporarily. The ultimate result of this stepping out of legal view, this stepping out of legal earshot, was a new direction in the law, and a bold instance of the voice of the judge, overriding the voice of the law. Evatt's dissent is now internationally regarded as one of our more significant judgments: and culturally, its resonance is only now beginning to be felt. It was recently enshrined as a classic of feminist jurisprudence – looking through the "eye of the mother" (Graycar and Morgan 1990), and is commended elsewhere as the one Australian literary allusion in all our legal literature: and for those interested in the problematic relationship between law and fact, it is a startling attempt to subvert the a priori tendencies in legal story-telling,[18] to let the telling of the facts play upon the writing of the law, rather than the shape of the law dictate the recounting of the facts.

What this chapter finally proposes, is a plea for a revival of rhetoric in legal training, for the critical analysis of such figures as personification (*prosopopaeia*, or *confirmatio*). The aim is not to eradicate all colour, all imagery, from our legal language. The proposition is not that if we stop invoking the eye and the voice of the law, a vigorous and "autochthonous" Australian legal culture will suddenly spring into being. The purpose is rather, through an exposure of turns of thinking secreted in turns of phrase, to deflect the tendency in Australia to "disembody" and disempower our legal thinking, in the very process of adding linguistic flesh and blood. It is an attempt to deflect the tendency, so coruscatingly exposed by Mr Justice Murphy, of abandoning the "real world" with its demands for imaginative legal adaptation, in mere submission to the imperial intonations of the law. Here, I speak not of "rhetoric" in the debased sense in which it is assailed in one Australian legal judgment after another: not "mere rhetoric", not "the stuff of mere rhetoric", not "empty rhetoric", not "unnecessary rhetoric", not "more rhetoric than meaning", nor of things "sounding more in rhetoric than in law" – all

18 On law and fact, and for a useful analytical model for Evatt J's judgement, see Professor William Twining's (1990) discussion of Lord Denning in "Lawyers' Stories", *Rethinking Evidence: Exploratory Essays,* Oxford, pp 232-7.

recent pronouncements on the subject from the Australian High Court. I speak rather of rhetoric, properly understood – rhetoric as recently revived and extended in modern critical theory – and rhetoric as the ancient analytical discipline, which for centuries taught us something of the ways we use language, and of the ways in which language uses us. A better understanding of the nature of language and its figurations will give us a better idea, legally, of what we think. The analytical resources of rhetoric and criticism will also give us a better sense of why it is that we think it. And above all – in relation to legal personification – it may remind us of who, in the end, should be doing the thinking.

BIBLIOGRAPHY

Bahktin, MM, 1981, "Discourse in the Novel", Emerson, C and Holquist, M (eds), *The Dialogic Imagination: Four Essays,* University of Texas Press, p 294.

Blackstone, Sir William, 1765, *Commentaries on the Laws of England*, I, III, IV, Oxford.

Carty, Anthony (ed), 1990, *Post-Modern Law: Enlightenment, Revolution and the Death of Man,* Edinburgh University Press.

Geertz, Clifford, 1983, "Local Knowledge: Fact and Law in Comparative Perspective", in *Local Knowledge: Further Essays in Interpretive Anthropology*, Basic Books, p 173.

Goodrich, Peter, *Languages of Law: From Logics of Memory to Nomadic Masks,* Weidenfeld & Nicholson.

Graycar, Regina and Morgan, Jenny, 1990, *The Hidden Gender of Law,* The Federation Press, pp 177-83.

Owen, WJB and Smyser, JB (eds), *Prose Works,* I, Clarendon Press, p 48.

Peller, Gary, 1985, "The Metaphysics of American Law", *California Law Review,* 73, p 1159.

Watson, Alan, 1985, *Evolution of Law*, Johns Hopkins University Press, pp 185-9.

Watson, Alan, 1988, *Failures of the Legal Imagination*, University of Pennsylvania Press, pp 22-7, 113 ff.

ANSWERS TO PRELIMINARY EXERCISE

A Dickens of a Legal Quiz – The Solution

KJA ASCHE

1. Fagin was not convicted of theft or receiving although both were capital offences and could have got him hanged. He was convicted of being an accessory in the murder of Nancy and thus a principal in the first degree.

2. The criminal law of the time adopted the same philosophy as the civil law, namely that a wife was the husband's inferior and not much different from a servant. Hence the presumption (albeit rebuttable) was that a wife who committed a crime (except treason or murder) in her husband's presence did so under his coercion. She was entitled to be acquitted and her husband convicted. On hearing that *he* could be convicted of her crimes, Mr Bumble, who was married to a nagging shrew who beat and bullied him unmercifully, expressed his amazement and indignation at the state of the law.

3. Almost certainly Murdstone would have succeeded and by Writ of Habeas Corpus. The first reason is admittedly conjectural because we have no evidence of it; but we can assume that Murdstone, being the sort of person he was, would probably have ensured that he was appointed guardian by the will of David's mother; and the rights of a guardian were as absolute as those of the father (Blackstone vol 1 p 442). However even without that evidence it is clear that Murdstone had already exercised sufficient authority over David (eg by sending him to school and then to the blacking factory), for the law to have recognised him as being in loco parentis. The authority for this is *Stone v Carr* (1797) 3 Esp 1; 170 ER 517. (Yes, I know Espinasse is a pretty weak reed to clutch at for support. The old joke was that he heard one half of the case and reported the other. But he must have been awake on this occasion for the case seems right on the prevailing principles at the time.) To be in loco parentis was to be, as Lord Eldon put it in *Ex p Pye* (1811) 18 Ves 140, "in the situation of the person described as father of the child". Hence Murdstone would have been in an almost unassailable position. The fact that he had

put David out to employment would have been regarded as no more than his right as a father and probably a prudent measure for his future. As for beating David, since he did not seriously maim him, his action would have been construed as rational correction. The fact that David hated him would have been quite irrelevant. The common law knew nothing of the doctrine of the welfare of the child being paramount, unless in the sense that it assumed the child's welfare was best with the father. Certainly equity was forming such a doctrine, but at this stage the expression "welfare" was mainly used in the sense of "financial welfare" if the child had property.

Finally, and conclusively, if David's aunt sought custody, she laboured under the obvious disadvantage of being a woman.

4. Although he was freed in Botany Bay, the sentence on Magwitch had been transportation for life. By returning to England without official permission, he committed a capital offence (Holdsworth vol XI, p 574: 5 Geo IV c 84).

5. Jaggers could not appear for Magwitch. Jaggers was an attorney. His reputation as an advocate was confined to the lower courts. An attorney had no right of audience in the higher courts. Hence Banjo Paterson's complaint many years later when the prohibition still prevailed, "The law won't allow me / (Attorneys are worms) / To appear in Gilhooley's Estate". In Australia solicitors gradually gained the right to audience in any court, although some states or colonies took longer than others to effect the change. It has only changed in England in very recent times and against some very vocal opposition from Bench and Bar. Jaggers briefed counsel.

6. Mr Pickwick insisted on seeing Serjeant Snubbin before the trial. He had his way, although it shocked the lawyers and was considered "a violation of all established rules and customs". The rule that counsel should not see parties or witnesses before trial was strictly applied. It has not operated in Australia for many years and I understand it has now been considerably relaxed in England.

7. The answer is interesting and proves Dickens made no mistake about his law. There was indeed a writ of execution of property *(fieri facias)* whereby property could be seized by the Sheriff and sold to satisfy debts. There was also the writ of execution on the person *(capias ad satisfaciendum)* whereby the person of the debtor could be arrested and lodged in prison until he paid. But if you used the latter you could not avail yourself of the former. Blackstone (Commentaries, bk III, p 415) is the authority:

> The writ of *capias ad satisfaciendum* is an execution of the highest nature, inasmuch as it deprives a man of his liberty, till he makes the satisfaction awarded; and therefore, when a man is once taken in execution upon this writ, no other process can be sued out against his lands or goods.

Dodson and Fogg obviously thought they could get immediate payment by frightening Mr Pickwick with imprisonment. Having misread their man they could not use the alternative process against him. So they arrested Mrs Bardell whom they had tricked into giving a *cognovit* for their costs "as a matter of form".

8. We cannot escape this by suggesting Dickens was ignorant of the prevailing rules because his account of the trial was checked by his friend Serjeant Talfourd. The answer to the question is, I think, twofold. First, by a very generous interpretation such as I doubt would be allowed by any judge today, it might be said that this was not a cross-examination but rather a very cross examination-in-chief.

That, however, seems a rather glib answer. I think the true reason is that the rules about hostile witnesses did not then have the precision they now have. Indeed in 1824 (and the Pickwick Papers commenced in 1836) in the case of *Clarke v Saffery* Ry & Mood 126; 171 ER 966, Best CJ had said:

> There is no fixed rule which binds a counsel calling a witness to a particular mode of examining him. If a witness, by his conduct, in the box, shows himself decidedly adverse, it is always in the discretion of the judge to allow a cross-examination; but if a witness called, stands in a situation which of necessity makes him adverse to the party calling him . . . the counsel may, as a matter of right, cross-examine him.

Once it is remembered that counsel could not call the person who would normally be the most important witness in proving the case, namely the party making the allegations, these observations of Best CJ become understandable. Obviously in many cases the only other witnesses to, say, the making of a contract or the occurrence of a tortious act would not always be favourable to the party relying upon such matters. Yet the essential elements of the cause had to be proved somehow. It is therefore not surprising that counsel were allowed much greater latitude in dealing with a witness who, to repeat the words of Best CJ stood "in a situation which of necessity makes him adverse to the party calling him".

The remarks of Best CJ in *Clarke v Safferey* were finally disapproved of in *Price v Manning* (1887) 42 Ch D 372; but by then parties in a civil suit were allowed to give evidence and the stricter rules against cross-examining one's own witness were being accepted along with the need to identify carefully a hostile witness.

9. I'm afraid this is one instance where Dickens was just plain wrong. Suicide was a felony and, as such, subject to the law that the property of a felon was forfeited to the Crown. Escheat or forfeiture for felony was not abolished until the *Forfeiture Act* 1870 (Eng).

Furthermore if Mrs Quilp *had* succeeded on intestacy she would have received only one half of the personalty. The situation was still governed by the *Statute of Distributions* 1670 whereby the wife of an intestate received one-third of the personal estate if there were children, and one half if there were not. As to real estate it would seem she only had her right of dower which was a life interest in one third of the real property. (See Hardingham 1978 pp 8-13 – dealing with the historical setting; see also Holdsworth vol XV p 377).

However, as Jaggers explains to Pip in *Great Expectations*, "there might be many cases in which the forfeiture was not exacted", and Mrs Quilp might have had the benefit of this. But, as the lawyers would say, we have no evidence of this.

10. "Bolt".

11. Your guess is as good as mine.

BIBLIOGRAPHY

Blackstone, Sir William, 1765, *Commentaries on the laws of England*, vol I, Oxford.

Hardingham, I, 1978, *The Law of Intestate Succession in Australia & New Zealand,* Law Book Company.

Holdsworth, WS, *History of English Law,* vols XI, XV.

Also from The Federation Press:

Plain Language for Lawyers

Michele Asprey

"I know that you believe you understand what you think I said, but I'm not sure you realise that what you heard is not what I meant."

Richard M Nixon, Quoted in *Australian Business*

This book explains what plain language is and what it isn't. It tells why lawyers need to use plain language, how they can profit from doing so and shows them how it can make them more efficient and more effective lawyers. It takes the readers step-by-step throughout the various elements of plain language writing, and it answers the most common questions that people ask about plain language writing.

Asprey, a former Consultant to the Centre for Plain Legal Language within the University of Sydney Law School, was previously the Director of Legal Precedents at Malleson Stephen Jaques in Sydney.

"By using plain language, not only will our clients know what they are reading, but we will better know what we are writing.

Every lawyer would do well to have a copy of this excellent book."

The New Gazette, Hong Kong

"This book should be read by all lawyers, particularly those who believe there is nothing wrong with their form of drafting and that they are good legal drafters. Those people in particular, will be in for some unpleasant surprises."

ACT Gazette

"Some stimulation to improve one's writing is always helpful, and this book certainly supplies that."

Queensland Bar News

"If any book is going to improve your writing, this is it. It doesn't preach. It doesn't contain long winded examples of bad drafting. An even if it doesn't improve your writing, it's entertaining to read.

There are numerous quotations, references to the work of others and a comprehensive 10 page index. The book will serve as an excellent reference book. Here is a textbook that is as easy to read as a newspaper."

Victorian Law Institute Journal

1991 PB ISBN 1862870632 $25.00

1991 HB ISBN 1862870640 $40.00

Also from The Federation Press:

Mabo
What the High Court Said
Peter Butt & Robert Eagleson

This book sets out in plain English the High Court decision in *Mabo*. It avoids repetition, translates legalese into English and gathers the judgment into chapters and themes.

It gives everyone the chance to read the case for themselves and make up their own minds. It enables all Australians to understand what our High Court has ruled in the *Mabo* Case and why.

"To understand what the High Court decided and why is to understand ... a fundamental part of Australia's identity as a nation.
... My hope is that this book, by bringing the debate back to the source, will make the High Court's decision itself more accessible and give Australians an insight to the heart of one of the most significant changes in this nation's history, a recognition of the truth about the history of the land itself, and a significant step in reconciling the indigenous and non-indigenous people of the nation."

The Hon Paul Keating MP
Prime Minister of Australia

"The Mabo decision will mean change in the political, economic and legal spheres ... Such changes will necessitate understanding.
It is towards this understanding that this publication makes a brilliant contribution. This plain English version of the Court's decision must find its way into the homes and schools of all Australians. So that all may understand the reasoning of the High Court, and the clear legal and historical basis for the decision."

Noel Pearson,
Director, Cape York Land Council

1993 ISBN 1862871183 PB 96pp $16.95

PO Box 45 Annandale NSW Australia 2038 Phone (02)552 2200 Fax (02)552 1681